A great time involved in rail

Visualisation of Hitachi Super Express Train for Intercity Express Programme.

Despite the challenges facing the UK economy, passenger numbers continue to rise on the railway network. The industry is well-placed as government sees investment in the rail network as key to economic growth. This has delivered plans for significant investment in electrification, and a focus on growth including cross-political party support for HS2 and Crossrail.

Particular highlights of 2012 were the London Olympic and Paralympic Games. The industry was challenged to deliver under the glare of the world's media - and the result was an outstanding success. The industry worked seamlessly together to deliver millions of British and international spectators to and from the games, allowing the nation to focus on the achievements in the sports arena and the many medals brought home by our athletes. Passenger feedback was excellent, which is a real testament to the great achievements possible through close collaboration.

The challenge moving forward is to develop growth whilst reducing the overall running cost of the network. 2012 was the starting point for the Intercity Express Programme, which involves the provision of almost 600 rail carriages into daily service over a period of 27.5 years. For the first time the rolling stock solution was based on whole-life costs, enabling the supplier to trade off investment in design considering whole-life maintenance and infrastructure maintenance costs including substantial investment in new depots. The contract also paves the way for a substantial investment in a new rolling stock manufacturing plant in the UK, which will increase competition, ultimately benefiting passengers as well.

Further evolutions in 2012 saw the drive to longer franchising, collaboration between train operating companies and Network Rail and a further drive to reduce infrastructure costs through investment in technology such as Traffic Management Systems and the European Train Control System. Whilst there have been some well-documented difficulties arising from the refranchising of the West Coast Main Line, it is important that the industry does not stand still for long as the refranchising process is essential to stimulate further investment in the industry.

Looking forward, the industry will benefit from the significant investment in the existing network and building HS2 and Crossrail, complemented by the investment in its people through the new National Skills Academy and renewed focus on apprenticeships.

2013 is a great time to be involved in the UK's rail industry.

Alistair Dormer
Chairman and Chief Executive Officer, Hitachi Rail Europe Ltd

3

Contents

3	Foreword by Alistair Dormer of Hitachi
6	Biggest modernisation in generations: Norman Baker, Rail Minister

SECTION 1 - SETTING THE AGENDA - INDUSTRY STRUCTURE

9	Collaboration is key: Jeremy Candfield, Director General, the Railway Industry Association
10	Growth and innovation in Rail Freight: Maggie Simpson, Executive Director, the Rail Freight Group
11	2013 - year of turmoil: business review by Roger Ford, Industry & Technology Editor of Modern Railways
14	RailRoute map of Britain's railways
16	Across the industry
	■ Department for Transport
	■ Scotland and Wales
	■ Network Rail
	■ Office of Rail Regulation
	■ Passenger Focus
	■ The privatised rail industry

SECTION 2 - FINANCE AND LEASING

28	Angel Trains
30	Porterbrook Leasing
31	Eversholt Rail Group
33	Britain's rolling stock - who owns it? The ROSCO fleets

SECTION 3 - TRAIN FLEET MANUFACTURE AND MAINTENANCE

40	GB rolling stock market - prospects reviewed by Roger Ford
46	Siemens
48	Bombardier
50	Hitachi
52	Alstom
54	CAF
56	GE Transportation
56	Electro-Motive Diesel
56	Vossloh
58	Wabtec

SECTION 4 - PASSENGER TRAIN OPERATORS

60	Train operating company index
62	Passenger operator finances: review by TAS's Chris Cheek
68	First Group:
68	First Great Western
70	First Capital Connect
71	ScotRail
73	First TransPennine Express
74	First Hull Trains
75	Govia:
75	Southern
76	Southeastern
78	London Midland
80	Stagecoach:
80	South West Trains
81	East Midlands Trains
83	Virgin Trains
85	Arriva:
85	Chiltern Railways
86	Arriva Trains Wales
88	CrossCountry
90	Grand Central
91	Serco and Abellio:
91	Northern
92	Merseyrail
94	Greater Anglia
96	c2c
97	East Coast
98	Eurostar
99	Eurotunnel
100	Heathrow Express

SECTION 5 - FREIGHT AND HAULAGE

103	Railfreight onward and upward! - we analyse the railfreight market
	■ Freight company accounts

The Modern Railway

Editor:	Ken Cordner
Production Editor:	David Lane
Contributors:	Roger Ford
	Alan Williams
	John Glover
	Chris Shilling
	Ken Harris
	Tony Miles
	Chris Cheek
	Keith Fender
Advertisement Manager:	Chris Shilling
Advertising Production:	Cheryl Thornburn
Graphic Design:	Matt Chapman
	Matt Fuller
Transport Publisher:	David Lane
Publishing Director:	Paul Appleton
Commercial Director:	Ann Saundry
Managing Director:	Adrian Cox
Executive Chairman:	Richard Cox

The Modern Railway is published by:
Key Publishing Limited, PO Box 100,
Stamford, Lincs PE9 1XP

The Modern Railway is supported by:

Printing:
Printed in England by Berforts Information Press Ltd,
Southfield Road, Eynsham, Oxford, OX29 4JB

Purchasing additional copies of *The Modern Railway*:
Please contact our Margaret Hayes on 01780 484 630
or by email at margaret.hayes@keypublishing.com
Corporate and bulk purchase discounts are available on
request.

Thank you!
We are very grateful to the many individuals from
businesses in all sectors of the railway who have kindly
provided help in compiling The Modern Railway.
Information contained in The Modern Railway
was believed correct at the time of going to press
in November 2012. We would be glad to receive
corrections and updates for the next edition.

© Key Publishing Ltd 2013

All rights reserved. No part of this publication may be reproduced or transmitted
in any form by any means, electronic or mechanical, including photocopying,
recording or by any information storage and retrieval system, without prior
permission in writing from the copyright owner. Multiple copying of the
contents of the publication without prior written approval is not permitted.

Cover photos: Hitachi, Crossrail,
Tony Miles and Brian Morrison
ISBN 978-0-9462-1938-4

- 108 DB Schenker
- 110 GB Railfreight
- 111 Direct Rail Services
- 112 Freightliner
- 114 Freight, haulage and rolling stock providers: Colas Rail, BARS, Riviera Trains, West Coast Railway

SECTION 6 - INNOVATION AND ENVIRONMENT
- 116 Alternative solutions? Modern Railways columnist Alan Williams examines an 'alternatives' strategy from a Community Rail perspective
- 119 Knorr-Bremse
- 120 The Railway Industry Innovation Awards
  - Golden Spanners focus on reliable trains
  - The Golden Whistles awards
  - The Fourth Friday Club
- 122 Railtex returns to Earls Court
- 122 Rail Vehicle Enhancements

SECTION 7 - KEY PROJECTS AND CONSULTANTS
- 124 Electrification - government sees the light. Roger Ford reviews the DfT's rolling programme
- 129 Key projects
  - London Crossrail
  - Intercity Express Programme
  - Thameslink Programme
  - High Speed 2
  - Scotland's rail projects
  - Great Western modernisation
  - Consultant files – supporting rail developments

SECTION 8 - INFRASTRUCTURE MAINTENANCE AND RENEWAL
- 139 Network Rail enters second decade
  - The capacity challenge
  - The main infrastructure contractors

SECTION 9 - SIGNALLING AND CONTROL
- 146 Invensys Rail
- 148 Signalling and Control: Traffic Management System and ETCS move ahead

SECTION 10 - LIGHT RAIL AND METRO
- 152 New generation trams in Blackpool
- 154 Light rail grows again:
  - GB light rail systems reviewed
- 159 Transport for London
  - London Underground
  - London Overground

SECTION 11 - INTO EUROPE
- 165 Into Europe - developments in European rail

- 169 **THE MODERN RAILWAY DIRECTORY**
  A compendium of some 2,000 UK Rail businesses, suppliers and industry bodies

5

Full speed ahead on Crossrail - Europe's largest crane lowers tunnelling machine 'Elizabeth' into the Crossrail tunnel shaft at Limmo peninsula near Canning Town on 25 October 2012. Crossrail

Biggest modernisation in generations

Building a stronger economy, a fairer society and a cleaner and greener environment - that is the triple-challenge faced by the Coalition Government. And to help meet that challenge, we are delivering the biggest rail modernisation programme in generations.

We know that economic growth and job creation are boosted when a country's rail networks are fast, reliable and affordable. We understand the social mobility bonus of high quality railways and the way they give people better access to employment opportunities and essential services. And we recognise the carbon-cutting benefits of rail travel, with its potential to attract people and freight away from less eco-friendly alternatives like long distance driving and short haul flying.

This Government is therefore a fully paid up member of the rail travel fan club. We are investing £18 billion in our railways during this Spending Review period. We have also set out £9.4 billion worth of projects in our recent announced plans for investment for the period 2014-2019. And, building on this, there is the £4.5 billion contract for a new generation of intercity trains that will roll out of a new purpose-built factory in County Durham.

We are going to electrify 850 miles of track: one in 9 miles compared to the paltry 9 miles electrified between 1997 and 2010. North, South, East and West the passenger experience is being transformed with new carriages and more seats, faster journeys and better services. We are pushing full speed ahead with landmark projects like Crossrail, Thameslink, the Northern Hub and HS2. We have given the green light to extensions to light rail systems in Birmingham, Manchester, Nottingham, and Sheffield. And we are reopening lines to unlock growth, such as the East West Rail project between Bedford and Oxford. At the same time, we're funding local authorities to develop new stations, such as Stratford-upon-Avon Parkway in Warwickshire and Kirkstall Forge in Yorkshire, and we are providing a further £200 million to develop the Strategic Freight Network.

Hand in hand with investing in our railways we are reforming our railways. We are working to cut the queues and the hassle by backing new technologies like smart ticketing. And in these tough economic times, we are helping passengers by limiting the rise in the average cap on regulated rail fares to 1% above inflation in 2013 and 2014. Beyond that, our plans for rail reform aim to build on the McNulty Report by driving down costs, improving value for money and giving fare-payers and taxpayers a better deal. And because local transport challenges are best met with local solutions, we are investigating opportunities to devolve greater responsibility for local rail services.

As Rail Minister I am convinced that a modern railway makes sense for our country's success and our children's future - economically, socially and environmentally. That is why I am proud to serve in a Department and a Government that, with the help of an incredibly talented industry, is renewing, rebuilding and reforming Britain's railways.

Norman Baker MP Parliamentary Under-Secretary of State for Transport

Setting the Agenda

In association with

HITACHI
Inspire the Next

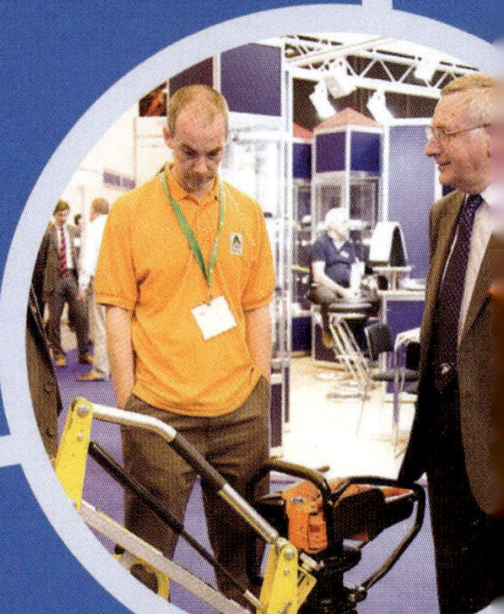

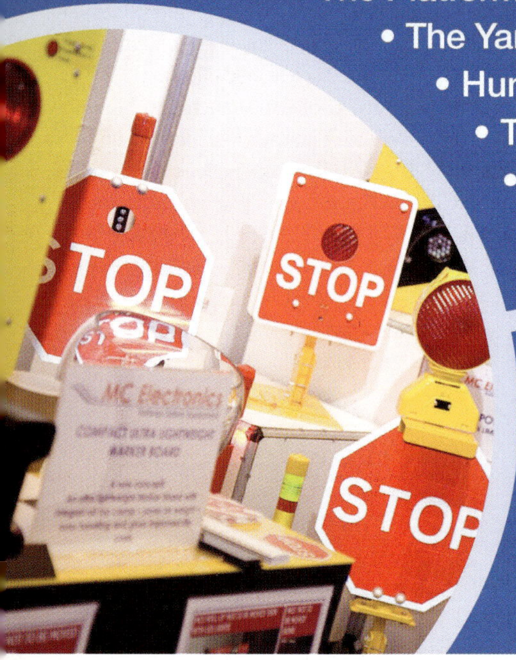

In association with HITACHI Inspire the Next

Maximum exploitation of track capacity is a theme of recent Network Rail and Crossrail contract awards for Traffic Management and Communications Based Train Control systems. Siemens

Collaboration is the key

As the UK's railways strive to meet the challenges of improving efficiency and reducing costs, while carrying ever more traffic, it becomes increasingly clear that we can only achieve success by working more closely together.

One of the key strategic themes that we in the Railway Industry Association have been pursuing for many years is the need to move away from the traditional adversarial supply-chain relationships to a much more collaborative and mutually beneficial approach. The 2011 McNulty Report, commissioned jointly by the British Government and the Office of Rail Regulation to look at potential efficiencies in the UK railway industry, identified this as a key objective, which has helped provide the necessary impetus for changes to be made.

A good example of this achieving tangible results in practice was the working together of Network Rail, the Association of Train Operating Companies (ATOC), freight operators and RIA in the production of the Initial Industry Plan, for the first time informing Government of the whole industry's views in advance of the process for determining funding levels for the next 5 year Control Period. Following the subsequent announcement by Government as to what high level outputs it expects the industry to deliver during the Control Period, those same industry partners have been working together to produce the more detailed Strategic Business Plan for publication early in 2013. This reflects a much more collaborative cross-industry approach than that adopted during the planning for the previous period.

Under the leadership of David Higgins and his team, Network Rail is becoming much more open to introducing new technologies and innovative processes, but especially to working in partnership. British Standard (BS) 11000 is the world's first collaborative framework standard and is applicable to all industries. It is relatively new and so still gaining traction. Nonetheless, NR and a number of RIA member suppliers have already achieved BS11000 accreditation in respect of a series of specific projects, with more to follow.

Joint working groups of NR and suppliers were instrumental in developing the business case for further main line electrification, rewarded by the programme recently announced by Government. Similar signs of increasing collaboration are also appearing with other key industry partners, such as Transport for London.

The hiatus in the franchising programme following the events around the West Coast franchise renewal must not be allowed to obstruct the continuing and vitally-high level of investment and steady progress in improvements. Major projects such as electrification clearly involve the franchised service operator, and capacity gains such as increased linespeeds and additional freight train paths will only be realised through close co-operation of all concerned. Many of the schemes depend heavily on cascades of rolling stock, so it is vital that the franchising programme gets 'back on the rails' as quickly as possible.

The continuing development of new technologies reinforces rail's already-green credentials and by working together we can ensure that railways contribute fully towards a sustainable future.

Jeremy Candfield
Director General,
Railway Industry Association

HITACHI Inspire the Next

9

Setting the Agenda

Growth and innovation in Rail Freight industry

For the rail freight sector, 2012 has been a good year, with continued growth despite difficult trading conditions in the economy. Investment in the network, and equipment has continued, and a number of new services have started up, including some innovative trials. On the back of this, what will 2013 have in store?

From a policy perspective, of course, there is still much at stake with the conclusions of the Periodic Review 2013 expected in the summer. The outcomes on freight access charges will have a material effect, positively or negatively, on freight operators, customers and the wider market. Coupled with that, the promised investment for rail freight in the DfT and Transport Scotland's High Level Output Statements must be secured, particularly if the crisis in passenger rail franchising impacts on the available funds.

On the ground, intermodal traffic has grown year on year for almost a decade now, and made significant efficiency improvements. Over 2013, a number of key schemes will help to further this, including the opening of the Nuneaton North Chord, gauge clearance of the second route from Southampton, between Water Orton and Doncaster, and up the East Coast. Private sector investments at ports and terminals are also progressing, with the new port at London Gateway expected to open in the first half of the year, and work at Felixstowe and at Southampton also progressing. Freightliner's new Shortliner wagons, developed and built by VTG Rail, are also expected to enter service, improving loading capability and efficiency again.

Domestic intermodal services have been growing slowly too, with Tesco setting the pace from their hub at Daventry. M&S's new rail linked warehouse at Castle Donnington is expected to come on line, and plans for new terminals, and further expansion at Daventry are likely to start their way through the planning system – noting that this remains a long, and expensive process with no guarantee of success.

The energy sector is becoming increasingly volatile, with OFGEM now warning of the potential for power shortages as some generation plants close. Indeed some power stations are expected to finish during 2013, with resulting impacts on rail freight flows and volumes. Other plants are continuing to investigate the potential for biomass generation, either entirely or as a fuel co-burnt with coal. The policy environment for biomass generation is still unsettled, but any increased use would have significant potential for rail freight. Biomass generation uses more raw fuel than coal, and therefore creates a greater demand for train paths from ports to power station. Wagon modifications are also necessary to keep the product dry. This could be a major challenge for the industry, but one which could deliver growth.

There are also positive signs for cross channel traffic, with piggyback trials and the Euro Carex express freight development amongst others, and continued progress with aggregates traffic, not least for Crossrail spoil, expected to keep operators busy during the year. We look forward to reporting continued progress and success over the 12 months ahead.

Maggie Simpson
Executive Director,
Rail Freight Group
(RFG)

Private sector pioneer - Aggregate Industries Class 59/1 No 59001 'Yeoman Endeavour' passes through Swindon on 26 July 2012, hauling the 13.30 Yeoman hoppers from Whatley to Dagenham, diverted via the Great Western main line. Brian Morrison

2013 – year of turmoil

In association with HITACHI Inspire the Next

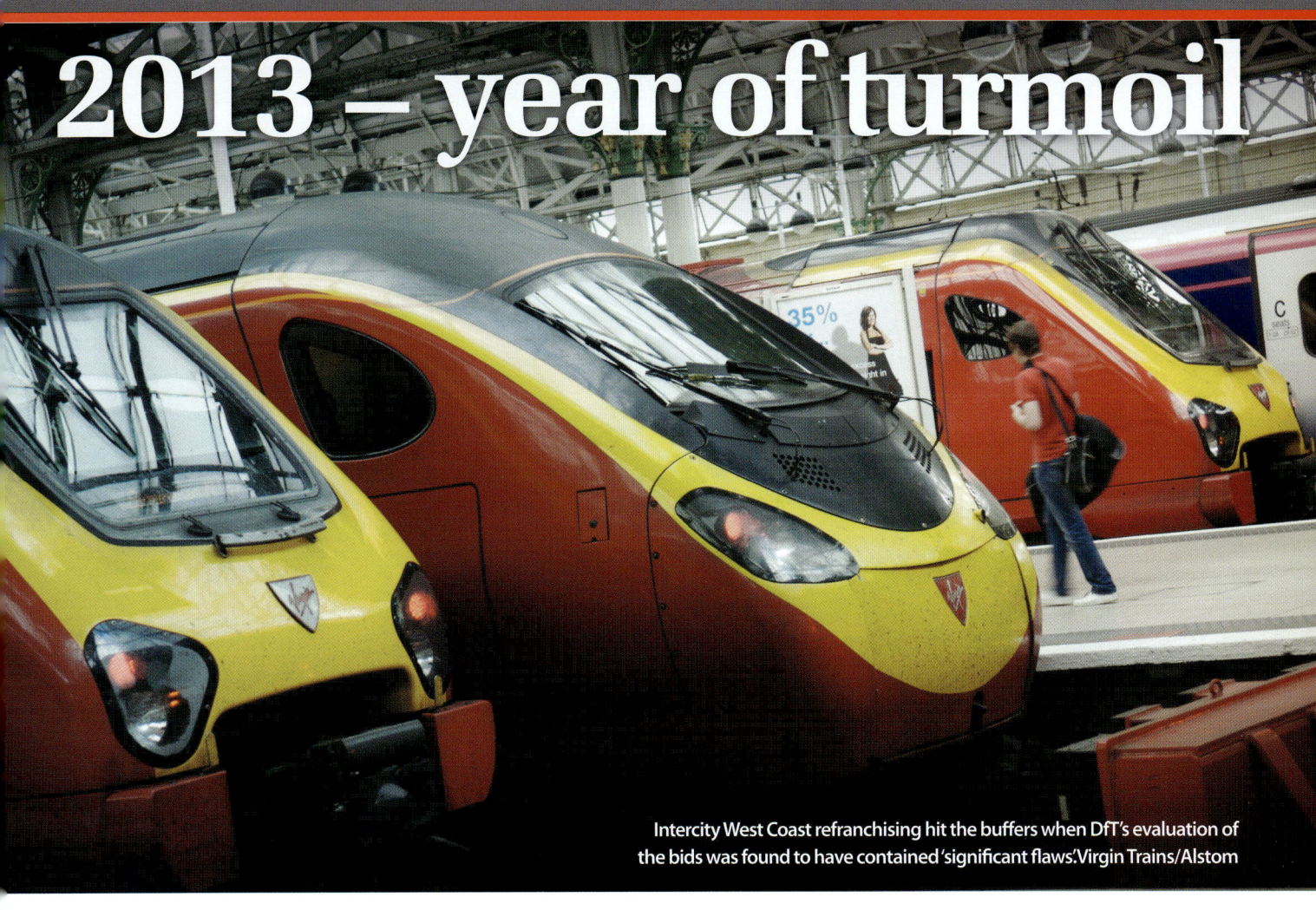

Intercity West Coast refranchising hit the buffers when DfT's evaluation of the bids was found to have contained 'significant flaws'. Virgin Trains/Alstom

Roger Ford, Industry & Technology Editor of *Modern Railways* magazine, says 2013 will be dominated by the franchising crisis

In 'The Modern Railway' last year we heralded 2012 as 'the year of decision'. We declared that 'one thing is clear: for the first time since TMR began, the railway industry should have a clearer idea of what it is expected to do, and the structure within which it will have to achieve the demands of its funders, by the time the next edition of our annual publication appears'.

Our optimistic conclusion was what while we should not expect complete clarity of intent, '2012 will be the year of several key decisions which will determine the long term nature of the industry'.

And it seemed that our optimism had been justified. The publication in July of the High Level Output Specifications (HLOS) and the associated Statements of Funds Available (SoFA) by the Westminster and Scottish governments revealed a growing confidence in the ability of the railway to deliver.

Meanwhile, the Office of Rail Regulation's (ORR's) Periodic Review, which will determine Network Rail's income for the new five-year Control Period (CP5), starting on 1 April 2014, was running to time, after an earlier delay to allow for the McNulty Report to be considered. The HLOS and SoFA are the governments' contribution to the Periodic Review – specifying what the industry has to deliver and how much of the taxpayer's money is available to fund it.

Franchise replacement was underway, with the new measures forecast in the Government's franchise reform proposals being included in Invitations to Tender (ITT). While there had been some slippage on the schedule published in The Modern Railway 2012, bidding was progressing, with four replacement franchises expected to start in 2013, including the return of the government-run East Coast franchise to the private sector.

More importantly, it was expected that new operators would take over the two most-demanding franchises on the network. Both Great Western and Thameslink involve the management of major new infrastructure upgrades and new rolling stock, while maintaining performance of the daily railway.

Economy

That said, franchise finances were suffering from the impact of the economy, with seven of the 10 franchises eligible under the 'Cap & Collar' provision in their franchise agreements receiving revenue support. But enthusiasm among bidders was undimmed, with strong competition for all four franchises.

On the rolling stock front there was also slippage, as the two multi-billion Train Service Provision contracts struggled to line up their financial packages. Agility Trains, the Hitachi-led consortium eventually signed the contract for the Great Western tranche of the Intercity Express Programme on 9 July 2012. But the 600-vehicle Thameslink rolling-stock deal continued to struggle, and by September the Department for Transport was hoping that the deal could be concluded 'around the turn of the year'.

And while the overall performance of the railway continued to improve, Network Rail was at odds with ORR over the Public Performance Measures figures for Intercity. Substantial fines were in prospect if, as was likely, Network Rail missed improvement targets by the end of the year. London & South East punctuality was also coming under scrutiny.

HITACHI Inspire the Next

11

Setting the Agenda

West Coast challenge

Thus, by the end of September, 2012 was turning out much as expected, with the industry growing in confidence. There had been only one out-of-course event. For the first time a franchise award had been challenged.

On 15 August, the Department for Transport announced that First Group had won the bidding for the replacement Intercity West Coast (ICWC) franchise. The new operator was due to take over on 9 December.

But on 26 August, ICWC incumbent Virgin Rail Group - the Virgin-Stagecoach joint venture which has held the franchise since 1996 - announced that it would challenge the award. Significantly, the challenge would not be against the decision, but the process on which it was based.

Virgin and First Group had offered similar bids in terms of investment and new services. However, where First had offered the classic straight-line constant-growth premium profile - with payment to Government topping £1 billion (2012 prices) in the final year - Virgin's was more complex.

While the Virgin bid offered more in the initial years, the company believed that the rebuilding of Euston station to accommodate High Speed 2 services would slow growth from around 2020 onward. Premium payments reflected this, with Virgin offering £6.5 billion (cash) over the franchise term, versus First's more optimistic £7.47 billion.

Virgin's primary challenge that the £190 million Subordinated Loan Facility (SLF), which First would forfeit if it defaulted on the franchise, was too small in relation to the size of the premium payments in the final years. The SLF is intended to mitigate the risk of a train operator walking away from a franchise which had been won with a heavily back-end-loaded premium profile. In the case of National Express East Coast in 2009, National Express had forfeited an SLF of £40 million.

Virgin calculated that the SLF for the First Group's winning premium profile should have been around £600 million rather than the £190 million calculated by DfT. However it was widely assumed that DfT would be able to justify the figure and that Virgin would lose its legal challenge.

PricewaterhouseCoopers was called in to check the government's response to the Virgin legal challenge. The accountants' checks revealed that DfT's evaluation of the bids had contained 'significant flaws'. Not only could PwC not replicate DfT's figures, DfT could not provide the calculations on which the franchise award decision had been based.

Reaction

Faced with the 'deeply regrettable and completely unacceptable' mistakes made by his department, recently appointed Transport Secretary Patrick McLoughlin had no choice but to cancel the ICWC competition and 'pause' bidding for the other franchises. Mr McLoughlin also ordered two urgent independent reviews.

One review, led by a DfT non-executive director, investigated what went wrong with the franchise bidding and award. This produced its initial report at the end of October.

But the really important review, in terms of the future of the railway, was being carried out by Eurostar Chairman Richard Brown. He was asked to report by the end of the year.

Mr Brown was tasked by the Secretary of State for Transport 'to look in detail at the implications for the remainder of the rail franchising programme, in particular, whether changes are needed to the way risk is assessed and to the bidding and evaluation processes, and at how to get the other franchise competitions back on track as soon as possible'.

While its remit clearly assumes a continuation of the current approach to franchising, the Brown Review had some latitude in its terms of reference. These include facilitating 'a clear and proportionate framework for franchising which balances Government's administrative and commercial judgements with the need for the market to have predictability, transparency and a proportionate application of legal rules'.

And while vested interests, such as the operator-dominated Rail Delivery Group (RDG), and the Association of Train Operating Companies have called for a rapid resumption of franchising business-as-usual, within wider industry

Thameslink - one of the most-demanding franchises on the network. The new overall roof at Blackfriars station, which now spans the Thames with access on both banks, is a striking symbol of the first stage of the Thameslink route improvement programme. Network Rail

Table 1: Franchise replacement status

Franchise	OJEU	ITT	Award	Current end date
Intercity West Coast	Issued	January 2012	Cancelled	January 2014(a)
Greater Western	Issued	July 2012	Paused	July 2013
Essex Thameside	Issued	May 2012	Paused	May 2013
Thameslink	Issued	October 2012	Paused	September 2013
Intercity East Coast	Deferred	January 2013 (b)	Summer 2013 (b)	December 2013
South Eastern	December 2012 (b)	May 2013 (b)	End 2013 (b)	April 2014
Trans Pennine Express Northern	December 2012 (b)	May 2013 (b)	End 2013 (b)	April 2014
Greater Anglia	December 2012 (b)	August 2013 (b)	Spring 2014 (b)	July 2014

(a) Extension to Virgin franchise (b) Previous schedule

Four priorities for the HLOS

- The 'Electric Spine'.
- Increased capacity and shorter journey times between 'key' cities.
- Facilitating commuting into 'major urban areas'.
- Improved rail inks to major ports and airports.

there is an appreciation that the ICWC cancellation represented a failure of the franchising concept, rather than just the process. Whether or not the Brown Review takes this wider view, it is unlikely that bidding for the three 'paused' franchises will be able to restart before the second half of 2013.

Paused

This will add to the problems faced by DfT, since both Essex Thameside (c2c) and Great Western have already been extended. In the case of Essex Thameside, there was a two year extension to May 2013, in part to maintain continuity up to and through the London Olympics.

First Great Western declined the option of an additional three year extension from 1 April 2013, but delays to the start of the bidding process meant that the end date had to be extended to 21 July 2013. With the need to incorporate any lessons from the Brown review in the ITT before restarting the 'paused' bidding, it is unlikely that the replacement Great Western franchise could be handed over before the end of 2013.

In the case of replacement Thameslink franchise, the ITT was due to have been issued in October 2012. However, the continuing delay in signing the train service provision deal with Siemens meant that the ITT would have had to have been delayed to early 2013, even without the 'pause'. This means that the replacement franchisee in unlikely to take over until the first quarter of 2014 at the earliest.

Further complicating Thameslink is the fact that the replacement franchise is expected take over the existing Southern franchise and incorporate Great Northern services plus some Southeastern services. The new franchise will also have to maintain services through the final stage of the Thameslink London Bridge works and manage the introduction of the new train fleet.

Even more demanding challenges will face the new Great Western franchisee, maintaining service on a route which is being electrified, resignalled with the European Train Control System, replacing its IC125 train fleet with the Intercity Express Programme, and interfacing with Crossrail between Paddington and Maidenhead.

In both cases, Network Rail had seen new franchises coming into effect in 2013 as making an important contribution to the management of the Thameslink upgrade and the Great Western route modernisation. In particular, the new franchise agreements would make allowance for the impact of the works in Schedule 4 of the track access agreement covering disruption.

Also affected by the pausing of franchises are the rolling stock manufacturers. This is examined in more detail in the article in the Train Fleet Manufacture and Maintenance section of this edition of The Modern Railway. However it means that the proposed orders for new 'Baby' Pendolinos or conventional electric multiple-units proposed in the First Group and Virgin bids for ICWC have been put back by at least an year and probably three.

Infrastructure

A rolling programme of electrification is at the heart of the HLOS published in July 2012. This will create an electrified 'Central Spine' running from the South Coast through Oxford, Bedford and via the Midland main line to the East Midlands and South Yorkshire, with a link from Oxford to the West Midlands and the Northwest.

Published with the HLOS, the SoFA confirmed support for infrastructure enhancements already committed, worth £5.2billion, and added new schemes worth a further £4.2billion. Total state funding for the five years of CP5 will be £16.84billion, which DfT emphasises is 'final'.

But, here too, the ICWC franchise casts a shadow. The £16.84 billion assumed that DfT would receive net premia from the franchised train operators totalling £1.49 billion. This would be deducted from the Direct Grants paid to Network Rail totalling £18.29 billion over the five years.

But following the errors in the ICWC evaluation process, which understated the risk mitigation associated with ambitious premium profiles, income from replacement franchises is likely to be less than expected. This could be reflected in cut-backs to the HLOS, the obvious candidate being the replacement of the existing 750V direct current electrification between Southampton and Reading with 25kV AC overhead line equipment.

A further drop in DfT income will result from the announcement, in October 2012, that fares rises will now be capped at RPI+1% for 2013 and 2014, instead of the RPI +3% announced in 2010. While DfT says that the revenue will be recouped by 'reprioritising existing budgets', this will create further pressure on the already squeezed SoFA.

Meanwhile, on 7 January 2013 the next major stage in the Periodic Review is due, as Network Rail publishes its Strategic Business Plan (SBP). This will represent the industry's estimates of the costs of meeting the HLOS.

Following consultation on the SBP, ORR publishes its draft determination, setting Network Rail's income for CP5 in June. And, once again following consultation, the final Determination is due to be published at the end of October.

But while the railway will keep on running, and the wheels of the regulatory machine turning, the dominant characteristic of 2013, will be not just uncertainty as to how the franchising crisis will pan out, but the sheer unpredictability facing almost all sectors of the railway industry.

Truly, a year of turmoil. ■

Table 2: Statement of funds available per year

£bn nominal	2010-11*	2014-15	2015-16	2016-17	2017-18	2018-19	Total CP5
Total funds available	3,124	3,165	3,382	3,385	3,516	3,394	16,842
Illustrative split of funding							
Franchise support	-170	-341	-166	-296	-254	-396	-1,453
Network Grant	3,294	3,506	3,548	3,681	3,770	3,789	18,294

Source: DfT, ORR *For comparison

Photo Paul Bigland

Setting the Agenda

Viewed from between the tracks of the East Coast main line, the 30 tonne main span of the new flyover at Hitchin is lifted into position on 30 June 2012. London-Cambridge trains will no longer have to cross the fast lines at Hitchin, increasing capacity and improving reliability. Network Rail

Across the Industry

Department for Transport

The Department for Transport is the Government body responsible for the transport industry. Its role in the running of the railways is to provide strategic direction and to procure rail services and projects that it specifies. Transport Scotland and the Welsh Government have devolved rail responsibilities.

The Secretary of State for Transport is responsible for determining the rail budget, setting the strategy and letting the passenger rail franchises in England and intercity services to and from Scotland and Wales. The Department also works with local and regional bodies, the rail industry and Passenger Transport Executives for major urban areas.

The McNulty Value for Money study of May 2011 put forward recommendations focused on cost reduction, new efficiencies, and methods of implementation. It estimated that annual savings of between £700m and £1bn could be made by 2019.

Justine Greening, then Secretary of State for Transport, in the Command Paper 'Reforming our Railways: Putting the Customer First' in March 2012, said, 'I believe that Government and the rail industry can and must do more for the passenger and the taxpayer.'

She said that the industry should aim to fully close the efficiency gap identified by the McNulty study by 2019. Above-inflation rises in average regulated fares would be reduced and then abolished, and the burden on the broader taxpayer purse lessened. Rail franchises would be reformed with greater transparency around costs and efficiency so that 'taxpayer subsidies are concentrated on the less profitable routes that remain crucial to communities'.

A more transparent, modern and flexible approach to fares and ticketing was promised, as well as investing in greater capacity and better connectivity, with a new national high speed rail network. A consultation was launched, inviting sub-national bodies to come forward with proposals for increased involvement in specifying and delivering rail services locally.

The five-year High Level Output Statement (HLOS) specifies what the government wants to buy from the railway in terms of safety, performance and capacity. This is accompanied by a Statement of Funds Available (SoFA) and a long term rail strategy (see article, p11). The timetable is shown in Table 1.

Transport Scotland

Transport Scotland is an agency of the Scottish Government and is accountable to Parliament and the public through Scottish Ministers. There are 350 stations in Scotland,

Table 1: Determination of outputs and funding
Control Period 5 (April 2014 to March 2019)

- September 2011: Rail industry published its proposals in the Initial Industry Plan (IIP) for Control Period 5 (CP5). This is to inform decisions to be made by the Office of Rail Regulation and governments (Westminster and Scotland).
- July 2012: HLOS and SoFA published in as part of the periodic review process.
- January 2013: Network Rail produces its Strategic Business Plan.
- June 2013: The ORR publishes its draft determination of what funds it thinks Network Rail will require to deliver what is required in CP5.
- October 2013: ORR publishes its final determination.
- March 2014: Network Rail publishes its Delivery Plan.

Moving the trains of the world.

Voith is a specialist for drive and cooling systems, control technology and Scharfenberg couplers. There is hardly a freight or passenger train that does not operate with our products, components and systems – up to complete locomotives or vehicle front ends. Be it higher speeds, more comfort, reduced fuel consumption or fewer emissions: with our wealth of experience we solve any task, however complex and challenging it may be, and offer you outstanding service – on the rails of the world.

voith.com

Setting the Agenda

used by 78.3million passengers annually. The Glasgow area is the largest commuter operation outside London and its users account for about 60pc of railway passengers in Scotland.

The Rail Directorate is responsible for securing, monitoring and managing the ScotRail franchise, which is due for renewal in 2014; long term strategic decisions about future investment; and funding and specification of where resources are targeted by Network Rail on track maintenance and investment in Scotland. Safety and the licensing of railway operators remain reserved for Westminster.

The Scottish High Level Output Statement (HLOS) runs concurrently with that for England & Wales for the period 2014-19. Aims include hourly services between Aberdeen and Inverness, taking around two hours, and a development of the Highland main line to provide an hourly service between Inverness and Perth with extensions to either Glasgow or Edinburgh. For its part, Network Rail is expected to electrify further parts of the network at a rate of 100 single track km per annum when EGIP work (see 'Key Projects' chapter) is finished. There are funding schemes for stations, freight, network improvements and level crossings, while passenger and train handling capacity at the main Edinburgh and Glasgow stations is clearly a concern.

The HLOS also includes this statement from ministers: 'It is our ambition that Scotland's railways are a source of pride, with an international reputation for efficiency and service, supporting sustainable economic growth to make Scotland a better place to live and a more competitive place to do business.

Transport Scotland also co-ordinates the National Transport Strategy and is responsible for the national concessionary travel scheme.
Transport Scotland Chief Executive David Middleton

Transport Wales
The Transport (Wales) Act 2006 conferred a general duty on the Welsh Government to promote and encourage integrated transport in Wales. Full responsibility for the Wales & Borders rail franchise became the Assembly's responsibility on 1 April 2006. The Welsh Government can specify services and regulate fares, and is responsible for the franchise's financial performance and for enhancements.

It is able to develop and fund infrastructure enhancement schemes, develop new passenger rail services, and invest in improving the journey experience for rail users. A National Transport Plan was published in December 2011.

Revenue support is given to rail links such as Cardiff-Holyhead which bring together south and north Wales and capital spending is allocated.
Director, Department for Transport Frances Duffy

Passenger Transport Executives
The six Passenger Transport Executives (PTEs) cover the former Metropolitan Counties of West Midlands (Centro), Greater Manchester, Merseyside (Merseytravel), South Yorkshire, West Yorkshire (Metro) and Tyne & Wear (Nexus).

These are statutory bodies, responsible for setting out policy and expenditure plans for public transport. They are funded by a combination of local council tax and grants from national government. They are responsible to Integrated Transport Authorities (ITAs), made up of elected representatives of the local councils.

PTEs are neither bus nor rail operators, but they do co-sign the Department for Transport's franchise agreements. They need to secure the agreement of the DfT for additional services, to be funded by themselves. Merseytravel itself lets and manages the concession for Merseyrail Electrics.

PTEs also contract for bus services which the private sector does not provide commercially, and provide local transport information.

PTEG, the Passenger Transport Executive Group, is a non-statutory body bringing together and promoting PTE and related interests.

The Northern and TransPennine franchises provide local rail services in all PTE areas other than Centro and are to be re-let in 2014/15. The PTEs have long argued for a bigger say in the planning and development of their local railways. The devolution of powers to local and accountable bodies under the Localism Act 2012 could allow a greater integration of rail with other modes - and unlock the opportunity for more investment by PTEs and others.

European Union
The common European transport policy has the objective of promoting the efficiency and competitiveness of railways through gradual liberalisation.

The First Railway Package aimed to open up the trans-European rail freight market for international goods services.

The Second Railway Package aimed to provide a legally and technically integrated European railway.

The Third Railway Package was aimed at revitalising international rail passenger services by extending competition, improving interoperability of the systems, and growing the rail freight market.

In January 2012 new regulations on interoperability affected both the conventional and high speed networks.

House of Commons Transport Committee
The Transport Committee is appointed by the House of Commons to examine the expenditure, administration and policy of the Department for Transport and its associated public bodies. It is chaired by Mrs Louise Ellman.

During the course of a year, the Committee will report on around 20 topics on which they will call formally for written evidence from interested parties. Formal reports are made to the House, which are published together with a verbatim

HS1 Ltd has the long term concession from the Government to operate, manage and maintain the high speed railway from St Pancras International to the Eurotunnel boundary. A Eurostar train crosses the Medway viaduct. Eurostar

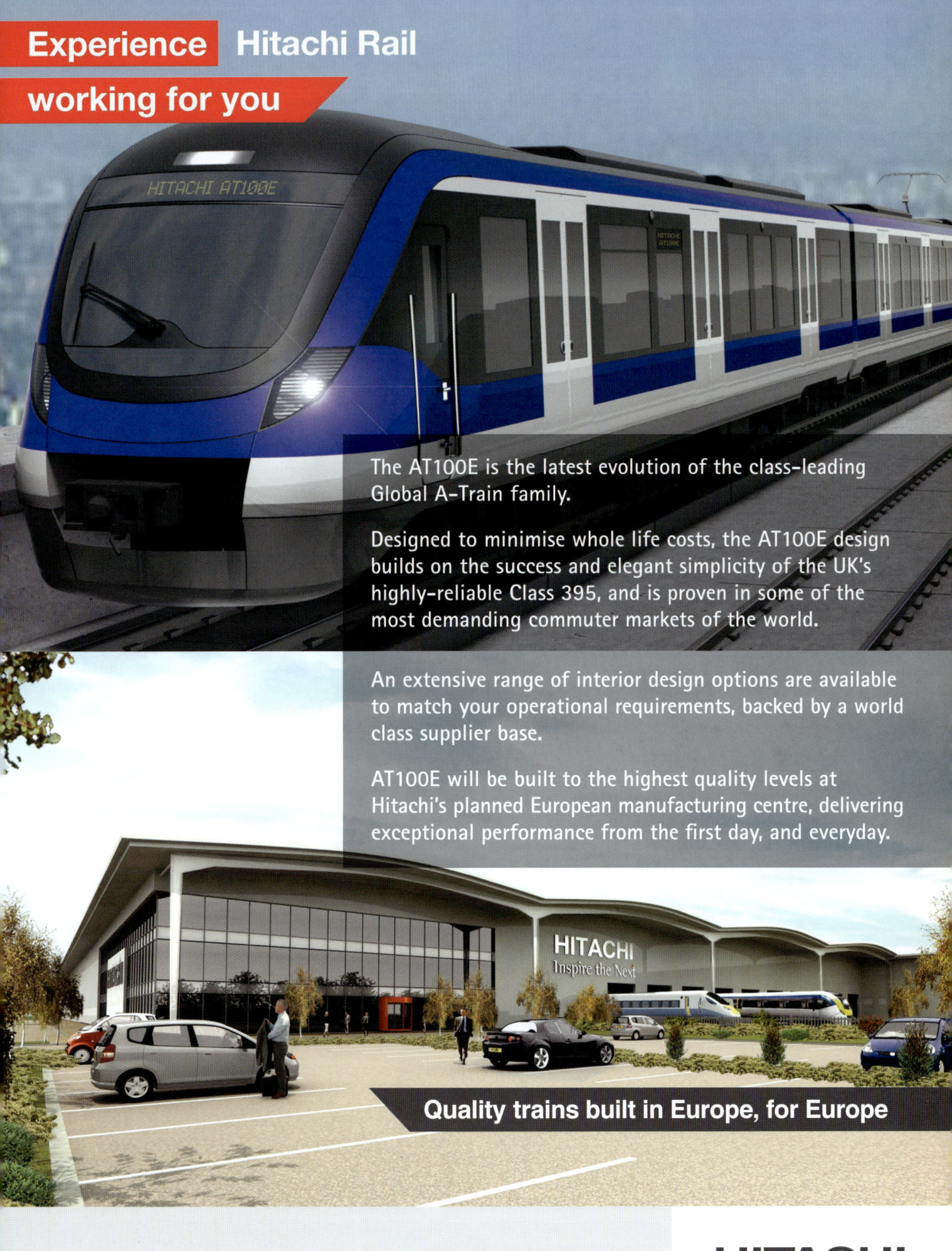

Setting the Agenda

A more transparent, modern and flexible approach to fares and ticketing is an aim of the government's rail policies. Masabi, Chiltern Railways and Atos won the Passenger Experience category of Modern Railways' Railway Industry Innovation Awards for 2012 for their m-ticketing system. An m-ticket barcode stored on a mobile phone is scanned at a station barrier. Masabi

report of the evidence sessions and the main written submissions.

Network Rail

Network Rail (NR) is the infrastructure manager. The company owns, operates, maintains and develops the railway infrastructure in Great Britain consisting of the track, signals, bridges, viaducts, level crossings and tunnels, of which it is the monopoly owner. It also owns and operates 17 large stations: with minor exceptions the others are owned by Network Rail, but are operated by the franchised train company which has the most train calls there.

The task is the delivery of a safe, reliable and efficient railway network. Network Rail is a company limited by guarantee, operating as a commercial business, but with members in place of shareholders. It aims to make surpluses from its operations, but its profits are re-invested in the infrastructure. The members do not have any financial or economic interest in the company.

Network Rail Ltd is licensed by the Secretary of State for Transport. The company is accountable to its train and freight operator customers through their access contracts and to the Office of Rail Regulation (ORR).

The company has decentralised management to its 10 Routes, each with its own Managing Director. It is also developing the practice of alliancing, forming closer bonds with its operator customers through joint management teams, but with each company retaining its own identity. This efficiency drive started with Network Rail Wessex and train operating company South West Trains.

The geographic Route Utilisation Strategies (RUSs) are being replaced by a more widely based Long Term Planning Process.

Chairman Richard Parry-Jones
Chief Executive Sir David Higgins

Office of Rail Regulation

The Office of Rail Regulation (ORR) is both an economic and safety regulator.

The principal economic regulatory functions are to regulate Network Rail's stewardship of the national rail network, to license operators of railway assets, and to approve track, station and light maintenance depot access arrangements.

Passenger train operating companies (TOCs) are granted franchises by the Department for Transport and apply to ORR for licences to operate. ORR also licenses freight train operators. TOCs and Network Rail undertake track and station access agreements and these require ORR approval. ORR also regulates High Speed 1.

The Periodic Review of the railway industry takes place every five years, the next in 2013 (PR13). Central to this is the ORR's assessment of what Network Rail must achieve, the money it requires so to do, and the incentives needed. This specifies the outputs and expenditure for Control Period 5 (2014-19).

The ORR has concurrent jurisdiction with the Office of Fair Trading to investigate potential breaches of the Competition Act 1998 in relation to the railways.

The ORR is the independent health and safety regulator for the railway industry, covering the safety of the travelling public and industry workers. HM Railway Inspectorate (HMRI) is part of ORR and its inspectors and policy advisors develop and deliver the safety strategy. ORR is the enforcing authority of the Health & Safety at Work Act 1974 and various railway specific legislation.

ORR is led by a Board appointed by the Secretary of State for Transport.

Chair Anna Walker
Chief Executive Richard Price

ATOC

ATOC's mission is to work for passenger rail operators in serving customers and supporting a prosperous railway. Set up after privatisation in 1993, ATOC (the Association of Train Operating Companies) brings together all train companies to preserve and enhance the benefits for passengers of Britain's national rail network.

ATOC provides a central clearing house for the train operators, allowing passengers to buy tickets to travel on any part of the rail network, from any station, through the Rail Settlement Plan.

A customer service operation provides information on train times, fares, reservations and service disruption across the country, through National Rail Enquiries (NRE).

A range of discounted and promotional railcards, cutting the cost of travelling by train for groups including young people, families, senior citizens and people with disabilities, are provided through Commercial activities.

Trade association activities include providing a national voice for Britain's train companies, and seeking to generate and shape policy on the railways, mainly through Policy, Operations and Engineering, together with Corporate Affairs.

Chairman Tom Smith
Chief Executive Michael Roberts

Rail Delivery Group

The creation of a Rail Delivery Group (RDG) was a recommendation of the McNulty report of May 2011. The purpose was to lead a substantial programme of change focused particularly on cost reduction, changing the industry culture, encouraging more integrated whole-system approaches where necessary, and improving the speed and effectiveness of cross-industry bodies.

Bringing industry leaders together on a voluntary basis, the RDG says it is focusing its efforts on identifying and delivering cross-industry efficiency opportunities through: collaboration in asset, programme and supply chain management; reform of contractual and regulatory arrangements; co-ordinated industry planning; production of a rail technical strategy; updating working practices by embracing advances in technology and innovation; and improvements in train procurement and utilisation.

RDG has stated that its voluntary basis may not be sustainable and it has decided that it should be formalised by creating a company limited by guarantee. An obligation would be placed on key industry players to participate in the RDG by the introduction of a licence condition requiring this.

Tim O'Toole, Chairman of the Rail Delivery Group said, 'Placing RDG on a more structured footing will enable it to take on a leadership role in which it will formulate strategies and policies for the whole industry'.

He continued, 'The Government's Command Paper expects the Rail Delivery Group to take a leadership role within the rail industry in order to drive efficiency and improve value for money for the passenger, freight customer and taxpayer. Formalising the Group will reinforce RDG's ability to fulfil this role'.

The ORR began consultation in July 2012, inviting views on the formalisation of the RDG and the

TRAM AND LIGHT RAIL COMPETENCE FOR THE UK

FLEXITY

The *BOMBARDIER* * *FLEXITY* * family encompasses the industry's most comprehensive portfolio of tram and light rail solutions, ranging from 100% low-floor trams to high-capacity light rail vehicles as well as dual-mode solutions. In the UK, operators in Blackpool, London and Manchester have opted for trams and light rail vehicles from the market leader.

The *FLEXITY* 2 trams, which have been in successful revenue service in Blackpool since April 2012, incorporate the 'best of the best', bringing the outstanding, proven features of Bombardier trams into one vehicle. In Manchester, tram operator, Transport for Greater Manchester has ordered 94 *FLEXITY SWIFT* light rail vehicles to date, which significantly ease congestion in the busy Greater Manchester city centre. In London, the Croydon Tramlink System operates 24 *FLEXITY* Swift light rail vehicles on its 28-km network. And linking the centre of London with the eastern Docklands area, the Docklands Light Railway is served by the first fully automated, driverless public transport system, operating 94 Bombardier-built vehicles proving enormously popular and reliable during the London Olympics 2012.

www.transportation.bombardier.com

*Trademark(s) of Bombardier Inc. or its subsidiaries.

BOMBARDIER
the evolution of mobility

Setting the Agenda

licence condition to enable this change.
Secretary Graham Smith

Rail Freight Group

The Rail Freight Group is the representative body of the UK rail freight industry. It has over 100 member companies, ranging from Maersk, the world's largest container shipping line, to high street retailer, Marks & Spencer. Members include customers, logistics providers, suppliers, terminal operators, ports and freight train operating companies.

RFG's aim is to promote cost effective rail solutions for freight. It is a company limited by guarantee, and all revenue is ploughed back into providing services to members. It was originally formed in 1991 to represent the views of those involved with the rail freight industry that were not British Rail.

The Rail Freight Group seeks to achieve its objectives by organising meetings and visits, by responding to consultation papers and by lobbying government, European Institutions, the Office of Rail Regulation and Network Rail.

Freight on Rail

Freight on Rail, a partnership between the rail trade unions, the rail freight industry and Campaign for Better Transport, works to promote the economic, social and environmental benefits of rail freight both nationally and locally. It advocates policy changes that support the shift to rail and provides information and help on freight related issues.

Deepsea containers remain the bedrock of the intermodal railfreight business, but domestic intermodal is growing strongly too. A DB Schenker Class 66 heads a train of low platform container wagons. Network Rail

High Speed 1

HS1 Ltd is the company with a long term concession from the Government to operate, manage and maintain HS1 as a high speed railway from St Pancras International to the Eurotunnel boundary. It must also preserve the nature and capacity of HS1.

In 2010, the Government sold the company for £2.1bn, with the concession in place. HS1 Ltd has the rights to sell access to track and stations on a commercial basis. The concession was awarded to Borealis Infrastructure and the Ontario Teachers' Pension Plan. HS1 Ltd is policed by the Office of Rail Regulation, which has concluded that it has performed well to date.

Network Rail (High Speed) is HS1 Ltd's contractor for maintenance and operation, apart from Ashford International station which is the responsibility of Eurostar International.

HS1 has physical connections with Eurotunnel, the DBS freight depot at Dollands Moor, and Network Rail at Ashford, Ebbsfleet, Ripple Lane and domestic lines north of London.

London & Continental Railways owns the infrastructure and is the freehold owner of the associated land, the company being owned directly by the Secretary of State for Transport.

In December 2040, the current concession ceases and ownership of the assets reverts to the Government. The concession may then be re-let.

A key objective of HS1 Ltd is to try attract new services, serving new destinations. Present operators are Eurostar, and Southeastern TOC for domestic services. The first revenue earning freight train was run by DB Schenker in 2011.

In 2010 Deutsche Bahn announced plans to run new services from Germany to St Pancras International using its ICE trains. Eurostar announced that it was purchasing 10 new e320 220km/h Velaro trains from Siemens, for delivery in 2014.

According to the National Audit Office, 'High Speed 1 has brought significant passenger benefits, but the assumptions on numbers were hugely optimistic. DfT is only now evaluating whether the project was value for money' (28 March 2012).

British Transport Police

British Transport Police (BTP) is the specialised police service for Britain's railways. BTP provides a service to rail operators, staff and passengers throughout England, Wales and Scotland, as well as on the London Underground, the Docklands Light Railway, Glasgow Subway, Midland Metro and London Tramlink.

Working closely with the rail industry and local police forces, BTP is divided into seven geographical areas. They oversee the daily journeys of six million passengers and 400,000 tonnes of freight over 10,000 miles of track and more than 3,000 railway stations and depots. There are over 2,800 Police Officers and 1,450 support staff.

The Force has four strategic objectives, set by its Police Authority: helping to keep the railway running, helping to make the railway safer and more secure, delivering value for money through continuous improvement, and promoting confidence in the use of the railway.
Chief Constable Andy Trotter

Railway Industry Association

The Railway Industry Association (RIA) is the trade association for UK-based suppliers of equipment and services to the rail industry world-wide. It has around 160 member companies across the whole range of railway supply. RIA is an active member of UNIFE, the trade association for the European railway supply industry.

RIA members represent the greater part of the UK railway supply industry. This includes the manufacture, leasing, component supply, maintenance and refurbishment of rolling stock, the design, manufacture, installation, maintenance and component supply of infrastructure, and specialist expertise in consultancy, training, project management and safety.
Director General: Jeremy Candfield

RSSB

RSSB is a not-for-profit company owned by the major industry stakeholders. Its primary purpose is to help the rail industry to improve continuously the level of safety where reasonably practicable; to drive out unnecessary cost; and to improve business performance.

RSSB supports the industry by managing system safety. This includes the development of the industry's Safety Risk Model (identifying all significant risks), a Precursor Indicator Model (risk from train accidents) and the SPAD ranking methodology (risk from passing signals at danger).

RSSB manages the industry's research and development programme, both of which are funded by the Department for Transport. Other activities are funded by levies on its members.

It also facilitates five System Interface Committees, which manage those between Vehicles and, respectively, Structures, Track, Train Energy, Train Control & Communications, and Other Vehicles.

Safe operation is supported by the Railway Group Standards (RGS), which are managed by RSSB on behalf of the industry. These define mandatory engineering and operational matters and include the national Rule Book. RSSB publishes an Annual Safety Performance Report.
Chief Executive Len Porter

Law Commission

Level crossings, of which there are around 8,000 in Britain, present the largest single risk of a catastrophic train accident. The Law Commission

Maintaining excellence

Day in, day out

Britain knows a thing or two about running great railways - and great trains. Luckily so does Siemens and so do the 700 highly skilled employees based at our UK traincare facilities who keep 10 fleets of Siemens trains operating at peak performance around Britain.

With trains that travel over 50 million miles nationwide each year, Siemens is proud to play its part in helping Britain maintain rail industry excellence and improve passenger comfort, day in, day out. So if you are looking for a partner that you can rely on, look no further.

Answers for mobility.

Setting the Agenda

The second phase of the Thameslink Programme, which will lead to a major capacity increase for the Thameslink cross-London route, was officially launched in October 2012. Here at London Bridge, a new viaduct (bottom right) was built in phase 1 to make two tracks available for each of the Charing Cross route and Thameslink through the Borough Market area: this will come into use when more through tracks are provided at London Bridge station. Network Rail

The privatised rail industry

Until 1994, the nationalised British Railways Board (BRB) operated what became known as the vertically integrated railway. The Board itself provided the infrastructure, owned the trains and operated the services.

Under the Railways Act 1993, these and other functions were separated. The ownership of the track went to a new company, Railtrack, which was subsequently privatised. All operators paid Railtrack access charges for the use of the track, signalling and electrification systems.

Passenger train operations were split into what initially were 26 separate franchises. They were the subject of competitive tendering, mostly for a seven year term. Franchise awards took into account the additional services and investment commitments of each bidder, and whether that company would require a subsidy or would pay a premium to the government over the franchise term.

The passenger stations were owned by Railtrack, but all except from the very largest were run by the Train Operating Companies (TOCs).

The passenger rolling stock became the property of three rolling stock companies (ROSCOs), which then leased the stock to the TOCs. This surmounted the problem of relatively short franchise terms and asset lives of around 30 years.

The freight companies were also privatised, and they owned the locomotives and any wagons which were not privately owned by customers.

Franchising was carried out by the Office of Passenger Rail Franchising (OPRAF) and various aspects of the industry including licensing were carried out by the independent Rail Regulator plus the Health & Safety Executive.

The Association of Train Operating Companies (ATOC) was created to manage passenger railway affairs such as running the National Rail Enquiry Service (NRES), Railcard schemes, and settling accounts between companies.

The last franchises were let very shortly before the 1997 General Election, which brought a change of government from Conservative to Labour. Labour said it wished to improve overall direction and planning in the industry, and created the short-lived Strategic Rail Authority (SRA). But other problems afflicted the industry, in particular the inability of some franchises to make the financial returns they had expected, plus the level and quality of maintenance and investment by Railtrack.

Rising traffic levels and the operation of many more trains led to performance problems.

These became chronic following the Hatfield derailment of 2001, caused by poor track quality. The result, according to Sir Alastair Morton, SRA Chairman at the time, was that 'the system suffered a collective nervous breakdown'. This led in turn to huge political and media driven criticism, the downfall of Railtrack, and a strong move to centralisation.

Over time, many of the franchises, including the management buy-outs, were acquired by groups active in the bus industry. More recently, franchise ownership has extended to companies from France, Germany, the Netherlands and Hong Kong.

The cost of the railway to the public purse rose fast, not least with the West Coast Route Modernisation. When the Rail Regulator ruled in 2003 on the level of access charges needed to fund Railtrack's successor, Network

and the Scottish Law Commission were expected to publish a report in 2013 recommending substantial reform of the law on this complex subject, together with a draft Bill.

Rail Accident Investigation Branch

The Rail Accident Investigation Branch (RAIB) is the UK's statutory but independent body for investigating accidents and incidents occurring on railways and tramways. It is part of the Department of Transport but functionally independent, and the Chief Inspector reports directly to the Secretary of State. An annual report is published.

The RAIB's aim is to improve the safety of the railways by determining the causes and circumstances, together with any other relevant factors. Its investigation reports are available on the web. These contain evidence based safety recommendations, aimed at reducing the likelihood of similar events in the future and mitigating their consequences.

The RAIB is not a prosecuting body and it does not apportion blame or liability. It investigates any serious railway accident, meaning those involving a derailment or collision which has an obvious impact on railway safety regulation or the management of safety. It includes those that result in the death of at least one person; that cause serious injuries to five or more persons; or that cause extensive damage to rolling stock, the infrastructure or the environment.

The RAIB may also investigate other accidents or incidents on railway property where it believes there may be significant safety lessons.

Chief Inspector Carolyn Griffiths

Passenger Focus

Passenger Focus is the consumer watchdog for Britain's rail passengers and England's bus, coach and tram passengers (outside London). Using research findings from, in particular, the Rail Passenger Survey and the Bus Passenger Survey, Passenger Focus seeks to drive change that will make a difference for passengers.

Passenger Focus is structured as an executive non-departmental public body. It is sponsored by the Department for Transport. The Scottish Executive, the Welsh Assembly Government and the Greater London Authority are each able to appoint a Board member. The organisation's independence is guaranteed by Act of Parliament.

Chief Executive Anthony Smith

The Association of Community Rail Partnerships

The Association of Community Rail Partnerships (ACoRP) is a federation of over 50 community rail partnerships and rail promotion groups, focused on practical initiatives to advance the local railway. Improved station facilities, better train services and improved integration with other forms of transport are central to the work of ACoRP and its members.

The government's Community Rail Development Strategy provides a framework in meeting social, environmental and economic objectives.

General Manager Neil Buxton

Derby & Derbyshire Rail Forum

The Derby & Derbyshire Rail Forum (DDRF) dates from 1993 and represents over 100 businesses across the East Midlands. These employ over 25,000 people and contribute £2.6bn to the local economy. The area is thought to contain the largest cluster of rail companies in the world.

As well as providing a collective voice and promoting the area's rail industry, DDRF holds quarterly networking meetings and an annual conference. DDRF has dedicated local support from local authorities and industry groups.

The Institution of Mechanical Engineers

The Railway Division of the Institution of Mechanical Engineers (IMechE) is one of eight divisions and was founded in 1969. Its scope covers research, design, development, procurement, manufacture, operation, maintenance and disposal of traction, rolling stock, fixed equipment and their components within rail, rapid transit and all forms of rail-borne guided surface transport.

Railway Civil Engineers Association

The Railway Civil Engineers Association (RCEA) is an Associated Society of the Institution of Civil Engineers, whose members are involved in the development, design, construction or maintenance of railway infrastructure. It exists to foster continuing professional development and the exchange of knowledge and experience. Presentations, meetings and visits take place on current projects and issues.

Permanent Way Institution

The Permanent Way Institution (PWI) promotes and encourages the acquisition and exchange of technical and general knowledge about the design, construction and maintenance of every type of railed track.

The PWI holds local meetings in all its geographically-based Sections, as well as arranging technical conferences and visits. Its textbooks have been the industry standard works for over half a century and members receive a widely consulted Journal.

Chief Executive Officer: David Packer

Institution of Railway Signal Engineers

The Institution of Railway Signal Engineers (IRSE) is an international organisation, active throughout the world. It is the professional institution for all those engaged or interested in railway signalling and telecommunications and allied disciplines. It aims to advance, for the public benefit, the science and practice of signal and telecommunications engineering within the industry and to maintain high standards of knowledge and competence within the profession.

Marking its centenary, '100 Years of Railway Signalling and Communications' was published by the IRSE in 2012.

Chief Executive & Secretary Colin Porter

Institution of Railway Operators

The Institution of Railway Operators (IRO) exists to advance and promote

---

Rail, this proved too much. This became a charge funded by government, since the TOCs were protected by an indemnity clause in their contracts.

The Railways Act 2005 abolished the SRA with most of its functions (including strategy, finance and the awarding of franchises) transferred to an enlarged Department for Transport. Safety policy, regulatory and enforcement functions are now the responsibility of the Office of Rail Regulation (ORR). Separately, the government set out what Network Rail was expected to deliver for the public money it receives in a High Level Output Statement (HLOS) plus a Statement of Funds Available (SoFA). The access charges review process was amended, and there was some transfer of powers and budgets to Scotland, Wales and London.

Political and public faith in the ability of the railway to contribute to capacity shortfalls in all modes, to regional economic growth, and the wellbeing of society in general, seems to be have been growing. It is now seen as a solution to problems which affect us all, rather than a problem in its own right.

High Speed 2 is being pursued by the Coalition Government, with its decision on the initial London-Birmingham section expected to be published by the end of 2012. Potentially, this leaves the existing network with greater capacity for the traffic which it can hardly accommodate at present, but completion will not be before 2026.

Localism has become a new political theme, with Network Rail pushing out more of its activities to its Route Directors, while further decentralisation of planning and perhaps some franchising has been consulted on by the DfT.

Setting the Agenda

A 21st century LED signal - the new lightweight signal head design from VMS - stands ready to replace semaphores at Yeovil Juction as part of Invensys Rail's resignalling of the Salisbury-Exeter line, commissioned in 2012. Invensys Rail

the safe and reliable operation of the railways by improving the technical and general skills, knowledge and competence of all those thus engaged.

As the industry's custodian of best practice, the IRO offers opportunities at all career stages.

At the heart of the IRO's educational provision is its Professional Development Programme, run in conjunction with Glasgow Caledonian University. This comprises the Certificate and Diploma of Higher Education in Railway Operational Management and the Degree in Railway Operational Management, all delivered through the combination of distance learning and direct tutorials. In 2012 the IRO launched a web-based lifelong learning product.

Through its seven Area Councils, the IRO also provides a full programme of local events and visits aimed at all members.
Chief Executive: Fiona Tordoff

Institution of Engineering and Technology
The Railway Network of the Institution of Engineering and Technology (IET) covers the electrical engineering aspects of the promotion, construction, regulation, operation, safety and maintenance of railways, metros, tramways and guided transport systems.

Chartered Institute of Logistics and Transport (UK)
The Chartered Institute of Logistics and Transport (CILT UK) is the professional body for individuals and organisations involved in all aspects of transport and logistics. It has some 18,000 members in many disciplines. As it is not a lobbying organisation, it is able to provide a considered and objective response on matters of transport policy. Through a structure of forums and regional groups, it provides a network for professionals to debate issues and disseminate good practice. There is a very active Strategic Rail Policy Committee in the Rail Forum, and another on Light Rail & Tram.
Chief Executive: Steve Agg

Young Railway Professionals
The Young Railway Professionals (YRP) was founded in 2009 by the appointed 'Young' representative of each Institute forming part of the Railway Engineers' Forum, who realised that there was a common interest in key events.

The intention of the YRPs is to reach out to young people who are looking at the railway as a career choice, and to those already in the industry. The aim is to inspire all of them to see the whole rail industry in context, to understand their own role, and to enable them to build links with those in other related fields.
Chairman Paul Cooper

REF
The REF (Railway Engineers' Forum) is an informal liaison grouping of the rail interest sections of eight professional institutions. The REF organises multi-disciplinary conferences, responds to consultation requests and produces statements on topical railway subjects. The REF produces a monthly resumé of professional meetings around Britain, which is available on the websites of its constituent bodies.

Railway Study Association
The Railway Study Association (RSA) was created to provide a forum for the exchange of experience, knowledge and opinion on issues relating to all aspects of the railway industry, and the part played by railways in the total transport scene. RSA membership is drawn from a wide range of backgrounds and expertise, embracing operations, engineering, business planning, project management, marketing and consultancy.

Typically, the Association holds a standard calendar of events including evening lecture style events in London, regional meetings in Birmingham, an Annual dinner, a Presidential address and an overseas study tour. These provide an arena for learning, professional development and networking.

The President for 2012/13 is Richard Morris, Director of Business and Service Continuity at Eurostar.

The annual subscription to the RSA includes copies of Modern Railways magazine. This is the house journal of the Association, which publishes papers, reports and a diary of forthcoming events.
Chairman: Jonathan Pugh

National Skills Academy for Railway Engineering (NSARE)
What skills will be required in future for those entering railway engineering as a profession? From where will they be recruited? Will there be enough of them? When will they be needed and where, in a geographical sense? At what level of expertise and in which disciplines? Who will do the training and accreditation? How will this be funded? Are these general requirements for the industry as a whole, or for specific large scale projects such as HS2 or ETCS?

These questions and a host of others are the concern of NSARE, which has a strategic role in their solution and ensuring that the industry has the necessary capabilities overall. For the two broad categories of infrastructure and rolling stock, there will always be the need for maintenance, renewal and enhancement.
Chief Executive: Gil Howarth

Rail Research UK Association
Rail Research UK Association (RRUK-A) is a partnership between the British rail industry and over 25 UK universities. It was set up in 2010 with the aims of: support and facilitation of railway research in academia; common understanding of research needs to support the rail network and its future development; identification of research, development and application opportunities in railway science and engineering; and provision of solutions to the rail industry.

Core activities are funded by RSSB and Network Rail.

Railway Research in Birmingham
The Birmingham Centre for Railway Research and Education brings together a multi-disciplinary team from across the University to tackle fundamental railway engineering problems. The team actively engage with industry, other Universities through RRUK-A, and international partners. Mission Statement: Providing fundamental scientific research, knowledge transfer and education to the international railway community.

Institute of Transport Studies, University of Leeds
The Institute of Transport Studies at Leeds is the largest of the UK academic groups involved in transport teaching and research. For more than two decades, a principal interest has been the economics of rail transport. Key research topics include demand forecasting and travel behaviour, infrastructure cost modelling, efficiency analysis and pricing, project appraisal methodology, off-track and on-track competition, and transport safety. Fostered by close links with British Rail, more recent projects have been undertaken for the European Commission, Network Rail, the DfT, ATOC, the Chinese Ministry of Railways, ORR, the World Bank, OECD and individual rail operators.

Finance and Leasing

In association with

angel Trains

Finance and Leasing

Angel Trains has been Britain's largest Rolling Stock Operating Company (ROSCO) since it was established as one of the original three ROSCOs at the time of rail privatisation. With an enviable record as a consistent, professional and innovative investor in trains, Angel Trains leases to all 21 train operating companies. It focuses its business solely on the UK, owning over 4,500 rolling stock vehicles in all. These are spread across a diverse range of vehicles, including regional, commuter and high speed passenger trains as well as freight locomotives. Angel Trains' portfolio of vehicles includes significant core fleets, including the Pendolino and Desiro, with Virgin West Coast and South West Trains respectively.

As a leading rolling stock provider, it has the ability to bring substantial private investment into the industry to finance new trains and to enhance existing stock. In keeping with its role as a whole life asset manager, the company bridges the worlds of finance and operations, and the composition of its people reflects this. Angel Trains has strength and depth in Finance, Engineering, Commercial and Customer Service. The company currently employs 111 people across its two offices in London and Derby, a third of whom are engineers.

Core services

Since 1996 the company has invested over £3bn in new trains and refurbishment programmes with an additional £70m a year spent on maintenance, working with suppliers and manufacturers such as Wabtec, Railcare and Bombardier. The company continues to support investment in new trains, and in recent years oversaw the delivery and acceptance of the 106 Pendolino vehicles for the West Coast main line and the introduction of 24 Class 172 vehicles for London Overground and Chiltern Railways. This ability to continue to provide investment and support in the UK rail industry was consolidated in 2011 with the completion of a debt refinancing programme, providing Angel Trains Group with a stable financial platform for the company to develop further. Angel Trains has already put this into practice and signed contracts to procure and finance 20 new Class 350 Desiro electric multiple-units (EMUs) worth a total of £131 million. The new rolling stock contract will see Siemens plc supply ten Class 350/3 units to strengthen the existing London Midland fleet and ten Class 350/4s to First TransPennine Express.

Whilst investing in new trains is a core part of the company's role, it is more than a leasing company. Angel Trains also manages the risks involved in the supply of rolling stock throughout its life, and the heavy maintenance, refurbishing and modernisation of existing stock. The company employs a strong and committed team whose rail experience, and depth of relationships within the industry, give it extensive trade knowledge. It is this skill, allied to innovative solutions through financing and asset management, which allows

Pendolino train on West Coast main line.

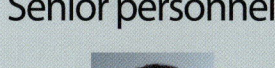

Angel Trains to add value by investing in existing fleets, to improve reliability and provide the performance and quality akin to a new build, but at significantly lower cost. As an example, Angel Trains has commenced a trial to re-traction a Class 317 unit and to undertake an interior refurbishment. The new traction equipment will improve the performance characteristics of the four car unit and improve the reliability and energy efficiency including a regenerative braking capability. The interior refurbishment will allow future operators and passengers to see and assess a modern metro-style layout. Another recent refurbishment project involved a £1.2m modification programme of the Class 180s on lease to First Great Western, First Hull Trains and Grand Central. The programme which increases the reliability of the fleets was completed in 2012.

With dedicated project managers and in-house teams of engineers with detailed knowledge of the trains, as well as development engineers able to consider future changes, Angel Trains is working on a number of projects with partners to enhance the long-term life of vehicles to the benefit of its customers. Plans include reducing wheel diameters across a range of diesel multiple-units and electric multiple-units to create longer lasting wheels, thereby reducing steel demand by around 10%, as well as exploring a number of modifications to improve track wear and improve ride performance, which is expected to result in a significant reduction in track charges for Train Operating Companies from Network Rail.

Rail for the future

Angel Trains continues to focus on delivering value for money in rolling stock procurement and whole-life asset management. This experience and knowledge has allowed it to be an active contributor to numerous industry groups and studies. Having taken a collaborative approach for many years, Angel Trains is continuing to work with stakeholders across the industry, including the Department for Transport, TOCs, manufacturers and other suppliers, Passenger Transport Executives, and the Office of Rail Regulation, to deliver sustainable value for money. This includes bringing about effective procurement of rolling stock, increased standardisation of trains and whole system cost reduction in the asset management of vehicles to the overall joint benefit of the industry. Angel Trains is also committed to looking at how their experience and technical expertise can reduce whole system and operating costs. The company is supporting the development of key modifications, including driver advisory systems, to help reduce a train's energy consumption, and is investing in projects, including energy metering for London Midland and South West Trains, to help improve energy efficiency. Over the next year these projects will form part of Angel's continuing commitment to working with partners across the rail industry to modernise and improve the UK's train fleet. ■

Senior personnel

Chief Executive Officer
Malcolm Brown

Chief Operating Officer
Kevin Tribley

Chief Financial Officer
Alan Lowe

Technical Director
Mark Hicks

Finance and Leasing

porterbrook

As one of the three major Rolling Stock Companies (ROSCOs), Porterbrook has owned and leased rolling stock and related equipment for more than 18 years and has invested over £2 billion in new equipment for the UK rail industry.

In addition Porterbrook has invested £300 million on existing fleet refurbishment and reliability work, having participated in some of the UK's most successful rolling stock enhancement programmes. This has resulted in the complete transformation of fleets such as the South West Trains-operated Class 455, giving a product that many customers believed to be equal to new trains. Although this work was undertaken a number of years ago the units still look bright and fresh but, with a programmed heavy maintenance exam due and the advent of 'Passengers of Reduced Mobility' (PRM) compliance, it is time for the Class 455s to be improved further for their continued operation beyond 2020. The work, starting at the end of 2012, is expected to be completed by November 2016.

Porterbrook's ability to provide substantial investment to the UK rail market was demonstrated by the recent announcement that it was awarded preferred bidder status for the funding of 130 new Electrostar vehicles for Southern. The vehicles will be classed 377/6 and will be configured as 5 car units; they will operate alongside the other 792 Electrostar vehicles Porterbrook already has on lease with Southern. The acquisition of these new trains will mean that since privatisation Porterbrook has either delivered or has on order more than 2,000 passenger rolling stock vehicles, giving a portfolio of almost 4,000 passenger vehicles and over 2,100 freight locomotives and wagons in use with the majority of train operators on the UK rail network.

In recognising the increasing environmental challenges being placed on the industry, Porterbrook has also been actively involved in the development of eco-friendly technologies. Initiatives include:
- trialling the installation of a Driver Advisory System (DAS) with a view to reducing energy consumption by optimising speed and power characteristics;
- trialling the deployment of a ZF Ecomat mechanical gearbox as a potential replacement fitment to quantify fuel savings, believed to be in the region of 10%; and
- the development of interior lighting technology to reduce energy consumption, maintainability and improve the internal ambience of the fleet.

Porterbrook is also involved in a joint ROSCO project to reduce the diversity of wheelset components and develop recovery procedures to significantly reduce material wastage/scrap.

As part of its continuing commitment to improving standards in the UK rail industry, Porterbrook gained accreditation to the RISAS scheme in October 2012. RISAS certification means that Porterbrook has proven its capabilities at the highest level, in the procurement of maintenance and other services needed to support its rolling stock.

The company employs a team of 90 professional staff with expertise in areas of Finance, Engineering, and Asset Management. Their extensive experience and knowledge of the rail industry gives Porterbrook a strong base to deliver value for money for the services which it offers.

Porterbrook also continues to support its accredited graduate training scheme, an arrangement which is helping bring new professionals into the UK rail industry. The scheme provides a comprehensive industry based training programme, giving a wider awareness of engineering management within the organisation.

Over the next few years further high levels of investment are required for the UK rail industry for new train projects and on-going vehicle enhancements. Porterbrook recognises that undertaking engineering improvement work and carrying out PRM compliance modification of existing stock will offer the industry substantial value for money benefits. In this context Porterbrook's aim in the coming years is to continue to develop its existing fleet and invest in new trains where the opportunity fits with its investment strategy - bearing out Porterbrook's commitment to the future of the UK rail industry. ∎

The 37 Class 350/2 EMUs operated by London Midland are leased from Porterbrook. Siemens

Among Porterbrook's newest fleets, Class 172 in service with London Midland. No 172342 arrives at Birmingham Moor Street on 17 May 2012. Tony Miles

In association with angel Trains

Eversholt owns approximately 29pc of the total current British rail fleet, with 19 main fleets of rolling stock leased to 11 passenger train operating companies. It provides a comprehensive range of rolling stock leases and asset management services for passenger and freight markets.

Eversholt Rail Group is owned by Eversholt Investment Group, a consortium consisting of investment funds managed by 3i Infrastructure plc, Morgan Stanley Infrastructure Partners, and STAR Capital Partners, which purchased the group from HSBC at the end of 2010. The transaction valued Eversholt's gross assets at approximately £2.1 billion.

The Eversholt Rail Group brand replaced that of HSBC Rail in 2010, and the business separated its maintenance, asset management and advisory services into different legal entities. The name echoes that originally given to the business - Eversholt Leasing - when privatised.

The most recent new fleet financed by Eversholt is the Class 380 electric multiple-units for ScotRail, valued at over £185m.

Transport Scotland funded the contract with Siemens and Eversholt to provide 130 new vehicles. Delivery to First ScotRail of all these trains, the first 'fly by wire' electric multiple-units in the country (using coded digital signals to control equipment), was completed in 2011, with Eversholt Rail intrinsically involved in the project management of the delivery and the acceptance of the trains.

The company is the funder (and project managed introduction) of the high profile Hitachi Class 395 trains for Southeastern high-speed services, under an investment programme worth some £260million. The trains' new depot at Ashford was developed by Eversholt in conjunction with its Depco partners in a project with an overall value of £87million, which also includes new depot facilities for existing fleets.

Another successful role for Hitachi traction on the Southeastern network is fitment of the Eversholt-owned 'Networker' Class 465/0 and 465/1 electric multiple-unit fleets with a reliable new traction system designed, built and maintained by Hitachi.

Other major Eversholt fleets include East Coast's electric trains of Class 91 locomotives and Mk4 coaches; First TransPennine Express's Class 185 Desiro diesel multiple-units; Southeastern's fleet of Class 375 and 376 Electrostars; the East Midlands Trains Class-222 'Meridian' trains built by Bombardier; and Freightliner and GB Railfreight Class-66s.

The company's portfolio also includes wagons for Freightliner and GB Railfreight, and Matisa tamping machines for Volker Rail.

Eversholt gained RISAS (Railway Industry Supplier Approval Scheme) certification in 2011.

Successful recent projects include:
- transfer of 155 Class 315 and 321 units to Abellio for the new Greater Anglia franchise.
- start of £12m Class 315 overhaul programme, including modifications to meet PRM (Persons of Reduced Mobility) legislation on the fleet by 2015.
- upgrade of CCTV system on Class 315 and 321 units, to support reliability with new equipment including remote viewing and download capability, and an innovative service contract to deliver guaranteed levels of reliability.
- early completion of Class-313 C6R overhaul and Class 465 half-life repair programmes ahead of the Olympics.
- the project to make the First ScotRail Class 320s fully compliant with the PRM requirements prior to the 2020 deadline is being delivered by Eversholt during overhauls, and includes the installation of a PRM compliant toilet. Performance post delivery has been excellent.
- Class-321 C6 overhaul has been completed to time and budget with its partners Wabtec.
- Northern - a new lease was agreed for five Class-322 units introduced on a phased basis during the second half of 2011, assisting Northern in delivering much needed additional capacity around Leeds.
- First TransPennine Express – a new lease has been agreed for leasing of 51 Class-185 units for the franchise extension until March 2015.
- Delivery of East Coast's Mk4 coaches OH2 overhaul is successfully progressing and due to finish in 2013.
- Successful award of a contract for overhaul of Class-365 C6X overhaul, including options for PRM modifications.
- Baselining the performance of Class 91 locomotives and improving them via 'glass case' examples.
- Continued delivery of bogies under a 10 year contract with Wabtec.

Senior personnel

Chief Executive Officer
Mary Kenny

Chief Financial Officer
Simon Purves

Head of Relationship Development
Steve Timothy

Head of Projects & Procurement
Richard Carrington

Head of Engineering
John Reddyhoff

Head of Asset Management
Kevin Limb

Head of Commercial and Business Services
Clive Thomas

A pair of Eversholt owned, First Capital Connect-operated Class 365s approaches Hitchin - a programme for major overhaul of the class is now under way. Network Rail

HITACHI Inspire the Next

Learn more about...

» Membership
» Area events
» Academic qualifications
» Professional Development
» CPD schemes

www.railwayoperators.co.uk

IRO The Institution of Railway Operators

**The Old Water Tower
Huddersfield Railway Station
St. Georges Square
HUDDERSFIELD
HD1 1JF**

E: info@acorp.uk.com   W: www.acorp.uk.com

'New Life for Local Lines'

In association with angel

Britain's rolling stock - who owns it?

Rolling stock allocation on the national network

All passenger rolling stock owned by the nationalised British Rail was transferred at railway privatisation to three rolling stock leasing companies (ROSCOs) in 1994. The ROSCOs were sold to the private sector two years later, with their initial leases in place.

The aim was for each ROSCO to have a reasonably diversified portfolio, with comparable fleets allocated to each ROSCO. Larger fleets of a single type were divided, and smaller fleets were allocated to a single ROSCO. This gave each ROSCO a range of customers and gave most train operating companies (TOCs) a relationship with at least two ROSCOs.

Table 1 shows how different types of passenger rolling stock were allocated to the three ROSCOs. Approximately 38 per cent of passenger rolling stock was allocated to Eversholt, 32 per cent to Angel and 30 per cent to Porterbrook. By 2009, ex-British Rail rolling stock formed approximately 60 per cent of the passenger fleet with the rest purchased since privatisation, and Angel had a 36 per cent share of the total rolling stock, Porterbrook 32 per cent and HSBC (now Eversholt) 29 per cent.

Details of passenger rolling stock ordered since privatisation are shown in the opening article in the Train Fleet Manufacture and Maintenance section of The Modern Railway.

Other rolling stock leasing companies

Another substantial lessor of rolling stock to franchised TOCs is Voyager Leasing, with a 3 per cent share of rolling stock. It was established to lease a new fleet of 'Voyager' trains to Virgin CrossCountry Trains. While it is a subsidiary of the Royal Bank of Scotland Group (RBS), ownership of the trains is equally split between the Lloyds Banking group (previously Halifax Bank of Scotland) and RBS.

Voyager Leasing originated when NatWest bank was appointed to arrange funding for the new fleet of 78 Voyager trains. The operating lease was arranged by a NatWest subsidiary, Lombard Leasing Contracts Ltd, later renamed Voyager Leasing. When NatWest was acquired by RBS (at that time the parent of Angel Trains), in order to reduce RBS's exposure to Virgin Trains, the CrossCountry fleet was evenly split and half the vehicles were sold to Halifax. RBS and Halifax then entered into head lease arrangements with Voyager Leasing.

Voyager Leasing has not undertaken any other leasing business. Though it had the same parent company as Angel Trains - RBS - it remained largely separate. It contracted Angel Trains to provide technical and other support, but these arrangements ended in 2008 when Angel was sold to a

Table 1 - Allocation of passenger vehicles at privatisation

ROSCO	DMU	EMU	HST vehicles*	Total
Angel	1,039	2,010	531	3,580
HSBC	0	2,864	1,366	4,230
Porterbrook	681	1,699	948	3,328
Total	1,720	6,573	2,845	11,138

*Diesel High Speed Trains - power cars and coaches. Source - Competition Commission

Angel Trains' Class 450 No 450011 passes a Porterbrook-owned Class 455, both operated by South West Trains, at Wimbledon. Paul Bigland

Finance and Leasing

The straight face of a Class 150/1 contrasts with the curvature of classes 185, 220 and 390 at Manchester Piccadilly (right to left). The trains are owned (respectively) by Angel Trains, Eversholt Rail Leasing, Voyager Leasing and Angel Trains, and operated by Northern, First TransPennine Express, CrossCountry and Virgin Trains.

consortium of investors. Part of the Voyager fleet is now leased by the new CrossCountry franchise, held by DB group company Arriva.

QW Rail Leasing, a joint venture between Sumitomo Mitsui Banking Corporation and National Australia Bank, leases Class 378 electric multiple units to London Overground Rail Operations Limited (LOROL) for Transport for London's London Rail Concession.

Some relatively small quantities of passenger rolling stock are owned by franchised train operating companies, most notably First Group which owns 12 HST power cars and 42 trailer vehicles, while Chiltern Railways has been acquiring around 40 Mk3 vehicles for use on London-Birmingham services.

Connex Leasing Limited purchased rolling stock for the Southeastern / SouthCentral franchises which its parent group originally won. These vehicles were subsequently purchased and leased by HSBC (now Eversholt). Wiltshire Leasing was a subsidiary of Great Western Holdings, set up to finance new Class 175s for its North Western franchise and new Class 180s for Great Western. These vehicles were subsequently purchased and leased by Angel.

Six Class 43 HST power cars and 24 trailers used by Grand Central were purchased in 2010 by Angel Trains from Sovereign Trains, a ROSCO within the same group as Grand Central.

Heathrow Express trains were purchased by the airports company BAA, including the five 5-car Class 360/2 electric multiple-units used for Heathrow Connect services. (In October 2012, the name BAA was dropped, and Heathrow airport operates as a standalone brand.)

Lloyds Banking group also owns the new £160 million fleet of 30 four-car Class-379 EMUs operated by Greater Anglia. Lloyds was also part of the consortium that purchased Porterbrook Leasing in 2008 but it exited from the consortium in 2010.

Other freight leasers

The three main ROSCOs lease out large fleets of freight and general purpose locomotives, as shown in the tables.

Other leasers are:
- Beacon Rail - leases 10 Class 66s to Freightliner and five to Direct Rail Services, and has worked with DRS on development of the 15 Class-68 'UKLight' version of Vossloh's Eurolight, ordered from Vossloh Espana in January 2012.
- Lloyds Banking group - leases the new Class 70s to Freightliner, 10 Class-66s to Freightliner, 23 Class-66s to Direct Rail Services, and is also owner of DB Schenker's Class-92s.

Ex-British Rail freight locomotives were transferred to the ownership of English, Welsh & Scottish Railway (now DB Schenker) or to Freightliner at privatisation. Direct Rail Services owns the majority of its own locomotives. In 2011, Class 66 locomotives were purchased from Eversholt Rail Leasing by GB Railfreight (4 locos) and Colas (5 locos), with five more purchased from Porterbrook by GBRf.

Several specialist companies including Harry Needle Railroad Company and Nemesis Rail also maintain smaller fleets of locomotives which are hired to UK freight and passenger operators and to Network Rail for infrastructure duties.

In continental Europe, CB Rail, a subsidiary of Lloyds Banking group, provides operating lease finance to regional passenger, freight wagon and passenger and freight locomotive rail operators. Alpha Trains - formerly Angel Trains International - manages a fleet of approximately 400 locomotives and 240 passenger trains in continental Europe.

Rolling stock - simplified guide to classes

Multiple units are self-propelled vehicles with their own driving cabs, usually comprised of one to five carriages. The main groups of ex- British Rail diesel multiple-unit (DMU) are:
- Class 142-144 'Pacers' - 4-wheeled bus-based trains.
- Class 150-159 'Sprinters'. Class 150 is the most basic, with Class 153 / 155 / 156 'Super Sprinters' for longer cross country services, and Class 158 / 159 Express units. Class 165 Networker Turbo and Class 166 Network Express fulfill similar roles.

Post privatisation, the main designs were Class 170-172 Turbostars (and similar Class 168) built by Bombardier Transportation, and less numerous Class 175 Coradia designed by Alstom. Class 180 is an Alstom design for express services, and Class 185 a Siemens design introduced for TransPennine Express. Class 220, 221 and 222 'Voyagers' and 'Meridians', built by Bombardier, also operate InterCity services.

Electric multiple-unit (EMU) Classes 313-315, 455, 456, 465, 466, 507 and 508 are ex-British Rail inner-suburban trains; Class 317-323, 365 and 442 are outer-suburban/long-distance types.

The main post-privatisation EMUs built by Alstom are Classes 334 and 458; by Bombardier, Classes 357, 375-379; and by Siemens, Classes 332, 333, 350, 380, 444 and 450.

The main electric locomotive designs are Class 91 built for East Coast high-speed services, designed for 140mph (225kph) running in semi-permanent 'InterCity225' formations; and Classes 86 and 90, used for both passenger and freight work.

The West Coast main line's Pendolino electric tilting trains are known as Class 390 and the new Southeastern high-speed trains using High Speed 1 are Class 395.

The dominant freight diesel locomotive type is the Class 66 from General Motors / Electro-Motive Diesel, designed for 75mph freight work. The Class 67 is an express locomotive from the same stable, and Class 57 is a rebuilt ex-British Rail freight and passenger locomotive. Class 70 is the new General Electric PowerHaul design for Freightliner.

Class 43 is the power car (locomotive) type used at both ends of diesel 'InterCity125' High Speed Trains: the ROSCOs also own substantial numbers of IC125 and IC225 passenger vehicles. ■

An Eversholt owned Class 185, in service with First TransPennine Express, is seen beneath the geometric patterns of Huddersfield station's roof on 8 May 2012. Paul Bigland

Finance and Leasing

Multiple-unit vehicles, HST power cars, and locomotives leased

porterbrook

Class	No of vehicles
Arriva Trains Wales	
Class 143	22
Class 150/2	52
Class 153	3
c2c Rail	
Class 357	184
Chiltern	
Class 168/0	20
Class 168/1	17
Class 168/2	21
CrossCountry	
Class 170 (2 Car)	26
Class 170 (3 Car)	48
Class 43 HST Power Car	5
East Coast	
Class 43 HST power car	9
East Midlands Trains	
Class 43 HST power car	24
Class 153	11
Class 156	22
Class 158	18

Class	No of vehicles
First Capital Connect	
Class 319/0	52
Class 319/2	28
Class 319/3	104
Class 319/4	160
Class 377	104*
*sub-leased from Southern	
First Great Western	
Class 43 HST Power Car	22
Class 57	4
Class 143	10
Class 150	34
Class 153	5
Class 158	43
First TransPennine	
Class 170 (2 Car)	18
Greater Anglia	
Class 153	5
Class 156	18
Class 170 (2 Car)	8
Class 170 (3 Car)	24
Class 90	15
London Midland	
Class 139	2

Class	No of vehicles
Class 153	8
Class 170 (2 car)	34
Class 170 (3 car)	18
Class 172 (2 car)	24
Class 172 (3 car)	45
Class 323	78
Class 350	148
Northern	
Class 144	56
Class 150	22
Class 153	8
Class 155	14
Class 156	36
Class 158	24
Class 323	51
ScotRail	
Class 158	80
Class 170 (3 car)	177
Southern	
Class 171 (2 car)	20
Class 171 (4 car)	24
Class 377	688
Class 456	48
Class 73	1

Class	No of vehicles
South West Trains	
Class 158	22
Class 159	90
Class 455	364
Class 458	120
Class 73	1
Virgin Trains	
Class 57	7
(incl. 4 sub-leased to Arriva Trains Wales)	
Freightliner	
Class 66	48
Class 86	13
Class 90	9
Network Rail	
Class 43 HST Power Car	3
Direct Rail Services	
Class 57	11
GB Railfreight	
Class 66	10

Southern's Class 455 fleet is owned by Eversholt Rail Group, whereas South West Trains Class 455s are owned by Porterbrook. Southern-operated No 455810 emerges from the elegant Knight's Hill tunnel portal as it approaches Tulse Hill on 14 June 2012. Paul Bigland

We're with the train for the entire journey.

At Angel Trains we don't just procure rolling stock, we manage it throughout its life. That's why over the last decade, we've invested £3 billion in our trains; reducing emissions, re-engineering components, modernising interiors, installing energy meters and championing such innovations as remote diagnostics. By taking this long term view, we strive to always offer the best value to our customers. No matter what the milometer says.

See what the UK's biggest rolling stock asset manager can do for you.

www.angeltrains.co.uk

Rail People
Real Expertise

Finance and Leasing

Class	No of vehicles
Chiltern	
Class 168	9
East Midlands Trains	
Class 222	143
First ScotRail	
Class 170	27
Class 318	63
Class 320	66
Class 334	120
Class 380	130
First Transpennine Express	
Class 185	153
First Capital Connect	
Class 313	132
Class 321	52
Class 365	160
Greater Anglia	
Class 315	244
Class 321	376
London Midland	
Class 321	28
Northern	
Class 158	20
Class 321	12
Class 322	20
Southeastern	
Class 375	438
Class 376	180
Class 395	174
Class 465	388
Southern	
Class 455	184
East Coast	
Class 91	31

Beacon Rail

Beacon Rail Leasing Limited was established in January 2009 by BTMU Capital Corporation as a wholly-owned subsidiary, to be its business entity for freight rolling stock leasing in the European market. Beacon Rail is a UK company headquartered in London and with an additional office in Rotterdam. The Beacon Rail portfolio at that time included 27 locomotives and 50 freight cars on lease in the UK and Belgium.

In addition, Beacon Rail ordered six new e4000 diesel electric locomotives from Vossloh Espana, for lease to CargoNet AS in Norway. Four similar Vossloh locos are leased to Eurotunnel subsidiary Europorte by Beacon.

In Britain, Beacon Rail leases ten low-emission Class 66s to Freightliner and five Class 66s to Direct Rail Services. It has worked with Direct Rail Services on the development of Vossloh Eurolight locomotives for the UK: 15 were ordered in January 2012 in a contract worth roughly Euro 50 million.

Beacon's first passenger trains were acquired in 2012 - twenty Class-313 dual-voltage electric multiple-units, retained by HSBC when it sold rolling stock company Eversholt Rail. Southern leases 19 of the Class 313s, and Network Rail has leased the 20th as the resident test train for the Hertford North Integration Facility, the new test track for different manufacturers' European Train Control system equipment.

BTMU Capital Corporation is a wholly-owned subsidiary of The Bank of Tokyo-Mitsubishi UFJ Ltd.

Class	No of vehicles
Freightliner	
Class 66	56
GB Railfreight	
Class 66	27

angel Trains

Class	No of vehicles
Arriva Trains Wales	
Class 142	30
Class 153	5
Class 158	48
Class 175 (2-car)	22
Class 175 (3-car)	48
c2c Rail	
Class 357/2	112
Chiltern	
165/0 (2-car)	56
165/0 (3-car)	33
CrossCountry	
Class 43 HST power car	5
East Coast	
Class 43 HST power car	22

Class	No of vehicles
East Midlands Trains	
Class 153	6
Class 156	8
Class 158	32
First Capital Connect	
Class 317	48
First Great Western	
Class 150	46
Class 153	9
Class 165/1 (2-car)	40
Class 165/1 (3-car)	48
Class 166	63
Class 43 HST power car	86
Grand Central	
Class 180	25
Class 43 HST power car	6
Greater Anglia	
Class 317/5	60
Class 317/6	96
Class 317/8	48
Class 360	84
Hull Trains	
Class 180	20

Class	No of vehicles
London Midland	
Class 150	6
Class 350/1	120
London Overground	
Class 172	16
Merseyrail	
Class 507	96
Class 508	81
Northern	
Class 142	158
Class 150	94
Class 153	11
Class 156	56
Class 158	52
Class 333	64
ScotRail	
Class 156	96
Class 158	14
Class 314	48
Southern	
Class 442	120
South West Trains	
Class 444	225
Class 450	508
Southeastern	
Class 465/2	64
Class 465/9	136
Class 466	86
Virgin Trains	
Class 390	574
DB Schenker	
Class 66	250
Class 67	30

The bulk of London Midland's fleet is leased from Porterbrook - including Class 170/6 Turbostar No 170634, seen descending the Lickey incline towards Bromsgrove and Worcester. Brian Morrison

Train Fleet Manufacture and Maintenance

In association with

FINNING

Train Fleet Manufacture and Maintenance

Finning (UK) Ltd
– trusted by experts

Located in Leeds with a state of the art laboratory and nearly 40 years experience, Finning fluid analysis reporting is now running at around 250,000 samples per year. Due to ongoing demand of our expertise we are ever expanding in terms of equipment, facilities and people.

Rail industries

The involvement within the rail sector has been a steady growth since the 1990s. We are now recognised as a premier supplier of fluid analysis reporting, with a rapid turnaround time and a highly skilled team, including staff who are very experienced within the rail industry.

It doesn't matter what your concept or level of complexity is "it will require lubrication and that's a fact!"

Modern Lubricants are designed to work harder for longer.

- Why do we still change oils at a set time or mileage and not on the actual condition of the oil?
- How many litres of serviceable oil have been discarded with all those costs?
- Let's make a change on how we can cut down on the amount of lubricants, man hours and have a better availability whilst retaining high standards of safety.

Condition Based Maintenance (CBM)

It has been recognised for some time that CBM is the way forward to help cut costs, spot problems early and help the environment.

Equipment Commander is a web based system that requires no additional software and is reliable and secure. The software is able to run a full CBM package to look at component wear (including wheel size and condition) component life cycles and plan your ongoing maintenance schedules. This will enable you to run your maintenance from one system covering all Oils, Fuel, Coolants and Transformers oils.

The CBM system is being looked at seriously by a number of TOCs and suppliers of maintenance and reliability monitoring systems. ∎

Finning fluid analysis reporting is now running at around 250,000 samples per year.

Component Rebuild Centre

The Finning national Component Rebuild Centre (CRC) at our Leeds site provides complete engine and power train overhaul solutions for both Cat® and other OEM products.

Our team of engineers are experts in component rebuild, from larger projects such high horsepower engine rebuilds through to fuel system and power train overhauls. We have a successful blend of time served experienced engineers and apprentices to create a high performance culture where learning is continuous. Our people are our most important asset and we employ individuals who have a positive attitude and are motivated to deliver excellent customer service. We have over 300 years of combined experience in our engineer team.

Contamination control is a critical part of our process and ensures our rebuilds maximise the life of your components and most importantly your investment. We're proud to be one of only a handful of Cat certified 5 star contamination control facilities in Europe.

All engine, hydraulic and power train units rebuilt at the CRC are tested to give you peace of mind that your unit is ready for action when it is needed. We can offer witness testing and provide a suite of testing services which now includes emissions certification.

For more information about our services and capability please call our Component Rebuild support team on 0113 201 2043.

In association with **FINNING**

The DfT contract for the Intercity Express Programme (IEP) was signed with Agility Trains, the Hitachi-led consortium, in July 2012. This impression shows a Hitachi Super Express Train at London Paddington. Hitachi

Rolling stock – investment switches to Continued Service Operation

Re-engineering of electric multiple-unit fleets is the likely focus of short term investment, writes Roger Ford

As 2012 ended, it was becoming clear that the immediate future of the rolling stock market is not about new trains but the 5,000 or so multiple-unit vehicles of the ex British Rail fleet. While the contract for the Intercity Express Programme (IEP) with Agility Trains, the Hitachi-led consortium, was eventually signed, on 25 July 2012, the procurement of the new fleet for Thameslink, also being run by the Department for Transport, dragged on through 2012. As The Modern Railway went to press, it was expected to be signed 'early in the new year'.

Throughout 2011, the rolling stock industry had appeared to be in a replay of the early years of privatisation with the number of days without a rolling stock order ticking up. Then, the hiatus lasted for 1,064 day. As the end of 2011 approached the question was whether that unhappy record would be beaten.

Clearly the government was sensitive to the likely media reaction, because on 28 December - day 1,000 - Southern ordered 26 five-car Class-377 Electrostar electric multiple-units (EMUs) from Bombardier. These were subsequently refinanced by Porterbrook Leasing, which already owns 792 Electrostar vehicles leased to Southern. The contract includes an option on a further 40 vehicles.

Prospects

With the Department for Transport declaring that in future responsibility for rolling stock procurement would return to the train operators, a number of prospective orders emerged during 2012. The most immediate was the proposal to add a pantograph car to the CrossCountry Class 220 'Voyager' diesel-electric multiple-units to create a dual mode train.

Known as e-Voyager, these trains would be able to exploit the extensive electrified mileage on the CrossCountry network where diesel traction currently runs under the wires. This proposal, which was first mooted in 2007, had subsequently become a means of providing design work for Bombardier's engineering department at Derby, following the loss of the Thameslink contract. The electric traction equipment would also provide work for Alstom's Preston factory.

However, rising costs of the conversion and falling numbers hit the business case. In September work stopped on the e-Voyager

HITACHI Inspire the Next

41

Train Fleet Manufacture and Maintenance

and it seemed unlikely to be revived in 2013.

Another proposal emerged in the Intercity West Coast (ICWC) franchise bidding. First Group planned to add 11 six-car electric trains to the fleet. These would have been either Alstom 'Baby' Pendolinos, or a new 110mph non-tilting EMU design from CAF of Spain.

Virgin's proposal was for 21 six-car 'Baby' Pendolinos to replace the 20 Class-221 tilting Voyager DEMUs in the fleet. For services beyond the electrified network, the Pendolinos would be hauled by new Vossloh diesel locomotives equipped for rapid coupling and push-pull working. It is unlikely that new rolling stock could now be procured before a new full length ICWC franchise is let in 2016.

Mentioned in our 2012 rolling stock review was the Merseyrail proposal to replace its fleet of Class 507 and 508 EMUs. A preliminary indicative notice (PIN) was issued some time ago but further progress waited until the appointment of a rolling stock director to lead procurement. An Official Journal of the European Union notice could start formal procurement later in 2013.

Crossrail

The hiatus leaves the new fleet of trains being procured by Crossrail as the only order outstanding. Procurement of the 600 vehicles was put on hold in August 2011 while the delivery schedule was revised with the aim of improving value for money.

Invitations to tender were issued to the shortlisted bidders in February 2012, with offers due to be returned during the 'Summer'. In the event bids were not submitted until 29 October, suggesting that procurement has slipped. Crossrail expects to award the contract in the second quarter of 2014.

Crossrail bidders

Bombardier Transportation (UK) Limited;
Construcciones y Auxiliar de Ferrocarriles SA (CAF);
Hitachi Rail Europe Limited;
Siemens plc.

Crossrail train fleet service introduction

Stage	Service	Date
1a	Test rolling stock, Liverpool St-Shenfield	From Dec 2016
1b	Passenger service starts, Liverpool St-Shenfield	May 2017
2	Paddington-Heathrow	May 2018
3	Paddington (Crossrail)-Abbey Wood	December 2018
4	Paddington (Crossrail)-Abbey Wood & Shenfield	May 2019
5	Maidenhead & Heathrow-Abbey Wood & Shenfield	December 2019

This fleet has been specified as a mix of 8-car and 12-car units. There are suggestions that the 12-car fixed formations could prove inflexible at less busy times.

Continued service

In the 2011 rolling stock review in The Modern Railway, we claimed that the prospects for Continued Service Operation (CSO) of the ex-British Rail fleets had 'never been brighter'. Two years on, the continued lack of new train orders has seen a growing willingness by the rolling stock companies (ROSCOs) to invest in re-engineering their EMU fleets in particular.

Such investment depends on having the confidence that the re-engineered vehicles will remain in service long enough to recoup the investment through increased rental charges. This confidence has been strengthened by the lifting of the threat of disability legislation taking fleets out of service.

Under the Disability Discrimination Act, all trains will have to comply with accessibility regulations from 1 January 2020. Initially this was seen as a 'drop-dead' date which would see large numbers of trains scrapped.

However, mass withdrawal became less likely when PRM TSI (the European Persons with Reduced Mobility Technical Specification for Interoperability) replaced the UK's Rail Vehicle Accessibility Regulations (RVAR). The less restrictive PRM TSI, particularly on certain dimensions such as door widths, reduced the cost of compliance.

Confidence

Another confidence-builder was the survey by the DfT Mobility Unit of all the ex-BR rolling stock fleets. This resulted in the creation of a schedule for each class specifying the modifications required for PRM TSI compliance.

Equally confidence-inducing was the decision by the Mobility Unit to adopt a pragmatic approach which focuses on what matters to passengers while tolerating minor discrepancies, such as a grab rail which fails to comply by a few millimetres.

As a result we are now seeing the ROSCOs combining PRM TSI compliance modifications with 'C6' heavy overhauls. For example, Porterbrook has two such programs underway, together worth over £26 million.

Under a £23 million contract, the 91 four-car Class 455 EMUs operated by South West Trains are undergoing a C6 overhaul. This follows the major refurbishment between 2004 and 2007 which featured an upgraded interior, corrosion repairs and reliability improvements.

Building on that upgrade, the C6 heavy overhaul will now prepare the Class 455 fleet for continued service operation beyond 2020. In fact, only minor changes are required because the vehicles are already largely PRM TSI compliant following earlier modifications and refurbishment.

External door sounders and internal door handles will be made compliant, and a 'call for aid' button will be fitted at both wheelchair

Eversholt Rail Group is investigating a traction system upgrade for its Class 321 and 322 EMUs. No 321903 is one of eight '321s' and '322s' operated by Northern for Metro (West Yorkshire PTE). Northern

42

EFFICIENT. TECHNOLOGY. WORLDWIDE.

LEADER®

... DRIVER ASSIST SYSTEM helps the driver operate the train in the most efficient way; saving energy by up to 20 %, reducing wear and environmental impact and maintaining better headways. | www.knorr-bremse.co.uk |

KNORR-BREMSE

Train Fleet Manufacture and Maintenance

Heavy overhaul will prepare the Porterbrook/South West Trains Class-455 fleet for continued service operation beyond 2020. SWT is carrying out the overhaul at its Bournemouth maintenance facility. Tony Miles

positions. Wheelchair ramps will also be provided.

SWT is carrying out the overhaul at its Bournemouth maintenance facility. Work will include a full exterior repaint, a major overhaul of the passenger and crew door systems, and a heavy interior clean. The programme will take four years.

A £3million upgrade of nine two-car Class 156 DMUs, leased by Porterbrook to Greater Anglia, similarly includes PRM TSI compliance modifications as part of the overhaul. A revised seating layout will provide priority seats plus two wheelchair spaces with 'call for aid' buttons. A new universal toilet is also being installed, together with a new, compliant, passenger information system. Access will be improved through the train, new external door sounders will be fitted and handrails replaced.

Three phase power

However the ultimate upgrade for the ex-British Rail EMUs is replacement of the existing traction packages with three-phase drive. This would enable regenerative braking, which on commuter services can reduce energy consumption by up to 20 per cent or more. Other benefits include lower maintenance costs and reduced time out of service for maintenance, which makes more units available. For example, regenerative braking, which uses the traction motors to slow the train minimises the use of the friction brakes. This in turn extends the life of brake pads, extending the time between changes.

Porterbrook has been developing a proposal to repower its Class 455 fleet with three-phase traction. My analysis suggests that that the energy costs savings from regenerative braking, typically about 15pc on 750 Volt third-rail electrification, will not cover the return on the investment in repowering this fleet.

This emphasises the need to quantify all the potential benefits from repowering, if the business case is to stand up. In addition to reduced maintenance costs, the improved availability could be important in a large fleet.

This potentially provides two or three additional sets for the same fleet lease rental. The key will be quantifying the value of these 'free' trains, which can be written into the repowering business case.

Eversholt Rail Group is also investigating a traction system upgrade for its fleet of Class 321 and 322 EMUs. These are 25kV AC units which, depending on the frequency of station stops, would

Table 1: Passenger train orders since 2007

Operator / financier	Class	Vehicles	Manufacturer	Delivered
London Midland / Porterbrook	350/2	148	Siemens	2009
Southern / Porterbrook	377/5	92	Bombardier	2009
Southeastern (HS1) / Eversholt	395	174	Hitachi	2009
London Overground / QW	378	228	Bombardier	2011
London Overground / Angel	172/0 DMU	16	Bombardier	2010
ScotRail / Eversholt	380	130	Siemens	2010
London Midland / Porterbrook	139*	2	Parry People Movers	2008
Virgin West Coast / Angel	390	106	Alstom	2012
Greater Anglia / Lloyds	379	120	Bombardier	2011
London Midland / Porterbrook	172/2 and /3 DMU	69	Bombardier	2011
Chiltern / Angel	172/1 DMU	8	Bombardier	2011
Southern / Porterbrook	377/6	130	Bombardier	2013
London Midland / Angel	350/3	40	Siemens	2014
TransPennine / Angel	350/4	40	Siemens	2014
DfT / Agility Trains**	IEP	596	Hitachi	2017**

*LPG/flywheel hybrid drive railcars.

**Intercity Express Programme contract provides for 369 electric and bi-mode vehicles for Great Western (first trains delivered 2017) and 227 vehicles for East Coast, with options for further 270 vehicles. Financial close announced July 2012 for Great Western elements, commercial close for East Coast. Agility Trains is DfT's contract partner for delivery, maintenance and service delivery, Hitachi is sub-contractor in charge of supplying trains and ensuring performance.

All are electric multiple-units except where shown (DMU - diesel multiple-unit)

A £3million upgrade of nine two-car Class 156 DMUs, leased by Porterbrook to Greater Anglia, includes PRM TSI compliance modifications. No 156416 forms a Sheringham-Norwich service at Cromer on 1 May 2012. Tony Miles

show a greater saving that the DC Class-455.

Vossloh Kiepe UK, formerly Transys Projects, has been awarded a feasibility study and is due to report by March 2013. ROSCO sources report that before its acquisition of Transys, Vossloh Kiepe was offering the most attractive repowering package. And Transys Projects was formed by engineers from Hunslet TPL, the company responsible for the Class 323, the first three-phase-drive EMU to gain a UK safety case.

Eversholt expects the feasibility study to take the design, safety case and associated processes for the repowering to a 'pre-concept' stage. This will enable a full evaluation of the new traction system, the installation design and certification. It will also provide accurate pricing for the re-tractioning of a pre-production Class 321 and, subsequently, fleet modification.

Angel Trains too is active in the traction upgrade field, commissioning Bombardier to convert a Class 317 EMU as a three phase traction demonstrator, with interior refurbishment to allow assessment of a modern metro-style layout.

Thus, although the new build rolling stock market is likely to remain dormant throughout 2013, the year could see the long forecast boom in Continued Service Operation become reality at last.

However, much depends on early support from the Department for Transport to underwrite the schemes, if a log-jam is to be avoided as 2020 approaches. ■

Table 2: Passenger train orders from privatisation (1994) to 2007

Original customer	Manufacturer	Type	No of vehicles	Delivery	Funder
Anglia Railways	Bombardier	Class 170 DMUs	32	2000	P
Arriva Tr Nthn	Siemens/CAF	16x4-car Class 333 EMUs	64	2000-04	A
c2c	Bombardier	74x4-car Electrostar EMUs	296	1999-2001	P,A
Central Trains[a]	Bombardier	23x2-car, 10x3-car Class 170 DMUs	76	2000-04	P
Central/Silverlink	Siemens	30x4-car Class 350/1 (West Coast route)	120	2004-05	A
Chiltern Railways	Bombardier	Class 168 DMUs	67	1998-2005	P, H
Connex (Southeastern)	Bombardier	Electrostar EMUs	618	2000-05	H
Connex / Southern	Bombardier	28x3-car, 154x4-car Electrostar EMUs	700	2002-05	P
First N Western	Alstom	16x3-car, 11x2-car Class 175 DMUs	70	2000	A
Gatwick Express	Alstom	8x8-car Juniper EMUs	64	1999	P
First Great Eastern	Siemens	21x4-car Desiro EMUs	84	2002	A
First Great Western	Alstom	14x5-car Class 180 DMUs	70	2000-01	A
Heathrow Connect	Siemens	5x5-car Class 360/2 EMUs	25	2005-06	T
Heathrow Express	CAF/Siemens	9x4-car, 5x5-car EMUs	61	1998-2002	T
Hull Trains	Bombardier	4x3-car Class 170 DMUs	12	2004	P
Hull Trains	Bombardier	4x4-car Class 222 DMUs	28	2005	H
Midland Mainline	Bombardier	17x2-car, 10x1-car Class 170 DMUs		2000-04	P
Midland Mainline	Bombardier	16x4-car, 7x9-car Class 222 DEMUs	127	2004-05	H
ScotRail	Alstom	40x3-car Class 334 Juniper EMUs	120	1999-2000	H
ScotRail	Bombardier	55x3-car Class 170 Turbostar DMUs	165	1999-2005	P, H
Southern	Bombardier	Class 170 DMUs	42	2003-04	P
South West Trains	Siemens	127 x 4-car Class 450 Desiro EMUs	508	2002-07	A
South West Trains	Bombardier	9x2-car Class 170 DMUs	18	2000-02	A
South West Trains	Siemens	45x5-car Class 444 Desiro EMUs	225	2002-05	A
TransPennine	Siemens	51x3-car Class 185 Desiro DMUs	153	2005-06	H
Virgin CrossCountry	Bombardier	40x5-car, 4x4-car tilting DEMUs	216	2001-03	V
Virgin CrossCountry	Bombardier	34x4-car non-tilting DEMUs	136	2000-02	V
Virgin West Coast	Alstom	53x9-car Pendolino trains	477	2001-05	A

Notes
[a] Plus 1x2-car and 2x3-car originally ordered by Porterbrook for spot hire
V   Halifax Bank of Scotland and Royal Bank of Scotland.
T   Owned by Heathrow Express.
A   Angel Trains
P   Porterbrook
H   HSBC Rail (Eversholt)

Train Fleet Manufacture and Maintenance

Siemens - evolution in motion

The reliable Class 350, in service with London Midland. Siemens

The railway system in the UK is the oldest in the world. Isolated local links expanded during the railway boom of the 1840s. Since that time the railway has continued to evolve: nationalisation, amalgamation, privatisation and significant changes in passenger numbers.

One thing that has remained constant is a desire for innovation and development, paving the way for greater capacity and improved services. That's where Siemens Rail Systems can make a real difference.

Siemens supplies trains to seven train operators and has built six rail depots to date in the UK. New trains are tested at Siemens' Test and Validation Centre in Germany under the same strict operating conditions found in the UK, helping to achieve seamless integration when they enter everyday operations and minimise disruption to the UK network.

Employing 700 highly skilled people across the UK, from such diverse backgrounds as yacht building and Formula 1 in addition to rail experts, Siemens currently maintains 10 fleets of trains - with more on order - that travel over 50 million miles a year in the UK.

Rolling stock service

With AC, DC and diesel variants in service across Britain, Siemens' Desiro trains regularly top the reliability league tables - the Class 350/2 fleet, operating London Midland services on the West Coast between Birmingham, Northampton and Euston, received a 'Golden Spanner' for the most reliable New Generation EMU at the end of 2011. The fleet also set a new UK record for a passenger train fleet in the four-week period to mid-September 2011, when it recorded no technical failures, equivalent to 382,240 miles between failures. Siemens also achieved the 'Supplier Excellence' award in the 2011 Rail Business Awards category that recognises 'outstanding business service to the rail industry'.

Key contributors to Siemens' ongoing success include the quality of the trains themselves; finding and valuing the right workforce; high availability of components; well designed and equipped depots; technical support teams; good collaborative relationships with train operating companies; and quality management techniques.

During 2012 a joint order for another 20 four-car Desiro sets was agreed with Siemens: 10 Class-350/3 units for London Midland and 10 Class-350/4 units for TransPennine Express's Manchester-Scotland service. Both fleets will be capable of running at 110mph.

This will bring the total number of Siemens main line

Siemens UK train fleets

Train	Configuration	Operator	Introduction
Class 332	4/5-car EMUs	Heathrow Express (14 trains)	1998
Class 333	4-car EMUs	Northern Rail (16 trains)	2000
Class 350/1	4-car Desiro EMUs	London Midland (30 trains)	2005
Class 350/2	4-car Desiro EMUs	London Midland (37 trains)	2008
Class 350/3	4-car Desiro EMUs	London Midland (10 trains)	2014
Class 350/4	4-car Desiro EMUs	First TPE (10 trains)	2013
Class 360/1	4-car Desiro EMUs	Greater Anglia (21 trains)	2003
Class 360/2	5-car Desiro EMUs	Heathrow Connect (5 trains)	2005
Class 444	5-car Desiro EMUs	South West Trains (45 trains)	2004
Class 450	4-car Desiro EMUs	South West Trains (127 trains)	2003
Class 185	3-car Desiro DMUs	First TPE (51 trains)	2006
Class 380	3/4-car Desiro EMUs	First ScotRail (38 trains)	2010
e320	16-car Velaro	Eurostar International (10 trains)	2014

Siemens and Cross London Trains were selected in June 2011 as preferred bidder for the Thameslink Rolling Stock Procurement Programme.
EMU - electric multiple-unit   DMU - diesel multiple-unit
Classes 332 and 333 were produced in conjunction with CAF.

46

commuter trains operating in the UK to over 400.

Depot evolution

Siemens trains are maintained at depots built / operated by Siemens in Acton, Northam, York, Manchester, Northampton and Glasgow, as well as in facilities shared with customers at Ilford, Neville Hill, Crewe and Strawberry Hill.

Committed to continuous improvement, and following the order placed by First TransPennine Express (FTPE) for 10 new Class 350/4 electric multiple units, Siemens has embarked on a project to electrify its depot in Ardwick, Manchester.

This will enable FTPE to introduce new services on the West Coast Main Line linking Manchester Airport to Edinburgh and Glasgow and for the trains to be maintained and accommodated at the same site as FTPE's existing diesel fleet. The electrification project and associated maintenance agreement is expected to create up to 50 new jobs in the local area.

LM 110 project

The need to improve capacity and timings on its West Coast services has seen London Midland leading an industry-wide collaborative project to make use of the Class 350 Desiro fleet's operational capability of 110mph - infrastructure issues previously restricted operation to 100mph. Siemens worked closely with Network Rail to test overhead line equipment and signalling, and with London Midland to modify on-train equipment to facilitate 110mph running. Trains of one to three 4-car units carried out a series of test runs to prove onboard systems and the interaction of pantographs and the overhead catenary. As a result London Midland will offer additional services from December 2012. By 2014, journey times will improve, such as reduction in the Nuneaton-Euston journey of 30min.

Class 380 Introduction

The 38 Class-380 Desiro EMUs supplied to ScotRail in 2010/11, have now completed over 6 million miles in service, with performance and MTIN figures showing continuous improvement. The continuing challenge for Siemens will be to meet and exceed performance predictions, by the continued development of predictive tools such as Com@ Desiro and Expert 2. These are enabling proactive fleet management, which assists the vehicle maintainer to remotely manage the effects of potential service failures. Vehicle software and hardware improvements are being developed with the collaboration of Siemens, First ScotRail and original equipment manufacturers, and improvements in fleet maintenance practices are being addressed via a programme of Reliability Centred Maintenance initiatives.

SWT partnership

A £3.2m partnership project between the South West Trains-Network Rail alliance and Siemens is expected to deliver significant performance improvements for the fleet of 45 Class 444 Desiros in service with SWT.

SWT was the first UK train operator to use state-of-the-art track 'listening' technology, RailBAM, which employs sensitive microphones at the side of the track to listen to every individual

Desiro City selected for Thameslink

Siemens and Cross London Trains (XLT) were selected in June 2011 as preferred bidder for the Thameslink Rolling Stock Procurement Programme, led by the Department for Transport.

The programme covers the delivery, maintenance and financing of around 1,200 vehicles and the construction and financing of two depots. When signed, this will represent the largest order in the commuter and regional market ever awarded to Siemens plc and the first for the Desiro City platform.

XLT is a consortium consisting of finance partners Siemens Project Ventures GmbH, Innisfree Limited and 3i Infrastructure plc.

Building on the success of the Desiro trains, Siemens has developed a new platform concept, Desiro City, for commuter, regional, and inter-regional services. The train will be environmentally friendly, with maximum flexibility, passenger safety, and comfort. The lightweight construction of the train and the bogies and an intelligent vehicle control system reduce the total energy consumption by up to 50pc compared with the predecessors.

The platform concept is a Siemens hallmark, with heavy investment in research and development of the advanced product platforms, with products then customised for each requirement.

SF7000 bogie

In December 2011 Siemens unveiled its new SF7000 bogie which is part of the Desiro City axle bearing on each train as it passes. It can detect axle defects or deterioration which can then be addressed more quickly. SWT was also first to introduce track-friendly hydraulic bushes which help reduce track damage, cut infrastructure maintenance costs and provide smoother journeys for passengers. The innovative engineering design - which combines conventional elastomer bushes with a hydraulic system - reduces the force between the wheel and the rail, ensuring better movement on curved track at low speeds.

Heathrow Express refurbishment

In May 2012 Heathrow Express unveiled the first of its refurbished Class 332 trains, manufactured by Siemens in conjunction with CAF.

The £15m upgrade of the fleet of 14 trains was aimed at making the passenger experience more like that of an airline and ensures the trains comply with new safety standards to be introduced in 2019. Heathrow Express worked closely with Siemens, Railcare and Interfleet to deliver improvements including 1+1 seating in First Class, new customer information systems, as well as updated toilets, and a new exterior livery was applied.

train design. The lighter weight bogie is optimised to meet the performance specification and functionality of the UK rail network and the requirements of the Thameslink route. The SF7000 has been under test at both the Graz plant in Austria and at Siemens' Wildenrath test centre in Germany, running on dedicated tracks night and day, accumulating one million miles of operation before passenger services commence. The SF7000 bogie has a welded bogie frame produced using state-of-the art robotic welding technology, and its lighter weight, combined with other features, is expected to contribute to reduced whole life, whole system costs and improved running behaviour for operators, including less track damage.

High speed trains

Established as a major supplier of high speed trains in Germany, Siemens has also supplied its Velaro family of high speed trains around the world - including Spain, China and Russia.

Deutsche Bahn intends to run services to London via High Speed 1 using the latest Velaros.

In October 2010, Eurostar announced that it had placed an order with Siemens for 10 Velaro e320 trainsets, to enable it to operate an expanded route network, including services from London to Cologne and Amsterdam, with a top speed of 320km/h (199mph) and total traction power of 16MW.

The new generation Velaro uses distributed traction, the modern technology now adopted by all manufacturers, with components housed beneath the train's carriages rather than in separate power cars at the end, freeing more space for passengers. To operate in new tunnels on high-speed routes in Switzerland and Italy as well as the Channel Tunnel, the Velaro needs to comply with a range of fire prevention and mitigation measures, and these are provided for as part of Siemens' basic design platform. ■

Train Fleet Manufacture and Maintenance

Leader in rail manufacturing and servicing

Bombardier Transportation is the global leader in the rail equipment manufacturing and servicing industry. It has a workforce of over 3,200 people and a presence at 31 locations throughout the UK. Bombardier has built, or has on order, around 60 per cent of the UK's rolling stock and is contracted to service over 5,200 vehicles (40 per cent of the current fleet) across the UK. Bombardier offers the broadest product portfolio in the rail industry and delivers innovative products and services that set new standards in sustainable mobility – conserve energy, protect the environment and help to improve total train performance for passengers and operators. Bombardier's global expertise ensures that the UK continues to benefit from the latest technology that the rail industry has to offer. Bombardier's rail transportation products are in operation in all major British regions, in the full range of rail services - intercity, urban and suburban, metros and light rail systems.

The award winning Bombardier ELECTROSTAR is the most successful post-privatisation EMU in the UK, with more than 2,000 vehicles entering service in the past decade. The proven ELECTROSTAR consistently excels in performance league tables, achieving some of the highest reliability figures in the country, with the star performers being the Class 357 ELECTROSTARS operated by c2c. ELECTROSTAR trains are also in operation on Southeastern, Southern, First Capital Connect, London Eastern Railways and London Overground railways, where they help to bring thousands of commuters to, from and around London daily. Bombardier also received supplier of the year award for the Global AirRail Awards for its provision of 120 state-of-the-art ELECTROSTAR cars for the Stansted Express services. In December 2011, Bombardier received a contract for the supply of 130 additional ELECTROSTAR trains for Southern to augment its existing fleet.

The Gautrain Rapid Rail Link, a brand new complete rail system in South Africa also operates UK ELECTROSTAR trains.

The CrossCountry and West Coast networks run Bombardier Voyager and Super Voyager diesel electric multiple-units (DEMUs). Bombardier Meridian DEMUs are also in daily passenger service with UK operator East Midlands Trains, and Bombardier's TURBOSTAR diesel multiple-units are in service with many operators, helping to connect towns and cities across Britain.

The 'greener' next generation TURBOSTARS are lighter and offer reduced CO2 emissions, improved fuel consumption and are over 90 per cent recyclable. More that 90 of the next-generation TURBOSTAR

ELECTROSTAR trains are in operation on London Overground, carrying thousands of commuters around London daily.

In association with **FINNING**

vehicles are now in service with Govia's London Midland franchise (these trains are owned by Porterbrook Leasing) and Transport for London and Chiltern Railways (trains owned by Angel Trains). London Midland's total *TURBOSTAR*-type fleet numbers over 120 vehicles and Chiltern's 75 vehicles.

Traffic congestion in Croydon has been significantly reduced through the use of Bombardier *FLEXITY* Swift light rail vehicles on Transport for London's Tramlink system, which are also supported by Bombardier's maintenance team, winners of an 'outstanding teamwork' award in 2012.

And linking the centre of London with the eastern Docklands area, the Docklands Light Railway is served by the first fully automated, driverless public transport system, operating 94 Bombardier-built vehicles proving enormously popular and reliable during the London Olympics 2012. Manchester's Metrolink System is benefiting from a new fleet of Bombardier *FLEXITY* Swift trams - a further 20 were ordered in 2012, which will bring the fleet to 94.

The *FLEXITY* 2 trams, which have been in successful revenue service in Blackpool since April 2012, incorporate the 'best of the best', bringing the outstanding, proven features of Bombardier trams into one vehicle.

Bombardier provides a complete portfolio of services from technical support and material solutions to total train care packages that are tailored to the needs of any operator. In the UK, Bombardier has total fleet management responsibility for, among other fleets, the diesel-electric trains operated by Arriva CrossCountry and Virgin West Coast, maintained at a purpose-built facility, Central Rivers, and a number of overnight out-station depots. Bombardier fleets throughout the UK are supported by highly skilled maintenance teams and also by *ORBITA* a leading edge predictive maintenance capability which helps operators to increase fleet utilisation, improve reliability and availability, reduce in-service failures and improve the passenger's overall journey experience.

During the Olympics, Bombardier's maintenance teams supported 800 trains on 9 key routes into London, ensuring that fleets ensuring optimum reliability and availability to meet increased demand and attracting praise from visitors, train operators and the mayor of London.

Major London Underground contract

Bombardier is a participant in the renewal of the London Underground (LU) network, as the supplier of 191 *MOVIA* metro trains for the Sub Surface Lines (SSL) upgrade, currently being built at Bombardier's production site at Derby. LU's Victoria line service has been provided entirely by new Bombardier *MOVIA* trains since July 2011 and Bombardier's system upgrade project for the line, which also includes replacement of the signalling system, will be completed in 2012.

Bombardier has also been awarded the major contract for the SSL automatic train control (ATC) signalling upgrade. The contract is valued at approximately £354million. Bombardier will provide the proven *CITYFLO* 650 ATC system, its innovative communication-based train control (CBTC) technology, similar to that running successfully on the Metro de Madrid in Spain.

The full scope of the contract is for the signalling renewal and provision of an ATC system for the four sub-surface lines (Metropolitan, District, Circle, Hammersmith & City) of the Underground network. Carrying 1.3million passengers a day, the lines comprise 40 per cent of the network and carry 25 per cent of the total ridership.

Bombardier will equip 310km of line (40km in tunnels), 113 stations, 191 trains, 49 engineering trains and six heritage trains by 2018, followed by a two-year warranty period.

Overall the upgrade will mean:
- 24 per cent more capacity on the District Line by providing space for an extra 10,000 passengers an hour.
- 27 per cent more capacity on the Metropolitan Line by providing space for an extra 9,500 passengers an hour.
- 65 per cent more capacity on the Circle and Hammersmith & City lines, delivered through new signalling, longer trains and recent improvements to service frequency. In total the upgrade will provide space for an extra 17,500 more passengers each hour.

CITYFLO 650 is a highly proven Bombardier ATC solution operating successfully around the world on 13 lines in North America, Europe and Asia. It is a moving block, CBTC system utilising modern radio-based wide-area networks to communicate between the control centre and the train. It can be installed without interruption to service and to tight timelines, provides interoperability with legacy train control systems and can be adapted to accommodate specific requirements of individual rail networks. This advanced solution is designed for improved safety, higher capacity and reliability, shorter headways between trains and reduced maintenance costs.

Recent major deliveries of *CITYFLO* 650 include Metro de Madrid Lines 1 and 6 in Spain, where a 30 per cent increase in passenger carrying capacity has been achieved, with further improvement expected, and Shenzhen Metro Line 3 in China, which was delivered in 22 months. Transit system projects are under way in Saudi Arabia and Brazil, where *CITYFLO* 650 is an integral part of the *BOMBARDIER INNOVIA* Monorail 300 system.

Bombardier Transportation's Rail Control Solutions portfolio covers the whole range of *CITYFLO* mass transit solutions, from manual to fully automatic, as well as communication-based systems. It also provides *BOMBARDIER INTERFLO* mainline solutions, from conventional to ERTMS Level 2 systems. Bombardier provides a complete palette of wayside and onboard signalling products. ■

Bombardier is a participant in the renewal of the London Underground (LU) network, as the supplier of 191 *MOVIA* metro trains for the Sub Surface Lines (SSL) upgrade. Bombardier has also been awarded the contract for the SSL automatic train control (ATC) signalling upgrade.

Train Fleet Manufacture and Maintenance

Hitachi - going for growth

Hitachi commuter train, visualised against a City of London backdrop.

2012 has been an excellent year for Hitachi Rail Europe. Over 2.4 million people from all over the world enjoyed the Hitachi Javelin® service at the London Olympic and Paralympic Games. The signing of the Intercity Express Programme marks the next phase of growth for Hitachi Rail Europe, in particular providing the green light for the new 500,000 sq ft rolling stock manufacturing facility in County Durham. Achieving breakthrough in the UK signalling and Traffic Management Systems markets provided further opportunities for growth moving forward.

The London Olympics focused the eyes of the world onto the London transport network. The Hitachi Javelin® trains provided the key shuttle service from London St Pancras directly to the games in just 7 minutes. During the Olympics approximately 1.4 million passenger journeys were made on the Class 395 trains, and around 1 million during the Paralympics. Through close partnership and co-operation with operator Southeastern and Network Rail, Hitachi's maintenance team based in Ashford, Kent, delivered 100% availability from the 29 trains and outstanding reliability to deliver the demanding Olympics and Paralympics schedule. The highly positive feedback was proof that this strategy paid off.

The growing team at Hitachi Rail Europe places the highest importance on entering true partnerships with customers, starting by listening carefully to their business requirements to delivering an end result that provides a reliable, pleasant travelling experience for passengers.

Capacity constraints remain an issue for the main railway routes in the UK and alleviating them is a main driver behind the Intercity Express Programme (IEP), which was successfully concluded between the Department for Transport (DfT) and Agility Trains in 2012.

The programme is set to bring major electrification to the Great Western Main Line. It will see Hitachi Rail Europe (as the main partner in Agility Trains) provide almost 600 Super Express Train carriages for the Great Western Main Line and the East Coast Main Line, through an agreement that focuses on reliability and availability.

The contract includes the provision of clean, reliable, and ready-for-service trains day in and day out over the contract duration of 27.5 years. To meet the very demanding reliability requirements, Hitachi will use a combination of new build maintenance facilities, for example in Bristol and Doncaster, and refurbished existing depots such as Swansea and the North Pole depot in West London.

In a major boost to the British rail industry, Hitachi Rail Europe is making a substantial investment in a rolling stock manufacturing and assembly facility in Newton Aycliffe, County Durham. The plant will be a 500,000 sq ft facility, employing over 700 people when fully operational. A part of the newly-opened European Rail Research Centre will be located within the factory to enable close collaboration.

Work on the construction of the facility starts in 2013 and the plant will be ready for the delivery of the first trains, set to go into service on the Great Western Main Line in 2017. The newly-appointed Manufacturing Plant Manager is currently focusing on ensuring that the necessary skills are available in the region to seamlessly integrate with Hitachi Rail Europe's own emphasis on training and development of staff.

The scope of the new Hitachi plant in England's North East will go well beyond delivering the Hitachi Super Express Trains for IEP. The company makes the investment with a view to its long-term strategy, which aims at

In association with **FINNING**

winning further contracts within the UK and Europe. The ideal platform for this is Hitachi's family of trains, which consists of the AT100, for inner city commuter services, the AT200, for regional requirements and the AT300, a high speed intercity train, which forms the basis for the Class 395 and the Hitachi Super Express Trains.

Rolling stock is not the only area of expertise for Hitachi Rail Europe. The company is successfully running a demonstration project for the European Train Control System (ERTCS). With regards to Traffic Management Systems (TMS), Hitachi has many years of experience of working closely with Japanese train operators to provide the technology that powers some of the busiest railway control rooms in the world. The TMS team at Hitachi Rail Europe is confident that they will be able to replicate the reliability demonstrated in other markets for the contract win to provide a prototype Traffic Management System for Network Rail. In both areas, Signalling and TMS, Hitachi Rail has many years of experience in other railway markets and is now bringing its expertise to Europe.

Alistair Dormer, Chairman and Chief Executive Officer of Hitachi Rail Europe comments: 'The year 2012 has been particularly successful for Hitachi Rail Europe. Successfully concluding the contract for the Intercity Express Programme, enables us to make a major investment in the UK, to expand our existing supplier base in Britain and continental Europe and to bid for further contracts – both here where we are headquartered and on the continent. In addition, the contract win for the prototype Traffic Management System proves that our capabilities go well beyond rolling stock.

'We are standing at the starting point of our ambitions in Europe. The IEP contract is a major enabler for us, but would be impossible without the great team, the dedication to delivering to the highest standards and of course providing outstanding technology that makes everybody proud.' ■

The AT100 train, for inner city commuter services.

The AT200, a train designed for regional requirements.

The AT300, a high speed intercity train design, which forms the basis for the Class 395 and the Hitachi Super Express Trains.

Train Fleet Manufacture and Maintenance

Alstom delivered in October 2012 the last coaches of the Pendolino capacity-increase order from the Department for Transport and Angel Trains, for the West Coast main line. The contract included the supply of four 11-car Pendolino trains and 62 additional coaches. Alstom

Alstom on track with trains and trams

Alstom has remained extremely busy as the company engages in work across its transport offering in the UK.

The H3 overhaul of the West Coast main line Pendolinos is a major engineering undertaking, and one that continues into the first half of 2013.

This is the third major overhaul that the Pendolino fleet has undergone - the first came after 750,000 miles, the second after a further 850,000, and this one comes after an additional 950,000. In order to carry out the work - which is seeing tens of thousands of components changed on each train - 100 extra staff were taken on in Longsight, Manchester. In addition the company invested in new lifting equipment and in improving the buildings and work areas.

The work is also seeing bogie overhaul on the Pendolinos. With each nine-car train having 18 bogies this was another major piece of work as the bogie workshop took them apart, overhauled them and then rebuilt them, ready to be returned to service.

In addition, the team at Longsight is also carrying out Virgin Trains''Extendolino' upgrade, with 62 carriages delivered to lengthen 31 nine-car trains into 11-car sets. The work has been going on in parallel with the H3 work. On top of that, Alstom also supplied four new 11-car Pendolinos (Nos 390154-157) for use on the West Coast main line, alongside the existing stock, with the final set arriving four months early in June.

Alstom teams have also been working hard as part of the Tramlink Nottingham consortium on the extension to the Nottingham tramway. Alstom is delivering 22 additional trams (which will be Citadis models) as well as designing and installing the track, power supply and signalling systems, with installation of the signalling equipment managed through the company's joint venture, Signalling Solutions Ltd (SSL).

Alstom's unique Appitrack machine has been brought in to help speed up the tracklaying work. The system allows for the insertion of fixings directly into slipform concrete in order to reduce tracklaying time, with the ability to lay up to 200 metres of track per day, compared with just 60-80 metres using conventional methods, reducing project timescales and disruption to local people.

Alongside the construction and design work, which is scheduled to be complete by the end of 2014, Alstom has also taken over responsibility for the maintenance of Nottingham's 15 existing trams, where the company has a 23-year maintenance contract.

Alstom has also been busy in the infrastructure market, bidding for major track and power projects on Crossrail in an ATC consortium with track specialist TSO and Costain, and bidding for Network Rail electrification works as ABC with Babcock and Costain.

In signalling, Alstom has had a successful year through SSL, picking up three of the Network Rail framework agreements, one of the ERTMS pilot studies, including the Class 313 trial vehicle fit, and one of the Traffic Management pilot studies, all of which will be delivered over the next few years.

In 2012's 'Summer of Sport', Alstom's Northern Line business helped to contribute to the success of the Olympic and Paralympic Games by working to ensure that trains ran smoothly, despite an 'extra' rush hour as spectators left the Olympic venues following the end of the events. With a reduced window of opportunity for maintenance work, the teams at Golders Green and at Morden were able to do their bit to keep the Games running smoothly.

Work at Longsight on the H3 overhaul of the Pendolinos will continue into 2013. The year will also see Appitrack in action in the UK for the first time, as work on laying the track for the 17.5km of the two extension lines in Nottingham begins in earnest. ∎

HITACHI Inspire the Next

RAIL DEPOT AND WORKSHOP EQUIPMENT

- Railcar Lifting Jacks
- Bogie Changing Systems
- Bogie Test Machines
- Under Car Handling
- Maintenance Machines
- Workshop Equipment

MECHAN
Strength Behind Technology

Davy Industrial Park
Prince of Wales Road
Sheffield S9 4EX

info@mechan.co.uk
www.mechan.co.uk
+44 (0)114 257 0563

MADE IN SHEFFIELD

Excellence In All We Do

WHEELS • AXLES • WHEELSET OVERHAUL • TYRES • GEARBOX OVERHAUL • WHEELPAN REPROFILING

LUCCHINI UK

Lucchini UK Ltd • Ashburton Industrial Park • Wheel Forge Way • Trafford Park • Manchester • M17 1EH
Tel: +44 (0)161 886 0300 • m.wood@lucchinirs.co.uk • www.lucchinirs.co.uk

LUCCHINI RS GROUP

Train Fleet Manufacture and Maintenance

CAF wins new orders

CAF - Construcciones y Auxiliar de Ferrocarriles, SA - has constructed several fleets of electric multiple-units and diesel multiple-units for railway operators in the UK and Ireland and, as we go to press, is soon to complete delivery of the final units for Edinburgh Tram, its first light-rail project in the UK.

CAF has followed this by being selected as the supplier of up to 25 five-car Urbos 3 trams for the Midland Metro in the West Midlands, in a deal worth in the region of £40 million.

The first new tram is scheduled to come into service – on the existing line – in February 2014. The city centre extension with the full new tram fleet is scheduled to be in service from March 2015. The five section air-conditioned trams will have a passenger capacity of approximately 200, with two dedicated spaces for wheelchair users, and its features will be fully compliant with the Disability Discrimination Act. Each section will have passenger information and CCTV, and passenger assistance units at each door. The trams will be similar to those commissioned in 2011 in Zaragoza: 30 metres long and 2.65 metres wide, with an aluminium body, 100% low floor access, and 70 km/h maximum speed.

Outside of light-rail the company is demonstrating its intentions for the UK market by adapting its Civity platform specifically to the UK, and being one of the pre-qualified bidders for the London Crossrail rolling stock procurement process.

CAF completed the delivery of 20 x 3 car diesel multiple-units to Translink, owner of Northern Ireland Railways, in July 2012 - under a new contract which includes maintenance by CAF Rail Services UK Ltd for a 15 year period. The new 100mph trains are arranged as 3 car units, like the Class 3000 series, but now with provision to increase the number of cars per unit in the future.

The Class 4000 is a development of the Class 3000 design, following a comprehensive review to produce a more environmentally-friendly train - adapting the traction system to meet new European emission regulations, cutting fuel consumption and maintenance costs.

Representing an investment of £105 million, the 20 Class-4000 trains are replacing 13 diesel-electric multiple-units and will operate alongside the existing fleet of 23 Class 3000 trains delivered by CAF in 2005.

Additionally CAF has also supplied 29 x 4 car Class 2900 diesel multiple-units for Iarnród Éireann (IE - Irish Rail). The most recent order supplied to IE was for 67 125mph Mk4 intercity vehicles, capable of 10 car operation but currently formed up as 8 car sets, including driving cars.

CAF provided the 14 electric multiple-unit trains for Heathrow Express, in conjunction with Siemens, and 16 trains based on that design were also supplied for West Yorkshire.

In a major research project, AVI-2015, CAF is heading a consortium of six companies to develop technologies to optimise high-speed interoperability between tracks with different signalling systems, power supplies and gauges. Major reduction in train weight, energy consumption and certification time are key aims. CAF's latest high-speed trains developed for Spanish Railways, RENFE, include adaptable bogies that can change from 1435mm standard gauge to 1664mm Spanish gauge in 3 seconds, whilst moving at up to 40km/h.

The company's products range from complete transportation systems for urban, suburban and long-distance routes and turnkey solutions, to custom-made parts and components. With several manufacturing plants in Spain, and others in North and South America, CAF has the capability and experience to manufacture using steel, aluminium or stainless steel. CAF also offers maintenance, upgrading and overhaul of vehicles and components.

A snapshot of other recent orders includes: a 400 vehicle framework contract for Civity EMU vehicles for Deutsche Bahn, 9 locos and 45 coaches for Saudi Arabian Railways (SAR) with 4 years maintenance, 16 x 6 car metro units for Metro Bucharest in Romania, 40 x 7 car trams for Tranvia Cuiaba, Brazil and 14 x 6 car metro units for Metro Calcuta, with an option for a further 7 units.

The company employs about 7,000 employees worldwide with profits for 2011 reaching 146.2 million euros, a 13% increase on 2010. ∎

An Urbos 3 tram, similar to those on order for Midland Metro.

CAF has adapted its Civity platform specifically to the UK.

urbos

NEW PLATFORM FOR CAF LIGHT METROS

Cities are a living entity that change over time. Now large cities need flexible and efficient transport services that also respect their historical and cultural traditions.

CAF meets these new demands with its **commitment to Technology**, where **Eco-design and energy savings** are essential mainstays for attaining sustainable urban transport that is well-integrated into the urban landscape.

The new range of CAF Light Metros includes technological innovations that allow for sustainability and perfect urban integration.

The **ACR System** is a CAF innovation based on ultra-capacitators that offers high speed recharge and is compatibile with other accumulation systems.

The Light Metro's energy system allows for the removal of the **catenary**, thus reducing visual impact to a minimum.

URBOS, THE TRANSPORT OF THE FUTURE THAT RESPECTS THE PAST.

CAF
www.caf.net

Train Fleet Manufacture and Maintenance

GE PowerHaul

GE Transportation unveiled its PowerHaul Series PH37ACai locomotive at InnoTrans 2012 in Berlin. It meets the latest interoperability requirements and has a full-width continental-gauge body, in contrast to Freightliner's UK-gauge version.

German open-access freight-hauler Heavy Haul Power International (HHPI) is to take delivery of a pilot batch of PowerHauls. Richard Painter, Group Chairman, 'HHPI is partnering with GE to produce a locomotive capable of operating more productive trains for bulk traffic than current technology. The focus is on "cost per tonne" which will be achieved by one train doing the job of three existing ones and therefore significantly benefiting the environment and the economy.'

The PH37ACai model, assembled by Turkish company Tülomsas, is equipped with GE's new Tempo ETCS solution, marking the first European Train Control System (ETCS) implementation on a PowerHaul Series locomotive, for 2013 deployment. The system is part of Tempo Railway Solutions, a comprehensive onboard and wayside signalling portfolio designed around a common failsafe, scalable, hardware and software platform as well as an integrated suite of engineering tools.

Freightliner Group in the United Kingdom placed the largest locomotive order in its history with GE for 30 locomotives in 2007, partnering with GE on the new design configured to take into account current and future requirements for efficiency, emissions control and safety.

The 129-ton PowerHaul Series locomotive for Freightliner is designed to generate more horsepower and tractive effort while lowering fuel consumption and greenhouse gas emissions than locomotives currently in use. The locomotive features several leading technologies to achieve this performance including the new V16-cylinder, twin-turbo PowerHaul series engine -- a product of Ecomagination, a GE-wide initiative to help meet customer demand for more energy-efficient products.

GE's unique AC individual-axle traction-control technology enables the PowerHaul Series to haul heavier loads by significantly reducing slippage on start-ups, inclines and sub-optimal track conditions. The PowerHaul Series also features dynamic braking in addition to air brakes to provide smoother handling when hauling heavier loads.

PowerHaul Series PH37ACai locomotive at InnoTrans 2012 in Berlin. GE

DRS order for Vossloh

Direct Rail Services announced in January 2012 an order for Vossloh España to supply 15 EuroLight Bo-Bo mixed traffic diesel-electric locomotives, with options for further orders.

The locomotives will have an axle load of 21.4 tonnes, and a 2,800 kW Caterpillar engine. The locomotives will be built at Vossloh's plant in Valencia, Spain, and are scheduled for delivery from late 2013.

The 'UKLight' design, developed in conjunction with Beacon Rail Leasing, is based on the EuroLight low-axleload freight and passenger locomotive design.

The locomotives will be fitted with AC traction equipment from ABB, will have a top speed of 100mph, and are designed for use on both intermodal and passenger trains. The locomotives are to meet Stage IIIA emission standards.

Vossloh España won an order from Eurotunnel rail freight subsidiary Europorte in 2011 for 12 Euro 4000 locomotives. The order has been placed by Eurosco, a subsidiary of Europorte responsible for the management of rolling stock.

The Euro 4000, designed and assembled in the Vossloh España plant in Albuixech (Valencia), is the most powerful diesel-electric locomotive manufactured in Europe, says Vossloh, specially designed to be able to run not only in France, but also in Belgium and Germany.

Equipped with an EMD (Electro-Motive Diesel) engine, the Euro 4000 can pull longer and heavier freight trains at a faster speed than competitors, says Vossloh, which substantially increases the operator's competitiveness and efficiency.

Vossloh Transportation Systems has two production plants - the Valencia location develops diesel-electric locomotives, metros, suburban trains, light rail vehicles, and train-trams. The Kiel location develops and builds diesel-hydraulic locomotives.

EMD

Bombardier Transportation's Savli rolling stock factory in Vadodara, India is to assemble locomotives for Electro-Motive Diesel, to be marketed as EMD products in southeast Asia and the Pacific. EMD expected the first locomotives to be completed in late 2013.

Electro-Motive Diesel was acquired by Progress Rail Services, a wholly-owned subsidiary of Caterpillar Inc, in August 2010 from previous owners Greenbriar Equity Group and Berkshire Partners. EMD became a wholly-owned subsidiary of Progress Rail, creating a global locomotive manufacturing and rail services company.

Progress Rail Services is one of the largest providers of rail and transit products and services in North America, including: locomotive upgrade and repair; railcar remanufacturing; trackwork; rail welding; rail repair and replacement; signal design and installation; maintenance of way equipment; parts reclamation and recycling.

EMD's Class 66 locomotive has become the UK standard, and gained acceptance more widely in Europe, with DB Schenker company Euro Cargo Rail using its Class 66 locomotives for cross-border operations between France, Belgium and Germany. They are equipped with safety systems and radios for all three countries, with automatic switching when crossing borders.

Moveright International

If you're buying a loco or wish to move a vehicle to a new railway, give us a call

Do you need to move a locomotive, coach, track machine or other item of rolling stock?
If the answer is yes, then we are who you are looking for...
We specialise in road haulage for the movement of railway vehicles and offer highly competitive rates

MOVERIGHT INTERNATIONAL LIMITED
Dunton Park, Dunton Lane, Wishaw, Sutton Coldfield, West Midlands B76 9QA
Tel: 01675 475590 (for the attention of Andrew Goodman)

We design and manufacture equipment for your trains, so who better to service it

- Engineering support
- Repairs & Overhauls
- Upgrades & Retrofits
- Reliability & LCC improvements

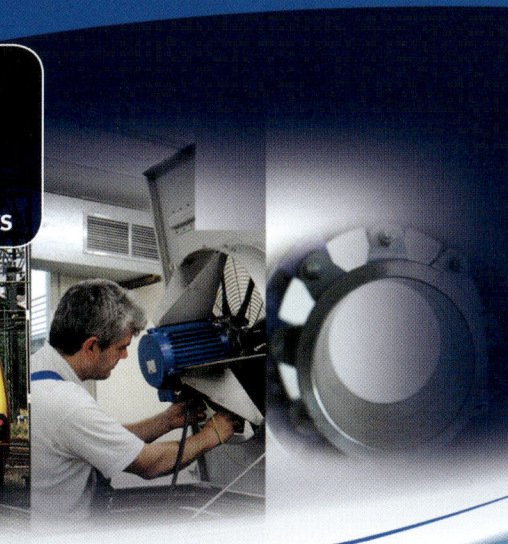

RANGE OF RAIL PRODUCTS
Brake Systems including WSP
Couplers
Doors
Pantographs
Platform Screen doors
HVAC
CCTV including DOO
Train Data Recorders
Wireless Systems

Faiveley Transport
Morpeth Wharf, Twelve Quays,
Birkenhead CH41 1LF
Tel: +44 (0) 151 649 5000
Fax: +44 (0) 151 649 5002
sales@faiveleytransport.com
www.faiveleytransport.com

Faiveley Transport
Unit 21/22 Darwell Park,
Mica Close, Amington
Tamworth
Staffordshire B774DR
Tel: +44 (0) 182 730 8430
Fax: +44 (0) 182 730 8431

For New Build Projects contact:
Kevin Smith
Sales & Marketing Manager
New Equipment & Maintenance
Tel: +44 (0)7808 364417
kevin.smith@faiveleytransport.com

For After Market Products & Services contact:
John Summers
Customer Services Manager
Tel: +44 (0)7778 590799
john.summers@faiveleytransport.com

Faiveley TRANSPORT

Train Fleet Manufacture and Maintenance

Wabtec Rail acquires LH Group

The Wabtec Rail Group, which includes Wabtec Rail Limited, Wabtec Rail Scotland and Brush Traction, has acquired LH Group, including the Hunslet Engine Company.

Based at Barton under Needwood in Staffordshire, LH is a leading supplier of multiple unit passenger rail products and services. A key part of the company's activities is the overhaul of rail vehicles, engines and transmission systems. Resources include a gear cutting and machining facility specialising in the manufacture of components, all types of gears, spiral bevels, castings, machining and reverse engineering. There is also a general fabrication facility offering a broad range of engineering capabilities.

The Hunslet Engine Company is renowned throughout the world as a designer and manufacturer of quality industrial shunting, tunnelling and specialised locomotives. With many operators finding the cost of new equipment to be prohibitive, the company also offers an extensive range of refurbishment, modernisation and repair services.

The acquisition of LH is complementary to Wabtec Rail Group's activities as one of the UK's leading rail vehicle engineering companies. Through Wabtec Rail Limited's works at Doncaster and Wabtec Rail Scotland's works at Kilmarnock in Scotland, the Group undertakes the refurbishment and maintenance of railway rolling stock, locomotives, passenger trains and freight wagons. Brush Traction's facilities at Loughborough provide locomotive overhauls, services and aftermarket components, including traction motors, electrical control systems and wheelsets.

With these acquisitions, the Wabtec Rail Group has the combined resources to provide an all-encompassing range of services to the UK rail industry.

Major refurbishment and overhaul contracts presently under way at Wabtec's works include creation of six additional Class 458 EMUs for Porterbrook, South West Trains and Alstom - reconfiguring the Class 458 fleet into 5-car units and incorporating equipment from the Class 460 fleet previously used on Gatwick Express.

Major coupler and brake interface modifications have been completed on Network Rail's Class 57/3 locomotives at Wabtec's Brush Traction facility, to enable the haulage of virtually every EMU class with full compliance to the Rule Book.

Other major contracts include the 'as new' refurbishment of the 90 Tyne & Wear Metrocars for DB Regio Tyne & Wear Ltd, and refurbishment of Mk3 vehicles for the new Chiltern Mainline services, fitting them with external sliding plug doors, with driving-van trailer vehicles also undergoing overhaul and modification. ∎

Work to reconfigure the Class 458 fleet is under way at Wabtec, Doncaster. Tony Miles

Faiveley

Faiveley Transport is a leading supplier of on-board railway systems. The group offers a complete scope of vehicle sub systems including on-board and platform screen doors, pantographs, air-conditioning, on-board electronics, brakes and coupler systems and a global Customer Service division focused on the life time support of the products.

Its product range is enhanced by on-train monitoring and recording equipment, energy metering, CCTV support equipment and passenger information systems. Hitachi chose Faiveley for the supply of the complete brake system and other equipment on the Class 395 trains for HS1.

Mechan

Mechan showcased the latest version of its Microlink jack control system at the Innotrans 2012 trade fair in Berlin, following a complete redesign to provide a technically and commercially viable solution for the synchronised lifting of multiple rail cars.

These recent upgrades to the patented jack controller have enabled Mechan to install the largest single system of lifting jacks in the UK at the Alstom Transport Traincare Centre near Manchester. Microlink's bespoke software is now operating a set of 44 jacks used to service the new 11-car Pendolino trains. It can be operated from anywhere in the chain, via a single cable, while a new touch screen panel provides constant feedback during the maintenance process.

Lucchini UK

Lucchini UK (LUK) is a wholly owned subsidiary of Lucchini RS of Italy, specialising in machining of train wheels and axles, assembly of complete wheelsets for new passenger carriages and overhaul of train wheelsets and gearboxes. Its continuous improvement programme called Lukomotion has supported the promotion of the high quality of its products, intensifying a close relationship between staff, customers and suppliers.

The company commitment is constantly to update its machining capability and non-destructive testing technology, and increase efficiency to keep up with customer demands for top quality, service and flexibility.

As well as being approved to ISO 9001, LUK is certified to IRIS and RISAS and in 2011 added ISO 14001 to its long list of approvals.

LUK is the wheelset overhaul contractor for Alstom for the Pendolino fleet.

Passenger Train Operators

In association with
SIEMENS

Passenger Train Operators

Train operating companies - index

Company	Owning group	Franchise start date	Nominal latest end date	Page no
(P) First Great Western	First	4/2006	5/2013	p69
(P) First Capital Connect	First	4/2006	9/2013	p70
*ScotRail	First	10/2004	10/2014	p71
First TransPennine Express	First/Keolis	2/2004	3/2015	p73
*First Hull Trains	First/Renaissance	-	-	p74
Southern	Govia	9/2009	7/2015	p75
Southeastern	Govia	4/2006	3/2014	p76
London Midland	Govia	11/2007	9/2015	p78
South West Trains	Stagecoach	2/2007	2/2017	p80
East Midlands Trains	Stagecoach	11/2007	3/2015	p81

A busy scene on the approaches to London Victoria: Southern's Nos 455829 and 377404 are arriving at the terminus while No 455830 and Gatwick Express Class 460 No 460006 depart. 2012 saw the last journeys for the distinctive Class 460, now being reformed with Class 458 to create a new fleet of 36 five-car units, known as Class 458/5, for South West Trains. Paul Bigland

(R) InterCity West Coast	Virgin/Stagecoach	-	-	p83
Chiltern Railways	Arriva	2/2002	12/2021	p85
Arriva Trains Wales (c)	Arriva	12/2003	10/2018	p86
Cross Country	Arriva	11/2007	3/2016	p88
*Grand Central	Arriva	-	-	p98
Northern Rail	Serco/Abellio	12/2004	4/2014	p91
*Merseyrail (a)	Serco/Abellio	7/2003	7/2028	p92
GreaterAnglia	Abellio	5/2012	7/2014	p94
(P) c2c	National Express	5/1996	5/2013	p96
East Coast	Directly Operated Railways (DfT)	11/2009	n/a	p94
*Heathrow Express	Heathrow airport	-	-	p100
*Eurostar	London & Continental (DfT)	-	-	p98
*Eurotunnel	-	-	-	p99
*London Overground Concession (b)	LOROL (MTR and Arriva)	11/2007	3/2016	p162

Notes:

(R) Interim 9 to 14 month franchise expected to begin December 2012 (award of new franchise due to start then was abandoned in October 2012).

(P) Refranchising process paused in October 2012. * Not franchised by Department for Transport.

(a) concession agreement with Merseytravel. (b) concession agreement with Transport for London.

(c) Management of franchise devolved to the Welsh Government, but DfT is the procuring authority. Many franchises can be extended by up to 28 weeks by the Department for Transport.

Passenger Train Operators

Passenger operator finances

Chris Cheek of passenger transport specialists TAS analyses train operating companies' financial performance, and finds that demand has proved robust

The past year has been another troubled one economically, but once more the passenger rail industry seems to have shrugged the downturn off in an apparently relentless rise in demand for its services – confounding those who expected history to repeat itself and deliver huge falls in patronage and revenue.

Indeed, the national figures seem to suggest that the number of people using the trains grew at a faster compound annual growth rate between 2008 and 2012 than it did in the five years before the recession. The result is that the national totals for the 12 months ended 31 March 2012 show yet another post war record, as the number of passenger kilometres rose by 5.3% to 56.9 billion. The number of passenger journeys rose by 7.9% to 1,460 million.

Looking at the individual sectors, passenger journeys on the London and South East routes grew at the fastest rate, winning another 76 million journeys – a rise of 8.3%, taking the total to 995 million. It is a sobering thought that this is higher than the total carried by the whole network as recently as a decade ago.

The longer distance operators won an extra 7.4 million passenger journeys, a rise of 6.2%, taking the total to 125 million. Outside the south east, the regional operators won another 23 million journeys, taking their total up by 7.1% to 341 million.

62

In association with SIEMENS

Results for operators in London and the South East improved quite sharply. Named after a reigning monarch, London Victoria was suitably attired for the Jubilee celebrations in June 2012. Network Rail

On the revenue front, all three sectors saw growth of 7% or more during 2011/12, as total railway revenue hit £7.2 billion – 9.2% up on the previous year. Commuter services gained 10.3%, regional routes 10.6% and InterCity services 7%. After taking rising inflation into account, revenue was ahead in real terms by around 5.6%.

This means that widespread predictions of financial problems amongst train operators have so far proved unfounded, though it is undoubtedly true that several operators continue to benefit from extra financial help from Government under the 'cap and collar' revenue sharing arrangements contained in franchise agreements.

Indeed, train operating company (TOC) profits actually rose by 7.3% in 2010/11, partially reversing previous declines, according to the latest research in the online Rail Industry Monitor publication from passenger transport specialists TAS. The figures are based on the accounts of the 19 franchised train operating companies, whose financial years ended between 31 December 2010 and 3 July 2011.

Across the TOCs as a whole, turnover was 4.4% higher at £8,801m, whilst operating profits totalled £274.6m (last year: £243m on £8,432m), to give an operating margin of 3.1% (last year: 2.9%).

Operating costs rose by 4.1% across the passenger TOCs, reaching a total of £8,527m, up from the 2009/10 total of £8,189m.

Rising wage and pension costs were one of the drivers of this, rising by 5.9% to top £2 billion for the first time. Unit labour costs rose by more than inflation, up 6.5% to £40,895. TAS estimates that labour costs in the train operating companies have risen by almost 65% in real terms since privatisation, with a workforce expanding by 12%. Unit labour costs have gone up by over 47%. However, the analysis also shows that real passenger revenue per employee has risen by almost 70% over the same period, suggesting that there have been some significant productivity gains.

The companies continued to be net earners of interest, though this figure includes pension scheme income. The total reached £45.2m, up from just £13.0m in 2009/10, but still way below the £80m or so regularly earned prior to the 2008 crash. Pre-tax profits were therefore 25.1% higher at £319.8m (2010: £255.6m). Pre-tax profit margins were 3.6% (last year: 3.0%).

Total capital expenditure by the TOCs during the year rose, from the previous year's £133.2m to £143.3m. Meanwhile, the value of net assets employed by the operators fell once again, by over 33% to just £152m, as the value of pension investments continued to fall in the wake of the ongoing economic uncertainties.

The analysis suggests that, as so often in the past, trends have not been uniform across the industry, with some sharp contrasts between sectors, and between different operators.

InterCity operators saw profits fall during the year. Total turnover rose by 2% to £3,131m, whilst operating costs were up by 2.2% to £3,100m. The resulting operating profit of £31.4m was 13.2% down on the £36m achieved in 2009/10, and was achieved at a margin of 1% (2009/10: 1.2%).

By contrast, results for operators in London and the South East improved quite sharply. Turnover growth by the companies was a hefty 7.7%, taking the total to £3,882m, whilst operating costs rose by 6.9% to £3,762m. The resulting operating profit of £121m compared with £87m in the previous year, at a margin of 3.1% (last year 2.4%).

The regional franchises (an industry category including the Wales and Scotland franchises) also show increased profit levels. Turnover rose by 1.8% to £1,788m, outstripping cost increases of 1.7%. Operating profits were 2.7% up at £122.5m (last year £119.3m), at a margin of 6.9% (6.8%).

The most profitable individual Train Operator in 2010/11 was once again TransPennine Express, the operator run by a joint venture between FirstGroup and Keolis. Next came Merseyrail Electrics, the urban railway run in joint venture by Serco and Dutch state railway company Abellio. Third came National Express Group's c2c Rail, which operates the London Tilbury & Southend franchise.

East Midlands Trains was the worst performing TOC. The Stagecoach Group business recorded an operating loss margin of 9%. Also in the red were Arriva's Cross Country operation (3.3%) and GOVIA's London Midland operation (0.9%).

In the summaries below, figures are extracted from accounts lodged at Companies House. Practice concerning the declaration and calculation of different cost and revenue items varies between train operators. This occasionally makes interpretation and reconciliation difficult: major issues are noted in the brief commentaries.

Long distance operators

Cross Country

The company's performance deteriorated sharply during the year, with operating losses increasing by more than 50%. Turnover in the business was reduced by a fall in subsidy from Government, which fell by almost £80m to £43.3m during the year. Passenger income rose by just under £20m. Operating costs were also reduced following

TAS - the Passenger Transport Specialists

For over 21 years, TAS has been providing research, analysis and advisory services to a huge range of organisations involved in passenger transport - including government at national, regional and local level, together with operators rail, light rail and bus and community transport services.

TAS's market-leading market intelligence reports have achieved a worldwide reputation for being the definitive analysis of the financial and market performance of the UK's rail, light rail and bus industries, being widely quoted by government, the media and academics. They are now available online in the hugely successful TAS Business Monitor subscription service.

Passenger transport in all its forms is about delivery providing services and networks that get customers to where they want to be quickly, comfortably and above all safely, whilst at the same time delivering value for money to customers and stakeholders.

Now an employee-owned company, TAS exists to help transport providers to deliver these services and to deliver continuous improvement in today's demanding and everchanging world.

For further details, visit www.tas.uk.net

Passenger Train Operators

Passengers throng the new western concourse at London King's Cross, completed in March 2012 after a £550m Network Rail scheme. Network Rail

the introduction of the new track access charging regime, but these were insufficient to prevent Arriva's operating losses from increasing sharply.

Period to:	31/12/2010	31/12/2009
	£000	£000
Turnover	396,470	446,172
Operating Costs	409,395	454,606
Operating Profit	(12,925)	(8,434)
Operating Margin	-3.3%	-1.9%
Turnover per Employee	£246,714	£276,267
Track Access	88,231	115,282
Rolling stock lease	45,373	44,075
Revenue Grant	43,268	111,942

First Great Western

The company saw profits improve sharply during the year, ahead of exceptional costs associated with the decision not to take advantage of the three year extension to the Greater Western franchise. The rise in profits was helped by receiving £141m worth of revenue support from the Government to offset the effects of the recession on modelled passenger revenue.

The largest increase in costs was the premium payable under the franchise agreement, which rose from £140.7m in 2009/10 to £249.9m in 2010/11. The decision not to extend the contract for a further three years and to terminate it in 2013 resulted in a provision for accelerated depreciation and other charges of £59.857m, for intangible amortisation of £7.429m and for interest costs of £5.335m.

Period to:	31/03/2011	31/03/2010
	£000	£000
Turnover	902,842	845,011
Operating Costs	887,829	834,968
Operating Profit	15,013	10,043
Operating Margin	1.7%	1.2%
Turnover per Employee	£188,721	£174,589
Track Access	132,317	131,443
Rolling stock lease	51,142	49,450
Revenue Grant	141,281	133,097

East Coast

The company improved its performance during this, the first full year of trading since taking over the East Coast franchise in November 2009.

On an estimated annualised basis, turnover was up by 4.8% and costs by around 4.6%. The growth in passenger revenue was restricted to 2% during the year, as a consequence of ongoing economic uncertainties and the effects of poor weather.

Period to:	31/03/2011	31/03/2010
	£000	£000
Turnover	644,646	231,595
Operating Costs	640,087	230,292
Operating Profit	4,559	1,303
Operating Margin	0.7%	0.6%
Turnover per Employee	£236,567	£85,712
Track Access	43,524	16,087
Rolling stock lease	83,132	31,407

West Coast

The company that has been at the heart of controversy during the autumn of 2012 saw profits fall sharply, primarily as a result of increased premium payments and reduced revenue support from the DfT. Turnover growth was driven by increased passenger revenue, whilst operating costs were affected by increased premium payments, amounting in total to £130m.

Period to:	05/03/2011	06/03/2010
	£000	£000
Turnover	876,714	848,921
Operating Costs	824,145	780,639
Operating Profit	52,569	68,282

In association with **SIEMENS**

Operating Margin	6.0 %	8.0 %
Turnover per Employee	£301,069	£283,446
Rolling stock lease	215,345	215,608
Track Access	136,700	170,552
Revenue Grant	44,791	68,120

East Midlands Trains

The company's performance deteriorated sharply during the year and substantial losses were recorded. A sharp increase in costs was driven by the premium paid to Government, coupled with a reduction in compensation payments from Network Rail, increased pension and property rental costs. Materials costs also rise, but this was offset by reduced rolling stock leasing charges. Together, these sharp rises outstripped otherwise strong revenue growth.

Period to:	30/04/2011	01/05/2010
	£000	£000
Turnover	310,180	289,232
Operating Costs	338,023	285,864
Operating Profit	(27,843)	3,368
Operating Margin	-9.0 %	1.2 %
Turnover per Employee	£152,124	£143,043
Track Access	69,294	65,378
Rolling stock lease	17,884	30,984

London and South East operators

First Capital Connect

The company recovered its position from the losses incurred in 2010, though margins remained very tight indeed. Revenue grew roughly in line with prevailing rates of inflation, whilst cost increases were restricted to below this level.

Period to:	31/03/2011	31/03/2010
	£000	£000
Turnover	497,688	481,085
Operating Costs	495,180	482,544
Operating Profit	2,508	(1,459)
Operating Margin	0.5 %	-0.3 %
Turnover per Employee	£219,536	£217,292
Rolling stock lease	39,805	38,636
Track Access	62,222	62,883
Revenue Grant	29,500	39,700

London Midland

The company's operating performance worsened during the year, as increased operating costs were recorded, resulting in operating and pre-tax losses. Turnover fell slightly, thanks largely to a £15m reduction in subsidy payments, whilst operating costs were also reduced, but by a lower amount.

Period to:	02/07/2011	03/07/2010
	£000	£000
Turnover	325,385	328,371
Operating Costs	328,405	329,882
Operating Profit	(3,020)	(1,511)
Operating Margin	-0.9 %	-0.5 %
Turnover per Employee	£138,935	£137,050
Track Access	73,559	76,159
Rolling stock lease	49,211	51,103
Revenue Grant	81,072	96,700

Southern

The company saw profits dip when compared with the previous year's summation of the results of the old and new franchises (the company having transferred in September 2009).

Turnover rose roughly in line with prevailing rates of inflation, but increased operating costs (including the premium payable to DfT, which rose by £41.1m), outstripped the growth.

Period to:	02/07/2011	03/07/2010
	£000	£000
Turnover	618,871	594,963
Operating Costs	600,390	569,218
Operating Profit	18,481	25,745
Operating Margin	3.0 %	4.3 %
Turnover per Employee	£153,224	£146,362
Track Access	123,957	135,755
Rolling stock lease	113,555	111,143

Southeastern

The company saw a strong improvement in results, returning trebled operating profits. Turnover increased sharply, thanks in part to a 6.3% rise in passenger income. Growing success on the new high speed service was reported, which helped boost the growth.

Period to:	02/07/2011	03/07/2010
	£000	£000
Turnover	728,675	631,146
Operating Costs	706,893	624,027
Operating Profit	21,782	7,119
Operating Margin	3.0 %	1.1 %
Turnover per Employee	£196,461	£168,261
Rail contracts	383,186	329,685

National Express East Anglia

The company saw a very small reduction in operating profits during the year, though this was offset by increased net finance earnings. This was the penultimate year of the franchise, which had started in 2004. The business was handed over to new operator Abellio in February 2012. In the year in question, cost increases – including a rise in the premium payable to DfT of around £12m - outstripped revenue growth, so that there was a small reduction in both cash operating profits and margins.

Period to:	31/12/2010	31/12/2009
	£000	£000
Turnover	526,281	510,265
Operating Costs	507,022	490,406
Operating Profit	19,259	19,859
Operating Margin	3.7 %	3.9 %
Turnover per Employee	£185,965	£173,089
Track Access	47,480	66,616
Rolling stock lease	107,025	102,675

c2c Rail

The company improved its performance sharply during the year, more than doubling operating and pre-tax profits. This occurred as revenue grew slightly faster than prevailing inflation, despite the ending of subsidy payments. Meanwhile, operating costs were reduced, thanks mainly to a cut in track access charges payable to Network Rail.

Period to:	31/12/2010	31/12/2009
	£000	£000
Turnover	116,095	111,464
Operating Costs	106,392	107,698
Operating Profit	9,703	3,766
Operating Margin	8.4 %	3.4 %
Turnover per Employee	£210,699	£192,511
Track Access	11,081	14,811
Rolling stock lease	22,034	22,033
Revenue Grant	0	1,095

Chiltern

The company returned to profitability in 2010, ahead of exceptional items, after several years of losses following the tunnel collapse at Beaconsfield in 2005. This was achieved despite the ending of subsidy payments during the year, and the payment of the first premium.

Meanwhile, though, the operating profit was reduced by exceptional items associated with the Evergreen 3 project of £57.4m and costs arising from the takeover of Dorridge and Solihull stations in November 2010. There were impairment charges against tangible assets £18.1m, though the company did receive project income of £56.0m.

Period to:	31/12/2010	09/01/2010
	£000	£000
Turnover	123,080	123,247
Operating Costs	119,441	127,564
Operating Profit	3,639	(4,317)
Operating Margin	3.0 %	-3.5 %
Turnover per Employee	£165,208	£166,550
Rolling stock lease	14,922	15,429
Track Access	22,814	33,092
Revenue Grant	0	4,662

London Overground

The company improved its results sharply during the year, returning an operating and pre-tax profit, compared with the previous year's pre-exceptional losses. The company continued to see huge growth in the use of its services following the opening of the new East London Line service in April 2010 – though the bulk of the revenue risk on this unique concession agreement is taken by Transport for London rather than the operator.

Period to:	31/03/2011	31/03/2010
	£000	£000
Turnover	126,253	95,889
Operating Costs	125,432	97,811
Operating Profit	821	(1,922)
Operating Margin	0.7 %	-2.0 %
Turnover per Employee	£111,827	£102,010
Track Access	10,464	11,462
Rolling stock lease	2,102	4,807
Revenue Grant	80,866	71,046

South West Trains

The company achieved a small improvement in performance during the year, with strong passenger revenue growth and £68m worth of revenue support from DfT. These offset the payment of a £177m premium as set down in the original franchise agreement. The figures vary from those shown in the statutory accounts: revenue support from the DfT is credited to the income account in this analysis, whereas the statutory accounts credit the amount received against operating costs. The different analysis is designed to make these

Passenger Train Operators

accounts comparable with other train operating companies.

Period to:	30/04/2011	01/05/2010
	£000	£000
Turnover	819,932	729,596
Operating Costs	772,393	689,457
Operating Profit	47,539	40,139
Operating Margin	5.8%	5.5%
Turnover per Employee	£188,360	£160,988
Track Access	76,396	76,957
Rolling stock lease	103,422	101,897
Revenue Grant	68,321	7,846

Regional operators

Arriva Trains Wales

The company recorded an increase of just under 11% in operating profits during the year, as the rise in operating costs was outstripped by increased turnover. The growth came from continuing patronage and revenue increases, coupled with a small £2.2m rise in subsidy payments.

Period to:	31/12/2010	31/12/2009
	£000	£000
Turnover	258,363	246,271
Operating Costs	243,026	232,444
Operating Profit	15,337	13,827
Operating Margin	5.9%	5.6%
Turnover per Employee	£128,603	£119,898
Rolling stock lease	36,650	36,426
Track Access	47,884	52,879
Revenue Grant	136,901	134,783

First ScotRail

The company saw a decline in operating profits during the year as increased costs outstripped otherwise strong revenue growth. The company saw costs rise as it introduced a fleet of new Class 380 electric trains during the year, and was involved in the reopening of the line between Airdrie and Bathgate to create a new electric train service between Edinburgh and Helensburgh Central and Milngavie, opening in December 2010.

Period to:	31/03/2011	31/03/2010
	£000	£000
Turnover	563,294	524,620
Operating Costs	547,647	504,333
Operating Profit	15,647	20,287
Operating Margin	2.8%	3.9%
Turnover per Employee	£130,001	£121,609
Rail contracts	200,175	192,482
Revenue Grant	270,029	249,163

First TransPennine

The company improved its performance further during the year, cementing its position as the UK's most profitable train operator. Revenue growth was strong at more than twice the prevailing rate of inflation, with around £12m coming from revenue and patronage growth and £10m from increased revenue grants. Meanwhile, cost increases were also substantial.

Period to:	31/03/2011	31/03/2010
	£000	£000
Turnover	268,329	246,434
Operating Costs	219,978	203,722
Operating Profit	48,351	42,712
Operating Margin	18.0%	17.3%
Turnover per Employee	£263,844	£242,077
Track Access	77,397	75,879
Rolling stock lease	47,424	37,901
Revenue Grant	109,922	99,495

Merseyrail Electrics

Revenue growth, though less than inflation, nevertheless outstripped a small rise in operating costs to produce an increase in operating and pre-tax profits during the year, ahead of exceptional costs associated with funding of the British Transport Police. Demand continues to grow strongly in Merseyside, and the company continues to deliver strong PPM and National Passenger Survey scores.

Passenger operator articles

In the following pages, statistics for train operating companies are drawn from data published by the Office of Rail Regulation and by companies themselves.

Punctuality figures are the Public Performance Measure annual average - for long distance operators, the percentage of trains arriving within ten minutes of planned arrival time at final destination; and for London & South East operators and regional, Scotland and Wales operators, the percentage arriving within 5min of planned arrival time.

For subsidy figures, negative values mean the Department for Transport was receiving payments.

Period to:	08/01/2011	09/01/2010
	£000	£000
Turnover	126,264	124,453
Operating Costs	114,352	113,913
Operating Profit	11,912	10,540
Operating Margin	9.4%	8.5%
Turnover per Employee	£107,459	£108,503
Track Access	10,613	13,814
Rolling stock lease	11,916	11,640

Northern Rail

Profits declined marginally in cash terms during the year, though it traded at slightly better margins. Revenue share continued to be paid to DfT despite the economic conditions. Turnover and costs both fell following a change in the Network Rail charging regime, which saw reductions in both grant revenue and track access charges of £53.1m. There was strong growth in passenger revenue and other income, largely from increased engineering sales to other train operating companies.

Period to:	08/01/2011	09/01/2010
	£000	£000
Turnover	571,930	614,694
Operating Costs	540,658	582,746
Operating Profit	31,272	31,948
Operating Margin	5.5%	5.2%
Turnover per Employee	£119,801	£129,355
Track Access	125,258	166,971
Rolling stock lease	34,340	35,531
Revenue Grant	339,883	390,069

Non franchised operators

Hull Trains

The company returned to profitability during the year, as income grew but costs were reduced sharply. The directors report that they continued to experience problems with the Class 180 train sets which were fully refurbished during the year. However the business did carry more than 750,000 passengers during the year - a new record and virtually a tenfold increase compared with the company's first year total of 80,000 a decade earlier.

Period to:	31/03/2011	31/03/2010
	£000	£000
Turnover	21,743	21,160
Operating Costs	20,008	23,034
Operating Profit	1,735	(1,874)
Operating Margin	8.0%	-8.9%
Turnover per Employee	£219,626	£218,144
Rolling stock lease	1,934	1,713

Eurostar

The accounts were drawn for the period to 30 August 2010 to reflect the major change in the nature and structure of the business which was completed at that date. Whereas the company previously only operated the UK share of the services, from 31 August 2010, Eurostar International Ltd owns and operates all the assets associated with the Eurostar train services, and is co-owned by London & Continental Railways (40%), SNCF (55%) and SNCB (5%). The company improved its performance during the first part of the year, recording reduced operating losses ahead of exceptional items. In its first trading period, the reconstructed business saw previous substantial losses all but eliminated.

Period to:	31/12/2010	30/08/2010
	£000	£000
Turnover	252,900	209,400
Operating Costs	253,400	243,500
Operating Profit	(600)	(34,100)
Operating Margin	-0.2%	-16.3%
Turnover per Employee	£148,765	£177,157

Period to:	30/08/2010	31/12/2009
	£000	£000
Turnover	209,400	316,200
Operating Costs	243,500	412,500
Operating Profit	(34,100)	(96,300)
Operating Margin	-16.3%	-30.5%
Turnover per Employee	£177,157	£243,418

Grand Central

The company achieved a further improvement in its results during the year, though it continued to make heavy losses. This was the first full year of operation of the full network of Bradford and Sunderland services. The company was purchased from its original owners by Arriva in November 2011.

Period to:	31/03/2011	31/12/2009
	£000	£000
Turnover	18,959	11,580
Operating Costs	25,762	18,006
Operating Profit	(6,803)	(6,426)
Operating Margin	-35.9%	-55.5%
Turnover per Employee	£151,673	£152,373
Rolling stock lease	5,236	1,185

Vossloh Kiepe UK

vossloh
KIEPE

It's not what we do.
It's the way that
we do it.

As the industry's leaders in integration engineering and rolling stock enhancement, our turnkey service gets enhanced trains back into service fast.

Just to reassure you, our RISAS certification gives Vossloh Kiepe UK the highest level of second party assurance of systems and competence available in the industry.

But it's our specialist expertise, and the calibre of our engineers themselves, that we're most proud of.

Our engineers have a detailed knowledge of new and legacy rolling stock that enables them to refine the design of even the most complex modifications. Your objectives become their objectives and they're single-mindedly focused on getting each project completed right first time.

To us, that's not difficult.

It's the way we've always done it.

Vossloh Kiepe UK Ltd
2 Priestley Wharf, Holt St, Aston, Birmingham B7 4BN
T +44 (0)121 359 7777 E enquiries@vkb.vossloh.com
www.vossloh-kiepe.co.uk

RISAS
Railway Industry Supplier Approval Scheme

BSI FS 30678

Link-up Registered

Passenger Train Operators

In association with **SIEMENS**

FirstGroup

FirstGroup is the largest rail operator in Britain, operating almost a quarter of the rail market. Its long distance, regional and commuter rail companies carry more than 300 million passengers a year (year to 31 March 2012), an increase of 40m since 2006/07 when the current franchise portfolio started operation.

The UK Rail division has some 13,000 employees and around 2,800 vehicles. The division includes four franchises: First Capital Connect; First Great Western; First ScotRail; and First TransPennine Express. Hull Trains is a non-franchised open-access operator, in which First has an 80pc share, resulting from the purchase of GB Railways in 2003. FirstGroup also operates London Tramlink on behalf of TfL, and operates passenger services in the Oresund region of Denmark in partnership with Danish State Railways. First's other major operations are in UK Bus and North America.

UK Rail revenue increased by 10.4pc in 2011/12 to £2,506.1m (2010/11: £2,269.8m) and operating profit was £110.5m (2010/11: £108.7m). Like-for-like passenger revenue increased by 8.4pc, reflecting strong volume growth across all its train companies.

FirstGroup has introduced nearly 750 new rolling stock vehicles, with punctuality and performance increasing across its franchises since they commenced operation.

The group companies played their part in the successful transport operation for the London 2012 Games, with First Great Western running a shuttle service connecting to buses at Slough station for rowing events, and First Capital Connect providing over a million extra seats during the Games and establishing a 24/7 customer support centre which has now become permanent.

FirstGroup was the only company shortlisted for all four franchises out to tender in 2012. UK Rail Managing Director is Vernon Barker, previously Managing Director of First TransPennine Express.

First Great Western

Seven year franchise from 1 April 2006

First Great Western runs services between London Paddington, the South and West of England and South Wales.

FirstGroup in 2011 decided not to take up a contractually permitted three-year extension to the franchise. This enabled the Department for Transport to develop plans for a longer term franchise taking account of major schemes, including electrification, Crossrail, and introduction of Intercity Express Programme trains. First was shortlisted for this longer term franchise.

The company has continued to work to improve performance and customer service and in the Spring 2012 National Passenger survey maintained overall customer satisfaction levels despite the extent of infrastructure projects. During the London 2012 Games, FGW transported about 10,000 people a day to London; 5,000 and 2,500 a day from Slough and Maidenhead respectively to rowing events at Eton Dorney; 10,000 to cycling events around Dorking, and 25,000 to football events at Cardiff.

FGW successfully provided 48 additional carriages as part of the third capacity upgrade agreed with the DfT in November 2011, designed to reduce crowding on peak services. FGW significantly reduced the number of trains carrying passengers in excess of capacity in 2012 and further improvements were expected.

15 former High Speed Train buffet cars were converted to Standard Class passenger vehicles, and by splitting one HST set, FGW has been able to add an extra Standard carriage to all HSTs that previously had seven coaches. Five Class 180 five-car trains have been reintroduced after extensive refurbishment and deployed on the North Cotswold line. Trains released are strengthening the busiest Thames Valley services. Two 3-car Class 150 DMUs previously with London Midland have also been leased for weekday commuter services between Reading and Basingstoke, increasing peak capacity by around 12pc. Two Class 150 vehicles were leased to provide additional capacity for Truro and Exeter commuting.

Prior to this, FGW and DfT agreed to enhance the size of the West Country fleet, retaining 24 vehicles cascaded from London Midland and London Overground. A further three 2-car units provide Exeter-Plymouth and Plymouth-Penzance capacity following withdrawal of CrossCountry and South West

The 14.00 First Great Western HST from Bristol Temple Meads to Paddington arrives at Swindon on 26 July 2012, led by Class 43 power car No 43179 'Pride of Laira', with No 43187 on the rear. Brian Morrison

HITACHI *Inspire the Next*

69

Passenger Train Operators

Key statistics
First Great Western

	2010-11	2011-12
Punctuality	90.3%	90.6%
Passenger journeys (millions)	90.6	95.6
Passenger km (millions)	5,519.8	5,840.4
Timetabled train km (millions)	42.9	42.7
Route km operated	2,090.5	1,997.2
Number of stations operated	211	210
Number of employees	4,431	4,874
Subsidy per passenger km (pence)	-1.9	-1.9

Senior personnel
First Great Western

Managing Director Mark Hopwood (in photo)
Engineering Director Andrew Mellors
Operations Director Kevin Gale
Projects and Planning Director Matthew Golton
Director of Communications Sue Evans
Finance Director Ben Caswell
Head of Sales & Marketing Diane Burke
Head of HR Sharon Johnston
Head of Safety & Environment Sharon Vye-Parminter

Trains services in 2008/09. In 2011, FGW and DfT agreed a deal for two 2-car Class-150s and two single-car Class-153s for peak services in the Bristol area.

Since the beginning of the franchise, the entire HST fleet has been completely overhauled with revamped interiors, more seats in the carriages, and more reliable, environmentally friendly engines in the power cars as part of a refurbishment programme, with new engines from MTU and cooler groups from Voith

A further £40m is being invested in improving stations. Major National Station Improvement Plan work has been under way at Didcot Parkway, with improvements also at Bristol Temple Meads, Truro, Penzance, Stroud and Plymouth.

Close working with Network Rail to tackle significant railway infrastructure challenges has continued with a number of initiatives introduced to improve punctuality and reliability. Right Time Railway Groups and particular focus by Network Rail are leading to improvements.

Heathrow Connect, the stopping service between Paddington and Heathrow Airport, is a joint venture with the airport company.

FGW has seven train maintenance and servicing depots; Old Oak Common, London; Laira, Plymouth; St Philips Marsh, Bristol; Long Rock, Penzance; Landore, Swansea, Exeter and Reading. The Bristol depot was re-equipped with new maintenance facilities for DMUs early in the franchise and the Exeter depot improved to cater for additional DMUs. A new replacement depot at Reading is due to open in Summer 2013, part of the infrastructure remodeling project.

Growth in rail travel has continued across the franchise and in particular on lines supported by Community Rail Partnerships, including work with Bristol City Council and the Severnside Community Rail Partnership to improve and promote services in the Bristol area.

FGW has achieved Investors in People silver status and extensive business and industry recognition, including several awards for its innovative driver advisory system and apprenticeship schemes.

The FGW diesel multiple-unit fleet consists has these 2-car units: Class 143 (8 units), Class 150/1 (17), Class 150/2 (20), Class 158 (3), Class 165/1 (20); and 3-car units: Class 150/0 (2), Class 158 (12), Class 165/1 (16), Class 166 (21); plus 14 Class-153 single-car units and one additional Class 158 vehicle. There are five Class 180 trains (25 vehicles).

The HST fleet has 119 Class 43 power cars (119) and 442 Mk3 coaches (442) (most leased from Porterbrook and Angel, but 12 power cars and 42 Mk3 vehicles are owned outright by FirstGroup).

There are 19 Mk3 Sleeper vehicles and four Class 57/6 locomotives mainly used on sleeper trains. ■

First Capital Connect
Thameslink Programme brings major changes

Thameslink/Great Northern, operated by First Capital Connect, was awarded as a six year franchise from 1 April 2006 with a possible extension to nine years. In August 2011 the Department for Transport announced a replacement franchise to commence from 15 September 2013, to facilitate the delivery of the Thameslink Programme and i introduction of new rolling stock. A revised timescale was expected to be announced in 2013.

First Capital Connect (FCC) has two groups of routes including some of the busiest sections of the UK's rail network.. The Thameslink service runs from Brighton and Gatwick Airport through London to Luton and Bedford, with a south London loop line via Wimbledon and Sutton. Great Northern runs from London King's Cross and Moorgate to Welwyn, Hertford, Stevenage, Peterborough, Cambridge and King's Lynn.

An increase in passenger journeys from 86m in 2006/07 to 100m in 2011/12 has been recorded, and a Public Performance Measure moving annual average score of over 90pc has been achieved for the first time.

Thameslink and Great Northern will be linked at St Pancras under the Thameslink Programme, which is providing major capacity improvements for the cross-London core of the Thameslink route.

In May 2012 the 'link' was put back into Thameslink when FCC began running across the centre of London again at nights and weekends, after over three years of engineering work. Longer trains, later trains and new services were also introduced. December 2012 marks the completion of FCC's three-year 'More Seats For You' campaign, providing extra capacity and relieving crowding.

Additional capacity on Thameslink was created through the transfer of the final eight Class 319 EMUs from Southern in March 2009 and the delivery of 23 new 4-car Class 377/5 Electrostars on a long sub-lease from Southern. From December 2011 FCC sub-leased a further three Electrostars from Southern to enable it to run 12-car trains on the Brighton line. A net gain since February 2009 of almost 5,000 seats per day in both morning and evening peaks combined has been achieved.

Further capacity has been created on the Great Northern route through transfer of 13 additional Class 321 four-car units and 3 Class-313 three-car sets. 12-car trains can now operate on Cambridge services.

Key statistics
First Capital Connect

	2010-11	2011-12
Punctuality (0-5min)	89.3%	90.0%
Passenger journeys (millions)	96.0	99.7
Passenger km (millions)	3,223.2	3,456.1
Timetabled train km (millions)	24.0	24.5
Route km operated	500.9	500.9
Number of stations operated	78	78
Number of employees	2,318	2,374
Subsidy per passenger km (pence)	-4.2	-4.7

In association with **SIEMENS**

Class 319/4 No 319430 (left) and Class 377/5 No 377521 stop beneath the new Farringdon station roof on 5 September 2011, forming, respectively, the 13.40 service from Bedford to Brighton and the 13.34 service from Brighton to Bedford.

FCC's main maintenance depot is at Hornsey in north London on the Great Northern route, where heavy maintenance of all of the company's trains is carried out. Bedford Cauldwell Walk is the main maintenance base for Class 319s. The completion of a £3.1m modification and renewal package for the Class 319 fleet has helped to resolve reliability issues.

The National Passenger Survey gave FCC a 79pc overall customer satisfaction rating in its spring 2012 report, one point up on 2011, whilst on the Great Northern route it rose by 9 points to 83pc.

FCC has made available a range of real time information tools to allow customers to make informed decisions before and during the journey. An improved free text and email alert system was rolled out in late 2012, automatically identifying relevant delays.

A customer service apprenticeship scheme - the first of its type in the rail industry - has bee launched. FCC's passenger safety levels have reached the highest levels nationally, and in 2012 it was awarded a Modern Railways 'Golden Whistle' for best passenger safety.

Secure Station status has been achieved at all 74 managed stations and crime is down by 41.4pc since the start of the franchise.

FCC plans to build on improvements already delivered, by increasing the number of 12-car trains still further. This follows the completion of supporting infrastructure works including at Finsbury Park. FCC will be investing in further station improvements in collaboration with DfT, NR and Local Authorities.

FCC played a major role in the London 2012 Games, responding to its own forecasts by adding 790,000 extra seats during the Olympics, far more than the 110,000 requested by the Olympic authorities. FCC redoubled its customer service efforts through a 24/7 Olympics Support Centre, with Twitter cover 07:00-23:00 to 13,500 followers. The centre will continue as a legacy of the games. Performance through the Games was very good, with a best-ever Public Performance Measure score of 94.4pc for Thameslink in the last period of the Games) and a second-best on Great Northern (94.9pc).

The train fleet is leased from all three major leasing companies, Angel, Eversholt, and Porterbrook. It comprises: Class 313 (44 trains); Class 317/1 (12), Class 319/0 (12); Class 319/3 (26); Class 319/4 (40); Class 321 (13); Class 365 (40); Class 377/5 (23); Class 377 (3). All are 4-car units apart from Class 313 (3-car). ■

Senior personnel
First Capital Connect

Managing Director Neal Lawson (in photo)
Commercial Director Laura Dunley
New Trains and Engineering Director Jonathan Bridgewood
Interim Projects Director Ian Duncan-Santiago
Operations Director Jackie Townsend
Finance Director Chris Cornthwaite
Customer Service Director Keith Jipps

ScotRail — Scotland's Railway

10 year franchise to November 2014

ScotRail operates passenger services within Scotland, as well as the cross-border Caledonian Sleeper service to London. In April 2004 the Scottish Government took on full funding responsibility for the rail franchise and in January 2006 Transport Scotland assumed responsibility for the majority of rail powers in Scotland and also for infrastructure projects, working in conjunction with regional transport partnerships. (The Strathclyde Partnership for Transport took over roles and functions of the Strathclyde Passenger Transport Authority and Executive, whose rail functions were transferred to Transport Scotland.) In April 2008 ScotRail's franchise was extended by three years to November 2014 by the Scottish Government, with the contract for the 10-year franchise valued at around £2.5billon. Following Transport Scotland's Rail 2014 consultation, the government announced in 2012 that the next franchise will be for 10 years with a half-way break point. The sleeper service will be let on a separate 15-year franchise, to oversee spending of the £100m jointly pledged by Westminster and Holyrood for modernisation of rolling stock.

Annual payments vary as they are linked to performance, monitored by a Service Quality Incentive Regime (SQUIRE) which focuses on 20 areas of station and 16 areas of train quality. Passenger numbers by 2011/12 had risen

Passenger Train Operators

Class 380 Desiro No 380007 has arrived at its Largs destination on 24 April 2012, leading the 17.20 ScotRail service from Glasgow Central. Brian Morrison

by 40pc since 2003/04, while the fine paid by the operator under SQUIRE was reduced significantly to £360,000.

Trains and stations are being rebranded with a new livery incorporating Scotland's flag, the Saltire, which will not change with any subsequent transfer to new operators.

ScotRail manages 346 stations but serves 363. The company achieved an overall rating of 89pc in the spring 2012 National Passenger Survey, outperforming the national average among UK train operators in 31 of 33 categories. ScotRail's Public Performance Measure score for train punctuality stood at 92.1pc on a moving annual average basis at the end of Period 7 of railway year 2012/12.

ScotRail's ban on visible alcohol between the hours of 21.00 and 10.00 has been well-received since its introduction in July 2012, with a 'softly-softly' implementation in conjunction with British Transport Police.

The completed Airdrie-Bathgate link was opened in December 2010 and following the completion of some outstanding work, the full four trains an hour timetable was introduced on 22 May 2011. Two services are express trains, with Drumgelloch the only stop between Airdrie and Bathgate, while the other two trains each hour call at all intermediate stations.

As reported in our Key Projects section, the Edinburgh Glasgow Improvements Programme and Borders rail link are now going ahead with revisions.

The Paisley Corridor Improvement project has delivered infrastructure capable of supporting future additional services between Glasgow, Inverclyde and Ayrshire, while the £12m project to electrify the Paisley Canal line was due for completion by December 2012.

Other projects likely to go ahead include a restored Platform 8 at Aberdeen, upgrading of the Aberdeen-Inverness line, with possible new stations at Kintore and Dalcross, and further electrification, to East Kilbride and Barrhead/Kilmarnock. Conon Bridge station, with lower costs achieved, is due to open in March, to ease congestion during resurfacing of the Kessock road bridge.

From December 2012 the Glasgow-Ayr timetable has been recast, following the Paisley Corridor work, to provide two additional fast trains an hour. Highland main line timings have been accelerated following line-speed improvements and selected additional calls have been inserted on the Perth-Aberdeen stretch. An extra early-morning train to Edinburgh and a Sunday service have been introduced on the Shotts route, with four new weekday trains between Edinburgh and Glasgow Central via Carstairs and Motherwell (and an extra late-night service from Edinburgh).

A £4m contract for refurbishment and overhaul of the Class 334 fleet is being carried out by Railway Projects Limited, Derby with much of the work sub-contracted to Kilmarnock-based Brodie Engineering, creating up to 20 new jobs. Work includes re-covering seats and flooring and upgrading the interiors as well as repainting in 'Saltire' livery. Overhaul of the Class 320 fleet, managed by Eversholt, is being carried out during routine maintenance cycles, with completion due in autumn 2013. Key elements address reliability, with enhancements including new accessible toilets.

The 16 Class 314 units have been put through an £800,000 improvement programme. The Class 380s have taken over services on the Ayrshire routes, releasing Class 334s for the Airdrie-Bathgate service.

Caledonian Sleeper services are hauled by locomotives hired from DBS (Class 90 electrics, usually carrying FirstGroup livery, for the main haul between London and Glasgow/Edinburgh, and Class 67 onwards to Aberdeen, Fort William and Inverness).

The ScotRail fleet has 2-car diesel multiple-units of Class 156 (48 trains) and Class 158 (48 trains). 3-car DMUs are of Class 170/3 (4 trains), and Class 170/4 (55). 3-car electric multiple-units are of Class 314 (16 trains), Class 318 (21), Class 320 (22), Class 334 (40). There are 22 three-car and 16 four-car Class 380s. ■

Key statistics

ScotRail

	2010-11	2011-12
Punctuality (0-5min)	90.1%	90.7%
Passenger journeys (millions)	78.3	81.1
Passenger km (millions)	2,641.8	2,681.6
Timetabled train km (millions)	41.9	43.8
Route km operated	3,065.8	3,065.8
Number of stations operated	346	346
Number of employees	4,392	4,585
Subsidy per passenger km (pence)	11.0	11.4

Senior personnel

ScotRail

Managing Director Steve Montgomery (in photo)
Finance Director & Deputy MD Kenny McPhail
Commercial Director Sean Duffy
Operations Director Jacqueline Dey
New Trains Director Nick Hortin
Engineering Director Kenny Scott
Human Resources Director Julie McComasky
Customer Services Director Jacqueline Taggart
Director of Business Planning Jerry Farquharson
Director of Facilities & Business Services Pat Callaghan

In association with **SIEMENS**

First TransPennine Express

Franchise extended to April 2015

First TransPennine Express (FTPE) is a joint operation by First Group (55pc share) and Keolis, a transport group in which French Railways (SNCF) is a major shareholder. Initially the franchise was awarded for eight years from 1 February 2004, with an optional five-year extension: in August 2011 the DfT announced an extension to April 2015, though it retains an option to roll this back to April 2014.

FTPE runs inter-city train services on three main routes, linking Liverpool and Manchester with Leeds, York and the Northeast; with Sheffield and Doncaster; and with Blackpool, the Lake District, and Glasgow and Edinburgh. It won a total of 57 industry awards in its first eight years, and in a recent National Passenger Survey scored 88pc for overall satisfaction. This has been supported by heavy investment in staff training, with £400,000 spent on providing 2,865 training days in 2011-12 alone. Staff are also encouraged to involve themselves in community work and over the last year FTPE delivered £100,000 of community investment with staff committing over 600 hours.

FTPE operates a fleet of 51 three-car, 100mph 'Desiro' diesel multiple-unit trains built by Siemens and leased from Eversholt. Additional capacity is provided by nine two-car Class 170 Turbostar sets, fully refurbished through Porterbrook by Transys Projects for use by FTPE in a £2million programme aimed at giving the trains a similar feel to the new Class 185s. Since the franchise began, passenger journeys have increased from 13.5 million to a record breaking 25 million: a year on year increase of 3.9pc. This equated to almost a billion passenger miles in 2010/11 and resulted in an 8.9pc increase in revenue for the company. Customers are clearly continuing to look for best value fares as FTPE has seen a 36pc improvement on advance purchase ticket sales since 2009/10.

In 2011/12 delay minutes caused by the company were reduced by 32pc and cancellations were reduced by 43pc compared with 2010/11.

The company is actively engaged with industry partners in helping to deliver the Northwest infrastructure electrification and the significant Northern Hub project. It has negotiated the purchase of ten new 4-car Class 350/4 Siemens Desiro electric trains to run between Manchester Airport and Glasgow/Edinburgh, as part of a larger order placed jointly with London Midland, which will be brought into traffic from late 2013. The £60m investment will increase capacity on the Anglo-Scottish services by 80pc; and with the entire diesel fleet remaining with the company, overall FTPE capacity will increase by some 30pc. Between Manchester and Leeds, an improved timetable will create much needed additional capacity.

Effective management of the fleet has already enabled 16pc more passenger miles to be delivered.

When FTPE took over Anglo-Scottish services, annual passenger journeys were just over 0.5 million, but this total has risen dramatically (with 7pc year on year growth in 2011-12) through significant improvements to the timetable, increasing the number of services (including a new Glasgow-Blackpool summer train), faster journey times, and more attractive departure times.

FTPE's Class 185 fleet continues to deliver effective fuel savings in the 'Eco Drive' project, which combines on-train fuel saving

Key statistics
First TransPennine Express

	2010-11	2011-12
Punctuality (0-10min)	91.1%	93.3%
Passenger Journeys (millions)	23.8	24.8
Passenger kilometres (millions)	1,508.2	1,575.8
Timetabled Train km (millions)	17.3	17.4
Route Kilometres operated	1,250.5	1,250.5
Number of Stations operated	30	30
Number of Employees	1,019	1,030
Subsidy per passenger km (pence)	5.2	5.0

TransPennine Express Class 185 No 185150, at York on 28 September 2012, forms the 16.48 from Scarborough to Liverpool. Brian Morrison

Passenger Train Operators

technology with structured driving techniques. Overall, FTPE is now achieving fuel burn 10pc to 11pc below the benchmark established before the project, saving over 14m litres of fuel in the first four years. FTPE has achieved certification to the ISO 14001 environmental performance standard - the first train company outside London to achieve this certification for all sections of the business.

A station improvement programme has continued with a total investment of around £20m, and FTPE has launched a number of leisure travel incentives, working closely with local attractions and businesses. ∎

Senior personnel
First TransPennine Express

Managing Director Nick Donovan (in photo)
Commercial Director Leo Goodwin
Engineering Director Paul Staples
Programme Director Chris Nutton
Operations Director Paul Watson
Finance Director Liz Collins
Head of HR Sue Whaley

First Hull Trains

Non-franchised intercity train company

First Hull Trains, the non-franchised ('open access') intercity train company operating between Hull and London King's Cross, began operation in 2000. From three trains a day at the outset, First Hull Trains grew to operate seven return services on weekdays, with five services each way on Saturday and Sunday. First Hull Trains carried about 80,000 passengers in its first year and 750,000 in 2011-12.

First Hull Trains (FHT) is 80pc owned by First Group, following the buyout of its previous parent company, GB Railways. The original promoter of Hull Trains, Renaissance Trains, set up by two former British Rail managers, John Nelson and Michael Jones, owns the remaining 20pc.

A new commercial strategy, launched in March 2012, has delivered a market share increase on FHT's route of 3pc. Client research, pro-active marketing, and ticketing innovation is credited with particular success well outside the 'Humberside' heartland, with growth at Retford and Grantham of 10pc and 21pc respectively.

In June 2012's National Rail Passenger Survey, FHT was one of the highest ranked train companies for customer service, for the second year running.

FHT has launched new M-ticketing technology, with 9pc of FHT-only advance tickets now retailed via smartphones. Paperless tickets are now available and a new website with greater functionality and real time train running information was due for launch in late 2012.

In June 2002, the company was awarded 10-year rights by the Rail Regulator, providing security of access at least until May 2010. Investment of some £36million saw a new fleet of 4-car Class 222 'Pioneer' trains come into use in 2005. After an agreement to release them for use by East Midlands Trains, FHT concluded a new leasing deal with Angel Trains to take four 5-car Class 180s in their place.

The change of fleet also enabled FHT to deal with overcrowding, which was becoming an issue on several services, as the Class 180s offer additional capacity (around half a million extra seats a year). In April 2009 the last Class 222 was released by Hull Trains.

An application for rights to be extended until 2018 was made to the Office of Rail Regulation (ORR) in 2008, along with an application to introduce a new four-trains-per-day open-access service between Harrogate and King's Cross via York. In February 2009 the ORR decided against the Harrogate service. Following a regulatory evaluation of East Coast main line capacity, First Hull Trains was granted firm rights for seven weekday and five weekend return services until December 2014. After further negotiations, the ORR offered an extension, with firm rights for all trains to operate during the week and weekdays, until the end of 2016, in exchange for a commitment by FHT to undertake a refurbishment programme for the Class 180 fleet and car park improvement work at Howden station.

The Class 180 refurbishment, which began in Summer 2010, was carried out by Brush-Barclay (now Wabtec) at Kilmarnock and saw the interiors returned to 'as new' condition, with installation of Wi-Fi equipment, at seat power points, leather seats in First class and new carpeting. Before returning to traffic all sets were repainted into a variant of the First Group 'Neon' livery and work was completed by end of December 2010.

Initially the Class 180s' reliability proved challenging, but significant performance improvement has been achieved following sustained investment in the company's engineering capability after the completion of the £4.5m overhaul of the fleet, and modifications implemented in conjunction with Angel Trains. By September 2012, FHT was one of the most reliable long distance train operating companies with Public Performance Measure reliability at 98.9pc, and unprecedented miles per casualty figures for the Class 180 were achieved (15,000mpc). ∎

Class 180 No 180110 passes Harringay at speed on 23 May 2011, forming the 09.48 First Hull Trains service from King's Cross to Hull. It is passing a First Capital Connect Class 313/0 (left) and a Class 321/4. Brian Morrison

Key statistics
Hull Trains

Punctuality (0-10min)	81.8 %
Passenger journeys	720,928
Timetabled train km (millions)	1.48
Route km operated	329.0
Number of stations operated	0
Staff employed	105

Senior personnel
Hull Trains

Managing Director Cath Bellamy [in photo]
Service Delivery Director Keith Doughty
Finance Manager Glenn McLeish-Longthorn
Head of Engineering Richard Elwen
Performance Manager Louise Mendham
On Board Standards Manager Katie Beckett
HR Manager Victoria Evans

Govia

Govia is a joint venture partnership between the Go-Ahead Group and Keolis. Go-Ahead, the 65pc majority partner, employs 23,000 people in UK rail and bus. More than one billion passenger journeys were undertaken on Go-Ahead's bus and rail companies in 2011-12. Keolis - in which French Railways (SNCF) is a major shareholder - operates trains, buses and metros across the world.

Rail has been a key element of Go-Ahead's transport strategy since privatisation and the businesses has continued to focus on strong London commuter rail links. Govia is responsible for nearly 30pc of national passenger rail journeys.

Go-Ahead operated the Thames Trains franchise from 1996 to 2004 and Govia the Thameslink franchise from 1997 to 2006. Govia took over the South Central franchise in 2001, later rebranding it as Southern. It retained the franchise in a new agreement from September 2009. In 2008, Gatwick Express became part of the franchise.

Govia was awarded the Integrated Kent franchise, now branded Southeastern, in 2006 and launched Britain's first domestic high-speed service in 2009. In November 2007 Govia began operating the new West Midlands franchise under the name London Midland.

GoAhead's pioneering smart card 'The Key' won the Excellence in Technology Award at the 2011 National Transport Awards, and is being deployed on its London Midland and Southern operations.

All three train companies were heavily involved in the successful delivery of transport for the 2012 Games, with around 2.4m passengers using Javelin services on Southeastern.

In 2012, Govia was shortlisted for the Thameslink, Southern and Great Northern rail franchise.

SOUTHERN

5 year 10 month franchise from September 2009

Southern provides train services in South London and connects central London to the South Coast, East and West Sussex, Surrey and parts of Kent and Hampshire, on one of the busiest British rail networks.

The South Central franchise from 20 September 2009 to 25 July 2015 was again won by Govia, which held the previous franchise from May 2003. The final year of the new franchise is subject to performance, with a possible two year extension at DfT discretion.

The company operates a mix of suburban commuter and main line routes, and strives to consistently improve its operating performance in punctuality and reliability, ticket buying facilities, car parking, security on stations and on trains, the cleanliness of its rolling stock and the helpfulness of staff. It has achieved high satisfaction scores in National Passenger Surveys.

Southern operates the non-stop Gatwick Express services from/to London Victoria using Class 442 trains, with some extended to Brighton in weekday peaks.

Southern sub-leases 23 dual-voltage Class-377 trains to First Capital Connect, helping to deliver key stages of the Thamslink Programme. In December 2011, Southern sub-leased a further three sets so that FCC could run 12-car trains on the Brighton line. Additional capacity at Southern has been created through reinstatement of the last five Class 442 trains from store, and transfer of 19 Class-313 units from London Overground. The '313s' are used on Coastway services from Brighton and all sets have been refreshed, with the installation of information systems and CCTV, enabling 3-car Class 377s to be transferred to strengthen services in London.

Class 455/8 EMU No 455816 arrives at Brockley on 25 September 2011, forming a Southern service from London Bridge to West Croydon. Brian Morrison

Passenger Train Operators

Key statistics
Southern

	2010-11	2011-12
Punctuality (0-5min)	89.6%	90.0%
Passenger journeys (millions)	166.0	174.1
Passenger km (millions)	4,132.8	4,395.4
Timetabled train km (millions)	37.5	38.0
Route km operated	666.3	666.3
Number of stations operated	157	158
Number of employees	4,047	4,104
Subsidy per passenger km (pence)	-2.5	-0.4

The new franchise includes commitments to deliver an additional 10pc capacity by December 2013, including the lengthening of eight car trains to 10 cars on key inner-suburban 'Metro' routes.

In December 2011 Southern announced an order worth £200m with Bombardier Transportation for an additional 26 five-car Class 377s, to be introduced from December 2013. Porterbrook is preferred funder, and there are options for up to 40 more vehicles.

A £76m investment programme includes £23m of interior and reliability improvements to trains and £28m to improve facilities at stations. Almost all Greater London stations are now staffed from first to last train, and there is a further focus on maintaining and improving punctuality during significant change (arising from the Thameslink programme and other major initiatives).

Improved passenger access and integration at stations, security, easier ticket buying, enhanced revenue protection and an improved overall passenger experience are also moving ahead. The company has upgraded information screens and all stations have been deep cleaned and repainted. An online passenger panel has over 5,000 members.

95pc of Southern's passengers pass through stations that have secure station status and the company aims to create a sustainable rail network with passengers' needs at the centre of its business. It is committed to making rail travel more accessible, more affordable and environmentally efficient. Southern has launched its new Smartcard system, 'The Key', with a view to rolling it out to the whole network by April 2013.

Revenue share applies from the start of the franchise, sharing with the DfT 50pc of incremental revenue above 102pc of the bid revenue, and 80pc above 106pc of bid. Revenue support applies from 21 September 2013, with the DfT to provide 50pc of any incremental shortfall in revenue below 98pc of bid revenue and 80pc support for any shortfall below 94pc of bid.

As part of the National Station Improvement programme (NSIP), new station buildings are being constructed at Hassocks, Ashtead and East Grinstead and major station improvement work has been completed at Balham, Norbury and Horsham stations. At East Croydon a new footbridge will create two new entrances.

Plans to provide over 1,000 additional car parking spaces are well underway, with double decking planned for Haywards Heath, East Grinstead and Upper Warlingham.

Southern continues to be recognised by industry peers having won numerous awards over the last 12 months, notably for many of its engineering initiatives, culminating in the award of Rail Business of the Year at the 2012 Rail Business Awards.

All Southern's Class 377 Electrostars now operate with third-rail regenerative braking, and are currently being refreshed inside and out. Southern's Class 455 trains is also currently being refreshed. Southern's driver simulators have been upgraded to enable energy efficient, eco-driving training to be carried out.

All of Southern's routes are electrified at 750V DC, except for Oxted-Uckfield and Ashford-Hastings, which are worked by Class 171 diesel units (six 4-car and ten 2- car).

Electric multiple-units are of: Class 313 (19 x 3-car); Class 377 (28 x 3-car, 154 x 4-car); Class 442 (24 x 5-car); Class 455 (46 x 4-car); Class 456 (24 x 2-car).

The main train depots are at Selhurst (also responsible for overhaul), Brighton, and Stewarts Lane, Battersea. ∎

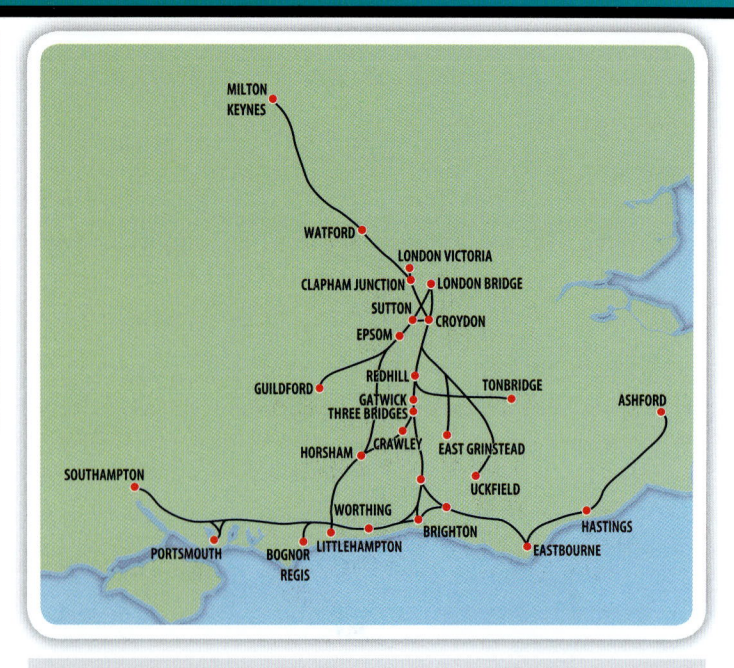

Senior personnel
Southern

Managing Director Chris Burchell (in photo)
Finance and Contracts Director Bob Mayne
Fleet Director Gerry McFadden
Service Delivery Director James Burt
Development Director Alex Foulds
Franchise Improvement Director David Scorey
Human Resources Director Matt Watson
Head of Safety and Operational Standards Steve Enright

southeastern.

Franchise from 1 April 2006 until 31 March 2014

The Southeastern franchise serves Kent, southeast London and part of East Sussex and includes high-speed domestic services on HS1 (the Channel Tunnel Rail Link). The automatic two-year extension from 31 March 2012 was granted following confirmation that performance targets had been met. Southeastern entered 80pc revenue support in April 2010, which the company says is a reflection of the recession and reduced passenger numbers against those predicted in 2005 when the Govia bid was submitted.

Southeastern is committed to lifting the number of trains arriving within 5min of schedule from 89.2pc in 2008 to 93.74pc in 2014. In mid-October 2012 its moving annual average Public Performance Measure (PPM) score stood at 92pc, while its four-week PPM score of 95.5pc, achieved in September, was higher than the national average and the best for the southeast network since PPM records began.

The Thameslink Programme has led to major timetable changes as has the start of the High Speed service: the December 2009 timetable

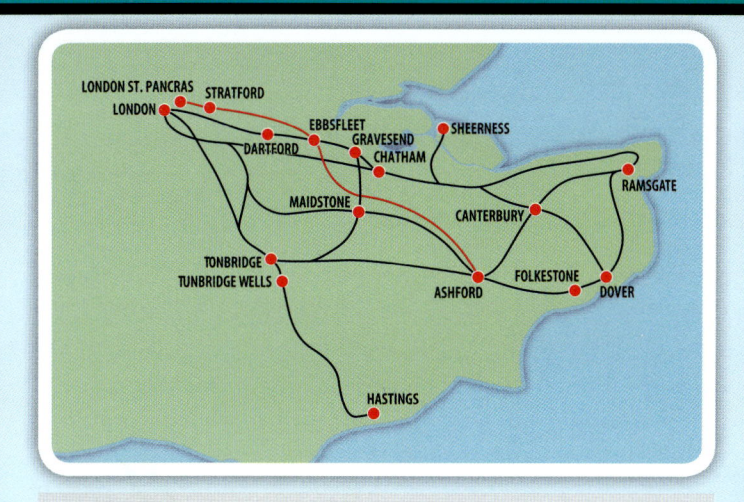

In association with SIEMENS

Senior personnel
Southeastern

Managing Director Charles Horton (in photo)
Finance Director Wilma Allan
Engineering Director Wayne Jenner
Human Resources Director Andy Bindon

Key statistics
Southeastern

	2010-11	2011-12
Punctuality (0-5min)	88.9%	91.8%
Passenger journeys (millions)	162.3	165.5
Passenger km (millions)	3,984.6	4,128.8
Timetabled train m (millions)	37.8	38.0
Route km operated	748.3	748.3
Number of stations operated	173	173
Number of employees	3,734	3,796
Subsidy per passenger km (pence)	5.5	2.1

brought a 5pc overall increase in capacity on peak services.

The High Speed service to St Pancras, worked exclusively by 29 six-car Class 395 trains, has brought dramatic reductions in journey times, including: London to Ashford in 37min, Canterbury in 59min. Peak services have seen trains running at around 80pc capacity, while from stations such as Canterbury West and Ashford International, 70pc of all journeys to London are on High Speed.

In May 2011 the High Speed service was extended to Maidstone West and in September 2011 to Sandwich and Deal with funding from Kent County Council.

Since its introduction, High Speed has consistently been recognised in the National Passenger Survey as the best commuter service in the country. Overall Southeastern has recently been seeing its highest ever levels of customer satisfaction since taking over the franchise in 2006, with year-on-year improvements. 95 stations are recognised with a Secure Station Award, while incidents of theft and assault are at record lows.

Southeastern formed an alliance with Network Rail in 2012, and together the companies have delivered upgrades to stations, weather-proofed the rail infrastructure and delivered the largest resignalling scheme in over 60 years. Punctuality performance has improved and emergency response times have shortened.

One of Southeastern's commitments was to invest in training and development of employees. Approximately 50pc of all employees now hold a National Vocational Qualification, the majority in customer services. Senior managers have also taken Institute of Learning Management qualifications, aiming to improve how the company manages and develops staff. In 2012 Southeastern was recognised with Investors in People Gold status, and hopes to achieve Champion status. The company was also awarded five stars in the European Foundation for Quality Management and Recognised for Excellence programme.

Southeastern launched its own internal professional social networking site, 'Workmate,' in 2012, allowing employees to communicate and share information in real time, leading to improvements in information passed to customers.

Southeastern's commitment to reducing traction energy has seen the increased use of regenerative breaking, the re-training of drivers and promotion of eco-driving techniques. The TOC's 'driving energy further' initiative has reduced carbon emissions by 42,000 tonnes of C02, saving around £6.2m. Southeastern was also the first stand alone train company to commit to '10:10', a carbon reduction commitment.

Class-395 No 395013 passes Singlewell, near Ebbsfleet, on 21 March 2012, forming the 12.44 Southeastern High-Speed service from Dover to St Pancras International. Brian Morrison

Passenger Train Operators

70pc of all waste is now recycled (up from only 10% in 2006).

Southeastern's engineering department has taken best practice and innovation from other industries to deliver improved train performance, efficiency savings, increased productivity and a more responsive workforce, helping in significant improvements to 'miles-per-casualty' figures. There is a completely electric train fleet, with units leased from Eversholt and Angel Trains. Maintenance is carried out at Slade Green near Dartford (suburban) and Ramsgate (main-line), with smaller depots at Ashford, Grove Park and Gillingham. A new Hitachi depot at Ashford maintains the 29 Class-395 six-car high-speed trains. The remainder of the fleet is made up of 10 three-car and 102 four-car Class 375s; 36 five-car Class 376s; 147 four-car Class 465s; and 43 two-car Class 466s.

Southeastern played a major part in the provision of transport for the London 2012 Games.

The operational plan involved hiring 1,000 extra customer service staff, running 200 extra trains a day, a 24 hour special Olympic control centre and 'a maintenance schedule that would rival a pit stop at the Formula One Grand Prix'. Southeastern served more Olympic venues than any other train company and ran the high speed Javelin service, the centrepiece of the Olympic Transport Plan.

Over the two events, 12.6m people travelled on Southeastern services, with 2.4m on the Javelin service worked by Class 395 trains. Southeastern achieved a PPM punctuality score of 95pc while operating at maximum capacity. ∎

london midland

7 year, 10 month franchise from November 2007

The London Midland franchise began on 11 November 2007, combining the Silverlink franchise's County routes and the major part of Central Trains.

London Midland City caters for the West Midlands conurbation and wider region, giving prominence to Centro's Network West Midlands brand. London Midland Express services connect London, the Midlands and the Northwest. LM is delivering investment of £300m in new trains, improvements at stations, information for passengers, better security and smartcard ticket technology.

A new London-Crewe service via the Trent Valley and Stoke-on-Trent, linked with the recast of the Virgin West Coast timetable, was the most significant of a series of changes in 2008, with through Birmingham-London services, increased Liverpool-Birmingham services, and improvements on West Midlands routes.

Other highlights have included introduction of 37 new four-car Siemens Class 350/2 Desiro electric trains, and the replacement of most Class 150 Sprinters with 12 two-car and 15 three-car Class 172 Bombardier Turbostars.

Agreement with the DfT also enabled LM to keep seven Class 321 EMUs to bolster capacity on peak services between Watford Junction, Harrow and London Euston.

Supported by the DfT and Network Rail, LM successfully tested its Class 350/1 trains at 110mph as part of a plan for additional and faster services on the Trent Valley route to Crewe. These are possible following the end of 'moderation of competition' protection for the Intercity West Coast franchise in March 2012. The Class 350/1 fleet has now been modified for 110mph, and an order has been placed with Siemens for 10 additional Class 350s to give additional capacity: these '350/3s' will also be capable of 110mph.

LM has fitted electricity meters on all Class 323 and Class 350s, monitoring electricity use and regeneration through the braking system. Data collected helps in work with drivers on energy efficient techniques. LM's £1m train driving simulator centre was opened in its Birmingham Customer Service Academy in 2009.

In June 2012 the National Passenger Survey gave LM an overall customer satisfaction score of 87pc, beating the national average of 83pc. An 83pc rating for provision of information at stations and 73pc for attitude and helpfulness of staff both outperformed national averages by 2pc. The company's investment in new rolling stock has also been recognised by customers where a satisfaction score of 84pc is well above both the national average of 75pc and the 63pc recorded at the start of the franchise.

Following successful Smartcard trials, the technology has been rolled out across the Birmingham Snow Hill lines. The company is also delivering a £1.7m project, using help points, public address and electronic visual displays to provide 'real time' train running information at stations. This is backed up by improved information to station staff to keep commuters informed, and the use of Twitter for social media presence and information distribution at times of disruption. As part of the National Stations Improvement Programme a multi-million pound programme of work is being delivered.

In April 2012 London Midland more than doubled its Sunday

Key statistics
London Midland

	2010-11	change on 2009-10 (%)
	2010-11	2011-12
Punctuality (0-5min)	89.4%	90.9%
Passenger journeys (millions)	56.6	59.5
Passenger km (millions)	1,852.3	2,090.5
Timetabled train km (millions)	24.4	24.7
Route km operated	861.0	861.0
Number of stations operated	147	147
Number of employees	2,340	2,315
Subsidy per passenger km (pence)	3.6	3.1

Senior personnel
London Midland

Managing Director Patrick Verwer (in photo)
Finance & Contracts Director Wilma Allan
Operations & Safety Director Wallace Weatherill
Commercial Director Richard Brooks
Engineering Director Neil Bamford
Human Resources Director Geraldine Goddard

London Midland's Class-350/2 Desiro No 350267 leaves London Euston for Birmingham New Street on 25 November 2011. Tony Miles

HITACHI Inspire the Next

In association with SIEMENS

service to and from London on the Trent Valley route to meet increased demand.

In the timetable from December 2012, London Midland scheduled faster journey times and extra services as part of Project 110. By running trains at 110mph on selected services, journey times to the capital will be reduced by up to 30min and capacity created for an additional service each hour, off-peak, between Milton Keynes, Rugby and London. From 2014 LM will introduce seven of the new Class 350/3s and, taking further advantage of the increased speed, will add eight new services during peak periods into and out of London, providing 4,474 extra seats each weekday. The remaining three new '350/3s' will provide extra services on the West Midlands CrossCity line, increasing peak and off-peak Redditch services from 2 to 3 trains per hour from December 2014, after installation of a passing loop at Alvechurch.

London Midland's diesel train fleet consists of: Class 172 Turbostars (12 two-car and 15 three-car), Class 170 Turbostars (17 two-car and six three-car), Class 150 Sprinters (3 two-car); Class 153 (8 single-car), Class 139 (2 single-car, LPG/flywheel-powered Parry People Movers).

The electric train fleet consists of 30 Class-350/1 and 37 Class-350/2 four-car Desiros, and 7 four-car Class-321 and 26 three-car Class-323 units.

London Midland's new £1.6m train washing plant is now in use at the Tyseley depot where it has introduced a pioneering liquid glass technology (Nanopool) which helps trains 'sparkle' after cleaning. ∎

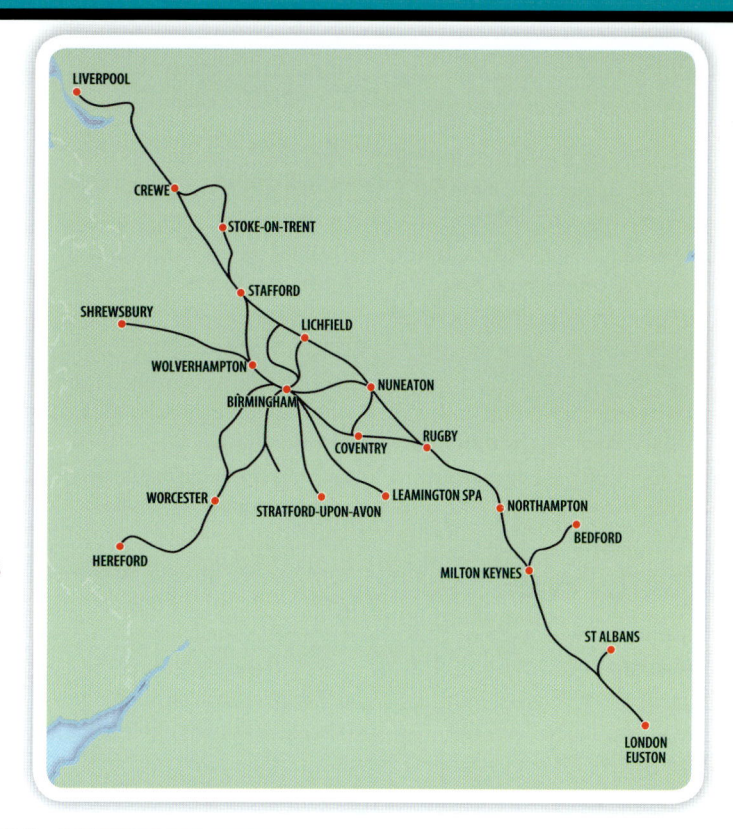

Passenger Train Operators

Stagecoach Group

Holder of the South West Trains franchise since it was first awarded in 1996, Stagecoach Group has extensive bus, rail and light rail operations in the UK and North America, employing around 35,000 people, over 7,000 of them in GB Rail. It is involved in running around 20pc of the GB passenger rail network. It was awarded the East Midlands rail franchise in 2007, and has a 49 per cent shareholding in Virgin Rail Group, operator of West Coast intercity. Stagecoach Supertram holds a 27-year concession until 2024 for Sheffield's 28km light rail network.

UK rail subsidiaries' revenue for the year to 30 April 2012 was up 6.6pc at £1,140.7m (2011: £1,070m). On a like-for-like basis, revenue, excluding tram operations, increased by 9.0pc. Operating profit was £27.1m (2011: £48.4m). The operating margin fell from 4.5 to 2.4pc.

Stagecoach's share of Virgin Rail Group's profit after tax in the year to 30 April was £15.9m (2011: £28.4m). This reduction was principally due to below-forecast revenue at East Midlands Trains, but from November 2011, the franchise has received revenue support payments from the DfT, returning it to profitability for the second half of the year. South West Trains, which also makes premium payments to the DfT, continued to receive revenue support. The wholly-owned franchises made net premium payments of £283.1m in 2011-12 to the DfT.

Stagecoach was shortlisted for Greater Western and Thameslink franchises in 2012 and stated, 'We will seek to add to our existing portfolio where we believe there is the right risk-reward profile and we can add value for our shareholders.'

SOUTH WEST TRAINS

10-year franchise from February 2007

A new alliance between South West Trains and Network Rail from 29 April 2012 put a single management team in charge of one of the busiest, most intensely used and complex railways in Europe. The alliance has 6,000 employees, who manage, operate and maintain the route. It has seven train depots, 334 trains, 4,626 signals and 1,373 sets of points, some moving up to 40,000 times a year, controlled through one integrated control centre.

Stagecoach holds the passenger rail franchise, running from 4 February 2007, which combined the previous South West Trains (SWT) and Island Line (Isle of Wight) franchises. Estimated in 2007 to generate £1,191 million (Net Present Value) in premium payments to the Department for Transport (DfT), the franchise was planned to see an approximate 20pc increase in peak capacity.

Some trains have been adapted to increase capacity, and agreements to source additional EMU vehicles have been concluded.

SWT committed to spend approximately £27m on further upgrading and improving stations between 2012 and 2014, ranging from small upgrades to new facilities, such as the new station at Wokingham.

The company has worked in partnership with Southampton airport to promote rail access, with rail information screens in the arrivals hall, and new station facilities including a new footbridge and lifts.

Last year SWT completed CCTV links from all stations to its control centre, for real time information monitoring. Other measures to improve the customer experience include investing in better information at stations and online, new technology, additional management resources, extra training, plus improved contingency and on-call arrangements - mobilising

The 09.58 South West Trains service from Guildford to Waterloo arrives at Effingham Junction on 31 May 2012, formed by Classes 455/8 & 455/7 EMUs Nos 5861 & 5712. Brian Morrison

In association with **SIEMENS**

Key statistics
South West Trains

	2010-11	2011-12
Punctuality (0-5min)	93.7%	92.3%
Passenger journeys (millions)	202.6	208.8
Passenger km (millions)	5,524.0	5,720.2
Timetabled train km (millions)	39.5	39.6
Route km operated	944.7	944.7
Number of stations operated	185	185
Number of employees	4,431	4,619
Subsidy per passenger km (pence)	-3.2	-4.0

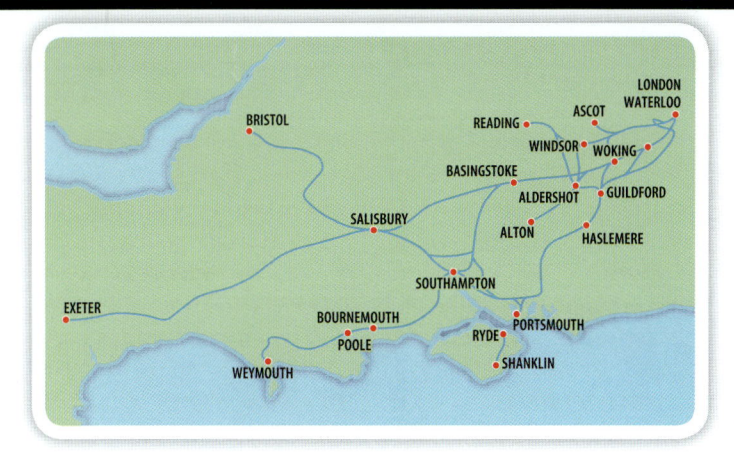

managers to provide assistance on trains and at stations. A more sophisticated information system at London Waterloo prioritises trains running during disruption over than those cancelled, and there is better communication with heavily-delayed trains. The company is working to ensure that delayed trains are brought into stations if reasonably practicable - or held at stations rather than sent into a blocked area. Bottled water is now held on the majority of trains. New forms of communicating with customers include a twitter account which has over 20,000 followers, with 'tweet the manager' sessions.

The company is delivering a greatly improved environmental performance: initiatives include regenerative braking on Class 450 and 458 rolling stock, metering of electricity use on four train classes, intelligent lighting at stations, and increased levels of waste recycling.

In many cases SWT is delivering 'best in class' fleet reliability, underpinning its train service performance. Work started in November 2012 on the £23m C6 overhaul of the Class 455 fleet at Bournemouth, with a new £3.2m paint shop at the depot.

The electric multiple-unit fleet has 45 Class 444 five-car Siemens Desiro trains (designed for longer distance services), 127 Class 450 four-car Desiros (28 of them converted for higher-capacity), 30 four-car Class 458 sets and 91 pre-privatisation Class 455 units.

A major increase in capacity will be delivered by 36 five-car Class 458/5 sets, created using 60 vehicles from former Gatwick Express Class 460s to lengthen the existing Class 458s, while adding six additional trains. New cabs will give the '458/5s' a similar appearance to the Desiros. 10-car trains on the Windsor line will result. Further capacity is being created through agreement with the DfT to transfer the 24 two-car Class 456s from Southern, from 2013.

SWT also operates 30 three-car Class 159s and 11 two-car Class 158s, diesel multiple-units used on the non-electrified routes from Southampton and Basingstoke to Salisbury and beyond.

Main train depots are at Wimbledon, Salisbury and, for the Siemens-built Desiro units, Northam near Southampton.

During the London 2012 Games, SWT achieved successful delivery of train services, with good performance and minimal disruption. Preparations included £16m of investment at Vauxhall, Weymouth, Wimbledon, Windsor & Eton Riverside, Southampton Central and Clapham Junction. The period saw some of the best performance delivered since the formation of the alliance, with Public Performance Measure punctuality at a record high of 95.8pc. A legacy is a management structure for the alliance to plan and deal with major events, and deal with incidents effectively and quickly, while improving performance. ∎

Senior personnel
South West Trains

Managing Director Tim Shoveller (in photo)
Customer Service Director Jake Kelly
Infrastructure Director Jim Morgan
Commercial Director Sam McCarthy
Operations Director Mark Steward
Safety & Environment Director Brian Cook
Finance Director Andy West
HR Director Kelly Barlow

EAST MIDLANDS TRAINS

Seven year, four month franchise from 11 November 2007

The East Midlands franchise began operations on 11 November 2007 and is due to continue until 1 April 2015. The DfT has the right to terminate it after six years if performance targets are not met. At the start of the franchise it was announced that a premium of £133m would be paid to the DfT over the full length of the franchise. Passenger numbers have continued to increase through the recession, but revenue growth has not met expectations, and EMT has been eligible for revenue support from the DfT from November 2011.

Early innovations an extra hourly Corby-Kettering-London service, a new London-Lincoln train, more frequent London-Sheffield trains, and a 9pc increase in peak capacity into and out of London St Pancras. New stations have opened at Corby and East Midlands Parkway - a £25m scheme near the M1 motorway at Ratcliffe-on-Soar.

The busy Liverpool-Norwich route saw significant increase in capacity from December 2011 when the transfer of four additional Class 156 sets from Northern Rail, funded by the DfT under its HLOS programme, enabled many services between Nottingham and Liverpool to be strengthened from 2-car to 4-car Class 158 sets.

East Midlands Trains continues to see demonstrable improvements in customer satisfaction, with the Spring 2012 National Passenger Survey (NPS) showing overall satisfaction at 87pc, and satisfaction increasing in 28 of the 33 categories judged by passengers.

EMT has consistently been the best performing long-distance train operator and in October 2012 the moving-annual-average punctuality score stood at

Key statistics
East Midlands Trains

	2010-11	2011-12
Punctuality	92.1%	93.6%
Passenger journeys (millions)	22.7	23.9
Passenger km (millions)	2,084.7	2,194.6
Timetabled train km (millions)	22.0	22.1
Route km operated	1,549.8	1,549.8
Number of stations operated	89	89
Number of employees	2,042	2,028
Subsidy per passenger km (pence)	-1.1	-1.8

Passenger Train Operators

The 11.17 East Midlands Trains service from Corby (Meridian No 222007 - right) arrives at London St Pancras on 13 June 2012, alongside Class 43 power car No 43047, which leads the 14.15 HST to Nottingham. Brian Morrison

93.4pc. EMT continues to focus on Right Time performance, not just the 'within 5 or 10min of time' yardsticks of the Public Performance Measure.

A £10m investment programme delivered improvements to most stations in 2012, including major schemes at Leicester and Loughborough (and the start of the multi-million pound transformation at Nottingham), solar-powered help-points, improved cycle facilities, a £2.2m joint scheme with Network Rail to install new real-time customer information screens at 26 stations, and improved passenger waiting facilities at large and small stations.

Smartcard technology has been exploited, with season tickets stored electronically on a StagecoachSmart travelcard, and card readers have been installed at 26 stations. 30 new collection-only ticket machines have been provided at key stations for tickets booked online.

EMT is leading an industry group developing measures to help make journeys easier during disruption, resulting in a new collaborative approach at London St Pancras International, King's Cross and Euston. Initiatives include new maps to show alternative routes, improved acceptance of train tickets on alternative services, and improved communication between station teams.

A £22million depot refurbishment at Derby (Etches Park), the centre of train maintenance operations, has provided increased maintenance capacity. A £1m wheel lathe has been provided, and synchronised jacks are capable of lifting a full seven-car Meridian train.

In September 2012, EMT completed the £30m programme to refurbish its entire fleet, which started in 2008 with the £10m refurbishment of the 25 two-car Class 158s. The 17 Class-153s and 11 two-car Class 156s were refurbished in a £5m project and then the four additional Class 156s. A 13 month, £9m programme for the 11 diesel high-speed trains saw 94 vehicles refurbished with updated interiors, new seat covers and carpets, with at seat power points installed in First class, and extensive technical modifications for reliability.

The final stage saw EMT's 27 Class-222 Meridian trains refurbished in a £6m project, which included the fitting of new leather seats in First class and new seat covers and carpeting throughout Standard.

An Energy Saving Mode on Meridian trains sees some engines turned off when the trains are sitting in stations, resulting in reduced noise and reduced emissions. Long-distance trains now offer improved wi-fi using a market-leading router which aggregates signals from multiple sources.

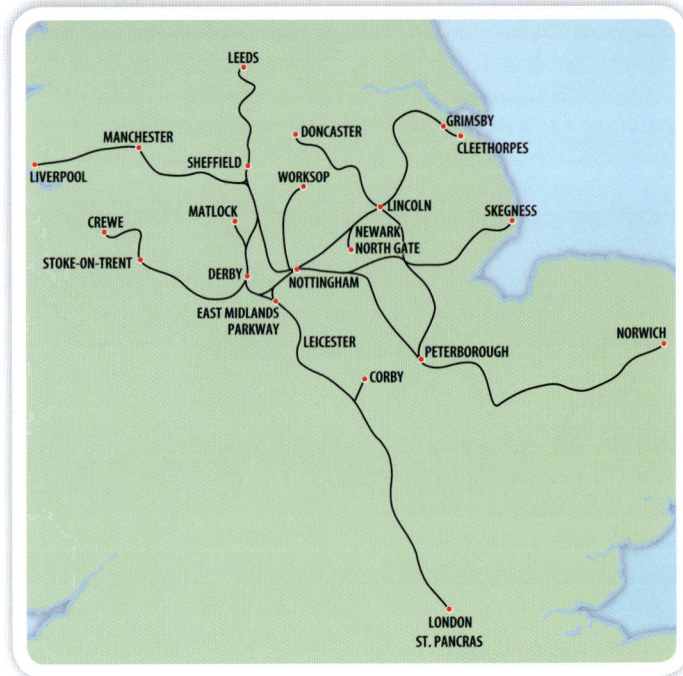

The investment in the comprehensive programme of fleet modification and depot improvement has paid off, with fleet reliability significantly improved. One of the highest increases in satisfaction in the NPS scores has related to the upkeep of EMT's trains. ∎

Senior personnel
East Midlands Trains

Managing Director David Horne (in photo)
Safety & Operations Director Ian Smith
Fleet Director Tim Sayer
Finance Director Tim Gledhill
HR Director Clare Burles
Customer Service & Commercial Director Neil Micklethwaite

82

HITACHI Inspire the Next

In association with SIEMENS

Virgin Trains

New franchise delayed

Virgin Rail Group (VRG) - a joint venture between Virgin Group (51pc) and Stagecoach Group (49pc) - runs the West Coast intercity franchise under the Virgin Trains banner. After changes to the West Coast Route Modernisation project affected the franchise agreement, revised terms were agreed in December 2006.

The 15-year franchise was due to end on 31 March 2012, but was extended to 8 December while the DfT revisited terms and specifications. The subsequent cancellation of the West Coast franchising process in October 2012, following what the Secretary of State for Transport, Patrick McLoughlin, called 'unacceptable mistakes' by his department, saw Virgin entering into discussions with the DfT to continue operating the franchise for between 9 and 14 months, until a short interim franchise could be let. This was intended as a precursor to the letting of a longer franchise once a full review of the franchising system has been completed.

In December 2008 Virgin introduced its Virgin High Frequency timetable recast which sees nine Virgin trains departing from London Euston every hour in the off-peak periods, and 11 in the peak. The number of trains on Sundays almost doubled. Virgin also runs the hourly Birmingham-Scotland service, taken over from the CrossCountry franchise in 2007. In December 2008 a daily Wrexham-London return train, via Chester, was introduced.

From December 2012, gaps in the London-Glasgow timetable will be filled with the introduction of two extra services in each direction to deliver a train every hour for the first time.

After projections of demand growth led the DfT to sanction capacity increases, train lessor Angel Trains signed contracts with Alstom in September 2008 for four new 11-car Pendolinos and two extra cars for 31 existing trains, in total some 106 additional vehicles, along with a 10-year maintenance regime, worth a total of £1.5bn. Virgin Rail Projects Ltd was chosen as service provider to support DfT throughout design, manufacture, delivery, testing and commissioning. The first of the new 11-car Pendolinos was delivered in December 2010 and all four were in passenger service by the end of April 2012. The first of the 31 nine-car units to be lengthened entered passenger service in April 2012, with all 31 lengthened sets due in service by the end of the year.

In November 2010 Virgin reformed its three 4-car Class 221 sets into two 5-car units, along with two spare driving vehicles, creating a uniform Class 221 fleet.

Following these changes Virgin's train fleet will comprise 35 eleven-car and 21 nine-car Pendolino electric tilting trains, and 20 five-car Class 221 diesel SuperVoyager units. These are supplemented by a 9-coach loco-hauled rake of Mk3 vehicles. The use of Pendolinos and double Voyager sets on the Birmingham-Scotland route and through London-Edinburgh via Birmingham services has continued, following the delivery of the additional Pendolino sets, enabling Virgin to provide adequate capacity on more popular services.

Virgin has achieved a customer satisfaction rating of 91pc, consistently delivering the best score across all long-distance franchise operators. Over the 15 years of its franchise, passenger numbers have more than doubled, from 13m to 31m, while rail's share of the Manchester-London rail-air market has increased from 30pc to 88pc.

During 2012, Virgin continued to work with Network Rail to drive up performance and, with infrastructure-related problems the major cause of delays on the West Coast main line, Chief operating officer, Chris Gibb, joined Network Rail on a temporary basis in a bid to improve performance.

Virgin's moving annual average score for punctuality stood at 86.1pc at the end of Period 7 in mid-October 2012, up from 84.4pc at the end of the same period in 2011.

Virgin also ran the CrossCountry franchise from 1997 until 2007, when the remapped franchise was won by Arriva. ∎

Key statistics
Virgin West Coast

	2010-11	2011-12
Punctuality (0-10min)	86.6%	85.9%
Passenger journeys (millions)	28.9	30.2
Passenger km (millions)	5,698.8	5,923.0
Timetabled train km (millions)	35.6	35.9
Route km operated	1,190.9	1,190.9
Number of stations operated	17	17
Number of employees	2,913	3,104
Subsidy per passenger km (pence)	-2.9	-2.8

Senior personnel

Chief Executive Tony Collins (in photo)
Chief Operating Officer Chris Gibb
Executive Director, Commercial Graham Leech
HR Director Patrick McGrath
Finance Director Phil Whittingham
Communications Director Arthur Leathley

Virgin Pendolino No 390040 heads north through Crewe. Tony Miles

Download Modern Railways
to your iPad or iPhone

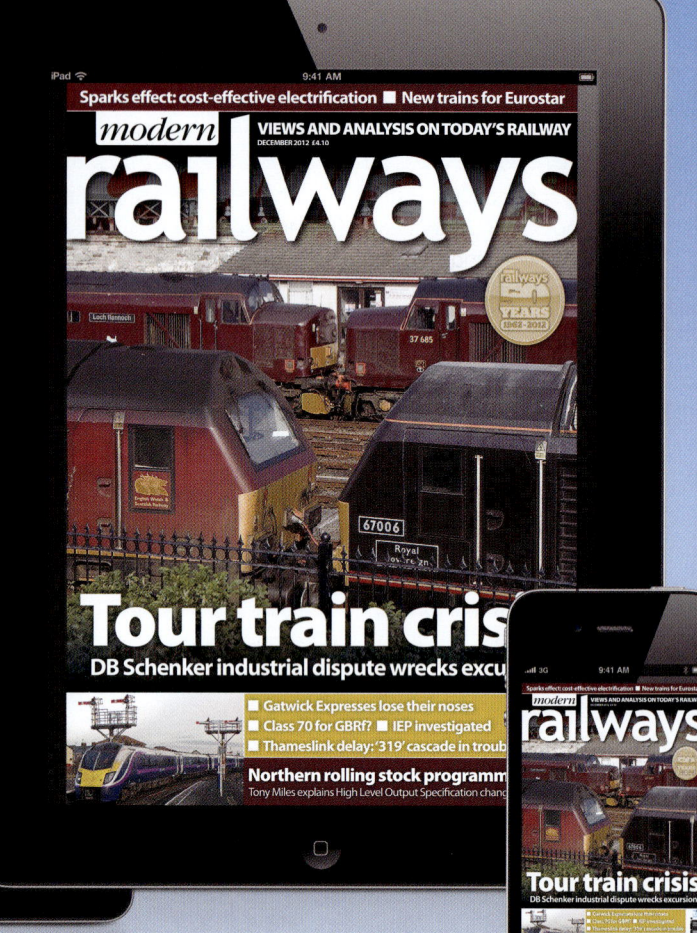

- Get your digital copy the same day as it's published
- An enhanced copy of the magazine in convenient digital format
- Six month trial subscription for only £15.99
- Back issues available
- Exclusive/extended features
- Download the App for just £1.49 and get a free issue!

Subscribe for 6 issues for just £15.99

Available on the App Store

Buy direct from
www.apple.com/itunes
www.pocketmags.com

modern railways

In association with SIEMENS

Arriva

A division of DB Bahn since Deutsche Bahn's acquisition of Arriva plc in August 2010, Arriva is responsible for regional passenger transport outside Germany. Active in 12 European countries, Arriva has 38,000 employees and revenue of over Euro 3bn.

Arriva UK Trains operates about 10pc of the UK passenger network through three franchises - CrossCountry and Arriva Trains Wales (Arriva plc held these two prior to the DB acquisition), and Chiltern Railways, which DB had run since acquiring its parent Laing Rail in 2008. Open Access train company Grand Central was acquired in November 2011.

The Laing acquisition also involved the London Rail concession for London Overground, awarded in 2007 to London Overground Rail Operations Ltd (LOROL), a joint venture of Laing with Hong Kong's MTR.

On the Tyne & Wear Metro, Arriva operates a seven-year contract on behalf of Nexus, the Passenger Transport Executive. It covers the train service, fleet maintenance and modernisation, plus day-to-day station management.

Arriva also owns rail maintenance business LNWR, based in Crewe and founded in 1996. It now also operates from depots in Gateshead, Bristol, Cambridge and Eastleigh, transferred from Axiom Rail (part of sister company DB Schenker Rail UK). This gave LNWR a combined turnover of £30million with a 210 strong workforce. The depots service CrossCountry trains on behalf of Bombardier.

Alliance Rail Holdings, acquired by DB in 2010, undertakes strategic development work for Grand Central as well as for its own open access services. On the West Coast main line this includes services between London and Bradford/Leeds, and London and Blackpool/Barrow. On the East Coast main line, Alliance is seeking to introduce London services for a new 'parkway' station at Micklefield as well as Leeds. It is also evaluating services to Scunthorpe, Grimsby and Cleethorpes, and Sheffield, Meadowhall, Barnsley and Huddersfield.

Laing Rail/Chiltern in 2006 joined Renaissance Trains in the Wrexham, Shropshire & Marylebone Railway open-access venture. Later run by Chiltern alone, it closed in 2011 after a loss of £2.8m was made in 2010.

In the first half of 2012, DB said, the UK Trains business improved noticeably, with volumes increased mainly due to acquisition of Grand Central.

Alongside higher revenue and positive exchange rates, government support payments commenced for the CrossCountry franchise, and the acquisition of Grand Central brought a 14 million Euro boost. Total revenues increased by 26.7pc.

Despite a significant increase in cost of materials, due mainly to exchange rate factors, and the acquisition of Grand Central, adjusted profit improved considerably. Adjusted earnings before interest and tax improved by Euro 28 million to Euro 19 million.

DB also plans to launch services through the Channel Tunnel, between London St Pancras and Brussels, Amsterdam (via Rotterdam), Cologne and Frankfurt.

Chiltern Railways

20 year franchise from February 2002

Chiltern Railways' unique 20-year franchise was awarded by the former Strategic Rail Authority in 2002, and is linked to delivery of investment.

Phase One of Chiltern's latest development package, 'Evergreen 3', created new London-Birmingham 'Chiltern Mainline' services from September 2011, with new fastest journey times to London Marylebone of 90min from Birmingham Moor Street, and 70min from Warwick Parkway. Over 50 miles of track were upgraded for 100mph, and key junctions were improved.

A year after the launch of Mainline, the train operator said its total Birmingham to London market had increased by 45.8 per cent, with a 33.6pc increase in journeys between the West Midlands and London.

Free Wi-Fi and a new Business Zone, designed as a cost efficient alternative to First class, are offered on key trains. The company has also restructured fares and restrictions, improved station facilities., Solihull and Warwick Parkway are the latest to have enlarged car parks.

Transport & Works Act approval for Phase 2 of Evergreen 3 was granted in October 2012. An Oxford-London Marylebone service via Bicester will be introduced by 2015 - involving upgrading and partial doubling of the Oxford-Bicester line, with a new link to the Chiltern line at Bicester, and a new multi-modal interchange station north of Oxford. Half hourly trains would take 66min from Oxford to Marylebone. Funding of about £259m for Evergreen 3 is coming from Network Rail, to be repaid by the train operator over 30 years. Chiltern took over operation of the existing Bicester-Oxford service from First Great Western in May 2011.

At the conclusion of the project, Chiltern Railways says a total of £600m will have been invested since the start of its original franchise in 1996 - passenger miles have increased threefold in the same period.

The Oxford service will dovetail with the planned East-West Rail services, which would run Oxford-Bicester-Bletchley-Bedford/Milton Keynes, with Chiltern services extended from Aylesbury to Bletchley and Milton Keynes.

The £80m 'Evergreen 2', completed in 2006, was a Design, Build, Finance & Transfer project, creating new station capacity, signalling and line enhancements, enabling 20 trains per peak hour to use Marylebone. A new £20m Wembley train depot was completed in 2005. 'Evergreen 1' doubled single track between Aynho Junction and Princes Risborough.

A Chiltern Mainline Mk3 train, refurbished with swing plug doors, is headed by Class 67 No 67014 at Birmingham Moor Street. Tony Miles

Passenger Train Operators

Senior personnel
Chiltern Railways

Managing Director Rob Brighouse (in photo)
Business Development Director Graham Cross
Customer Services Director Jennifer Payne
Engineering Director Kate Marjoribanks
Finance Director Duncan Rimmer
Operations and Safety Director Andrew Munden
Commercial Director Thomas Ableman

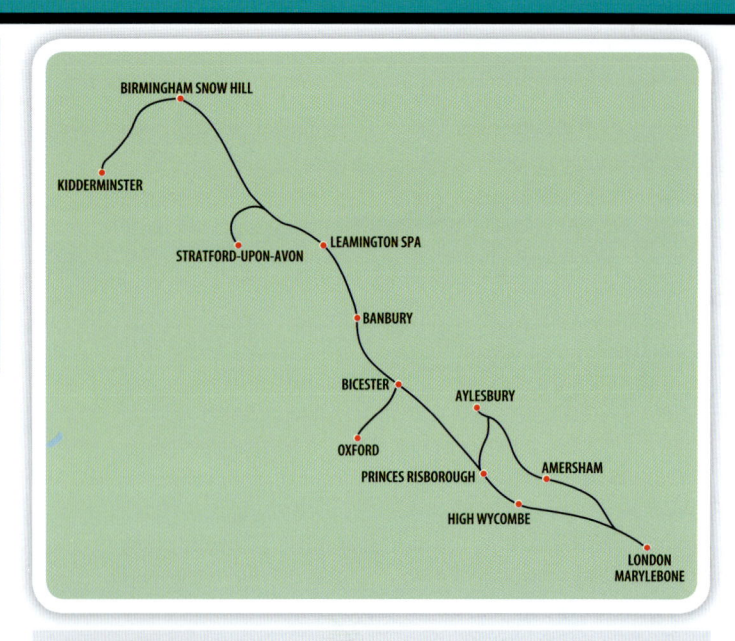

Aylesbury Vale Parkway, a new station 3km north of Aylesbury, designed to serve housing development and park-and-ride, opened in 2008, with a 20 year, £13m concession jointly funded by the Community Infrastructure Fund, Buckinghamshire County Council and John Laing. Chiltern and Laing were responsible for Warwick Parkway, the first non-Railtrack station delivered on the rail network, in 2000.

Chiltern's collaboration with Masabi, Atos, and Access IS to become the first rail operator to go live with the full barcode ticket system was the winner of a Modern Railways Railway Industry Innovation award in 2012. Ticketing by mobile phone was introduced by Chiltern in 2007 and 'print at home' ticketing is also available.

Locomotive-hauled trains of Mk3 coaches have been introduced to London-Birmingham services. A major refurbishment by Wabtec includes power-operated bodyside doors replacing slam doors, and new controlled-emission toilets. From late 2012 the company planned to use three lengthened 6-car sets of refurbished Mk3 coaches, with another set used on a Banbury commuter service.

Up to 13 100mph diesel locomotives featured in an invitation to suppliers in 2012. Currently, Chiltern leases six Class 67s from DB Schenker, which come off lease at the end of 2014. Bids will be compared against continued use of Class 67s.

Four new two-car Class 172 diesel multiple-units from Bombardier went into service in June 2011. The Bombardier-built Class 168 'Clubman' fleet, for longer distance services, has ten 4-car and nine 3-car units. There are 28 two-car and 11 three-car Class 165 'Turbo' trains. Two refurbished Class-121 single-car diesels are used on Aylesbury-Princes Risborough shuttles. Chiltern's main maintenance depot is at Aylesbury. ∎

Key statistics
Chiltern Railways

	2010-11	2011-12
Punctuality (0-5min)	94.0%	93.0%
Passenger journeys (millions)	18.6	19.7
Passenger km (millions)	924.5	1,000.9
Timetabled train km (millions)	9.6	10.3
Route km operated	341.2	341.2
Number of stations operated	30	30
Number of employees	789	750
Subsidy per passenger km (pence)	-1.8	0.65

ARRIVA Trains Wales / Trenau Arriva Cymru

15 year franchise from December 2003

Arriva Trains Wales/Trenau Arriva Cymru (ATW) includes national, regional and local routes within Wales; through services to Birmingham, Manchester and Cheltenham; and the 'Borders' route via Hereford and Shrewsbury.

The 15-year Wales & Borders franchise commenced on 7 December 2003, and in April 2006 the Welsh Government took responsibility for it, gaining powers to fund improvements.

While the franchise was let on assumptions of little growth, there has been 40 per cent growth in journeys since 2003. The business has invested more than £30m in train maintenance and improvements, station upgrades, improved ticketing, information and security, while government investment has included funding of additional trains on routes such as Shrewsbury-Aberystwyth, Holyhead-Cardiff, the Cardiff Valleys and Wrexham-Bidston.

Major changes are expected in South Wales, with electrification of the route between London, Cardiff and Swansea set to take place by 2018, and the entire Valley Lines network around Cardiff to follow by about 2019.

Capacity of 340,000 extra seats a year was added on the Arriva Trains Wales network with the timetable change in May 2012, improvements over and above the requirements set out in ATW's franchise.

Services gaining capacity included Shrewsbury-Telford-Birmingham in the morning commuter period, Birmingham-Aberystwyth in the mid-morning period, Chester-Llandudno Junction in the mid-afternoon and evening commuter period. There were more services between West Wales, Swansea and Cardiff, and improved connections with Irish Sea ferries at Holyhead.

Another 125,000 seats a year were added from September 2012, benefiting several commuter flows, and a revised north-south express service was also introduced. Instead of a twice-daily service, there is a single Holyhead to Cardiff and return service, via Wrexham instead of Crewe, receiving an annual subsidy of about £1.9m. Mk3 vehicles were refurbished by Pullman Rail in Cardiff for the train, which is powered by a Class

Key statistics
Arriva Trains Wales

	2010-11	2011-12
Punctuality (0-5min)	93.9%	94.2%
Passenger Journeys (millions)	27.8	28.4
Passenger km (millions)	1,100.9	1,142.0
Timetabled train km (millions)	23.8	23.6
Route km operated	1,840.8	1,840.8
Number of stations operated	244	243
Number of employees	1,990	2,012
Subsidy per passenger km (pence)	11.8	11.98

Senior personnel
Arriva Trains Wales

Managing Director Tim Bell (in photo)
Operations and Safety Director Mike Tapscott
Customer Services Director Ian Bullock
Commercial Director Mike Bagshaw
Finance Director Rob Phillips
Fleet Director Peter North

67 locomotive, and uses a driving van trailer to enable reversal at Chester. Other trains were rescheduled covering part of the second Holyhead-Cardiff and return service.

The Welsh Government provided £1.4m funding annually to provide five extra daily return trains for Fishguard, from September 2011. A review of the extra services will be carried out after the third year of the scheme.

From May 2011, timetable improvements included faster services between west and south Wales and Manchester, with Cardiff-Manchester journeys accelerated by 15min, bringing them close to 3hr, by exploiting the capability of Class 175 trains.

Current network enhancements include proposals for additional platforms at Cardiff Central, Queen Street, Pontypridd, Caerphilly and Barry; and daytime hourly services between Aberystwyth and Shrewsbury (with details to be confirmed). As part of the National Stations Improvement Plan (NSIP), major enhancements to stations have been completed at Swansea and Chester, in addition to the provision of real time customer information screens and improved access for the disabled.

Redoubling the railway between Chester and Wrexham and between Gowerton and Loughor, and a new station at Energlyn, are also to go ahead. A new station at Ebbw Vale town is also planned for the period beyond 2015.

A complete upgrade of ATW's Class 158 and 153 trains (carried out by LNWR) is in progress, with the Welsh Government providing £7.5m. The Class 175 fleet has also recently been refurbished.

Apart from the Holyhead-Cardiff express train, long-distance services use Class 158 diesel multiple-units (24 trains) and Class 175 'Coradias' (27 trains). A fleet of 30 Class-142/143 Pacer railbuses is mainly used in the Cardiff area, and a refurbished Class 121 railcar works a Cardiff Bay shuttle. There are also 36 Class-150s and 8 single-car Class-153s in the fleet.

The majority of the fleet is based at Cardiff Canton depot, with a £3million purpose-built train care facility at Machynlleth servicing Class 158s, while Class 175s are maintained at manufacturer Alstom's Chester depot. Servicing is also undertaken at Holyhead depot. ∎

An Arriva Trains Wales Class 175 train on the Cardiff-Shrewsbury line passes Stokesay Castle near Craven Arms. ATW

Passenger Train Operators

crosscountry

Franchise from November 2007 to March 2016

The CrossCountry (XC) network is the most extensive GB rail franchise, stretching from Aberdeen to Penzance, and from Stansted to Cardiff. Arriva's franchise started on 11 November 2007 and runs until 31 March 2016.

There are regular half-hourly services on key route sections, including Birmingham to Bristol, Reading, Manchester, Sheffield and Leicester; hourly direct services between Bristol and Manchester; hourly through services for all destinations between Plymouth and Edinburgh (via Leeds), Reading and Newcastle (via Doncaster), Bournemouth and Manchester, Cardiff and Nottingham, Birmingham and Stansted Airport.

CrossCountry is now the main operator of Edinburgh-Motherwell-Glasgow trains. It runs 18 trains each weekday and 12 on Sundays, connecting Glasgow with Northeast England, Yorkshire, the Midlands and Southwest. From December 2010 six Newcastle-Reading services, on alternate hours, were extended to Southampton, resulting in reduction in crowding on Manchester-Bournemouth services.

Work in conjunction with Nomad Digital to equip all High Speed Trains and Voyagers with wi-fi was completed in 2012.

CrossCountry has continued to develop innovations to generate new business and retain existing customers. It has pioneered print-at-home rail e-tickets in the UK, and by 2012, almost 20 per cent of all tickets bought online were e-tickets. XC actively markets attractive fares on lightly used services, with advance purchase tickets on sale until midnight the day before travel.

CrossCountry's Train Tickets app, developed by Masabi, offers a one-stop shop to look up train times, check real-time running information, get prices and buy train tickets on smartphones. XC Advance tickets can be delivered to the app and displayed for inspection, while other tickets can be collected from a self service ticket machine at the station. The app is free to download and there is no booking fee.

The app now includes a journey manager which allows travellers to check real-time train information, platforms and connections.

Business travellers can register for alerts as soon as advance purchase tickets become available for their journeys. Students holding an 'NUS Extra' card receive an extra 10pc discount on CrossCountry Advance tickets, regardless of other discounts.

A new last-minute seat reservation facility has been introduced on all main routes. Passengers can reserve a seat by mobile phone or online through CrossCountry's website up to 10min before train departure.

CrossCountry operates 34 Class-220 (4-car) and 23 Class-221 Voyager trains (22 x 5-car, 1 x 4-car); 29 Class-170 Turbostar diesel multiple-units (16 x 3-car, 13 x 2-car) and 5 HST sets, currently running in 7+2 configuration. The Voyagers have been reconfigured to provide additional seating and luggage space. Each four-car unit now has 202 seats, the five-car sets 264 seats. Work has been carried out to refresh the Voyager interiors, with seat covers

CrossCountry Voyager No 220028 at Penzance on 13 October 2011. Tony Miles

88

In association with SIEMENS

Senior personnel
CrossCountry

Managing Director Andy Cooper (in photo)
Commercial Director David Watkin
Finance Director Jonathan Roberts
Customer Service Director Jeremy Higgins
Production Director Helen Waters
HR Director Maria Zywica
Head of Safety Des Lowe

Key statistics
Cross Country

	2010-11	2011-12
Punctuality (0-10min)	88.2%	89.6%
Passenger journeys (millions)	31.3	33.0
Passenger km (millions)	3,078.5	3,252.4
Timetabled train km (millions)	32.0	32.7
Route km operated	2,661.9	2,661.9
Number of stations operated	0	0
Number of employees	1,610	1,700
Subsidy per passenger km (pence)	1.0	0.21

and carpets being replaced. Improvements to the Voyager's reliability have seen them with the coveted Modern Railways 'Golden Spanner' for the most reliable InterCity train for three consecutive years.

The five HSTs were fully refurbished by Wabtec at Doncaster, with a number of additional trailers converted from loco-hauled vehicles. MTU engines were fitted to the HST power cars. In 2011 CrossCountry's HSTs were awarded the 'Golden Spanner' for the most reliable InterCity 125 Fleet. The HSTs offer either 457 or 462 seats and operate on the main Northeast-Southwest route, releasing Voyagers to strengthen services on other routes. In total the HST programme, along with reconfiguration of the Voyagers, delivered a 35% increase in capacity on principal routes in the evening peaks.

The five HST sets are used on the busiest services between the Northeast and Plymouth. From December 2011 the number in service each weekday has been varied in response to demand.

The Class 170 Turbostars were refreshed by Transys Projects with exterior repainting by Axiom Rail. The various sub-classes inherited from a variety of operators are configured to a standard layout (120 seats in the two-car and 200 in three-car units). The Class 170s operate on Cardiff/Birmingham-Nottingham, Birmingham to Stansted Airport/Leicester routes.

A trial of more frequent stops at Chepstow and Lydney on the Nottingham-Cardiff service concluded in 2012. XC is only required to stop two trains at these stations in each direction, but the trial proved sufficient demand existed for the extra services to be included in future timetables. ■

Passenger Train Operators

A Grand Central HST led by No 43465 heads towards King's Cross at Stevenage on 28 September 2012. Tony Miles

Open access company

Grand Central Railway's first open access services from Sunderland/Hartlepool to London via York were launched in December 2007. A series of changes in ownership culminated in the company being acquired by Arriva in November 2011.

After some early reliability problems, a full timetable of three return trains every day between Sunderland and King's Cross, now branded the 'North Eastern' service, began in 2008. A successful application for a fourth path on weekdays and Saturdays enabled Grand Central to introduce an additional morning departure from Sunderland and mid-evening return from London King's Cross in 2009, both of which are generating significant numbers of new passenger. From December 2012, Grand Central is introducing a fifth return service on this route.

At the end of 2011/12 Grand Central's moving annual average punctuality score was 84.1pc. Despite the economic situation, by October 2012, journey growth was 24pc since the start of the year.

In February 2009 the Office of Rail Regulation (ORR) granted access rights for three return services between London King's Cross and Bradford Interchange, and the new 'West Riding' service started in May 2010, calling at Halifax, Brighouse, Wakefield Kirkgate, Pontefract and Doncaster. While access rights for the North Eastern service were originally granted until December 2014, these were extended to December 2016, the end date for the current West Riding rights, on condition that Grand Central delivered improvements at stations, including CCTV, and information systems.

For the additional Sunderland and West Riding trains, Grand Central leased five Class 180 diesel trains from Angel Trains. All West Riding services are worked by these, while North Eastern duties are shared with three diesel high-speed trains. In March 2010 the 21 HST vehicles (6 Class-43 power cars and 15 Mk3 coaches) were sold by Sovereign Trains Ltd, a sister company of Grand Central, to Angel Trains. As part of the deal Angel agreed to a substantial programme of engineering works to improve performance and reliability. This included installation of new MTU engines, and various reliability and interior modifications for passenger vehicles. Grand Central agreed to lease the sets until at least December 2016.

The Class 180s have also been refreshed with installation of Wi-Fi and at-seat power sockets. A programme of reliability modifications on all operators' Class 180 sets commenced in autumn 2011. Northern Rail maintains Grand Central's trains at Heaton depot in Newcastle and provides Riding Inspectors to check on trains en route. Additionally, the two West Riding Class 180s are serviced overnight at Crofton depot, Wakefield, by Bombardier.

Grand Central believes passengers should not be penalised for last minute decisions to travel, and offers competitive, easy to understand fares which can be bought at the same price whether on line, on train or at a staffed station. The company has offered special pricing to encourage travellers to sample its services, and introduced an advance purchase offer via its website. Seat reservations are free of charge for passengers to/from London.

The company is working with industry partners and local authorities to help improve passenger information, and has introduced station ambassadors at Hartlepool to improve r information and assistance when the station is unstaffed on Sundays. It is undertaking a similar scheme for Eaglescliffe, where a ticket office and improved passenger facilities have been opened.

To date Grand Central has invested over £40 million of private capital in trains and people, as well as covering its start-up costs, and will have completed a £400,000 programme of investment in stations by the end of 2013. It continues to develop plans for station investment in conjunction with other industry partners.

With a total staff of 121, Grand Central has created more than 55 new jobs in Sunderland, 35 new jobs in Bradford and 20 in York - skilled, permanent positions which it believes make a real contribution to economic development.

Grand Central has confirmed that it will continue to focus on developing its services on the East Coast main line by introducing additional services on each of its routes. The company has introduced calls at Mirfield, and is also seeking to reduce overall journey times to London by around 20min. ∎

Senior personnel

Grand Central

Chairman Bob Holland
Managing Director Richard McClean (in photo)
Marketing Manager David Crocker
Fleet Engineer Dave Hatfield
Operations Director Sean English

HITACHI Inspire the Next

In association with **SIEMENS**

Serco and Abellio

A 50-50 partnership of Serco and Abellio (formerly NedRailways) holds the Northern Rail and Merseyrail rail franchises. Abellio alone has the Greater Anglia franchise.

Serco, an international service company, also operates, maintains and supports the Docklands Light Railway in London under a seven-year franchise agreement from March 2006, and began operating and maintaining the new Dubai Metro in September 2009. Serco Rail Technologies specialises in design, development, and provision of infrastructure measurement and assessment services. Operations in transport and local authority direct services account for approximately 35pc of UK & Europe revenues.

Abellio is an international public transport company which delivers rail and bus services to over one million passengers every day across the UK, Germany and the Czech Republic. With a stated philosophy of working in partnership with clients and all other stakeholders, it aims to consistently exceed expectations of passengers and stakeholders. The group's international best practice programme facilitates a structured exchange of expertise between staff in all Abellio's subsidiaries and its parent company Netherlands Railways.

northern

Franchise extended until 1 April 2014

The Department for Transport in 2012 granted a continuation of Northern Rail's franchise from 15 September 2013 until 1 April 2014. The franchise began in December 2004.

Northern runs local and regional train services for northwest and northeast England, Yorkshire, and Humberside, and had already secured a two-year extension in 2010, triggered by improved punctuality and reliability. The new end date coincides with the earliest possible termination of the First TransPennine Express franchise: re-mapping is an option being considered for new franchises.

Since its franchise began, Northern has provided a more punctual and reliable railway, increasing the number of trains arriving on time from 83.7pc to 91.9pc in early 2012; and it has attracted over 40pc growth in passenger demand. Against a 'no growth, no investment' franchise specification, it has attracted over £100m of external investment, and Serco and Abellio have invested £30m to deliver more trains, better stations and new services. Northern and its partners have also welcomed additional carriages, new stations, as well as improved station facilities and employee accommodation, and Northern said its trains were 60pc more reliable by mid 2012 than at the start of the franchise.

In the additional franchise period, Northern pledged to upgrade washing plants to improve cleanliness of trains; improve facilities at a number of stations; and work with partners to install more customer information screens.

Research estimates that, each year, Northern services generate at least £650m of economic and other benefits for the north of England, providing a 2:1 return on subsidy.

December 2011 saw an additional 8,550 seats every day on services into main urban destinations (Leeds, Liverpool, Manchester, Newcastle and Sheffield), with over 5,200 of these in peak hours. The improvement marks completion of an agreement with the DfT which added over 60 vehicles to Northern's fleet. Class 142 and Class 150 DMUs came from First Great Western and London Midland, and a small number of Class 156 and 180 trains left for other operators. Five 4-car Class 322 EMUs were transferred from ScotRail.

Allerton depot, operational since December 2011, is home to Northern's fleet of additional '156' trains. The depot was made as 'green' as possible by, for example, using recycled concrete walkways; rain water harvesting and a train washer which recycles up to 80pc of water; and energy efficient lighting and radiant heaters. Delivered in partnership with Network Rail at a cost of £10.6mn,

A Northern Class 158 diesel multiple-unit at Nottingham. Tony Miles

HITACHI Inspire the Next

91

Passenger Train Operators

Key statistics
Northern

	2010-11	2011-12
Punctuality (0-5min)	90.8%	91.8%
Passenger journeys (millions)	86.8	91.5
Passenger km (millions)	2,026.3	2,132.9
Timetabled train km (millions)	44.4	44.6
Route km operated	2,745.5	2,745.5
Number of stations operated	462	464
Number of employees	4,790	4,853
Subsidy per passenger km (pence)	3.4	4.5

time and cost savings were made by partially running design and construction work in parallel. As a result, the depot was operational within six months. Further EMUs will be added to Northern's fleet by 2019 period as part of the Northwest electrification: some are likely to be based at Allerton.

As part of its review of franchising, the DfT launched consultation in 2012 on rail decentralisation and governance of future north of England franchises. Options included transfer of responsibility for all services to a single franchising organisation; maintaining the status quo; or allocating control over groups of services to local bodies.

Local authorities have been considering a proposal for a new executive body, formed by Greater Manchester, South Yorkshire, West Yorkshire and York council, to assume responsibility for a franchise made up from much of the present Northern and TransPennine franchises. Over 80pc of services in a Northern/TPE franchise would be within the four local authorities' boundaries. Merseyside and Tyne & Wear have been considering different arrangements, possibly working alongside the executive body.

Northern Rail and Network Rail signed a framework agreement for an alliance in 2012. It focuses on seeking ways to improve industry efficiency and reduce costs to deliver improved facilities and services for passengers.

Northern supports community rail partnerships on many of its routes, and many other community rail groups including over 60 station partnerships.

Northern operates a diverse fleet of diesel multiple-units: 79 Class-142, and 13 two-car and 10 three-car Class 144 'Pacers'; 58 Class-150s; 7 Class-155s; 42 Class-156s; 37 two-car and 8 three-car Class-158s; and 18 single car Class-153s. There are eight Class-321/322 electric multiple-units (EMUs) and 16 Class-333s operated in West Yorkshire, with 17 Class-323s used mainly in Greater Manchester.

The main maintenance depots are at Newcastle (Heaton), Manchester (Newton Heath), and Leeds (Neville Hill) and Liverpool (Allerton). Concentrating maintenance of each type of train at particular depots has helped to improve reliability. Alstom's West Coast Traincare maintains the Class 323s at Manchester. ∎

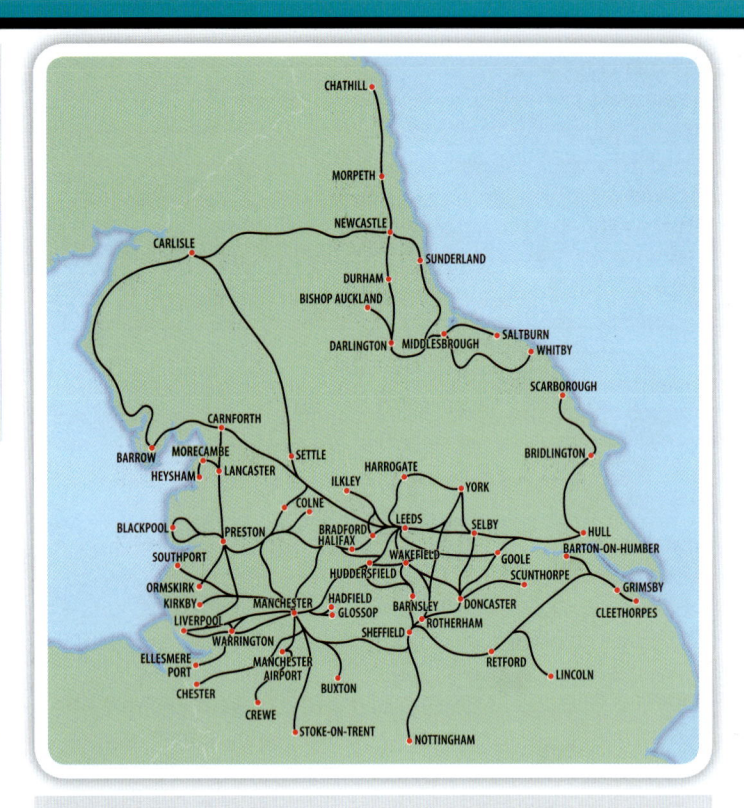

Senior personnel
Northern

Managing Director Ian Bevan (in photo)
Chief Operating Officer Alan Chaplin
Commercial Director Jonathan Stewart
Engineering Director Stuart Draper
Performance and Planning Director Rob Warnes
Safety and Assurance Director Gary Stewart
HR Director Adrian Thompson
Area Directors Lee Wasnidge, Richard Allan

Merseyrail

25-year concession from 20 July 2003

Merseytravel, the Merseyside Public Transport Executive, manages the unique operating concession for this 75-mile, self-contained network of 750V DC, third-rail electrified railway. The 25-year contract, with a total value of £3.6bn, was awarded in 2003 to the Serco and Abellio joint venture, subject to five-yearly reviews. Merseytravel livery is carried on trains and stations.

Merseyrail is one of the most heavily used networks outside London, with almost 800 trains per weekday carrying 110,000 passengers a day, on 15min train frequencies, increasing to 5min on city centre sections.

The Northern Line serves Southport/Ormskirk/Kirkby to Hunts Cross, and the Wirral Line serves West Kirby/New Brighton/Chester/Ellesmere Port and a central Liverpool loop line - 6.5 miles in tunnel with four underground stations in Liverpool and one in Birkenhead. Three of these five stations are getting a £40m-plus overhaul, starting with £20m of improvements completed in October 2012 at the network's busiest station, Liverpool Central, which served 17.9m passengers in 2010/11.

The funding package is shared between Network Rail, Merseytravel and the European Rail Development Fund. Work began in September 2012 at James Street, with Lime Street to follow in 2013.

At Central, transformation of the concourse was carried out by Merseyrail and contractor Strategic Team Group, while Network Rail and contractor Morgan Sindall improved the platforms, escalators and passageways. The station has gained an additional lift, replacement escalators to

Senior personnel
Merseyrail

Managing Director Maarten Spaargaren (in photo)
Operations Director Andy Heath
Engineering Director Mike Roe
Finance and Commercial Director Paul Bowen
Head of Marketing & Commercial Revenue Matt Roche
Head of Property and Programme Management Simon Olorenshaw

In association with **SIEMENS**

Key statistics
Merseyrail

	2010-11	2011-12
Punctuality (0-5min)	94.9%	95.2%
Passenger journeys (millions)	44.9	43.5
Passenger km (millions)	545.1	634.3
Timetabled train km (millions)	6.1	6.4
Route km operated	120.7	120.7
Number of stations operated	66	66
Number of employees	1,200	1,220

the Northern Line; additional platform space; and improved toilets and waiting areas. A clear glazed roof and glass external walls allow natural lighting.

Merseytravel has asked manufacturers for expressions of interest in supplying a new train fleet - the current fleet of Class 507 and Class 508 trains was built in 1978-79. Trains are maintained and stabled at Kirkdale and Birkenhead North depots.

In previous years, Merseytravel has invested more than £100m in Merseyrail, refurbished eight stations and built six new ones, with £32m invested in refurbishing rolling stock.

Nearly half of Merseyrail passengers are daily users. Performance is consistently good, and a Public Performance Measure figure of over 95pc is consistently achieved. In 2012 Merseyrail achieved an overall satisfaction rating in the National Passenger Survey of 96pc, the highest score for any train company.

In recent years, six-car trains were introduced on more peak time services, achieved through timetable and train engineering improvements. Merseyrail introduced more services between Liverpool and Chester from December 2010, running every 15min throughout the day.

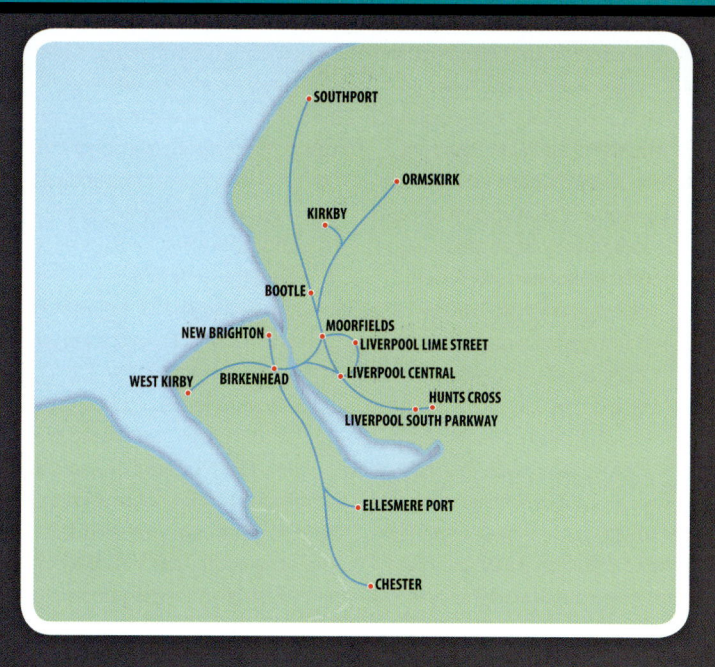

Electrification and integration into Merseyrail of the Bidston-Wrexham, Kirkby-Wigan and Ormskirk-Preston lines are ambitions of Merseytravel, as are a number of new lines and stations.

Merseyrail in 2010 became the first 'fully secure' rail network in the UK with all 66 stations and 36 car parks accredited by the British Transport Police. Merseyrail staff, police and partners such as byelaw enforcement officers work together to create a consistent high visibility presence to counter anti-social behaviour and ticketless travel. A penalty fare scheme covers all stations. Security improvements has seen reduction in fare evasion from 15pc to 3.5pc, in passenger assaults by more than 60pc, and staff assaults by 50pc.

Merseyrail Class 508 EMU No 508123 stops at Moorfields, working a service to Kirkby on 30 April 2012. Fred Kerr

Passenger Train Operators

Liverpool South Parkway, a £32m new station, was opened in 2006 at the intersection of the Merseyrail electric and Liverpool-Crewe routes. It has a bus shuttle to Liverpool John Lennon Airport, acts as a hub for local bus routes, and offers park-and-ride.

Merseyrail's latest 'MtoGo' stores are at Maghull and Lime Street. The first of these combined retail outlet and ticket units opened at Moorfields in 2006, and others are at Hamilton Square, Southport, Liverpool Central, Hooton, and Waterloo - tailored to suit both large and smaller locations.

Merseytravel began introduction of smartcard technology in 2011, investing a 'seven-figure' sum in the technology, after receiving a £2.2m grant from government.

After trials in 2012 of a smartcard 'ticket at home' system, Merseytravel aimed to develop the system alongside full roll-out of its Walrus smartcard in 2013. The new system allows customers to download products such as travel tickets onto their card through a reader attached to their PC.

Merseytravel, in partnership with the European Regional Development Fund (ERDF), was in late 2012 completing two new park and ride facilities on the Wirral Line at Bidston and Birkenhead North stations, providing 464 parking spaces. Both are on former brownfield land made available through Wirral MBC. ∎

GreaterAnglia

29 month franchise from 5 February 2012

The Greater Anglia (GA) franchise was awarded to Abellio, running from 5 February 2012 for 29 months. The government then expects to let a significantly longer franchise.

The previous franchise, held by National Express East Anglia, ran from April 2004, and a programme of improvements and capacity enhancement had been progressed in conjunction with the DfT. Since the commencement of the new franchise, Greater Anglia has installed new ticket machines at key stations, introduced mobile-phone and print-at-home ticketing and complimentary refreshments in First Class on London-Norwich and Stansted Express trains. It installed new information desks at stations, and equipped 1,600 frontline customer service employees with Blackberrys to improve communication.

Greater Anglia has made consistent improvements in punctuality, working closely with Network Rail through an alliance to deliver improved performance. A revised approach to engineering work will mean far fewer disruptive possessions (and bus replacements). The moving annual average PPM punctuality scores for GA as a whole in autumn 2012 showed that the main line (including intercity services) and the Metro/Southend services had reached their highest levels of performance for over 12 years, with the figure of 94pc among the highest ever achieved.

The company has worked with a region-wide alliance of stakeholders supporting an East Anglian Rail Prospectus, to help influence and increase rail investment in the region.

Greater Anglia made a great success of delivering services during the 2012 Olympic and Paralympic Games, carrying 7.7m passengers into London during this period, with 94.9pc of trains on time and around 1.3m additional passenger journeys made.

The company has continued to develop and promote its rural 'community' railways and a new Hereward Community Rail Partnership was launched in October 2012 to promote services between Peterborough

Key statistics
Greater Anglia

	2010-11	2011-12
Punctuality	90.2%	90.9%
Passenger journeys (millions)	115.0	122.8
Passenger km (millions)	3,886.5	4,035.6
Timetabled train km (millions)	32.7	33.3
Route km operated	1,611.0	1,611.0
Number of stations operated	167	167
Number of employees	2,869	2,878
Subsidy per passenger km (pence)	-2.8	-2.22

(Figures until 5 February 2012 for National Express East Anglia)

and Ely. GA has doubled the cash contribution to existing CRPs and has contributed towards the starting up of the Hereward CRP, while innovative projects like the App for the Bittern and Wherry lines are also being introduced.

From December 2012, Greater Anglia has scheduled an hourly Ipswich-Lowestoft service, enabled by a new passing loop at Beccles. In 2013, and for the rest of the franchise, further improvement plans include Oyster pay-as-you-go extended to more stations, and improved car park and cycle facilities at a number of locations including Cambridge and Chelmsford. Plans are being progressed to develop a scheduled bus service trial linking Saffron Walden with Audley End station. Station improvement schemes will continue and colour-coded timetables are to be introduced, providing information on train loadings.

A renewed focus on marketing is encouraging more passenger journeys. An innovative partnership with Visit East Anglia has seen significant joint initiatives developed with the tourist industry to promote regional attractions and visits by train, with 2 for 1 and other incentives. Greater Anglia is also extending advance tickets, already available on its intercity services, to stations on the Clacton / Walton line, and also Ely and Cambridge, to attract leisure and off-peak travellers.

Greater Anglia operates 30 new Class 379 four-car electric multiple-units (EMUs), built by Bombardier and used on Stansted Express and some Cambridge services, as part of a capacity enhancement initiative, together with 17 four-car Class 321 EMUs that were transferred from London Midland. These '321s' are being refurbished during the short franchise. The fleet of Class 153s has been upgraded, and a programme to improve and refurbish Class 156s is underway, including installation of accessible toilet facilities. All trains in the fleet were deep cleaned in advance of the Olympics.

Main train depots are at Ilford, Norwich and Clacton, with cleaning and stabling at other locations. The fleet of four-car electric multiple-units, based at Ilford, is made up of: 61 Class-315s, 51 Class-317s, 94 Class-321 s, 21 Class-360s, and 30 Class 379s.

The diesel fleet is made up of: five single-car Class-153s, nine Class-156s, four two-car Class-170s and eight three-car Class-170s. The locomotive-hauled fleet is comprised of 15 Class-90 locomotives and 15 Mk3 Driving Van Trailers along with 119 Mk3 coaches. Two Class 08 shunters are hired; and also Class 47 diesel locomotives for 'Thunderbird' rescue duties and to power the Norwich-Great Yarmouth legs of high season London-Great Yarmouth services, as well as additional trains for special events. ■

Propelled by Class 90 No 90009 'Diamond Jubilee' in Jubilee livery, the 12.00 London Liverpool Street to Norwich approaches Stratford on 4 May 2012. Brian Morrison

Senior personnel
Greater Anglia

Managing Director Ruud Haket (in photo)
Operations Director Nanouke van't Riet
Customer Service Director Andrew Goodrum
Finance Director Adam Golton
Engineering Director John Ratcliffe
Asset Management Director Simone Bailey
HR & Safety Director Michelle Smart
Projects Director TJ Noomen
Commercial Director Andy Camp

Passenger Train Operators

c2c

London, Tilbury & Southend franchise

National Express became responsible for c2c in 2000, when it took over Prism Rail after financial problems at other Prism franchises. The London, Tilbury & Southend (LTS) route franchise had been awarded in May 1996 in a 15-year deal.

The company name was changed to c2c in July 2002, as part of a £400million investment programme including a £300million fleet of 74 new trains. According to company statements at the time, 'c2c' could indicate 'coast to capital' or 'commitment to customers'.

The franchise is the only one currently held by National Express. It was extended for two years, to 26 May 2013, as the Department for Transport prepared for revisions in franchising policy. The deal included key commitments on additional trains and staffing during the 2012 Olympic and Paralympic Games, with further station improvements, and an improved frequency of service at West Ham, for connections to Canary Wharf.

Passenger demand broke records for c2c during the London 2012 Games, with 1.96m journeys during the 17 days of the Games. An estimated 425,000 travellers were going to Games events. Leigh-on-Sea station had its busiest ever weekend during the mountain bike event. 30,000 journeys to and from the station were almost four times as many as the average for a summer holiday weekend. Almost 380,000 journeys were made on c2c to and from West Ham, a main station for the Olympic Park. 98.8 per cent of c2c trains were on time during the Games, despite the extra passengers.

c2c's timetable from December 2011 introduced 22 more weekday stops at West Ham in morning and evening peak periods, following upgrading of signalling equipment. The timetable from May 2011 featured almost 6,000 additional seats each weekday, following completion of a train refurbishment programme. The upgrade for c2c's Class 357 fleet saw all 74 four-car trains refreshed in a new livery as part of the scheduled maintenance programme.

c2c started a new alliance with Network Rail in 2012, building on an established partnership, which included joint signalling and operating control based at Upminster. Better management of stations, better planning of engineering work, and further improvements to punctuality are key aspirations. c2c set up a new security team in 2012 to tackle any anti social behaviour issues on stations or trains.

Over the year to 15 September 2012, 97.2 per cent of c2c trains were on time - a new GB record, and the 10th successive time that c2c had finished top of the moving annual average punctuality table.

c2c Class 357/0 Electrostar No 357006 'Diamond Jubilee 1952-2012' passes Shadwell on 4 May 2012 - one of five c2c Electrostars in Jubilee livery, with the Union Jack on one carriage and the official Diamond Jubilee emblem on the train doors. Brian Morrison

Senior personnel

Managing Director Julian Drury (in photo)
Operations Director Kevin Frazer
Finance Director Richard Bowley
Engineering Director Ben Ackroyd
Head of Retail Hugh Jennings

c2c also held the UK record for any 4-week performance period at 98.8pc, and came close to matching this, at 98.7pc, in the four weeks ending 15 September 2012 - the best result for any train operating company in the period, which included the Paralympic Games.

The company has also recorded good customer satisfaction results, at 91pc in six successive Passenger Focus surveys up to June 2012, when it was the joint-second highest score.

All maintenance and servicing on the Class 357 fleet are performed, in partnership with manufacturer Bombardier, at East Ham depot, along with some heavy maintenance, with other heavy repairs including tyre turning, bogie overhauls, corrosion repairs, and painting at Bombardier's Ilford heavy maintenance depot. Stabling also takes place at Shoeburyness. The company switched its entire fleet to regenerative braking in 2007.

Infrastructure works, including platform extensions, have been completed for 12-car trains. Driver-only operation is used for trains of up to 8 cars.

New platforms were to be constructed at Benfleet station in a major project over the Christmas 2012 period, during which the rail bridge was to be replaced. ■

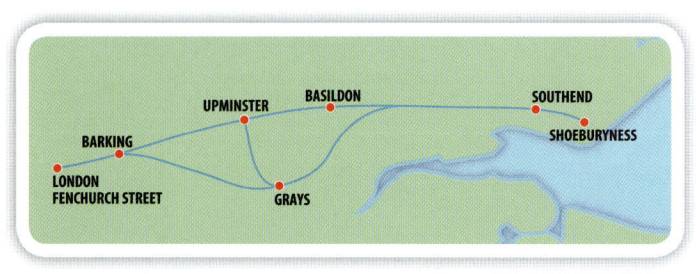

Key statistics

c2c

	2010-11	2011-12
Punctuality	94.8%	96.8%
Passenger journeys (millions)	35.3	36.4
Passenger km (millions)	957.8	988.8
Timetabled train km (millions)	6.4	6.5
Route km operated	129.6	115.5
Number of stations operated	24	25
Number of employees	586	779
Subsidy per passenger km (pence):	-0.7	-1.22

EAST COAST

Publicly-owned operator since 2009

East Coast's trains link London with Scotland, serving York, Newcastle, Edinburgh, Aberdeen and Inverness, and also link London and Leeds, with less frequent services to Hull, Lincoln, Harrogate, Skipton, Bradford and Glasgow. A subsidiary of government-owned holding company Directly Operated Railways, East Coast Main Line Company Limited is responsible for the route's intercity services until a new franchise is let to the private sector.

Services were transferred to the new company when National Express's East Coast franchise was terminated in November 2009. Total premiums of £1.4bn were due over the franchise from December 2007 to March 2015, but revenue was undermined by the economic downturn.

Turnover for the year to 31 March 2012 was £665.8m (2011: £645.5m), while operating expenditure was £661.0m (2011: £641.3m), generating an operating profit before DfT service payments and taxation of £195.7m (2011: £182.8m), and an operating profit after DfT service payments before taxation of £7.1m (2011: £6.5m).

Year on year growth was 3 per cent, slightly behind overall industry comparators - East Coast said this weaker performance reflected economic conditions in regions it serves.

A major timetable change was introduced in May 2011, accompanied by a new First-class complimentary food and drinks offer. Some £10.2m was invested in depots, trains and equipment. The company went from serving typically 100,000 meals a year to over a million.

The new timetable provided 19 additional services each weekday, and 3m extra seats per year. Highlights are the early morning 4hr 'Flying Scotsman' from Edinburgh to London, calling only at Newcastle, and a 2hr non-stop train from Leeds to London. One new daily Lincoln-London return train was introduced, instead of the two-hourly service previously proposed - a change estimated to save £9m a year, avoiding acquisition of additional trains. Most East Coast services to Glasgow were replaced by extra CrossCountry trains on the Edinburgh-Glasgow section.

Following the changes, passenger numbers increased overall by 21pc in First Class in 2011-12, with numbers on the flagship London-Edinburgh route increasing by as much as 39pc. Other initiatives included print-at-home ticketing and a £0.5m upgrade of on-board Wi-Fi systems.

With typically four-fifths or more of delays still caused by external factors, East Coast has been examining with Network Rail ways to ensure a sustainable step-change in reliability. DOR said it was encouraged by Network Rail's new devolved management structure, with closer joint working beginning to deliver better operational performance, and plans for renewal of essential equipment starting to be addressed.

The train fleet is comprised of 31 Class-91 electric locomotives which power 30 rakes of Mk4 coaches to make up InterCity225 trains; and 13 diesel HST sets (refurbished with new MTU engines), with a 14th transferred from East Midlands Trains in 2011.

The DfT in the summer of 2012 announced the replacement of the HST fleet under the InterCity Express Programme. East Coast was looking at options for the IC225 electric fleet - life extension, replacing the locomotives, or entire replacement. Existing fleet leases terminate by 2015. East Coast in 2012 appointed asset and maintenance management experts Vetasi to provide a new engineering maintenance management system, a £1.5 million investment to provide more visible and readily-available maintenance and defect information. ■

Key statistics
East Coast

	2010-11	2011-12
Punctuality (0-10min)	83.3%	86.6%
Passenger Journeys (millions)	18.5	18.9
Passenger km (millions)	4,771.5	4,893.3
Timetabled train km (millions)	19.9	21.7
Route km operated	1,429.1	1,480.6
Number of stations operated	12	12
Number of employees	2,807	2,876
Subsidy per passenger km (pence)	-3.6	-3.84

Senior personnel
East Coast

Managing Director Karen Boswell (in photo)
Operations Director Danny Williams
Finance Director Tim Kavanagh
Commercial and Customer Service Director Peter Williams
Engineering Director Jack Commandeur
Business Planning Director Phil Cameron
Stations and Property Director Tim Hedley-Jones

Passenger Train Operators

Eurostar train at London St Pancras International. Eurostar

EUROSTAR™

International inter-city trains

Since its launch in 1994, Eurostar's trains have carried more than 115 million passengers on the high-speed service linking Britain with France and Belgium via the Channel Tunnel.

Eurostar was official international rail services provider to the London 2012 Olympic and Paralympic Games, and carried hundreds of thousands of fans and competitors from the continent to London. Two trains were adapted to carry up to 18 wheelchair users unable to transfer from a wheelchair to a seat, as well as many other wheelchair users, and other Paralympic athletes with special travel needs.

Eurostar reported a net profit of over £20m in 2011, its first full year of operation as a standalone company. Total sales revenue grew by 6pc to £803m, with particularly strong growth in the second half of the year. On a like for like basis, after adjusting the 2010 results for the volcanic ash cloud impact on airlines, sales revenues grew by 10pc. Passenger numbers rose 2pc to 9.7million.

Eurostar was launched by the three countries' state railways, with the British interest sold by the government in 1996 to its chosen Channel Tunnel Rail Link development group, London & Continental Railways (LCR). As it prepared to sell the Channel Tunnel Rail Link (High Speed 1 - HS1), the government took control of LCR in June 2009, and in September 2010, a new standalone joint venture company, Eurostar International (EI), replaced the unincorporated joint venture of the three national companies. The UK has a 40 per cent shareholding, SNCF (French Railways) 55pc, and SNCB (Belgian Railways) 5pc.

European Commission approval for EI was subject to conditions including access to stations, information systems and maintenance services for competitors, as new EU rules encourage greater international rail competition - train paths would be released if competitors could not obtain them through allocation procedures.

Eurostar announced in October 2010, as the new access rules were introduced, that it was to buy a new fleet of 10 Siemens Velaro-based 320km/h trains (named 'e320'), to be delivered in 2014. A £700m rolling stock programme also covers overhaul and refurbishment of existing trains by 2013, and rebranding. Nomad Digital in autumn 2011 was awarded a contract to supply onboard wi-fi connectivity and state-of-the-art infotainment on the existing fleet.

The new trains will be equipped for multi-voltage, multi-signalling-system operation, to possible new destinations including Amsterdam (under 4hr) and Geneva (around 5hr). Though the same length as existing trains, the e320 will have about 150 more seats.

Following major disruption to services during adverse winter weather in December 2009, new investment of £28m was committed, to improve resilience of trains in severe winter conditions, as well as passenger care during disruption, and customer communication inside and outside the Channel Tunnel.

The opening in 2007 of HS1, the new line from London to the Channel Tunnel, with its new London St Pancras terminal, saw journey times cut by about 20min, with a new station opened at Ebbsfleet, north Kent, joining the established Ashford, east Kent. The London-Paris non-stop timing is now 2hr 16min.

Record journey times were achieved on special runs before normal services began on HS1 in 2007: Paris-London, 2hr 3min, and Brussels-London, 1hr 43min.

Travel on Eurostar continues to be a major attraction for international travellers coming to London, says the company, with the number of passengers originating outside Europe growing by 11% in the first half of 2012 compared with last year. This was attributed in part to a strong increase in the number of passengers originating from the US and the Far East who see Eurostar as an integral part of the European tour – particularly in an Olympic year.

Eurostar introduced a new quiet coach facility from September 2012. In 2011 the flagship Business Premier class was enhanced, with new menus, a new guaranteed boarding service; a mobile app for iPhone and Android users including new, mobile ticketing; on-board taxi bookings; and enhancements to business traveller facilities in Paris and Brussels. Standard Premier is a 'mid-class' designed for cost-conscious business travellers, and others who want extra space and service.

Under its Tread Lightly environmental plan launched in April 2007, Eurostar set a target of reducing carbon dioxide emissions per traveller journey by 35pc over five years. A new target was also set of a 25pc cut in wider Eurostar business emissions by 2015, alongside studies of Eurostar's direct and indirect carbon footprint, and new Sustainable Travel Awards to promote local initiatives in the UK, France and Belgium.

Eurostar operates a fleet of 28 trains - each 400 metres long, weighing 750 tonnes and carrying 750 passengers in 18 carriages. Three more 'Three Capitals' trains (and seven 14-car trains built for aborted UK regional services) are used only on French domestic services. ■

Senior personnel

Chief Executive Officer Nicolas Petrovic (in photo)
Operations Director Delphine Couzi
Director of Stations Mikaël Lemarchand
Chief Information Officer Christophe Lemaire
Director of Strategy Kara Livingston
Commercial Director Nicholas Mercer
Director of Business and Service Continuity Richard Morris
Service and People Director Marc Noaro
Director of Regulatory Affairs & Company Secretary Gareth Williams
Director of Marketing and Brand Lionel Benbassat

In association with **SIEMENS**

EURO TUNNEL

Cross-Channel and rail freight group

In just under 18 years up to 2011, 284 million people and 57 million vehicles travelled through the Channel Tunnel, which consists of twin railway tunnels and a service tunnel.

Operated by Eurotunnel under a 100-year concession signed in 1986 with the French and British governments, the Tunnel opened in 1994. Terminals at Folkestone and Coquelles provide car, coach and lorry access to shuttle trains. International passenger and freight trains also run through the Tunnel.

Traffic boomed during the London 2012 Games: 15,152 vehicles travelled by shuttle (in both directions) on 11 August 2012, a new daily record.

Group revenues for 2011 grew to Euro 845 million (11 per cent up on 2010, like for like), generating a net profit of Euro 11m. Group debt stood at Euro 3.6bn (compared with Euro 4.3bn in 2007, following restructuring that wiped out Euro 5 billion of debt).

Eurotunnel's international rail freight subsidiary, Europorte, includes operations in France, and the British operator GBRf. It is responsible for UK-France freight haulage for operators other than DB Schenker (successor to British Rail's freight business).

Tests on a new-generation Alstom Prima II locomotive were conducted in September 2012 to check compatibility with Tunnel systems and safety standards. Eurotunnel is pursuing application of European Interoperability Specifications, one aim being that standard rail freight services can run in the Tunnel without needing the specialised Class 92 locomotives.

Europorte owns 16 Class-92 locomotives (though not all are in use), equipped for North of London, Tunnel and North of France 25kV 50Hz pantograph supply; and for the UK 750V-DC third-rail network. Locos such as Prima II can use four different power supplies (25kV, 15kV, 1500V and 3,000V) and run on all European freight corridors.

Europorte also plans a piggyback railway network to carry lorry trailers across Europe and into Britain. The Modalohr piggyback wagon has been authorised for use in the Tunnel, and a test of lorry trailers on rail between Antwerp and Barking in May 2012 used 6-axle 'Sdggmrss Twin' pocket wagons.

Eurotunnel has bought the three ferries previously used by Sea France for Euro 65million, with financial support from French local authorities. The ferries are leased to independent operating company MyFerryLink.

Europorte revenues increased in 2011 to Euro 157.8m (+26pc like for like) as a result of the signature of new contracts and the maintenance of all the established Europorte France contracts.

The number of through Channel Tunnel freight trains increased by 14 per cent in 2011 and tonnage by 17 per cent. The growth included new intermodal services and short term transportation of steel. Freight shuttle traffic experienced 16pc growth, increasing market share by 3.5pc.

A European Railway Agency report in March 2011 found passenger trains with distributed traction (rather than power cars at train ends) could be permitted in the Tunnel, as required in Deutsche Bahn and Eurostar plans for new international passenger services.

Installation of four SAFE fire-fighting points was completed in 2011 - they are designed to suppress fires on lorry shuttles, and hot-spot detectors are used on every lorry before a shuttle departs. SAFE delivers water at high pressure to produce a mist of micro-droplets.

The tunnel's radio system has been upgraded to digital GSM-R (Global System for Mobile Communications - Railways), and mobile phone reception was being added, under Euro 21.5m and Euro 14m contracts with Alcatel-Lucent.

Eurotunnel has nine passenger shuttles for cars and coaches (one was restored in 2012 after being out of use), and 15 lorry shuttles. Each 800-metre long shuttle has two locomotives, one at each end.

Shuttle locomotives have three bogies, each with two motorised axles, giving excellent wheel/rail adhesion. After upgrading of most of the initial 5.6MW locomotives, 43 of 7MW rating were in service, with 13 expected to remain at 5.6MW. There are also seven Krupp/MaK diesel locomotives - including an additional two purchased in conjunction with Eurostar, for rescue of broken-down trains, after severe problems during winter 2009-10.

Eurotunnel increased the top speed of its shuttle services from 140km/h to 160km/h in 2012, shortening crossing times and creating more capacity.

A joint venture with STAR Capital - ElecLink - to develop a 500MW electrical interconnector between Great Britain and France was announced by Eurotunnel in 2011, with investment envisaged of about Euro 250m. ∎

Senior personnel

Chairman and Chief Executive Jacques Gounon (in photo)
Chairman of Europorte Pascal Sainson
Deputy Chief Executive, Channel Tunnel Michel Boudoussier
Deputy Chief Executive, Corporate Claude Lienard
Commercial Director Jo Willacy
Business Services Director Patrick Etienne

A Eurotunnel shuttle locomotive in one of the Channel Tunnel's running tunnels. Eurotunnel

Passenger Train Operators

The first refurbished Class 332 Heathrow Express multiple-unit, No 332002, at Terminal 5 on 28 May 2012, awaiting departure with the 19.03 service to Paddington. Unit No 332008 is on the rear. Brian Morrison

Heathrow Express

High-speed air-rail link

Heathrow Express launched new branding, corporate colours, staff uniforms and a train refurbishment programme in 2012 - a £16million investment in the business.

A fast and frequent service between Heathrow and London Paddington, Heathrow Express carries more than six million passengers a year. 150 trains each day depart every 15min to and from Heathrow taking just 15min to/from Terminals 1 - 3. Since its launch in 1998, Heathrow Express has shuttled over 60m passengers between the airport and the city, with an average reliability rate of 99.37pc.

Trains reach the airport on a dedicated line tunnelling from near Hayes & Harlington on the Great Western main line, for about 3.5km to Heathrow Central (Terminals 1 - 3) and about 6.5km to Terminal 4.

The full service to Terminals 1 - 4 was opened in 1998, and an 1.8km extension to the new Terminal 5 opened in 2008. Terminal 5 station has two platform faces in reserve for possible western rail links: funding for a link towards Reading via the Great Western main line was pledged by government in 2012, subject to business case and agreements. A proposed link via Staines was dropped in 2011.

A private train operating company owned by Heathrow, Heathrow Express's infrastructure within the airport was built as part of a long-term strategy to increase public transport use for airport access. (In October 2012, the former airport group name BAA was dropped, and Heathrow airport operates as a standalone brand).

Terminals 1 - 3 station and the extension to Terminal 5 are served direct by Heathrow Express. A regular shuttle service runs between Terminal 4 and Terminals 1 - 3.

Heathrow Express's Class 332 electric trains, the first Siemens train fleet in the UK, are owned (under a leaseback arrangement) by Heathrow, and were built by Siemens in partnership with CAF of Spain.

The major, £15m refurbishment of rolling stock is being undertaken at Railcare, Wolverton, with input from Siemens and Interfleet Technology. The designs by the Tangerine agency aim to create an 'airliner ambience. In First class, seats are all 1 + 1, in Express class there is a mixed bay and face-to-back layout. Seats have new covers by Replin, upholstered by ProStyle.

LED lighting throughout improves energy efficiency. Coloured mood-lighting under seats intensifies (with all lighting) when the train arrives in stations. New glazing (with additional window positions to improve views), new bespoke Axminster carpets, and updated toilets are also part of the revamp. Over 1,300 new components have been introduced from over 200 suppliers.

A Wi-Fi HotSpot service provided by T-Mobile and Nomad Digital enables internet and e-mail access throughout the journey. Heathrow Express was the first UK train company to launch a Blackberry and Android app which allows users to buy a ticket and receive it direct to their phone. An iPhone version quickly followed. Print-at-home ticketing is also provided.

Full single fares (late 2012) for Express Class are £18 online, £19 at station; or £26 / £28 First Class. Full fare tickets can be purchased on-board trains, with a £5 premium for Express Class. Flight information screens and self-service check-in machines for selected airlines are provided at Paddington.

The Heathrow Connect train service runs half-hourly between Paddington and Heathrow Central (32min journey), calling at Ealing Broadway, West Ealing, Southall, Hanwell and Hayes & Harlington. Introduced in 2005, it represented a £35m investment by Heathrow, in partnership with FirstGroup. Trains and on-board staff are supplied by Heathrow Express, and between Paddington and Hayes & Harlington, operation is by First Great Western. Between Hayes & Harlington and Airport Junction, open-access rights apply. Heathrow Connect uses five 5-car Class 360/2 trains built by Siemens.

Heathrow Connect is aimed at providing access to the airport for London and Thames Valley residents and airport workers, with fares aligned with price-sensitive and local markets. The London-Heathrow single fare (late 2012) is £9.10.

The 14 Class-332 Heathrow Express trains generally run in pairs, making up eight or nine-car trains. (Five additional carriages, valued at £6m, increased five trains to five-car length.) Distance travelled between major overhauls has been more than doubled from the originally expected 450,000 miles to one million miles.

Siemens carries out train maintenance, with reliability standards specified in the contract. A purpose-built depot is at Old Oak Common, near Paddington. The total value of the original train order, including a 10-year maintenance element, was about £70m. A new, 19-year maintenance contract valued at £70m was awarded in 2005, covering both Heathrow Connect and Heathrow Express.

In the year 2011, Heathrow Express's sales totalled £174m (4.8pc down on 2010), gross profit from operations was £62m (a 12pc increase), with Heathrow Express passenger numbers increasing 5.1pc to 6.2 m (2010: 5.92m). Heathrow Express has 460 staff. ■

Senior personnel

Managing director
Keith Greenfield (in photo)
Operations director
Keith Harding
Head of commercial
Joanne Gowing
Head of engineering
Daniel Smith

Freight and Haulage

In association with

RFG
Rail Freight Group

HNRC

Nowadays, when controlling your costs is more important than ever, hiring rather than owning your own locomotive can be a major factor in ensuring that your rail freight operation remains within budget. Of course, selecting a partner to supply the ideal locomotive for your site isn't just a matter of going to the phone book. You need a specialist with a proven record of delivering and maintaining locomotives throughout the UK.

With a fleet of over fifty modern diesel locomotives, the Harry Needle Railroad Company is a leader in the field of locomotive hire, and trusted by many leading railfreight users.

HNRC provides –
- locos from 28tons to 120tons, 200-2750hp
- main line registered and/or NR approved
- With or without crewing and maintenance
- full support from competent personnel and extensive parts holding
- Available in client liveries for longer term contracts
- Locomotives overhauled in HNRC's own NR-approved workshops
- Radio (remote) control, speed limiting and other features incorporated to client requirements

So whether your requirement is short term to cover breakdown or major outage, or long term to stabilise your railfreight budget, talk to HNRC for the specialist solution.

HARRY NEEDLE RAILROAD Co Ltd

Barrow Hill Depot, Campbell Drive, Barrow Hill, Chesterfield S43 2PR
Tel: 01246 477001
E-mail: hnrcbh@aol.com
Website: www.harryneedlerail.com

In association with RFG Rail Freight Group

Railfreight: onward and upward!

The Modern Railway's review of the railfreight market (now with added sparks, with electrification for railfreight planned!)

2012 will, understandably, be remembered as the year of a tremendously successful London Olympics due, in no small measure, to the contribution of Britain's railways – primarily 'on the day', but also during the construction phase when millions of tonnes of materials were moved into East London without fuss or disruption.

Behind the scenes, however, some notable, encouraging and, in some cases, downright remarkable things occurred in the railfreight sector. Indeed, as the year ends, it is hard to find an indicator which is not pointing in a strongly positive direction. In spite of Britain's economy still being mired in recession, almost all commodities showed increased carryings, new locomotive and wagon types were introduced, new terminals opened and – perhaps most significant of all for the long term – government announced major investment in new infrastructure during Control Period 5 (CP5 - 2014 to 2019), not least in electrification.

Battle-hardened veterans of the 1970s and 1980s could be forgiven for thinking they have died and woken in heaven. Compared with that road-dominated, motorway era, when railfreight was seen as an irrelevance to most parts of the economy, government policy has changed beyond recognition. That, within the rail industry, freight matters, and is seen as a key long player term, is in stark contrast to a time when its only strategic significance was the small matter of generating a £100m annual surplus for the British Railways Board to fund the next generation of Inter City or Network SouthEast rolling stock!

Competition

A decade of intense competition between freight operators has seen those profits disappear as, in spite of major strides in efficiency, prices – especially for classic heavy trainload flows - have reduced substantially. In effect, cash has been transferred from the railway to such deserving causes as the electricity and steel industries. But in spite of the much reduced margins on offer, freight operators continue to invest heavily in additional locos and wagons – to the extent that delivery times for new wagons remain a concern, and the lack of a heavy haul diesel loco compliant with forthcoming Euro emissions requirements is a real worry, for some operators at least.

True, Freightliner's Class 70s meet current legislation, but now, it appears, even tighter rules are fast approaching from Brussels. Direct Rail Services's (DRS's) new Class 68, due for delivery in 2013, is better placed, but is clearly not a heavy haul machine, being intended for passenger and fast intermodal trains rather than heavy bulk traffic – a Class 67 rather than a 66, as it were, although with rather more grunt than the former.

In parallel, a US-style market in refurbished second hand locos (with grandfather rights re emissions) is now starting to emerge – very few of the last batch of Class 56s sold by DB Schenker (DBS) have ended up at the scrap yard, and are instead going back into service with smaller operators such Colas and Devon & Cornwall Railways (DCR). Meanwhile, DBS itself continues to overhaul and return to service the definitive 1990s Trainload Freight Class 60s, as their value in hauling super-heavy trains is once again appreciated. The situation with electric locos is also starting to assume more significance, as we shall see later.

Fast growth

Why the concern about traction? Quite simply, traffic volumes are very healthy, recession notwithstanding – 2011/12 was all but 10 per cent up on 2010/11. That bears repetition: with the UK economy at best flat-lining, rail carryings grew faster than almost any year in living memory. All commodities, with the exception of petroleum, increased – coal continues to rebound and was up 17pc, while domestic intermodal marches ever upward, increasing 12pc to a new high, having virtually doubled since 2003. Construction, too, hit a new record, having risen by 25pc in two years and 8pc in the year, in spite of Olympic construction work coming to an end. As an aside, the surge in Coal took it (just) back above Intermodal, at least for the moment.

The trend continued in the first quarter of 2012/13, with volumes up by 6.8pc on the comparable quarter in the previous year. A slackening in some commodities - Metals down 18pc on an abnormally high Q1 in 2011/12, when interworks traffic was

Colas Rail' has successfully expanded timber haulage for Kronospan. Class 66/8 No 66850 at Langwathby Moor on the Settle & Carlisle line on 26 April 2012, hauling the 12.44 Carlisle Yard-Chirk timber. Brian Morrison

Freight and Haulage

Short Sea intermodal traffic - Direct Rail Services' No 66304 approaches Copmanthorpe, York on the East Coast main line, heading south with a train of P&O containers on SuperLow wagons. Colin Irwin

buoyant due to plant problems, and International traffic 7pc down for the same reason – was more than offset by a 24pc increase in coal, reflecting how the high price of gas results in a much greater coal burn at the power stations. Domestic intermodal showed a further 4pc rise while the, admittedly much smaller, 'Other' category grew by 22pc, reflecting encouraging advances in automotive and timber traffic. Even Petroleum recovered, posting a 5pc rise on the same quarter in 2011/12.

Coal

Growth in a recession implies improving market share, and so it is in this instance. Granted, in the case of Coal it is the railborne fuel's share of the electricity generating market that has increased, but with every other commodity, rail growth in a recession is business won from another mode of transport – generally road haulage.

Even in Coal, flows which could move by road – such as blending coal moving between production sites or coal to industrial users – is moving by rail as the mode of choice. Notable movements in recent months have been flows in both directions between South Wales and Scotland, usually for blending - but also, in the southbound direction, to Tata Steel at Port Talbot. Within Scotland, a new opencast site on the Methil branch – which has not seen traffic for many years - is loading coal trains to Hunterston for blending with imported fuel before despatch to Longannet (a location they have passed en route!) and to English power stations.

Quite what will happen over the coming years in the core power station market is matter of considerable conjecture. On the one hand, government is under pressure to reduce carbon emissions but, on the other, nuclear capacity seems more likely to shrink than increase, and gas prices keep on heading north at a rapid rate. Meanwhile, the coal-fired stations are seeing higher levels of activity than they have for a number of years, and yet are slated for closure, sooner rather than later in some cases. There was more than

Freight operator finances

The freight industry recovered from the immediate impact of the recession in 2010/11, with a return to pre-tax profits after the previous year's losses, according to analysis undertaken by consultants TAS in Rail Industry Monitor.

Cash operating profits improved by a factor of six, from below £4.9m to just above £24.7m, with margins improving from a tiny 0.6% to 3.1%.

The combined turnover of the companies analysed was 3% higher at £795.5m, whilst the rise in operating costs was kept to just 0.5%, taking the total to £770.9m. Combined net interest costs climbed by 13% to reach £7.0m, but even so there was a pre-tax profit of £17.7m at a margin of 2.2%, compared with last year's loss of £1.2m.

TAS also reports on market share, as measured by turnover. DB Schenker retains the lion's share of the business, with 54.6%, up from 54.3% last year (compared with over 80% in the late 1990s). Freightliner was next with 32.7%, up by 0.3%. Post privatisation new entrants, Eurotunnel's GB Railfreight subsidiary and Direct Rail Services, have steadily built up their market shares over the last decade, reaching 7.3% and 5.4% respectively. Both saw small reductions in their share in this continuingly difficult market.

G B Railfreight

The company changed ownership during the year, being acquired from FirstGroup by Europorte SAS, a subsidiary of Eurotunnel. The company traded at reduced margins in a shortened financial period, since the company's financial year end was changed to 31 December, so shortening this accounting period to nine months. On an estimated annualised basis, turnover was up by 1% but operating costs were 5.6% higher.

Period to:	31/12/2010	31/03/2010
	£000	£000
Turnover	43,596	57,242
Operating Costs	42,109	52,977
Operating Profit	1,487	4,265
Operating Margin	3.4%	7.5%
Turnover per Employee	£142,938	£188,917
Rolling stock lease	6,702	8,390

Direct Rail Services

The company saw profits fall during the year, as turnover fell but was not matched by reductions in operating costs. The directors report that the business mix changed during the year, with a wider customer base and entry into new business sectors.

Period to:	31/03/2011	31/03/2010
	£000	£000
Turnover	43,311	45,034
Operating Costs	41,634	42,465
Operating Profit	1,677	2,569
Operating Margin	3.9%	5.7%

a little irony in National Power's announcement that Didcot's closure was to be brought forward from 2015 to April 2013 - this at a time when the station is generating almost continuously and coal trains keep rolling up the Great Western main line: much head scratching in the marsh! With UK energy policy in disarray and a second dash for (now very expensive) gas in prospect, where is the R&D into carbon capture and storage that would square the circle for coal-fired generation – and is needed in any event for gas? Answers on a postcard to Downing Street – either No 10 or 11 will do.

Metals

In Metals, it has been a case of 'one in, one out', with the former fortunately bigger than the latter. Thames Steel at Sheerness in Kent went into liquidation during 2011/12, meaning the end of inbound flows of scrap by rail – this was third time the works has gone bust, previously having brought down ASW and Sheerness Steel. Creditors of Thames Steel are understandably taking a fairly jaundiced view of plans to restart the plant yet again. Conversely, steel making recommenced at Lackenby on Teesside, generating flows of raw materials (lime and limestone) from Shap and the Peak District. Virtually all of the slab produced at the plant is shipped directly from Tees Dock and sees only the internal rail network.

Meanwhile, to cover a blast furnace rebuild at Port Talbot (itself a major commitment to steel making for the next decade), Tata is importing significant tonnages of slab (and some coil) through Cardiff Docks and Bird Port, a coaster-size facility on the Uskmouth branch at Newport. Having seen off a major challenge from GBRf for Tata's South Wales traffic, DB Schenker has further strengthened its hold by winning back from Colas the twice weekly flow of coil through the Channel Tunnel to Mauberge in France. An interesting alternative route to the Continent is used for export tinplate, which is sent by a twice weekly train from Trostre to Tilbury where it is transhipped into road trailers for delivery, principally in Benelux.

Construction

In Construction, there has been little change in the network of quarries, wharves and receiving depots, but an encouraging across-the-board increase in throughput. Mendip limestone and Leicestershire granite quarries continue to supply the Southeast with substantial tonnages of aggregate, supplemented by sea-dredged sand and gravel landed at Angerstein wharf and Cliffe quay for movement to a range of depots in the Home Counties. In the north, rail movements of limestone from the Peak District and Rylstone (near Skipton) to depots across Lancashire and Yorkshire – and further afield – continue to expand. In this context, Aggregate Industries plans to open a major new rail-fed plant at Tinsley in 2013, with 80pc of aggregates supplied by rail from Leicestershire and the Peak, the remaining 20pc being recycled material from the local Sheffield area.

Auto and timber

Moving on from the traditional bulk commodities, two long-standing businesses that had suffered severe cutbacks in rail activity are seeing a welcome resurgence: automotive and timber. The success of the 'new' British motor industry has seen car production back up at two million cars a year – levels not seen since the demise of volume car production by Leyland and Ford. Jaguar at Halewood and Castle Bromwich is enjoying considerable export success, as is BMW at Oxford. As a result, up to five trains a day are running to Southampton for Jaguar and one a day to each of Southampton and Purfleet for BMW.

In spite of the consequent ready availability of empty car carriers heading north from Southampton, and a substantial import flow of foreign cars through the port, few if any imported cars are sent by rail. Onerous performance requirements to get the empties back to the factories for reloading are said to be the reason for this, but it does seem a missed opportunity, particularly as several of the car importers have stated an interest in using rail from Southampton. Given the trains are running anyway, it is unfortunate that, for the sake of perhaps half a set of wagons to cover longer cycle times, cars imported at Southampton for sale in the North and Scotland are not being moved by rail.

That this makes sense is demonstrated by the fact that Ford cars imported through Dagenham are, indeed, sent to England's Northwest and Scotland by rail on a daily basis – and the wagons return south empty. A similar picture emerges at Portbury – along with Southampton, the UK's major car importing facility. Rail features to some degree, with a thrice weekly DB Schenker train to Warrington, from where connecting services provide links to Doncaster and Mossend. However, this accounts for but a small proportion of Portbury's throughput and there is much more to go at. The same applies with the three Japanese manufacturers – Honda at Swindon, Nissan at Sunderland

---

DB Schenker

Period to:	31/12/2010	31/12/2009
	£000	£000
Turnover	401,000	395,000
Operating Costs	391,000	398,000
Operating Profit:	10,000	(3,000)
Operating Margin:	2.5 %	-0.8 %
Turnover per Employee	£129,690	£115,972
Turnover per Employee	£148,325	£148,138
Rolling stock lease	5,502	6,056
Revenue Grant	1,203	1,193

The company improved its operating result during the year ahead of exceptional items, returning to a small operating and pre-tax profit after the previous year's losses. Turnover was slightly ahead, though the increase fell well short of prevailing rates of inflation, whilst operating costs were reduced and the workforce cut.

EWS International

Period to:	31/12/2010	31/12/2009
	£000	£000
Turnover	33,078	24,486
Operating Costs:	42,979	37,393
Operating Profit:	(9,901)	(12,907)

This DB Schenker Channel Tunnel through-freight operation improved its results during the year on the back of a hefty one-third-plus increase in turnover. Even so, the business continued to record substantial operating and pre-tax losses as the cross-channel railfreight market continues to struggle.

Freightliner

Period to:	26/03/2011	27/03/2010
	£000	£000
Turnover	163,504	148,333
Operating Costs:	154,995	144,263
Operating Profit:	8,509	4,070
Operating Margin:	5.2 %	2.7 %
Turnover per Employee	£148,236	£134,360
Operating Margin:	-29.9 %	-52.7 %
Turnover per Employee	£187,943	£130,245
Revenue Grant	100	0

The intermodal company improved its performance during the year, as turnover grew following a recovery in volumes of container traffic. As a result, profits more than doubled, though margins remained well short of pre-recession levels.

Freightliner Heavy Haul

Period to:	26/03/2011	27/03/2010
	£000	£000
Turnover	96,711	101,906
Operating Costs:	84,307	91,958
Operating Profit:	12,404	9,948
Operating Margin:	12.8 %	9.8 %
Turnover per Employee	£155,985	£158,239
Rolling stock lease	13,869	14,598
Rolling stock lease	9,361	9,368

The trading environment continued to be challenging for the coal, aggregates and infrastructure division of the Freightliner Group. This was reflected in a fall in turnover during the year. However, the company managed to reduce costs at a faster rate, so improving profitability.

Freight and Haulage

and Toyota at Burnaston near Derby – none of whom have despatched any cars by rail for some years (in the case of Toyota, never). With concentrated volumes on offer at both import and export locations, the automotive market would seem to be crying out for a determined marketing campaign by rail operators.

Timber is benefiting from just such an approach by Colas Rail. Working with Kronospan at Chirk, the French-owned operator has progressively introduced trains from Carlisle, Ribblehead, Teigngrace (near Newton Abbot) and, most recently, Baglan Bay in South Wales. In each case logs harvested in local forests are roaded to the railhead and stockpiled for the next train – daily from Carlisle and at least weekly from the other locations. Having built the business using converted wagons, Colas is now adding extra capacity to the fleet with wagons brought in from the Continent. Interestingly, the motive power for the new flows is often a refurbished Class 56, demonstrating how imaginative use of existing resources can provide a suitable cost base for traffic that would struggle to cover the cost of new equipment.

Intermodal

And so to Intermodal, where deep-sea containers remain the bedrock of the business. An hour or so spent within sight of the main routes from Felixstowe or Southampton provides ample evidence of just how big the business has become. Trains are frequent, they are longer than ever and they are well-loaded, often virtually to capacity. Any remaining sceptics would do well to observe one of DB Schenker's 34-wagon trains from Southampton passing through Oxford – around 100 SLUs (21ft standard length units) running at 75mph with hardly a spare slot on the train: somewhat more efficient than 50 plus lorries staggering from jam to jam on the A34 ... and making money for the freight operator.

With longer trains behind the same Class 66 (or 70 in the case of Freightliner) and better use of capacity due to gauge enhancement, it is indeed finally possible to start making money from intermodal. Unit cost reduction is reinforced by rising road haulage rates – always rock bottom in container haulage – due to higher fuel prices, and by more enlightened policies from shipping lines and their customers, who are now realising the logistical, as well as environmental, benefits of using rail.

Additional inland terminals are coming on stream, notably in the East Midlands at Castle Donington, adjacent to Marks & Spencer's new distribution centre, and at Ashby-de-la-Zouch, where the former Lounge opencast coal loading point is being converted into an 850,000 sq ft warehouse and intermodal terminal by Gazeley and UK Coal.

At the ports, Felixstowe has already rebuilt the southern terminal and work on a new north terminal is underway. Similarly, albeit on a smaller scale, Southampton is rebuilding two berths to take the very largest container carriers. Both ports are setting out their stall to take the latest 16,000 TEU (20ft equivalent unit) vessels. It remains to be seen what proportion of the two ports' trade will switch to London Gateway (nee Shellhaven) when it opens in 2014. Nearer to the London market it is, but further up river, and thus necessitating longer sailing times which, with the new behemoths of the shipping world and the need for maximum utilisation, is probably undesirable.

For sure, the massive rail-served logistics park behind the port will prove popular, but perhaps as much for Southeast regional distribution centres as for port-centric distribution hubs. While some (probably smaller) lines may well switch to London Gateway (not least as there will presumably a initial price incentive), the mega carriers will, more than likely, remain at Felixstowe and Southampton. Accordingly, it would not be a surprise to see trains running from these ports to London Gateway with boxes for the distribution centres located there.

There is an element of déjà vu here, since Freightliner used to run a Southampton-Barking service, and still operates from Felixstowe to Tilbury. Speaking of Tilbury, Freightliner recently posted record weekly container numbers from the port, which specialises in particular trades such as fruit. As such, it will hope to weather the competition from Gateway just downriver, but the future for Thameshaven on the Isle of Grain, with poor road and rail links, doesn't look too bright.

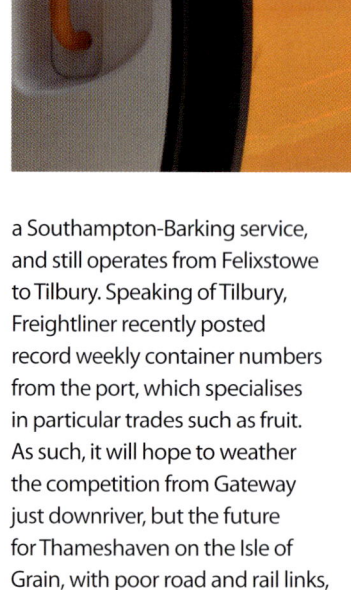

Short Sea

In contrast to the very positive picture with Deep Sea, the nascent Short Sea rail revival may be in danger, particularly on the Tees. The WH Malcolm service to Scotland, launched with great optimism, struggled to find a regular traffic base, and the P&O European service to Widnes was not attracting extra business over and above the base-load Proctor & Gamble volume. Suspended during the 2012 leaf-fall season to release Direct Rail Services crews for Rail Head Treatment Trains, it could be rerouted and possibly combined with other flows.

The situation on the Thames has been brighter, and JG Russell has added a new link to Purfleet, the key southern short-sea facility. Linking into Russell's Daventry and Anglo-Scottish service at Barking, the new service was loading well. Perhaps the lesson is that, with inherently smaller volumes, a dedicated short-sea train service is likely to struggle and needs to be combined with other business – most obviously domestic intermodal – to be viable.

Retail cutting edge

Which brings us neatly to the cutting edge of rail freight. Of all the big investments in rail infrastructure that are happening, arguably the most significant is barely visible from the railway and is operated by a retailer and a road haulier. Tesco's one million square foot rail-connected distribution centre at Daventry shows what can be done and exactly how to make rail-based logistics work. Swap bodies loaded at the warehouse are taken by internal tractor & trailer units to the on-site intermodal terminal, to be lifted onto trains. In consequence,

A Tesco intermodal train passes a London Overground Class 172 diesel multiple-unit on the congested North London Line on 27 April 2012. Electrification of the Gospel Oak-Barking line has been the subject of jousting between the Department for Transport and Transport for London. Tony Miles

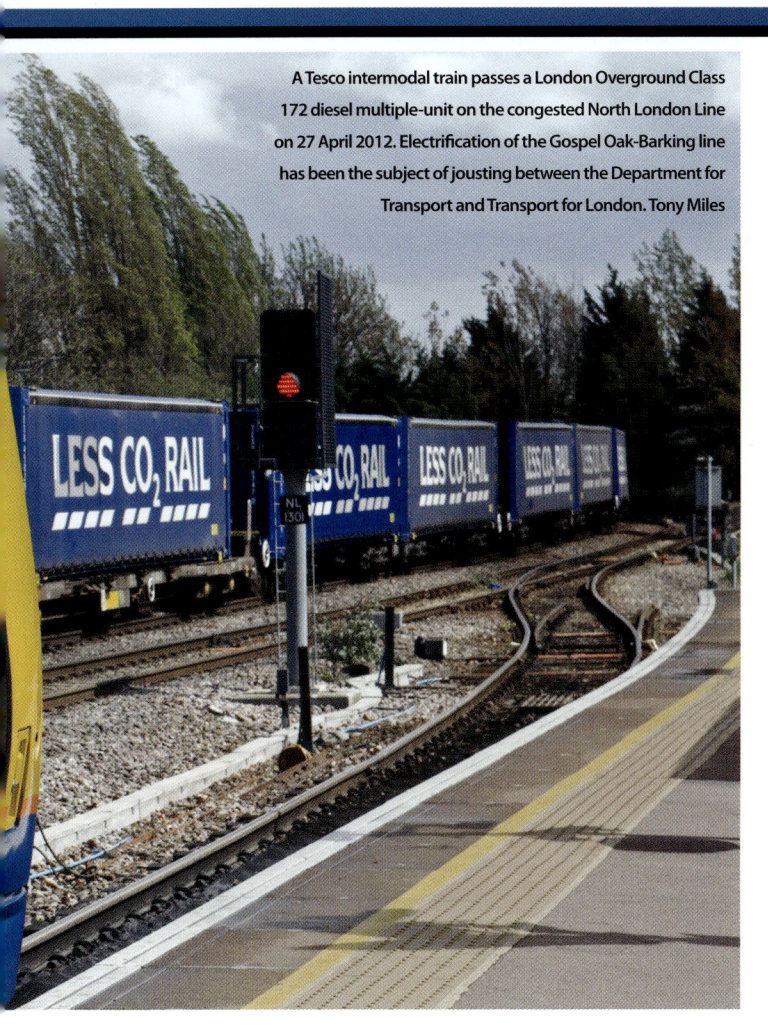

the normal cost of hauling the container on public roads (say, £60 minimum) and a lift at a third-party terminal (c£25) can be reduced to probably £30ish – a saving of £50 on each and every load. This permits rail to be competitive over much shorter distances, and Tesco takes advantage of this by using rail to Barking/Tilbury and to Cardiff – flows which would not be viable with higher on-costs.

It is salutary that warehouse location is of greater significance than almost any rail cost or efficiency improvement - hence the crucial importance of developing rail-connected distribution facilities at key national and regional centres. This applies both to inbound traffic flows, such as import containers from the ports, and to outbound flows of picked product to customers and stores. Indeed, the Tesco trains return from Thameside and Cardiff with goods from suppliers located in those areas, which are then fed into the supply chain at Daventry – the saving in cost and lorry miles and carbon multiplies. Having a railhead at (or immediately adjacent to) the distribution centre is the most significant thing a company can do to get onto rail – period.

Infrastructure

Finally, to infrastructure – probably the most visible manifestation of a growing freight railway. The pipeline of schemes – and movement along it – is impressive. Nuneaton North Chord – the link from Felixstowe onto the WCML – was due to be commissioned in late 2012. Gauge enhancement of the second route (via Andover) to Southampton was to be implemented around the same time. Ipswich North Curve, allowing trains to run directly from Felixstowe to Peterborough without run round in Ipswich Yard, received approval in September 2012. Gauge enhancement to W10 (9ft 6in high boxes on standard wagons) of the ECML is due in early 2013, and of the NE-SW route from Birmingham to Doncaster later that year or early 2014. Electrification of the Great Western main line will bring W10 or even W12 to Bristol and South Wales by 2016/17.

Ah, electrification. The Department for Transport's High Level Output Statement (HLOS) proposal for an 'Electric Spine' from Southampton via Oxford, Bletchley and the Midland Main Line (plus Oxford – Coventry – Nuneaton) caught most observers napping, but there is a powerful logic to it. The reopening, including electrification, of the East-West route is especially welcome, creating a direct link from Daventry, Corby and Milton Keynes to the South and Southwest. Worth noting in this context is that both Freightliner's Southampton-Daventry service and Tesco's Daventry-Cardiff train currently have to run via Birmingham – not an attractive option due to the considerable excess mileage, through a congested area to boot.

And yet, questions remain. There is a puzzling gap in the wiring proposals between Sheffield and Leeds/Doncaster. Further, given passenger service density through Derby and Sheffield, it is barely conceivable that long/heavy freights will follow the wires through these stations. The only practical solution is to electrify the freight route from Trent, through Chesterfield and Rotherham (the 'Old Road') to Doncaster and South Kirkby. There is then the issue of terminal access. In the Midlands, the wires will need to extend to (at least) Lawley Street and Hams Hall; in Yorkshire, to Stourton and Wakefield. There is HLOS provision for 'minor freight schemes' but the above shopping list would quickly exhaust the available pot - and more. Perhaps, DfT is jousting with South and West Yorks Passenger Transport Executives about Sheffield-Doncaster/Leeds in the same way as they are with Transport for London about Gospel Oak-Barking electrification, but it hardly seems like joined up thinking.

Electric traction

Much air has been expelled, and column inches written, about the freight operators investing in electric traction to take advantage of the 'Electric Spine'.

In reality, both DB Schenker and Freightliner have more electric locos at their disposal than they will be able to use in the immediate future. In the latter's case, diversion of Felixstowe trains via Peterborough and away from London will mean that the proportion of electrically-hauled trains will actually reduce. It follows that Freightliner has Class 90s spare, and DB Schenker has Class 90s, plus the massively underused but highly capable Class 92s, to deploy on Southampton trains when the wires are available. GBRf, too, has access to Class 92s, although with a container business based on Felixstowe rather than Southampton, it is not hard to see why John Smith thinks the Ipswich-Peterborough-Nuneaton route should be electrified before the 'Spine'! Furthermore, at some stage the Class 90s used on Liverpool Street-Norwich services will, no doubt, be replaced by EMUs, throwing up more locos for freight work. Nevertheless, it is perhaps unfortunate that all the Class 87s have recently been exported to Bulgaria – while not purpose-built freight locos, they could well have found a role in the same way as the Class 56 diesels are.

The freight companies can afford to play a long game when it comes to new electric locos. The reality is that there is no UK-gauge electric freight loco available off the shelf, and electrification will take some years to come to fruition. Word has it that they are working together (wonders will never cease, as some have remarked) to produce a specification for a heavy(ish)-haul freight loco. The question will, no doubt, be: is a manufacturer prepared to work up the design, and at what cost given the relatively small market on offer, and what will be the price of the resultant machine? Prices quoted for express passenger locos are certainly not a viable basis for switching to electric traction.

With ministers beginning to suggest that carbon reduction targets might be achieved more easily in the transport sector (by reducing heavy lorry mileage) than in electricity generation, it could just be that there is both a need and a logic for incentivising the freight companies to go electric. ∎

Freight and Haulage

DB Schenker Class 60 No 60015 rounds the curve between Bromley South and Shortlands on 30 May 2012. Brian Morrison

DB SCHENKER

Largest rail freight operator

DB Schenker Rail UK Ltd is Britain's largest rail freight operator. Formerly English, Welsh & Scottish Railway (EWS), the company was acquired in 2007 by Deutsche Bahn (DB - German Rail), becoming part of its DB Schenker Rail business.

Employing around 32,500 people, DB Schenker Rail operates in 15 countries. It operates a fleet totalling nearly 3,600 locomotives and 109,000 wagons, generating revenues of 4.9billion Euros in 2011. The company has subsidiaries in Bulgaria, Poland and Romania in its Region East, while DB Schenker Rail Deutschland in Germany plus subsidiaries in Denmark, Italy, the Netherlands, Scandinavia and Switzerland are among operations forming Region Germany/Central.

DB Schenker Rail UK is part of Region West, along with Euro Cargo Rail (ECR), created in France by EWS in 2005, and Transfesa/ECR in Spain. It employs around 4,000 people, and as well as undertaking rail freight operations provides a range of passenger haulage, engineering support, technical and hire services nationwide.

DB Schenker Rail UK group companies include Axiom Rail, a supplier of rolling stock construction, maintenance and refurbishment services and a manufacturer of vehicle suspension systems and components. Also part of the group is Transeo, a strategic alliance with Thales providing information technology services to the transport sector.

DB Schenker Rail UK structures its main business in three divisions:
- Industrial moves coal and other fuels and heavy industrial materials, such as metals and petroleum products.
- Construction conveys products for the construction and infrastructure markets, operating waste trains and providing rail industry services for Network Rail, infrastructure contractors and other train operating companies.
- Logistics provides intermodal, international and logistics services.

A highlight for the company in 2012 was the successful development of freight traffic using the HS1 high-speed line, enabling continental gauge wagons to reach London on a regular basis for the first time. In October 2012 a second weekly service began between Barking and Wroclaw in Poland, conveying manufactured retail goods in curtain-sided swapbodies. This follows the launch of an initial service in November 2011 after successful tests with Class 92 electric locomotives modified to operate over HS1. The 1,250-mile journey to Poland takes around 50 hours.

DB Schenker runs a weekly intermodal service between Hams Hall in the West Midlands and Padua, Italy. Continental traffic flows also include intermodal services between Hams Hall and Domodossola, Italy, steel slabs for rail manufacture from Scunthorpe to Ebange in France for Tata Steel and bottled water from France to Daventry, plus a weekly train of china clay slurry for paper-making from Antwerp to Irvine in Scotland. In addition there is a service three times a week linking Trafford Park, Manchester, and Duisburg in Germany and a long-established flow of Ford car components between Valencia and Dagenham.

Among Logistics activities in the domestic market are rail freight services for Stobart Rail, with electric locomotives used between Daventry and Mossend, carrying Tesco goods. DB Schenker is also active in the automotive sector, which has been creating significant levels of traffic. Successes include movements for export of new Jaguar Land Rover and BMW Mini vehicles, with output from Halewood and Cowley plants respectively generating additional trains.

DB Schenker runs regular trains of deep sea containers from Southampton and Felixstowe. The number of containers passing though Southampton that it now carries has increased to more than 60,000 per year, leading to the establishment of a new office facility in the city that also handles bookings for all intermodal services operated by DB Schenker Rail UK.

In July 2012 DB Schenker and DP World London Gateway jointly announced an agreement to provide rail services from the start of operations at the new deep-sea port and Europe's largest logistics park. The development is taking place on the north bank of the Thames estuary, with opening planned in late 2013. The agreement will see DB Schenker introduce at least four pairs of rail freight services a day, subject to volumes, and will serve a range of inland terminals including potential new UK locations. DB Schenker says it will also pursue the development of rail freight services from London Gateway to mainland Europe using the Channel Tunnel.

The company continues to fulfil the Ministry of Defence's Strategic Rail Capability and Mainline Rail Freight Services haulage contract. This covers the supply of locomotives for haulage of the MoD's own wagons, as well as providing specialist services utilising its own wagon fleet. Some movements are combined with other traffic forming a residual wagonload network.

DB Schenker operates Royal Mail postal trains, running seven services a day between London, Warrington and Glasgow using Class 325 mail EMUs. It also holds the Network Rail Infrastructure Monitoring contract, operating test trains across the system, in some cases using Network Rail's own traction. The operation is managed by a separate entity, DB Schenker Infrastructure Monitoring, part of the Construction business.

In its Industrial market segment, up to 600 DB Schenker trains a week move heavy raw materials, such as metals, iron ore and petroleum products. In the last-mentioned category there are significant flows from complexes on Humberside and Robeston in Wales. The company also operates more than 700 trains per week for the power generation industry and has contracts with British Energy, Drax Power, E.ON, EDF Energy, RWE npower, Scottish & Southern Energy and ScottishPower. Recent agreements include a three-year renewed deal signed in 2011 with Drax Power to convey coal from ATH Resources and Keir Mining in Scotland and from the Port of Immingham. Services to be operated under the contract also include coal traffic from Hull Docks and limestone from Tunstead. In 2012 coal traffic commenced from a new opencast coal development at Earlseat Hall in central Fife.

DB Schenker provides a shuttle service for Tata Steel connecting its steelworks at IJmuiden in the Netherlands with its Trostre plant in South Wales to convey steel coils for the packaging industry. The wagons return to Tata Steel's Llanwern site for back-loading with traffic for IJmuiden.

The Construction business operates up to 400 trains a week for the construction and waste industries. A contract with Mendip Rail covers operation of trains carrying up to 4,000 tonnes of stone from the Mendips quarries of Aggregates Industries (Merehead) and HeidelbergCement subsidiary Hanson (Whatley), some of these using the shippers' own locomotives and wagons. DB Schenker has a contract with Cemex UK covering its rail freight haulage requirements for aggregates and coal. Traffic includes substantial flows from the Peak District. The Lafarge quarry at Mountsorrel in Leicestershire is also served and sea-dredged aggregates are moved from Thames-side terminals for Brett and Marcon.

Other commodities carried include china clay from production sites in Cornwall for Imerys and cement. In addition, a seven-year infrastructure haulage contract with Network Rail generates heavy traffic volumes through both scheduled movements of materials such as ballast and rail and trains run in association with infrastructure maintenance and renewals.

The company is also active in the passenger sector. In 2012 it continued to provide locomotives for overnight sleeper trains operated by ScotRail, with Class 90 electrics handling the Anglo-Scottish legs and Class 67s undertaking domestic haulage in Scotland. Class 67s are also hired to ScotRail for scheduled peak hour trains serving Edinburgh and to Chiltern Railways for its London Marylebone-Birmingham Moor Street 'Mainline' services. And since December 2011 locomotives of this type have been employed by Arriva Trains Wales on its weekday locomotive-hauled services. DB Schenker additionally supplies traction for the Orient Express luxury train, as well as for charter services and as standby power for the East Coast franchise. In March 2012 it unveiled a specially repainted Class 67 locomotive for use on Royal Train duties during the Queen's Diamond Jubilee celebrations.

The core of the traction fleet is formed of some 250 EMD-built Class 66 locomotives leased from Angel Trains, although some of these have been despatched for use by Euro Cargo Rail and other DB Schenker companies in continental Europe, notably in Poland. Also leased from Angel Trains are 30 Class-67 125mph locomotives originally acquired mainly for express mail duties. They are used on charter passenger services or hired out to franchised TOCs as well as being used to a limited extent for light freight duties.

Changes in traffic patterns have led to reduced use of the main element of ex-BR diesel fleet, the heavy-haul Class 60 locomotives. However, DB Schenker sees a continuing role for the class and in 2011 it embarked on a £3million programme to submit 21 machines to heavy overhaul and refurbishment. Around half had been returned to traffic by late 2012. There are also six Class 59/2s used mainly on Mendips aggregates traffic.

Electric traction comprises 30 Class 92 dual-voltage machines and 25 Class 90s, although the number of both of these in service is dictated by traffic demands and some may not see further use. The Class 92s operate freight services through the Channel Tunnel as well as over DC- and AC-electrified networks. DB Schenker has implemented a programme to modify six Class 92s to enable them to operate on the HS1 high-speed line. One example of the type was despatched to Bulgaria in 2012 to enable it to be evaluated by DB Schenker's subsidiary there. ■

No 325016 heads a train of three Royal Mail multiple-units north through Crewe. Tony Miles

Senior personnel

Chief Executive
Alain Thauvette (in photo)
Chief Financial Officer
Andreas Lübs
MD, Logistics Dr Carsten Hinne
MD, Industrial Neil McDonald
MD, Construction Nigel Smith

Freight and Haulage

Special pocket wagons were used for the pilot train of unaccompanied trailers between Antwerp and Barking via HS1, operated for Ewals Intermodal and Ewals Cargo Care and conveying goods for the Vauxhall group on 22 May 2012. After shunting, containers are being unloaded at the Russell Barking terminal, next to the trunk haul loco, GBRf's Class 92 No 92032. Brian Morrison

GB Railfreight
PART OF EUROPORTE

Since its formation in 1999, GB Railfreight (GBRf) has grown into the UK's third largest freight operator in terms of the number of trains run. The company is now part of Eurotunnel subsidiary Europorte, having been acquired from FirstGroup in 2010. In 2012 it employed 446 people.

GBRf operations encompass a diverse mix that includes the provision of maritime container services linking Felixstowe with Doncaster, Selby and Birmingham Intermodal Freight Terminal at Hams Hall. September 2011 saw the start of an additional service between Felixstowe and Manchester Trafford Park, contributing to the company's claim to operate almost 20pc of trains out of Felixstowe. GBRf says the strategic vision for its intermodal network is to expand to other ports including Tilbury and Southampton, as well as those in northwest and northeast England.

In 2011 GBRf and Europorte Channel commenced a contract with container shipper DFDS to operate a mixed goods intermodal service from Daventry through the Channel Tunnel to France and then on to Novarro in northern Italy. A seasonal weekly train on behalf of Stobart group carrying fruit and vegetables from Silla in Spain to Ripple Lane, east London, has also been operated.

The potential for additional Continental traffic was demonstrated in May 2012 with the pilot run by Europorte Channel of an unaccompanied trailer transport service between Antwerp and Barking via HS1.

In the coal haulage market GBRf has built a share of around one-third of traffic, with British Energy, Drax Power and EDF Energy among its clients. In 2010 GBRf became the first UK rail freight operator to move renewable biomass material, operating four trains a day for Drax Power from the Port of Tyne to Drax power station near Selby, using specially adapted HYA coal hoppers.

Other bulk products handled include containerised desulphogypsum, carried under a five-year contract signed with British Gypsum in 2008 to serve facilities at East Leake and Robertsbridge. Although aluminium smelting ended in March 2012 at Lynemouth in Northumberland, GBRf continues to move alumina from there to Rio Tinto Alcan's aluminium smelter in Fort William.

An existing contract with Petrochem Carless for the haulage of gas condensate from North Walsham to Harwich and mud oil from Harwich to Aberdeen was renewed in 2010 for a further five years. In late 2011 a three-year contract was signed with Greenergy, the supplier of petrol, biofuel and diesel, to haul petroleum products.

Scrap metal traffic is conveyed from the Midlands to a Celsa plant at Cardiff, where GBRf also provides shunting services within the steelworks. At the end of 2011 a ten-year contract was secured to undertake all rail operations within the revived Lackenby steelworks on Tees-side. Thai-based Sahaviriya Steel Industries restarted the blast furnace in April 2012 to produce steel for export to Thailand. By autumn 2012, SSI had manufactured and shipped one million tonnes since the contract started, with GBRf hauling every ounce.

From its inception GBRf has been active in the haulage of infrastructure trains out of Eastleigh, Hoo Junction and Whitemoor yards for Network Rail. It also continues to fulfil a ten-year £80million contract awarded in 2006 to provide infrastructure haulage services for Metronet, now part of London Underground - much of it concentrated on a dedicated materials depot operated by the company at Wellingborough.

In February 2012 GBRf won a two-year contract with Crossrail tunnelling contractor BFK (BAM/Ferrovial/Kier joint venture) to move over one million tonnes of excavated material from a tunnel portal at Westbourne Park to Northfleet in Kent - involving more than 860 Class 66-hauled trains of JNA bogie ballast box wagons hired from VTG.

A five-year contract with Bombardier Transportation to deliver new 'S' stock trains for London Underground started in 2010. They go first from Bombardier's Derby facility to the Asfordby test track near Melton Mowbray, then after a period of fault-free running are moved by GBRf to London.

Other rail industry services range from movements of rolling stock for overhaul or refurbishment to the provision of drivers for new train commissioning. Recent work includes haulage of 465 and 466 EMUs to Wabtec, Doncaster, for overhaul, and movements of ScotRail Class 320 EMUs under their own power, also to Doncaster.

The core of GBRf's locomotive fleet comprises 45 Class 66/7s. Of these, 27 are leased from Eversholt Rail, nine from Porterbrook and the remainder owned outright. Four are equipped with RETB equipment for the West Highland Line.

To haul London Underground 'S' stock, GBRf has taken on nine Class 20 locomotives from various sources, operated in 'top'n'tail' pairs with translator vehicles to ensure continuous braking.

Nine Class 73 electro-diesels were available in 2012 for infrastructure duties on the third rail network. GBRf is also responsible for five Europorte Channel Class 92 dual-voltage electric locomotives in the UK - handling traffic through the Channel Tunnel, and used on the Dollands Moor-Daventry DFDS service. 10 Class Di8 diesel locomotives acquired from Norwegian State Railways are used at Lackenby steelworks. ■

Senior personnel

Managing Director
John Smith (in photo)
Director of Finance
David Simons
Operations Director
Dave Knowles
Commercial Director
Phil Webster
Head of Production Lee Bayliss
Head of Business Development Mike Higgins

In association with RFG Rail Freight Group

DRS Class 37/4 No 37423 with inspection saloon No 975025 awaits departure from Southampton Central on 4 April 2011, heading for Nuneaton with VIPs to travel the route upgraded by Network Rail for larger containers. Brian Morrison

Direct Rail Services Limited
Safe Secure Reliable

Logistics and industry services

A wholly owned subsidiary of the Nuclear Decommissioning Authority (NDA), Direct Rail Services Limited (DRS) was established in 1995 to provide British Nuclear Fuels Limited with a strategic rail transport service.

In addition to its core business of moving nuclear materials from power stations and other sources to the NDA's facilities at Sellafield, Cumbria, DRS runs intermodal freight services. Recent innovations include trains operated for Tesco in conjunction with Stobart Rail from Daventry to Tilbury and to Wentloog near Cardiff. Both run six days per week. This followed the launch in October 2011 of a service that runs five days per week from PD Ports' Teesport terminal to Stobart Group's Widnes depot on behalf of P&O Ferrymasters. This uses IDA 'Super Lowliner' twin wagons from WH Davis to allow high-cube containers to be carried over routes that have not seen gauge enhancement.

Long-distance logistics operations include a Mossend-Daventry service running five days per week for The Malcolm Group. In addition, two weekday Daventry-Coatbridge intermodal services are operated in collaboration with Scottish-based logistics firm John G Russell. There is also a Daventry-Grangemouth service six days a week run in conjunction with The Malcolm Group.

In Scotland DRS operates two intermodal services out of Grangemouth – a short-haul consist of shipping containers to Elderslie running five days a week and an Aberdeen train six days a week carrying mainly Asda supermarket traffic. In partnership with John G Russell, there is also a weekday service between Coatbridge and Needlefield intermodal terminal, Inverness.

Scotland features too in the operator's nuclear traffic sector. A terminal was constructed at Georgemas Junction in 2012 to enable DRS to load material destined for Sellafield from the Dounreay complex, which is being demolished.

Rail industry services form a significant part of DRS activities. Among these are seasonal operations for Network Rail that include running autumn railhead treatment trains, crewing MPVs for weed control, winter snow clearance using its own snowplough-fitted locomotives and overhead line 'ice breaking' with Network Rail-owned Class 86/9 electric locomotives. The company also provides traction for trains operated for Network Rail to monitor its infrastructure.

In the passenger sector, DRS continues to provide traction for the Northern Belle luxury train under a five-year contract signed with Orient-Express Hotels Ltd in April 2011. More than 85 trips per year are handled, with traction usually provided by Class 47s painted in Northern Belle livery. Also ongoing is the operation of trains for Cruise Saver Travel conveying passengers joining cruise ships at the Port of Southampton. These run from Glasgow Central or Edinburgh Waverley, calling at intermediate points, with services also provided for returning passengers.

Class 47 locomotives are provided to Greater Anglia for 'Thunderbird' standby services for the London-Norwich route, with these machines also used between Norwich and Great Yarmouth on summer Saturday London-Great Yarmouth through services.

DRS is poised to introduce a newcomer to the British traction scene following the 2012 award of an order for 15 Vossloh Eurolight Bo-Bo diesel locomotives, with an option for 10 additional examples. Adapted specifically for the UK network from a design unveiled for European operations in 2010, the DRS machines will be powered by a Caterpillar C175-16, 3,755hp engine with ABB transmission featuring AC traction motors. With a top speed of 100mph and an electric train heating capability, they are intended for passenger traffic as well as freight operations. Deliveries are due from Vossloh's Valencia plant in 2013-14. They will be designated Class 68.

Until their arrival, the most modern locomotives in the company's fleet are 19 Class 66s, mostly leased from Lloyds Banking Group, but also including five ex-Fastline machines hired from Beacon Rail. They are used principally for long-distance intermodal services. In addition there are nine Class 57s (eight leased from Porterbrook and one owned) plus three ex-Virgin Class 57/3s leased for three years from Porterbrook in April 2012, and ten active Class 47s.

The operational Class 37 fleet totals 24, with more stored or under refurbishment including some of 13 redundant Class 37/4s acquired from DB Schenker Rail. There were also seven Class 20s in service, with more in store.

Traction maintenance is carried out at DRS's headquarters depot at Carlisle Kingmoor and at its Crewe Gresty Bridge facility. ∎

Senior personnel

Managing Director
Neil McNicholas

Commercial and Business Development Director
Chris Connelly

Operations and Compliance Director Jeff Marshall

Engineering and Terminals Director Tony Bush

Finance and Resources Director John Bamforth

HITACHI Inspire the Next

111

Freight and Haulage

Freightliner

Intermodal and heavy haul

Freightliner Group is owned by Bahrain-based investment firm Arcapita, which in 2008 acquired the company from previous owners 3i, Electra Private Equity and Freightliner management and staff. It has two rail operating subsidiaries in Britain: Freightliner Ltd the leading intermodal rail freight haulier with 81pc of the UK deep-sea rail-borne container market, and Freightliner Heavy Haul (FHH), specialising in bulk commodities. Established in 2006, Freightliner Maintenance Ltd is the Group's third UK subsidiary, dedicated to the maintenance and repair of the traction and rolling stock. UK subdivisions also include Logico, a division of Freightliner Ltd established in 2004, offering bespoke rail space to new markets.

Internationally there is an Australian subsidiary, Freightliner Australia, created in 2009, and Freightliner Poland Ltd, set up in 2005. The group employs more than 1,900 people, and in Britain operates some 3,200 wagons and around 160 locomotives.

Freightliner Limited

Freightliner Ltd is the largest rail carrier of maritime containers in the UK, operating from the major deep-sea ports of Felixstowe, Seaforth, Southampton, Thamesport and Tilbury. These run to 14 strategically located rail freight interchanges, nine of which are terminals owned and operated by Freightliner and also offer with secure container storage facilities. Operating a road fleet of more than 300 vehicles, the company offers port-to-door and door-to-port services around the clock. It moves around 3,000 containers per day on more than 100 services to and from deep sea ports, with 37 direct route offerings.

Main locations are:
- Ports: Felixstowe, Seaforth (Liverpool), Southampton, Thamesport (Isle of Grain) and Tilbury.
- Inland terminals: Birmingham, Bristol, Wentloog (Cardiff), Wilton (Cleveland), Coatbridge (Glasgow), Doncaster, Leeds, Liverpool and Manchester.
- Independent terminals served include Birch Coppice (Birmingham International Freight Terminal), Daventry (DIRFT), Scunthorpe and Ditton (Widnes).

Logico provides bespoke intermodal haulage to freight movers, manufacturers, retailers, import/exporters, tank operators, freight forwarders, NVOCCs and transport operators. It offers regular space on services without the need to make a long-term commitment. Logico can provide its customers with the Complete Logistics Package of rail, road and terminal operations moving import/export services or domestically throughout the UK.

Maritime traffic at Southampton has benefited from completion by Network Rail in 2011 of W10 gauge enhancements to clear the route from the port to the West Midlands for 9ft 6in containers. The first Southampton-bound Freightliner service conveying 9ft 6in containers on conventional wagons ran from Manchester Trafford Park on 23 February 2011. By October 2012 the number of containers of this size handled by Freightliner at Southampton Maritime had risen by 76pc since the route was gauge cleared. Similar work continues to clear the Felixstowe to Nuneaton (F2N) route for W10, which will boost traffic opportunities at the Suffolk port.

Freightliner maintains relationships with a number of the world's leading shipping lines including OOCL, Hamburg Sud, Evergreen, Hapag-Lloyd, MSC, China Shipping and ZIM. It has the largest intermodal contract in the UK with Maersk, the container arm of the Danish conglomerate A P Moller-Maersk. In April 2011 Freightliner Limited signed a new multi-year contract with Maersk Line to provide committed space for the transport of containers over its network from Felixstowe. In September 2011 Freightliner also announced its second landmark 10-year contract with shipping line OOCL.

An increase in container volumes by rail to northwest England is covered in a contract renewed in January 2012 between Freightliner and MSC (UK) Ltd. This represents an expansion of the existing service which moves 30,000 container moves annually. It followed a late 2011 agreement with logistics company CMA CGM to convey containers for the

Freightliner's No 66577 heads an intermodal train through Ely station. Tony Miles

Asda supermarket chain, initially between Southampton and Wilton in Cleveland.

October 2012 saw the inauguration of two new container cranes at Freightliner's Southampton Maritime Terminal. Costing £9m, the company says this represents its largest single-item capital investment by Freightliner in terminal or ports infrastructure since privatisation of the business in 1996.

In January 2012 Freightliner was named the UK's best performing rail freight operator at the Golden Whistle Awards.

Freightliner Heavy Haul

Established in 1999, Freightliner Heavy Haul (FHH) has a turnover of over £100million, with more than 600 employees. It operates around 1,200 trains per week using a fleet of 83 locomotives and more than 1,400 wagons. Sectors served include aggregates and minerals, cement, petroleum, scrap metal, domestic waste and infrastructure services, securing approximately 30pc of the bulk rail freight market and moving more than 20 million tonnes annually.

The company's largest bulk market is coal. It serves all of the UK's rail-connected coal-fired power stations from opencast sites and collieries in Britain, and from import terminals including Ellesmere Port, Hunterston, Immingham, Liverpool and Portbury. In early 2012 a revised long-term agreement was reached with EDF Energy to transport coal to its power stations at Cottam and West Burton. FHH has also been anticipating power generators' future needs: at the end of 2011 it unveiled a HHA coal hopper wagon modified by WH Davis to carry biomass. The vehicle has covers fitted to ensure the product is kept dry during transit.

In the aggregates sector, FHH's clients include Tarmac, Lafarge, Aggregate Industries and Hanson. Significant volumes for Aggregate Industries are carried from the quarry at Bardon Hill quarry and from Neath Abbey Wharf, as well as sand from Wool to Neasden. Limestone is also conveyed from Tunstead in the Peak District to several coal-fired power stations to be used in emissions cleaning processes.

Regular flows of bulk cement from Lafarge Cement's Hope plant are conveyed to Dewsbury, Moorswater, Theale, West Thurrock and Westbury, and from the company's works at Oxwellmains in East Lothian to Aberdeen, Inverness and Uddingston in Scotland and to Seaham. Wagons conveying bagged cement are added to bulk cement flows from Oxwellmains to the three destinations north of the Border and Carlisle. Pulverised fuel ash is also carried for Lafarge Cement.

FHH continues to work with Greater Manchester Waste Disposal Authority (GMWDA) and Viridor moving municipal waste to a landfill site at Roxby Gullet, Scunthorpe. At a future date, FHH will take Solid Recovered Fuel from new facility at Longley Lane, Manchester, to a Combined Heat and Power plant at Runcorn, following a move away from the use of landfill by GMWDA. FHH also runs a containerised household waste service from Cricklewood in north London to Calvert.

Potash and rock salt are moved between a mine at Boulby, on the Cleveland coast, and Tees Dock and Middlesbrough. April 2011 FHH commenced a contract to convey sand on behalf of Quinn Glass from Sibelco UK's Middleton Towers quarry to Quality Freight's facility at Ellesmere Port. The sand is used in the manufacture of glass containers for the food and beverage industries at Quinn's plant at Elton, Cheshire. Also signed in 2011 was multi-year contract with steelmaker Celsa to transport scrap metal from Dagenham to Cardiff, generating three trains per week.

In the infrastructure sector, Freightliner provides support for Network Rail, including haulage of high-output ballast cleaning and track renewal systems, ballast movements and operation of the major distribution centre at Basford Hall, Crewe. Activities include support for infrastructure renewals and maintenance programmes.

International

Freightliner Australia Pty Ltd began operation in 2009, providing rail haulage services in New South Wales for Namoi Cotton Cooperative Ltd under a long term agreement. In 2011 it began a 10-year contract with Xstrata Coal, moving coal from the company's Hunter Valley mines in New South Wales to the port of Newcastle. For this traffic Xstrata acquired 10 XRN Class (Type C44ACi) locomotives from United Group Rail and 300 hoppers. These are operated by Freightliner Australia as three formations comprising three locomotives and 90 wagons, hauling up to 12million tonnes of coal a year. Other traffic is handled by GE-engined Class FLA C30-MMi locomotives and a fleet of container flats.

Freightliner Poland (FPL), commenced operations in 2007, running coal trains to Kozienice power station, followed by a multi-year contract with the heat and power plant PGE Zespół Elektrociepłowni Bydgoszcz SA. It was the first rail freight company in Poland to use Class 66s, which are equipped for cross-border operations into Germany. In 2012 the fleet had grown to 17 of these locomotives, together with three leased Bombardier TRAXX F140MS three-voltage electrics. Since its initial coal contracts, FPL has diversified into other markets, providing cross-border aggregates services into Germany, hazardous products haulage, 'hook and haul' services and the operation of private terminals and sidings.

Freightliner Maintenance Limited

Freightliner Maintenance Ltd (FML) was established in April 2006, when it took over the assets and staff of LNWR's former Leeds Midland Road depot, together with field engineering support across the UK. FML operates as a separate entity dedicated to the repair and maintenance of traction and rolling stock. As well as carrying out maintenance and repairs on the entire Freightliner locomotive fleet, FML also maintains its HHA and HXA coal wagons and Lafarge cement wagons. Supplementary facilities are located at Crewe, Dunbar, Hope and York. Dedicated traction and rolling stock maintenance facilities for Freightliner Limited are located at Southampton.

Freightliner's overall UK fleet totals 137 Class-66 and 19 Class-70 diesels – with electric locomotives of Class 86 (16), and Class 90 (10), plus locomotives used for shunting. The 19 Class-70 PowerHaul diesel locomotives are part of an order for 30 from GE Transportation. They are divided between the intermodal (8) and FHH (11) businesses.

The UK wagon fleet totals more than 3,000, of which some 1,700 are container flats. In 2012 Freightliner placed an order with wagon hire company VTG for an undisclosed number of 43 twin-platform Ecofret 'Shortliner' wagons, each comprising a twin sent of two 40ft deck length wagons. These are intended to provide more capacity for increasingly common containers of that size and to eliminate the incidence of unused space on the 60ft wagons that currently make up the bulk of the fleet. Their manufacture is being undertaken by Greenbrier in Poland. ■

Senior personnel

Chief Executive Officer, Freightliner Group Peter Maybury (in photo)
Finance Director, Freightliner Group Russell Mears
Managing Director, Freightliner Ltd Adam Cunliffe
Managing Director, Freightliner Heavy Haul Paul Smart
Engineering Director, Freightliner Group Tim Shakerley
Corporate Development Director, Freightliner Group Dom McKenna
Managing Director, Freightliner PL Rafal Milczarski
Managing Director, Freightliner Australia John McArthur
General Manager Freightliner Maintenance Dave Curtis

Freight and Haulage

Devon & Cornwall Railways Class 56/3 No 56311 passes Undy, Monmouthshire, on 27 April 2012, hauling Cardiff Tidal to Shipley empty scrap metal hoppers. Brian Morrison

Colas Rail Freight

Colas Rail Freight is part of the Colas Group, a subsidiary of the French-based multinational Bouygues construction and services conglomerate. Operations began in 2007 and have included running the UK legs of trains for Freight Europe UK, a French National Railways subsidiary. Commodities carried currently include inbound consignments of steel for the automotive industry. Originating at Dunkerque, France, these are shipped to Boston docks for onward transfer in covered wagons to Washwood Heath in Birmingham. The service is operated several days each week.

In 2011 Colas began moving coal in HHA wagons for UK Coal from its Park Wall opencast mine, near Wolsingham, County Durham, to Tata Steel at Scunthorpe and Ratcliffe Power Station for E.ON. The trains were the first freight services to use the Weardale Railway since 1983.

In May 2012 the company commenced a 12-month contract for Air BP moving aviation fuel from the INEIOS refinery at Grangemouth in Scotland to Prestwick Airport, Linkswood in Fife and the Rolls Royce factory in Derby. Two-axle tank wagons leased by Air BP from VTG are used for these flows.

Also undertaken is the haulage of timber for building materials maker Kronospan under a five-year contract signed in 2007. The original flow between Carlisle and Chirk has been supplemented by regular trains from Baglan Bay in South Wales and Teigngrace near Newton Abbot, as well as occasional loads from Ribblehead. In August 2012, 30 Dutch-registered IWA wagons converted from former CargoWaggons arrived in the UK for this traffic. In addition, Colas has occasionally provided traction for trains operated in connection with Network Rail engineering work.

The traction fleet comprises five Class 66s, three Class 47s and operational members of a pool of five Class 56s. By late 2012 two of the last-mentioned had been returned to traffic. In 2012 Colas acquired Cardiff-based vehicle maintenance company Pullman Rail, strengthening its capability to maintain its own fleet and to expand group services for other rolling stock owners and operators.

Devon & Cornwall Railways Limited

Devon & Cornwall Railways is an embryonic open access freight operator owned by British American Railway Services Limited, itself formed by Iowa Pacific Holdings, an American shortline railroad holding company. Other BARS subsidiaries include locomotive hire and track maintenance company RMS Locotec, the Weardale Railway linking Bishop Auckland with Wolsingham and Eastgate, and the Dartmoor Railway between Yeoford and Meldon. BARS acquired Hanson Traction Ltd, the provider of main line railway locomotives, engineering and maintenance services during 2010.

While it was created initially with a view to handling movements between private infrastructure and Network Rail-controlled lines, DCR has mostly operated irregular or short term flows such as scrap metal traffic from Shipley and Stockton on Tees to the Celsa plant at Cardiff and aggregates from Peak Forest to Leeds. It also handles rolling stock movements on behalf of other operators and supplies locomotives on hire.

The operational fleet in late 2012 included three Class 56 locomotives and two Class 31s.

West Coast Railway Company

West Coast Railway Company (WCR) has been a licensed train operating company since 1998, when it became the first privately-owned company to obtain a licence, under rail privatisation, allowing it to co-ordinate and run its own trains without third-party involvement. With its main base at Carnforth, Lancashire, it specialises in operating charter trains, both in its own right and on behalf of tour operators, using classic and modern diesels and historic steam locomotives.

It runs regular steam-hauled trains including the 'Jacobite' (Fort William-Mallaig) and the 'Scarborough Spa Express' (York-Scarborough).

WCR owns, maintains and operates diesel locomotives and over 80 passenger vehicles (including the last 10 Pullman carriages to be built, in 1965). Steam locomotives it operates include GWR 'Hall' No 5972 'Olton Hall' - 'Hogwarts Castle' in the Harry Potter films.

Riviera Trains

Riviera Trains Ltd, formed in 1996, is a prominent independent charter train provider, working closely with leading charter operating companies, and it also provides quality locomotives and coaching stock to support the additional requirements of train operating companies. It operates from a main base at Crewe, and has a sizeable fleet of coaches.

Riviera Trains operates with DB Schenker as part of the Charter Alliance, which was launched in April 2007, as a 'one stop shop' for the provision of coaching stock for franchised train operating companies and charter trains.

Charter trains include mixed rakes of First and Standard Class coaches for enthusiast and 'days out' railtours, and full rakes of First Class vehicles with at-seat dining for luxury VIP charters. The company has six Class 47 diesel locomotives.

Senior personnel

Colas Rail

Chief Executive Officer Charles-Albert Giral
Finance Director Colin Evans
Head of Freight Simon Ball

Innovation and Environment

In association with
KNORR-BREMSE

Innovation and Environment

Alternative solutions?

'Modern Railways' columnist Alan Williams casts a critical eye over the second draft Network Rail Alternative Solutions RUS from a Community Rail perspective

It has long been the contention of many community rail supporters that the ideal of an improved service, at lower cost, could be achieved on secondary lines by adopting differing standards of operation and maintenance to those required on main lines. One of the main recommendations of the McNulty Report in 2011 was that the railway industry should consider alternative solutions to conventional heavy rail approaches to provide lower whole life cost options. Network Rail subsequently set up an 'Alternative Solutions' Network-wide Route Utilisation Strategy (RUS), and in October 2012 the All Party Parliamentary Light Rail Group called for a revision of 'unnecessarily high' safety standards which lead to projects being over-engineered and thus over-expensive. The community rail fraternity welcomed these interventions.

The first draft of the Alternative Solutions RUS Consultation was published early in 2012, and a second draft, also for consultation, was published in September 2012.

This RUS is overseen by a Stakeholder Management Group (SMG) consisting of representatives from the Association of Train Operating Companies, Department for Transport, freight operating companies, Freight Transport Association, London Travelwatch, Passenger Focus, Passenger Transport Executive Group, Rail Industry Association, Rail Freight Group, rolling stock companies, Transport for London, Transport Scotland, and Welsh Government. The Office of Rail Regulation (ORR) also has a seat in the capacity of observer.

So a heavy emphasis on urban and freight representation, but disappointingly not a single voice in support of the 33 designated Community Rail Partnerships, or the much greater number of other supporting groups.

The SMG identified those elements of strategy which it wished to include, and set up a working group composed of some of the SMG members, but also including Transport for Greater Manchester. But still no specific representative of community rail, even though it does not fall into the sphere of interest of any of the rail members of the Group and indeed some, like freight operators, have on occasion been opposed to community rail proposals.

The group proposed that the RUS should consider:
■ The replacement of self-powered rolling stock;
■ Aspirations for lighter vehicles on less heavily used parts of the network;
■ A desire to identify innovative lower cost forms of electric traction;
■ Aspirations to operate more frequent services on routes currently limited by infrastructure constraints (e.g. single lines with passing loops);
■ Aspirations for greater connectivity through enhanced city centre penetration;
■ Increased community involvement in operating the railway.

But despite these seemingly quite catholic terms of reference, at least four of which are also central to community rail objectives, it soon emerged that the Alternative Solutions RUS would be looking at just three quite specific issues – tram or tram train conversion of heavy rail infrastructure and services, alternative methods of delivery of electric traction on lower traffic density routes and, slightly bizarrely, the community rail proposition itself. It seems that the McNulty report recommendation that

In association with **KNORR-BREMSE**

Low cost electrification for branches

A study prepared by Delta Rail in July 2010 for a Department for Transport (DfT) Research Project on Low Cost Electrification examined whether it can be economically feasible to electrify low usage branch lines. It was published by the DfT in May 2012.

Assessment of electrification options, which considered various operating voltages and methods of current collection, concluded that a 750V DC overhead line system would provide the most economic solution for branch line spurs remote from existing electrification. Primary factors for this conclusion are comparative ease of installation/integration of low voltage overhead with existing infrastructure, and relative ease of grid supply connections.

The study found a number of factors that would substantially reduce electrification costs for a rural branch line scheme, compared to the high usage situations where electrification schemes are normally applied. Those factors include comparatively low service speeds, requiring limited dynamic current collection performance, that allow the use of lower cost tram style overhead equipment; low service frequency enabling operation from comparatively few sub-stations, aided by increasing nominal system voltage to 850V DC; inherently reduced power requirement of energy efficient light rail vehicles; and reduced requirement to relocate/modify buried services for electrical reasons.

In addition to these inherent cost reduction factors, the study also considered how new technologies and innovative designs/solutions may be applied to achieve further cost reductions, including: alternative materials, low cost design of overhead equipment; energy recovery/storage solutions; low power (low cost) substations; and wireless monitoring and control.

Two branch line electrification conversion scenarios, based on real routes, were assessed to provide an understanding of notional costs.

Case 1 was a nine-mile single-track community line operating approximately an hourly service at low speed (30mph). Estimated cost for provision of low cost electrification infrastructure was £4.0 million.

Case 2 was a 25 mile route operating a community service over a 20 mile mixed traffic branch line, and an additional five mile section of main line. Estimated cost for provision of low cost electrification infrastructure was £9.8 million. (Both cases exclude vehicle costs and servicing facilities).

The first Northern service across Thorneywaite bridge on the Esk Valley community rail line to Whitby on 18 June 2012, after bridge replacement. Network Rail

the industry consider alternative solutions to traditional heavy rail approaches has been quietly downdialled, because the draft makes it clear that there is to be no consideration of community rail thinking (or anybody else's!) on alternative methods of operation or maintenance. In a paragraph headed 'Infrastructure and rolling stock', the draft Alternative Solutions RUS states 'The Community rail concept also includes achieving cost reductions in infrastructure and train operation and [I think this should be "but"] has focused on revenue generation and community involvement and not on cost savings to a great extent'. Is this really true?

Certainly CRPs have been more successful in promoting existing services and boosting revenue than in achieving cost savings on their lines. But it is not for the want of trying. Despite being constantly encouraged by DfT to be entrepreneurial and to 'think outside the box', I suspect almost every one of the 33 designated CRPs could point to proposals for operational or maintenance cost savings which have been rejected without any serious consideration - either because they required changes in conventional railway methods of operation, or changes to Network Rail standards for heavy rail signalling or infrastructure. This whole issue, which many believe is the main stumbling block to major reductions in the cost of operating community style lines, is dismissed in a single sentence: 'this document has not considered this issue because it has network wide implications broader than this strategy'. But wasn't this supposed to be a network-wide search for alternative solutions? What could be broader than that?

Almost by way of apology, the draft continues 'the other alternative solutions under consideration in this strategy, namely tram train, tram conversion and energy storage, all have the potential to contribute directly or indirectly to the rolling stock and infrastructure cost of community rail routes'. But do they?

Tram and tram train

The draft RUS examines conversion of heavy rail infrastructure and services for trams or tram trains in considerable and sometimes highly theoretical detail, although there is no exploration of why the tram train concept is perceived to be so much more expensive or difficult to implement in Britain compared to mainland Europe, where tram trains have been in successful operation for more than 20 years. Coloured by urban transport interests, there is an assumption that tram trains will be electrically powered and diesel tram trains get short shrift on grounds of cost, weight and environmental issues. We are told that a bi-mode (electric plus diesel powered) tram train would be more expensive than a conventional new diesel multiple-unit, but that seems to be comparing apples with pears unless savings that could then be made by switching to simpler methods of operation are factored into the equation. There is no estimate of the comparative cost of a pure diesel tram train, which realistically is what most community lines are likely to be able to use, or consideration of making heavy rail trains more able to work in light rail or tramway style by, for example, fitting them with track brakes to enable line of sight operation. As a result, very little of this part of the draft has any relevance to any existing community rail operations, concentrating instead on possible conversions to tramway style operation in urban areas - and in particular extensions to the existing tram networks in Greater Manchester, the West Midlands, South Yorkshire, Edinburgh, Nottingham and London, as well as identifying aspirations for possible entirely new tram train services around Glasgow, Aberdeen and - intriguingly, in view of the recent decision to go ahead with a trolleybus network rather than trams - Leeds.

Alternative electrification – or not

So, if the future is to be electric, what promise does it hold for community lines? The draft examines three electrification options which it describes as 'coasting', 'discontinuous' and 'discrete'. Coasting involves trains running without power through extended neutral sections in an otherwise conventional electrification to avoid the costs of gauge clearance at bridges and other structures. It is not particularly novel, but it is important because gauge clearance is estimated to account for as much

HITACHI *Inspire the Next*

117

Innovation and Environment

as 30 or even 40 per cent of the cost of any electrification scheme. Its use is obviously restricted, both in terms of length to a few tens of metres, and in location, which has to be well away from stations, junctions, signals or any other place where a train might have to stop and thus become immobilised.

Discontinuous electrification, as its name implies, envisages actual gaps in the overhead line equipment of up to about 2km to avoid wiring through tunnels or at locations with complicated track layouts. Again there would be expected savings on gauge clearance, and by avoiding the provision of overhead line equipment: but bespoke rolling stock with on board energy storage would be required, which is estimated to be more rather than less expensive overall. And there must be real questions about the operational feasibility of working a route with several large gaps in the overhead line.

Discrete electrification is essentially a polite phrase for 'no electrification'. It envisages very little new overhead line, involving instead the extensive use of bi-mode trains (or tram trains), perhaps radiating from a central electrified modal area around a major city or conurbation. This would seem the most likely form of electrification to suit community lines, but the form of alternative power is challenging. With the cost of an electric/diesel bi-mode estimated at more than a conventional diesel multiple-unit, the draft examines battery operation instead, proposes an off-wire operational radius of 75 miles, and provides a map of routes analysed for battery-powered train operation. This is not reassuring: one of the community lines identified, the 40 mile Bishop Auckland-Saltburn route, is currently electrified for just a few hundred yards through Darlington station on the East Coast main line. Would a brief station stop there be sufficient to recharge batteries? Surprisingly, despite detailed investigation of these somewhat novel proposals, there is no similar examination of the feasibility or comparative cost of straightforward single 'trolley wire' electrification. The report merely notes that it 'may be possible for routes with line speeds of less than 60mph' – which encompasses the entire length of some community lines and most of the remainder!

Community rail

The third and final part of the 'Alternative Solutions' RUS is the shortest and in many ways the most disappointing, at times a contradictory description of what community rail is rather than what it might be able to do. It makes great play of the fact that 'community rail lines tend to have a lower share of season tickets than the national average' and that 'this suggests that the majority of journeys are taken for leisure journeys rather than commuting' - without recognising that on many community lines the service is so sparse that any sensible commuting is at best difficult, and at worst (as for example on the Whitby-Middlesbrough Esk Valley line) virtually impossible. Noting that 'much of the community rail market is for leisure purposes' and is 'highly seasonal' with 'stations in holiday locations', the draft then contradicts itself in listing the five community lines which have grown in excess of 80 per cent. Top of the list is the Severn Beach line, which despite its holiday-sounding name connects the centre of Bristol with the urban areas of Sea Mills and Shirehampton and the industrial area of Avonmouth. A holiday location it is not, and most of the growth has been from commuter traffic thanks to, as the draft notes, 'major changes to the service provision to increase frequencies'. Exactly.

There are now 33 Community Rail Partnerships, the latest having been designated by the DfT just a couple of months ago, and there are 16 other partnerships which are not yet designated, together with 126 formally recognised station adoption groups. The one thing they all have in common is an enthusiasm to kick over traditional traces and try new ways of improving the railway, and certainly none of them are short of ideas. So you might think that between them they would provide the ideal place to both look for and then trial alternatives. But the 14 page long 'Emerging Solutions' section of the draft has just two paragraphs on community rail.

This Alternative Solutions RUS has unusually had a second published draft, but clearly still requiring much more work to even begin to justify its title. It needs to be much more realistic and far wider ranging than just three very narrow subjects. It needs to spend less time on esoteric discussions of the types of tram train conversion that might or might not be possible in urban locations, and more on the alternatives for replacing the present large fleet of heavy rail diesel units, two thirds of which are already over 20 years old, which currently provide services on almost all community and other rural lines. We know that, thanks to latest EU emission regulations, replacement with conventional heavy-rail diesel multiple-units is likely to be significantly more expensive and less fuel efficient. Equally, it is clear that electrification is unlikely to reach anywhere near most community lines in the next 30 years. Yet there is no exploration in the RUS of the obvious alternative, a lighter weight diesel train or tram train, or of the accompanying need to make significant cost savings by breaking away from 'heavy rail' methods of operation. So despite its hard work on other subjects, as far as Community Rail goes, this draft report certainly 'must try harder'. ■

> "No organisation has a monopoly on good ideas. Indeed, we believe that there may be other areas where alternative approaches or technologies have the potential to drive costs down." - Paul Plummer, Group Strategy Director, Network Rail, in Foreword to Draft for Consultation of the Network Route Utilisation Strategy: Alternative Solutions September 2012.

Saltire-liveried Class 156 No 156506 near Maybole, on the Ayr-Stranraer community rail line, on 25 April 2012, forming the 11.05 ScotRail service from Kilmarnock to Girvan. Brian Morrison

In association with KNORR-BREMSE

Knorr-Bremse... Innovation Delivering Real Benefits

Mechanical innovation; the Knorr-Bremse Oil-free Compressor delivers environmental benefits, lower life cycle costs and requires some 20% less operational energy against conventional compressors.

Knorr-Bremse continue to demonstrate leadership in rail systems innovation through the development and introduction of a range of products and systems designed to offer train builders and operators technology which delivers real benefits whilst benefiting the environment.

Innovation in Brake Systems

The well established and Queen's Award for Innovation winning EP2002 mechatronic brake control system, which is lighter and smaller than conventional brake control systems, is now joined by the new EP1001 system. EP1001 has been specially developed for freight wagons and addresses the major issue of wheel locking which result in expensive wheel flats and rail damage. EP1001 is self-powered, requiring no additional electrical supply and can be retrofitted to most existing freight wagon types. Wheel flats can also affect energy consumption and cause environmentally damaging noise problems near affected rail lines.

Within the braking system portfolio of Knorr-Bremse another example of an innovative and environmentally friendly product is the Oil-free compressor. Knorr-Bremse was first with oil-free compressor technology and with less noise and vibration there are now some 8,000 Knorr-Bremse Oil-free compressors in service around the world.

However, the real success of the Oil-free compressor stems from the use of its cleaner and more efficient technology. Oil-free means there is no environmentally harmful waste oil, contaminated filters or air dryer granulate to dispose of. This, together with the low-friction design of the compressor means lower life cycle costs and the consumption of some 20% less operational energy against conventional compressors.

Innovation in HVAC

Knorr-Bremse has a wide rail portfolio in addition to its braking products and systems and the other areas of the portfolio are not left behind in the Group's approach of continuous technological development.

Merak, the Knorr-Bremse specialist rail HVAC Company for example, has developed air-conditioning systems which operate with the new, ultra eco-friendly refrigerant HFO1234yf. The use of this refrigerant represents a major advance with The Global Warming Potential (GWP) of this fluorinated solution used being only 4 compared to 1,300 for R134a solution. This means that the average time that HFQ1234yf solution, as used in the Merak system, stays in the air is 11 days compared to 13.8 years of, for example, the older R134a type!

Innovation in Energy and Condition Management

However, there are even more graphic examples of how Knorr-Bremse is offering new technology to help train builders and operators. Recognising that the cost of energy will not decrease, Knorr-Bremse has developed two key energy management systems to help to save costs for operators and to deliver substantial environmental benefits.

Knorr-Bremse LEADER is the first of these innovative new systems. LEADER is an advanced driver assist system which improves schedule adherence whilst delivering significant energy savings and environmental benefits.

The system helps the driver to anticipate what actions are required and to operate the train in a more efficient way. Using real time information about the train's dynamics, the timetable and the route details, including specific features and speed limits, LEADER calculates an optimum speed profile whilst a clear cab display shows the driver in advance how he can adapt his driving style to optimise the energy required along a particular route.

Energy metering is another area where Knorr-Bremse can support train operators and help to drive down environmental damage, waste and cost through its Eurometer system. The Knorr-Bremse Eurometer system enables operators to more fully understand what energy is being used (and wasted) and how various styles of driving and operational conditions affect specific energy usage. The Eurometer system provides a perfect partner with LEADER to empower operators in the management of expensive energy.

Ensuring that the train systems are operating as they should is also essential for efficient and cost effective operation. New from Knorr-Bremse is COMORAN, a monitoring and diagnostic system for powered and unpowered bogies and their components. Integrated into the braking system, COMORAN identifies critical and safety-relevant conditions such as damage to wheelset bearings and hot axle boxes, unstable running or derailment, all according to TSI requirements. The system provides comprehensive data which enables condition-based maintenance work to be carried out economically.

Knorr-Bremse is committed to continuous innovation which brings drives out cost and waste and brings real benefits to train builders and operators and the environment.

For more information on all Knorr-Bremse products and systems please contact Paul Smith on 01225 898826 or email paul.smith@knorr.bremse.com
www.knorr-bremse.co.uk

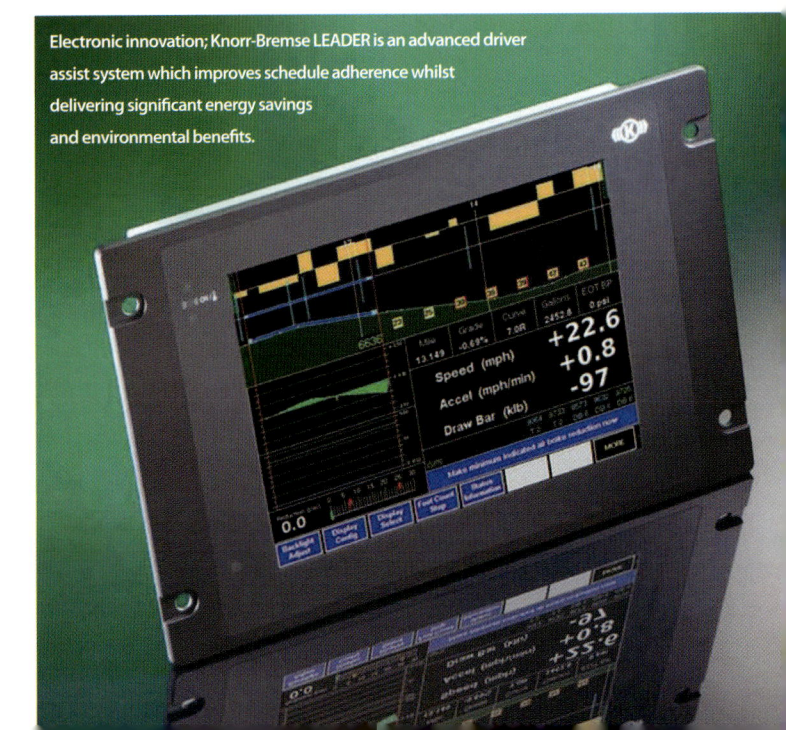

Electronic innovation; Knorr-Bremse LEADER is an advanced driver assist system which improves schedule adherence whilst delivering significant energy savings and environmental benefits.

Innovation and Environment

Railway Industry Innovation Awards - Blackfriars takes major prize

Left to right: Richard Price, ORR Chief Executive, who presented the 2012 Railway Industry Innovation Awards. Claiming the Environment award are Mark Parsons and Mark Wardell, Energy Efficiency Engineer and Project Manager (Operations) with First Group; on the right is Tim Mason, Group Account Director - Services, with award sponsor, Bombardier. Tony Miles

The Railway Industry Innovation Awards, run by Modern Railways magazine, is the longest running award scheme in the rail industry, and one of the most prestigious. Observers and participants in the industry, ranging from Rail Value for Money study author, Sir Roy McNulty, to Network Rail's Technical Director, Steve Yianni, have called for more attention to be paid to innovation. With innovation climbing up the industry's agenda, the Railway Industry Innovation Awards scheme has come into its own.

Richard Price, Chief Executive of the Office of Rail Regulation, gave the keynote speech at the 2012 awards, held at the Paddington Hilton. 'The exposure Modern Railways gives to innovation is all the more relevant now that the industry has moved out of the long phase of managed decline of the late 20th century, and into a period of remarkable sustained growth not seen since Victorian times', he commented.

'There are still a number of barriers to innovation which we are working with the industry to resolve', he said. 'For what it's worth, I think that the industry can be very risk averse - where type approvals and changes to standards can sometimes be a drawn out process; and archaic work practices can stifle innovation.

'We will keep pushing for more transparency about cost data, better asset knowledge, management and whole-life costings, and better smarter procurement and relationships with the supply chain.

'And of course we want to free the industry's leaders and innovators from the constraints of excessive involvement in the detail and micro-specification from government and regulators.

The Periodic Review of industry spending will look in substance to the next steps on rolling out innovation in areas like signalling, passenger information, and asset knowledge and management. 'More and more the industry will need to increase its efficiency, to find new and better ways of doing things. And you will need to develop new products that will satisfy the demand for higher standards and lower costs', he told the audience at the Hilton.

'The conventional wisdom for decades has said that Britain has fallen behind in the innovation race. What I see in rail – not just new ideas but real delivery on the ground – makes me optimistic. And my role is to help to create the environment in which innovation can thrive and make a big difference for the better.'

Blackfriars takes top prize

The Major Project award for 2012 went to the London Blackfriars development project team - including Network Rail, designers Jacobs and Tony Gee & Partners, principal contractor Balfour Beatty, and First Capital Connect. They pioneered a number of successful innovations to minimise project risk, protect programme timing, and minimise impact on live railway operations. These included pre-cast pier extensions to widen the Thames bridge structure; slipform construction for shafts and stairs near the London Underground lines; and a track protection structure above those lines.

Trophies for the Modern Railways-organised Innovation Awards. Tony Miles

In the Environment category, sponsored by Bombardier, the winning entry was the driver advisory system developed by First Great Western, supplied by TTG Transportation Technology, and installed in 119 high-speed train power cars, to offer drivers advice on optimum driving speeds to meet timetable requirements, and improve fuel usage.

The Engineering & Safety award, sponsored by the Railway Industry Association, went to OmniVision, the system designed to replace basic visual inspection of plain line track by a combination of image acquisition, track geometry measurement, processing and reporting technology. Developed for Network Rail by Omnicom Engineering, the system's key benefits are a reduction in the risk to staff undertaking inspection on the live network, creation of a standardised consistent method of delivering track inspection across the network, and a reduction in the cost of track inspection activities.

The Passenger Experience award, sponsored by Modern Railways' publishers Key Publishing, went to Chiltern Railways, Masabi, Atos, and Access IS. Chiltern was the first rail operator to go live with a full barcode ticket system. The mTicketing application allows commuters to securely purchase and display rail tickets on most mass-market handsets, which are then available for pick up at the station, or displayed in the app as a barcode or readable ticket which can be checked visually, with handheld scanners, or at station gates.

Winner of the Operations & Performance award, sponsored by Informatica, was Tube Lines' new generation electronic programme machine. Senior Technical Officer, Nick Healey, designed an electronic programme machine which can take the place of the mechanical machines in interlocking machine rooms. This has significantly improved reliability, led to better passenger services and fewer delays, with a projected saving of £342,241 after three years.

Winning entry in the Small Scale project category was Northern Rail's community ambassadors scheme, created to promote the use of local rail services with black and minority ethnic and socially excluded groups around Blackburn, Brierfield, Rochdale and Farnworth stations. A full-time project manager and four part-time ambassadors have worked from within the communities to understand, and then overcome, barriers to local rail travel.

The Cross Industry Partnership award, sponsored by Modern Railways' publishers Key Publishing, was won by Comply Serve for its new approach to project compliance. Early adoption of a new approach to compliance by projects like Crossrail, sharing virtual documents across many hundreds of users, is delivering significant advantage in both performance and cost savings. The introduction of new collaborative, cloud-based approaches by Comply Serve has extended well understood systems integration principles and processes into the domain of project management and delivery. Projects are benefiting from joined up project teams and unprecedented visibility of delivery compliance.

New look for 'Golden Spanners'

The tenth annual review of traction and rolling stock fleet reliability is published in the January 2013 issue of Modern Railways magazine. An awards luncheon the previous November - one of the Modern Railways Fourth Friday Club events - sees 'Golden Spanners' awarded to the best performers.

The brainchild of Roger Ford, Industry & Technology Editor of Modern Railways, the awards now reflect major changes in the data used by the rail industry to measure reliability.

The previous Miles per 5 Minutes Delay (MP5MD) measure is now replaced by Miles per Technical Incident (MTIN). This is a more demanding measure because TINs are triggered by a 3min delay. In addition the monthly reports now include Primary Delay Minutes per Incident (DPI) for each fleet - thus rating rolling stock fleets for delay to service when a failure occurs.

Golden Whistles Awards!

Skilful operators can make the trains run safely and on time – and the best operators deserve recognition.

For this reason the Institution of Railway Operators and Modern Railways magazine joined forces to launch the Golden Whistles Awards. These awards acknowledge best practice and congratulate railway operators that have done a good job by rewarding them with that ultimate symbol of smart operating – a whistle!

The Golden Whistles, based on objective data, emulate the successful Golden Spanners Awards already run by Modern Railways. There are categories for: Operational Safety, Operational Performance, and Managing Disruption, with awards for best performance and most improved performance in several categories. A panel of senior railway executives interpret the data and ensure fair play.

The 2013 Golden Whistles Awards will be presented at the January meeting of the Modern Railways Fourth Friday Club.

The Fourth Friday Club

The Modern Railways Fourth Friday Club provides a unique networking forum for executives from all sectors in the railway industry. There are club meetings on five Fridays in each year, the season running from September to June. The club was the idea of 'Modern Railways' Editor, James Abbott who is also Club Secretary.

Since the first meeting in 2003, the growing reputation of the Club for attracting senior policy makers and top railway managers as guest speakers has seen membership expand rapidly.

For more information, contact modern.railways@googlemail.com ∎

A special event on 28 September 2012 marked 50 years since Modern Railways magazine was published under this name, after changing from 'Trains Illustrated'. GBRf's Managing Director John Smith (left) kindly invited Industry & Technology Editor, Roger Ford (centre), and Editor, James Abbott, to name loco No 66745 'Modern Railways - The First 50 years' at a ceremony at the National Railway Museum. GBRf and UK Railtours operated a special train from London King's Cross, with the return run hauled by the newly named locomotive. Tony Miles

Innovation and Environment

Railtex returns to Earls Court

The industry's entire supply chain will be represented at Railtex 2013.

Railtex, the UK's leading event for the rail industry, returns to Earl's Court in London in 2013. Taking place from 30 April to 2 May, this will be the 11th of these popular shows organised by Mack Brooks Exhibitions, serving as a showcase for the entire range of railway equipment, systems and services, embracing both rolling stock and infrastructure and representing the industry's entire supply chain.

Railtex 2013 will include features familiar to visitors to previous events and to Infrarail – plus some innovations. One of these will be The Yard, a dedicated display area in the exhibition hall for large plant and machinery used for railway construction and maintenance. Following its highly successful introduction at Infrarail 2012 at the NEC in Birmingham, The Yard will now be a key part of Railtex 2013 too. Supported by the Rail Plant Association, The Yard enables companies in this key sector of the rail market to display vehicles and machines that were previously difficult to exhibit.

In another new development, the 2013 event will see the first-ever Railtex Awards Dinner. Devised to recognise exhibitors' achievements, this will take place on 1 May 2013 at the capital's Copthorne Tara Hotel, and will bring together show participants and VIPs for a social evening that will include entertainment and networking opportunities.

Railtex always attracts the leading companies supplying the needs of the UK's rail market and the 2013 event will be no exception. As well as individual company stands the show will feature the Rail Alliance Hub, a dedicated area for members of the alliance to promote their products and services, and similarly a section of the exhibition for members of the Derby & Derbyshire Rail Forum cluster of industry suppliers.

And while the main aim of visitors will be to meet exhibitors and to learn more about their products, services and innovations, there will be a broad programme of activities intended to provide insights into industry developments and trends in both technology and policy.

Running throughout Railtex 2013 will be a full seminar programme with daily keynote speeches by industry leaders. Attendance will be free and open to all. Also open to visitors will be the Project Update Theatre, where industry managers and engineers will outline the status of major rail schemes taking place or planned across the UK.

A new development will be The Platform, where for the first time Railtex in partnership with Rail Champions will host an interactive discussion forum with a panel of industry experts on themes of topical relevance. People attending the event will also be able to learn about exhibitors' employment opportunities via the Recruitment Wall at the show.

The 2013 exhibition will take place against the background of an upbeat mood in the UK rail supply industry, with the government giving its very clear support for development of the national network through major investment projects. Exhibition Manager Heidi Cotsworth commented: 'This really sets the scene for Railtex 2013. The underlying message is that the government has a positive long-term vision for rail and is backing that up with investment funding. Railtex will provide a great opportunity for companies from all sectors of the market to demonstrate their products and capabilities and for the industry to meet and discuss the ongoing projects and opportunities.'

More than 400 exhibitors took part in the last Railtex in 2011, attracting some 9,200 industry professionals from 49 countries. Among organisations supporting the 2013 exhibition are the Railway Industry Association, the Rail Alliance, the Institution of Engineering and Technology, the Chartered Institute of Logistics & Transport, the Permanent Way Institution and the Rail Plant Association. Also endorsing the event are the National Skills Academy for Railway Engineering, and Young Railway Professionals.

More information on Railtex 2013, including a regularly updated exhibitor list, details of seminar programmes and all other visitor activities, can be found on the show website: (www.railtex.co.uk). Entry to the show for pre-registered visitors will be free. A registration form will appear on the website closer to the exhibition. ∎

Rail Vehicle Enhancements

Visitors to the Rail Vehicle Enhancements show in London and Derby in October 2012 were able to:
- drive the Cubris GreenSpeed driver simulator;
- see the h2gogo DMU hydrogen generator;
- witness live video feeds from R2P CCTV equipment on service trains;
- feel the chill of DC Airco cab cooling equipment;
- experience the Volo in-train entertainment and advanced passenger information systems;
- evaluate the Westermo data coms equipment;
- talk to staff about Infodev's advanced passenger counting technology; and
- gain information about McGeoch energy saving LED lighting solutions.

RVE was organised by Onyxrail and sponsored by *Modern Railways*.

Onyxrail is an installer of technical enhancements and was able to display UIC castings produced by sister company Brentto Industry.

The web site www.rve2012.co.uk will be live until RVE2013.

HITACHI Inspire the Next

Key Projects

In association with

COSTAIN

Key Projects

The first of the new wave of electrification schemes will see TransPennine Express services between Manchester and Scotland switch to electric traction. Passengers throng Manchester Piccadilly, with a Class 185 diesel train forming a service for Edinburgh. Tony Miles

Electrification
government sees the light

Roger Ford, Industry & Technology Editor of *Modern Railways* magazine, reports on the implications of government commitment to a rolling programme of electrification

An economic recession at the end of the 1980s, combined with the subsequent fragmentation of the railways, spelt the end of new electrification of the British rail network. With track and train separated, there was no incentive for infrastructure owner Network Rail to introduce costly and complex equipment, where it would bear the cost and risk while train operators gained the benefit.

Equally, while train operators would gain from replacing existing electrified fleets with more energy-efficient and more reliable multiple units which cost less to maintain, that did not apply to replacing diesel traction with electric trains. The average franchise length meant that an incumbent operator would suffer from the disruption of wiring a route and introducing new rolling stock, only to lose the franchise when it expired and see another firm reap the benefits.

Then, the collapse of Railtrack saw the costs to the taxpayer of the railway soar. Network Rail spent its first five years restoring order. During this time there was little scope, or funding for major projects.

And an overly expensive railway played into the hands of the civil servants at the Department for Transport who had historically always been opposed to investment in electrification despite past success.

Anti

By 2007, however, the railway was back to 'business as usual' and electrification was creeping up the investment agenda. But the government's 2007 White Paper 'Delivering a sustainable railway', which also contained the High Level Output Specification (HLOS) for the five year Control Period starting on 1 April 2009, showed that DfT was clinging to its historic opposition to modern traction.

According to the White Paper, 'It would not be prudent to commit now to "all-or-nothing" projects, such as network-wide electrification or a high-speed line, for which the longer-term benefits are currently uncertain and which could delay

Table 1: Rail network electrification statistics

	Current	After Already Committed Schemes	After Expected HLOS Schemes
% of network electrified (single track miles)	40.5%	48%	53%
% of passenger vehicle miles operated electrically *	64%	72%	76%

* excludes service lengthening, frequency increases and service pattern changes as a result of electrification
Source: Network Rail

124

HITACHI Inspire the Next

tackling the current strategic priorities such as capacity.' Even as this was published, the tide was turning, and at the end of that year this policy was publicly challenged by the train operators and Network Rail. DfT backed down.

Positive

It was not an overnight victory. But in July 2009, an immediate start on electrification of the Great Western main line (GWML), including the routes to Oxford and Newbury, was announced by then Prime Minister, Gordon Brown, and his Transport Secretary, Lord Adonis. At the same time Network Rail was instructed to start planning for the 'urgent' electrification of the Liverpool-Manchester route via Newton-le-Willows. Combined cost of the two schemes was put at £1 billion.

Network Rail, whose Electrification Route Utilisation Strategy (RUS) included a notional rolling programme, was already investigating ways of reducing the cost of electrification based on the use of modular 'factory trains' capable of wiring line at the rate of one mile of track per night. This gave additional confidence in the ability of industry to deliver.

Rolling

And when the HLOS for the Control Period 5 (CP5), starting on 1 April 2014, was published in July 2012, the change in policy compared with 2007 was marked. It declared, 'The Government's strategy for CP5 is built around a rolling programme of electrification, making continued use of 'cascaded' modern electric rolling stock and exploiting synergies between schemes in order to efficiently meet forecast demand growth, support economic growth and better environmental outcomes, and secure cost efficiencies for both passenger and freight operators'.

As Table 1 shows, in terms of single track miles, around 40.5pc of the rail network is electrified. This is broken down into approximately 5,000 track miles at 25kV AC overhead line and 2,775 at 750V DC third-rail. Note that while only 40pc of the network is electrified, these are business routes generating 64pc of traffic. Under the DfT's new rolling programme, a further 1,700 track miles will be electrified at 25kV AC (Tables 2 and 3).

It should be noted that the schemes already authorised or listed in the HLOS are seen as the start of a rolling programme. Schemes such as the Great Western main line electrification are due to be completed before the end of CP5 in March 2019, and the essence of a rolling programme is continuity for the workforce and the expensive installation equipment. This is recognised by DfT which, when the HLOS was published in 2012, called on the industry to identify the 'most

This shows Network Rail's core electrification strategy of 2009 - it has largely been fulfilled, and heavily supplemented by the HLOS schemes. But, in late 2012, Barking-Gospel Oak and London Gateway port remain to be approved, and Scotland's EGIP has been curtailed (see later in 'Key Projects' chapter)

Table 2: Committed electrification projects (pre-HLOS)

- West Coast main line power supply upgrade.
- Great Western main line to Cardiff, Oxford and Newbury.
- North West Triangle (Manchester-Liverpool via Chat Moss, Huyton-Wigan, Manchester-Euxton Junction and Blackpool North-Preston).
- North trans-Pennine (Manchester Victoria and Guide Bridge-Huddersfield-Leeds-Colton Junction.

125

Key Projects

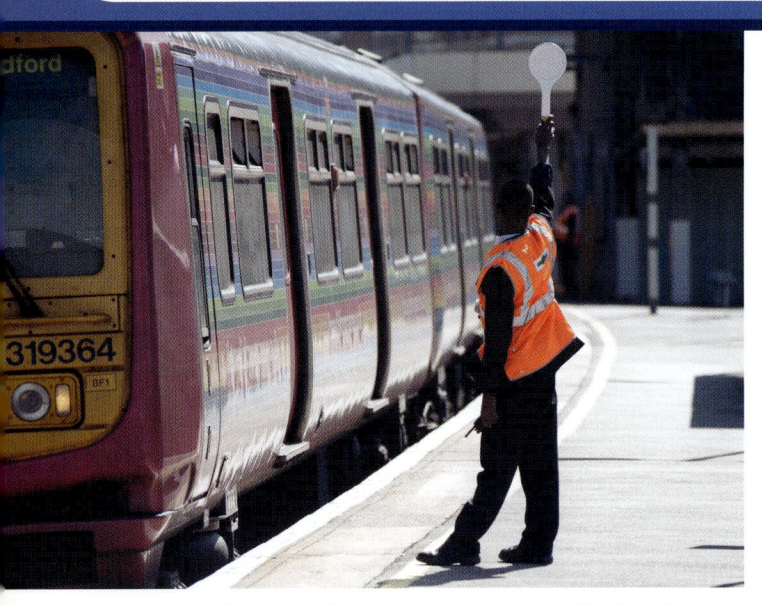

Release of Thameslink Class 319s for the Great Western main line and Northern Triangle electrification schemes is in doubt. The all clear is given for a Class 319 train to depart from East Croydon for Bedford. Tony Miles

efficient strategic' electrification schemes for consideration in CP6 which runs from 2019 to 2024. According to DfT, these follow-on schemes 'should include' freight linkages in South Yorkshire, plus the Derby-Birmingham-Bristol cross-country route. This highlights the role of political imperatives in scheduling the rolling programme.

Politics

While the Great Western main line electrification was overdue, the Midland main line (MML) had shown the best business case in an assessment of potential schemes by the Association of Train Operating Companies. Similarly, Network Rail analysis highlighted tn of the Gospel Oak-Barking line and its extension to serve the new London Gateway container port as the best 'strategic infill'.

In the event, Lord Adonis gave the Northern Triangle priority over the MML. Similarly, in 2011, when further electrification was authorised in the Chancellor's Autumn Statement, the trans-Pennine route from Manchester to Leeds and onwards to join the East Coast main line at Colton Junction was the preferred route.

Table 3: New schemes in HLOS

Electric Spine:
Southampton Port-Basingstoke (conversion from 750V DC),
Basingstoke-Reading;
Oxford-Leamington-Coventry;
Coventry-Nuneaton;
Oxford-Bletchley-Bedford (East West Rail core route).

Midland main line (forms part of Electric Spine):
Bedford-Nottingham and Derby;
Derby-Sheffield;
Kettering-Corby.

South Wales:
Great Western main line extended from Cardiff to Swansea;
Cardiff Valleys lines (to all terminus stations, including Ebbw Vale and Maesteg), Cardiff City Line, Vale of Glamorgan.

Great Western main line:
Acton-Willesden;
Slough-Windsor;
Maidenhead-Marlow;
Twyford-Henley on Thames.

Under Network Rail's provisional electrification programme, the trans-Pennine Route had been scheduled to follow MML, which not only had a strong business case but had been developed to the pre-feasibility stage of Network Rail investment appraisal. In addition, the strong business case meant that MML could fund the provision of an additional connection to the National Grid at its northern end. The ability to share this supply point would have improved the business case for the trans-Pennine scheme.

In the case of the Gospel Oak-Barking infill which would give electrically hauled container trains from the new port access to the East and West Coast main lines, the scheme appears to have been the victim of a power struggle between Whitehall and the Mayor of London. The Department of Transport required the mayor to take all the risk on what is, in effect, a project of national interest.

Contracts

For the supply industry, the rolling programme is already generating orders. Network Rail has ordered a 'factory train' from Windhoff at a cost of £35m which is scheduled to start work on the Great Western main line in 2013.

European electrical contractors have already identified the UK as a rising market. For example, Alstom has formed a new consortium with Babcock and Costain which has put in bids for 11 schemes, including North West triangle and the Edinburgh-Glasgow Improvement Project.

It is hard to estimate the total value of the rolling programme, since civil engineering and signalling costs depend on the existing infrastructure of each route. Installation of the overhead line equipment alone for the schemes in the HLOS is likely to be worth around £900 million.

Network Rail has valued the package combining the North trans-Pennine route electrification with the ECML power supply upgrade at £500m-800m. Total cost of the GWML electrification has risen to over £1 billion as a result of incorporating work for the Reading remodelling. And DfT has valued the Northern Hub schemes already approved at £447 million. This includes the North trans-Pennine electrification.

Missing traction

However, as the rolling programme ramps up, a key element is missing - the 'cascaded modern electric rolling stock', referred to in the HLOS. In particular, the business cases for the GWML and Northern Triangle schemes, authorised in 2009, assumed that Class 319 electric multiple-units released by the new Thameslink fleet would be used to replace diesels when commuter services were electrified.

This expectation has been overtaken by events. As The Modern Railway closed for press, further delays to signing the contract with Siemens for the new Thameslink fleet meant that the deal was not expected to be concluded until February or March 2013.

In November 2012, a proposal was revealed for Southern in conjunction with the DfT to procure 116 electric multiple-unit vehicles, with an option for 100 more, to form part of rolling stock cascades linked with the Thameslink Programme. The new, dual-voltage trains would be capable of 110mph and could be aimed at the new electrified lines, due to be energised from 2016.

While the industry has achieved its aim of government commitment to a rolling programme of electrification, the definitions of the schemes to go ahead in CP5 are likely to be refined during 2013. And if the rail budget tightens following the cancellation of the Intercity West Coast franchise, the conversion of Southampton-Reading from 750V DC to 25kV AC could be sacrificed. ■

Table 4: Northern triangle electrification schedule

December 2013	Manchester-Newton le Willows
December 2014	Manchester-Liverpool, and Huyton-Wigan
May 2016	Preston-Blackpool
December 2016	Manchester-Preston

East meets West

As part of the team delivering East West Rail we have:

- Delivered a business case and outline design for the Western section of the route for the East West Rail Consortium, and
- Worked with Chiltern Railways to develop the Bicester to Oxford section of the East West route under the banner of Project Evergreen 3.

Want to know more?
Contact Jez Baldock
jeremy.baldock@atkinsglobal.com

www.atkinsglobal.com
www.eastwestrail.org.uk
www.chilternrailways.co.uk

Plan Design Enable

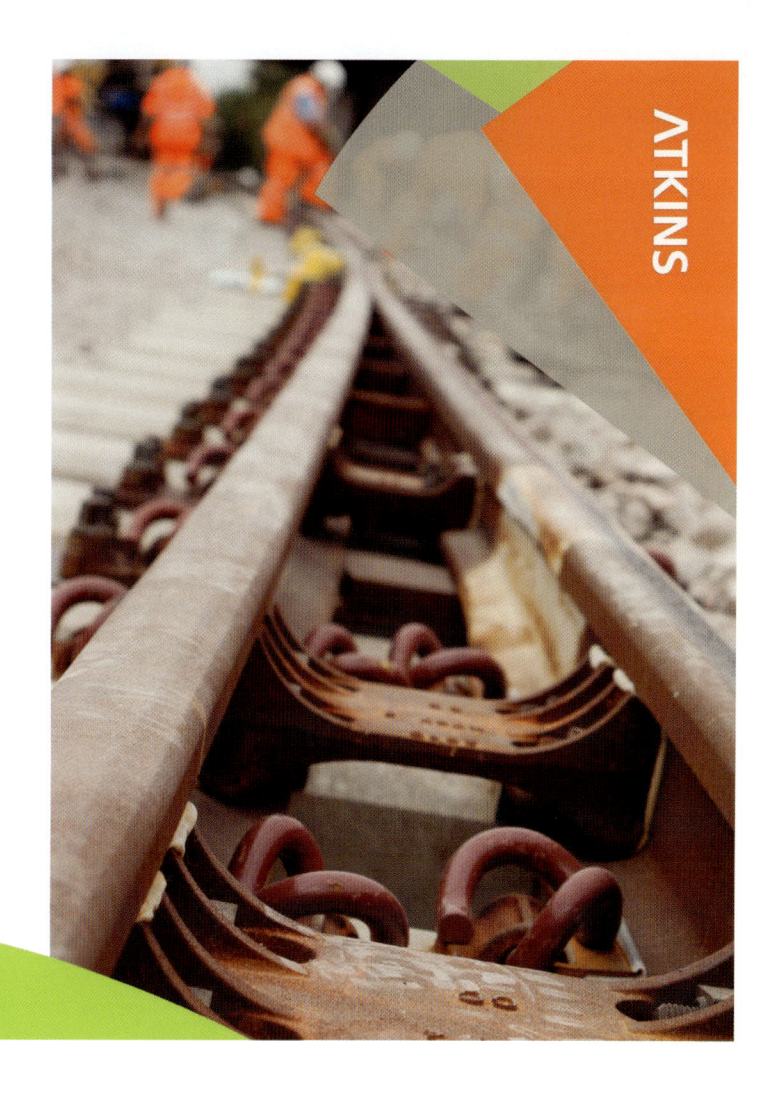

ATKINS

UNIQUELY INTERFLEET

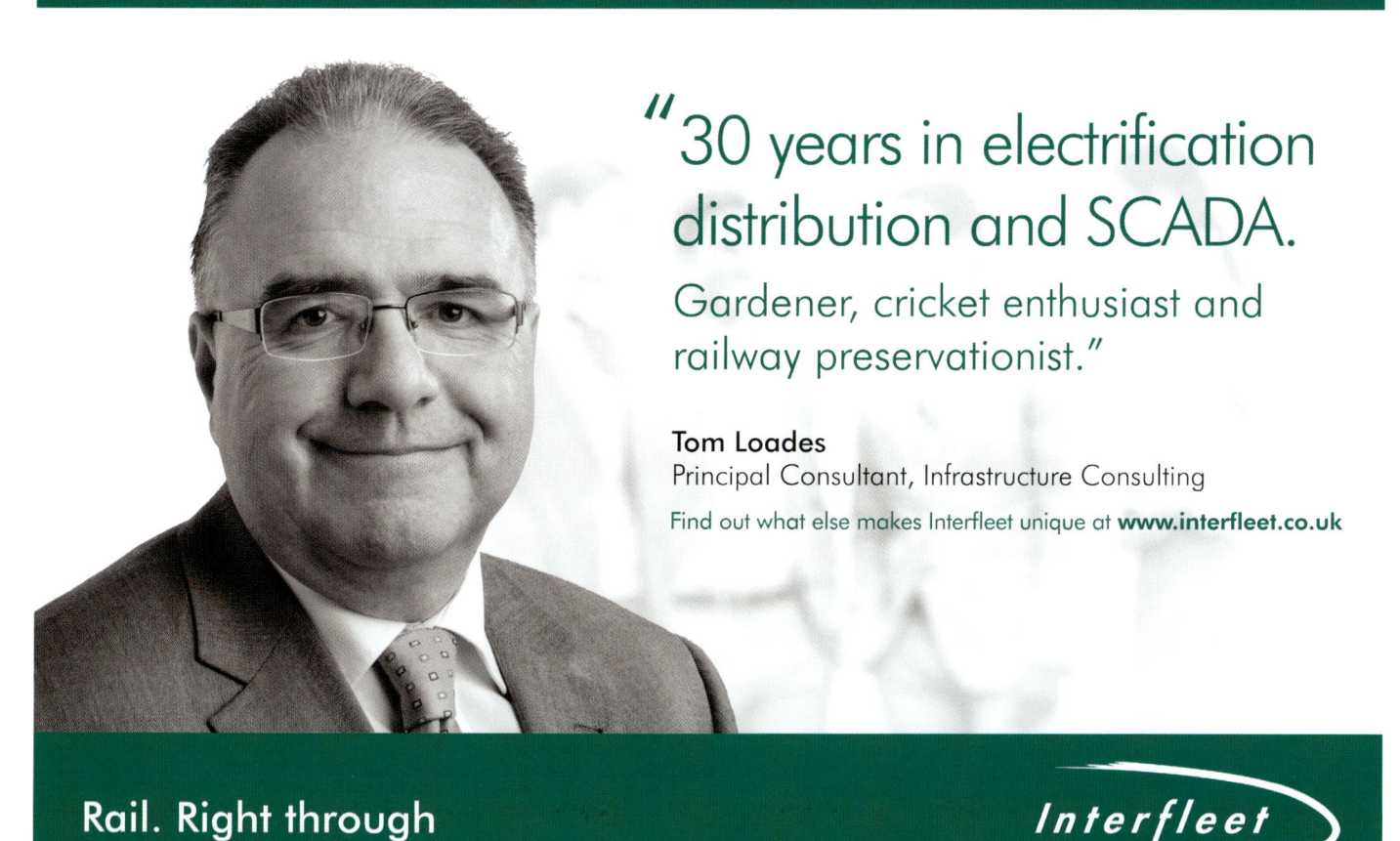

"30 years in electrification distribution and SCADA.

Gardener, cricket enthusiast and railway preservationist."

Tom Loades
Principal Consultant, Infrastructure Consulting

Find out what else makes Interfleet unique at **www.interfleet.co.uk**

Rail. Right through

Member of the SNC·LAVALIN Group

Interfleet Technology

HITACHI
Inspire the Next

127

Costain.
Solutions Provider for Rail.

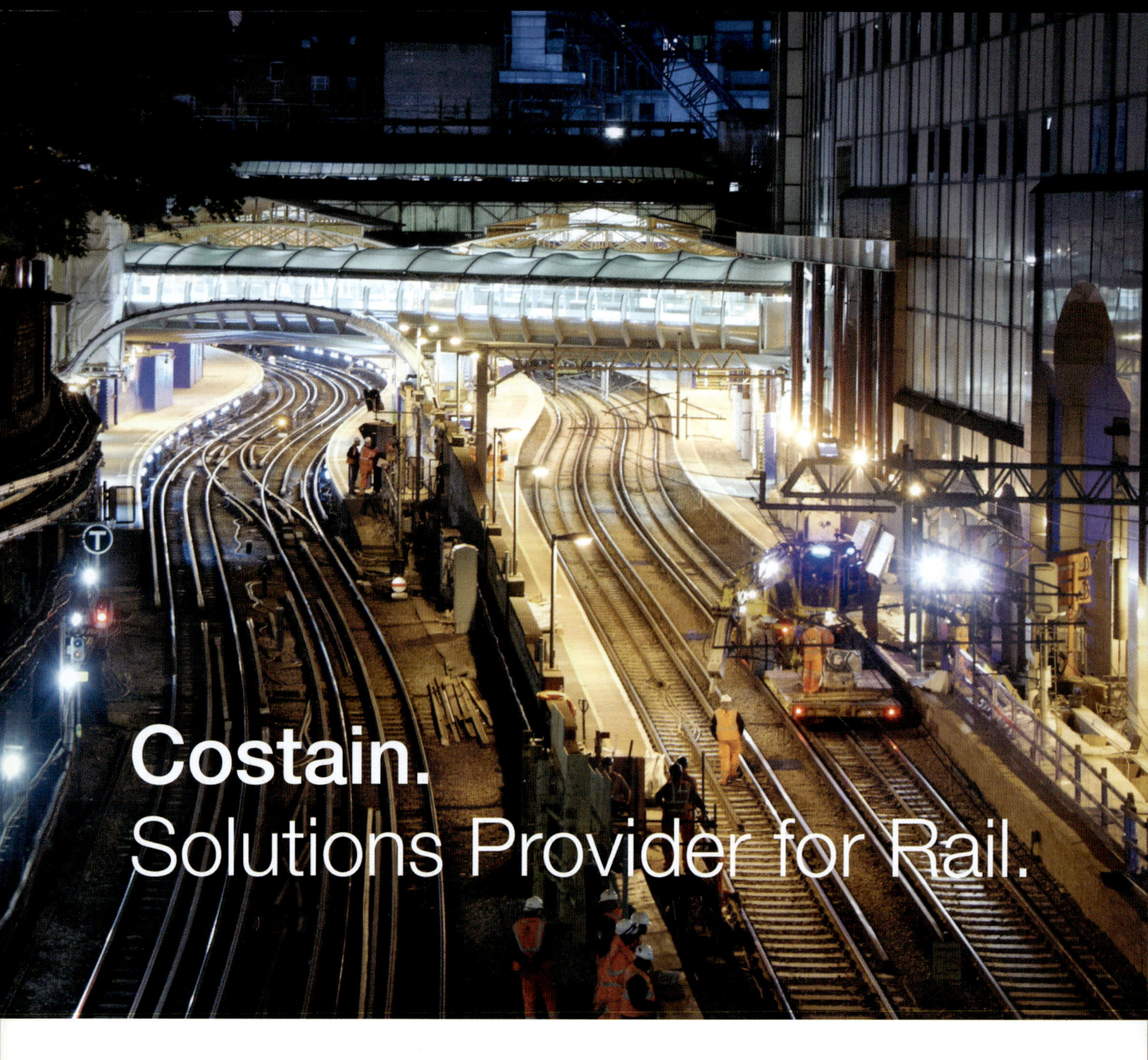

Contractors of the Year 2010 nce
Contractor of the Decade winner

Costain, one of the UK's leading engineering solutions providers, will deliver your major rail network needs:

- Expert programme management
- Front end engineering and design
- Rail Systems
- Construction
- Financial engineering
- Major multi disciplinary projects
- Lifecycle maintenance

COSTAIN

Contact: 01628 842444
www.costain.com

In association with COSTAIN

Phase 1 of the Thameslink Programme was completed in 2012, with the new Blackfriars station spanning the Thames with entrances both here on the north bank and also on the south. Attention now shifts to reconstruction at London Bridge. Network Rail

Key Projects

Western electrification, signalling, and Reading project

Major modernisation now under way on the Great Western main line includes the Reading, resignalling and electrification projects, plus the Intercity Express Programme and Crossrail.

Network Rail in conjunction with Reading Borough Council is enlarging and modernising Reading station, building two new entrances connected by a new footbridge. There will be new lifts and escalators and five extra platforms to enhance station capacity.

A grade-separated junction west of the station will enable freight flows (in particular) to and from Basingstoke to cross to the relief lines towards Didcot without obstructing the fast lines. The diesel unit depot has been relocated and the new signalling centre at Didcot was commissioned in 2011. The project is due for completion in 2015.

The first drive to install the European Rail Traffic Management System is due to take place on the Great Western main line starting in 2016 - overlaid on conventional resignalling planned for Didcot-Oxford/Swindon (2012); Swindon-Chippenham, Swindon-Gloucester, Swindon-Hullavington (2014); and Reading-Newbury, Oxford area, Hullavington-Bristol Parkway, Bath-Bristol Temple Meads-Parson Street (2015).

This work will centralise signalling control and is associated with the revision of track layouts for the forthcoming electrification, with structural work to provide overhead clearances. Filament signal heads will be replaced with LED heads.

Intercity Express Programme (IEP)

'The Intercity Express programme comprises the infrastructure, rolling stock and franchise changes needed to replace services operated by the ageing fleet of HST sets. The new trains will be faster, with higher capacity, more comfortable and more environmentally friendly services that will support growth on some of the busiest main line routes'. This is how the Department for Transport described in July 2012 its £4.5bn contract with Agility Trains (a consortium of Hitachi Rail (Europe) Ltd and John Laing plc) as part of the Intercity Express Programme.

The IEP fleet will include some all electric trains and some with a combination of electric and diesel power (bi-modes). One aim of the bi-mode approach is to preserve through services beyond the electrified network without operating diesel traction under the wires for appreciable distances.

Key Projects

Agility Trains will be responsible for construction of 92 complete trains (596 vehicles), with a significant proportion of the work at a new factory in Newton Aycliffe. 369 vehicles are for the Great Western, 227 vehicles for the East Coast, and there are further options for 270 vehicles. There will be maintenance depots in Bristol, Swansea, west London and Doncaster. Agility will also maintain the trains, with the train operating company responsible for operations and paying Agility Trains a set availability payment for trains in operation. The DfT is providing Agility with a usage guarantee.

The DfT said that the first phase could operate on London-Cardiff-Swansea; London-Oxford-Worcester-Hereford; London-Gloucester-Cheltenham Spa; and London-Bath-Bristol; then London-Leeds, and London-York-Newcastle-Edinburgh-Aberdeen/Inverness.

The Newton Aycliffe factory is expected to be fully operational by 2015, with the first IEP trains entering revenue earning service in 2017 on Great Western and 2018 on the East Coast. The fleet will be a mixture of 5-car sets (able to work in pairs) and 9-car sets.

There are also options for ordering further trains, which could operate on London-Exeter-Penzance; and as East Coast replacement of IC225 stock.

Thameslink

The Thameslink Programme is a £6bn project to deliver a high capacity, north-south spine railway through central London. With scheduled completion in 2018, Thameslink will provide greater capacity, higher frequencies, new services and improved access to central London from a range of destinations within London and across southeast England.

Major benefits include a capacity increase in the core section between Farringdon and Blackfriars to 24 trains per hour, mostly 12-cars. Large-scale works include the rebuilding of Blackfriars station, completed in 2012. This is the first station to span the Thames, providing direct passenger access to both north and south banks. Farringdon's rebuilding for Thameslink is also complete; in future it will become a major interchange with Crossrail as well

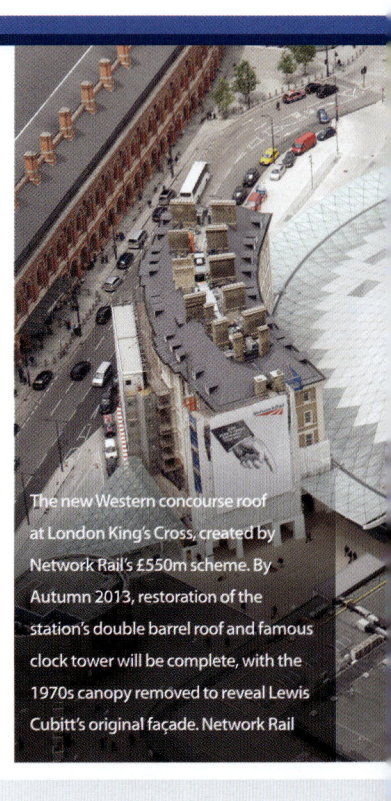

The new Western concourse roof at London King's Cross, created by Network Rail's £550m scheme. By Autumn 2013, restoration of the station's double barrel roof and famous clock tower will be complete, with the 1970s canopy removed to reveal Lewis Cubitt's original façade. Network Rail

Consultant files: Supporting rail developments

AECOM
AECOM is a global provider of professional technical and management support services, with international experience of a wide range of rail disciplines, such as network and systems enhancements, operations, infrastructure maintenance, rail engineering and policy and strategy. AECOM is a 40 per cent partner in the Transcend joint-venture team, providing strategic management services for the London Crossrail project.

Atkins
Atkins is the UK's largest engineering consultancy and the 13th largest international design firm. Atkins is a leader in rail engineering and systems design, providing expertise from experience and in-depth knowledge. From development and maintenance of existing systems to the implementation of new schemes, it helps clients through the entire project lifecycle to maximise value and outcomes.

Key rail projects include providing architectural and engineering design services on Crossrail, and civil and structural design services and environmental impact assessments for sections of HS2.

Arup
Arup is a global firm of designers, engineers, planners and business consultants which provides a full range of professional services to the rail industry. Arup's portfolio includes all modes of rail, ranging from high speed through to metros and urban transport systems. Services provided to the rail sector incorporate everything to ensure the successful planning, design and completion of economic, state of the art, sustainable rail systems.

HS2 Ltd appointed Arup, supported by Grimshaw and Costain, to produce preliminary designs for Euston station, and Arup is also carrying out civil and structural design and environmental work for HS2.

Bechtel
Founded in 1898, Bechtel is a major engineering, construction, and project management corporation, active around the world. Major UK projects in which Bechtel has been involved include the West Coast route modernisation, and the Jubilee Line Extension. It was part of the Rail Link Engineering consortium creating High Speed 1, part of the Tube Lines consortium modernising London Underground lines; and has been appointed as part of the Project Delivery Partner team for the central tunnel section of Crossrail, and as Network Rail's Delivery Partner for its Crossrail and Reading programmes.

Capita Symonds
Capita Symonds provides a multidisciplinary service for guided transport systems. With a core of experienced rail engineers it focuses on providing the specialist skills required by major railway clients. Design management expertise is supported by railway specific design skills in permanent way, railway bridges and structural engineering.

A Capita Symonds / Ineco joint venture has won a design contract for HS2 covering approximately 78km of route.

CH2M Hill and Halcrow
CH2M Hill, a global leader in infrastructure programme and project management, recently acquired Halcrow, one of the leading UK engineering and environmental consultants. CH2M Hill is HS2 Ltd's development partner for the current phase of engineering, design and environmental work.

As well as Halcrow's experience with HS1 and Crossrail, and the skills and expertise that CH2M Hill demonstrated they could bring to the project, CH2M Hill also successfully delivered the construction for the 2012 London Olympics as the Olympic Delivery Authority's delivery partner, and provides programme management services for Crossrail.

DeltaRail
DeltaRail is a software and technology company dedicated to the needs of the rail industry, with its principal activity in signalling control software. The company's strategy focusses on its three core areas of 'On Operations', 'On Track' and 'On Train'.

On Operations activity includes signalling, with the next generation signalling control system IECC Scalable, as well as operational planning software and management services.

On Track includes world class products such as TracklineTwo for track geometry measurement, with solution partners in Spain, the USA, India, China and Australia actively promoting these products.

On Train activity includes the train maintenance optimisation and structures consultancy, disciplines which align well with the VIEW and XVPlus products in the train maintenance market.

ESG
ESG is an international railway rolling stock engineering consultancy business of around

In association with COSTAIN

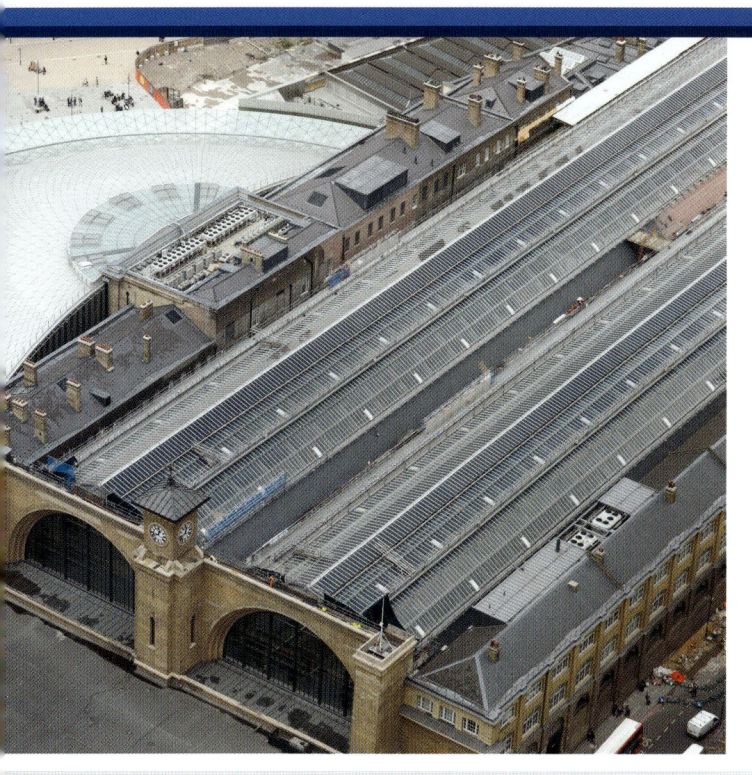

as London Underground. London Bridge is being rebuilt significantly.

The enhanced route will serve around a threefold increase in the number of stations and provide significant relief to existing systems, with capacity for future growth.

The Thameslink programme includes major infrastructure works to provide platforms to accommodate trains of 12-car 20 metre vehicles and the removal of key capacity bottlenecks; plus specification and procurement of new rolling stock; and changes to operating franchises to accommodate the new Thameslink services.

Following the permanent closure of the Farringdon-Moorgate section in 2009, AC electrification has been extended to City Thameslink. After 12-car platform lengthening, a 16 trains per hour service through central London at peak times is offered by First Capital Connect.

The aim of the major works at London Bridge is to remove bottlenecks, improve passenger facilities and significantly improve passenger capacity. Six high-level through platforms and nine low-level terminal platforms are to be converted to nine high-level through and six low-level terminal. A new approach viaduct and two-track bridge over Borough High Street will feed the new high-level station tracks. A new station concourse, 70m wide and 150m deep, will be built underneath the tracks at street level. Track layout and signalling renewals will allow metro-style operation,

---

50 permanent and associate engineers. Since an inter-group transfer in 2011 from previous parent DB Schenker, ESG and related company Railway Approvals Limited (RAL) are now subsidiaries of DB Systemtechnik (DBST) in Germany, with offices in the UK, France and Germany, but with capabilities and skills that extend cross-border throughout Europe and are increasingly recognised as applicable worldwide.

ESG has first-hand experience as a train operator, and a legacy of success born from its hands on, innovative approach. It has access to parent company technical expertise, facilities and products (650 engineers and 18 test laboratories across Germany), combining the responsiveness of a smaller business with large company leverage and international coverage. RAL offers new train homologation and the range of RISAB, NoBo, EOQA (heavy and light rail) and VAB certification services.

Interfleet Technology

A member of the SNC-Lavalin group of companies, Interfleet Technology is an international rail technology consultancy group. Founded in 1994, it delivers business benefits for our clients in the areas of rolling stock, railway systems and strategic railway management.

Interfleet's rolling-stock engineering expertise is established world-wide, with strength-in-depth across all areas from strategy to technical. It has significantly augmented its capabilities in rail infrastructure and train-control systems, to offer integrated cross-sector consultancy support. New capabilities in areas such as Track, Electrification & Power, the Built Environment and Signalling are being applied to several new projects, such as shaping the national delivery plan for ERTMS.

Jacobs Consultancy

Jacobs UK Ltd, a subsidiary of Jacobs Engineering Group Inc, is a leading international consultancy, providing railway privatisation and restructuring advice, business case development, funding advice, traffic forecasts, route selection studies, parliamentary procedures and public consultations. It also offers a full range of engineering services, including civil engineering design, signalling and electrification systems integration, contract documentation, project management and supervision of construction. Operational expertise includes train planning, timetable analysis and capacity studies.

Lloyd's Register

Lloyd's Register's transportation business covers a complete range of services to help manage the safety, functional and business performance of new and existing rail systems and projects. Its multifunctional specialist rail consultancy companies operate in Europe, Asia and Australia.

They specialise in rail systems integration and safety assurance founded on core rail skills in all of the key rail disciplines, including rolling stock, infrastructure and their interfaces, signalling, telecommunications, power systems and operations.

Mott MacDonald

In its global transport business Mott MacDonald has some 3,000 professional staff from a wide range of related disciplines. It provides rail engineering consultancy services through teams based in the UK and internationally. Its technical engineering disciplines cover all aspects of railway systems and infrastructure. It also specialises in applying advanced simulation techniques.

The project portfolio includes the Channel Tunnel, West Coast route modernisation, London Underground, high-speed rail including High Speed 1, and light rapid transit in cities such as London, Birmingham, and Manchester.

Network Rail Consulting

The new international rail consultancy business, Network Rail Consulting, has set out to harness the vast range of skills and experience available within Network Rail to demonstrate British expertise overseas, and to be an international ambassador for Britain's rail industry. It will also help channel innovation back into Network Rail's core business, helping deliver a better value railway for Britain.

It offers consultancy services across the full spectrum of Network Rail's expertise, including institutional and policy advice, strategic planning, asset management, operations and maintenance, and infrastructure projects.

Nichols Group

The Nichols Group is a UK consultancy specialising in areas including strategy, programme management and project management. Since its formation in 1975, Nichols has been involved in many transport schemes including the Docklands Light Railway, London Luton Airport and Jubilee Line Extension. The

Key Projects

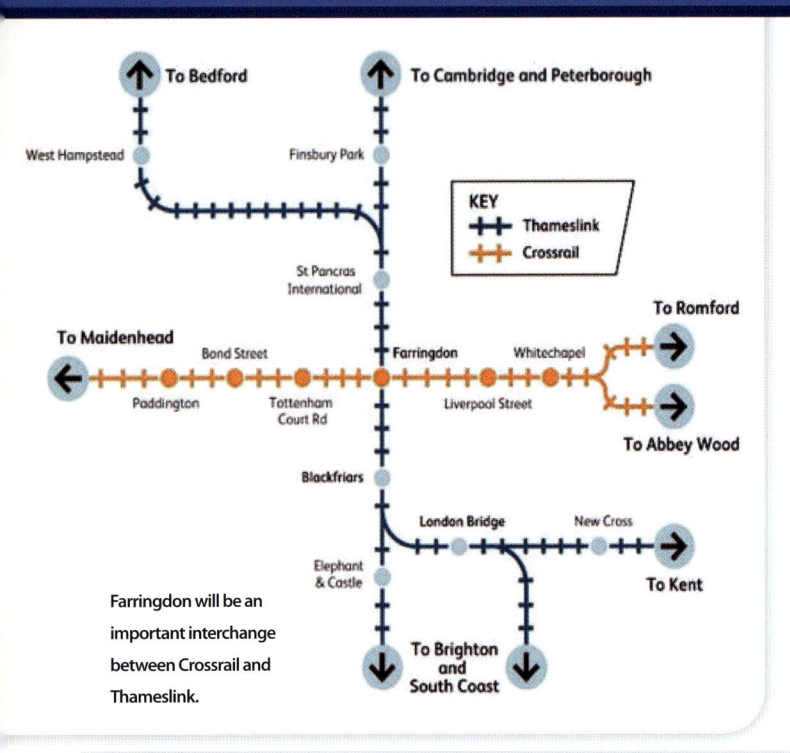

Farringdon will be an important interchange between Crossrail and Thameslink.

with telecoms and power supplies upgraded. AC overhead line equipment north of London is being reconfigured and power supply strengthened.

To allow trains to proceed at closer intervals, there is now bi-directional signalling throughout between Kentish Town and Blackfriars. The European Train Control System will be overlaid to provide automatic operation when infrastructure work in the London Bridge area is completed.

In 2011, Siemens was declared by the Department for Transport as the preferred bidder to build, own, finance and maintain approximately 100 new dual-voltage 12-car trains, with new depots to be constructed at Three Bridges and Hornsey.

Network Rail in the route strategy for London & South East in 2011 published an indicative Thameslink service pattern for 2018, with 14 of the 24 trains per hour originating on the Brighton lines, and 10 on the South Eastern. Similarly, 16 terminate on the Midland, and 8 on the Great Northern.

This omitted previously mooted destinations - north of Cambridge (due to power supply problems and short platforms), and also Dartford, Eastbourne, Guildford and Littlehampton. The Wimbledon/Sutton services at 4tph were shown as terminating in the bay platforms at Blackfriars.

The merging of train services to access the central area between St Pancras International and Blackfriars will take place at

Consultant files (continued)

group has advised and assisted in implementing programme management and in restructuring major capital rail investment programmes. Nichols is a partner in the Transcend team working in programme management for the London Crossrail project.

Onyxrail
Onyxrail Ltd is an independent turnkey enhancement and maintenance provider to the rail traction and rolling stock industry, providing high quality managed solutions at its own facilities or client depots, enabling a complete service at the line of route.

Project management and procurement teams, with technology partners, provide comprehensive projects delivered locally at the point of need. Onyxrail also assists higher technology OEMs with route to market services in the UK, and through its sister company provides a range of castings, forgings, fabrications and machined components.

Optimum
Optimum's track record has been developed over a continuous 15 year period of involvement in the rail sector. Optimum delivers independent construction and management consultancy support services to public and private clients and is fully familiar with the complex and challenging nature of the operational environment. Optimum has worked on some of the largest and most prestigious rail programmes and projects in recent years reporting to stakeholders at all levels. This has included commissions on high speed, classic, underground and light rail systems in stations, depots, signalling, electrification, telecommunications and permanent way.

Optimum is fully conversant with industry procedures including Network Rail's GRIP development process, and is capable of delivering a 'one stop shop' service on projects that includes full design services and IT project management.

Parsons Brinckerhoff
Parsons Brinckerhoff is a leader in developing and operating infrastructure around the world, offering skills and resources in strategic consulting, planning, engineering, program/construction management, and operations for all modes of infrastructure, including transportation, power, buildings and infrastructure, water and the environment. Parsons Brinckerhoff is part of Balfour Beatty plc, the international infrastructure group operating in professional services, construction services support services and infrastructure investments.

Steer Davies Gleave
Steer Davies Gleave is a leading independent transport consultancy providing services to government, operators, regulators, promoters, financiers and other interest groups.

Expertise includes rail demand and revenue forecasting, financial modelling, rail operations & costing, rail strategy development & implementation, business case preparation, public consultation, outreach & stakeholder engagement, rail project delivery & appraisal, procurement, rail franchise bidding, specification & evaluation, performance regime design, rail pricing & fares.

Steer Davies Gleave supported the DfT from the outset of the Intercity Express Programme as economic advisors.

Vossloh Kiepe UK
Transys Projects has changed its name to Vossloh Kiepe UK, further strengthening the brand's position in the UK rail market after being acquired by Vossloh Kiepe GmbH.

Vossloh Kiepe UK offers a broad range of engineering expertise, encompassing its existing UK services as well as new capabilities brought in from the Vossloh Kiepe Group. These include engineering, consultancy and design packages, turnkey solutions, technology enhancements, product support, refurbishment of rail vehicles, and traincare.

URS/Scott Wilson
Scott Wilson is now part of URS Corporation. With its headquarters in San Francisco, URS is a leading provider of engineering, construction and technical services.

Scott Wilson offers consultancy services that cover all aspects of rail infrastructure planning, design, project management, construction supervision and asset maintenance. Specialist multi-disciplinary railway engineering skills are combined with extensive planning, environment and management expertise.

York EMC Services
York EMC Services Ltd is the well established market leader for the provision of EMC services to the railway industry.

York EMC Services offers a range of consultancy, testing and training services, specifically designed for the railway industry. The company has a solid track record of solving EMC problems and demonstrating EMC for major railway projects around the world.

Midland Road Junction (between the Midland and Great Northern lines north of St Pancras, and built during construction of High Speed 1). A new grade-separated junction at Bermondsey will facilitate separation of Brighton and South Eastern services. Trains will generally be of up to 12 cars, but 8 cars will be the maximum for trains calling at Hendon, Cricklewood and Kentish Town.

A new Thameslink franchise is planned, absorbing Southern services and some Southeastern services.

Crossrail

The Crossrail bill became law on 22 July 2008. Following the then Prime Minister Gordon Brown's announcement in October 2007 that the £15.9bn funding package had been secured, the project was expected to become operational in 2017. The Act granted all the necessary powers.

Crossrail will run from Maidenhead and Heathrow in the west, through tunnels under central London, with stations at Paddington, Bond Street, Tottenham Court Road, Farringdon, Liverpool Street and Whitechapel, then to Stratford and on out to Shenfield north of the Thames, and to Canary Wharf, Custom House, Woolwich and Abbey Wood to the south. With 24 trains an hour during peak times throughout the central section, and 12 an hour off-peak, an estimated 160,000 passengers will be carried in the morning rush hour. The total length of the Crossrail system is 118.5km, including 31.5km in tunnels. 38 stations will be served directly.

Crossrail is justified as underpinning the most rapid economic growth areas of London and will be a very significant capacity addition to the transport network. It will also offer significant crowding relief on the Underground generally, and the Docklands Light Railway. Overall, the benefits of Crossrail are now estimated to be worth at least £42bn in current prices to the national GDP over the next 60 years.

Crossrail will use a 21km tunnel under the centre of London, and construction started on 15 May 2009 with the Canary Wharf station site. The station is built below the water of North Dock and will have pedestrian links to Poplar and Canary Wharf DLR stations, and the Jubilee Line station.

The five pairs of tunnels to be constructed are Royal Oak to Farringdon west (6.1km); Limmo Peninsula (Royal Docks) to Farringdon east (8.3km); Stepney Green to Pudding Mill Lane (2.7km); Limmo Peninsula to Victoria Dock Portal (0.9km); Plumstead to North Woolwich (2.6km). This amounts to about 21km of twin bore tunnel drives.

Of the eight Tunnel Boring Machines (TBMs), six are of the earth pressure balance type for use in clay, the other two of the slurry type for boring through the chalk of the 2.6km tunnel under the Thames.

The main civil engineering construction works are now planned for completion in 2017. All tunnel drives are expected to be complete by the end of 2014, tunnel portals and shafts in 2016, with stations at various times up to 2018.

The station works are co-ordinated with works needed at existing stations where there are interchanges.

Network Rail is responsible for the design, development and delivery of those parts of Crossrail on the existing network. This includes upgrading 70km of track, redeveloping 28 stations and renewing 15 bridges. One scheme of particular note is the complete reconstruction of the Airport Junction flyovers, where services to Heathrow diverge.

Crossrail will employ up to 14,000 people at the peak of construction during 2013-2015 and provide an estimated 1,000 jobs directly when fully operational. The company's skills strategy supports the use of local labour and a tunnelling academy.

Crossrail Ltd is a wholly-owned TfL subsidiary. The company manages the programme for project sponsors, the Department for Transport and Transport for London.

Over 60pc of Crossrail funding comes from Londoners and London-based business through direct contributions from the City of London, Heathrow airport, Canary Wharf Group and a London Business Rates Supplement and planning development levy. The government is providing about £5bn by means of a grant from the Department for Transport. The funding package is designed to strike a fair balance between businesses, passengers and taxpayers.

To ensure value for money, says Crossrail, its intention is that the new trains are based upon technology already developed by the worldwide rolling stock market for deployment on other railways. In the running are Bombardier, CAF, Hitachi and Siemens. It is anticipated that the £1bn contract for the 57 trains and the Old Oak Common depot will be let in 2014.

Each train will be a maximum length of 205m. With ten 20m vehicles, the requirement for around 450 seats is a modest 45 per car, but overall capacity including standing will be 1,500. Acceleration will be up to 1 metre/sec, comparable with metro standards. Trains will be air-conditioned. They will be powered at 25kV AC, but with potential for fitment with third-rail pick up.

Crossrail's trains will operate in Automatic Train Operation mode with Automatic Train Protection in the central section, but will need to feature existing train protection systems until the European Train Control System (ETCS) is installed at either end on Network Rail.

Crossrail route control will be based at Liverpool Street in the first instance, and later at a new centre at Romford.

The Prime Minister, David Cameron and Spanish Prime Minister, Mariano Rajoy, visited Crossrail's Westbourne Park site in west London to view the tunnel boring machines (TBMs) in February 2012, just before tunnelling commenced. Construction of tunnels between Royal Oak and Farringdon is being undertaken by a joint venture of BAM Nuttal, Kier Construction and Ferrovial Agroman - the UK subsidiary of Spanish multinational Ferrovial. Crossrail

Table 1: Comparative journey times

Journey	Crossrail	London Underground
Heathrow-Canary Wharf	43min	70min
Heathrow-Tottenham Court Road	31min	52min
Ealing Broadway-Liverpool Street	20min	37min
Abbey Wood-Tottenham Court Road	22mn	45min*

*also using Southeastern trains

Key Projects

The first half of the new concourse at Birmingham New Street is to open to passengers in April 2013 - marking the half way point in the Birmingham Gateway redevelopment. Network Rail

Operation of Crossrail services will be let as a concession similar to London Overground

Some projected comparative journey times are shown in Table 1.

Crossrail signalling and control systems will enable a 24tph service to be operated during the peak between Paddington and Whitechapel, but they must be designed to support enhancement to 30tph through this section at a later date.

Full Crossrail operation is expected to start in December 2019.

High Speed 2

The previous, Labour government set up HS2 Ltd, with a remit to examine the detailed case for a High Speed line from London to the West Midlands, and the broad case for extensions further north on each side of the Pennines.

The outcome in 2010 favoured a line from London Euston to Birmingham Curzon Street with intermediate stations at Old Oak Common (interchange to Crossrail and the various terminals at Heathrow Airport) and Birmingham NEC.

HS2 Ltd also proposed that the initial core network should proceed further north, to Manchester and, separately, to an East Midlands station, South Yorkshire and Leeds. There would be connections for onward travel to both the West and East Coast Main Lines. The coalition government broadly endorsed this approach, a so-called 'Y' network. The Secretary of State set out the government's final preferred route for consultation in 2010, to be followed later by the line of route to Leeds and Manchester.

A complex matter which was not fully resolved was a link between HS2 and HS1.

The use of a single hybrid bill to allow construction of HS2 all the way from London to Manchester and to Leeds was ruled out by the government as it could add three years to the time needed to prepare the Bill. In late 2012, the current intention is to put a hybrid bill for the London-West Midlands phase before parliament in 2013.

Edinburgh-Glasgow Improvements Programme (EGIP)

In 2012 the Scottish Government announced an updated version of EGIP, providing 'almost all of the benefits' of the original plan for 65% of the originally estimated cost. The Edinburgh-Glasgow line via Falkirk High will be electrified, plus the line to Cumbernauld in time for the Glasgow Commonwealth Games in 2014.

Glasgow-Edinburgh expresses are to remain at four trains per hour (rather than increasing to six as in the original plan), but with longer, 8-car trains, enabled by longer platforms at Glasgow Queen Street, and a journey time of around 42min. Electrification to Stirling and Alloa/Dunblane, and via Falkirk Grahamston, has been deferred - along with junction improvements, and the Dalmeny chord, intended to provide an extra link between Glasgow and Edinburgh via the Edinburgh Gateway tram interchange for the airport.

A commitment to a further 100km of electrification every year for five years has been repeated. The electrification of the Paisley Canal line is being completed in December 2012.

Northern Hub

The Northern Hub is intended to stimulate economic growth by upgrading the rail network. After proposals were launched by Network Rail in 2010, piecemeal authorisation took place, with the scheme fully funded by July 2012.

Main improvements include two additional through platforms on the Oxford Road lines at Manchester Piccadilly, construction of the Ordsall Curve to provide a direct route between Manchester Piccadilly and Manchester Victoria, selective track doubling to increase capacity between Leeds and Liverpool and between Sheffield and Manchester, and rebuilding Manchester Victoria as a single transport interchange.

The result will be an ability to run more and faster trains on key routes, thus also reducing journey times, plus scope for more direct rail services to Manchester Airport.

The plan is linked with electrification of several routes, as reported in the introductory article in this section.

Borders Railway

This project is to reinstate a 35 mile rail link from Edinburgh through Midlothian to Tweedbank in the Scottish Borders, the northern part of the Waverley route which was closed completely in January 1969. The line is to rejoin the existing network at Newcraighall, and seven new stations are being built. This is to be a mainly single track railway, with dynamic passing loops.

In September 2011, Network Rail agreed to take on the Borders Railway project, the previous bidders having withdrawn, with a contract announced in November 2012. The target date for opening is now 2015.

The throughout journey time between Edinburgh Waverley and Tweedbank is estimated at 55min.

Birmingham New Street

Birmingham New Street is used by 140,000 passengers a day, more than twice the number for which it was designed.

The station buildings are being completely renewed. The £600m project doubles passenger capacity and delivers a hugely larger concourse, with platforms made accessible by over 30 escalators and 15 lifts. There will be a new station façade, with eight new entrances.

The New Street Gateway project is funded by Network Rail, Birmingham City Council, Advantage West Midlands, Centro and the Department for Transport. The scheme is being delivered by Network Rail in partnership with Mace.

The first half of the new concourse is expected to open in April 2013, with the project due to be completed in 2015.

Stratford station, next to the Olympic Park, was transformed for the London 2012 Games. Network Rail

After the Olympics - a summer like no other

The arrangements for the London 2012 Olympic and Paralympic Games were a success for the transport industry in general - and rail in particular. Over the same 101 day period, the Notting Hill Carnival and The Queen's Diamond Jubilee celebrations took place. What lessons can be learned from these events, according to London Underground?

This was to be perhaps the largest ever peacetime exercise, with nine million spectators for London 2012 and two and a half million for the Paralympics.

Regular meetings took place at senior level between all bodies involved, ensuring that the challenges of the Games were addressed. There was prior engagement with spectators, London businesses and the general public.

Stratford station, next to the Olympic Park, was transformed. It now has 19 platforms, additional entrances and exits, and train services at peak total 192 per hour.

Planning

Venues were scattered widely, which meant that access was a network and not a point specific issue. Detailed day-by-day planning took place on the level of service and staffing requirements. Every 15 minute period was modelled and location specific impacts identified.

The mantra that 'events run late' was true for both the openings and the first closing ceremony, but the closing ceremony for the Paralympics finished 10 minutes early! Generally, the Underground ran one hour later than normal at night.

The main travel modes between central London and the Olympic Park were the Jubilee Line, Central Line, or Olympic Javelin from Stratford International to St Pancras via High Speed 1. This amounted to some overprovision, but calculations showed that if only two out of the three were working, it might just about have been enough.

The use of magenta signage to help spectators find their way worked well. Over 40 stations were equipped with more than 35,000 signs: 'the bigger and bolder the better'.

Encouraging people to use West Ham station as an alternative access, by a walk along The Greenway, worked well, and about 25pc of spectators did so.

Collaboration with the British Transport Police saw the Underground's Emergency Response Unit vehicles given police vehicle status with police officer drivers. This cut the times needed to reach sites by 50pc for both parties, who on arrival were able to hit the ground running.

Operations

Over 50 tried and tested timetables were used at various times on the network, 14 of which were for the Jubilee Line alone. There was a third peak period in the late evenings, to get spectators away as events finished. As many as 28pc of normal users changed their journey patterns in one way or another.

Reducing night time

135

Key Projects

Spectators leave the Olympic Park and head for Stratford station after a morning of Paralympic games on 4 September 2012. John Glover

maintenance wherever possible had the benefit of reducing risk to delays with service provision the next morning. Additional technical support which could be called upon when things did go wrong was also valuable.

The provision of a Games Travelcard with the venue tickets did encourage people to come by public transport. At the same time, it avoided huge queues at ticket offices, particularly at interchanges.

There was however a large failure rate of the tickets' magnetic strips, which open the Underground ticket gates.

The previous maximum passenger total in one day on the Underground was 4.22 million. This record was well and truly broken with a staggering 4.57 million being recorded on Tuesday 7 August. Overall, 11pc more train service km were run over a longer operating day, and crowding was not excessive. Stratford saw 250,000 passengers a day, plus the shoppers, which was termed 'quite scary'!

Staff
There was large scale employee engagement, through a series of meetings well before the event, creating a certain buzz around the Olympics. After all, the reputation of London was at stake and maybe that of the country as well.

Flexibility in staff duty lengths, times of breaks and deployment to other sites all helped, with attendance rates reaching 98/99pc. This had to be paid for, but the staff performed brilliantly. Senior staff were out on the front line too, and seen to be there.

The use of office staff in support worked well. The job of the Underground is to get people from A to B, with consistent and reliable travel information being given out at all times. There have been few occasions with such a high proportion of visitors to the capital.

Overall customer satisfaction for Games transport arrangements was 87% for attendees and 85% for other users.

The London Legacy Development Corporation is to reopens progressively what will become the Queen Elizabeth Olympic Park. It is expected to be a top tourist attraction, with more than nine million visitors a year. With its sporting venues, together with 8,000 new homes and commercial developments, Stratford station will see huge and permanent increases in passenger usage.

The Javelin shuttle was a key part of the Olympic transport plan. Here a Class 395 is seen at Stratford International on 18 March 2010. Paul Bigland

Infrastructure Maintenance and Renewal

Infrastructure Maintenance and Renewal

The major role of minor works

You may be surprised to learn that the UK's largest engineering design consultancy delivers minor works, but for the past 12 months Atkins has been doing just that. Using an experienced team who have a proven record in delivering major projects, Atkins can now provide 'a one stop shop' for a wide portfolio of minor works projects.

As the name suggests, minor works are smaller tasks that need to be completed as part of larger projects such as platform extensions, level crossing safety enhancements and minor signalling SWTH (Signalling Works Testing Handbook) schemes. Minor works also cover small renewal projects which are critical to ensuring the network remains reliable and efficient.

No job too big or too small!

Atkins turned its attention to minor works a year ago after the business reviewed the work it was doing. It found that by offering minor works as a capability it could supplement the National Signalling Framework schemes it was undertaking and at the same time provide its engineers with the opportunity to do something different, learning new skills and increasing their competency in a variety of projects to enhance their technical skills.

So far the response to this new initiative has been very positive especially because of the wide-ranging services Atkins provides including project management, signalling, telecom, electrification & plant design, installation and test. To date Atkins has supported Multi Asset Framework Agreement (MAFA) contractors and Network Rail in a range of schemes by delivering everything from million pound projects to simply providing a testing team to supplement the client's teams. The success of Atkins' minor works offering is evident through the praise it has received from its clients.

Andy Little, Programme Manager of the Infrastructure Minor Works team said: 'We pride ourselves on providing our clients with high quality, professional support so it's great to see the likes of Network Rail and the MAFA contractors benefiting from this service. Our strength lies in the fact that we have very experienced engineers in a number of rail disciplines, not to mention specialist support from the wider Atkins Group. When it comes to minor works no job is too small, we've picked up projects from both ends of the price scale and our expertise and flexibility means that we can deliver a wide range of different services across the UK.'

Looking to the future, Atkins is striving to diversify the work it undertakes whether it be developing new engineering solutions or taking a more innovative approach to delivering important rail infrastructure projects. From the encouraging feedback Atkins has received from its clients there appears to be a great opportunity for major players to undertake minor works projects by adding value and efficiency to the rail industry in the delivery of smaller schemes.

For further information contact Andy Little (andy.little@atkinsglobal.com) or visit www.atkinsglobal.com ■

Atkins can now provide 'a one stop shop' for a wide portfolio of minor works projects.

Network Rail enters second decade

In 2012, Network Rail entered its second decade. Ten years earlier, following Hatfield and other fatal accidents, the railway was facing a crisis of confidence, said Chief Executive, David Higgins: but now 'the challenge is different – dealing with success'.

'Public confidence in and demand for the railway has meant that, on many of our key corridors, there are simply too many trains trying to use too little track', he continued. 'There are now over 1.3 billion journeys a year – the busiest the network has been since World War Two. This "capacity crunch" is the defining challenge of Network Rail's second decade, alongside the quite legitimate demand that, as an industry, we need to become more efficient.'

Multiple changes had taken place at Network Rail, but 'as we change, we must also maintain a level of excellence in what we do – and particularly as regards safety,' said Sir David.

The devolution of power to all Network Rail's ten routes – completed in November 2011 – was a watershed, continued Sir David. 'This means decisions can be made more quickly, closer to the customer, resulting in benefits to passengers and cost savings. Let me be clear, this is about quicker decision making and cutting costs, not cutting corners.'

In a further initiative, at the beginning of 2012 Network Rail announced discussions with several train operating companies about new ways of working ever closer - 'alliances', which Network Rail hopes to develop with every willing train operator, but taking different forms depending on the kind of railway in each area and the views of the operator.

An early example is a deep alliance with South West Trains (SWT) - going further than any other arrangements envisaged so far, and enabled by a strong geographic overlap between the Network Rail management unit and the train operator. An alliance governance board was set up with representatives from both SWT and Network Rail, and SWT's Tim Shoveller as Managing Director of the alliance team. Train and infrastructure operations answer to one boss.

Key accountabilities for infrastructure operator and train operator will not change, Sir David Higgins stressed: Network Rail and the train operator will remain separate entities, employees will continue to have their current employer, and the interests of other passenger rail companies and freight operators are protected.

Network Rail has also moved to a new, commercially focused, regionally based projects delivery business – Network Rail Infrastructure Projects – with four regional Directors and three programme Directors responsible for delivery of major renewal and enhancement work in their area.

139

Infrastructure Maintenance and Renewal

They will manage their own profit and loss and will be charged with winning work under a proposed new competitive structure.

There is also a focus on developing the client capability within Network Rail to clearly define project outputs and work with delivery organisations much earlier in the project lifecycle. These changes should enable improved specification of output requirements, better integration of these into route plans, and greater discipline in the interface with the delivery team. This in turn should help to facilitate greater innovation, including through earlier engagement with the supply chain and through improved project-based partnerships with customers.

Where appropriate, says Network Rail, it will invite other organisations to tender for work in competition with Infrastructure Projects, enabling benchmarking of capital project delivery.

Network Rail Infrastructure Projects will become a separate legal entity in 2013. Network Rail Consulting was established in 2012, bringing further skills into the company, with further opportunities to benchmark against market competitors.

Network Rail has become the first company in the rail industry – and only the 13th nationwide – to achieve the award of BS11000, the new British Standard for collaborative working, which Sir David Higgins sees as 'a concrete demonstration of the cultural change we are making in this part of our business'.

Route organisation

Network Rail's operation of the railway is organised by ten geographic zones or 'Routes' under an organisation structure first implemented in May 2004. The tenth route, covering Wales, was announced in March 2011.

Each route managing director in effect runs their own infrastructure railway business with significant annual turnover and resources, with a supporting centre to help make the most of economies of scale. 'The railway still needs to be planned and operated as a network which operates seamlessly. And we must maintain the company's focus on efficient and effective management of long-life railway assets,' said Chief Executive, Sir David Higgins.

The route managing directors have responsibility for issues including safety; all customer service matters; asset management outputs and spend; operations; planning and delivering maintenance; and delivery of some renewals and enhancements.

A new National Centre in Milton Keynes unites many of Network Rail's national teams and functions under one roof to support the new, more powerful business units.

Network Rail is installing more access humps at stations on the Cumbria coast line - this is a low-cost solution to the problem of low platforms, raising a small section of the platform to correspond with the disabled access doors on the trains. Network Rail

Asset management savings

Network Rail plans a series of changes in asset policies to improve the value for money of the railway in Control Period 5 (CP5 - April 2014 until March 2019):

- Track - less complete renewal, more refurbishment, more preventative maintenance and more track treated for an overall reduction in whole life cost and spend in CP5.
- Signalling - targeted approach to renewal rather than full resignalling; integration of the renewal work bank with operating strategy and the European Rail Traffic Management System.
- Telecoms - more effective obsolescence management and technology change; greater use of partial renewal intervention where appropriate.
- Electrical Power & Fixed Plant - prioritised based on condition and criticality in terms of impact on service outputs.
- Drainage - improved drainage asset condition on high criticality routes, maintained condition elsewhere and contribution to improved track quality with consequent reduction in delay minutes; improvements in overall track quality by reduced track maintenance interventions and savings in abortive renewal costs; reduced flooding leading to improved safety and reduced delay minutes.
- Buildings - the ability to target the required CP5 performance outcomes - less spend on major station train sheds, buildings and platforms and more spend on canopies; key assets are managed in a sustainable manner, maintaining long term condition and thereby securing the long term functionality of the asset.
- Structures - improved consistency in managing bridge strength & critical condition risks; increased emphasis on maintenance and minor works.

Project partnerships

Network Rail has developed a new approach to small and medium-sized projects, aiming to deliver them more quickly, with suppliers 'on standby' rather than having to enter another bid process.

The time it takes to deliver 'multi asset framework agreement' (MAFA) projects – which combine signalling, track and civils – is cut significantly.

Six suppliers were selected. They are:
- Balfour Beatty Rail (Scotland),
- Buckingham (London North Western),
- Carillion (London North Eastern),
- Colas/Morgan Sindall (West),
- C Spencer (South East - shared portfolio),

Over £6 million has been invested to improve Leicester station, funded jointly by Network Rail, the Department for Transport's National Stations Improvement Programme, and East Midlands Trains. An improved station entrance, retail area, and ticket office; a refurbished concourse and overbridge, and improved station access are included in the revamp. Network Rail

We deliver
modern solutions for the modern railways

Find out how we can help you deliver, visit
www.invensysrail.com or call **+44 (0) 1249 441441**

invensys
Rail

Infrastructure Maintenance and Renewal

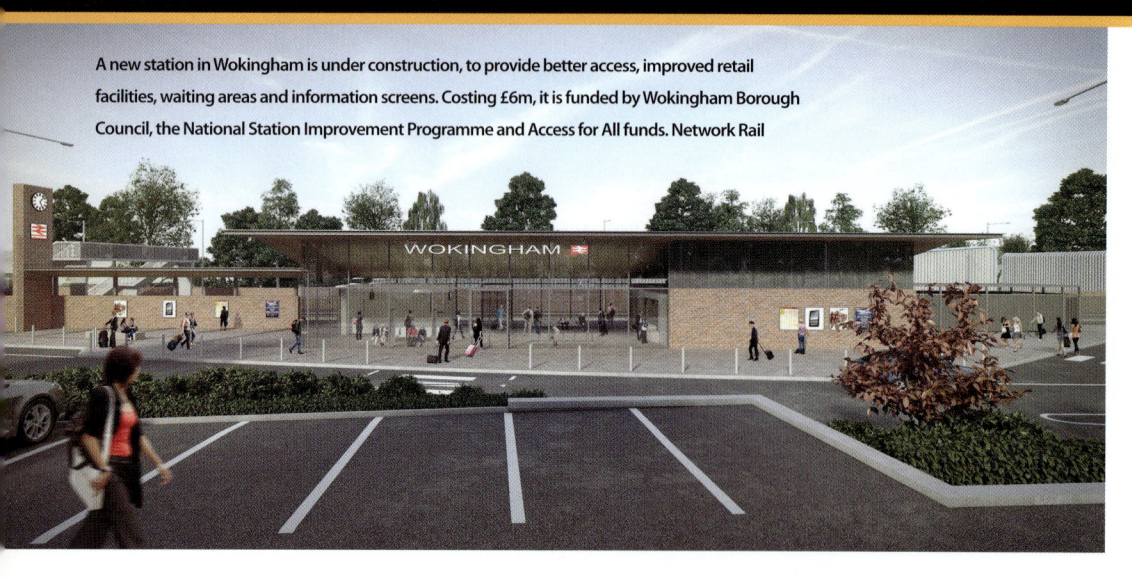

A new station in Wokingham is under construction, to provide better access, improved retail facilities, waiting areas and information screens. Costing £6m, it is funded by Wokingham Borough Council, the National Station Improvement Programme and Access for All funds. Network Rail

- Volker Fitzpatrick (South East - shared portfolio).

Track enhancement contractors

NR's track enhancement contractors were selected in January 2009, including all three current track renewals contractors (Amey Colas, Balfour Beatty, Babcock Rail) who were awarded contract extensions in April 2010 (a fourth, Jarvis, ceased to trade in early 2010). The other three track enhancement contractors are Carillion, VolkerRail and Trackwork.

Amey Colas was awarded the contract to operate and maintain NR's fleet of high-tech, high-output track renewal systems for four years from 2010.

Infrastructure contractors

While Network Rail carries out maintenance work in-house, it relies on contractors for track renewals and infrastructure projects work, and work on stations and structures, and is now reinvigorating relationships with suppliers, with out-sourcing of maintenance work under consideration. Some of the main contractors are featured below.

Amey

Amey's rail sector services include design, advisory and inspection services in signalling, electrification and power, track and civil engineering structures, as well as installation, renewals and enhancements services. Amey is part of Grupo Ferrovial, the major European services and construction group.

In 2012 Amey won a £700m contract for electrification of the Great Western main line. The contract covers Maidenhead to Bristol and Cardiff, Newbury and Oxford.

Working with partner Colas, Amey brings together planning, design and operations skills for track renewals and in 2009 won Network Rail's five-year High Output Track Renewals contract.

Amey was awarded responsibility for Network Rail's Civil Examination Framework Agreement throughout the network, worth about £250m over five years from 2009. This made it the largest provider of consultancy services to Network Rail. Amey also has specialist skills in customer information, telecoms and security.

In 2010 Amey and Bechtel sold their interests in Underground infrastructure company Tube Lines to Transport for London. Amey will continue to manage around £300m of maintenance services for Tube Lines per year for 7.5 years.

Babcock Rail

Babcock Rail - formerly First Engineering - is a leading player in the UK rail infrastructure market and the largest conventional track renewals company in the UK.

It carries out a wide of range of rail infrastructure work, including track renewal, power and signalling contracts throughout Great Britain.

Babcock reached an agreement with Network Rail in 2010 to deliver Plain Line and Switch & Crossing (S&C) track renewals in London North Eastern and Midland, extending its track renewals coverage down the east coast of England into London. This was a significant addition to Babcock Rail's workload, and doubled its track renewals activity.

The company will deliver track renewals in Scotland, the North West and LNE until 2014.

Babcock collected two major industry awards at the Network Rail Partnership Awards 2012, winning the highly prestigious Supplier of the Year Award, and the Best Medium Project award for the Boston to Skegness track renewals campaign, achieving record breaking output.

Babcock also supported the successful first deployment of Network Rail's Modular S&C Tilting Delivery wagons, working with Babcock's Kirow 250 cranes, and has been involved in further successful installations.

A joint venture of Babcock, Costain and Alstom was formed in 2011 to bid for major contracts associated with upcoming electrification projects.

Balfour Beatty

Balfour Beatty Rail plans, integrates and delivers multi-disciplinary design and construction projects, and works with specialist partners where necessary to complements its own expert services in five capabilities: multi-disciplinary solutions; power and electrification; track; signalling; and asset management

Network Rail awarded Balfour Beatty the £50m North West Electrification Phase 2 Contract in October 2012. The project will be led by Balfour Beatty Rail in joint venture with Balfour Beatty Engineering Services who will be undertaking the power and distribution works. Balfour Beatty Rail was awarded Phase 1 of the North West Electrification project in November 2011.

This includes deploying innovative high output train based solutions such as the high output concrete train which was developed for Phase 1.

Balfour Beatty was also awarded the Electrical Distribution works of Phase 3a of the West Coast Power Supply Upgrade project.

Balfour Beatty's track renewal framework contract - to deliver plain line rail and switches and crossings at junctions - extends to 2014. Worth approximately £56 million in the first year of the contract, a further £115 million is to be awarded should agreed targets be met.

In Scotland, Balfour Beatty won the contract to construct a new third line and associated overhead electrification additions as part of the Paisley corridor improvement project in Glasgow. This contract, worth £27 million, was completed in 2012.

Balfour Beatty has an approximate 30pc share of the joint venture awarded the £235m Whitechapel and Liverpool Street Station tunnels contract as part of the Crossrail project. The joint venture partners comprise Balfour Beatty, Alpine BeMo Tunnelling, Morgan Sindall and Vinci Construction.

Group company Birse Metro was awarded a £75m contract by Transport for London in 2011 to build the final part of the London Overground rail network, from Surrey Quays to Clapham Junction. London Underground has awarded a £220m, five-year contract to carry out track renewal work to Balfour Beatty.

Balfour Beatty Rail will deliver the track remodelling for the redevelopment of the London Bridge area as part of

In association with **HGI GENERATORS**

Major fuel saving for Class 66

A Department for Transport report on Rail Powertrain Efficiency Improvements, published in March 2012, highlights the results of research work carried out by Ricardo and TRL on how improvements in fuel efficiency could be realised within the UK rail network.

The Class 66 was selected as the focus of the research for freight locomotives as this forms the backbone of the country's rail freight network, representing 48% of the freight locomotive fleet, and 87% of overall freight distance travelled.

Although the report evaluates many options for potential improvements, only one is recommended as appropriate to retrofit to the existing fleet.

This includes the addition of a new stop/start lead-acid battery system; gas exchange system upgrade; and a new 30kW lightweight diesel genset, for uses such as cabin air conditioning. Potential fuel economy benefit over baseline is 30% on the freight duty cycle.

Overall, this technology package is the most attractive retrofitting solution for improving the efficiency of the GB rail fleet if applied to all 450 Class-66 freight locomotives. The payback period is less than one year, it could save 89 million litres of diesel per year, and save the operator millions of pounds in fuel costs.

HGI (Harrington) Generators is the ideal supply partner for such a product - with unparalleled expertise and experience in the design, manufacture and supply of rail-vehicle generators, HGI have become the No 1 supplier in the UK for vehicle-mounted power generation.

Powering over 97% of the Network Rail NDS infrastructure maintenance and monitoring fleet, HGI have amassed a wealth of understanding and capability which is second to none in the industry. Familiar, rugged equipment such as the Auto-ballasters, the bulk side-tippers and the RDT all carry HGI power.

The most sophisticated Network Rail measurement vehicles – SGT, DBS, UTU and the prestigious NMT all operate on HGI power. New Network Rail vehicles – SITT (Snow and Ice Treatment Trains) and PLPR (Plain Line Pattern Recognition) will all use HGI power.

When Chiltern Railways needed a unique and bespoke solution to a particular noise problem, HGI responded with an equally unique and innovative 250kW, 850V DC system, installed in a Mk3 DVT and with a ground-breaking noise signature of only 65dB (A) at 1 metre – quieter that the average office environment and also allowing shutdown of the Class 67 loco, otherwise idling at zero mpg!

Class 66 - backbone of the freight fleet.

HGI GENERATORS

On-Board Power - we deliver!

HGI is the No 1 provider of vehicle--mounted power generaton to the UK rail industry.

For over ten years, HGI have worked in close collaboraton with Network Rail and other operators to provide a range of power solutons dedicated to unique and often challenging requirements.

HGI generators deliver over 97% of Network Rail NDS vehicle power requirements.

From the arduous world of ballast tippers to the latest super--silent Chiltern Railways DVT installation, HGI deliver solutions to exactly meet your needs.

We are unique and have an unparalleled understanding of the industry and its requirements with a wealth of experience that delivers!

Harrington Generators International (HGI)
Ravenstor Road
Wirksworth
Derbyshire
DE4 4FY

Tel: +44 (0)1629 824284

www.HGIgenerators.com

143

Infrastructure Maintenance and Renewal

the Thameslink programme, a contract worth circa £50m.

Carillion

Carillion plc is one of the UK's leading support services and construction companies, employing around 50,000 people.

Carillion has also been selected by Network Rail as one the contractors to deliver infrastructure services under a £750 million multi asset framework agreement. It expects to deliver services for 19 projects worth some £250m in the London North Eastern area.

The contract for track work for the upgrade of Reading station and the surrounding railway, worth in the region of £20m, was awarded to Carillion in 2011. Network Rail has also awarded Carillion the contract to carry out a £43m expansion of Peterborough station.

Bombardier Transportation and Carillion have launched a new UK joint venture, named Infrasig. It combines Bombardier technology for both conventional and ETCS signalling solutions, with the UK rail experience of Carillion to deliver signalling and multi-disciplinary projects.

Carillion started work in 2012 on the Stockley Interchange in west London to allow Crossrail services to operate to and from Heathrow. Carillion will also be responsible for improvements to depots and stabling sites to allow the introduction of the new 12-car fleet on Thameslink.

Network Rail has also awarded Carillion a £15.6m contract to replace Loughor viaduct between Swansea and Gowerton.

Colas Rail

Colas Rail Ltd was created in May 2007 after Amec Spie Rail was taken over by the French infrastructure company Colas, part of the Bouygues group.

Colas Rail combines the engineering skills of specialist businesses to provide total solutions in all aspects of railway infrastructure, from high speed rail systems to light and urban rail. It is also active in freight train operation (see 'Freight and Haulage' section).

The AmeyColas joint venture commenced work under the Network Rail's new high output track renewals contract in 2010 and also delivers conventional track renewals.

The arrival of a Plasser 08 4x4 Unimat Switch & Crossing tamper in 2011 increased Colas's fleet to 14 principal S&C machines, which with additional compact and plain line machines provided Colas with what it believes to be the largest modern on-track plant fleet in Europe.

Under the new enhancements multi asset framework agreement, with joint venture partner Morgan Sindall, Colas will deliver works in the Western region, with anticipated turnover of c£200m.

Colas runs an extensive suite of courses for personnel who work on Network Rail infrastructure, including track safety and permanent way, electrification, safety training, and railway operations.

A new division, Colas Rail Europe, was formed in 2011, incorporating all Colas Rail businesses across Europe (excluding France) with the purpose of exploring new opportunities.

Costain

Costain Ltd will carry out the station redevelopment at London Bridge as part of the congestion-busting Thameslink programme, a contract worth circa £400m.

The Costain Skanska joint venture (CSJV) won Crossrail's first 'Whole Project Award' under the CEEQUAL sustainability in civil engineering award scheme for the Royal Oak Portal contract in west London. CSJV also recently won a contract to provide intermediate tunnel shafts for Crossrail, its fifth contract on Crossrail.

A Costain/Hochtief joint venture is principal contractor for the station work as part of Network Rail's Reading remodelling.

A Costain and Laing O'Rourke Joint Venture excelled in a 2012 Considerate Constructors Scheme assessment, achieving a total score of 38 out of a possible 40 points for its work on the Bond Street Station Upgrade for London Underground.

Costain delivers solutions across infrastructure (highways, rail and airports); environment (water and waste); energy & process (nuclear, power, and hydrocarbons and chemicals). Increasingly it provides consultancy and maintenance as well as construction.

VolkerRail

VolkerRail, part of the Netherlands-based Volker Wessels group, is a comprehensive multi-disciplinary rail infrastructure contractor. Capabilities include design, manufacture and construction; life time maintenance and asset inspection management; heavy rail rigid and ballasted track systems; light rail on-street track systems; signalling design, installation and testing; electrification, overhead line and line side civil engineering works; and high and low voltage power distribution systems. These disciplines can be delivered individually or as part of a fully integrated project requiring full interdisciplinary design and construction project management.

The overall railway capability is enhanced by the plant and welding division, and the fleet of on-track plant consists of beaver lightweight, On Track Machines and S&C tampers, Kirow rail mounted cranes, ballast regulators, rail mounted excavators, mobile work platforms, Colmar lifting machines, an array of rail mounted support and inspection vehicles, and specialist welding equipment including flash butt and gauge corner restoration.

VolkerRail, as part of the M-Pact Thales consortium with Laing O'Rourke and Thales UK, was awarded contracts to provide Manchester Metrolink Phase 3a and 3b extensions. A joint venture with Skanska won two contracts for the Docklands Light Railway's Stratford International extension.

In 2011 VolkerRail was awarded a seven year framework contract for the supply of 11 on-track machines, worth c£67 million over seven years, in the London North East territory.

Network Rail has awarded VolkerRail a £15.5m contract to remodel Acton yard, including a diveunder, as part of the Crossrail programme. ■

Slough station's upgrade, completed in time for the London 2012 Games, includes station forecourt improvements delivered by Slough Borough Council; a new footbridge and lifts to provide step-free access to all platforms, delivered by Network Rail; and major improvements to the station building, delivered by First Great Western. Network Rail

Signalling and Control

In association with

invensys
Rail

Signalling and Control

Invensys Rail
Successful project delivery

Invensys Rail's recent successful mainline project deliveries include the commissioning of phases one, two and three of Thameslink Key Output 1 (KO1). A new signal stands guard at Farringdon as a Thameslink train heads towards London St Pancras International. Paul Bigland

Invensys Rail is a world leader in the design, supply, installation, testing and commissioning of signalling and control solutions for mainline and mass transit railways. With over 140 years' experience, the company has an enviable reputation for successful project delivery and its systems are proven at the heart of many of the world's railways, providing reliable, robust and safe operation for operators, infrastructure owners and the travelling public.

The company's recent roll call of successful mainline project deliveries includes the commissioning of phases one, two and three of Thameslink Key Output 1 (KO1), phases one and two of the Water Orton resignalling project, Salisbury to Exeter resignalling, the final phase of the Paisley Corridor Improvement Programme, the Reading Southern Lines project and Leicester re-control scheme. A number of mass transit programmes have been successfully delivered in the same period, most notably the Victoria Line Upgrade project on London Underground.

The key requirement of the Thameslink project is to deliver a state of the art, high volume, high capacity railway through the City of London – working within the constraints of Victorian infrastructure. Across three phases, Thameslink KO1 covered the resignalling of Kentish Town to Loughborough Junction, for which Invensys commissioned two WESTLOCK systems controlled via WESTCAD control centres.

The solutions developed by the KO1 project team (Network Rail, Invensys and the major civils contractors) revolved around some extremely novel designs, with the high quality design work a feature of the programme. With over 300 signalling equivalent units and 13 large relocatable equipment buildings installed, testing and commissioning were carried out in a controlled manner, despite the fact that by the very nature of the project, testing times were squeezed. As a result of the work, the railway now operates through the Thameslink core area with a capacity of up to 20 trains per hour.

At the same time as the Thameslink commissioning and following a 98 hour possession, the second and final phase of the Water Orton Corridor Resignalling Programme in the West Midlands was also delivered, within possession constraints. The project saw the replacement and renewal of life-expired signalling equipment, enabling significantly improved traffic flows in and through the Water Orton area. This was the largest of the two project commissionings, covering 273 track circuits, 103 signals, 58 point ends and four fringes, as well as an extension to the WESTLOCK system that was commissioned as part of phase one.

The Salisbury to Exeter resignalling programme saw the replacement of all life-expired mechanical signal boxes along the 90 mile route from Salisbury to Exmouth Junction with three solid state interlockings and a new push button panel to control the route from the Basingstoke Area Signalling Centre. The works also included the renewal and recontrol of three manually controlled barrier (MCB) level crossings to CCTV and the recontrol of a further existing MCB (CCTV). As part of a value engineering exercise carried out by the project team, lightweight signals from VMS were also installed along the route, allowing considerable savings in installation time.

The multi-disciplinary programme was completed in a remarkably short period of just 11 months, with commissioning taking place across six consecutive weekends with three discrete phases, plus enabling works.

This was a particularly challenging scheme given the tight timescale, the geographical spread of the work and the technical challenge of interfacing the new signalling with the old. The fact that the programme was delivered on schedule was a tremendous achievement, with great credit going to the entire project team.

These projects were all part of a particularly intense commissioning period. To have successfully delivered such a breadth and depth of projects is an extraordinary achievement and a great reflection of the commitment, dedication skill and expertise of those involved in the work. ∎

HITACHI
Inspire the Next

In association with invensys Rail

Siemens and Invensys win Crossrail signalling contract

Crossrail has awarded the signalling system contract for the railway's central section to a consortium comprising Siemens PLC and Invensys Rail Limited.

The November 2012 contract covers the design, manufacture, supply, installation, testing and commissioning of a train control system for Crossrail's central section. The value of the contract, No C620, is in the region of £50m.

Andrew Wolstenholme, Crossrail's Chief Executive said: 'Crossrail is now in a position to award the main signalling contract which is the first of our railway systems contracts. Crossrail will operate up to 24 trains per hour during the peak between Whitechapel and Paddington. The new signalling system will incorporate Automatic Train Operation to support the delivery of a high-frequency metro service and will also be capable of enhancement to 30 trains per hour through the central section at a later date.'

The contract also includes commitments to provide apprenticeships and job opportunities for Londoners. Siemens will be required to create around 20 apprenticeships and new job start roles for individuals who are long-term unemployed or out of education or training for six months or more during the life of their contract.

It is a requirement that all of the new job starts be taken up by individuals living within Greater London or within one mile of the Crossrail route. Siemens will also be required to provide 500 days of work experience and placement opportunities for young people.

Crossrail said it 'will be adopting a Communications Based Train Control (CBTC) signalling system as it is technically and operationally proven and is successfully used by many metro systems around the world'.

Having prequalified for the C620 contract as separate entities in September 2011, Invensys Rail Limited and Siemens PLC submitted a combined bid which was a permissible approach under the procurement rules for all bidders.

The new signalling system will be installed along the Crossrail route between Portobello Junction (west of Paddington) on the Great Western main line, Pudding Mill Lane Junction (west of Stratford) on the Great Eastern main line in the east, and Abbey Wood in the southeast.

Crossrail's services will operate in Automatic Train Operation (ATO) mode with Automatic Train Protection (ATP) in the central operating section from Portobello Junction to Pudding Mill Lane / Abbey Wood.

Due to the integration of Crossrail's central section with the existing National Rail network, Crossrail services will need to operate with existing signalling and safety systems installed at either end of the Crossrail tunnels.

The successful contractor will work closely with the future rolling stock provider to deliver compatible on-board equipment. The rolling stock will also be capable of operating with the European standard ETCS (European Train Control System) Level 2 signalling system and with the principal legacy signalling systems found on British rail infrastructure.

As Crossrail's central section is subject to the Railways (Interoperability) Regulations 2006, Crossrail sought non-application of the Technical Specification for Interoperability (TSI). This was conditionally granted with a Commission Implementing Decision in January 2012 followed by a UK decision the following month. Provision has been made to plan for the migration from the CBTC system that will be installed to the European Rail Traffic Management System system / ETCS level 3.

Crossrail trains will be equipped for Communications Based Train Control (CBTC), and also be capable of operating with the ETCS Level 2 signalling system and with the principal legacy signalling systems found on British rail infrastructure. Provision has been made for migration from CBTC to the European Rail Traffic Management System / ETCS level 3. Copyright Crossrail Ltd

Signalling and Control

Signalling displays at Manchester South signalling centre. Network Rail

Traffic management system contracts awarded

The shape of signalling on Britain's railways for future decades is set to be influenced by contracts awarded by Network Rail in 2012.

Design and development of a new nationwide traffic management system for Britain's rail network is covered by contracts awarded in August 2012. Development of a new, European-standard, signalling system for Britain's railways is covered by framework agreements signed in March 2012.

Traffic management technology forms an integral part of Network Rail's operating strategy, which seeks to consolidate control of Britain's rail network from more than 800 signalboxes into 14 state-of-the-art rail operating centres over the next 30 years. Once fully implemented, Network Rail expects this strategy to cut the cost of Britain's railways by £250m each year, improve industry efficiency, reduce delays and provide more accurate and timely information to staff and passengers.

Now working with Network Rail to design and develop a traffic management software prototype, due for completion in December 2013, are:
- Hitachi Rail Europe,
- Signalling Solutions (the joint venture between Alstom Transport and Balfour Beatty Rail),
- Thales UK.

The prototype will be subject to vigorous testing and evaluation before being rolled out across the network from 2014.

Robin Gisby, managing director of network operations, Network Rail, said: 'As the number of people and businesses relying on rail continues to grow, it is vital we have the technology to make the best use of Britain's rail infrastructure. Working with our suppliers, our focus is on developing a system which meets the needs of Network Rail, our customers and passengers, helping deliver a leaner, more efficient and reliable railway'.

This new, highly automated system will allow larger areas of the network to be controlled from fewer locations and will help increase capacity and improve reliability. For instance, it will be able to include real-time planning, prediction and resolution of conflicts, areas of control will be easily reconfigured when operational needs dictate and it will include a single operational information system, providing real-time information to train companies and passengers, particularly during times of disruption.

Traffic management systems are used extensively, and successfully, around the world on a number of rail networks. Network Rail has analysed and compared best practice from these different systems in order to develop a reliable product which will suit the varied demands of Britain's complex rail network.

A working group of future users of the system – including signallers, control centre and other operations staff and passenger and freight operating company staff, plus trade union representatives – is helping shape the system, roles and ways of working.

Network Rail has over 800 operating locations, with aging and inconsistent equipment and different ways of working. Many of these locations already need replacing. By upgrading signalling at a faster than usual pace, Network Rail believes it can deliver savings sooner and for longer.

At the heart of the strategy are rail operating centres – 14 centres which will become the central hub for all aspects of operating the railway, where Network Rail works with train and freight operators to deliver a better railway for Britain using leading technology. By 2015, Network Rail plans to have built six new operating centres (Basingstoke, Manchester, Romford, Rugby, Three Bridges, York), in addition to eight existing locations (Ashford, Cardiff, Derby, Edinburgh, Gillingham, Saltley, with further upgrade required at Didcot and Glasgow)

The total value of the prototype contracts awarded is approximately £20m.

ETCS framework contracts

Network Rail announced framework agreements in March 2012 with four suppliers for the development and design of a European Train Control System (ETCS) Level 2 signalling system. The successful suppliers are:
- Signalling Solutions Ltd,
- Invensys Rail,
- Infrasig (Bombardier and Carillion joint venture),
- Ansaldo STS.

The collaborative agreements cover a one-year development phase until March 2013, which will confirm the suppliers' design of a European Train Control System (ETCS) Level 2 signalling system. These will then be demonstrated on Network Rail's new testing facility on the Hertford loop with contracts for the delivery of the programme to be awarded in 2014.

ETCS is part of the European Rail Traffic Management System (ERTMS) which will replace traditional line-side railway signals with a computer display inside every train cab, reducing the costs of maintaining the railway, improving performance and enhancing safety.

Andrew Simmons, Network Rail director, future trains and operation control systems, said: 'ETCS is now a crucial part of our plans for resignalling the railway – our focus now is on building confidence and experience in the technology

Signalling excellence

We have the knowledge and experience to deliver any signalling programme from minor works through to major remodelling schemes such as the North London Railway Infrastructure Project.

Want to know more?
Contact Steve Higham on
+44 (0)207 121 2686
or steve.higham@atkinsglobal.com

www.atkinsglobal.com

ATKINS

Plan Design Enable

Designed to deliver

ESG
Consultancy
Turnkey Solutions
Enhancement Products

Designed to deliver

www.esg-rail.com | 01332 383565

- Engineering
- Design
- Structures
- Maintenance
- Enhancements
- Approvals

- RISAB
- Continuous Service Operation
- PRM and TSI
- Cab Air Con
- ERTMS
- Refurbishment

149

Signalling and Control

The trusty filament colour light signal - lineside signals could soon be a thing of the past on several main lines. Tony Miles

Route-based signalling frameworks

Framework area	Primary contractor	Secondary contractor
Scotland	Invensys	SSL
Central (west)	Invensys	SSL
Central (east)	SSL	Invensys
Wales & West	Invensys	SSL
Great Western (inner)	SSL	Invensys
Great Western (outer)	SSL	Invensys
Anglia & Kent	Atkins	SSL
Sussex & Wessex	Atkins	Invensys

so that future schemes can be delivered seamlessly. These new frameworks are the building blocks to developing this capability and will allow us to work closely with our chosen suppliers to develop long-term plans for work to be carried out more quickly and efficiently.'

The first drive to install ERTMS will take place on the Great Western main line starting in 2016 as part of the large-scale resignalling of the line, coinciding with the arrival of new trains and electrification between London Paddington and Heathrow Airport, Oxford, Newbury and Bristol. The East Coast main line (commencing 2018) and Midland main line (commencing 2020) are scheduled to follow soon after.

Network Rail says it is seeking to use technology which delivers the lowest whole-life asset costs, with the aim of providing a safe, reliable and efficient rail infrastructure for freight and passenger operators. ETCS level 2 does not require lineside signals and is cheaper to install than conventional re-signalling, says Network Rail, adding that it and its industry partners have chosen ETCS as one of its recommended methods of resignalling and have developed a plan for its deployment across the network.

Schemes in the near future include the Great Western main line between Paddington and Bristol, Oxford, Newbury and Heathrow Airport where the technology will be installed from 2016 and operated in parallel with conventional lineside signals until they are removed in 2025. It will be installed on the East Coast main line between King's Cross and Doncaster from 2018 and then the Midland main line between Farringdon/St Pancras and Derby from 2020. There are also a number of smaller schemes to be carried out in association with the main line routes.

The plans for wider national rollout are being developed consistent with a targeted signalling renewal policy, Network Rail's operational strategy and the industry's train fleet fitment programme.

Signalling renewals and enhancements

Network Rail in 2012 awarded new framework agreements of up to seven years to deliver railway signalling projects worth approximately £1.5bn. This is part of wider reforms to its infrastructure business, says Network Rail, with a greater focus on partnership with suppliers and a restructuring of the way the company delivers capital projects.

The frameworks, which cover the majority of signalling renewals and enhancements across England, Scotland and Wales, were awarded to:

- Invensys Rail,
- Signalling Solutions (SSL),
- Atkins.

The agreements will operate until then end of Control Period 4 (March 2014) and can be extended by Network Rail to cover the whole of Period 5 (2014-19).

The new framework agreements form the backbone of a programme to modernise and maintain safety-critical railway signalling systems and are designed to deliver efficiency savings across the company's signalling work bank over the next seven years, through further reductions in unit costs.

Simon Kirby, Network Rail managing director, infrastructure projects, said: 'These new frameworks represent a seven-year commitment by suppliers, allowing us to work closely with them to develop long-term plans for work to be carried out more quickly and efficiently. The length of the agreements, coupled with a visible workload, will provide much-needed stability throughout the supply chain and drive further cost savings and innovation across our signalling renewals and enhancements activities.'

In line with Network Rail's new approach to supplier engagement, the frameworks incorporate collaborative working in order to deliver the necessary efficiencies. Integrated design teams and a reduction in man-marking will remove costly duplication of effort, while smoothing of peaks and troughs in Network Rail's work bank will allow better use of suppliers' resources.

The new frameworks appoint both a primary and secondary supplier for each area. This provides the flexibility needed to meet the significant increase in volumes required over the life of the framework and provides an alternative in each area if the primary supplier does not have the capacity. The agreements also provide the option to competitively tender up to 20pc of the predicted workload each year.

IECC Scalable pilot

September 2012 saw the pilot of DeltaRail's IECC Scalable at Swindon B signalbox come to a conclusion. This first installation of IECC Scalable was commissioned in March 2012, and had been controlling the railway with no significant issues, said DeltaRail.

The system's new and permanent home is at the Thames Valley Signalling Centre.

The system offers: reduced hardware cost and equipment room space requirements, reduced maintenance expenditure, re-configurable workstations that can be matched to traffic levels, workstations and signalling interfaces that can be located remotely using open communications, interfaces to ERTMS/ETCS and strategic traffic management tools, all of the functionality of the Classic IECC system.

The system has also been installed at Cambridge and Harrogate. A contract has also been awarded by Network Rail to re-control the Slough power signalbox on to a new IECC Scalable at the Thames Valley Signalling Centre.

A programme of upgrading at 21 Classic IECCs throughout the UK has now been completed. DeltaRail's IECC now has 53 workstations operating in the UK from 27 IECCs at 12 signalling locations. ∎

Light Rail and Metro

In association with

BOMBARDIER
the evolution of mobility

Light Rail and Metro

Latest international technology for Blackpool

The beginning of the an exciting future for the next generation of tramways worldwide

In April 2012 sixteen BOMBARDIER FLEXITY 2 trams went into revenue service in Blackpool proving an instant success with tram passengers. Blackpool and Lancashire County Councils have purchased the world's most advanced tram technology from Bombardier to revitalise Britain's most traditional tram system and is operating the new vehicles on the Blackpool and Fleetwood tramway.

At the 2012 Light Rail Awards, Bombardier Transportation received the award for Worldwide Manufacturer of the Year and Honourable Mention for Worldwide Supplier of the Year or the third year running. 'This award underscores our capability as a provider of light rail solutions and as a reliable partner for transport operators in the UK, which is a core market for Bombardier Transportation. Our vehicles are already in successful revenue service in Manchester, London-Docklands, London-Croydon and Nottingham, and we have just recently launched our FLEXITY 2 tram in Blackpool,' said Germar Wacker, President Light Rail Vehicles, Bombardier Transportation.

The FLEXITY 2 tram combines 'the best of the best' in global tram technology and Bombardier's experience in delivering more than 3,500 trams and light rail vehicles to around 100 cities in more than 20 countries. FLEXITY 2 is based on the very successful BOMBARDIER FLEXITY family of light rail vehicles and combines proven technology with continuous improvement and innovation.

With 126 years of service, Blackpool has the UK's longest running tram operation. As a popular tourist destination, 4 million passengers use the tram annually, with the majority travelling during the busy summer period. While the heritage trams that still operate remain a popular tourist attraction for visitors, with new accessibility regulations coming into effect in 2019, Blackpool and Lancashire County Council began an extensive programme to identify a supplier for a new fleet of vehicles, which would enable ease of access and comfort for all passengers.

The new FLEXITY 2 tram is equipped with Bombardier's industry-leading BOMBARDIER ECO4 range of technologies, making it an energy efficient and low carbon means of transit.

Combining 100 percent low-floor technology with conventional wheel-set bogies, the FLEXITY 2 tram not only guarantees a smooth ride, but also includes some new advanced features, such as touch-screens in the driver's cab, reflecting the latest developments in intelligent digital technology.

'We travelled to every part of Europe to visit both vehicle manufacturers and other tram operations,' Paul Grocott, Programme Manager for Blackpool Council explained. 'We were keen to look at everything the market had to offer and thereby ensure that we got the most competitive and best solution available. Ultimately we narrowed our search and selected Bombardier with the FLEXITY 2 tram.'

'In the end the technical message from Bombardier was extremely strong,' Mr Grocott added. 'The company has a lot of experience, particularly in the UK, and whilst this is a new vehicle type it is a derivative of what is best in the FLEXITY family.'

Following Bombardier's contract success in Blackpool and Lancashire, the Queensland Government in Australia ordered 14 high-capacity 45 m long, seven-module FLEXITY 2 trams for its Gold Coast Rapid Transit system in 2011. As part of the GoldlinQ consortium, Bombardier will also design, build and operate the system. The Basel Transport Authority BVB placed an order for 60 FLEXITY trams in January 2012, the biggest order in its 116-year history. Bombardier Transportation will supply 48 FLEXITY 2 trams for the cities of Ghent and Antwerp to the Flemish operator De Lijn. The total number of FLEXITY 2 trams ordered to date now stands at 138.

Based on the highly successful FLEXITY platform, with a strong reputation for performance and reliability and 1,224 100% low floor FLEXITY trams sold worldwide to date, the FLEXITY 2 tram combines proven features and innovation in a single vehicle. It sets the highest standards in the areas of comfort, safety and environmental protection.

Each Blackpool tram is 32.2 m long and 2.65 m wide, with five sections and three bogies. The trams can carry approximately 74 seated passengers, with additional wheelchair and pushchair space plus standing room.

The technical advantages include an improved carbody concept, with good corrosion protection (essential for the seafront environment in which the vehicles operate) and an enhanced bogie design, the BOMBARDIER FLEXX Urban 3000 bogie.

Principal features are as follows:
- Leading-Edge Technology - The combination of 100% low-floor technology and conventional wheel-set bogies ensures a low unsuspended mass on the bogie, which results in
  - ultra-smooth running qualities
  - low noise levels and vibrations
  - a more comfortable ride for passengers
  - reduced track maintenance costs for the operator

  Furthermore an advanced Intelligent Driver's Desk includes 2 touch screen displays.
- Enhanced Safety - The FLEXITY 2 tram provides the best possible protection for both passengers and driver with vehicles equipped to the highest standards for collision and fire damage.
- Customised design - The FLEXITY 2 tram provides operators with the opportunity to individually shape cityscapes and get good value for money: creative customisation based on standardised components.
- Environmental Excellence - The latest flagship tram in the Bombardier portfolio is equipped with energy-saving technologies from the ECO4 portfolio.
- Improved repairabilty - An intelligent repairability concept and various smart functions make the FLEXITY 2 tram easier to repair. This means significant savings of time and money for the operator.

The exciting future of the next generation of trams worldwide has begun. ■

New FLEXITY 2 tram in service in Blackpool. Bombardier

RAILWAY SYSTEMS ENGINEERING & INTEGRATION (RSEI) AT THE UNIVERSITY OF BIRMINGHAM

Continuous Educational Development for Railway Professionals

400 years after their invention, railways are transporting more and more people and goods ever faster and over greater distances. Railway systems engineers ensure the reliability and safety of 5 km long iron ore trains in Australia, of a 574.8 km/h world record train in France and of peak flows of 40,000 passengers per hour on MTRC in Hong Kong. In Britain, they are building Crossrail and they have started the design of a high speed railway for 400 km/h between London, Manchester and Leeds.

The postgraduate programme in Railway Systems Engineering and Integration at the University of Birmingham allows participants to acquire the skills and know-how to become recognised leaders and experts in the railway field, ready to tackle the challenges of climate change and economic volatility! The modular rogramme is suitable for experienced railway staff as well as new entrants to the industry, in both part-time and full-time modes of study. It leads to the degree of MSc, the Postgraduate Diploma or a Postgraduate Certificate of the University.

Our Master of Research (MRes) programme in RSI (Railway Systems Integration) has been running since 2011/12. This one year period of postgraduate study involves the equivalent of 2 months of taught courses 2 months of research training and 8 months of research under the guidance of one of our experts. Some MRes projects are supported by major international sponsors and research bodies. Alumni of the taught postgraduate programmes at Birmingham can be found in senior positions in railways and railway consultancies around the world. MRes graduates will join this select group on successful completion of their studies.

The University of Birmingham encourages equality of opportunity for all and offers railway engineering studies as part of its provision of higher education in a research-led environment.

UNIVERSITY OF BIRMINGHAM

Further information and registration: contact Joy Grey (0121 414 4342, j.grey@bham.ac.uk)

or in writing to Administrator RSEI, BCRRE, Gisbert Kapp, University of Birmingham, B15 2TT.

Research and technical consultancy enquiries to f.schmid@bham.ac.uk.

CONTINUOUS PROFESSIONAL DEVELOPMENT

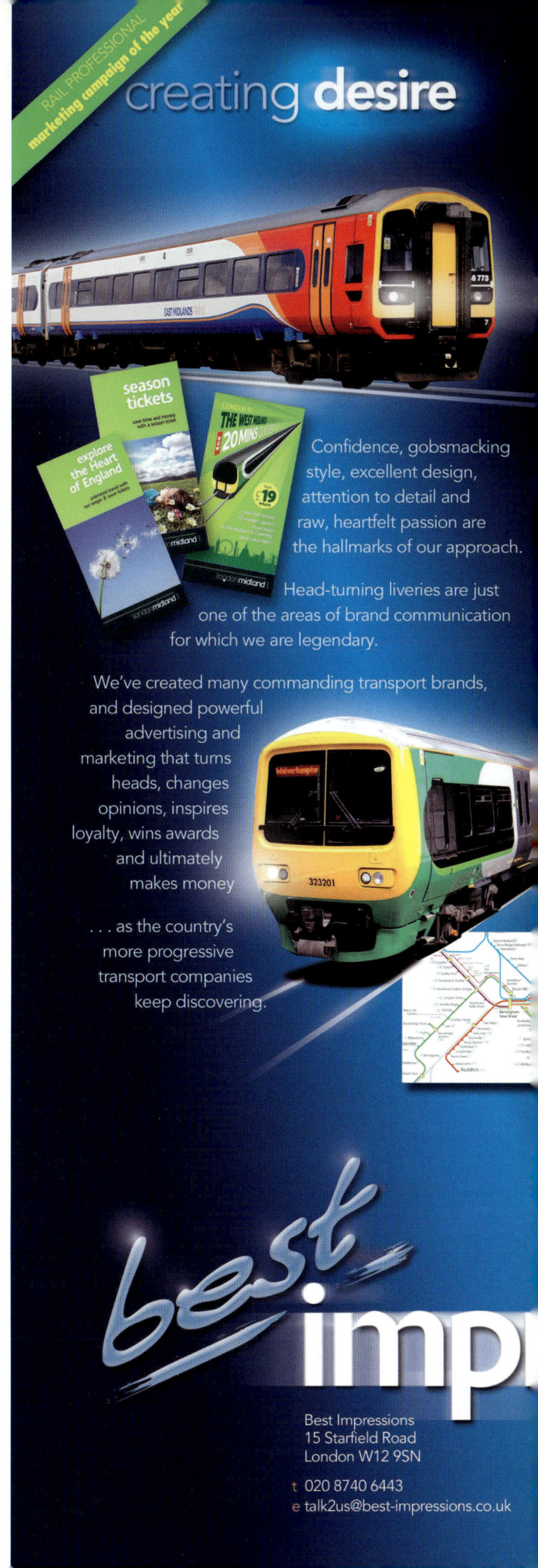

RAIL PROFESSIONAL marketing campaign of the year

creating desire

Confidence, gobsmacking style, excellent design, attention to detail and raw, heartfelt passion are the hallmarks of our approach.

Head-turning liveries are just one of the areas of brand communication for which we are legendary.

We've created many commanding transport brands, and designed powerful advertising and marketing that turns heads, changes opinions, inspires loyalty, wins awards and ultimately makes money

...as the country's more progressive transport companies keep discovering.

best impr

Best Impressions
15 Starfield Road
London W12 9SN

t 020 8740 6443
e talk2us@best-impressions.co.uk

Light Rail and Metro

Light rail grows again

London Tramlink: New five-section Stadler Variobahn tram No 2554 is in special 'Love Croydon' livery and vinyls, with a hopeful future route indication for Crystal Palace. It stands at East Croydon on 25 June 2012, alongside classmate No 2555, on a service between West Croydon and Elmers End. Brian Morrison

New construction and modernisation is under way on light rail systems across Britain

A modest rise in overall journeys from 2010/11 to 2011/12 of 3.6 per cent was recorded for light rail and metro networks, excluding London Underground. The results were however uneven, with the Docklands Light Railway outperforming all others.

System expansion has continued, notably in Manchester, and Nottingham has two lines under construction, Midland Metro is being extended, and Edinburgh Trams should commence operation in 2014. Blackpool meanwhile has seen total reconstruction, and the Glasgow Subway is beginning major modernisation.

Several systems are seeing new tram deliveries, in some cases replacing existing fleets of vehicles which are far from life expired. The second refurbishment of the 1980s Tyne & Wear Metrocars is in contrast with some of the approaches found elsewhere.

Traditional approaches are also being challenged by the use of light-rail-type vehicles on conventional heavy railway, presently at Stourbridge, but also with the Sheffield tram-train experiment.

Light rail and metro networks

Blackpool Tramway key statistics

Key statistics	2011/12	2010/11
Passenger journeys (millions)	1.1	1.6
Passenger km (millions)	3.3	4.9
Passenger revenue (£m 2011/12 prices)	1.7	2.5

Blackpool trams run on 17km of reserved track and seafront promenade, with street running in Fleetwood. With the £100m upgrade to the system launched in the spring of 2012, the question now is whether patronage will return to anywhere near the levels the system once enjoyed.

The infrastructure and trams are owned by Blackpool Borough Council, operated under contract by the municipally-owned Blackpool Transport Services Ltd.

Extensive reconstruction included complete trackwork replacement, overhead supply renewal, power voltage increase to 600V DC, new substation equipment, level access platforms, tram-priority road signals, and a new depot at Starr Gate. Stops were reduced in number.

Two thirds of the £102m package came from the government, the rest equally from Blackpool Borough and Lancashire County councils. Roughly £33m was for the new trams.

Sixteen Bombardier 'Flexity 2' trams commenced fleet operation on 4 April 2012. The aluminium-bodied cars have five articulated sections and are a substantial 32.2m long. Each has 74 seats and a standing capacity of 148; they are fully accessible. End-to-end journey time has been reduced from 70 to 55min. 16 of the old fleet have been retained for seasonal and heritage operations.

Docklands Light Railway key statistics

Key statistics	2011/12	2010/11
Passenger journeys (millions)	86.1	78.3
Passenger km (millions)	455.5	414.0
Passenger revenue (£m 2011/12 prices)	105.3	90.9

23 August 2012 marked 25 years since the original section of the Docklands Light Railway in London opened. It has been extended progressively, most recently in 2011 from Canning Town to Stratford International, in readiness for a key role in the London 2012 Games.

The DLR is double track throughout with many grade separated junctions, keeping conflicts to the minimum. The 750V DC third rail system uses underside contact.

A new Control Centre for the network opened at Beckton in February 2012, introducing the first third-generation installation of Thales' Seltrac communications-based train control system.

Usage is rising fast, 10pc more passengers being carried in 2011/12 than 2010/11, with 13pc growth for the two years before that. This is expected to continue until the opening of Crossrail.

Most trains are now formed of three pairs of articulated units, each 28.8m long. The main Beckton depot now has to accommodate 149 vehicles.

Serco Docklands operates and maintains the DLR under a franchise running until May 2013. The company is paid a set fee for operating the railway to agreed levels of service and is entitled to part of the revenue received.

The DLR has been supported by concessionaires who have designed, financed, built and maintained some of the extensions. In 2011, Transport for London announced it was to take over the concessionaires for the City Airport London City Airport and Woolwich extensions, as replacing private with public-sector borrowing was expected to bring 'ongoing savings' of up to £250m over the remaining life of the concessions. City Greenwich Lewisham (CGL) Rail manages the Lewisham extension.

There is further scope to extend the DLR network in the longer term to improve orbital links and connectivity in the Thames Estuary. There has also been discussion of a western extension from Bank and options south of Lewisham and north of Stratford International.

Edinburgh Trams

Route km under construction	14
Stops to be served	16

The Edinburgh tram route will now run between Edinburgh Airport, Haymarket, St Andrew Square (for Waverley) and York Place. Project management is now being overseen by Transport Scotland

and Turner & Townsend. The overall budget is £776m, compared with £512m when contracts for a considerably larger system were signed in May 2008.

Bilfinger Berger, Siemens and CAF are responsible for civil engineering, tracklaying, tram stop construction, electrification, and communications. CAF was due to deliver the last of 27 seven-section trams by December 2012. At 42.8m, they are the longest in Britain.

Opening is now expected in 2014. End-to-end journey time will be about 30min, and the council was exploring options for trams that are surplus to the reduced network's requirements.

Glasgow Subway key statistics

Key statistics	2011/12	2010/11
Passenger journeys (millions)	12.9	13.0
Passenger km (millions)	41.6	41.4
Passenger revenue (£m 2011/12 prices)	14.3	14.5

The Subway opened in 1896, with cable-hauled trains, and runs for 10.6km in a circle, with 15 stations. Only Broomloan depot is above ground. Two running tunnels (inner circle and outer circle) are to the restrictive diameter of 3.35 metres, and track gauge is a highly unusual 1,220mm (4ft 0in).

The Subway was electrified in 1935, with large scale reconstruction and renewal in 1980, and Strathclyde Partnership for Transport has started a new full-scale modernisation programme, to include fully automated trains, resignalling with communications-based train control, refurbished stations, a new smartcard ticketing system, and improvements to the tunnels and track infrastructure.

£246m towards the £289m project is being paid by the Scottish Government. Systra has been appointed as client technical advisor for procurement.

London Tramlink key statistics

Key statistics	2011/12	2010/11
Passenger journeys (millions)	28.6	27.9
Passenger km (millions)	148.4	144.9
Passenger revenue (£m 2011/12 prices)	21.2	19.6

Tramlink converted four under-used or disused railways around Croydon to light rail and became fully operational in 2000. A continuing strong market position was emphasised by the 2.5pc growth to a new record high in patronage in 2011/12.

The assets are now owned by Transport for London, and the 28km system is operated by Tram Operations Ltd (a First Group subsidiary).

The fleet consists of 24 'K4000' pairs of articulated cars built in Austria by Bombardier, each 30.1m long. An additional six Variobahn trams were delivered by Stadler in 2012, to provide more frequent services (up to 50pc increase in on the busiest section) to meet passenger growth. The longer (32.4m) vehicles have required stop and depot modifications.

Twin tracking of the Mitcham-Mitcham Junction section has been carried out to improve reliability, and to enable a new Willow Way tram stop to be built when funded. A second platform at Wimbledon is also proposed (for about £25m including four additional trams) to enable a 5min service to be operated.

Medium term extension proposals are to Crystal Palace, Morden and Sutton. The Beckenham Junction spur could also be extended to Bromley.

Metrolink

Manchester Metrolink key statistics

Key statistics	2011/12	2010/11
Passenger journeys (millions)	21.8	19.2
Passenger km (millions)	228.0	200.8
Passenger revenue (£m 2011/12 prices)	33.7	28.1

Transport for Greater Manchester's Metrolink system was created by the linking of the heavy rail lines from Manchester to Bury and Altrincham through the city centre, creating a 31km network opened in phases through 1992. A 6km route through Salford Quays to Eccles opened in 2000. A 'Big-Bang' expansion, with four new lines taking the network from from 37 to 97km by 2016, began in 2009. The expansion is financed through a special fund of £1.5 billion agreed in 2009 to deliver 15 transport schemes in Greater Manchester. The money will come from increased council tax, contributions from Manchester Airport, increased ticket revenue, and early release of central government money already allocated for transport improvements. The first new section, the 400m spur to the MediaCityUK development in Salford Quays, opened in 2010 and in July 2011 the Chorlton route from Trafford Bar to St Werburgh's Road opened.

The section from the City Centre to Oldham Mumps opened in June 2012. Work continues on a diversion through Oldham town centre and the rest of the route to Rochdale.

The East Manchester extension to Droylsden was expected to open by the end of 2012 continuing to Ashton-under-Lyne - scheduled to open in 2014.

The extension from St Werburgh's Road to Didsbury, due to open in summer 2013, could be advanced if progress is made with the new Tram Management System. The route from St Werburgh's Road to Manchester Airport is planned to open in summer 2016, though an additional line to the Trafford Centre retail complex is being discussed.

To handle the significantly increased flow of trams through the city centre once the expansion has been completed, a Second City Crossing is to be constructed for 1.6km between Deansgate-Castlefield and Victoria station, via St Peters Square. A Transport & Works Act application was submitted in May 2012.

In 2011 Stagecoach completed the sale of the Metrolink operating concession (due to run until 2017) to to RATP Dev UK, a wholly owned subsidiary of RATP Développement, part of the French state-owned company which runs the Paris Metro. The name of the business was changed to Metrolink RATP Dev Ltd. Metrolink continues to

Light Rail and Metro

be owned by Transport for Greater Manchester.

A total of 62 new Bombardier M5000 'Flexity Swift' trams was ordered for the new routes and to provide additional capacity. The 28.4m long articulated units are being built in conjunction with Vossloh Kiepe. In 2011 the Greater Manchester Combined Authority (GMCA) announced plans to retire the first of the original 32-strong fleet of T68 and T68a trams, and order an additional 12 M5000s, and in July 2012 it was decided that the rest of the original trams would also be replaced by a 20 more M5000s, bringing the fleet to 94. Better reliability, reduced maintenance costs, and (through lighter weight) reduced energy costs and prolonged rail life are expected.

Midland Metro key statistics

Key statistics	2011/12	2010/11
Passenger journeys (millions)	4.9	4.8
Passenger km (millions)	50.9	50.4
Passenger revenue (£m 2011/12 prices)	7.4	7.2

Patronage on the Midland Metro route grew in 2011/12, though it remains short of the 5 million previously achieved.

The line was built almost entirely on the disused trackbed of the Birmingham Snow Hill to Wolverhampton line of the former Great Western Railway. On this 20.4km route, only the last 2.3km into Wolverhampton St George's are on street. Promoted by the West Midlands transport authority and its Executive, now known as Centro, Line 1 opened in 1999 and is operated by Travel West Midlands Ltd, part of the National Express Group. A fleet of 16 two-section 24m articulated cars was built by Ansaldo. Electrification is 750V DC overhead.

A 1.3km extension now under construction runs from Birmingham Snow Hill to Stephenson Street (outside New Street station), using a new £9m viaduct already built by developer Ballymore. There will be four new stops, one of which replaces the existing Snow Hill terminus. The government has made £72m available towards the £128m scheme, with the remainder provided by Centro.

A completely new fleet of 20 Urbos-3 trams is being built by CAF, and extensive depot alteration is being undertaken by Morgan Sindall. There will also be electrification and telecoms upgrades.

The new trams will each carry around 200 people, rather than the 150 of the present fleet. New trams will enter service from February 2014, with the line extension completed in March 2015.

In the longer term, Centro proposes other rapid transit projects, in the Black Country, on the Birmingham City Centre-Birmingham Airport corridor, a loop in Wolverhampton and in Coventry.

Nottingham Express Transit key statistics

Key statistics	2011/12	2010/11
Passenger journeys (millions)	9.0	9.7
Passenger km (millions)	40.1	41.3
Passenger revenue (£m 2011/12 prices)	8.4	9.2

Nottingham Express Transit's (NET's) Line 1 opened in 2004 and runs from Nottingham main line station to Hucknall via the city centre. A short branch leads to Phoenix Park. Patronage suffered another setback in 2011/12, slipping well below the peaks of 2007 and 2008.

The fleet consists of 15 articulated cars of 22m built by Bombardier in Derby. Electrification is at 750V DC and each car has 58 seats. About a quarter of all passenger journeys are to/from one of five park & ride sites.

Powers to construct two further lines (Phase 2) were approved, for which government announced a grant of £480m. Separately, Regional Funding Allocations included £7.8m for preparation works. Approval was linked to a workplace parking levy.

Phase 2 will continue across Nottingham station on a new bridge. Line 2 will run 7.6km to Clifton and Line 3 will run 9.8km to Chilwell, both terminating at new park-and-ride facilities.

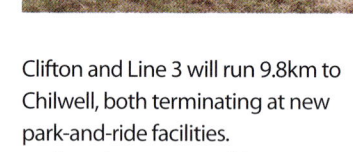

The 31km system will be more than double the length of the original Line 1. The PFI concession to finance, build, operate and maintain Phase 2 (and take over operation and maintenance of Phase 1) for 22 years, was awarded to the Tramlink Nottingham consortium. This consists of tram builder Alstom, operators Keolis and Wellglade (parent of bus company Trent Barton), Vinci Construction UK, and investors OFI Infravia and Meridiam Infrastructure. 22 Alstom Citadis trams are being built for the extensions, due to open in late 2014.

Sheffield Supertram key statistics

Key statistics	2011/12	2010/11
Passenger journeys (millions)	15.0	15.0
Passenger km (millions)	97.0	97.3
Passenger revenue (£m 2011/12 prices)	15.4	15.6

Supertram, operated by Stagecoach, has maintained passenger numbers at a record high of 15 million. It was completed in 1995 over a 29km network, roundly half is fully segregated. There is some tight geometry, with a minimum horizontal curve radius of 25m and vertical curve of 100m. Maximum gradients are 10pc.

Services run from the City Centre to Middlewood in the north with a spur to Meadowhall Interchange. In the south the route is to Halfway, with a spur to Herdings Park.

The fleet of three-section, 34.8m cars built by Siemens/Duewag is 25 strong. The large cars were chosen to avoid multiple working and hence obstruction of other traffic, or excessively frequent services. Vehicles have 88 seats, with space for around 200 standing.

A £58m pilot scheme of the tram-train concept is to take place in Sheffield: this sees city trams also running on the heavy rail network, reducing the need for passenger interchange.

Services will originate in Rotherham Parkgate Retail Park and use the freight-only railway towards Sheffield, joining the Supertram network via a 400 metre

In association with **BOMBARDIER**

A Manchester Metrolink T68-type tram (left) passes a new M5000 vehicle at Trafford Bar. Tony Miles

link at Meadowhall South. Network Rail will electrify its part of the route at 750V DC overhead.

The new tram-trains will make the eight mile journey to Sheffield City Centre in about 25min. Seven vehicles are to be procured from Vossloh.

Issues to be studied in the pilot include wheel-rail interface, variations in technical standards, signalling detection of vehicles, and use of sanders and magnetic track brakes.

The trials are to be conducted by the Department for Transport in conjunction with Northern Rail (and its successors), Network Rail, South Yorkshire PTE and Stagecoach. Services are to be operational from 2015 for two years, with an expectation of permanent operation.

Tyne & Wear Metro key statistics

Key statistics	2011/12	2010/11
Passenger journeys (millions)	37.9	39.9
Passenger km (millions)	303.9	315.1
Passenger revenue (£m 2011/12 prices)	42.2	42.6

Work is now in full swing on the major £385m programme to refurbish and upgrade the Metro system, with new ticket barriers and machines being installed in 2012, as well as track upgrades and station refurbishment.

The Tyne & Wear Metro pioneered modern light rail operation in Britain and the first stage opened in 1980. Subsequent extensions were to Newcastle Airport in 1991, and Sunderland/South Hylton in 2002, to make 78km of route. There is mixed running with National Rail trains between Pelaw and Sunderland.

The Metro uses former British Rail lines on north and south sides of the Tyne, coupled with new underground sections in the central area.

The 90-strong fleet of six-axle Metrocars was built by Metro-Cammell. Each unit is 27.4m long, seating 68. Electrification is at 1,500V DC overhead and the depot is a Gosforth.

A high of 59.1m passenger journeys was reached in 1985, but then suffered a serious decline. The low was 32.1m journeys in 2000/01. In the subsequent recovery journey levels exceeded 40 million, but in 2011/12 dropped below 38 million for the first time since 2007.

Government confirmed a £580m modernisation package in February 2010, conditional upon operations being put out to tender. It consisted of £350m for the 11 year Metro 'All Change' renewal and modernisation programme, plus £230m for operating subsidy for 2010-19.

Nexus split Metro into operations and infrastructure companies. The operating concession, which requires the use of more than 80 cars at peak times, was won by DB Regio Tyne & Wear, commencing commenced on 1 April 2010 for seven years, extendable by two years.

For completion in 2015, the Metrocars are undergoing a 'three-quarter life' refurbishment by Wabtec at Doncaster. This sees a complete rebuild of the vehicle interiors.

Nexus continues to own the Metro and sets fares and services, paying DB Regio a fee related to service quality and revenue protection targets. The Nexus Rail subsidiary's duties include letting contracts covering new communication systems, comprehensive improvements for 45 of the 60 stations, and undertaking a wide ranging overhaul of overhead lines, track and structures. In 2019, the entire fleet is planned to be replaced, as will the signaling.

The Local Transport Plan 2011-21 identifies challenges and opportunities for further changes and improvements, improved integration with other modes; and considers the long term direction - perhaps including further extension of Metro and joint running.

Abbey Line

In October 2009, plans were announced by the Department for Transport and Hertfordshire County Council for the council to lease the 10.5km Watford Junction-St Albans 'Abbey Line' from Network Rail, converting it to light rail.

Presently electrified at 25kV AC, the intention was to offer at least a half hourly service in place of the present 45min frequency. Usage is about 450,000 passengers a year and traffic at intermediate stations is modest.

Issues being discussed included land ownership and responsibilities for maintaining and renewing bridges; fares and ticketing; and depot location, vehicle procurement and infrastructure works.

Extensions into the centres of Watford and/or St Albans could be considered if the scheme proceeds and suitable funding can be found.

Parry People Mover, Stourbridge

Service provision on the 1km Stourbridge Junction-Stourbridge Town National Rail branch is by Pre-Metro Operations Ltd. The company runs Parry People Mover railcars for franchise holder London Midland, employs operating staff and maintains the vehicles.

Two Class-139 PPM-60 units use flywheel stored energy charged by a small Ford engine. The 24 seat (and one wheelchair space) vehicles are 9.6m long and weigh a modest 12.5 tonnes. Carrying capacity is about 60 and they have a maximum speed of 40mph. With a running time of 3min, one train makes six return trips in the hour. Reliability is better than 99pc. Parry People Movers is examining the technical practicalities of doubling the passenger capacity by using a longer bogie vehicle.

UKTram Ltd

UKTram Ltd represents the light-rail industry in dealings with government and statutory bodies in developing a co-ordinated and structured approach to regulation, procurement and standardisation. The company is limited by guarantee and is owned in equal shares by London Bus Services Ltd, the Confederation of Passenger Transport UK, PTEG Ltd (the Passenger Transport Executive Group) and the Light Rapid Transit Forum.

Subjects addressed include the Network Rail interface, tram design standards and accessibility issues, protection and diversion of utilities, operational performance measures, noise and vibration, and traction power supplies.

Light Rail and Metro

Serving the City: a London Underground Hammersmith & City Line train to Hammersmith arrives at Barbican, C Stock Driving Motor No 5525 leading. Brian Morrison

In association with **BOMBARDIER**

A District Line service from Wimbledon to Edgware Road arrives at Southfields on a sweltering 24 May 2012, the C Stock train led by Driving Motor No 5730. Brian Morrison

Transport for London

Finding capacity for four million passengers a day

Transport for London (TfL), created in 2000, is directly accountable to Mayor Boris Johnson, and responsible for implementing the Mayor's transport strategy and managing transport services in various modes across the capital.

Senior personnel
Transport for London

Commissioner Peter Hendy (in photo)
Managing Director, London Underground and London Rail Mike Brown
Managing Director, Finance Steve Allen
Managing Director, Planning Michele Dix

London is growing quickly, with 1.2 million more people living in the capital by 2031, plus a forecast 800,000 new jobs. In the 2011/12 year, the Underground carried 1,171 million people, up from 1,107 million in 2010/11. This was another record figure. Growth in passenger journeys has more than doubled over the past 30 years, with an increase of 52 per cent over the previous 15 years, and 13 per cent over the last five.

London Underground expects demand to reach 1.2bn journeys a year quite soon. Something over four million passengers a day is thus likely to become the norm. This gives an additional urgency to the upgrade programme of replacing life-expired assets with modern technology, which in turn allows capacity to be increased.

TfL companies

Several TfL companies have public transport responsibilities related to rail. London Underground (LU) Ltd is responsible for operating the Underground network and serves 270 stations. Docklands Light Railway (DLR) Ltd owns the land on which the DLR is built and is responsible for the operation of the railway.

Transport Trading Ltd is the holding company for all TfL's operating transport companies, and receives revenues from sales. TfL can only carry out certain activities through a limited liability subsidiary, or a subsidiary which TfL formed alone or with others. Rail for London Ltd (London Rail), Docklands Light Railway Ltd and Crossrail Ltd are three such subsidiaries; others include the London Transport Museum.

London Rail deals with the National Rail network in London and has the main responsibilities of overseeing major new rail projects, including those relating to London Overground; managing the London Rail concession, DLR and Tramlink; supporting and developing Crossrail, and Thameslink improvements.

It also influences and supports National Rail's contribution to an integrated public transport system; works with the Department for Transport and the rail industry to improve National Rail services in London; and liaises with the freight industry to support sustainable movement of goods and promotion of rail freight with respect to London's needs.

Light Rail and Metro

Key statistics
London Underground

	2011/12	2010/11
Passenger journeys (millions)	1,171	1,107
Passenger km (millions)	9,519	8,876
Passenger revenue £m 2011/12 prices)	1,982	1,801
Scheduled service operated	97.0%	95.6%
No of staff (LU)	17,839	n/a
No of staff (Tube Lines)	2,546	n/a

London Underground

London Underground's operational structure is based on the network's lines. The Chief Operating Officer is responsible for the running of the Underground and for nearly 12,000 operational and support staff across the network. The Chief Operating Officer leads a team with Line General Managers responsible for day to day management and performance of their respective lines. The Network Services division aims to deliver long-term improvements to operating performance, while Operational Upgrades staff are the Chief Operating Officer's representatives for all matters affecting the operational railway, to ensure that what is delivered is fit for purpose and that he is ready to accept new assets and systems into use.

LU's fundamental objective is to provide a safe and reliable service. This means assets that consistently perform well, correctly trained staff, and the ability to recover swiftly from delays when they do occur.

This results in challenges, to deliver a safe service day-in, day-out, irrespective of the reliability of ageing and often obsolete assets; to use the investment programme to make good deficiencies in asset quality and to build in sufficient new capacity to meet future demand expectations; and to maintain customer service during the biggest rebuilding programme that the Underground has ever seen.

Table 1 shows the 15 busiest stations on the system, in descending order. The figures represent the annual usage during 2011, being the totals of entry and exit counts taken on different days throughout the year. Passengers interchanging between lines and who thus do not pass through the ticket barriers are excluded.

The total of 821.78m passengers for the top 15 stations in 2011 compares with 768.71 for the top 15 in 2010 and represents a continuing pattern of growth. The 2011 figures were 6.9% higher than the previous year; those for 2012 will include the results of the London 2012 Games.

Of the top 15, Canary Wharf alone has a single Underground line (the DLR station is completely separate); this and Stratford are the only top 15 stations outside the central area.

Thus total usage of all four Piccadilly Line Heathrow airport stations (Table 2), at 16.32 million, is very similar to that of the inner-suburban station of Highbury & Islington, with 16.26 million users. Hatton Cross is used mainly by airport workers. LU services are of course supplemented by the Heathrow Express/Heathrow Connect services to Paddington, but Underground airport traffic is hardly overwhelming.

Peak and off peak

Table 3 sets out the maximum number of trains in service: noticeable is the varying extent to which the numbers required reduce from the Monday to Friday peak to the midday period: overall, 81 per cent are still running. The Saturday service requires slightly more trains but there are reduced operations on Sundays.

Train loadings have thus become more constant, with the variations between peak and off-peak diminishing. Encouraging off peak travel is no longer the solution to capacity problems.

The 12.05 London Overground service from Gospel Oak to Barking arrives at Woodgrange Park on 2 July 2011, formed by Class 172/0 Turbostar No 172003. Waiting at Woodgrange Park Junction on the other side of the bridge is Freightliner Class 66/5 No 66587 hauling an intermodal train to Tilbury. Brian Morrison

Table 1: LU station usage - top 15

Station	millions of passengers, 2011
Waterloo	84.12
Victoria	82.25
King's Cross St Pancras	77.11
Oxford Circus	77.09
London Bridge	65.44
Liverpool Street	63.65
Stratford	48.57
Bank & Monument	47.80
Canary Wharf	46.59
Paddington	46.48
Piccadilly Circus	40.58
Leicester Square	38.78
Bond Street	36.02
Euston	35.32
Holborn	31.98
Total, top 15 stations	**821.78**

(LU station annual usage, 2011)

Table 2: LU passengers at Heathrow

Heathrow Terminals 1,2,3	7.72m
Heathrow Terminal 4	2.46m
Heathrow Terminal 5	3.21m
Hatton Cross	2.93m
Total, LU Heathrow stations	**16.32m**

(LU annual station usage 2011 – millions of passengers)

In association with BOMBARDIER

Where Automatic Train Operation has been introduced, overall journey times have been shortened. This allows the same number of trains to offer a more intensive service. Throughout LU, train formations remain constant for each line.

The Asset Performance team manages the upkeep and repair of the eight lines (including their trains) formerly part of the Metronet Public-Private Partnership (PPP) consortium. The remaining Jubilee, Northern and Piccadilly lines are maintained by the wholly owned Tube Lines subsidiary (formerly a PPP consortium).

Transformation of the Tube

The key elements of the 'Transforming the Tube' programme are to replace most train fleets to increase fleet reliability and capacity; replace signalling assets to reduce service delays and increase network capacity; reduce the backlog of track investment to reduce safety risks and increase capacity by removing speed restrictions; renew infrastructure assets to maintain a safe service, reduce the risks of flooding, and the service limitations caused by speed or weight restrictions; and modernise stations by replacing fire systems, public address, CCTV, and lifts and escalators.

A critical feature of line upgrades is to enable LU to provide capacity for future (or even present) demands. By the end of the current programme, the Underground will have delivered up to an additional 30 per cent capacity. Beyond this, there is a continuous requirement to keep assets in a state of good repair.

Work on this scale inevitably requires some service disruptions. Total blockades are now seen as an efficient way of delivering upgrades while minimising disruption to passengers, and are likely to become more common. Balfour Beatty has a £220m contract lasting until 2016 to carry out track renewal work on the Bakerloo, Central and all sub-surface lines.

LU and Crossrail have awarded a major contract to Otis for the procurement and management of 107 escalators throughout their life. Of these, 50 heavy duty metro-type escalators will be installed on LU over the next 10 years.

LU is ending a Private Finance Initiative contract for operation and maintenance of its high voltage electrical power network, aimed at reducing financing costs.

More trains

The Metropolitan Line ran a full service using the new Bombardier-built 'S8' stock for the first time on 28 July 2012. The first 'S7' train made its debut on the Hammersmith & City service on 6 July. Once complete, the S stock upgrade will have delivered 191 new trains to these, the Circle and the District lines. (S8 and S7 refer to the number of vehicles per train).

The signalling equipment for the whole of the sub-surface railway will eventually be housed in a new service control centre at Hammersmith.

New trains will be needed for the Bakerloo (1972 stock) and Piccadilly Line (1973 stock) and it is intended that these will be to a common design, with bogies shared between cars, allowing for walk-through gangways. Fleet replacement is to be accompanied by installation of moving block signalling. The new trains will

Table 3: LU lines - trains required

Line	AM peak	midday	Saturday	Sunday
Bakerloo	33	29	29	27
Central	77	67	67	58
Circle/Hammersmith & City	32	30	30	30
District	76	59	61	58
Jubilee	57	42	49	41
Metropolitan	49	35	35	35
Northern	91	72	72	72
Piccadilly	79	68	69	68
Victoria	36	30	29	29
Waterloo & City	5	3	3	no service
Total trains	**535**	**435**	**444**	**418**
As index	**100**	**81**	**83**	**78**

(LU maximum number of trains required, 2012)

Light Rail and Metro

be lighter and offer greater passenger capacity; even with air conditioning, they could be 17 per cent more energy-efficient than recent designs.

Platform cooling at Green Park (cool water from boreholes below the park used in platform air cooling units) and Oxford Circus (cooling units using air provided by chilling units of top of an adjacent building) were installed before London 2012.

Ticketing

The fares system on all TfL services is now dominated by the Oyster smartcard, with prepaid credit. Oysters can be loaded with Travelcards, or they can be used on a pay as you go basis.

Cash fares are still available, at typically twice the Oyster levels. Ticket office use by passengers has been falling steadily due mainly to the use of Oyster cards, and ticket office utilisation was reported to have dropped by 28% in the five years to 2011.

London Overground

London Overground services are operated by London Overground Rail Operations Ltd (LOROL) under a concession (not a franchise) until 2014. An extension to 2016 is possible. The company is a 50/50 consortium of the Mass Transit Railway of Hong Kong and Deutsche Bahn. The concession was awarded by Transport for London, and has been presented as a first step in relation to National Rail services around the capital generally. The aim is to offer a similar style of frequency and service quality to that of the Underground. TfL sets fares, procures rolling stock and decides service levels

All electric services operated by London Overground use four-car multiple units. Those requiring dual voltage AC/DC units (Class 378/2) are Stratford-Richmond, plus Willesden Junction-Clapham Junction. Those not requiring an AC capability (Class 378/1), services Highbury & Islington to New Cross, Clapham Junction, West Croydon and Crystal Palace, also Euston to Watford.

The Gospel Oak-Barking line uses Class 172/0 2-car diesel trains.

With East London services extended to from Surrey Quays to Clapham Junction via Peckham Rye in December 2012, the London orbital rail network map is complete. Rapid demand growth has resulted in plans to strengthen trains from four to five cars (from two to three cars on Gospel Oak-Barking). Further infrastructure work would also be needed.

Extensions and improvements

Beyond the current investment programme, crowding on the LU network is likely to remain. Improvement schemes are subject to value for money and feasibility analysis and funding constraints, but several longer-term enhancements and extensions have been proposed by the Mayor.

A Northern Line extension to Battersea, with an intermediate station at Nine Elms, is favoured by the Mayor, starting from Kennington, and funding has been promised by the developers of the Battersea power station site.

Senior personnel
London Overground

Managing Director Steve Murphy (in photo)
Operations Director Stuart Griffin
Fleet Director Peter Daw
Customer Service Director David Wornham
Finance Director Peter Austin
Human Resources Director Darren Hockaday
Concession Director Mark Eaton

Key statistics
London Overground

	2010-11	2011-12
Punctuality (0-5min)	94.8	96.6
Passenger journeys (millions)	53.6	102.6
Passenger km (millions)	606.2	644.9
Timetabled train km (millions)	5.5	7.0
Route km operated	113.1	113.1
Number of stations operated	55	55
Number of employees	1,142	1,171

percentage point change

Northern Line Upgrade 2 would include separation of the Charing Cross and City routes to increase capacity significantly. Various possible destinations have been canvassed for a Bakerloo Line southern extension, but this seems unlikely in the short term.

More generally, the Mayor's planning (as opposed to transport) document says he will work with strategic partners to improve the public transport system, including cross-London and orbital rail links to support development and regeneration priorities.

He will also aim to increase capacity by implementing Crossrail, completing Thameslink, developing Chelsea–Hackney, completing London Underground upgrades, and improving local services on national rail.

National Rail devolution

With a number of National Rail franchises due for re-letting, the Mayor has argued for the devolution of decision making and funding allocation on London's National Rail services to TfL, arguing that London Overground has demonstrated TfL's ability to leverage extra investment, increase service levels and make sizeable gains in passenger satisfaction.

The Mayor said inner-suburban services in new franchises should be specified by TfL to London Overground standards, with all fares within London set by the Mayor.

The complication that London's political boundaries do not match railway geography is addressed by referring to the example of the Metropolitan Line in Buckinghamshire and Hertfordshire, and appealing for a degree of flexibility to ensure the potential of devolution is maximised.

Chelsea-Hackney

Also known as Crossrail 2, the Chelsea-Hackney line is being rethought. Besides the original proposal of Epping via Tottenham Court Road to Wimbledon (cost £12bn-£15bn), alternatives on the same general northeast to southwest axis are now under consideration. Option A is a London focused metro scheme between Seven Sisters and Clapham Junction via Euston and Victoria (£9bn-£11bn).

Option B is a broader regional scheme, with a similar alignment to Option A, but extending onto National Rail routes - perhaps the Lea Valley lines to Cheshunt and 'beyond', and suburban services to Epsom, Chessington, Woking, Shepperton and Twickenham (£13bn-£16bn).

A critical issue is the need for the amendment of route safeguarding by DfT. Construction start in 2023 is postulated (apart from an earlier station box at Euston as part of HS2), with opening in 2033.

Croxley plan

The Croxley rail link will re-route the Watford branch of the Metropolitan Line via a new viaduct to join the disused Croxley Green branch and reach Watford Junction.

Government funding was allocated in December 2011 and a public hearing for a Transport & Works Act order took place in October 2012. The £117m scheme is mainly to be funded by DfT (65 per cent) and Hertfordshire County Council (29pc). Hertfordshire and London Underground are joint promoters.

The new service could become operational in 2016.

London Travelwatch

This statutory consumer body deals with services operated or licenced by TfL, National Rail services in an area somewhat larger than Greater London, Heathrow Express, and Eurostar. It is sponsored and funded by the London Assembly.
www.londontravelwatch.org.uk
Chief Executive: Janet Cooke

Into Europe

In association with
CAF

Into Europe

Italian private high speed operator Nuovo Trasporto Viaggiatori (NTV) started services using Alstom built 187.5mph AGV high speed trains in April 2012. Alstom

An Alstom-built TGV Lyria Euroduplex on the LGV Rhin-Rhône near Mulhouse in July 2012. Alstom

Into Europe

Keith Fender, Europe Editor of Modern Railways magazine, reviews developments on the continent's railways.

The continuing poor economic outlook is set to impact Europe's rail industry in 2013. Reductions in government expenditure have already resulted in passenger service reductions in many EU countries. While long term infrastructure investment in countries such as France, Germany and Switzerland has continued, in others such as Spain it has slowed down. Some major projects, like both Portuguese high speed lines, have been cancelled altogether.

The rail supply industry is experiencing much reduced demand for freight locomotives, although new and replacement wagons continue to be ordered. Orders for passenger trains appear to be slowing - refurbished regional trains are cheaper, and very large orders in several countries are now being delivered (but, in most cases, unlikely to be repeated for years). Some big orders of high speed trains are being manufactured in Germany (Velaro for Germany, Eurostar and Russia; and ICx for Germany), in France (Duplex TGV for French Railways - SNCF), and Italy (Zefiro for Trenitalia). Development of new light rail and metro systems continues in many countries, with renewal of older train fleets also in several cities.

Competition - mixed signals

Despite the country's economic woes, Italian private high speed operator Nuovo Trasporto Viaggiatori (NTV) started services using Alstom built 187.5 mph AGV high speed trains in April 2012. In mid October the company welcomed its millionth passenger and was running 18 trains each way per day on the Salerno-Naples-Rome-Florence-Milan/Venice route, with further services planned as more of its 25 trains are ready for use. In Slovakia the first tendering of regional passenger services resulted in Czech operator RegioJet replacing national operator ZSSK, using leased diesel trains: in the Czech Republic, RegioJet's open access intercity service between Prague and Ostrava, competing with Czech Railways (ČD) since late 2011, has continued to grow, with over 80 per cent occupancy reported: planned expansion has been delayed by non delivery of coaches being built in Romania. Plans for RegioJet to replace ČD as Berlin-Prague Eurocity operator, in conjunction with DB in Germany, have been deferred to December 2013. Competition on the Prague-Ostrava route was scheduled to further increase in December 2012 when a third operator, Leo Express, starts services with a new fleet of three-class Flirt electric multiple-units (EMUs) purpose built by Stadler: as part of its response ČD has ordered seven Viaggio (Railjet) push-pull sets from Siemens (having previously ordered and then cancelled 16 similar sets!).

In Germany, open access operator Hamburg Köln Express (HKX) started services in mid 2012 although another operator (MSM) on the same route delayed launch to 2013. The longer established Vogtlandexpress open-access service (Plauen-Berlin), started by Arriva then operated by Netinera, ceased. In Austria, Salzburg-Vienna Westbahn services, using new Stadler Kiss EMUs, have experienced growth: legal disputes with national operator ÖBB appear resolved. In France, SNCF announced a new budget TGV brand, from April 2013, operating from Paris suburban stations and clearly aimed at attracting budget conscious travellers from low cost airlines.

One of the European Court of Justice's own Advocate General legal advisors in September 2012 questioned the validity of legal action taken by the EC against Germany and Austria, over failure to create independent rail infrastructure management companies: the argument that such separation is required by EU Directive was rejected in the 'non-binding opinion'. The Court of Justice is to make a

165

Into Europe

final judgment in 2013: this will be closely watched in several EU countries where the debate on separation versus 'holding company' continues - most notably in France, where SNCF has lobbied for infrastructure manager RFF to be merged within it (a view the new government is more receptive to than its predecessor).

The EC and many Members of the European Parliament (plus many private rail operators) had argued that the DB / ÖBB style holding company model was not compatible with the directive. The EC was expected to publish proposals for the 'fourth railway package' to extend and consolidate legislation in late 2012 - specifically non-discriminatory access to infrastructure and essential facilities, simplification of cross border vehicle acceptance (safety case) processes, and, most controversially, opening up domestic passenger rail services to competition.

Freight consolidation

Railfreight volumes have continued to increase or at least remain steady in most EU countries: in Germany rail had a 17.7 per cent market share in 2011, and growth from the recessionary lows of 2009 has continued. Freight train noise continues to be a very emotive topic in Germany and Switzerland, and DB has unveiled a range of mitigation measures, aiming to reduce freight train noise by 50pc by 2020. From 2013, track access charge discounts will be available for 'quiet' freight wagons: DB Schenker has started to retrofit all its 60,000 wagons not already fitted with composite 'whisper' brakes rather than cast iron brake blocks, and DB has also developed disc-braked bogies for freight wagons to replace the ubiquitous Y25 design widely used in Europe. Other manufacturers are experimenting with disc-brake-fitted Y25 bogies.

In France, overall, rail freight fell by 4.3pc in 2011: large-scale infrastructure improvement programmes were blamed by operators. The election of the new socialist government encouraged SNCF trade unions to initiate an 'economic warning procedure' which could lead to changes in policy direction: the policy of substantially reducing wagonload traffic is to be challenged by new entrant Régiorail, owned by the US based Railroad Development Corporation and Belgian operator Eurorail. They aim to focus on a wagonload offer for customers currently unable to use Fret SNCF services. The loss of much of the major Gefco contract for transport of new cars to a variety of private operators caused a further drop in Fret SNCF traffic during 2012. The planned acquisition of 75% of Gefco by Russian Railways (RZD) from its owner PSA Peugeot Citroën for a reported Euro 800million could result in RZD's

Siemens announced during 2012 that it would no longer build the Eurorunner ER20 design loco - the new Vectron DE having replaced it. One of the last ER20s to be delivered to Austrian open access freight operator LTE, No 2016 909, is seen passing Hrušovany u Brna in the Czech Republic (on the main line from Brno to Vienna /Bratislava) with a southbound oil train bound for Vienna on 21 June 2012. Keith Fender

Siemens has achieved full approval for its new Vectron family of locos in Poland and Romania. Siemens

'strategic partner' SNCF regaining some traffic: likely to be finalised in early 2013, this is RZD's first significant step into EU logistics.

Governments in several countries have sought to sell all or part of (profitable) rail freight companies, normally to fund other expenditure: in Bulgaria, sale of the rail freight business was planned to finance the rest of the state railway, which has been at risk of bankruptcy for most of 2012; it was cancelled due to lack of bidders although a new attempt to sell is expected in 2013. Privatisation of Georgian Railways was cancelled at an advanced stage, reportedly because of concerns that it could be bought by a foreign operator.

The Spanish government announced major restructuring of the railway industry, with privatisation planned for parts of RENFE in 2013, and regional metre gauge operator FEVE absorbed into RENFE and infrastructure manager ADIF.

A joint Alstom/Eurotunnel test of an Alstom Prima II electric loco in the Channel Tunnel in September 2012 could lead to locos other than Class 92 being used for Chunnel freight traffic; tests earlier in 2012 saw Europorte operating a train of UIC gauge wagons to London for the first time via HS1, regular operation is planned from 2013. Eurotunnel has criticised the decision of RFF in France to levy a Euro 600 security charge on every UK bound freight train.

Infrastructure development variations

Construction of high speed lines in Germany and Spain has continued during 2012; in Spain, despite wide-scale government austerity programmes, Euro 4.7 billion has been assigned to rail infrastructure projects in 2013, most of this (Euro 3.3 billion) going to existing high speed projects. Euro 270m has been assigned to lay 1,435mm / 1,668mm dual-gauge track on existing coastal routes between Barcelona and Valencia. In France, construction of several significant extensions of high-speed lines is under way simultaneously; the Tours-Bordeaux, Le Mans-Rennes and Nîmes-Montpellier lines are all being built under Public Private Partnership-type long-term concessions; extension of LGV Est Européenne to Strasbourg is also under construction. In Sweden, significant sections of new faster line have opened on the west coast route to Boden; new Bombardier built 250km/h Regina EMUs are now entering service on this route.

Years of Austrian infrastructure investment will come together in December 2012 when the last major high-speed section of the Salzburg-Vienna Westbahn opens, with the Lainzer Tunnel under the western suburbs of Vienna and the first stage of the new central station. Construction work for both planned Austrian alpine base tunnels (Semmering and Koralm) is now underway: in neighbouring Switzerland the new Gotthard base tunnel is largely complete.

In the Netherlands, opening of the new Lelystad-Zwolle line in December 2012, was due to lead to a complete re-cast of services to the north of the country as trains to Groningen/Leeuwarden are diverted via this route.

Russia's preparation for the 2014 Winter Olympics in Sochi includes the construction of a new airport line in Sochi that opened in 2012 plus another new 48 km line and the delivery of 38 Siemens built Desiro-Rus EMUs being built in Germany. Plans for a high speed line from Moscow to St Petersburg are still under discussion with central government and this is now unlikely to be built in time for the 2018 FIFA World Cup.

Implementation of the European Train Control System (ETCS) continues, especially on the trans-Europe network defined by the EU. Thales has been particularly successful winning contracts in Denmark (for half the network), Hungary and Slovenia; while an Alstom-led consortium won contracts for rebuilding the only electrified line from Romania to Hungary with ETCS. In Germany the national infrastructure manager, supported by government, has resisted implementation of ETCS on cost and other grounds - despite neighbouring Switzerland and Denmark being committed to full implementation.

Train builders - mixed fortunes

The reduction in orders for freight locomotives has led the German Railway Industry Association (VDB) to call for tax reductions to enable operators to trade in older noisy and polluting diesel locos for new locos meeting modern environmental standards. German diesel loco specialists have been busy fulfilling previous orders (130 Voith Gravita locos for DB Schenker, and Vossloh G6 shunters for several customers), but have smaller order books for 2013 and beyond. Vossloh also builds locos in Albuixech near Valencia and has delivered Euro 3000 and Euro 4000 locos to Israel, plus Euro 4000 locos to Eurotunnel subsidiary Europorte during 2012; the only major order for construction in 2013 is the 15 UKlight Class 68 locos for UK operator DRS.

At the Innotrans trade fair in September 2012 a variety of manufacturers were displaying electric locos fitted with 'last mile' diesel engines - Bombardier Traxx, Siemens Vectron and Stadler electric shunting locos are all now also offered with this capability. Polish manufacturers Pesa and ZNLE have unveiled new 5,600kW electric locos, as competition intensifies for renewal of large fleets in Eastern Europe – both targeting the same market as Siemens and Bombardier. GE unveiled the first of its Powerhaul series designed for Europe, assembled from a kit by Turkish partner company Tülomsas and destined for use in German by Heavy Haul Power International (HHPI).

New electric loco orders are rare, but Siemens achieved full approval for its new Vectron family of locos in Poland and Romania with passenger train testing conducted by PKP Intercity in Poland and ÖBB in Austria during 2012. The first Vectrons built for leasing company Railpool should enter service in 2013. In Russia both Alstom and Siemens working with their local partners (Transmashholding and Sinara respectively) have started deliveries of potentially

Into Europe

New Pesa-built ELF electric multiple-unit at the new Warsaw Stadion station on 14 May 2012. Keith Fender

hundreds of new locos for Russian Railways; over the next two decades around 20,000 new locos are anticipated to be bought in Russia. Ukrainian Railways is also renewing its Soviet era loco fleet and ordered 300 electric locos from Transmashholding: orders for more than another 500 are likely to follow in 2013/14. In autumn 2012 Estonia took delivery of its first DF7G diesel, the first loco imported to an EU state from China.

The success of Polish manufacturers, especially Pesa, in challenging for both diesel multiple-unit train and light rail orders in Germany (building on success in Italy) is a trend that is likely to grow. With the continuing rise in orders for Stadler, which won its first electric multiple-unit (EMU) supply contract from DB in 2011 (along with CAF from Spain and Alstom), Siemens, Bombardier and Alstom now have serious mass market competition from eastern as well as western Europe. Polish rail operators benefited from infrastructure and station upgrades plus many new commuter EMUs for Warsaw, coinciding with the Euro 2012 football tournament.

Siemens has led the industry in choosing to use partners for delivery of major projects, rather than working in consortia demanded by customers or governments as was historically the case. Siemens has sub-contracted Bombardier to build many vehicles and bogies for DB's new ICx high speed train, the new Inspiro metro trains for Warsaw are being mostly built by Newag in Poland, and in Germany Siemens has agreed to bid with Stadler on S-Bahn trains for Berlin when tendered in 2013 - no doubt hoping that German electrical equipment from Siemens, in trains built in Stadler's Berlin factories, will be a successful offering. Siemens announced investments in 2012 to expand the Krefeld (EMU / high speed) and Vienna (Metro and light rail) factories to cope with orders. Hitachi Europe has also started to bid for European projects and is in discussion with DB about EMUs for S-Bahn systems: Hitachi says it would build these trains in the UK.

Light Rail and Metro thrives

Polish manufacturers achieved export success in Germany in 2012, with Solaris selling its Tramino trams to both Braunschweig and Jena. Siemens received the first order for its new Avenio tram design from HTM in The Hague while Bombardier continued to sell its Flexity design to German operators renewing their fleets (such as Essen and Mülheim), and received major orders for the newer Flexity 2 design from Basel in Switzerland, plus Antwerp and Ghent in Belgium. Light rail development

Czech company RegioJet took over operation of some diesel worked regional services from the Slovak Capital during 2012. One of RegioJet's Bombardier Talent DMUs is seen in Bratislava. Keith Fender

in France has continued with the opening of new tramways in Dijon, Brest and Le Havre during 2012, with construction of others proceeding in several cities, all involving fleets of Alstom Citadis trams. Tram-train operation using SNCF operated Citadis Dualis vehicles began in Nantes and Lyon during 2012. The change of French government during 2012 has resulted in the orbital metro plans for the Greater Paris area being re-examined. Planning approval for the extension of automatic Metro Line 14 west of Paris St Lazare was granted in Autumn 2012, on the Paris RER system delivery of 60 new MI09 double deck EMUs for Line A started in 2012.

One item of positive news for Portugal is the Lisbon metro's airport extension opened in 2012: in Spain an entire new airport metro line is under construction in Barcelona. Metro construction in eastern Europe, aided by large-scale EU grants, has continued, in Prague, Budapest, Warsaw, Sofia and Bucharest. Siemens has sold its new Inspiro train to Warsaw for the new Metro Line 2 under construction (the first trains built in Vienna with the majority in Poland by partner Newag). In Sofia, new metro trains built in Russia by Metrovagonmash entered service. In Budapest, 22 Metropolis trains built by Alstom in 2008-10 have finally started entering service after a long running approval and legal dispute. ∎

Directory
The UK Rail Industry in your hands

In association with

ATKINS

360 Vision Technology Ltd
Unit 7, Seymour Court, Runcorn, Cheshire WA7 1SY
T: 0870 903 3601
F: 0870 903 3602
W: www.360visiontechnology.com

3D Laser Mapping
1a Church St, Bingham, Nottingham NG13 8AL
T: 0870 442 9400
F: 0870 121 4605
E: info@3dlasermapping.com
W: www.3dlasermapping.com

3M CPPD
Standard Way, Northallerton, N.Yorks DL6 2XA
T: 01609 780170
F: 01609 777905
W: www.copon.co.uk

3M United Kingdom PLC
3M Centre, Cain Rd, Bracknell, Berks RG12 8HT
T: 01344 858704
E: railsolutions@mmm.com
W: www.3m.co.uk/railsolutions

A Belco Engineering
Jubilee Ind. Est., Ashington, Northumberland NE63 8UG
T: 01670 813275
F: 01670 851141
E: sales@a-belco.co.uk
W: www.a-belco.co.uk

A J Wells & Sons Vitreous Enamellers
Bishop's Way, Newport, IOW PO30 5WS
T: 01983 537766
F: 01983 537788
E: enamel@ajwells.co.uk
W: www.ajwells.com

A N Wallis & Co Ltd
Greasley St, Bulwell, Nottingham NG6 8NG
T: 0115 927 1721
F: 0115 875 6630
E: carl.ford@an-wallis.com
W: www.an-wallis.com

A Plant
See Ashtead

A S Peck Engineering
116 Whitby Rd, Ruislip, Middx HA4 9DR
T: 01895 621398
F: 01895 613761
E: markjones@aspeckeng.co.uk
W: www.aspeckeng.co.uk

Aardvark Site Investigations Ltd
See Screwfast

AATI
See Antislip Antiwear

AB Connectors Ltd
Abercynon, Mountain Ash, Rhondda Cynon Taff CF45 4SF
T: 01443 740331
F: 01443 741676
E: sales@ttabconnectors.com
W: www.ttabconnectors.com

AB Hoses & Fittings Ltd
Units 6-7, Warwick St Ind Est., Chesterfield, Derbys S40 2TT
T: 01246 208831
F: 01246 209302
E: info@abhoses.com
W: www.abhoses.com

ABA Surveying
Lansbury Est., Lower Guildford St, Knaphill, Woking, Surrey GU21 2EP
T: 01483 797111
F: 01483 797211
W: www.abasurveying.co.uk

Abacus Lighting Ltd
Oddicroft Lane, Sutton in Ashfield, Notts NG17 5FT
T: 01623 511111
F: 01623 552133
E: sales@abacuslighting.com
W: www.abacuslighting.com

ABB Ltd
Daresbury Park, Daresbury, Warrington WA4 4BT
T: 01925 741111
F: 01925 741212
E: karen.strong@gb.abb.com
W: www.abb.com/railway

Abbey Pynford Foundation Systems Ltd
Second Floor, Hille House, 132 St Albans Rd, Watford WD24 4AQ
T: 0870 085 8400
F: 0870 085 8401
E: info@abbeypynford.co.uk
W: www.abbeypynford.co.uk

Abbeydale Training Ltd
26 Stonewood Grove, Sheffield S10 5SS
T: 0114 230 4400
E: abbeydale.training@btconnect.com
W: www.abbeydaletraining.co.uk

Abbott Risk Consulting Ltd
10 Greycoat Place, London SW1P 1SB
T: 020 7960 6087
F: 020 7960 6100
E: rail@consultarc.com
W: www.consultarc.com

Abellio
1 Ely Place, 2nd Floor, London EC1N 6RY
T: 020 7430 8270
F: 020 7430 2239
E: info@abellio.com
W: www.abellio.com

ABET Ltd
70 Roding Rd, London Ind. Park, London E6 4LS
T: 020 7473 6910
F: 020 7476 6935
E: sales@abet.ltd.uk
W: www.abetuk.com

Abloy UK
Portobello Works, School St, Willenhall, West Midlands WV13 3PW
T: 01902 364500
E: sales@abloy.co.uk
W: www.abloy.co.uk

ABM Precast Solutions Ltd
Ollerton Rd, Tuxford, Newark, Notts NG22 0PQ
T: 01777 872233
F: 01777 872772
E: precast@abmeurope.com
W: www.abmeurope.co.uk

Abracs Ltd
Glaisdale Rd, Northminster Business Park, Upper Poppleton, York YO26 6QT
T: 01904 789997
F: 01904 789996
E: abracs@abracs.com
W: www.abracs.com

ABS Consulting
EQE House, The Beacons, Warrington Rd, Birchwood, Warrington WA3 6WJ
T: 01925 287300
F: 01925 287301
E: enquiriesuk@absconsulting.com
W: www.eqe.co.uk

Abtus Ltd
Falconer Rd, Haverhill, Suffolk CB9 7XU
T: 01440 702938
F: 01440 702961
E: chris.welsh@abtus.com
W: www.abtus.com

Access IS
18 Suttons Business Park, Reading, Berks RG6 1AZ
T: 0118 966 3333
F: 0118 926 7281
E: carol.harraway@access-is.com
W: www.access-is.com

Accolade Associates
63 Elgar Drove, Shefford, Beds SG17 5RZ
T: 01462 709854
F: 01462 709854
W: www.accoladeassociates.com

Acetech Personnel Ltd
Pembroke House, Pegasus Bus. Park, Castle Donnington, Derby DE74 2TZ
T: 01509 676962
F: 01509 676867
E: rail@acetech.co.uk
W: www.acetech.co.uk

Achilles Information Ltd (Link-Up)
30 Park Gate, Milton Park, Abingdon, Oxon OX14 4SH
T: 01235 820813
F: 01235 838156
E: link-up@achilles.com
W: www.achilles.com

ACIC International Ltd
14 Blacknest Business Park, Blacknest, Nr Alton Hants GU34 4PX
T: 01420 23930
F: 01420 23921
E: sales@acic.co.uk
W: www.acic.co.uk

ACM Bearings Ltd
Derwent Way, Wath West Ind Est, Rotherham, S Yorks S63 6EX
T: 01709 874951
F: 01709 878818
E: sales@acmbearings.co.uk
W: www.acmbearings.co.uk

ACOREL S.A.S
Technopar Pole 2000, 3 Rue Paul Langevin, 07130 St Peray, France
T: 0033 475 405979
F: 0033 475 405771
E: info@acorel.com
W: www.acorel.com

ACT Informatics Ltd
One St Peters Rd, Maidenhead, Berks SL6 1QU
T: 0870 114 9800
F: 0870 114 9801
E: admin@act-consultancy.com

Acumen Design Associates Ltd
1 Sekforde St, Clerkenwell, London EC1R 0BE
T: 020 7107 2900
F: 020 7107 2901
E: info@acumen-da.com
W: www.acumen-da.com

Adaptaflex
Station Rd, Coleshill, Birmingham B46 1HT
T: 01675 468222
F: 01675 464276
E: sales@adaptaflex.co.uk
W: www.adaptaflex.com

ADAS UK Ltd
Woodthorn, Wergs Rd, Wolverhampton WV6 8TQ
T: 01902 754190
E: david.middleditch@adas.co.uk
W: www.adas.co.uk

Adeo Construction Consultants
Unit 16, Oakhurst Business Park, Wilberforce Way, Southwater, Horsham RH13 9RT
T: 01403 821770
F: 01403 733405
E: enquiries@adeo.uk.com
W: www.adeo.uk.com

Adien Ltd
Delta Court, Sky Business Park, Robin Hood Airport, Doncaster DN9 3GB
T: 01302 802200
F: 01302 802201
E: info@adien.com
W: www.adien.com

ADT Fire & Security
Security House, The Summit, Hanworth Rd, Sunbury on Thames TW16 5DB
T: 01932 743229
F: 01932 743047
W: www.tycoint.com

Advance Training & Recruitment Services
2nd Floor, Woodbridge Chambers, 89 Woodbridge Rd, Guildford GU1 4QD
T: 01483 968851
F: 01483 431958
M: 07786 968851
E: info@advance-trs.com
W: www.advance-trs.com

Advanced Handling Ltd
Northfields Ind. Est, Market Deeping, Peterborough PE6 8LD
T: 01778 345365
F: 01778 341654
E: sales@advancedhandling.co.uk
W: www.advancedhandling.co.uk

Advanced Selection Ltd
Cooper House, The Horsefair, Romsey, Hants SO51 8JZ
T: 02380 744455
F: 01794 518549
E: sam@advancedselect.co.uk
W: www.advancedselect.co.uk

Advantage Technical Consulting
See Atkins

Advante Strategic Site Services
4th Floor, Phoenix House, Christopher Martin Rd, Basildon SS14 3HG
T: 01268 280500
F: 01268 293454
E: sales@advante.co.uk
W: www.advante.co.uk

AECOM
AECOM House, 63-77 Victoria St, St Albans, Herts AL1 3ER
T: 01727 535000
F: 01727 535099
E: pippa.baker@aecom.com
W: www.aecom.com

Aedas Group Ltd
5-8 Hardwick St, London EC1R 4RG
T: 020 7837 9789
F: 020 7837 9678
E: london@aedas.com
W: www.aedas.com

AEG Power Solutions Ltd
Vision 25, Electric Ave, Enfield, Middx EN3 7GD
T: 01992 719200
F: 01992 702151
E: kevin.pateman@aegps.com
W: www.aegps.com

Aegis Engineering Systems Ltd
29 Brunel Parkway, Pride Park, Derby DE24 8HR
T: 01332 384302
F: 01332 384307
E: info@aegisengineering.co.uk
W: www.aegisengineering.co.uk

AEI Cables Ltd
Durham Rd, Birtley, Chester-le-Street, Co. Durham DH3 2RA
T: 0191 410 3111
F: 0191 410 8312
E: info@aeicables.co.uk
W: www.aeicables.co.uk

Aerco Ltd
17, Lawson Hunt Ind. Park, Broadbridge Heath, Horsham, W. Sussex RH12 3JR
T: 01403 260206
F: 01403 259760
E: chenderson@aerco.co.uk
W: www.aerco.co.uk

Aerial Facilities Ltd
Aerial House, Asheridge Rd, Chesham, Bucks HP5 2QD
T: 01494 777000
F: 01494 777002
E: sales@aerial.co.uk
W: www.aerialfacilities.com

Aerosystems International
See BAE Systems

AECOM

AECOM offers a one-stop capability in rail planning, engineering and consultancy. We combine integrated services with value for money. Global reach with local knowledge.

AECOM House, 63-77 Victoria Street, St Albans, Herts, AL1 3ER

T: 01727-535000

E: pippa.baker@aecom.com

www.aecom.com

AES
The Old Warehouse, Park St, Worcester WR5 1AA
T: 01905 363520
E: contact@aesco.co.uk
W: www.aesco.co.uk

Agant Ltd
T: 020 8123 9401
E: contactus@agant.com
W: www.agant.com

AGD Equipment Ltd
Avonbrook House, Masons Rd, Stratford upon Avon, Warks CV37 9LQ
T: 01789 292227
F: 01789 268350
E: info@agd-equipment.co.uk
W: www.agd-equipment.co.uk

Aggregate Industries UK Ltd
Bardon Hill, Coalville, Leics LE67 1TL
T: 01530 510066
F: 01530 510123
W: www.aggregate-uk.com

Aggreko
4 Station Court, Girton Rd, Cannock, Staffs WS11 0EJ
T: 08458 247365
F: 01543 437772
E: nrcsales@aggreko.co.uk
W: www.aggreko.co.uk

Agility Trains
7th Floor, 40 Holborn Viaduct, London EC1N 2PB
T: 020 7970 2700
E: enquiries@agilitytrains.com
W: www.agilitytrains.co.uk

Aikona Management Ltd
Windsor House, Lodge Place, Sutton SM1 4AU
T: 020 8770 9393
F: 020 8770 9555
E: training@aikona.com
W: www.aikonatraining.com

Ainscough
Bradley Hall, Bradley Lane, Standish, Lancs WN6 0XQ
T: 01257 473423
F: 01257 473286
E: heavy.cranes@ainscough.co.uk
W: www.ainscough.co.uk

Airdrie Bathgate Rail Link
Network Rail, Buchanan House, 58 Port Dundas Rd, Glasgow G4 0LQ
T: 0141 555 4108
E: info@airdriebathgaterailink.co.uk
W: www.airdriebathgaterailink.co.uk

Airquick (Newark) Ltd
Brunel Business Park, Jessop Close, Newark, Notts NG24 2A
T: 01636 640480
F: 01636 701216
E: info@airquick.co.uk
W: www.airquick.co.uk

Airscrew Ltd
See Ametek

Airtec International Ltd
40, Couper St, Glasgow G4 0DL
T: 0141 552 5591
F: 0141 552 5064
E: akilpatrick@airtecintl.co.uk
W: www.airtecinternational.com

Alan Dick UK Ltd
The Barlands, London Rd, Cheltenham GL52 6UT
T: 01242 518500
F: 01242 510191
E: contact-uk@alandick.com
W: www.alandick.com

Albashaw Ltd (t/a Vacuum Reflex Ltd)
Unit 2, Gamma Terrace, West Rd, Ransomes Euro Park, Ipswich IP3 9SX
E: info@vacuum-reflex.com
W: www.vacuum-reflex.com

Albatros UK
Unit 9, Garamonde Drive, Clarendon Ind Park, Wymbush, Milton Keynes MK8 8DF
T: 01908 305740
F: 01908 577899
E: sales@raildoorsolutions.co.uk
W: www.raildoorsolutions.co.uk

Alcad
1st Floor, Unit 5, Astra Centre, Edinburgh Way, Harlow, Essex CM20 2BN
T: 01279 772555
E: carter.sarah@alcad.com
W: www.alcad.com

Alcoa Fastening Systems (Huck)
Unit 7, Stafford Park 7, Telford TF3 3BQ
T: 01952 204603
E: matthew.dowd@alcoa.com
W: www.afsglobal.net

Alcontrol
Units 7&8, Hawarden Business Park, Manor Rd, Hawarden, Deeside, Cheshire CH5 3LD
T: 01244 528700
F: 01244 528791
W: www.alcontrol.com

Alert Safety Technologies
Nasmyth Buildings, Nasmyth Ave, East Kilbride, Glasgow G75 0QR
T: 01355 272828
F: 01355 272788
E: sales@alertsafety.net
W: www.alertsafety.net

Alfred Bagnall & Sons (North)
6, Manor Lane, Shipley, West Yorks BD18 3RD
T: 01274 714800
F: 01274 530171
E: info@bagnalls.co.uk
W: www.bagnalls.co.uk

The 2013 Modern Railway Directory - The most comprehensive directory of businesses involved in the operation of the UK rail industry

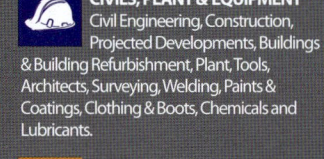

KEY TO SYMBOLS

TRAIN OPERATORS
Passenger and Freight Train Operators, TOC Owning Groups, Railway, Metro and Tramway Operators, Rail Tour Operators, Passenger Transport Authorities/Executives.

ROLLING STOCK MANUFACTURE, SUPPLY AND DELIVERY
Locomotive, Carriage and Wagon Manufacture, Locomotive, Wagon and Coaching Stock Hire, Chartering, Rolling Stock Leasing Companies, Heavy Haulage, Replacement Buses and Vehicle Hire.

CIVILS, PLANT & EQUIPMENT
Civil Engineering, Construction, Projected Developments, Buildings & Building Refurbishment, Plant, Tools, Architects, Surveying, Welding, Paints & Coatings, Clothing & Boots, Chemicals and Lubricants.

INFRASTRUCTURE
Infrastructure Maintenance and Renewal, Workshop Equipment, Carriage Washing, Weighing & Lifting, Fencing & Security, Lighting (except rolling stock), Platforms, Cable Management, Power Supply, Freight Terminals, Car Parking, Cleaning, Grafitti Removal, Pest Control Ticketing, CCTV, Test Facilities, Fares and Collection.

ROLLING STOCK MAINTENANCE/PARTS
Locomotive, Carriage and Wagon Maintenance, Component supply, Lighting and Cabling, Decals and Transfers, De-Icing, Sanding, Upholstery, Disposal, Textiles, Fuel Technology and Carpeting.

CONSULTING
Consultants, Legal Services, Economists, Industry Reporting, Insurance, Accreditation & Compliance, Verification & Validation, Assessment, Test & Development, Systems & Software, IT Services, Data Management, Financial Services, Solutions and Turnkey Providers, Vehicle Acceptance and Project Management.

SIGNAL & TELECOMMUNICATION
S&T Installation and Equipment, Wireless Technology and Datacoms.

PERSONNEL SERVICES, TRAINING & HEALTH
Recruitment and Training Companies/Consultancies, Personnel Supply, Retirement and Convalescence, Training Simulators, Medical Services and Religious/Spiritual support.

INDUSTRY BODIES
Trade Associations, Alliances and Authorities, Advisory Boards, Government Departments, Customer Organisations, Accident Investigators, Campaigning Organisations, Passenger Watchdogs, Trade Unions, Port Authorities and Development Agencies.

MISCELLANEOUS
Conferences & Exhibitions, Catering, Property, Journey Planning, In-Train Entertainment, Photography, Mapping, Lost Property and Video & Film Production.

HITACHI
Inspire the Next

In association with ATKINS

Alfred Mc Alpine Plc
See Carillion

ALH Rail Coatings
Station Rd, Birch Vale, High Peak,
Derbys SK22 1BR
T: 01663 746518
F: 01663 746605
E: help@dowhyperlast.com
W: www.hyperlast.com

All Clothing & Protection Ltd
Units 6&7, Manor Park Ind Est,
Station Rd South, Totton, Hants SO40 9HP
T: 02380 428003
F: 02380 869333
E: sales@allclothing.co.uk
W: www.allclothing.co.uk

Allelys Heavy Haulage
The Slough, Studley,
Warks B80 7EN
T: 01527 857621
F: 01527 857623
E: robert@allelys.co.uk
W: www.allelys.co.uk

Allen & Douglas Corporate Clothing
See Sartoria

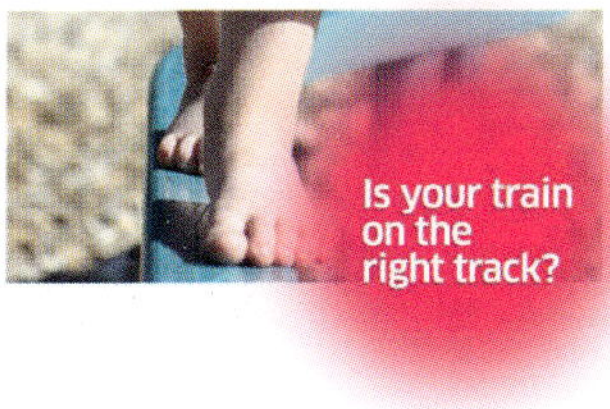

Alcatel-Lucent
Voyager Place, Shoppenhangers Rd,
Maidenhead SL5 2PJ
T: 01628 428221
E: olivier.andre@alcatel-lucent.com
W: www.alcatel-lucent.com/railways

Alliance Rail Holdings
88 The Mount, York YO24 1AR
T: 01904 628904
E: info@alliancerail.co.uk
W: www.alliancerail.co.uk

Alltype Fencing Specialists Ltd
Ye Wentes Wayes, High Rd, Langdon Hills,
Essex SS16 6HY
T: 01268 545192
F: 01268 545260
E: alltypefencing@btinternet.com
W: www.alltypefencing.com

Alpha Adhesives & Sealants Ltd
Llewellyn Close, Sandy Lane Ind. Est.,
Stourport-on-Severn, Worcs DY13 9RH
T: 01299 828626
F: 01299 828666
E: sales@alpha-adhesives.co.uk
W: www.alpha-adhesives.co.uk

Alpha Trains (UK) Ltd
Egginton House, 25-28 Buckingham Gate,
London SW1E 6LD
T: 0207073 9026
F: 0207073 9046
E: info@alphatrains.eu
W: www.alphatrains.eu

Alphatek Hyperformance Coatings Ltd
Head Office & Works, Unit A5, Cuba Ind. Est,
Bolton Rd North, Ramsbottom,
Lancs BL0 0NE
T: 01706 821021
F: 01706 821023
E: railcoatings@alphatek.co.uk
W: www.alphatek.co.uk

Alstom Transport
PO Box 70, Newbold Rd,
Rugby, Warks
CV21 2WR
T: 01788 577111
F: 01788 546440
E: helen.connolly@transport.alstom.com
W: www.transport.alstom.com

Altran Praxis Ltd
2nd Floor, Shaddleton House,
4 Battle Bridge Lane,
London SE1 2HP
T: 020 3117 0880
F: 020 3117 0881
E: info@altran-praxis.com
W: www.altran-praxis.com

Alucast Ltd
Western Way, Wednesbury,
W.Midlands
WS10 7BW
T: 0121 556 6111
F: 0121 556 6111
E: aes@alucast.co.uk
W: www.alucast.co.uk

Ametek Airscrew
111 Windmill Rd,
Sunbury-on-Thames TW16 7EF
T: 01932 765822
F: 01932 761098
E: mail.airscrew@ametek.co.uk
W: www.ametekaerodefense.com

Aluminium Special Projects Ltd (ASP Group)
Unit 39, Second Ave, The Pensnett Estate,
Kingswinford, W.Midlands
DY6 7UW
T: 01384 291900
F: 01384 400344
E: david@aspgroup.co.uk
W: www.aspgroup.co.uk

Aluminium Structures
Unit 5a, Aviation Park,
Flint Rd, Saltney Ferry,
Chester CH4 0GZ
T: 01244 531889
F: 01244 539412
E: info@allystructures.co.uk
W: www.allystructures.co.uk

Amicus
See Unite – The Union

AMOT
Western Way, Bury St Edmunds,
Suffolk IP33 3SZ
T: 01284 762222
F: 01284 760256
E: info@amot.com
W: www.amot.com

Amphenol Ltd
Thanet Way, Whitstable,
Kent CT5 3JF
T: 01227 773200
F: 01227 276571
E: www.amphenol.com

Amalgamated Construction Ltd (AMCO)
Whaley Rd, Barugh, Barnsley, S.Yorks S75 1HT
T: 01226 243413
F: 01226 320202
E: info@amco.co.uk
W: www.amco.co.uk

AMPL Ltd
See Carillion

AMT Sybex Ltd
The Spirella Building, Bridge Rd,
Letchworth Garden City,
Herts SG6 4ET
T: 01462 476400
F: 01462 476401
E: info@amt-sybex.com
W: www.amt-sybex.com

Ambassador Train Travel
PO Box 79, Ventnor PO38 9BP
T: 01983 853708
E: info@ambassadortraintravel.co.uk
W: www.ambassadortraintravel.co.uk

Amber Composites
94 Station Rd, Langley Mill,
Nottingham NG16 4BP
T: 01773 530899
F: 01773 768687
E: sales@ambercomposites.co.uk
W: www.ambercomposites.co.uk

AMCL Systems Engineering Ltd
221 St John St,
Clerkenwell, London EC1V 4LY
T: 020 7688 2561
F: 020 7688 2829
E: sky.crockford@amcl.com
W: www.amcl.com

Ameron UK Ltd
Bankside,
Hull HU5 1SQ
T: 01482 341441
F: 01482 348350
E: sales.uk@ameron-bv.com
W: www.ameron-bv.com

Amery Construction Ltd
Amery House, Thirdway,
Wembley, Middx
HA9 0EL
T: 020 8903 1020
F: 020 8903 1560
E: reception@ameryrail.co.uk
W: www.ameryrail.co.uk

Amey
The Sherard Building, Edmund Halley Rd,
Oxford OX4 4DQ
T: 01865 713100
F: 01865 713357
E: ais@amey.co.uk
W: www.amey.co.uk

Amtrain Midlands Ltd
A38 Southbound, Fradley, Lichfield,
Staffs WS13 8RD
T: 01283 792633
F: 01283 792622
E: info@amtrain.co.uk
W: www.amtrain.co.uk

Anders Elite Ltd
Dashwood House, 69,
Old Broad St,
London EC2M 1NQ
T: 020 7256 5555
F: 020 7256 9898
E: rail@anderselite.com
W: www.anderselite.com

Anderson Precision Gearing Ltd
Flemington Industrial Park,
Motherwell ML1 2NT
T: 01698 260000
F: 01698 252010
E: enquiries@apg-gears.com
W: www.apg-gears.com

Anderton Concrete Products Ltd
Anderton Wharf,
Soot Hill, Anderton,
Northwich,
Cheshire CW9 6AA
T: 01606 79436
F: 01606 871590
E: sales@andertonconcrete.co.uk
W: www.andertonconcrete.co.uk

Andrew Muirhead & Son Ltd
273-289 Dunn St, Glasgow G40 3EA
T: 0141 554 3724
F: 0141 554 3724
E: sales@muirhead.co.uk
W: www.muirhead.co.uk

APB Group Ltd
Ryandra House, Ryandra Business Park,
Cheadle, Stoke-on-Trent ST10 1SR
T: 01538 755377
F: 01538 755010
E: apbgroup@aol.com

APD Communications Ltd
Newlands Centre, Inglemire Lane,
Hull HU6 7TQ
T: 01482 808300
F: 01482 803901
E: info@apdcomms.com
W: www.apdcomms.com

Aperio Ltd
See Fugro Aperio

Apex Cables Ltd
St Johns Rd, Meadowfield Ind Est,
Durham DH7 8RJ
T: 0191 378 7908
F: 0191 378 7809
E: apex@apexcables.co.uk
W: www.apexcables.co.uk

Appleyards Consulting
72, Brighton Rd, Horsham, West Sussex
RH13 5BU
T: 08705 275201
F: 08705 143047
E: mail@appleyards.co.uk
W: www.appleyards.co.uk

Application Solutions (Safety & Security) Ltd
Unit 17, Cliffe Ind. Est, Lewes, E Sussex BN8 6JL
T: 01273 405411
F: 01273 405415
E: contactus@asl-control.co.uk
W: www.asl-control.co.uk

Applied Inspection Ltd
Bridge House, Bond St,
Burton upon Trent
DE14 3RZ
T: 01283 515163
F: 01283 539729
E: ted@appliedinspection.co.uk
W: www.appliedinspection.co.uk

APT Skidata Ltd
The Power House, Chantry Place,
Headstone Lane, Harrow,
Middlesex HA3 6NY
T: 020 8421 2211
F: 020 8428 6622
E: d.murphy@aptskidata.co.uk
W: www.aptcontrols-group.co.uk

Ansaldo STS
8-10 Great George St, London SW1P 3EA
T: 020 7340 6100
E: dcollins@ansaldo-signal.co.uk
W: www.ansaldo-signal.com

Ansec
Ansec Business Park, Burma Rd, Blidworth,
Notts NG21 0RT
T: 01623 491422
F: 01623 798958
W: www.ansecuk.com

Antagrade Electrical Ltd
Victoria Building, Lewin St, Middlewich,
Cheshire CW10 9AT
T: 01606 833299
F: 01606 836959
E: enquiries@antagrade.co.uk
W: www.antagrade.co.uk

Antal International Network
170 Lanark Rd West, Currie,
Edinburgh EH14 5NY
T: 0870 428 1745
F: 0870 428 1745
E: edinburgh@antal.com
W: www.antal.com

Antislip Antiwear Treads Int.
11 Swinbome Drive,
Springwood Ind. Est,
Braintree, Essex, CM7 2YP
T: 01376 346248
F: 01376 348480
E: mgeorge@aati.co.uk
W: www.aati.co.uk

AP Webb Plant Hire Ltd
Common Rd,
Stafford ST16 3DQ
T: 01785 241335
F: 01785 255178
E: mail@apwebbplanthire.co.uk
W: www.apwebbplanthire.co.uk

Anixter (UK) Ltd
Unit A, The Beacons, Warrington Rd, Risley,
Warrington WA3 6GB
T: 0870 242 2822
F: 01925 848006
E: railsales@anixter.com
W: www.anixter.com

Anixter Adhesives
3 Edmund St, Sheffield S2 4EB
T: 0114 275 5884
F: 0114 275 7169
E: enquiries@anixteradhesives.com
W: www.infast.com

Aqua Fabrications Ltd
Belmont House, Garnett Place,
Skelmersdale,
Lancs WN8 9UB
T: 01695 51933
F: 01695 51891
W: www.aquafab.co.uk

Aquarius Railroad Technologies Ltd
Old Slenningford Farm,
Mickley, Ripon,
N Yorks HG4 3JB
T: 01765 635021
F: 01765 635022
E: enquiries@railrover.com
W: www.railrover.com

Arbil Lifting Gear
Providence St, Lye, Stourbridge,
West Midlands DY9 8HS
T: 01384 424006
F: 01384 898814
E: info@arbil.co.uk
W: www.arbil.co.uk

Arcadis UK
10 Furnival St,
London EC4A 1YH
T: 020 7216 1000
E: john.ryder@arcadis-uk.com
W: www.arcadis-uk.com

Archer Signs & Panels Ltd
Unit 6 Daniels Way, Hucknall, Nottingham
NG15 7LL
T: 0115 927 3100
F: 0115 976 1110
E: brian@archersigns.co.uk
W: www.archersigns.co.uk

Areva Risk Management Consulting Ltd
Suite 7, Hitching Court, Abingdon Business Park,
Abingdon, Oxon OX14 1RA
T: 01235 555755
F: 01235 525143
E: abingdon@arevarmc.com
W: www.arevarmc.com

Aries Power Solutions Ltd
Oaklands, Flordon Rd, Creeting St Mary,
Ipswich IP6 8NH
T: 01449 720842
F: 01449 722846
E: john@ariesgen.co.uk
W: www.generating-sets.co.uk

Arlington Fleet Services Ltd
Railway Works, Campbell Rd, Eastleigh,
Hants SO50 5AD
T: 02380 696789
F: 02380 629118
E: info@arlington-fleet.co.uk
W: www.arlington-fleet.co.uk

ARM Engineering
Langstone Technology Park, Langstone Rd,
Havant, Hants PO9 1SA
T: 02392 228228
F: 02392 228229
E: marketing@arm.co.uk
W: www.arm.co.uk

Arriva CrossCountry
See Crosscountry Trains

Arriva plc
1 Admiral Way,
Doxford International Business Park,
Sunderland SR3 3XP
T: 0191 520 4000
F: 0191 520 4001
E: enquiries@arriva.co.uk
W: www.arriva.co.uk

Arriva Trains Wales
St Mary's House, 47 Penarth Rd,
Cardiff CF10 5DJ
T: 0845 606 1660
E: customer.relations@arrivatrainswales.co.uk
W: www.arrivatrainswales.co.uk

Arrow Cleaning & Hygeine Solutions
Rawdon Rd, Moira, Swadlincote,
Derbys DE12 6DA
T: 01283 221044
F: 01283 225731
E: sales@arrowchem.com
W: www.arrowchem.com

Arrowvale Electronics
Arrow Business Park, Shawbank Rd,
Lakeside, Redditch,
Worcs B98 8YN
T: 01527 514151
F: 01527 514321
E: sales@arrowvale.co.uk
W: www.arrowvale.co.uk

Artel Rubber Company
Unit 11, Waterloo Park,
Wellington Rd, Bidford on Avon,
Warks B50 4JH
T: 01789 774099
F: 01789 774599
E: sales@artelrubber.com

Is your train on the right track?

Alcatel-Lucent's Dynamic Communications for Rail keeps your train on track for operational excellence, ensuring on-time, safe and connected journeys.

Learn more, visit
www.alcatel-lucent.com/railways

Alcatel·Lucent

Angel Trains Limited
Portland House
Bressenden Place
London SW1E 5BH
T: +44 20 7592 0500
E: communications@angeltrains.co.uk
www.angeltrains.co.uk

**Rail People
Real Expertise**

angel Trains

Angel Trains Limited
Portland House, Bressenden Place, London
SW1E 5BH
T: 020 7592 0500
F: 020 7592 0520
E: communications@angeltrains.co.uk
W: www.angeltrains.co.uk

Atkins is a leader in the industry, driving transport forward in the UK and overseas.

We use our knowledge and experience to deliver technical excellence to programme and budget.

Our services:

- Multidisciplinary Design Solutions
- Asset Management
- Civil Engineering
- Electrification and Plant
- Fleet Consultancy
- Signalling
- Stations and Property
- Telecommunications

BS11000 Accreditation

rail@atkinsglobal.com
www.atkinsglobal.com

Plan Design Enable

HITACHI
Inspire the Next

Directory

Arthur D Little Ltd
Unit 300, Science Park, Milton Rd, Cambridge CB4 0XL
T: 01223 427100
F: 01223 427101
E: enquiries.uk@adlittle.com
W: www.adl.com

Arthur Flury AG
CH-4543 Deitingen, Switzerland
T: 0041 32613 3366
F: 0041 32613 3368
E: info@aflury.ch
W: www.aflury.ch

Arup
The Arup Campus, Blythe Gate, Blythe Valley Park, Solihull, West Midlands B90 8AE
T: 0121 213 3412
F: 0121 213 3001
E: rail@arup.com
W: www.arup.com/rail

Ashley Group
704 London Rd, North Cheam, Sutton, Surrey SM3 9BY
T: 020 8644 4416
F: 020 8644 4417
E: colin@ashleygroup.co.uk
W: www.ashleygroup.co.uk

Ashtead Plant Hire Co Ltd (APlant)
102 Dalton Ave, Birchwood Park, Birchwood, Warrington WA3 6YE
T: 0870 050 0797
F: 01925 281005
E: enquiries@aplant.com
W: www.aplant.com

Ashurst
Broadwalk House, 5 Appold St, London EC2A 2HA
T: 020 7859 1897
F: 020 7638 1112
W: www.ashurst.com

ASL Contracts
See Pitchmastic

ASLEF
75-77 St Johns St, Clerkenwell, London EC1M 4NN
T: 020 7324 2400
F: 020 7490 8697
E: info@aslef.org.uk
W: www.aslef.org.uk

Aspin Foundations Ltd
The Freight Yard, Hemel Station, London Rd, Hemel Hempstead, Herts HP3 9BE
T: 01442 236507
F: 01442 239096
E: barry.mcmahon@aspingroup.com
W: www.aspingroup.com

Aspire Rail Consultants
See Keltbray Aspire

Asset international Structured Solutions
Stephenson St, Newport NP19 4XH
T: 01633 637505
F: 01633 290519
E: koh@assetint.co.uk
W: www.assetint.co.uk

Asset-Pro Ltd
Concorde House, 24 Cecil Pashley Way, Shoreham Airport, W.Sussex BN43 5FF
T: 0845 120 2046
F: 01444 448071
E: info@asset-pro.com
W: www.asset-pro.com

Associated British Ports
150 Holborn, London EC1N 2LR
T: 0207 430 1177
F: 020 7430 1384
E: pr@abports.co.uk
W: www.abports.co.uk

Associated Rewinds (Ireland) Ltd
Tallaght Business Park, Whitestown, Dublin 24, Ireland
T: 00353 1 452 0033
F: 00353 1 452 0476
E: sales@associatedrewinds.com
W: www.associatedrewinds.com

Associated Train Crew Union
PO Box 647, S72 8XU
T: 01226 716417
E: admin@atcu.org.uk
W: www.atcu.org.uk

Association for Project Management
150 West Wycombe Rd, High Wycombe, Bucks HP12 3AE
T: 01494 460246
F: 01494 528937
E: info@apm.org.uk
W: www.apm.org.uk

ACoRP
Association of Community Rail Partnerships

The Old Water Tower
Huddersfield Railway Station
St. Georges Square
HUDDERSFIELD
HD1 1JF
E: info@acorp.uk.com W: www.acorp.uk.com
'New Life for Local Lines'

Association of Community Rail Partnerships (ACORP)
The Old Water Tower, Huddersfield Railway Station, St Georges Sq, Huddersfield HD1 1JF
T: 01484 847790
F: 01484 847877
E: office@acorp.uk.com
W: www.acorp.uk.com
tel change 9/11

Association of Railway Training Providers (ARTP)
Russell Square House, 10-12 Russell Square, London WC1B 5LF
T: 020 7201 0778
E: info@artp.co.uk
W: www.artp.co.uk

Association of Train Operating Companies (ATOC)
3rd Floor, 40 Bernard St, London WC1N 1BY
T: 020 7841 8000
F: 020 7841 8263
E: enquiry@atoc.org
W: www.atoc.org

AST Recruitment Ltd
Ascot Suite 5, Keys Business Village, Keys Park Rd, Hednesford, Cannock, Staffs WS12 2HA
T: 01543 273850
F: 01543 273851
E: ian.perry@astr.co.uk
W: www.astrecruitment.co.uk

Astrac Safety Training Solutions Ltd
Unit 2, Victoria Rd, Stoke on Trent ST4 2HS
T: 07878 041285
F: 01782 411490
E: train@astractraining.co.uk
W: www.astractraining.co.uk

At Source QX Ltd
18 Eve St, Louth, Lincs LN11 0JJ
T: 01507 604322
F: 01507 608513
E: mick@sourceqx.com
W: www.protecthear.co.uk

ATA Rail
See Catalis

ATEIS UK Ltd
10 Hacche Lane Business Park, Pathfields, South Molton, Devon EX36 3LH
T: 0845 652 1511
F: 0845 652 2527
E: neil.voce@ateis.co.uk
W: www.ateis.co.uk

Atkins
Euston Tower, 286 Euston Road, London NW1 3AT
T: 020 7121 2000
F: 020 7121 2111
E: rail@atkinsglobal.com
W: www.atkinsglobal.com

Atlantic Design Projects Limited
Branch Hill Mews, Branch Hill, London NW3 7LT
T: 020 7435 1777
E: cg@atlanticdesign.uk.com
W: www.atlanticdesign.uk.com

Atlantis International Ltd
See Karcher

Atlas Copco Compressors Ltd
Swallowdale Lane, Hemel Hempstead, Herts HP2 7HA
T: 01442 261201
F: 01442 234791
E: gba.info@uk.atlascopco.com
W: www.atlascopco.co.uk

Atlas Copco Tools
Swallowdale Lane, Hemel Hempstead, Herts HP2 7EA
T: 01442 261202
F: 01442 240596
E: toolsuk_info@uk.atlascopco.com
W: www.atlascopco.com

Atlas Rail Components
3.14 Warwick Mill, Warwick Bridge, Carlisle, Cumbria CA4 8RR
T: 01228 210167
F: 01228 510965
E: rpotter@atlasrail.co.uk
W: www.atlasrail.co.uk

ATOS Origin
4 Triton Square, Regents Place, London NW1 3HG
T: 020 7830 4447
E: ukwebenquiries@atos.net
W: www.atos.net/transport

AUS Ltd
1 Deanne Park Ind Est, Park Mill Way, Clayton West, Huddersfield HD8 9XJ
T: 01484 860575
F: 01484 860576
E: sales@aus.co.uk
W: www.aus.co.uk

Austin Reynolds Signs
Augustine House, Gogmore Lane, Chertsey, Surrey KT16 9AP
T: 01932 568888
F: 01932 566600
E: sales@austinreynolds.co.uk
W: www.austinreynolds.com

Autobuild Ltd
See Pelma Services And Autobuild Ltd

Autoclenz Holdings Plc
Stanhope Rd, Swadlincote, Derbys DE11 9BE
T: 08707 510410
F: 01283 552272
E: sales@autoclenz.co.uk
W: www.autoclenz.co.uk

Autodrain
Wakefield Rd, Rothwell Haigh, Leeds LS26 0SB
T: 0113 205 9332
F: 0113 288 0999
E: mark@autodrain.net
W: www.autodrain.net

Autoglass
1 Priory Business Park, Cardington, Bedford MK44 3US
T: 01234 273636
E: debbie.barnes@autoglass.co.uk
W: www.autoglass.co.uk

Autoglym PSV
Letchworth Garden City, Herts SG6 1LU
T: 01462 677766
F: 01462 686565
E: npro@autoglym.com
W: www.autoglym.com

Autolift GmbH
Mayrwiesstasse 16, 5300 Hallwang - Salzburg
T: 0043 662 450588 11
F: 0043 662 450588 18
E: a.foelsce@autolift.info
W: www.autolift.info

AVE Rail Products
See Compin UK

Avoidatrench Ltd
Brookes Lane, Middlewich, Cheshire CW10 0JQ
T: 01606 831600
F: 01606 831260
W: www.pochins.plc.uk/avoidatrench

Avondale Environmental Services Ltd
Fort Horsted, Primrose Close, Chatham, Kent ME4 6HZ
T: 01634 823200
F: 01634 844485
E: info@avondaleuk.com
W: www.avondaleuk.com

Axiom Rail
Lakeside Business Park, Carolina Way, Doncaster DN4 5PN
T: 0870 140 5000
F: 0870 140 5009
E: sales@axiomrail.com
W: www.axiomrail.com

Axion Technologies
Lokesvej 7-9, 3400 Hilleroed, Denmark
T: 0045 7219 3500
F: 0045 7219 3501
E: info@axiontech.dk
W: www.axiontech.dk

Axis Communications (UK) Ltd
Ground Floor, Gleneagles, Belfry Business Centre, Colonial Way, Watford WD24 4WH
T: 01923 211417
F: 01923 205589
W: www.axis.com/trains

Axminster Carpets Ltd
Woodmead Rd, Axminster, Devon EX13 5PQ
T: 01297 630686
F: 01297 35241
E: sales@axminster-carpets.co.uk
W: www.axminster-carpets.co.uk

Axon Bywater
See Bywater Training

Aztec Chemicals
Gateway, Crewe CW1 6YY
T: 01270 655500
F: 01270 655501
E: info@aztecchemicals.com
W: www.aztecchemicals.com

B3 Cable Solutions
Delaunays House, Delaunays Rd, Blackley, Manchester M9 8FP
T: 0161 740 9151
F: 0161 795 8393
E: info@b3cables.com
W: www.b3cables.com

Babcock Rail
Kintail House, 3 Lister Way, Hamilton International Park, Blantyre G72 0FT
T: 01698 203005
F: 01698 203006
E: shona.jamieson@babcock.co.uk
W: www.babcock.co.uk/rail

Bache Pallets Ltd
Bromley St, Lye, Stourbridge DY9 8HU
T: 01384 897799
F: 01384 410306
E: mike@bache-palletsltd.co.uk
W: www.bache-pallets.co.uk

BAE Systems
Marconi Way, Rochester, Kent ME1 5XX
T: 01634 844400
F: 01634 205100
E: john.hawkins@baesystems.com
W: www.baesystems.com/hybridrive

Bailey Rail
Forder Way, Hampton, Peterborough PE7 8GX
T: 01733 425700
F: 01733 425701
E: andy.holt@baileyrail.co.uk
W: www.baileyrail.co.uk

Baker Bellfield Ltd
Display House, Hortonwood 7, Telford, Shropshire TF1 7GP
T: 01952 677411
F: 01952 670188
E: sales@bakerbellfield.co.uk
W: www.bakerbellfield.co.uk

Bakerail Services
4 Green Lane, Hail Weston, St Neots, Cambs PE19 5JZ
T: 01480 471349
F: 01480 218044
E: info@bakerailservices.co.uk
W: www.bakerailservices.co.uk

Baldwin & Francis Ltd
President Park, President Way, Sheffield S4 7UR
T: 0114 286 6000
F: 0114 286 6059
E: sales@baldwinandfrancis.com
W: www.baldwinandfrancis.com

Balfour Beatty Ground Engineering
Pavilion C2, Ashwood Park, Ashwood Way, Basingstoke, Hants RG23 8BG
T: 01256 366000
F: 01256 366001
E: neil.beresford@bbge.com
W: www.bbge.com

Balfour Beatty Rail
86 Station Road, Redhill, Surrey RH1 1PQ
T: 01737 785000
F: 01737 785100
E: info@bbrail.com
W: www.bbrail.com

Balfour Kilpatrick Ltd
Lumina Building, 40 Ailsie Rd, Hillington Park, Glasgow G52 4RU
T: 0141 880 2001
F: 0141 880 2201
E: enquiry@balfourkilpatrick.com
W: www.balfourkilpatrick.com

Ballast Tools (UK) Ltd
7 Pure Offices, Kembrey Park, Swindon SN2 8BW
T: 01793 697800
F: 01793 527020
E: sales@btukltd.com
W: www.btukltd.com

BAM Nuttall Ltd
St James House, Knoll Rd, Camberley, Surrey GU15 3XW
T: 01276 63484
F: 01276 66060
E: headoffice@bamnuttall.co.uk
W: www.bamnuttall.co.uk

Bam Ritchies
Glasgow Rd, Kilsyth, Glasgow G65 9BL
T: 01236 467000
F: 01236 467030
E: ritchies@bamritchies.co.uk
W: www.bamritchies.co.uk

Bance
Cockrow Hill House, St Mary's Rd, Surbiton, Surrey KT6 5HE
T: 020 8398 7141
F: 020 8398 4765
E: admin@bance.com
W: www.bance.com

Bank of Scotland Corporate
155 Bishopsgate, London EC2M 3YB
T: 020 7012 8001
F: 020 7012 9455
W: www.bankofscotland.co.uk/corporate

Baqus Group Plc
2/3 North Mews, London WC1N 2JP
T: 020 7831 1283
F: 020 7242 9512
E: enquiries@baqus.co.uk
W: www.baqus.co.uk

Barclays
1 Churchill Place, London E14 5HP
T: 020 7116 5214
F: 020 7116 7653
E: rob.riddleston@barclayscorporate.com
W: www.barclays.co.uk/logistics_transport

Barcodes For Business Ltd
Buckland House, 56 Packhorse Rd, Gerrards Cross SL9 8EF
T: 01753 888833
F: 01753 888834
E: info@barcodesforbusiness.co.uk
W: www.barcodesforbusiness.co.uk

Bardon Aggregates
See Aggregate Industries

Barhale Construction Plc
Unit 3, The Orient Centre, Greycaine Rd, Watford, Herts WD24 7JT
T: 0844 736 0090
F: 01923 474501
M: 07939 997529
E: samantha.davis@barhale.co.uk
W: www.barhale.co.uk

Barker Ross Recruitment
24 De Montford St, Leicester LE1 7GB
T: 0800 0288 693
F: 0116 2550 811
E: people@barkerross.co.uk
W: www.barkerross.co.uk

Basic Solutions Ltd
See Lnt Solutions Ltd

BATT Cables
The Belfry, Fraser Rd, Erith, Kent DA8 1QH
T: 01322 441166
F: 01322 440492
E: battindustrial.sales@batt.co.uk
W: www.batt.co.uk

BCM Glass Reinforced Concrete
Unit 22, Civic Industrial Park, Whitchurch, Shropshire SY13 1TT
T: 01948 665321
F: 01948 666381
E: info@bcmgrc.com
W: www.bcmgrc.com/railhome

Beacon Rail Leasing Ltd
Floor 28, 30 St Mary Ave,London EC3A 8BF
T: 020 7015 0030
F: 020 7015 0001
E: rail@beaconrail.com
W: www.beaconrail.com

Beakbane Bellows Ltd
Stourport Rd, Kidderminster, Worcs DY11 7QT
T: 01562 820561
F: 01562 820560
E: amd@beakbane.co.uk
W: www.beakbane.co.uk

Bechtel Ltd
Bechtel House, 245 Hammersmith Rd, Hammersmith, London W6 3DP
T: 020 8846 5111
F: 020 8846 4938
E: jgreen2@bechtel.com
W: www.bechtel.com

Becorit GmbH
PO Box 189, Congleton, Cheshire CW4 7FB
T: 01270 269000
M: 07866 424869
E: becorit@btinternet.com
W: www.becorit.de

Beejay Rail Ltd
79 Charles St, Springburn, Glasgow G21 2PS
T: 0141 553 1133
F: 0141 552 5333
E: info@beejayrewinds.com
W: www.beejayrewinds.com

Belden Solutions
Suite 13, Styal Rd, Manchester M22 5WB
T: 0161 498 3724
F: 0161 498 3762
E: info@belden.com
W: www.belden.com

Bell & Webster Concrete Ltd
Alma Park Rd, Grantham, Lincs NG31 9SE
T: 01476 562277
E: bellandwebster@eleco.com
W: www.eleco.com/bellandwebster

Bender UK Ltd
Low Mill Business Park, Ulverston, Cumbria LA12 9EE
T: 01229 480123
F: 01229 480345
E: info@bender-uk.com
W: www.bender.org.uk

Bentley Systems UK Ltd
North Heath Lane, Horsham, W Sussex RH12 5QE
T: 01403 259511
W: www.bentley.com

Bernstein Ltd
Unit One, Tintagel Way, Westgate, Aldridge, West Midlands WS9 8ER
T: 01922 744999
F: 01922 457555
E: sales@bernstein-ltd.co.uk
W: www.bernstein-ltd.co.uk

Berry Sytems
Springvale Business & Industrial Park, Bilston, Wolverhampton WV14 0QL
T: 01902 491100
F: 01902 494080
E: sales@berrysystems.co.uk
W: www.berrysystems.co.uk

Best Impressions
15 Starfield Rd, London W12 9SN
T: 020 8740 6443
F: 020 8740 9134
E: talk2us@best-impressions.co.uk
W: www.best-impressions.co.uk

Bestchart Ltd
6A, Mays Yard, Down Rd, Horndean, Waterlooville, Hants PO8 0YP
T: 023 9259 7707
F: 023 9259 1700
E: info@bestchart.co.uk
W: www.bestchart.co.uk

Beta Cable Management Systems Ltd
Nothway Lane, Newtown Trading Est, Tewkesbury GL20 8JG
T: 01684 274274
F: 01684 276266
W: www.betacable.com

Bevan Brittan
Fleet Place House, 2 Fleet Place, Holborn Viaduct, London EC4M 7RF
T: 0870 194 7710
F: 0870 194 7800
E: martin.fleetwood@bevanbrittan.com
W: www.bevanbrittan.com

Bewator Ltd
See Siemens

Bex Railstaff Services
Bex House, Crabtree Manorway South, Belvedere, Kent DA17 6BJ
T: 020 8311 2992
F: 020 8311 2303
E: mking@bexplc.com
W: www.bexplc.com

BF Technology Ltd
Unit 6, Cobham Centre, Westmead Industrial Est, Westlea, Swindon SN5 7UJ
T: 01793 498020
E: sales@bftechnology.co.uk
W: www.bftechnology.co.uk

Bideem Rail
Bideem Maintenance, Jubilee House, Jubilee Way, Avonmouth, Bristol BS11 9HU
T: 0117 916 3800
F: 0117 916 3801
W: www.bideem.co.uk

Bierrum International Ltd
Bierrum House, High St, Houghton Regis, Dunstable, Beds LU5 5BJ
T: 01582 845745
F: 01582 845746
E: solutions@bierrum.co.uk
W: www.bierrum.co.uk

Bijur Delimon International
Business Innovation Centre, 1 Electric Ave, Innova Science Park, Enfield EN3 7XU
T: 01992 782415
F: 01992 782425
E: chris.riley@bijurdelimon.co.uk
W: www.bijurdelimon.co.uk

Bingham Rail
Barrow Rd, Wincobank, Sheffield S9 1JZ
T: 0870 774 5422
F: 0870 774 5423
E: info@trainwash.co.uk
W: www.trainwash.co.uk

Bircham Dyson Bell LLP
50 Broadway, London SW1H 0BL
T: 020 7227 7000
F: 020 7222 3480
E: enquirieslondon@bdb-law.co.uk
W: www.bdb-law.co.uk

Birchwood Price Tools
Birch Park, Park Lodge Rd, Giltbrook, Nottingham NG16 2AR
T: 0115 938 9000
F: 0115 938 9010
W: www.birdwoodpricetools.com

Birley Manufacturing Ltd
Birley Vale Ave, Sheffield S12 2AX
T: 0114 280 3200
E: info@birleyml.com
W: www.birleyml.com/rail

Birmingham Centre for Railway Research and Education
University of Birmingham, Gisbert Kapp Building, Edgbaston, Birmingham B15 2TT
F: 0121 414 4291
E: j.grey@bham.ac.uk
W: www.railway.bham.ac.uk or www.rruka.org.uk

Birmingham Centre for Railway Research and Education
Rail Technology Unit, Manchester Metropolitan University, John Dalton Building, Chester St, Manchester M1 5GD
T: 0161 247 6247
F: 0161 247 6840
E: j.grey@bham.ac.uk
W: www.rtu.mmu.ac.uk or rruka.org.uk

Birse Rail Ltd
15th Floor, Lyndon House, 58-62, Hagley Rd, Edgbaston, Birmingham B16 8PE
T: 0121 456 4200
F: 0121 456 3880
E: marketing@birse.co.uk
W: www.birserail.co.uk

Blackpool Transport Services
Rigby Rd, Blackpool,Lancs FY1 5DD
T: 01253 473001
F: 01253 473101
E: enquiries@blackpooltransport.com
W: www.blackpooltransport.com

Blom Aerofilms Ltd
The Astrolabe, Cheddar Business Park, Cheddar, Somerset BS27 3EB
T: 01934 745820
F: 01934 745825
E: uk.info@blomasa.com
W: www.blomasa.com

Blue I UK Ltd
See Peli

BMAC Ltd
Units 13-14, Shepley Ind. Est., South Shepley Road, Audenshaw, Manchester M34 5PW
T: 0161 337 3070
F: 0161 336 5691
E: enquiries@bmac.ltd.uk
W: www.bmac.ltd.uk

HITACHI
Inspire the Next

In association with ATKINS

BMT Fleet Technology Ltd
12 Little Park Farm Rd, Fareham, Hants PO15 7JE
T: 01489 553200
F: 01489 553101
E: uk@fleetech.com
W: www.fleetech.com / www.bmrail.com

BNP Paribas Real Estate
One Redcliff St, Bristol BS1 6NP
T: 0117 984 8480
F: 0117 984 8401
W: www.realestate.bnpparibas.co.uk

BOC
Customer Service Centre, Priestley Rd, Worsley, Manchester M28 2UT
T: 0800 111 333
F: 0800 111 555
E: custserv@boc.com
W: www.bocindustrial.co.uk

Boddingtons Electrical
Prospect House, Queenborough Lane, Great Notley, Essex CM77 7AG
T: 01376 567490
F: 01376 567495
E: info@boddingtons-electrical.com
W: www.boddingtons-electrical.com

Boden Rail Engineering
16 Taplin Close, Holmcroft, Stafford ST16 1NW

Bodycote Materials Testing
See Exova

Bodyguard Workwear Ltd
Adams St, Birmingham B7 4LS
T: 0121 380 1308
E: sales@bodyguardworkwear.co.uk
W: www.bodyguardworkwear.co.uk / www.railclothing.co.uk

Bombardier is a world -leading manufacturer of innovative transportation solutions, from commercial aircraft and business jets to rail transportation equipment, systems and service

Litchurch Lane,
Derby, DE24 8AD
T: 01332 344 666
F: 01332 289 271
www.bombardier.com

BOMBARDIER
the evolution of mobility

Bombardier Transportation UK Ltd
Litchurch Lane, Derby DE24 8AD
T: 01332 344666
F: 01332 289271
W: www.bombardier.com

Bonar Floors Ltd
See Forbo Flooring Ltd

Bond Insurance Services
Salisbury House, 81 High St, Potters Bar, Herts EN6 5AS
T: 01707 291200
F: 01707 291202
W: www.bond-insurance.co.uk

Borders Railway Project
Transport Scotland, 7th Floor, Buchanan House, 58 Port Dundas Rd, Glasgow G4 0HS
T: 0141 272 7100
E: bordersrailway@transportscotland.gsi.gov.uk
W: www.bordersrailway.com

Bosch Security Systems
PO Box 750, Uxbridge, Middx UB9 5ZJ
T: 01895 878088
F: 01895 878089
E: uk.securitysystems@bosch.com
W: www.boschsecurity.co.uk

Bott Ltd
Bude-Stratton Business Park, Bude, Cornwall EX23 8LY
T: 01288 357788
F: 01288 352692
E: i-sales@bottltd.co.uk
W: www.bott-group.com

Bovis Lend Lease Consulting
142 Northolt Rd, Harrow, Middx HA2 0EE
T: 020 8271 8000
F: 020 8271 8026
E: peter.lawrence@eu.bovislendlease.com
W: www.bovislendlease.com

Bowen Projects Ltd
1 Portway Close, Coventry CV4 9UY
T: 02476 695550
F: 02476 695040
E: s.bowen@bowenprojects.co.uk
W: www.bowenprojects.co.uk

Boxwood Ltd
15 Old Bailey, London EC4M 7EF
T: 020 3170 7240
F: 020 3170 7241
E: info@boxwoodgroup.com
W: www.boxwoodgroup.com

Bradgate Containers
Leicester Rd, Shepshed, Leics LE12 9EG
T: 01509 508678
F: 01509 504350
E: sales@bradgate.co.uk
W: www.bradgate.co.uk

Branch Line Society
37 Osberton Place, Hunters Bar, Sheffield S11 8XL
T: 0114 275 2303
E: info@branchline.org.uk
W: www.branchline.org.uk

Brand-Rex Ltd
Specialty Cabling Solutions, West Bridgewater St, Leigh, Lancs WN7 4HB
T: 01942 265500
F: 01942 265576
E: specialty@brand-rex.com
W: www.brand-rex.com

Bratts Ladders
Abbeyfield Rd, Nottingham NG7 2SZ
T: 0115 986 6851/2221
F: 0115 986 1991
E: stephen@brattsladders.com
W: www.brattsladders.co.uk

BRB (Residuary) Ltd
4th Floor, One Kemble St, London WC2B 4AN
T: 020 7904 5026
F: 020 7904 5114
W: www.brb.gov.uk

Brecknell, Willis & Co Ltd
PO Box 10, Chard, Somerset TA20 2DE
T: 01460 64941
F: 01460 66122
E: sales@brecknellwillis.com
W: www.brecknellwillis.com

Bridgeway Consulting Ltd
Bridgeway House, Beeston Business Park, Technology Drive, Beeston, Nottingham NG9 1LA
T: 0115 919 1111
F: 0115 919 1112
E: enquiries@bridgeway-consulting.co.uk
W: www.bridgeway-consulting.co.uk

Bridgezone
22 Lower Town, Sampford Peverell, Tiverton, Devon EX16 7BT
T: 01884 822899
E: info@bridgezoneltd.co.uk
W: www.bridgezoneltd.co.uk

Bright Bond (BAC Group)
Stafford Park 11, Telford, Shropshire TF3 3AY
T: 01952 208524
F: 01952 290325
E: brightbond@bacgroup.com
W: www.brightbond.com

Britannia Washing Systems
See Smith Bros. & Webb

British American Railway Services (BARS)
Stanhope Station, Stanhope, Bishop Auckland, Co Durham DL13 2YS
T: 01388 526203
E: mfairburn@britamrail.com
W: www.rmslocotec.com

British Geological Survey
Kingsley Dunham Centre, Keyworth, Nottingham NG12 5GG
T: 0115 936 3100
F: 0115 936 3200
E: enquiries@bgs.ac.uk
W: www.bgs.ac.uk

British Springs
See GME Springs

British Transport Police (BTP)
25 Camden Rd, London NW1 9LN
T: 020 7830 8800
F: 020 7023 6952
E: first_contact@btp.pnn.police.uk
W: www.btp.police.uk

Briton Fabricators Ltd
Fulwood Rd South, Huthwaite, Sutton-in-Ashfield, Notts NG17 2JW
T: 0115 963 2901
F: 0115 968 0335
E: sales@britonsltd.co.uk
W: www.britonsltd.co.uk

Brixworth Engineering Co Ltd
Cracton Rd, Brixworth, Northampton NN6 9BW
T: 01604 880338
F: 01604 880252
E: sales@benco.co.uk
W: www.benco.co.uk

Broadland Rail
7 York Rd, Woking, Surrey GU22 7XH
T: 01483 725999
W: www.broadlandrail.com

Brockhouse Forgings Ltd
Howard St, West Bromwich, West Midlands B70 0SN
T: 0121 556 1241
F: 0121 502 3076
W: www.brockhouse.co.uk

Brown & Mason Ltd
Schooner Court, Crossways Business Park, Dartford DA2 6QG
T: 01322 277731
F: 01322 284152
E: b&m@brownandmason.ltd.uk
W: www.brownandmason.com

Browse Bion Architectural Signs
Unit 19/20, Lakeside Park, Medway City Est, Rochester, Kent ME2 4LT
T: 01634 710063
F: 01634 290112
E: sales@browsebion.com
W: www.browsebion.com

BRP Ltd
See Keltbray

Brush Barclay
Caledonia Works, West Longlands St, Kilmarnock KA1 2QD
T: 01563 523573
F: 01563 541076
E: sales@brushtraction.com
W: www.brushtraction.com

Brush Traction
PO Box 17, Loughborough, Leics LE11 1HS
T: 01509 617000
F: 01509 617001
E: sales@brushtraction.com
W: www.brushtraction.com

Bruton Knowles
Greybrook House, 28 Brook St, London W1
T: 0845 200 6489
F: 020 7499 8435
E: patrick.downes@brutonknowles.co.uk
W: www.brutonknowles.co.uk

Bryn Thomas Cranes Ltd
421 Chester Rd, Flint CH6 5SE
T: 01352 733984
F: 01352 733990
E: dylan.thomas@brynthomascranes.com
W: www.brynthomascranes.com

BSP Consulting
12 Oxford St, Nottingham NG1 5BG
T: 0115 840 2227
F: 0115 840 2228
E: info@bsp-consulting.co.uk
W: www.bsp-consulting.co.uk

BTMU Capital Corporation
See Beacon Rail

Buck and Hickman
Siskin Parkway East, Middlemarch Business Park, Coventry CV3 4FJ
T: 02476 306444
F: 02476 514214
E: enquiries@buckandhickman.com
W: www.buckandhickman.com

Buckingham Group Contracting Ltd
Silverstone Rd, Stowe, Bucks MK18 5LJ
T: 01280 823355
F: 01280 812830
E: mail@buckinghamgroup.co.uk
W: www.buckinghamgroup.co.uk

Buildbase
Gemini One, 5520 Oxford Business Park, Cowley, Oxford OX4 2LL
T: 01865 871700
E: tony.newcombe@buildbase.co.uk

Bumar SP ZOO
Al Jana Pawla 11, no 11, PL-00-828 Warsaw, Poland
T: 0048 22 311 2512
F: 0048 22 311 2642
E: bumar@bumar.com
W: www.bumar.com

Bupa – Health Care Service Delivery
Battle Bridge House, 300 Grays Inn Rd, London WC1X 8DU
T: 020 7800 6459/0845 600 3476
F: 020 7800 6461
E: lampkine@bupa.com
W: www.bupa.co.uk/business/large-business/occupational-health/railways

Bureau Veritas Weeks
Tower Bridge Court, 224-226 Tower Bridge Rd, London SE1 2TX
T: 020 7550 8900
F: 020 7403 1590
E: transport.logistics@bureauveritas.com
W: www.bureauveritas.com

Burges Salmon LLP
Narrow Quay House, Narrow Quay, Bristol BS1 4AH
T: 0117 939 2000
F: 0117 902 4400
E: email@burges-salmon.com
W: www.burges-salmon.com

Burns Carlton Plc
Simpson House, Windsor Court, Clarence Drive, Harrogate HG1 2PE
T: 01423 792000
F: 01423 792001
E: contactus@burnscarlton.com
W: www.burnscarlton.com

Butler & Young (BYL) Ltd
Unit 3-4 Jansel House, Hitchin Road, Luton LU2 7XH
T: 01582 404 113
F: 01582 483 420
E: debbie.clark@byl.co.uk
W: www.byl.co.uk

Bywater Training Ltd
3 Furtho Manor, Northampton, Old Stratford MK19 6NR
T: 01908 543900
F: 01908 543999
E: sales@bywatertraining.co.uk
W: www.bywatertraining.co.uk

C & S Equipment Ltd
9d Wingbury Courtyard, Leighton Rd, Wingrave HP22 4LW
T: 01296 688500
F: 020 3070 0055
E: info@candsequipment.co.uk
W: www.candsequipment.co.uk

C A P Productions Ltd
The Crescent, Hockley, Birmingham B18 5NL
T: 0121 554 9811
F: 0121 554 3791
E: sales@capproductions.co.uk
W: www.capproductions.co.uk

C Buchanan
See Colin Buchanan

C F Booth Ltd
Armer St, Rotherham, S.Yorks S60 1AF
T: 01709 559198
F: 01709 561859
E: info@cfbooth.com
W: www.cfbooth.com

C P Plus Ltd
10 Flask Walk, Camden, London NW3 1HE
T: 020 7431 4001
F: 020 7435 3280
E: info@cp-plus.co.uk
W: www.cp-plus.co.uk

C Spencer
Mill Lane, Barrow upon Humber DN19 7DB
T: 01469 532266
F: 01469 532233
E: mailbox@cspencerltd.co.uk
W: www.cspencerltd.co.uk

C2C Rail Ltd
2nd Floor, Cutlers Court, 115 Houndsditch, London EC3A 7BR
T: 020 7444 1800
F: 020 7444 1803
E: c2c.customerrelations@nationalexpress.com
W: www.c2c-online.co.uk

C2e Consulting
Ludlow House, The Avenue, Stratford upon Avon, Warks CV37 0RH
M: 07813 616939
E: ed.sharman@c2econsulting.co.uk
W: www.c2econsulting.co.uk

C3S Projects
Canal Mills, Elland Bridge, Elland, Halifax HX5 0SQ
T: 01422 313800
E: info@c3s.com
W: www.c3s.com

C4 Industries Ltd
Unit 3-5, Yardley Rd, Knowsley Ind Park, Kirkby, Liverpool L33 7SS
T: 0151 548 7900
F: 0151 548 7184
E: paul.lighton@c4-industries.com
W: www.c4-industries.com

Cable & Wireless UK
Lakeside House, Cain Rd, Bracknell, Berks RG12 1XL
T: 01908 845000
F: 01344 713961
W: www.cw.com

Cable Detection Ltd
Unit 1, Blythe Park, Sandon Rd, Cresswell, Stoke on Trent ST11 9RD
T: 01782 384630
F: 01782 388048
W: www.cabledetection.co.uk

Cable Management Products Ltd - Thomas & Betts Ltd
CMG House, Station Rd, Coleshill, Birmingham B46 1HT
T: 01675 468 200
F: 01675 464930
E: info@cm-products.com
W: www.cm-products.com

Cablecraft Ltd
Cablecraft House, Unit 3, Circle Business Centre, Blackburn Rd, Houghton Regis, Beds LU5 5DD
T: 01582 606033
F: 01582 475419
E: claire@cablecraft.co.uk
W: www.cablecraft-rail.co.uk

Cabletec ICS Ltd
Sunnyside Rd, Weston Super Mare BS23 3PZ
T: 01934 424900
F: 01934 636632
E: sales@cabletec.com
W: www.cabletec.com

CAF
See Construcciones

CAF

CAF is one of the international market leaders in the design, manufacture, maintenance and supply of equipment and components for railway systems.

Construcciones y Auxiliar de Ferrocarriles (CAF)
A The TechnoCentre, Puma Way, Coventry, CV1 2TT
T +44 2476158195
F +34 914366008
E caf@caf.net

www.caf.net

Calco Services Ltd
Melrose House, 42 Dingwall Rd, Croydon CR0 2NE
T: 020 8655 1600
F: 020 8655 1588
E: careers@calco.co.uk
W: www.calco.co.uk

Calmet Laboratory Services
Hampton House, 1 Vicarage Rd, Hampton Wick, Kingston upon Thames KT1 4EB
T: 0845 658 0770
F: 020 8614 8048
E: sales@lazgill.co.uk
W: www.calmet.co.uk

Campaign for Better Transport
12-18 Hoxton St, London N1 6NG
T: 020 7613 0743
F: 020 7613 5280
E: info@bettertransport.org.uk
W: www.bettertransport.org.uk

Campbell Collins Ltd
Boulton Rd, Pin Green Ind. Area, Stevenage, Herts SG1 4QX
T: 01438 369466
F: 01438 314665
E: sales@camcol.co.uk
W: www.camcol.co.uk

CAN Geotechnical
Smeckley Wood Close, Chesterfield Trading Est., Chesterfield S40 3JW
T: 01246 261111
F: 01246 261626
E: info@can.ltd.uk
W: www.can.ltd.uk

Cannon Technologies Ltd
Head Office, Queensway, Stem Lane, New Milton, Hants BH25 5NU
T: 01425 638148
F: 01425 619276
E: sales@cannontech.co.uk
W: www.cannontech.co.uk

Capita Architecture
90-98 Goswell Rd, London EC1V 7DF
T: 020 7251 6004
F: 020 7253 3568
E: mervyn.franklin@capita.co.uk
W: www.capitaarchitecture.co.uk

Capita Symonds
Capita Symonds House, Wood St, East Grinstead, W. Sussex RH19 1UU
T: 01342 327161
F: 01342 315927
E: john.mayne@capita.co.uk
W: www.capitasymonds.co.uk

Capital Project Consultancy Ltd (CPC)
See CPC

Capital Safety Group
Unit 7, Christleton Court, Manor Park, Runcorn, Cheshire WA7 1ST
T: 01928 571324
F: 01928 571325
E: csgne@csgne.co.uk
W: www.ucsafetysystems.com

Captec Ltd
11 Brunel Way, Segensworth, Fareham, Hants PO15 5TX
T: 01489 866066
F: 01489 866088
E: sales@captec.co.uk
W: www.captec.co.uk

Captrain UK Ltd
Asra House, 2nd Floor, 1 Long Lane, London SE1 4PG
T: 020 7939 1900
F: 020 7939 1901
E: sales@captrain.co.uk
W: www.captrain.co.uk

Cardev International
See Ecolube

Cargo-D Ltd
32 Sydney Rd, Haywards Heath, West Sussex RH16 1QA
T: 01444 300160
F: 0845 051 8771
E: dirk.ottermans@cargo-d.co.uk
W: www.cargo-d.co.uk

Carillion Rail
24 Birch St, Wolverhampton WV1 4HY
T: 01902 422431
F: 01902 316165
E: railenquiries@carillionplc.com
W: www.carillionrail.com

Carlbro Group
See Grontmij

Carlisle Support Services
Wallace House, 4 Falcon Way, Shire Park, Welwyn Garden City AL7 1TW
T: 01707 824200
E: info@carlislesupportservices.com
W: www.carlislesupportservices.com

Carlow Precast Tanks UK Ltd
Gunnery House, The Royal Arsenal, Woolwich, London SE18 6SW
T: 01538 753333
F: 0870 493 1409
E: sales@carlowprecasttanks.com
W: www.carlowprecasttanks.com

Carlton Technologies Ltd
Unit 4, Church View Business Park, Coney Green Rd, Clay Cross, Chesterfield, Derbys S45 9HA
T: 01246 861330
F: 01246 251466
E: sales@carltontech.co.uk
W: www.carltontech.co.uk

Carson Industries Ltd
IDA Industrial Est., Racecourse Rd, Roscommon, Ireland
T: 00353 9066 25922
F: 00353 9066 25921
E: sales@carsoneurope.com
W: www.carsoneurope.com / www.multiduc.com

Carver Engineering Services Ltd
11 Brunel Close, Brunel Ind. Est, Blyth Rd, Harworth, Doncaster DN11 8QA
T: 01302 751900
F: 01302 757026
E: alan@carvereng.co.uk
W: www.carvereng.co.uk

Cass Hayward LLP
York House, Welsh St, Chepstow, Monmouthshire NP16 5UW
T: 01291 626994
F: 01291 626306
E: office@casshayward.com
W: www.casshayward.com

Catalis
See TQ Catalis

Caterpillar (Progress Rail Services)
Eastfield, Peterborough PE1 5NA
T: 01733 583000
E: mcdonald_michael@cat.com
W: www.progressrail.com

Cats Solutions Ltd
Two Rushy Platt, Caen View, Swindon, Wilts SN5 8WQ
T: 01793 432913
F: 01793 490270
E: sales@cats-solutions.co.uk
W: www.cats-solutions.com

CB Frost & Co Ltd
Green St, Digbeth, Birmingham B12 0NE
T: 0121 773 8494
F: 0121 772 3584
E: info@cbfrost-rubber.com
W: www.cbfrost-rubber.com

CB Rail S.a.r.l
6 Rue Jean Monnet, L2180 Luxembourg
T: 07595 123440
F: 020 7158 2701
W: www.cbrail.com

CCD Design and Ergonomics
95 Southwark St, London SE1 0HX
T: 0207 593 2900
F: 020 7593 2909
E: info@ccd.org.uk
W: www.ccd.org.uk

CCL Rail Training
Scope House, Weston Rd, Crewe CW1 6DD
T: 01270 252400
E: info@ccltraining.com
W: www.ccltraining.com

CCP Composites
16/32 Rue Henri Regnault, La Defense 6, 92062 Paris La Defense cedex, France
T: 00331 4796 9850
F: 00331 4796 9986
M: 07896 094628
E: kevin.louis@ccpcomposites.com
W: www.ccpcomposites.com

CDC Draincare Ltd
Unit 1, Chatsworth Ind. Est, Percy St, Leeds LS12 1EL
T: 0845 644 6130
E: enquiries@cdc-draincare.co.uk
W: www.cdc-draincare.co.uk

HITACHI
Inspire the Next

CDL (Collinson Dutton Ltd)
See GHD

CDM-UK
PO Box 7035, Melton Mowbray, Leics LE13 1WG
T: 01664 482486
F: 01664 482487
E: info@cdm-uk.co.uk
W: www.cdm-uk.co.uk

CDS Rail Ltd
1570, Parkway, Solent Business Park, Portsmouth PO15 7AG
T: 01489 571771
F: 01489 571555
E: sales@cdsrail.com
W: www.cdsrail.com

Cembre Ltd
Dunton Park, Kingsbury Rd, Curdworth, Sutton Coldfield B76 9EB
T: 01675 470440
F: 01675 470220
E: sales@cembre.co.uk
W: www.cembre.co.uk

Cemex Rail Products
Aston Church Rd, Washwood Heath, Saltley, Birmingham B8 1QF
T: 0121 327 0844
F: 0121 327 7545
W: www.cemex.co.uk

Centregreat Rail Ltd
Ynys Bridge, Heol yr Ynys, Tongwynlais, Cardiff CF15 7NT
T: 02920 815661
F: 02920 815660
E: rail@centregreat.net
W: www.centregreatrail.co.uk

Centro
Customer Relations, 16 Summer Lane, Birmingham B19 3SD
T: 0121 200 2787
W: www.centro.org.uk

Ch2m Hill
Avon House, Kensington Village, Avonmore Rd, West Kensington, London W14 8TS
T: 020 7471 6100
F: 020 7471 6101
E: sharon.marsh@ch2m.com
W: www.ch2m.com

Charcon
See Aggregate Industries

Charles Endirect Ltd
Wessex Way, Wincanton Business Park, Wincanton, Somerset BA9 9RR
T: 01963 828400
F: 01963 828401
E: info@charlesendirect.com
W: www.charlesendirect.com

Charter Security Plc
Cambridge House, Cambridge Rd, Barking, Essex IG11 8NR
T: 020 7507 7717
E: info@charter-security.co.uk
W: www.charter-security.co.uk

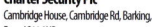

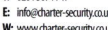

CHB & W Buildings & Railway Contractors
Unit 9, Skein Enterprises, Hodsall St, Sevenoaks, Kent TN15 7LM
T: 01732 824687
F: 01732 823285
E: admin@chbw.co.uk
W: www.chbw.co.uk

Chela Ltd
78 Bilton Way, Enfield, Middx EN3 7LW
T: 020 8805 2150
F: 020 8443 1868
E: tony.philippou@chela.co.uk
W: www.chela.co.uk

Chester le Track Ltd
See The Trainline

Chieftain Trailers Ltd
207 Coalisland Rd, Dungannon, Co Tyrone BT71 4DP
T: 028 8774 7531
F: 028 8774 7530
E: sales@chieftaintrailers.com
W: www.chieftaintrailers.com

Chiltern Railways
2nd Floor, Western House, Rickfords Hill, Aylesbury, Bucks
T: 08456 005165
F: 01296 332126
E: marketing@chilternrailways.co.uk
W: www.chilternrailways.co.uk

Chloride Power Protection
See Emerson Network Power

Chubb Systems Ltd
Shadsworth Rd, Blackburn BB1 2PR
T: 0844 561 1316
F: 01254 667663
E: systems-sales@chubb.co.uk
W: www.chubbsystems.co.uk

Cintec International Ltd
Cintec House, 11 Gold Tops, Newport, S.Wales NP20 4PH
T: 01633 246614
F: 01633 246110
E: johnbrooks@cintec.co.uk
W: www.cintec.co.uk

CIRAS
Block 2, Angel Square, 1 Torrens St, London EC1V 1NY
T: 0800 410 1101
E: info@ciras.org.uk
W: www.ciras.org.uk

CITI
Lovat Bank, Silver St, Newport Pagnell, Bucks MK16 0EJ
T: 01908 283600
F: 01908 283601
E: bdu@citi.co.uk
W: www.citi.co.uk

Cityspace Ltd
Astley House, 33 Notting Hill Gate, London W11 3JQ
T: 020 7313 8400
F: 020 7313 8401
E: enquiries@cityspace.com
W: www.cityspace.com

CJ Architecture
Earl Business Centre, Office 20, E3, Dowry St, Oldham OL8 2PF
T: 0161 620 8834
M: 07845 571351
E: enquiries@cjarchitecture.co.uk
W: www.cjarchitecture.co.uk

CJ Associates Ltd
26 Upper Brook St, London W1K 7QE
T: 020 7529 4900
F: 020 7529 4929
E: nharrison@cjassociates.co.uk
W: www.cjassociates.co.uk

Clancy Docwra
Clare House, Coppermill Lane, Harefield, Middx UB9 6HZ
T: 01895 823711
F: 01895 825263
E: enquiries@theclancygroup.co.uk
W: www.theclancygroup.co.uk

Class 40 Preservation Society
38 Watkins Drive, Prestwich, Manchester M25 0DS
T: 07500 040145
E: chairman@cfps.co.uk
W: www.cfps.co.uk

CLD Fencing Systems
Unit 11, Springvale Business Centre, Millbuck Way, Sandbach, Cheshire CW11 3HY
T: 01270 764751
F: 01270 757503
E: sales@cld-fencing.com
W: www.cld-fencing.com

CLD Services
170 Brooker Rd, Waltham Abbey EN9 1JH
T: 01992 702300
E: contact@cld-services.co.uk
W: www.cld-services.co.uk

Cleartrack
Salcey-EVL Ltd, The Old Woodyard, Forest Rd, Hanslope, Milton Keynes MK19 7DE
T: 01908 516250
E: info@cleartrack.co.uk
W: www.cleartrack.co.uk

Clemtech Rail
9 The Spinney, Parklands Business Pk, Forest Rd, Denmead, Waterlooville, Hants PO7 6AR
T: 0845 223 5303
F: 0845 223 5313
E: rail@clemtech.co.uk
W: www.clemtech.co.uk

Cleshar Contract Services Ltd
Heather Park House, North Circular Rd, Stonebridge, London NW10 7NN
T: 020 8733 8888
F: 020 8733 8899
E: info@cleshar.co.uk
W: www.cleshar.co.uk

Cleveland Bridge Uk
PO Box 27, Yarm Rd, Darlington DL1 4DE
T: 01325 381188
F: 01325 382320
W: www.clevelandbridge.com

Clyde Process Ltd
Carolina Court, Lakeside, Doncaster DN4 5RA
T: 01302 321313
F: 01302 554400
E: dbogovac@clydeprocess.co.uk
W: www.clydeprocess.co.uk

CMCR Ltd
See Survey First Ltd

CMS Cameron McKenna
Mitre House, 160 Aldersgate St, London EC1A 4DD
T: 020 7367 2113
F: 020 7367 2000
E: jonathan.beckitt@cms-cmck.com
W: www.law-now.com

Co Channel Electronics
Victoria Rd, Avonmouth, Bristol BS11 9DB
T: 0117 982 0578
F: 0117 982 6166
E: sales@co-channel.co.uk
W: www.co-channel.co.uk

Cobham Technical Services (ERA Technology Ltd)
Cleeve Rd, Leatherhead, Surrey KT22 7SA
T: 01372 367030
F: 01372 367102
E: era.rail@cobham.com
W: www.cobham.com/technicalservices

COE Ltd
Photon House, Percy St, Leeds LS12 1EG
T: 0113 230 8800
F: 0113 279 9229
E: sales@coe.co.uk
W: www.coe.co.uk

Coffey Geotechnics
Atlantic House, Atlas Business Park, Simonsway, Manchester M22 5PR
T: 0161 499 6800
F: 0161 499 6802
E: julia_cartmell@coffey.com
W: www.coffey.com

COLAS Rail
Dacre House, 19 Dacre Street, London SW1H 0DQ
T: 020 7593 5353
F: 020 7593 5343
E: enquiries@colasrail.co.uk
W: www.colasrail.co.uk

Colin Buchanan
See SKM Colin Buchanan

Collis Engineering Civils Division
Salcombe Rd, Meadow Lane Ind. Est, Alfreton, Derbys DE55 7RG
T: 01773 833255
F: 01773 520693
E: sales@collis.co.uk
W: www.signalhousegroup.co.uk

Collis Engineering Ltd
Salcombe Rd, Meadow Lane Ind. Est, Alfreton, Derbys DE55 7RG
T: 01773 833255
F: 01773 520693
E: sales@collis.co.uk
W: www.collis.co.uk

Comech Metrology Ltd
Castings Rd, Derby DE23 8YL
T: 01332 867700
F: 01332 867707
E: sales@comech.co.uk
W: www.comech.co.uk

Commend UK Ltd
Commend House, Unit 20, M11 Business Link, Parsonage Lane, Stansted, Essex CM24 8GF
T: 01279 872020
F: 01279 814735
M: 07584 474988
E: sales@commend.co.uk
W: www.commend.co.uk

Compass Group
Rivermead, Oxford Rd, Denham, Uxbridge UB9 4BF
T: 01895 554554
F: 01895 554555
W: www.compass-group.co.uk

Compass Performance Software
Loughborough Technology Centre, Epinal Way, Loughborough LE11 3GE
T: 01509 632625
E: enquiries@sis-limited.co.uk
W: www.sis-limited.co.uk

Compass Tours
46 Hallville Rd, Liverpool L18 0HR
T: 0151 722 1147
F: 0151 722 0297
E: info@compasstoursbyrail.co.uk
W: www.compasstoursbyrail.co.uk

Competence Assurance Solutions Ltd
221 St John St, Clerkenwell, London EC1V 4LY
T: 020 7688 2840
F: 020 7688 2829
E: info@casolutions.co.uk
W: www.casolutions.co.uk

Complete Drain Clearance
49 Weeping Cross, Stafford ST17 0DG
T: 01785 665909
F: 01785 664944
E: completedrainclearance@yahoo.co.uk
W: www.completedrainclearance.co.uk

Complus Teltronic
See Commend UK Ltd

Comply Serve Ltd
Number 1, The Courtyard, 707 Warwick Rd, Solihull B91 3DA
T: 0121 711 2185
M: 07547 120619
E: chris.angus@complyserve.com
W: www.complyserve.com

Concept Rail Limited
Unit 5, Hailey Rd, Hailey Rd. Business Park, Erith, Kent DA18 4AA
T: 020 8311 3950
F: 020 8312 2066
E: info@conceptrail.com
W: www.conceptrail.com

Conductix-Wampfler Ltd (Insul 8)
1 Michigan Ave, Salford M50 2GY
T: 0161 848 0161
F: 0161 873 7017
E: info.uk@conductix.co.uk
W: www.conductix.co.uk

Confederation of Passenger Transport UK
Drury House, 34-43 Russell St, London WC2B 5HA
T: 020 7240 3131
F: 020 7240 6565
E: admin@cpt-uk.org
W: www.cpt-uk.org

Consillia Ltd
See Donfabs and Consillia Ltd

Construcciones y Auxiliar de Ferrocarriles SA (CAF)
The TechnoCentre, Puma Way, Coventry CV1 2TT
T: 02476 158195
F: 0034 914 366008
E: caf@caf.net
W: www.caf.net

Containerlift
PO Box 582, Great Dunmow, Essex CM6 3QX
T: 0800 174 546
F: 0800 174 547
E: joostbaker@containerlift.co.uk
W: www.containerlift.com

Continental Contitech
Chestnut Field House, Chestnut Field, Rugby, Warks CV21 2PA
T: 01788 571482
F: 01788 542245
W: www.contitech.co.uk

Cook Rail
See William Cook

Cooper and Turner Ltd
Templeborough Works, Sheffield Rd, Sheffield S9 1RS
T: 0114 256 0057
F: 0114 244 5529
E: sales@cooperandturner.co.uk
W: www.cooperandturner.com

Cooper B-Line
Walrow Ind. Est, Highbridge, Somerset TA9 4AQ
T: 01278 783371
F: 01278 789037
E: sales@cooperbline.co.uk
W: www.cooperbline.co.uk

Cooper Bussmann (UK) Ltd
Burton-on-the-Wolds, Leics LE12 5TH
T: 01509 882600
W: www.cooperbussmann.com

Copon E Wood Ltd
See 3M PPD

Cordek Ltd
Spring Copse Business Park, Slinfold, West Sussex RH13 0SZ
T: 01403 799600
F: 01403 791718
E: sales@cordek.com
W: www.cordek.com

Corehard Ltd
Viewpoint, Babbage Rd, Stevenage, Herts SG1 2EQ
T: 01438 225102
F: 01438 213721
E: info@corehard.com
W: www.corehard.com

Coronet Rail Ltd
See Portec Rail

Corporate College
Derby College, Prince Charles Ave, Derby DE22 4LR
T: 01332 520145
E: enquiries@derby-college.ac.uk
W: www.corporatecollege.co.uk

Correl Rail Ltd
See SGS Correl Rail

Corus Cogifer
See VTS Track Technology

Corus Rail Infrastructure Services
See Tata Steel Products

Corys T.E.S.S
74 Rue des Martyrs, 38027 Grenoble, France
T: 0033 476 288200
F: 0033 476 288211
W: www.corys.com

Cosalt Ltd
Banner House, Greg St, Reddish, Stockport SK5 7BT
T: 0161 429 1100
F: 0161 429 1103
E: graham.robinson@cosalt.com
W: www.cosalt.com

Costain Ltd - Rail Sector
Costain House, Vanwall Business Park, Maidenhead, Berks SL6 4UB
T: 01628 842310
E: gren.edwards@costain.com
W: www.costain.com

Covtec Ltd
Allens West, Eaglescliffe Logistics Centre, Durham Rd, Eaglescliffe, Stockton on Tees TS16 0RW
M: 07776 148839
E: info@covtec.co.uk
W: www.covtec.co.uk

Cowans Sheldon
The Clarke Chapman Group Ltd, PO Box 9, Saltmeadows Rd, Gateshead NE8 1SW
T: 0191 477 2271
F: 0191 477 1009
E: martin.howell@clarkechapman.co.uk
W: www.cowanssheldon.co.uk

Coyle Personnel Plc
Hygeia, 66-68 College Rd, Harrow, Middx HA1 1BE
T: 020 8901 6619
F: 020 8901 6706
M: 07899 074370
E: roger@coyles.co.uk
W: www.coylerail.co.uk

CP Films Solutia (UK) Ltd
13 Acorn Business Centre, Northarbour Rd, Cosham PO6 3TH
T: 02392 219112
F: 02392 219102
W: www.llumar.eu.com

CPC Project Services LLP
5th Floor, Quality House, 6-9 Quality Court, Chancery Lane, London WC2A 1HP
T: 020 7539 4750
F: 020 7539 4751
E: andy.norris@cpcprojectservices.com
W: www.cpcprojectservices.com

Craig & Derricott Ltd
Hall Lane, Walsall Wood, Walsall WS9 9DP
T: 01543 375541
F: 01543 452610
E: sales@craiganderricott.com
W: www.craiganderricott.com

Cranfield University
College Rd, Cranfield, Beds MK43 0AL
T: 01234 750111
E: info@cranfield.ac.uk
W: www.cranfield.ac.uk/soe/rail-investgation

Creactive Design
22 New St, Leamington, Warks CV31 1HP
T: 01926 833113
F: 01926 832788
E: neil@creactive-design.co.uk
W: www.creactive-design.co.uk

Creative Rail Dining
PO Box 10375, Little Waltham, Chelmsford, Essex CM1 9JW
T: 01255 556222
E: graham@creativeraildining.co.uk
W: www.creativeraildining.co.uk

Critical Power Supplies Ltd
Unit F, Howlands Business Park, Thame, Oxon OX9 3GQ
T: 01844 340122
E: sales@critical.co.uk
W: www.criticalpowersupplies.co.uk

Critical Project Resourcing Ltd
6 Blighs Rd, Blighs Meadow, Sevenoaks, Kent TN13 1DA
T: 01732 455300
F: 01732 458447
E: rail@cpresourcing.co.uk
W: www.cpresourcing.co.uk

Cross Services Group
Cross House, Portland Centre, Sutton Rd, St Helens WA9 3DR
T: 01744 458000
F: 01744 458099
E: martindementson@crossgroup.co.uk
W: www.crossgroup.co.uk

CrossCountry
5th Floor, Cannon House, 18 Priory Queensway, Birmingham B4 6BS
T: 0121 200 6000
F: 0121 200 6003
E: richard.gibson@crosscountrytrains.co.uk
W: www.crosscountrytrains.co.uk

Crossrail Ltd
25 Canada Square, Canary Wharf, London E14 5LQ
T: 0845 602 3813
E: helpdesk@crossrail.co.uk
W: www.crossrail.co.uk

Crouch Waterfall & Partners Ltd
Solly's Mill, Mill Lane, Godalming, Surrey GU7 1EY
T: 01483 425314
F: 01483 425814
E: office@cwp.co.uk
W: www.cwp.co.uk

Crowd Dynamics
21 Station Rd West, Oxted, Surrey RH8 9EE
T: 01883 718690
F: 08700 516196
E: enquiries@crowddynamics.com
W: www.crowddynamics.com

Croylek Ltd
23 Ullswater Cres, Coulsdon, Surrey CR5 2UY
T: 020 8668 1481
F: 020 8660 0750
E: sales@croylek.co.uk
W: www.croylek.co.uk

CSC
Royal Pavilion, Wellesley Rd, Aldershot GU11 1PZ
T: 01252 534000
F: 01252 534100
E: uk-consumer@csc.com
W: www.csc.com

CSE International Ltd
Sovereign House, Queensway Court Business Park, Scunthorpe, N.Lincs DN16 1AD
T: 01724 862169
F: 01724 846256
E: info@cse-international.com
W: www.cse-international.com

CSRE Ltd
78 York St, London W1H 1DF
T: 0207 193 7351
F: 0203 514 2989
E: info@csre.co.uk
W: www.csre.co.uk

Cubic Transportation Systems
AFC House, Honeycrock Lane, Salfords, Redhill, Surrey RH1 5LA
T: 01737 782362
F: 01737 789759
E: jennifer.newell@cubic.com
W: www.cubic.com/cts

Cubis Industries
Lurgan, Co Armagh BT66 6LN
T: 0151 548 7900
F: 0151 548 7184
E: info@cubisindustries.com
W: www.cubisindustries.com

Cudis Ltd
Power House, Parker St, Bury BL9 0RJ
T: 0161 765 3000
F: 0161 705 2900
E: sales@cudis.co.uk
W: www.cudis.co.uk

Cummins
Yarm Rd, Darlington DL1 4PW
T: 01327 886464
F: 0870 241 3180
E: cabo.customerassistance@cummins.com
W: www.everytime.cummins.com

Cyril Sweett
60 Grays Inn Rd, London W1X 8AQ
T: 020 7061 9000
F: 020 7430 0603
E: eryl.evans@sweettgroup.com
W: www.sweettgroup.com

D&D Rail Ltd
Time House, Time Square, Basildon, Essex SS14 1DJ
T: 01268 520000
F: 01268 520011
E: info@ddrail.com
W: www.ddrail.com

DAC Ltd
Unit 28, Lomeshaye Business Village, Turner Rd, Nelson, Lancs BB9 7DR
T: 01282 447000
F: 0845 280 1915
E: sales@daclimited.co.uk
W: www.daclimited.co.uk

Dailys UK Ltd
See Novah

Dalkia Rail
5 Limeharbour Court, Limeharbour, London E14 9RH
T: 01784 496200
F: 01784 496222
E: carol.taylor@dalkia.co.uk
W: www.dalkia.co.uk

Dallmeier Electronic UK Ltd
Dallmeier House, 3 Beaufort Trade Park, Pucklechurch, Bristol BS16 9QH
T: 0117 303 9303
F: 0117 303 9302
E: dallmeieruk@dallmeier-electronic.com
W: www.dallmeier-electronic.com

Dartford Composites Ltd
Unit 1, Ness Rd, Erith, Kent DA8 2LD
T: 01322 350097
F: 01322 359438
E: sales@dartfordcomposites.co.uk
W: www.dartfordcomposites.co.uk

Data Display UK Ltd
3 The Meadows, Waterberry Drive, Waterlooville, Hants PO7 7XX
T: 023 9224 7500
F: 023 9224 7519
E: sales@datadisplayuk.com
W: www.datadisplayuk.com

Data Systems & Solutions
See Optimized Systems & Solutions

David Brice Consultancy
11 Sebastian Ave, Shenfield, Brentwood, Essex CM15 8PN
T: 01277 221422
F: 01277 263614
E: davidpbrice@aol.com
W: www.bricerail.co.uk

David Brown Gear Systems Ltd
Park Gear Works, Lockwood, Huddersfield HD4 5DD
T: 01484 465664
F: 01484 465587
E: soldroyd@davidbrown.com
W: www.davidbrown.com

David Simmonds Consultancy
Suite 14, Millers Yard, Mill Lane, Cambridge CB2 1RQ
T: 01223 316098
F: 01223 313893
E: dsc@davidsimmonds.com
W: www.davidsimmonds.com

David Simmonds Consultancy
7-9 North St. David St, Edinburgh EH2 1AW
T: 0131 524 9475

Davis Langdon – an AECOM Company
MidCity Place, 71 High Holborn, London WC1V 6QS
T: 020 7061 7000
E: railways@davislangdon.com
W: www.davislangdon.com/eme

Davis Pneumatic Systems Ltd
Huxley Close, Newnham Ind Est, Plympton, Plymouth PL7 4BQ
T: 01752 336421
F: 01752 345828
E: sales@davispneumatic.co.uk
W: www.davispneumatic.co.uk

DB Schenker
Lakeside Business Park, Carolina Way, Doncaster DN4 5PN
F: 0870 140 5000
W: www.rail.dbschenker.com

dBD Communications
4 Furlongs, Basildon, Essex SS16 4BW
T: 01268 449871
F: 01268 442390
E: npurcell@dbdcom.co.uk
W: www.dbdcom.co.uk

In association with ATKINS

DBK Technitherm Ltd
Unit 11, Llantrisant Business Park,
Llantrisant CF72 8LF
T: 01443 237927
F: 01443 237867
E: dbk@dbkt.co.uk
W: www.dbktechnitherm.ltd.co.uk

DC Airco
Flemingstraat 17, 1704 SI Heerhugowaard,
Netherlands
T: 0031 72533 6540
F: 0031 72533 9393
E: info@dcairco.com
W: www.dcairco.com

DCA Design International
19, Church St, Warwick CV34 4AB
T: 01926 499461
F: 01926 401134
E: transport@dca-design.com
W: www.dcatransport.co.uk

DCA For transport design

Everyday over a quarter of a million people worldwide complete journeys using our designs by road, air and rail.

Can we help solve your transport design issues?

19 Church Street Warwick CV34 4AB
T +44 (0)1926 499461
E transport@dca-design.com
W www.dcatransport.com

Dean & Dyball Rail Ltd
Unit 8,
Viewpoint Office Village,
Babbage Rd, Stevenage SG1 2EQ
T: 01438 765360
F: 01438 765361
E: enquiries@deandyball.co.uk
W: www.deandyball.co.uk

Dedicated Micros
1200 Unit,
Daresbury Park,
Daresbury,
Warrington WA4 4HS
T: 0845 600 9500
F: 0845 600 9504
E: customerservices@dmicros.com
W: www.dedicatedmicros.com/uk

DEG Signal Ltd
Aspect House, Crusader Park,
Warminster,
Wilts BA12 8BT
T: 01985 212020
F: 01985 212053
E: info@degsignal.co.uk
W: www.degsignal.co.uk

Delimon Denco Lubrication
See Bijur Delimon International

Dellner Couplers UK Ltd
Heathcote Rd,
Swadlincote,
Derbys DE11 9DX
T: 01283 221122
F: info@dellner.com
W: www.dellner.com

Delta Rail Group Ltd
Hudson House,
2 Hudson Way,
Pride Park,
Derby DE24 8HS
T: 01332 221 000
F: 01332 221 008
E: enquiries@deltarail.com
W: www.deltarail.com

Deltix Transport Consulting
4 Church Hill Drive,
Edinburgh EH10 4BT
T: 0131 447 7764
M: 07917 877 319
E: david@deltix.co.uk
W: www.deltix.co.uk

Deltone Training Consultants
Ground Floor, 42-48 High Rd, South Woodford,
London E18 2QL
T: 020 8532 2208
F: 020 8532 2206
E: sales@deltonetraining.com
W: www.deltonetraining.com

Demco
Heyford Close, Aldermans Green Ind. Est.,
Coventry CV2 2GB
T: 02476 602323
F: 02476 602116
E: info@mgs.co.uk
W: www.demco.co.uk

Denton Wilde Sapte
One Fleet Place, London EC4M 7WS
T: 020 7242 1212
F: 020 7246 7777
E: info@dentonwildesapte.com
W: www.dentonwildesapte.com

Det Norske Veritas
See DNV

Deuta-Werke GmbH
Paffrather Str. 140,
D-51465 Bergisch Gladbach,
Germany
T: 0049 2202 958 100
F: 0049 2202 958 145
E: support@deuta.de
W: www.deuta.de

Deutsche Bahn UK
DB Vertrieb GmbH,
Suite 6/7, The Sanctuary,
23 Oakhill Grove, Surbiton,
Surrey KT6 6DU
W: www.bahn.co.uk

Deutz AG UK & Ireland
Unit 3, Willow Park,
Burdock Close, Cannock,
Staffs WS11 7FQ
T: 01543 438900
F: 01543 438932
E: admin.uk@deutz.com
W: www.deutzuk.com / www.deutz.driven.co.uk

Software and technology for the rail industry.

DeltaRail

Signalling Control Systems
Operational Software
Asset Management

Hudson House
2, Hudson Way
Pride Park
DERBY
DE24 8HS

Tel: 01332 221000
Fax: 01332 221008

e-mail: enquiries@deltarail.com
website: www.deltarail.com

Department for Transport
Great Minster House, 76 Marsham St, London
SW1P 4DR
T: 020 7944 5409
F: 020 7944 2158
E: fax9643@dft.gsi.gov.uk
W: www.dft.gov.uk

Depot Rail ltd
Mercury House, Willoughton Drive,
Gainsborough, Lincs DN21 1DY
T: 01427 619512
F: 01427 619501
E: sales@drail.co.uk
W: www.depotrail.com

Derby & Derbyshire Rail Forum
Saxon Rise, Friar Gate, Derby DE1 1XD
T: 01332 642395
F: 01332 225408
M: 07812 300067
E: debbie.cook@derby.gov.uk
W: www.derbyrailforum.org.uk

Derby Engineering Unit Ltd
Unit 22, Riverside Park, East Service Rd,
Raynesway, Derby DE21 7RW
T: 01332 660364
F: 01332 675191
E: enquiries@derbyengineeringunit.co.uk
W: www.derbyengineeringunit.co.uk

Design & Projects Int Ltd
2 Manor Farm,
Flexford Rd,
North Baddesley,
Hants SO52 9FD
T: 02380 277910
F: 02380 277920
E: colin.brooks@designandprojects.net
W: www.railwaymaintenance.com

Design Triangle Ltd
The Maltings, Burwell,
Cambridge CB25 0HB
T: 01638 743070
F: 01638 743493
E: mail@designtriangle.co.uk
W: www.designtriangle.co.uk

Det Norske Veritas
See DNV

DIEM Ltd
Merseyside Office, 11 Jubilee Rd, Formby,
Merseyside L37 2HN
T: 01704 870461
M: 07737 194686
E: davidinman@diemltd.co.uk
W: www.diemltd.co.uk

Diesel Trains Ltd
Great Minster House, 76 Marsham St,
London SW1P 4DR
T: 020 7944 5409
F: 020 7944 2158
W: www.dft.gov.uk

Difuria Ltd
Wood Lane, Beckingham, Doncaster
DN10 4NR
T: 01427 848712
F: 01427 848056
W: www.difuria.co.uk

Dilax Systems Ltd
3 Calico House, Plantation Wharf,
London SW11 3TN
T: 020 7326 9821
F: 020 7223 2011
E: nigel.fountain@dilax.com
W: www.dilax.co.uk

Direct Link North
56 Beverley Gardens, Wembley, Middx
HA9 9QZ
T: 020 8908 0638
E: keith.gerry@virgin.net
W: www.directlinknorth.com

Direct Rail Services (DRS)
Kingmoor Depot, Etterby Rd, Carlisle CA3 9NZ
T: 01228 406600
F: 01228 406601
E: enquiries@drsl.co.uk
W: www.directrailservices.com

Direct Track Solutions Ltd
Unit C, Midland Place, Midland Way,
Barlborough Links, Barlborough,
Chesterfield S43 4FR
T: 01246 810198
F: 01246 570926
E: info@directtracksolutions.co.uk
W: www.directtracksolutions.co.uk

Directly Operated Railways
4th Floor, One Kemble St,
London WC2B 4AN
T: 020 7904 5043
E: enquiries@directlyoperatedrailways.co.uk
W: www.directlyoperatedrailways.co.uk

Discover LEDs
PO Box 222, Evesham,
Worcs WR11 4WT
T: 0844 578 3000
F: 0844 578 1111
E: sales@mobilecentre.co.uk
W: www.mobilecentre.co.uk

DIAMOND POINT INTERNATIONAL

25 years' experience building **Rugged computers** to Rail industry standards to EN50155, EN50121, RIA12/18. Trackside, on train, under train, WiFi, 3G, Streaming video, Data acquisition and control.

A: Suite 13, Ashford House, Beaufort Court
Sir Thomas Longley Road, Rochester ME2 4FA
T: +44 (0) 1634 300900
E: john.vaines@dpie.com

www.dpie.com

Diamond Point
Suite 13, Ashford House, Beaufort Court, Sir
Thomas Longley Rd, Rochester ME2 4FA
T: 01634 300900
F: 01634 722398
E: john.vaines@dpie.com
W: www.dpie.com

Discovery Drilling Ltd
32 West Station Yard, Maldon,
Essex CM9 6TS
T: 01621 851300
F: 01621 851305
E: enquiries@discoverydrilling.co.uk
W: www.discoverydrilling.co.uk

DLA Piper UK LLP
Princes Exchange,
Princes Square,
Leeds LS1 4BY
T: 0113 369 2468
F: 0113 369 2999
E: neil.mclean@dlapiper.com
W: www.dlapiper.com

DMC Group
Unit 17,
The Capstan Centre,
Thurrock Park Way,
Tilbury,
Essex RM18 7HH
T: 01375 845070
F: 01375 841333
E: office@dmccontracts.co.uk
W: www.dmccontracts.co.uk

DML Group
See Babcock

<image: DILAX pedestrians>

DILAX is your partner for fully automated people counting and passenger counting systems. Our priority is on customer satisfaction, which is based on far more than the sum of the individual parts.

A: Dilax Systems UK Ltd, 3 Calico House
Plantation Wharf, London SW11 3TN
T: 0207 326 9821
F: 0207 223 2011
E: nigel.fountain@dilax.com

www.dilax.co.uk

Direct Link North

Britain's affordable High Speed Passenger and Fast Freight Railway for the 21st Century

Contact Keith Gerry (Bsc, CEng, CMILT)
56 Beverley Gardens, Wembley,
Middlesex HA9 9QZ
T: 020 8908 0638
E: keith.gerry@virgin.net
W: www.directlinknorth.com

DMS Technologies
Belbin's Business Park, Cupernham Lane,
Romsey, Hants SO51 7JF
T: 01794 525463
F: 01794 525450
E: info@dmstech.co.uk
W: www.dmstech.co.uk

DNH WW Ltd
31 Clarke Rd, Mount Farm, Bletchley,
Milton Keynes MK1 1LG
T: 01908 275000
F: 01908 275100
E: dnh@dnh.co.uk
W: www.dnh.co.uk

DNV (Det Norske Veritas)
Palace House, 3 Cathedral St, London SE1 9DE
T: 020 7716 6593
F: 020 7716 6738
E: david.salmon@dnv.com
W: www.dnv.com

Docklands Light Railway
Castor Lane, Poplar, London E14 0DX
T: 020 7363 9898
F: 020 7363 9708
E: enquire@tfl.gov.uk
W: www.dlr.co.uk

Docmate Services Ltd
15 Millside Rd, Petercultter,
Aberdeen AB14 0WE
T: 01224 732780
F: 01224 732780
E: info@docmates.co.uk
W: www.docmates.co.uk

Dold Industries Ltd
11 Hamberts Rd, Blackall Ind Est,
South Woodham Ferrers, Essex CM3 5UW
T: 01245 324432
F: 01245 325570
E: admin@dold.com
W: www.dold.co.uk

Domnick Hunter Industrial Operations
Dukesway, Team Valley Trading Est.,
Gateshead, Tyne & Wear NE11 0PZ
T: 0191 402 9000
F: 0191 482 6296
E: dhindsales@parker.com
W: www.domnickhunter.com

Donaldson Associates
Eastfield, Church St, Uttoxeter, Staffs ST14 8AA
T: 01889 563680
F: 01889 562586
E: tunnels@donaldsonassociates.com
W: www.donaldsonassociates.com

Donfabs and Consillia Ltd
The Old Iron Warehouse, The Wharf, Shardlow,
Derby DE72 2GH
T: 01332 792483
F: 01332 799209
E: ian.moss@consillia.com
W: www.trackgeometry.co.uk

Donyal Engineering Ltd
Hobsin Ind Est, Burnopfield,
Newcastle upon Tyne NE16 6EA
T: 01207 270909
F: 01207 270333
E: mike@donyal.co.uk
W: www.donyal.co.uk

Dorman
Wennington Rd, Southport, Merseyside
PR9 7TN
T: 01704 518000
F: 01704 518001
E: info@dorman.co.uk
W: www.dorman.co.uk

Dow Hyperlast
Station Rd, Birch Vale, High Peak SK22 1BR
T: 01663 746518
F: 01663 746605
W: www.dowhyperlast.com

DP Consulting
Unit 4, Tygan House,
The Broadway, Cheam,
Surrey
T: 0845 094 2380
F: 0700 341 8557
E: info@dpconsulting.org.uk
W: www.dpconsulting.org.uk

DPSS Cabling Services Ltd
Unit 16, Chiltern Business Village,
Arundel Rd, Uxbridge UB2 2SN
T: 01895 251010
F: 01895 813133
E: airon.duke@dpsscabling.co.uk
W: www.dpsscabling.co.uk

DRail
See Depot Rail

Drum Cussac
8 Hill St, St. Helier,
Jersey JE4 9XB
T: 0870 429 6944
E: risk@drum-cussac.com
W: www.drum-cussac.com

Dual Inventive
27 Royal Scot Rd, Pride Park,
Derby DE24 8AJ
T: 01332 346026
E: info@dualinventive.com
W: www.dualinventive.com

DuPont (UK) Ltd
Wedgwood Way, Stevenage, Herts SG1 4QN
T: 01438 734061
F: 01438 734836
W: www.rail.dupont.com

The UK's leading designer and supplier of LED signalling to Network Rail

**Wennington Road,
Southport, Merseyside
PR9 7TN**

T: +44 (0) 1704 518000
F: +44 (0) 1704 518001
E: info@dorman.co.uk
W: www.dorman.co.uk

DORMAN

Dura Composites
Unit 14, Telford Rd, Clacton-on-Sea,
Essex CO15 4LP
T: 01255 423601
F: 01255 435426
E: info@duracomposites.com
W: www.duracomposites.com

Durapipe
Walsall Rd, Norton Canes, Cannock,
Staffs WS11 9NS
T: 01543 279909
E: enquiries@durapipe.co.uk
W: www.durapipe.co.uk

Dyer & Butler Ltd
Mead House, Station Rd, Nursling,
Southampton SO16 0AH
T: 02380 742222
F: 02380 742200
E: enquiries@dyerandbutler.co.uk
W: www.dyerandbutler.co.uk

Dyer Engineering Ltd
Solution House, Unit 3,
Morrison & Busty North Ind Est,
Annfield Plain, Stanley, Co Durham DH9 7RU
T: 01207 234315
F: 01207 282834
E: paul.dyer@dyer.co.uk
W: www.dyer.co.uk

Dynex Semiconductor Ltd
Doddington Rd, Lincoln LN6 3LF
T: 01522 500500
F: 01522 500020
E: power_solutions@dynexsemi.com
W: www.dynexsemi.com

Dywidag-Systems International Ltd
Northfield Rd, Southam, Warks CV47 0FG
T: 01926 813980
F: 01926 813817
E: sales@dywidag.co.uk
W: www.dywidag-systems.co.uk

E A Technology
Capenhurst Technology Park, Capenhurst,
Chester CH1 6ES
T: 0151 339 4181
F: 0151 347 2404
E: john.hartford@eatechnology.com
W: www.eatechnology.com

E C Harris
ECHQ, 34 York Way,
London N1 9AB
T: 020 7812 2000
F: 020 7812 2001
W: www.echarris.com

Eagle Pest Control Services UK Ltd
1 King Alfred Way, Cheltenham GL52 6QP
T: 01242 696969
F: 01242 696970
E: sales.eagle@mitie.co.uk
W: www.epest.demon.co.uk

EAO Ltd
Highland House, Albert Drive,
Burgess Hill RH15 9TN
T: 01444 236000
F: 01444 236641
E: sales.euk@eao.com
W: www.eao.com

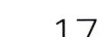

HITACHI Inspire the Next

175

Directory

East Coast Main Line Company Ltd
1/18, Great Minster House,
76 Marsham St,
London SW1 4DR
T: 020 7904 5043
E: dorenquiries@dor.gsi.gov.uk
W: www.dft.gov.uk/dor

East Lancashire Railway
Bolton St Station, Bury,
Lancs BL9 0EY
T: 0161 763 4340
F: 0161 763 4481
E: general.manager@east-lancs-rly.co.uk
W: www.eastlancsrailway.org.uk

East Midlands Trains
Stagecoach Group,
10 Dunkeld Way,
Perth PH1 5TW
T: 01738 442111
F: 01738 643648
E: mail@stagecoachgroup.com
W: www.stagecoachgroup.com

Eaton Electrical Ltd
Reddings Lane, Tyseley,
Birmingham B11 3EZ
T: 0121 685 2346
M: 07803 740082
E: chrisswales@eaton.com
W: www.eaton.com

EcarbonUK
See Electrical Carbon UK

Ecolube
Cardev International Ltd, Ripon Way,
Harrogate HG1 2AU
T: 01423 817200
F: 01423 817400
E: admin@ecolube.co.uk
W: www.ecolube.co.uk

ECT Group
See British American Railway Services

Eden Brown
222 Bishopsgate,
London EC2M 4QD
T: 020 7422 7300
F: 0845 434 9573
E: london@edenbrown.com
W: www.edenbrown.com

Eden Business Analysis Ltd
23 Station Rd, Upper Poppleton,
York YO26 6PX
T: 01904 780781
E: neil@edenba.co.uk
W: www.edenba.co.uk

EDF Energy
See UK Power Networks

Edgar Allen
See Balfour Beatty

Edilon Sedra
See Tiflex

Edmund Nuttall Ltd
See Bam Nuttall

EFD Corporate
Blackhill Drive, Wolverton Mill,
Milton Keynes MK12 5TS
T: 08451 285174
E: enquiries@efd-corporate.com
W: www.efd-corporate.com

EFi Heavy Vehicle Brakes
6/7 Bonville Rd, Brislington, Bristol BS4 5NZ
T: 0117 977 7859
F: 0117 971 0573
E: tonyp@efiltd.co.uk
W: www.efiltd.co.uk

Eglin Concourse International
Globe Works, Victoria Rd, Sowerby Bridge,
West Yorks HX6 3AE
T: 01422 317601
F: 01422 833857
E: sales@eglinconcourse.com
W: www.eglinconcourse.com

Elan Public Transport Consultancy Ltd
8 The Grange, Chesterfield S42 7PS
T: 0845 123 5733
E: george.watson@elanptc.com
W: www.elanptc.com

Eland Cables
120 Highgate Studios, 53-79 Highgate Rd,
London NW5 1TL
T: 020 7241 8787
F: 020 7241 8700
E: sales@eland.co.uk
W: www.eland.co.uk

Elcot Environmental
The Nursery, Kingsdown Lane, Blunsdon,
Swindon SN25
T: 01793 700100
F: 01793 722221
E: peterw@elcotenviro.com
W: www.elcotenviro.com

Eldapoint Ltd
Charleywood Rd, Knowsley Ind. Est.,
Knowsley, Merseyside L32 2BL
T: 0151 548 9838
F: 0151 546 4120
E: paul.wyatt@eldapoint.co.uk
W: www.eldapoint.co.uk

Electrical Carbon UK Ltd
Office 100, Devonshire House, 49 Eldon St,
Sheffield S1 4NR
T: 0114 231 6454
F: 0114 238 5464
E: sales@ecarbonuk.com
W: www.ecarbonuk.com

Electro Motive
9301 W.55th St, LaGrange, Illinois 60525, USA
T: 001 800 255 5355
F: 001 708 387 6626
E: scott.garman@emdiesels.com
W: www.emdiesels.com

Electromagnetic Testing Services Ltd (ETS)
Pratts Fields, Lubberhedges Lane, Stebbing,
Dunmow, Essex CM6 3BT
T: 01371 856061
F: 01371 856144
E: info@etsemc.co.uk
W: www.etsemc.co.uk

Eltek Valere UK Ltd
Eltek House, Maxted Rd, Hemel Hempstead,
Herts HP2 7DX
T: 01442 219355
F: 01442 245894
E: steve.pusey@eltekvalere.com
W: www.eltekvalere.com

Eltherm UK Ltd
Liberta House, Scotland Hill, Sandhurst,
Berks GU47 8JR
T: 01252 749910
E: sales@eltherm.uk.com
W: www.eltherm.uk.com

Embedded Rail Technology Ltd
Rose Hill House, Derby DE23 8GG
M: 07967 667020
E: cp@charlespenny.com

EMEG Electrical Ltd
Unit 3, Dunston Place, Whittington Moor,
Chesterfield, Derbys S41 8XA
T: 01246 268678
F: 01246 268679
E: enq@emeg.co.uk
W: www.emeg.co.uk

Emergency Power Systems
See Emerson Network Power

Emergi-Lite - Thomas & Betts Ltd
Bruntcliffe Lane, Morley, Leeds LS27 9LL
T: 0113 281 0600
F: 0113 281 0601
E: emergi-lite.sales@tnb.com
W: www.emergi-lite.co.uk

Emerson Crane Hire
Emerson House, Freshwater House,
Dagenham, Essex RM8 1RX
T: 020 8548 3900
F: 020 8548 3999
E: liam@emersoncranes.co.uk
W: www.emersoncranes.co.uk

Emerson Network Power
Carley Drive Business Area, Westfield,
Sheffield S20 8NQ
T: 0114 247 8369
F: 0114 247 8367
E: uk.rail@emerson.com
W: www.emerson.com

Emerson Network Power Chloride Products & Services
George Curl Way, Southampton SO18 2RY
T: 02380 610311
F: 02380 610852
E: uk.enquiries.chloride@emerson.com
W: www.emersonnetworkpower.com

Emico
Able House, 1 Figtree Hill, Hemel Hempstead,
Herts HP2 5XL
T: 01442 213111
F: 01442 236945
E: contact@emico-rail.com
W: www.emico-rail.com

Enerpac
Bentley Rd South, Darlaston, West Midlands
WS10 8LQ
T: 0121 505 0787
F: 0121 505 0799
E: info@enerpac.com
W: www.enerpac.com

Enersys Ltd
Rake Lane, Clifton Junction, Swinton,
Manchester M27 8LR
T: 0161 794 4611
F: 0161 727 3809
E: robert.marshall@uk.enersys.com
W: www.enersysinc.com

Engineering Support Group
See ESG

Ennstone Johnston
See FP McCann

ENOTRAC UK Ltd
Chancery House, St Nicholas Way, Sutton,
Surrey SM1 4AF
T: 020 8770 3501
F: 020 8770 3502
E: sebastien.lechelle@enotrac.com
W: www.enotrac.com

Enplex
310 Green Lane, Ilford,
Essex IG1 1LQ
T: 0870 763 6059
F: 0870 763 6064
E: info@enplex.co.uk
W: www.enplex.co.uk

Entec UK Ltd
Atlantic House,
Imperial Way,
Reading RG2 0TP
T: 01189 036686
F: 01189 036261
E: whitr@entecuk.co.uk
W: www.entecuk.com

Entech Technical Solutions Ltd
1st Floor, Hamilton House, 111 Marlowes,
Hemel Hempstead,
Herts HP1 1BB
T: 01442 898900
F: 01442 898990
E: info@entechts.co.uk
W: www.entechts.co.uk

Entech Technical Solutions Ltd
4th Floor, York House, Empire Way,
Wembley, Middx HA9 0PA
T: 020 8900 9390
F: 020 8900 9490
E: saul@entechts.co.uk
W: www.entechts.co.uk

Enterprise
Trident 1, Trident Park, Basil Hill, Didcot,
Oxon OX11 7HJ
T: 01772 819000
F: 01235 515888
E: john.davies@enterprise.plc.uk
W: www.enterprise.plc.uk

Enterprise Informatics
Old Bridge House, 40 Church St, Staines,
Middx TW18 4EP
T: 01784 426600
F: 01784 426601
E: info@enterpriseinformatics.com
W: www.enterpriseinformatics.com

Enterprise Managed Services Ltd
Endeavour House, 1 Lyonsdown Rd,
New Barnet, Herts EN5 1HR
T: 020 8275 8000
F: 020 8449 6536
E: evin.harcombe@enterprise.plc.uk
W: www.enterprise.plc.uk

Environment Hygeine Services (EHS)
32 Clay Hill,
Enfield EN2 9AA
T: 020 8367 7350
E: info@pigeonglide.com
W: www.pigeonglide.com

Environmental Management Solutions Group Holdings Ltd (EMS)
Global House, Geddings Rd, Hoddesden,
Herts EN11 0NT
T: 01992 535445
F: 01992 456435
W: www.emsgroup.org

Environmental Scientifics Group Ltd (ESG)
ESG House, Bretby Business Park, Ashby Rd,
Burton upon Trent DE15 0YZ
T: 01283 554400
F: 01283 554401
E: sales@esg.co.uk
W: www.esg.co.uk

Envirotech
See LH Group Services

EPC Global
See Talascend

ERA Technology Ltd
Cleeve Road, Leatherhead, Surrey KT22 7SA
T: 01372 367 345
F: 01372 367359
E: info@era.co.uk
W: www.era.co.uk

ERA
TECHNOLOGY

ERA Technology provides cost-effective and pragmatic solutions to the rail industry:

- Safety Engineering
- Safety Assessment
- EMC Assurance
- Power Systems
- Software Assurance
- Failure Analysis

A: Cleeve Rd, Leatherhead, Surrey, KT22 7SA
T: 01372 367 345
F: 01372 367 359
E: info@era.co.uk

www.era.co.uk

ERG Transit Systems (UK) Ltd
Unit 1, Riverside, Waters Meeting Rd,
The Valley, Bolton BL1 8TU
T: 01204 384709
F: 01204 384806
E: tim.burke@vix-erg.com
W: www.vix-erg.com

Ergonomics & Safety Research Institute (ESRI)
Holywell Building, Holywell Way,
Loughborough,
Leics LE11 3UZ
T: 01509 226900
F: 01509 226960
E: esri@lboro.ac.uk
W: www.lboro.ac.uk

ERM Ltd
2nd Floor, Exchequer Court,
33 St Mary Axe,
London EC3 8LL
T: 020 3206 5401
F: 020 7465 7272
E: nick.cottam@erm.com
W: www.erm.com

Ernst & Young LLP
1 More London Place,
London SE1 2AF
T: 020 7951 1113
F: 020 7951 3167
E: gfavaloro@uk.ey.com
W: www.ey.com/uk

ESAB (UK) Ltd
Hanover House,
Queensgate,
Britannia Rd,
Waltham Cross EN8 7TF
T: 01992 768515
F: 01992 788053
E: info@esab.co.uk
W: www.esab.co.uk

ESG
Derwent House,
RTC Business Park,
London Rd,
Derby DE24 8UP
T: 01332 483800
F: 01332 383565
E: sales@esg-rail.com
W: www.esg-rail.com

Esmerk Ltd
County House,
3rd Floor, Friar St,
Reading RG1 1DB
T: 0118 956 5836
F: 0118 956 5850
E: response@esmerk.com
W: www.esmerk.com

ESR Technology Ltd
410 Birchwood Park,
Warrington,
Cheshire WA3 6FW
T: 01925 582491
E: info@esrtechnology.com
W: www.esrtechnology.com

ESS Rail
3rd Floor, Regal House,
70 London Rd,
Twickenham TW1 3QS
T: 0845 245 3000
F: 0845 245 3061
E: john.lynch@essengineering.com
W: www.essengineering.com

Essempy
1 Phoebe Lane, Church End, Wavendon,
Bucks MK17 8LR
T: 01908 582491
M: 07967 398431
E: norman.price@essempy.co.uk
W: www.essempy.co.uk

ETS Cable Components
Units 4/5, Red Lion Business Park, Red Lion Rd,
Tolworth KT6 7QD
T: 020 8405 6789
F: 020 8405 6790
E: sales@etscc.co.uk
W: www.etscc.co.uk

Eurailscout GB Ltd
Unit 2, Kimberley Court, Kimberley Rd,
Queens Park, London NW6 7SL
T: 020 7372 2973
F: 020 7372 5444
E: info@eurailscout.com
W: www.eurailscout.com

Euro Cargo Rail SAS
Immeuble la Palacio, 25-29 Place de la
Madelaine, 75008 Paris France
T: 0033 977 400 000
F: 0033 977 400 200
E: info@eurocargorail.com
W: www.eurocargorail.com

Eurochemi
Kingsbury Park, Midland Rd, Swadlincote,
Derbys DE11 0AN
T: 01283 222111
F: 01283 550177
W: www.eurochemi.co.uk

Eurocom Ltd
1 Glyn St, Vauxhall, London SE11 5HT
T: 020 7820 8344
E: comms@eurocomltd.co.uk
W: www.eurocomltd.co.uk

Eurolog Ltd
Orlando House, 3 High St,
Teddington TW11 8NP
T: 020 8977 4407
F: 020 8977 3714
E: info@eurolog.co.uk
W: www.eurolog.co.uk

Europe Rail Consultancy Ltd
North Court, Hassocks, West Sussex BN6 8JS
T: 01273 845583
E: chris.dugdale@europerailconsultancy.com
W: www.europerailconsultancy.com

European Friction Industries Ltd (EFI)
6/7 Bonville Rd, Brislington, Bristol BS4 5NZ
T: 0117 977 7859
E: rail@efiltd.co.uk
W: www.efiltd.co.uk

Europhoenix
W: www.europhoenix.eu

Eurostar International Ltd
Times House, Bravingtons Walk,
Regent Quarter, London N1 9AW
E: press.office@eurostar.co.uk
W: www.eurostar.com

Eurotech Ltd
3 Clifton Court, Cambridge CB1 7BN
T: 01223 403410
F: 01223 410457
E: sales@eurotech-ltd.co.uk
W: www.eurotech-ltd.co.uk

Eurotunnel
The Channel Tunnel Group Ltd, UK Terminal,
Ashford Rd, Folkestone, Kent CT18 8XX
T: 08443 353535
F: 01303 288784
E: communication.internet@eurotunnel.com
W: www.eurotunnel.com

Eurox
Aqua House, Buttress Way,
Smethwick B66 3DL
T: 0121 555 7167
F: 0121 555 7168
E: neil@eurox.co.uk
W: www.eurox.co.uk

Eve Trakway Ltd
Bramley Vale, Chesterfield,
Derbys S44 5GA
T: 08700 767676
F: 08700 737373
E: mail@evetrakway.co.uk
W: www.evetrakway.co.uk

Evergrip Ltd
Unit 4, Flaxley Rd, Selby YO8 4BG
T: 01757 212744
F: 01757 212749
E: sales@evergrip.com
W: www.evergrip.com

Eversholt Rail Ltd
PO Box 68166,
210 Pentonville Rd,
London N1P 2AR
T: 020 7380 5040
F: 020 7380 5148
E: wendy.filer@eversholtrail.co.uk
W: www.eversholtrail.co.uk

EWS
See DB Schenker

Excalibur Screwbolts Ltd
Gate 3, Newhall Nursery,
Lower Rd, Hockley,
Essex SS5 5JU
T: 01702 206962/207909
F: 01702 207918
E: charles.bickford@screwbolt.com
W: www.excaliburscrewbolts.com

Exide Technologies
see gnb industrial power

Exova (UK) Ltd
6 Coronet Way, Centenary Park,
Salford M50 1RE
T: 0161 787 3291
F: 0161 787 3251
E: steve.hughes@exova.com
W: www.exova.com

Expamet Security Products
PO Box 14, Longhill Ind. Est. (North),
Hartlepool TS25 1PR
T: 01429 867366
F: 01429 867355
E: sales@exmesh.co.uk
W: www.expandedmetalfencing.com

Eldapoint Ltd
Charleywood Road,
Knowsley Ind. Park North,
Knowsley, L33 7SG
Tel: - 0151 548 9838
Fax: - 0151 546 4120

Eldapoint manufacture Re-locatable Equipment Buildings (REB's) all manufactured to the BR1615D Specification, Specialist Housing's, Fire Rated Units, Blast Resistant Units, Modular Buildings, Secure Steel Accommodation Units, Secure Stores, Changing Rooms, Toilet Blocks, Shower Blocks, Mobile Welfare Units, Sleeper Units & Welfare Units. We pride ourselves in being the leaders in quality and innovation in the manufacture of Re-locatable Equipment Buildings (REB's) and Portable Accommodation Units.

We are an accredited ISO9001:2008 company and Link-up approved for the supply of Re-locatable Equipment Buildings (REB's) to the Rail Network, we are also members of the Modular & Portable Buildings Association (MPBA) and the Knowsley Chamber of Commerce.

We offer proven capability supported by our team of skilled management and AUTOCAD LT2009 designers. In addition we can provide turnkey projects from design concept through to manufacture, fitting out and final installation/delivery on site.

www.eldapoint.co.uk

Eldapoint Ltd
Manufacturing Division

HITACHI
Inspire the Next

In association with ATKINS

Express Electrical
37 Cable Depot Rd, Riverside Ind Est, Clydebank G81 1UY
T: 0141 941 3689
F: 0141 952 8155
E: sales@expresselectrical.co.uk
W: www.expresselectrical.co.uk

Express Medicals Ltd
8, City Business Centre, Lower Rd, London SE16 2XB
T: 020 7500 6900
F: 020 7500 6910
E: workhealth@expressmedicals.co.uk
W: www.expressmedicals.co.uk

Express Rail Alliance
W: www.expressrailalliance.com

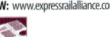

External Solutions Ltd
Unit 1, Queensway Business Centre, Dunlop Way, Scunthorpe, North Lincs DN16 3RN
T: 01724 847770
F: 01724 289051
E: enquiries@external-solutions.co.uk
W: www.external-solutions.co.uk

Exxell (Acorn People)
7 York Rd, Woking, Surrey GU22 7XH
T: 01483 654463
F: 01483 723080
E: sarah.griffiths@acornpeople.com
W: www.acornpeople.com

Factair Ltd
49 Boss Hall Rd, Ipswich, Suffolk IP1 5BN
T: 01473 746400
F: 01473 747123
E: enquiries@factair.co.uk
W: www.factair.co.uk

Faithful & Gould
Euston Tower, 286, Euston Rd, London NW1 3AT
T: 020 7121 2121
F: 020 7121 2020
E: info@fgould.com
W: www.fgould.com

Faiveley Transport Birkenhead Ltd.
Morpeth Wharf, Twelve Quays, Birkenhead, Wirral CH41 1LW
T: 0151 649 5000
F: 0151 649 5001
E: kevin.smith@faiveleytransport.com
W: www.faiveleytransport.com

Faiveley Transport Tamworth Ltd
Darwell Park, Mica Close, Amington, Tamworth, Staffs B77 4DR
T: 01827 308430
F: 01827 308431
E: brian.harvey@faiveleytransport.com
W: www.faiveleytransport.com

Falcon Electrical Engineering Ltd
Falcon House, Main St, Fallin, Stirlingshire FK7 7HT
T: 01786 819920
F: 01786 814381
E: sales@falconelectrical.com
W: www.falconelectrical.com

Fantuzzi Noell (UK) Ltd
Units 3&4, Oldham West Business Centre, Watts Green, Chadderton, Manchester OL9 9LH
T: 0161 785 7870
F: 0161 670 6582
E: info@fantuzzi.co.uk
W: www.fantuzzi.co.uk

Farrer Consulting Ltd
See MWH Global Ltd

Fastrack (Expamet Security Products)
PO Box 14, Longhill Ind. Est. (North), Hartlepool TS25 1PR
T: 01429 867366
F: 01429 867355
E: sales@exmesh.co.uk
W: www.expandedmetalcompany.co.uk

Federal Mogul Friction Products (Ferodo)
Chapel-en-le-Frith, Derbys SK23 0JP
T: 01298 811689
F: 01298 811580
W: www.federal.mogul.com

Fencing & Lighting Contractors Ltd
Unit 21, Amber Drive, Bailey Brook Ind Est, Langley Mill, Derbys NG16 4BE
T: 01773 531383
F: 01773 531921
E: info@fencingandlighting.co.uk

Fenton UK
Merlin Way, North Weald, Essex CM16 6HR
T: 01992 522555
F: 01992 523444
E: info@fenton.com
W: www.fentonuk.com

Feonic Technology
3a, Newlands Science Park, Inglemire Lane, Hull HU6 7TQ
T: 01482 806688
F: 01482 806654
E: info@feonic.com
W: www.feonic.com

Faiveley Transport Birkenhead Ltd:
Morpeth Wharf, Twelve Quays, Birkenhead, Wirral CH41 1LF
T: 0151 649 5000 F: 0151 649 5001
E: kevin.smith@faiveleytransport.com
Faiveley Transport Tamworth Ltd:
Darwell Park, Mica Close, Amington, Tamworth, Staffordshire B77 4DR
T: 01827 308430 F: 01827 308431
E: brian.harvey@faiveleytransport.com
W: www.faiveleytransport.com
Faiveley Transport UK provides a comprehensive range of services and products. Operating out of two facilities in Birkenhead and Tamworth, we provide customer service operations and original equipment supply, to UK and Ireland.
Faiveley TRANSPORT

Ferrabyrne Ltd
Fort Rd Ind. Est, Littlehampton BN17 7QU
T: 01903 721317
F: 01903 430452
E: sales@ferrabyrne.co.uk
W: www.ferrabyrne.co.uk

Ferrograph Ltd
Unit 1, New York Way, New York Ind Park, Newcastle Upon Tyne NE27 0QF
T: 0191 280 8800
F: 0191 280 8810
E: info@ferrograph.com
W: www.ferrograph.com

Fibergrate Composite Structures
5151 Beltline Rd, Ste 1212, Dallas, TX 75254 USA
T: 00 800 527 4043
F: 00 972 250 1530
E: info@fibergrate.com
W: www.fibergrate.com

Fibreglass Grating Ltd
Unit 14, Telford Rd, Gorse Lane Ind. Est, Clacton on Sea, Essex CO15 4LP
T: 01255 423601
F: 01255 436428
E: info@fibreglassgrating.co.uk
W: www.fibreglassgrating.co.uk

Field Fisher Waterhouse LLP
35 Vine St, London EC3N 2AA
T: 020 7861 4000
F: 020 7488 0084
E: nicholas.thompsell@ffw.com
W: www.ffw.com

Fifth Dimension Associates Ltd (FDAL)
Suite 18411, 145-157, St John St, London EC1V 4PW
T: 020 7060 2332
F: 020 7060 3325
E: london@fdal.co.uk
W: www.fdal.co.uk

Findlay Irvine Ltd
Bog Rd, Penicuik, Midlothian EH26 9BU
T: 01968 671200
F: 01968 671237
E: sales@findlayirvine.com
W: www.findlayirvine.com

Finning (UK) Ltd
Gelderd Road, Gildersome, Leeds LS27 7JS
T: 0113 201 2065
F: 0113 201 2051
E: oillab@finning.co.uk
W: www.finning.co.uk

Fircroft
Trinity House, 114 Northenden Rd, Sale, Cheshire M33 3FZ
T: 0161 905 2020
F: 0161 969 1743
E: hq@fircroft.co.uk
W: www.fircroft.co.uk

First Capital Connect
Hertford House, 1 Cranwood St, London EC1V 9QS
T: 0845 026 4700
E: customer.relations.fcc@firstgroup.com
W: www.firstcapitalconnect.co.uk

First Choice Protection
See Portwest

First Class Partnerships
148 Lawrence St, York YO10 3EB
T: 01904 870792
F: 01904 424499
E: info@firstclasspartnerships.com
W: www.firstclasspartnerships.com

First Components Ltd
Wallows Ind Est, Wallows Rd, Brierley Hill, DY5 1QA
T: 01384 262068
F: 01384 482383
E: info@firstcomponents.co.uk
W: www.firstcomponents.co.uk

First Engineering Ltd
See Babcock Rail

First Great Western
Milford House, 1 Milford St, Swindon SN1 1HL
T: 08457 000125
E: fgwfeedback@firstgroup.com
W: www.firstgreatwestern.co.uk

First Group Plc
395 King St, Aberdeen AB24 5RP
T: 01224 650100
F: 01224 650140
W: www.firstgroup.com/corporate

First Hull Trains
Europa House, 184 Ferensway, Hull HU1 3UT
T: 01482 215746
E: customer.services@hulltrains.co.uk
W: www.hulltrains.co.uk

First Procurement Associates
See FPA Consulting Ltd

First Rail Support Ltd
Unit 20, Time Technology Park, Blackburn Rd, Simonstone, Lancs BB12 7TG
T: 01282 688110
F: 01282 688141
E: rail.support@firstgroup.com
W: www.firstgroup.com/firstrailsupport

First Scotrail
Customer Relations, PO Box 7030, Fort William PH33 6WX
T: 0845 601 5929
E: scotrailcustomer.relations@firstgroup.com
W: www.firstgroup.com/scotrail

First Trans Pennine Express
Bridgewater House, 60 Whitworth St, Manchester M1 6LT
T: 08700 005 151
F: 0161 228 8120
E: tpecustomer.relations@firstgroup.com
W: www.tpexpress.co.uk

Firstco Ltd
4 Celbridge Mews, London W2 6EU
T: 020 7034 0833
F: 020 7229 8002
E: info@firstco.uk.com
W: www.firstco.uk.com

Fishbone Solutions Ltd
25 Statham St, Darley, Derbys DE22 1HR
T: 0115 714 3444
F: 020 7942 0701
E: go-fish@fishbonesolutions.co.uk
W: www.fishbonesolutions.co.uk

Fitzpatrick Contractors Ltd
See Volker Fitzpatrick

FKI Switchgear
See Hawker Siddeley

Fleetech Ltd
12 Little Park Farm Rd, Fareham, Hants PO15 7JE
T: 01489 553200
F: 01489 553101
E: uk@fleetech.com
W: www.fleetech.com/ www.bmrail.com

Flexible & Specialist (FS) Cables
Alban Point, Alban Park, Hatfield Rd, St Albans AL4 6JX
T: 01727 840841
F: 01727 840842
E: sales@fscables.com
W: www.fscables.com

Flexicon Ltd
Roman Way, Coleshill, Birmingham B46 1HG
T: 01675 466900
F: 01675 466901
E: rail@flexicon.uk.com
W: www.flexicon.uk.com

FLI Structures
Francis & Lewis International, Waterwells Drive, Waterwells Business Park, Gloucester GL2 2AA
T: 01452 722200
F: 01452 722244
E: j.sparkes@fli.co.uk
W: www.fliscrewpiles.co.uk

Flint Bishop Solicitors
St Michaels Court, St Michaels Lane, Derby DE1 3HQ
T: 01332 340211
E: info@flintbishop.co.uk
W: www.flintbishop.co.uk

Flir Systems Ltd (UK)
2 Kings Hill Ave, West Malling, Kent ME19 4AQ
T: 01732 220011
F: 01732 220014
E: sales@flir.uk.com
W: www.flir.uk.com

Flowcrete UK Ltd
The Flooring Technology Centre, Booth Lane, Sandbach, Cheshire CW11 3QF
T: 01270 753000
F: 01270 753333
E: uk@flowcrete.com
W: www.flowcrete.co.uk

Fluke UK Ltd (Tracklink)
52 Hurricane Way, Norwich NR6 6JB
T: 020 7942 0700
F: 020 7942 0701
E: industrial@uk.fluke.nl
W: www.fluke.co.uk

Fluor Ltd
Fluor Centre, Riverside Way, Camberley, Surrey GU15 3YL
T: 01276 62424
F: 01276 26762
W: www.fluor.com

Focus 2000 Infrared Ltd
5a Lodge Hill Business Park, Westbury-sub-Mendip, Somerset BA5 1EY
T: 01749 870620
F: 01749 870622
E: sales@focus2k.co.uk
W: www.focus2k.co.uk

Fone Alarm Installations Ltd
59 Albert Rd North, Reigate RH2 9EL
T: 01737 223673
F: 01737 224349
E: enquiries@fonealarm.co.uk
W: www.fonealarm.co.uk

Forbo Flooring Ltd
High Holborn Rd, Ripley, Derbys DE5 3NT
T: 01773 740615
F: 01773 744142
E: bob.summers@forbo.com
W: www.uk.bonarfloors.com

Ford Components Manufacturing Ltd
Unit 2, Monkton Business Park North, Mill Lane, Hebburn, Tyne & Wear NE31 2JZ
T: 0191 428 6600
F: 0191 428 6620
E: steve.lum@ford-components.com
W: www.ford-components.com

Foremost Logan Ltd
Kersey Hall, Tannery Rd, Combs, Stowmarket, Suffolk
T: 01449 742450
F: 01449 771207
E: info@foremostlogan.com
W: www.foremostlogan.com

ForgeTrack Ltd
Thistle House, St Andrew St, Hertford SG14 1JA
T: 01992 500900
F: 01992 589495
E: sales@forgetrack.co.uk
W: www.forgetrack.co.uk

Forward Chemicals Ltd
PO Box 12, Tanhouse Lane, Widnes, Cheshire WA8 0RD
T: 0151 422 1000
F: 0151 422 1011
E: salesandservice@forwardchem.com
W: www.forwardchem.com

Fourway Communications Ltd
Delamere Rd, Cheshunt, Herts EN8 9SH
T: 01992 629182
F: 01992 639227
E: enquiries@fourway.co.uk
W: www.fourway.co.uk

FP McCann
Brascote Lane, Cadeby, Nuneaton, Warks CV13 0BE
T: 01455 290780
F: 01455 292189
E: kjones@fpmccann.co.uk
W: www.fpmccann.co.uk

FP McCann
Brascote Lane, Cadeby, Nuneaton, Warks CV13 0BE
T: 01455 290780
F: 01455 292189
E: scarson@fpmccann.co.uk
W: www.fpmccann.co.uk

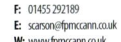

FPA Consulting Ltd
1 St Andrew's House, Vernon Gate, Derby DE1 1UJ
T: 01332 604321
F: 01332 604322
E: johnb@fpaconsulting.co.uk
W: www.fpaconsulting.co.uk

Frankham Consulting Group Ltd
Irene House, Five Arches Business Park, Maidstone Rd, Sidcup, Kent DA14 5AE
T: 020 8309 7777
F: 020 8306 7890
E: enquiries@frankham.com
W: www.frankham.com

Franklin + Andrews
Sea Containers House, 20 Upper Ground, London SE1 9LZ
T: 020 7633 9966
F: 020 7928 2471
E: enquiries@franklinandrews.com
W: www.franklinandrews.com

Frauscher Selectrail (UK) Ltd
Unit 58, Basepoint Business Centre, Isidore Rd, Bromsgrove B60 3ET
T: 01527 834670
F: 01527 834671
E: info@frauscher-selectrail.com
W: www.frauscher-selectrail.com

Frauscher UK
Suite 5, Yeovil Innovation Centre, Barracks Close, Copse Rd, Yeovil, BA22 8RN
T: 01935 385905
E: richard.colman@uk.frauscher.com
W: www.frauscher.com

Frazer Nash Consultancy Ltd
Stonebridge House, Dorking Business Park, Station Rd, Dorking, Surrey RH4 1HJ
T: 01306 885050
F: 01306 886464
E: r.jones@fnc.co.uk
W: www.fnc.co.uk

Freeman Williams Language Solutions Ltd
College Business Centre, Uttoxeter New Rd, Derby DE22 3WZ
T: 01332 869342
F: 01332 869344
E: abi@freemanwilliams.co.uk
W: www.freemanwilliams.co.uk

Freeth Cartwright LLP
2nd Floor, West Point, Cardinal Square, 10 Nottingham Rd, Derby DE1 3QT
T: 0845 634 9804
F: 0845 634 1732
E: mike.copestake@freethcartwright.co.uk
W: www.freethcartwright.co.uk

Freight Europe (UK) Ltd
See Captrain UK Ltd

Freightarranger
West View, Brownshill, Stroud, Glos GL6 8AQ
T: 01453 883186
E: enquiries@freightarranger.co.uk
W: www.freightarranger.co.uk

Freightliner Group Ltd
3rd Floor, The Podium, 1 Eversholt St, London NW1 2FL
T: 020 7200 3900
F: 020 7200 3975
E: pressoffice@freightliner.co.uk
W: www.freightliner.co.uk

Frequentis UK Ltd
Gainsborough Business Centre, 2 Sheen Rd, Richmond upon Thames TW9 1AE
T: 020 8973 2616
E: marketing@frequentis.com
W: www.frequentis.com

Fresh Approach Solutions Ltd
Ground Floor, Norfolk House, Smallbrook Queensway, Birmingham B5 4LJ
T: 0121 633 5035
F: 0871 431 6083
W: www.freshapproachsolutions.com

Freshfields Bruckhaus Deringer LLP
65 Fleet St, London EC4Y 1HT
T: 020 7936 4000
F: 020 7832 7001
W: www.freshfields.com

Frimstone
Ashcraft Farm, Main Rd, Crimplesham, Norfolk PE33 9EB
T: 0845 177 9900
E: enquiries@frimstone.co.uk
W: www.frimstone.co.uk

FS Cables
See Flexible & Specialist

Fuchs Lubricants (UK) Plc
New Century St, Hanley, Stoke on Trent ST1 5HU
T: 08701 203700
F: 01782 202072
E: contact-uk@fuchs-oil.com
W: www.fuchslubricants.com

FINNING
Fluid & Condition Monitoring Services
The number one fluid analysis service for all your oils, coolants, fuels and transformer testing requirements.
Dedicated interpretation staff offering reliability and consultancy.
To find out more call 0113 201 2065
Immediate Results.
Expert Advice.
It's What We Do.
www.maintain-it.co.uk

HITACHI Inspire the Next
177

Directory

Fuelcare Ltd
Suite 1, The Hayloft, Blakenhall Park, Barton under Needwood, Staffs DE13 8AJ
T: 01283 712263
F: 01283 262263
E: sales@fuelcare.com
W: www.fuelcare.com

Fugro Aperio Ltd
Focal Point, Newmarket Rd, Bottisham, Cambridge CB25 9BD
T: 0870 600 8050
F: 0870 800 8040
E: info@fugro-aperio.com
W: www.fugro-aperio.com

Fujikura Europe Ltd
C51 Barwell Business Park, Leatherhead Rd, Chessington, Surrey KT9 2NY
T: 020 8240 2000
F: 020 8240 2010
E: sales@fujikura.co.uk
W: www.fujikura.co.uk

Fujitsu
W: www.fujitsu.com/uk/industries/rail

Funkwerk Information Technologies York Ltd
Middleham House, 6 St Mary's Court, Blossom St, York YO24 1AH
T: 01904 639091
F: 01904 639092
E: sales@funkwerk-it.com
W: www.funkwerk-it.com

Furneaux Riddall & Co Ltd
Alchorne Place, Portsmouth, Hants PO3 5PA
T: 02392 668624
F: 02392 668625
E: info@furneauxriddall.com
W: www.furneauxriddall.com

Furrer + Frey
Thunstrasse 35, PO Box 182, CH-3000 Berne 6, Switzerland
T: 0041 31357 6111
F: 0041 31357 6100
E: adm@furrerfrey.ch
W: www.furrerfrey.ch

Furse - Thomas & Betts Ltd
Wilford Rd, Nottingham NG2 1EB
T: 0115 964 3700
F: 0115 986 0538
E: enquiry@furse.com
W: www.furse.com

Furtex
See Holdsworth

Fusion People Ltd
2nd/3rd Floor, Aldermary House, 10-15 Queen St, London EC4N 1TX
T: 020 7653 1070
F: 020 7653 1071
E: rail@fusionpeople.com
W: www.fusionpeople.com

Future Rail (formerly Future Welding)
The Rowe, Stableford, Staffs ST5 4EN
T: 01782 411800
E: futureraildesign@gmail.com
W: www.futurerail.com

Gabriel & Co Ltd
1 Cromwell Rd, Smethwick, West Midlands B66 2JT
T: 0121 555 7615
F: 0121 555 1922
E: john.gabriel@gabrielco.com
W: www.gabrielco.com

GAI Tronics (Hubbel Ltd)
Brunel Dr., Stretton Business Park, Burton upon Trent DE13 0BZ
T: 01283 500500
F: 01283 500400
E: sales@gai-tronics.co.uk
W: www.gai-tronics.co.uk

Gallifford Try Rail
Crab Lane, Fearnhead, Warrington WA2 0XR
T: 01925 822821
F: 01925 812323
E: ron.stevenson@gallifordtry.co.uk
W: www.gallifordtry.co.uk

Gamble Rail
See Keltbray

Ganymede Solutions Ltd
26 Hershel St, Slough SL1 1PA
T: 01753 820810
F: 0870 890 1894
E: gary.hewett@ganymedesolutions.co.uk
W: www.ganymedesolutions.co.uk

Gardiner & Theobald
32, Bedford Square, London WC1B 3JT
T: 020 7209 3000
F: 020 7209 3359
E: p.armstrong@gardiner.com
W: www.gardiner.com

Gardner Denver Ltd
Claybrook Drive, Washford Ind. Est, Redditch, Worcs B98 0DS
T: 01527 838200
F: 01527 521140
E: hydrovane-info.uk@gardnerdenver.com
W: www.hydrovane.co.uk

Garic Ltd
Kingfisher Park, Aviation Rd, Pilsworth, Bury BL9 8GD
T: 0161 766 8808
E: sales@garic-ltd.co.uk
W: www.garic-ltd.co.uk

Garrandale Ltd
Alfreton Rd, Derby DE21 4AP
T: 01332 291676
F: 01332 291677
E: info@garrandale.co.uk
W: www.garrandale.co.uk

GarrettCom Europe Ltd
Haslar Marine Technology Park, Haslar Rd, Gosport PO12 2AU
T: 0870 382 5777
F: 0870 382 5098
E: john.ward@garrettcom.co.uk
W: www.garrettcom.co.uk

Gates Power Transmission
Tinwald Downs Rd, Heath Hall, Dumfries DG1 1TS
T: 01387 242000
F: 01387 242010
E: mediaeurope@gates.com
W: www.gates.com

Gatwick Express
See Southern

Gatwick Plant Ltd
Woodside Works, The Close, Horley, Surrey RH6 9EB
T: 01293 824777
F: 01293 824077
E: transport@gatwickgroup.com
W: www.gatwickgroup.com

GAV Access Covers
PO Box 85, Nuneaton, Warks CV11 9ZT
T: 02476 381090
F: 02476 373577
E: gavmet@aol.com
W: www.gav-solutions.com

GB Railfreight
15-25 Artillery Lane, London E1 7HA
T: 020 7983 5177
F: 020 7983 5170
E: gbrfinfo@gbrailfreight.com
W: www.gbrailfreight.com

modern
railways
You too can join the Fourth Friday Club!
The *Modern Railways* Fourth Friday Club is a convivial meeting place for railway industry executives, giving the opportunity for valuable networking and a chance to hear an after-lunch speech from one of the industry's leading figures. Roger Ford of *Modern Railways* gives a pre-lunch starter speech in his own inimitable style, followed by a guest speaker from the rail industry.
FREE FIRST-TIME TRIAL FOR RAILWAY INDUSTRY PERSONNEL
If you have not attended the club before, your first meeting is free! E-mail modern.railways@googlemail.com to secure a place.
More details on www.modern-railways.com

GE Transportation Systems
Inspira House, Martinfield, Welwyn Garden City, Herts AL7 1GW
T: 01707 383700
F: 01707 383701
W: www.getransportation.com

Geatech S.p.a
Via Del Plazzino 6, 40051 Altedo (BO) Italy
T: 0039 051 6601514
F: 0039 051 6601309
E: info@geatech.it
W: www.geatech.it

Geismar UK Ltd
Salthouse Rd, Brackmills Ind. Est., Northampton NN4 7EX
T: 01604 769191
F: 01604 763154
E: sales@geismar.co.uk
W: www.geismar.com

Geldards LLP
Number One, Pride Place, Pride Park, Derby DE24 8QR
T: 01332 331631
F: 01332 294295
E: roman.surma@geldards.co.uk
W: www.geldards.co.uk

Gemma Lighting
Victoria St, Mansfield, Notts NG18 5RW
T: 01623 415601
F: 01623 420484
E: marketing@gemmalighting.com
W: www.gemmagroup.com

GenQuip Plc
Aberafan Rd, Baglan Ind. Park, Port Talbot SA12 7DJ
T: 01639 823484
F: 01639 822533
E: sales@genquip.co.uk
W: www.genquip.co.uk

Genwork Ltd
See Bache Pallets

Geodesign Barriers Ltd
2 Montgomery Ave, Pinehurst, Swindon SN2 1LE
T: 01793 538565
M: 07890 983239
E: britt.warg@palletbarrier.com
W: www.geodesignbarriers.com

Geoff Brown Signalling Ltd
The Cottage, Old Lodge, Minchinhampton, Stroud GL6 9AQ
T: 07977 265721
E: geoffbrownsignalling@btinternet.com

GeoRope
Arumindarrich, West Laroch, Ballachulish, Argyll PH49 4JG
T: 01855 811224
E: kam@geo-rope.com
W: www.geo-rope.com

Geosynthetics Ltd
Fleming Rd, Harrowbrook Ind.Est., Hinckley, Leics LE10 3DU
T: 01455 617139
F: 01455 617140
E: sales@geosyn.co.uk
W: www.geosyn.co.uk

Geotechnical Engineering Ltd
Centurion House, Olympus Park, Quedgeley, Glos GL2 4NF
T: 01452 527743
F: 01452 729314
E: geotech@geoeng.co.uk
W: www.geoeng.co.uk

Geotechnics Ltd
The Geotechnical Centre, 203 Torrington Ave, Tile Hill, Coventry CV4 9AP
T: 02476 694664
F: 02476 694642
E: mail@geotechnics.co.uk
W: www.geotechnics.co.uk

Getzner Werkstoffe GmbH
Herrenaus, A-6706 Burs, Austria
T: 0043 5552 2010
F: 0043 5552 201899
E: sylomer@getzner.at
W: www.getzner.at

GGB UK
Wellington House, Starley Way, Birmingham Int. Park, Birmingham B37 7HB
T: 0845 230 0442
F: 0121 781 7313
E: greatbritain@ggbearings.com

GGR Group Ltd
Broadway Business Park, Broadgate, Chadderton, Oldham OL9 0JA
T: 0161 683 2580
F: 0161 683 4444
E: info@ggrgroup.com
W: www.ggrail.com

GGS Engineering (Derby) Ltd
Atlas Works, Litchurch Lane, Derby DE24 8AQ
T: 01332 299345
F: 01332 299678
E: sales@ggseng.com
W: www.ggseng.com

GHD
6th Floor, 10 Fetter Lane, London EC4A 1BR
T: 020 3077 7900
E: sue.jackson@ghd.com
W: www.ghd.com

Gifford
See Ramboll Uk Ltd

Giken Europe BV
Room 302, Burnhill Bus. Centre, Kingfisher House, Elmfield Rd, Bromley, Kent BR1 1LT
T: 0845 260 8001
F: 0845 260 8002
E: info@giken.co.uk
W: www.giken.com

Gilbarco Veeder-Root
Crompton Close, Basildon, Essex SS14 3BA
T: 0870 010 1136
F: 0870 010 1137
E: uksales@gilbarco.com
W: www.gilbarco.com

Gioconda Limited
Unit 10, Woodfalls, Gravelly Lane, Laddingford, Maidstone, Kent ME18 6DA
T: 01622 872512
E: mail@gioconda.co.uk
W: www.gioconda.co.uk

Glasdon UK Ltd
Preston New Rd, Blackpool, Lancs FY4 4UL
T: 01253 600412
F: 01253 792558
E: sales@glasdon-uk.co.uk
W: www.glasdon.com

Glenair UK Ltd
40 Lower Oakham Way, Mansfield, Notts NG18 5BY
T: 01623 638100
F: 01623 638111
E: cbaker@glenair.co.uk
W: www.glenair.com

Glentworth Rail Ltd
Long Lane, Hawthorn Hill, Maidenhead, Berks SL6 3TA
T: 01628 639823
F: 01628 639823
E: alistair.forsyth@glentworth.co.uk
W: www.glentworth.co.uk

Global Crossing (UK) Telecommunications Ltd
1 London Bridge, 4th Floor, London SE1 9BG
T: 020 7904 2607
E: christian.evans@globalcrossing.com
W: www.globalcrossing.com

Global House Training Services Ltd
35a Astbury Rd, London SE15 2NL
T: 020 7639 3322
E: contact@globalhouse.co.uk
W: www.globalhouse.co.uk

Global Rail Support
8 Curzon Lane, Alvaston, Derby DE24 8QS
T: 01332 601596
F: 01332 727494
E: ask@globalrailsupport.com
W: www.globalrailsupport.com

Globalforce UK Ltd
The Willows, College Avenue, Grays, Essex RM17 5UN
T: 01375 380629
F: 01375 381995
E: graham@globalforceuk.co.uk
W: www.globalforceuk.co.uk

GM Rail Services Ltd
65 Somers Rd, Rugby, Warks CV22 7DG
T: 01788 573777
F: 01788 551138
E: dwhitley@gmrail.co.uk
W: www.gmrail.co.uk

GME Springs
Boston Place, Foleshill, Coventry CV6 5NN
T: 02476 664911
F: 02476 663020
E: sales@gmesprings.co.uk
W: www.gmesprings.co.uk

GMPTE
2 Piccadilly Place, Manchester M1 3BG
T: 0871 200 2233
E: publicity@gmpte.gov.uk
W: www.gmpte.com

GMT Manufacturing Ltd
Old Gorsey Lane, Wallasey CH44 4AH
T: 0151 630 1545
F: 0151 630 8555
E: info@gmt.co.uk
W: www.gmt.co.uk

GMT Rubber-Metal-Technic Ltd
The Sidings, Station Rd, Guiseley, Leeds LS20 8BX
T: 01943 870670
F: 01943 870631
E: sales@gmt.gb.com
W: www.gmt-gb.com

GNB Industrial Power (UK) Ltd
Mansell House, Aspinall Close, Middlebrook, Horwich, Bolton BL6 6QQ
T: 0845 606 4111
F: 0845 606 4112
E: sales-uk@eu.exide.com
W: www.gnb.com

GNER
See Alliance Rail Holdings

GNWR
See Alliance Rail Holdings

Go Ahead Group plc
Head Office, 4 Matthew Parker St, Westminster, London SW1H 9NP
T: 020 7821 3939
F: 020 7821 3938
E: enquiries@go-ahead.com
W: www.go-ahead.com

Goldline Bearings Ltd
Stafford Park 17, Telford, Shropshire TF3 3DG
T: 01952 292401
F: 01952 292403
E: sales@goldlinebearings.co.uk
W: www.goldlinebearings.com

Gordon Services Ltd
Unit 8, Daws Farm, Ivy Barn Lane, Ingatestone, Essex CM4 0PX
T: 01277 352895
F: 01277 356115
E: enquiries@gordonservicesltd.co.uk
W: www.gordonservicesltd.co.uk

GOS Tool & Engineering Services Ltd
Heritage Court Rd, Gilchrist Thomas ind. Est, Blaenavon, Torfaen NP4 9RL
T: 01495 790230
F: 01495 792757
E: enquiries@gosengineering.co.uk
W: www.gosengineering.co.uk

Goskills
See People 1st

Go-Tel Communications Ltd
See Samsung Electronics

Govia
Go-ahead Group Rail, Go-ahead House, 26-28 Addiscombe Rd, Croydon, Surrey CR9 5GA
E: contact@go-ahead-rail.com
W: www.govia.info

Gradus Ltd
Park Green, Macclesfield, Cheshire SK11 7LZ
T: 01625 428922
F: 01625 433949
E: imail@gradusworld.com
W: www.gradusworld.com

Gramm Interlink
17-19 High St, Ditchling, East Sussex BN6 8SY
T: 07827 947086
F: 01275 846397
W: www.gramminerlinkrail.co.uk

Grammer Seating Systems Ltd
Willenhall Lane Ind. Est., Bloxwich, Walsall WS3 2XN
T: 01922 407035
F: 01922 710552
E: david.bignell@grammer.com
W: www.grammer.com

Gramos Applied Ltd
Spring Rd, Smethwick, West Midlands B66 1PT
T: 0121 525 4000
F: 0121 525 4950
E: info@gramos-applied.com
W: www.gramos-applied.com

Grand Central Railway Co. Ltd.
River House, 17 Museum Street, York YO1 7DJ
T: 01904 633307
F: 01904 466066
E: customer.services@grandcentralrail.com
W: www.grandcentralrail.co.uk

Grant Rail Group
See Volker Rail

Grant Thornton UK LLP
Melton St, Euston Square, London NW1 2EP
T: 0141 223 0731
E: taylor.ferguson@uk.gt.com
W: www.grant-thornton.co.uk

Grass Concrete Ltd
Duncan House, 142 Thornes Lane, Thornes, Wakefield WF2 7RE
T: 01924 379443
F: 01924 290289
E: info@grasscrete.com
W: www.grasscrete.com

Graybar Ltd
10 Fleming Close, Park Farm Ind. Est, Wellingborough, Northants NN8 6QF
T: 01933 676700
F: 01933 676800
E: sales@graybar.co.uk
W: www.graybar.co.uk

Greater Anglia
Floor 2, East Anglia House, 12-34 Great Eastern St, Shoreditch, London EC2A 3EH
T: 020 7904 4031
F: 020 7549 5999
E: firstname.surname@greateranglia.co.uk
W: www.greateranglia.co.uk

Green Leader Ltd
21 Foxmoor Close, Oakley, Basingstoke, Hants RG23 7BQ
T: 01256 781739
M: 07944 855611
E: nmoore@greenleader.co.uk
W: www.greenleader.co.uk

Hafren
security fasteners
specialists in security and vandal deterrent fixings
T: +44 (0)1686 621 300
E: security@hafrenfasteners.com
W: www.hafrenfasteners.com

Greenbrier Europe/Wagony Swidnica SA
Ul Strzelinska 35, 58-100 Swidnica, Poland
T: 0048 74 856 2000
F: 0048 74 856 2035
E: europeansales@gbrx.com
W: www.gbrx.com

GreenMech Ltd
Mill Ind. Park, Kings Coughton, Alcester, Warks B49 5QG
T: 01789 400044
F: 01789 400167
E: sales@greenmech.co.uk
W: www.greenmech.co.uk

Grimshaw Architects
57 Clerkenwell Rd, London EC1M 5NG
T: 0207 291 4141
E: info@grimshaw-architects.com
W: www.grimshaw-architects.com

Grontmij
Grove House, Mansion Gate Drive, Leeds LS7 4DN
T: 0113 262 0000
F: 0113 262 0737
E: enquiries@grontmij.co.uk
W: www.grontmij.co.uk

Groundwise Searches Ltd
Suite 8, Chichester House, 45 Chichester Rd, Southend on Sea SS1 2JU
T: 01702 615566
F: 01702 460239
E: mail@groundwise.com
W: www.groundwise.com

GroupCytek
The Oast House, 5 Maed Lane, Farnham, Surrey GU9 7DY
T: 01252 715171
F: 01252 713271
E: projects@groupcytek.com
W: www.groupcytek.com

Gummiwerk
See Strail

Gunnebo UK Ltd
PO Box 61, Woden Rd, Wolverhampton WV10 0BY
T: 01902 455111
F: 01902 351961
E: marketing@gunnebo.com
W: www.gunnebo.com

H S Bassett
Coronet Way, Enterprise Park, Morriston, Swansea SA6 8RH
T: 01792 790022
F: 01792 790033
E: info@hsbassett.co.uk
W: www.hsbassett.co.uk

h2gogo Ltd
T: 01494 817174
E: info@h2gogo.com
W: www.h2gogo.com

Hadleigh Castings Ltd
Pond Hall Rd, Hadleigh, Ipswich, Suffolk IP7 5PW
T: 01473 827281
F: 01473 827879
E: data@hadleighcastings.com
W: www.hadleighcastings.com

Hafren Security Fasteners
Unit 23, Mochdre Industrial Park, Newtown, Powys SY16 4LE
T: 01686 621300
F: 01686 621800
E: security@hafrenfasteners.com
W: www.hafrenfasteners.com

Haigh Rail Ltd
60 Grange Drive, Hoghton, Preston PR5 0LP
M: 07875 847602
E: haighrailltd@ymail.com
W: www.haighrail.com

Haki Ltd
Magnus, Tame Valley Ind. Est, Tamworth, Staffs B77 5BY
T: 01827 282525
F: 01827 250329
E: info@haki.co.uk
W: www.haki.co.uk

Hako Machines Ltd
Eldon Close, Crick, Northants NN6 7SL
T: 01788 825600
F: 01788 823969
E: sales@hako.co.uk
W: www.hako.co.uk

Halcrow Group Ltd
Quammill House, Stores Road, Derby DE21 4XF
T: 01332 222620
E: hansonc@halcrow.com
W: www.halcrow.com

Halfen Ltd
Humphrys Rd, Woodside Est., Dunstable, Beds LU5 4TP
T: 0870 531 6300
F: 0870 531 6304
E: info@halfen.co.uk
W: www.halfen.co.uk

HallRail
Lyons Ind Est, Hetton le Hole, Tyne & Wear DH5 0RF
T: 0191 526 2114
F: 0191 517 0112
E: enquiries@hallrail.co.uk
W: www.hallrail.co.uk

Halo Rail
See Stewart Signs

Harmill Systems Ltd
Unit B1, Cherrycourt Way, Leighton Buzzard, Beds LU7 4UH
T: 01525 851133
F: 01525 850661
E: david.flint@harmill.co.uk
W: www.harmill.co.uk

HITACHI
Inspire the Next

Harp Visual Communications Solutions
Unit 7, Swanwick Business Centre, Bridge Rd, Lower Swanwick, Southampton SO31 7GB
T: 01489 580011
F: 01489 580022
E: sales@harpvisual.co.uk
W: www.passengerinformation.com

Harrington Generators International (HGI)
Ravenstor Rd, Wirksworth, Matlock, Derbys DE4 4FY
T: 01629 824284
F: 01629 824613
E: sales@hgigenerators.com
W: www.hgigenerators.com

Harry Fairclough Construction
Howley Lane, Howley, Warrington WA1 2DN
T: 01925 628300
F: 01925 628301
E: post@harryfairclough.co.uk
W: www.harryfairclough.co.uk

Harry Needle Railroad Company
Barrow Hill Depot, Campbell Drive, Barrow Hill, Chesterfield S43 2PR
T: 01246 477001
F: 01246 477208
M: 07917 777871
E: hnrcbh@aol.com
W: www.harryneedlerail.com

Harsco Rail Ltd
Unit 1, Chewton St, Eastwood, Notts NG16 3HB
T: 01773 539480
F: 01773 539481
E: uksales@harsco.com
W: www.permaquip.com

Harting Limited
Caswell Rd, Brackmills Ind. Est, Northampton NN4 7PW
T: 01604 827500
F: 01604 706777
E: gb@harting.com
W: www.harting.com

Halcrow
A CH2M HILL COMPANY
Excellence in Traction and Rolling Stock
- Rolling Stock Technical and Procurement Advice
- Lenders' Technical Advice
- Turnkey Project Management
- Rail Approvals & Certification
- Fleet maintenance support
- Independent Safety Assessment

Halcrow Group Ltd
Quarnmill House
Stores Road
Derby
DE21 4XF
T: 01332 222620
E: hansonc@halcrow.com
W: www.halcrow.com
sustaining and improving the quality of people's lives

Hawker Siddeley
Switchgear Ltd, Unit 3, Blackwood Ind. Est., Newport Rd, S.Wales NP12 2XH
T: 01495 223001
F: 01495 225674
E: nigel.jones@hss-ltd.com
W: www.hss-ltd.com

Hawkgrove Ltd
Bloomfield, Coalpit Lane, Stoke St Michael, Somerset BA3 5JT
T: 01373 837900
F: 08700 518155
E: mike.duberry@hawkgrove.co.uk
W: www.hawkgrove.co.uk

Hayley Rail
48-50 Westbrook Rd, Trafford Park, Manchester M17 1AY
T: 0161 877 3005
F: 0161 755 3425
E: phil.mccabe@hayley-group.co.uk
W: www.hayley-group.co.uk

HBM Test & Measurement
58 Station Rd, North Harrow, Middx HA2 7SA
T: 020 8515 6100
F: 020 8515 6159
E: info@uk.hbm.com
W: www.hbm.com

Health, Safety & Engineering Consultants Ltd (HSEC)
70 Tamworth Rd, Ashby de la Zouch, Leics LE65 2PR
T: 01530 412777
F: 01530 415992
E: hsec@hsec.co.uk
W: www.hsec.co.uk

Healthcare Connections Ltd
Nashleigh Court, 188 Severalls Ave, Chesham, Bucks HP5 3EN
T: 08456 773002
F: 08456 773004
E: sales@healthcare-connections.com
W: www.healthcare-connections.com

Heath Lambert Group
Transportation Division, 133 Houndsditch, London EC3A 7AW
T: 020 7560 3819
F: 020 7560 3294
E: mhawkes@heathlambert.com
W: www.heathlambert.com/projects

Heathrow Connect
6th Floor, 50 Eastbourne Terrace, Paddington, London W2 6LX
T: 020 8750 6600
F: 020 8750 6615
W: www.heathrowconnect.com

Heathrow Express
See Heathrow Connect
W: www.heathrowexpress.com

Heavy Haul Power International GmbH
Steigerstrasse 9, 99096 Erfurt, Germany
T: 0049 361 43046714
F: 0049 361 2629971
E: richard.painter@hhpi.eu
W: www.hhpi.eu

Hedra
See Mouchel

Hegenscheidt MFD GmbH & CO KG
Hegenscheidt Platz, D-41812 Erkelenz, Germany
T: 0049 2431 86279
F: 0049 2431 86480
E: fadler@niles-simmons.de
W: www.hegenscheidt-mfd.de

Hellermann Tyton
1 Robeson Way, Altrincham Road, Wythenshawe, Manchester M22 4TY
T: 0161 947 2200
F: 0161 9472220
E: sales@hellermanntyton.co.uk
W: www.hellermanntyton.co.uk

Henkel Loctite
Technologies House, Wood Lane End, Hemel Hempstead, Herts HP2 4RQ
T: 01442 278100
F: 01442 278293
W: www.loctite.com

Henry Williams Ltd
Dodsworth St, Darlington, Co. Durham DL1 2NJ
T: 01325 462722
F: 01325 381744
E: info@hwilliams.co.uk
W: www.hwilliams.co.uk

Hepworth Rail International
4 Merse Rd, North Moons Moat, Redditch, Worcs B98 9HL
T: 01527 60146
F: 01527 66836
E: markjones@b-hepworth.com
W: www.b-hepworth.com

Hering UK LLP
Wessex House, Oxford Rd, Newbury, Berks RG14 1PA
T: 01635 814490
F: 01635 814491
W: www.heringinternational.com

Hertford Controls Ltd
14 Ermine Point, Gentlemens Field, Westmill Rd, Ware, Herts SG12 0EF
T: 01920 467578
F: 01920 487037
E: info@hertfordcontrols.co.uk
W: www.hertfordcontrols.co.uk

Hexagon Metrology Ltd
Halesfield 13, Telford, Shropshire TF7 4PL
T: 0870 446 2667
F: 0870 446 2668
E: enquiry.uk@hexagonmetrology.com
W: www.hexagonmetrology.com/uk

Hiflex Fluidpower
Howley Park Rd, Morley, Leeds LS27 0BN
T: 0113 281 0031
F: 0113 307 5918
E: sales@hiflex-europe.com
W: www.dunlophiflex.com

High Speed 1 Ltd
73 Collier St, London N1 9BE
T: 020 7014 2700
F: 07717 151070
E: ben.ruse@highspeed1.co.uk
W: www.highspeed1.com

High Voltage Maintenance Services Ltd
Unit A, Faraday Court, Faraday Rd, Crawley, West Sussex RH10 9PU
T: 0845 604 0336
F: 01293 537739
E: enquiries@hvms.co.uk
W: www.hvms.co.uk

High-Point Rendel Limited
61 Southwark St, London SE1 1SA
T: 020 7654 0400
F: 020 7654 0401
E: london@hprworld.com
W: www.hprworld.com

Hill Cannon (UK) LLP
Royal Chambers, Station Parade, Harrogate HG1 1EP
T: 01423 562571
F: 01423 530018
E: harrogate@hillcannon.com
W: www.hillcannon.com

HellermannTyton
HellermannTyton is a Global manufacturer and supplier of cable management solutions. Ranges include Cable ties, Rail Industry approved Thermal printers and associated tags & markers.
A: 1 Robeson Way, Altrincham Rd, Wythenshawe, Manchester M22 4TY.
T: +44 (0) 161 947 2200
F: +44 (0) 161 947 2220
E: sales@hellermanntyton.co.uk
www.hellermanntyton.co.uk

Hill McGlynn
See Ranstadt CPE

Hillfort Communications Ltd
3 Campion Way, Lymington, Hants SO41 9LS
T: 01590 670912
F: 01590 688341
E: hillfort@doc2prod.demon.co.uk

Hilti (GB) Ltd
No1 Trafford Wharf Rd, Trafford Park, Manchester M17 1BY
T: 0800 886 100
F: 0800 886 200
E: gbsales@hilti.com
W: www.hilti.co.uk

HIMA-SELLA
Infrastructure & Mobile Solutions
Contact Hima-Sella for any of the following:
- Train Control & Protection
- Customer Information (CIS & PA)
- Selective Door Opening (SDO & CSDE)
- Integrated Communication Management
- CCTV (Driver Only & Front Facing)
- GSM-R Communications
- Panel & Electrical Build
- SCADA

Hima-Sella Ltd
Carrington Field Street
Stockport Cheshire SK1 3JN
T: 0161 429 4500
F: 0161 476 3095
W: www.hima-sella.co.uk
E: sales@hima-sella.co.uk
Link-up Qualified via Audit Link-up ID 3633
The Logical Solution for Safety

Hima-Sella Ltd
Carrington Field St, Stockport SK1 3JN
T: 0161 429 4500
F: 0161 476 3095
E: sales@hima-sella.co.uk
W: www.hima-sella.co.uk

Hiremasters
See Quickbuild

Hiremee Ltd
York Way, Royston, Herts SG8 5HJ
T: 01763 247111
F: 01763 247222
E: info@hiremee.co.uk
W: www.hiremee.co.uk

Hitachi Capital Vehicle Solutions Ltd
Kiln House, Kiln Rd, Newbury, Berks RG14 2NU
T: 01635 574640
W: www.hitachicapitalvehiclesolutions.co.uk

Hitachi Rail Europe Ltd
70 Holborn Viaduct, London EC1N 2PB
T: 020 7970 2700
F: 020 7970 2799
E: rail.enquiries@hitachi-eu.com
W: www.hitachi-rail.com

HJ Skelton & Co Ltd
9 The Broadway, Thatcham, Berks RG19 3JA
T: 01635 865256
F: 01635 865710
E: email@hjskelton.com
W: www.hjskelton.co.uk

HOCHTIEF (UK)Construction Ltd
Epsilon, Windmill Hill Business Park, Whitehill Way, Swindon SN5 6NX
T: 01793 755555
F: 01793 755556
E: enquiries@hochtief.co.uk
W: www.hochtief.co.uk

Hodge Clemco Ltd
Orgreave Drive, Sheffield S13 9NR
T: 0114 254 8811
F: 0114 254 0250
E: sales@hodgeclemco.co.uk
W: www.hdgeclemco.co.uk

Hodgson & Hodgson Group Ltd
Crown Business Park, Old Dalby, Melton Mowbray, Leics LE14 3NQ
T: 01376 555200
E: info@hodgsongroup.co.uk
W: www.acoustic.co.uk/h&h/rail

Hogia Transport Systems Ltd
St James House, 13 Kensington Square, London W8 5HD
T: 020 7795 8156
E: gary.umpleby@hogia.com
W: www.hogia.com

Holdfast Level Crossings Ltd
Brockenhurst, Cheap St, Chedworth, Cheltenham, Glos GL54 4AA
T: 01242 578801
F: 01285 720748
M: 07970 656143
E: request@railcrossings.co.uk
W: www.railcrossings.co.uk

Hitachi is a railway system supplier. Products include trains, traction equipment, signalling, maintenance, and traffic systems. Hitachi has delivered the Class 395 High Speed trains.
40 Holburn Viaduct
EC1N 2PB
Tel: 0207 970 2700
Fax: 0207 970 2799
rail.enquiries@hitachirail-eu.com
www.hitachirail-eu.com
HITACHI
Inspire the Next

Holdsworth Fabrics Ltd
Hopton Mills, Mirfield, West Yorks WF14 8HE
T: 01924 490591
F: 01924 495605
E: info@camirafabrics.com
W: www.holdsworthfabrics.com

Holland Company
1000 Holland Drive, Crete, Illinois 60417 USA
T: 001 708 672 2300
F: 001 708 672 0119
E: sales@hollandco.com
W: www.hollandco.com

Holmar Rail Services
Kendal House, The Street, Shadoxhurst, Ashford, Kent TN26 1LU
T: 01233 731007
F: 01233 733221
W: www.holmar.co.uk

Holophane Rail Solutions
T: 01908 649292
F: 01908 367618
E: info@holophane.co.uk
W: www.holophane.co.uk

Homegrown Timber (Rail) Ltd
Courtlands, Antlands Lane, Shipley Br, Surrey RH6 9TE
T: 01293 821321
F: 01293 772319
E: rail@homegrowntimber.com
W: www.homegrowntimber.com

Hoppecke Industrial Batteries Ltd
2 Lowfield Drive, Centre 500, Newcastle, Staffs ST5 0UU
T: 01782 667300
W: www.hoppecke.com

Hosiden Besson Ltd
11 St Josephs Close, Hove, East Sussex BN3 7EZ
T: 01273 861166
F: 01273 777501
E: info@hbl.co.uk
W: www.hbl.co.uk

Houghton International
Fisher St, Walker, Newcastle upon Tyne NE6 4LT
T: 0191 234 3000
F: 0191 263 7873
E: info@houghtoninternational.com
W: www.houghton-international.com

Howells Railway Products Ltd
Longley Lane, Sharston Ind. Est., Wythenshawe, Manchester M22 4SS
T: 0161 945 5567
F: 0161 945 5597
E: info@howells-railway.co.uk
W: www.howells-railway.co.uk

HP Information Security
3200 Daresbury Park, Daresbury, Warrington WA4 4BU
T: 01925 665500
F: 01925 667200
E: salessupport.infosec@hp.com
W: www.hp.com

HPR Consult
See High Point Rendel

HS Carlsteel Engineering Ltd
Crabtree Manorway South, Belvedere, Kent DA17 6BH
T: 020 8312 1879
F: 020 8320 9480
E: sales@hscarlsteel.co.uk
W: www.hscarlsteel.co.uk

HSBC Rail (UK)
See Eversholt Rail Ltd

HSS Training Ltd
Circle House, Lostock Rd, Davyhulme, Manchester M41 0HS
T: 0845 766 7799
F: 0161 877 9074
E: training@hss.com
W: www.hsstraining.com

Huber + Suhner (UK) Ltd
Telford Rd, Bicester, Oxon OX26 4LA
T: 01869 364100
F: 01869 249046
E: info.uk@hubersuhner.com
W: www.hubersuhner.co.uk

Hull Trains
See First Hull Trains

Human Engineering Ltd
Shore House, 68, Westbury Hill, Westbury-on-Trym, Bristol BS9 3AA
T: 0117 962 0888
F: 0117 962 9888
E: barry.davies@humaneng.co.uk
W: www.humaneng.net

Human Reliability
1 School House, Higher Lane, Dalton, Lancs WN8 7RP
T: 01257 463121
F: 01257 463810
E: dembrey@humanreliability.com
W: www.humanreliability.com

Hunslet Barclay
See Brush Barclay

Hunslet Engine Co
See LH Group Services

Husqvarna Construction Products
Unit 4, Pearce Way, Bristol Rd, Gloucester GL2 5YD
T: 0844 844 4570
E: husqvarna.construction@husqvarna.com
W: www.husqvarna.co.uk

Hutchinson Team Telecom Ltd
See Indigo Telecom Group

HV Wooding Ltd
Range Rd, Hythe, Kent CT21 6HG
T: 01303 264471
F: 01303 262408
E: sales@hvwooding.co.uk
W: www.hvwooding.co.uk

Hyder Consulting (UK) Ltd
Manning House, 22 Carlisle Place, London SW1P 1JA
T: 020 3014 9000
F: 020 7828 8428
E: mahmoud.alghita@hyderconsulting.com
W: www.hyderconsulting.com

Hydrex Equipment UK Ltd
Hydrex House, Serbert Way, Portishead, Bristol BS20 7GD
T: 01275 399400
F: 01275 399500
E: enquiries@hydrex.co.uk
W: www.hydrex.co.uk

Hydro Aluminium Extrusions Ltd
Pantglas Ind. Est., Bedwas, Caerphilly CF83 8DR
T: 0870 777 2262
F: 02920 863728
E: sales.haeuk@hydro.com
W: www.hydro.com/extrusion/uk

Hydrotech Europe Ltd
Beaufort Court, 11 Roebuck Way, Knowlhill, Milton Keynes MK5 8HL
T: 01908 675244
F: 01908 397513
W: www.hydro-usl.com

Hydrotechnik UK Ltd
Unit 10, Easter Lane, Lenton, Nottingham NG7 2PX
T: 01159 003550
F: 01159 705597
E: sales@hydrotechnik.co.uk
W: www.hydrotechnik.co.uk

Hypertac UK
36-38 Waterloo Rd, London NW2 7UH
T: 020 8450 8033
F: 020 8208 3455
E: info@hypertac.co.uk
W: www.hypertac.co.uk

I C Consultants Ltd
58 Prince's Gate, Exhibition Rd, London SW7 2QA
T: 020 7594 6565
F: 020 7594 6570
E: consultants@imperial.ac.uk
W: www.imperial-consultants.co.uk

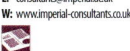

IAD Rail Systems
See Network Rail

Ian Catling Consultancy
Ash Meadow, Bridge Way, Chipstead CR5 3PX
T: 01737 552225
F: 01737 556669
E: info@catling.com
W: www.catling.com

Ian Riley
See Riley & Son

IBI Group
Kemp House, 152-160 City Rd, London EC1V 2NP
T: 020 7017 1850
F: 020 7251 8339
E: enquiriesuk@ibigroup.com
W: www.ibigroup.com

ICEE
20 Arnside Rd, Waterlooville, Hants PO7 7UP
T: 02392 230604
F: 02392 230605
E: sales@icee.co.uk
W: www.icee.co.uk

Icomera UK
1092 Galley Drive, Kent Science Park, Sittingbourne, Kent ME9 8GA
T: 01884 860 799
E: information@icomera.com
W: www.icomera.com

Icon Silentbloc UK Ltd
Wellington Rd, Burton upon Trent, Staffs DE14 2AP
T: 01283 741700
F: 01283 741742
E: info@iconpolymer.com
W: www.iconpolymer.com

Icore International Ltd
220 Bedford Avenue, Slough SL1 4RY
T: 01753 896600
F: 01753 896601
E: cristophebigare@zodiacaerospace.com
W: www.zodiacaerospace.com

ID Computing Ltd
ID Centre, Lathkill House, rtc Business Park, London Rd, Derby DE24 8UP
T: 01332 258880
F: 01332 258823
E: info@idcomputing.co.uk
W: www.idcomputing.co.uk

Ideas Limited (Integration Design Ergonomics Applications Solutions)
PO Box 193, Thame, Oxon OX9 0BR
T: 01844 216896
F: 0970 460 6190
E: info@ideas.ltd.uk
W: www.ideas.ltd.uk

IET
See Institution of Engineering & Technology

IETG Ltd
Cross Green Way, Cross Green Ind. Est., Leeds LS9 0SE
T: 0113 201 9700
F: 0113 201 9701
W: www.ietg.co.uk

HITACHI
Inspire the Next

Directory

Ilecsys
Tring Ind. Est, Upper Icknield Way, Tring,
Herts HP23 4JX
T: 08444 770990
F: 01442 828399
E: pjd@ilecsys.co.uk
W: www.ilecsys.co.uk

ILME UK Ltd
50 Evans Rd, Venture Point, Speke,
Merseyside L24 9PB
T: 0151 336 9321
F: 0151 336 9326
E: sales@ilmeuk.co.uk
W: www.ilmeuk.co.uk

Imagerail
Reservoir House, Wetheral Pasture,
Carlisle CA4 8HR
T: 01768 800208
E: andrew@imagerail.com
W: www.imagerail.com

In2rail Ltd
Hobbs Hill, Rothwell,
Northants NN14 6YG
T: 01536 711804
M: 07980 104571
E: pm@in2rail.co.uk
W: www.in2rail.co.uk

Inbis Ltd
Club St, Bamber Bridge, Preston,
Lancs PR5 6FN
T: 01772 645000
F: 01772 645001
W: www.inbis.com

Inchmere Design
Inchmere Studios, Grange Park, Chacombe,
Banbury, Oxon OX17 2EL
T: 01295 711801
E: mark@inchmere.co.uk
W: www.inchmere.co.uk

Incorporatewear
Edison Rd,
Hams Hall National Distribution Park,
Coleshill B46 1DA
T: 0844 257 0530
F: 0844 257 0591
E: info@incorporatewear.co.uk
W: www.incorporatewear.co.uk

Independent Glass Co Ltd
540-550 Lawnmoor St, Dixons Blazes Ind. Est,
Glasgow G5 0UA
T: 0141 429 8700
F: 0141 429 8524
E: toughened@ig-glass.co.uk
W: www.independentglass.co.uk

Independent Rail Consultancy Group (IRCG)
E: info@ircg.co.uk
W: www.ircg.co.uk

Indigo Telecom Group
Field House, Uttoxeter Old Rd,
Derby DE1 1NH
T: 01332 375570
F: 01332 375673
E: sales@indigotelecomgroup.com
W: www.indigotelecomgroup.com

Industrial Door Services Ltd
Adelaide St, Crindau Park, Newport,
Gwent NP20 5NF
T: 01633 853335
F: 01633 851989
E: enquiries@indoorserv.co.uk
W: www.indoorserv.co.uk

Industrial Flow Control Ltd
Unit 1, Askews Farm Lane, Grays,
Essex RM17 5XR
T: 01375 387155
F: 01375 387420
E: sales@inflow.co.uk
W: www.inflow.co.uk

Inflow
See Industrial Flow Control Ltd

Infodev EDI Inc.
1995 Rue Frank-Carrel, Suite 202,
Quebec G1N 4H9 Canada
T: 001 418 681 3529
F: 001 418 681 1209
E: info@infodev.ca
W: www.infodev.ca

Infor
1 Lakeside Rd, Farnborough,
Hants GU14 6XP
T: 0800 376 9633
F: 0121 615 8255
E: ukmarketing@infor.com
W: www.infor.co.uk

Informatica Software Ltd
6 Waltham Park, Waltham Rd,
White Waltham, Maidenhead,
Berks SL6 3JN
T: 01628 511311
F: 01628 511411
E: ukinfo@informatica.com
W: www.informatica.com

Informatiq
Gresham House, 53 Clarendon Rd,
Watford WD17 1LA
T: 01923 224481
F: 01923 224493
E: permanent@informatiq.co.uk
W: www.informatiq.co.uk

Infotec Ltd
The Maltings, Tamworth Rd,
Ashby De La Zouch,
Leics LE65 2PS
T: 01530 560600
F: 01530 560111
E: sales@infotec.co.uk
W: www.infotec.co.uk

Infra Safety Services
See ISS Labour

INIT Innovations in Transportation Ltd
49 Stoney St,
The Lace Market,
Nottingham NG1 1LX
T: 0870 890 4648
F: 0115 989 5461
W: www.init.co.uk

Initial Facilities - Transport Sector
Victoria House, 1-3 College Hill,
London EC4R 2RA
T: 0800 0778963
E: if-contact-uk@rentokil-initial.com
W: www.initial.co.uk

Initiate Consulting Ltd
9 Gainsford St,
Tower Bridge,
London SE1 2NE
T: 020 7357 9600
F: 020 7357 9604
E: info@initiate.uk.com
W: www.initiate.uk.com

Inline Track Welding Ltd
Ashmill Business Park,
Ashford Rd, Lenham,
Maidstone ME17 2GQ
T: 01622 854730
F: 01622 854731
E: david.thomson@fsmail.net

InnoTrans – a trade fair organised by Messe Berlin GmbH,
Messedamm 22,
D-14055 Berlin,
Germany
T: 0049 303038 2376
F: 0049 303038 2190
E: innotrans@messe-berlin.de
W: www.innotrans.com

Innovative Support Systems Ltd (ISS)
15 Fountain Parade,
Mapplewell,
Barnsley,
S Yorks S75 6FW
T: 01226 381155
F: 01226 381177
E: enquiries@iss-eng.com
W: www.iss-eng.com

Insight Security
Unit 2, Cliffe Ind. Est,
Lewes,
E Sussex BN8 6JL
T: 01273 475500
F: 01273 478800
E: info@insight-security.com
W: www.insight-security.com

Insituform Technologies Ltd
Roundwood Ind. Est., Ossett,
West Yorks WF5 9SQ
T: 01924 277076
F: 01924 265107
E: jbeech@insituform.com
W: www.insituform.co.uk

Inspectahire Instrument Co. Ltd
Unit 11, Whitemyres Business Centre,
Whitemyres Ave,
Aberdeen AB16 6HQ
T: 01224 789692
F: 01224 789462
E: enquiries@inspectahire.com
W: www.inspectahire.com

Install CCTV Ltd
10 Rochester Court,
Anthonys Way,
Rochester,
Kent ME2 4NW
T: 01634 717784
F: 01634 718085
W: www.installcctv.co.uk

Institution of Railway Operators
PO Box 375, Burgess Hill,
West Sussex RH15 5BX
T: 01444 246379
F: 01444 246392
E: admin@railwayoperators.org
W: www.railwayoperators.org

Institution of Railway Signal Engineers (IRSE)
4th Floor, 1 Birdcage Walk,
Westminster,
London SW1H 9JJ
T: 020 7808 1180
F: 020 7808 1196
E: hq@irse.org
W: www.irse.org

Intamech Ltd
see Arbil

Intec (UK) Ltd
York House, 76-78 Lancaster Rd,
Morecambe,
Lancs LA4 5QN
T: 01524 426777
F: 01524 426888
E: intec@inteconline.co.uk
W: www.inteconline.co.uk

Integrated Transport Planning Ltd
50 North Thirtieth St,
Milton Keynes MK9 3PP
T: 01908 259718
F: 01908 605747
E: wheway@itpworld.net
W: www.itpworld.net

Integrated Utility Services
16 Toft Green,
York YO1 6JT
T: 01904 685678
F: 01904 685671
E: railenquiries@ius.biz
W: www.ius.biz

Integrated Water Services Ltd
Park Lane West, Tipton,
Dudley DY4 8LH
T: 0121 520 1006
F: 0121 521 2811
E: nickitasmith@integrated-water.co.uk
W: www.integrated-water.co.uk

Intelligent Locking Systems
Bordesley Hall, Alvechurch,
Birmingham B48 7QA
T: 01527 66885
F: 01527 66681
E: info@islocks.co.uk
W: www.islocks.co.uk

Intelligent Radio Solutions (IRIS) Ltd
Networks House, 32 Stephenson Rd, St Ives,
Cambs PE27 3WT
T: 01438 767359
F: 01438 767305
E: cthomason@theiet.org
W: www.theiet.org

Institution of Mechanical Engineers (I Mech E)
1 Birdcage Walk, Westminster,
London SW1H 9JJ
T: 020 7222 7899
F: 020 7222 4557
E: railway@imeche.org.uk
W: www.imeche.org.uk

Institution of Engineering & Technology
Michael Faraday House,
Six Hills Way,
Stevenage SG1 2AY
T: 01438 767359
F: 01438 767305
E: cthomason@theiet.org
W: www.theiet.org

Intelligent Radio Solutions (IRIS) Ltd
Networks House, 32 Stephenson Rd, St Ives,
Cambs PE27 3WT
T: 01223 906052
E: info@intelligentradiosolutions.com
W: www.intelligentradiosolutions.com

Interface Fabrics Ltd
See Holdsworth

Interfaces
2 Valley Close,
Hertford SG13 8BD
T: 01992 422042
E: reg.harman@ntlworld.com

Interfleet Technology Ltd - a member of the SNC-Lavalin Group
Interfleet House, Pride Parkway, Derby
DE24 8HX
T: 01332 223 000
F: 01332 223 001
E: grace.m@interfleet.co.uk
W: www.interfleet.co.uk

Intermodal Logistics
Cedar House, Glade Rd, Marlow, Bucks
SL7 1DQ
T: 01234 822821
F: 01628 486800
E: derekbliss@intermodallogistics.co.uk
W: www.intermodallogistics.co.uk

Intermodality LLP
6 Belmont Business Centre,
East Hoathly, Lewes,
East Sussex BN8 6QL
T: 0845 130 4388
F: 01825 841449
W: www.intermodality.com

International Transport Intermediaries Club Ltd
See Leigh Fisher

Intertrain (UK) Ltd
Intertrain House, Union St,
Doncaster DN1 3AE
T: 01302 815530
F: 01302 815531
E: intertrain@intertrain.biz
W: www.intertrain.biz

Invensys Rail Ltd
PO Box 79, Langley Park, Pew Hill,
Chippenham, Wilts SN15 1JD
T: 01249 441441
F: 01249 441442
E: marketing@invensysrail.com
W: www.invensysrail.com

Institution of Civil Engineers (ICE)
One Great George St,
Westminster,
London SW1P 3AA
T: 020 7222 7722
E: communications@ice.org.uk
W: www.ice.org.uk

Installation Project Services Ltd
53 Ullswater Crescent, Coulsdon,
Surrey CR5 2HR
T: 020 8655 6060
F: 020 8655 6070
E: sales@ips-ltd.co.uk
W: www.ips-ltd.co.uk

Institute of Rail Welding
Granta Park, Great Abingdon,
Cambridge CB21 6AL
T: 01223 899000
F: 01223 894219
E: tim.jessop@twi.co.uk
W: www.iorw.co.uk

Ionbond Ltd
Unit 36, Number One Ind Est, Medomsley Rd,
Consett DH7 6TS
T: 01207 500823
F: 01207 590254
E: maria.beadle@ionbond.com
W: www.ionbond.com

Iosis Associates
15 Good Shepherd Close, Bishop Rd,
Bristol BS7 8NF
T: 0117 370 6313
M: 07968 947021
E: pwt@iosis.org.uk
W: www.iosis.org.uk

Ipex Consulting
Rose Cottage, Woodcroft Lane, Woodcroft,
Chepstow NP16 7QB
M: 07767 436467
E: info@ipexconsulting.com
W: www.ipexconsulting.com

I-Plas Ltd
Ridings Business Park, Hopwood Lane,
Halifax HX1 3TT
T: 0845 459 9352
F: 0845 459 9354
E: enquiries@i-plas.co.uk
W: www.i-plas.co.uk

IQPC
Anchor House, 15-19 Bitten St,
London SW3 3QL
T: 020 7368 2363
F: 020 7368 9301
E: enquire@iqpc.co.uk
W: www.iqpc.co.uk

Iridium Onboard
Clue House, Petherton Rd,
Hengrove,
Bristol BS14 9BZ
T: 01275 890140
E: info@iridiumonboard.com
W: www.iridiumonboard.com

Irish Traction Group
31 Hayfield Rd, Bredbury,
Stockport SK6 1DE
M: 07713 159869
E: info@irishtractiongroup.com
W: www.irishtractiongroup.com

IRL Group Ltd
Unit C1, Swingbridge Rd,
Loughborough,
Leics LE11 5JD
T: 01509 217101
F: 01509 611004
E: info@irlgroup.com
W: www.irlgroup.com

Ironside Farrar
111 McDonald Rd,
Edinburgh EH7 4NW
T: 0131 550 6500
E: mail@ironsidefarrar.com
W: www.ironsidefarrar.com

ISC Best Practice Consultancy Ltd
Lower Market Hall Offices,
Market St, Okehampton, Devon EX20 1HN
T: 01837 54555
E: isc.bestpractice@btconnect.com
W: www.isc-bestpracticeconsultancy.co.uk

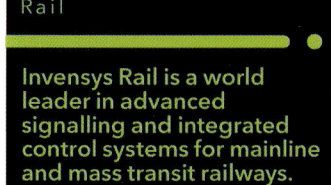

Ischebeck Titan
John Dean House, Wellington Rd,
Burton upon Trent DE14 2TG
T: 01283 515677
F: 01283 516126
E: sales@ischebeck-titan.co.uk
W: www.ischebeck-titan.co.uk

IS-Rayfast Ltd
Unit 2, Westmead, Swindon SN5 7SY
T: 01793 616700
F: 01793 644304
E: sales@israyfast.com
W: www.israyfast.com

ISS Labour
5/6, Acorn Place, Alfreton Rd,
Derby DE21 4AS
T: 01332 542800
F: 01332 542829
E: info@isslabour.co.uk
W: www.isslabour.co.uk

ITIC
90 Fenchurch St, London EC3M 4ST
T: 020 7338 0150
F: 020 7338 0151
E: itic@thomasmiller.com
W: www.itic-insure.com

itmsoil Group Ltd
Bell Lane, Uckfield, E Sussex TN22 1QL
T: 01825 765044
F: 01825 744398
E: sales@itmsoil.com
W: www.itmsoil.com

ITS United Kingdom
Suite 312, Tower Bridge Business Centre,
46-48 East Smithfield, London E1W 1AW
T: 020 7709 3003
F: 020 7709 3007
E: mailbox@its-uk.org.uk
W: www.its-uk.org.uk

ITSO Ltd
Luminaire House, Deltic Way, Milton Keynes
MK13 8LW
T: 01908 255455
F: 01908 255450
E: info@itso.org.uk
W: www.itso.org

ITT Water & Wastewater UK Ltd
Colwick, Nottingham NG4 2AN
T: 0115 940 0111
F: 0115 940 0444
W: www.ittwww.co.uk

ITW Plexus
Unit 3, Shipton Way, Express Business Park,
Northampton Rd, Rushden,
Northants NN10 6GL
T: 01933 354550
F: 01933 354555
E: sales@itwppe.eu
W: www.staput.co.uk

J Murphy & Sons Ltd
Hiview House, 81 Highgate Rd,
London NW5 1TN
T: 020 7692 9540
F: 020 7692 9539
E: info@murphygroup.co.uk
W: www.murphygroup.co.uk

J.A.B Services (UK)
September Cottage,
Haven Rd,
Rudgwick,
Horsham
RH12 3JH
T: 01403 822326
M: 07786 636495
E: baggsja@hotmail.com

J.Boyle Associates Ltd
Bunch Meadows,
Woodway,
Princes Risborough,
Bucks
HP27 0NW
F: 0870 4602044
M: 07919 386100
E: info@jba.net
W: www.jba.net

Jacobs Consultancy UK Ltd
See Leigh Fisher

Jacobs UK Ltd
95 Bothwell St,
Glasgow
G2 7HX
T: 0141 204 2511
F: 0141 226 3109
W: www.jacobsbabtie.com

180

In association with ATKINS

Jafco Tools Ltd
Access House, Great Western St, Wednesbury, West Midlands WS10 7LE
T: 0121 556 7700
F: 0121 556 7788
E: info@jafcotools.com
W: www.jafcotools.com

JB Corrie & Co Ltd
Frenchmans Rd, Petersfield, Hants GU32 3AP
T: 01730 237129
F: 01730 264915
E: mhickman@jbcorrie.co.uk
W: www.jbcorrie.co.uk

JBA Management Consultants
See J Boyle Associates Ltd

JCB
World Headquarters, Rocester, Staffs ST14 5JP
T: 01889 590312
F: 01889 593455
W: www.jcb.co.uk

Jefferson Sheard Architects
Fulcrum, 2 Sidney St, Sheffield S1 4RH
T: 0114 276 1651
F: 0114 279 9191
E: katrin.milano@jeffersonsheard.com
W: www.jeffersonsheard.com

Jewers Doors td
Stratton Business Park, Biggleswade, Beds SG18 8QB
T: 01767 317090
F: 01767 312305
E: mjewers@jewersdoors.co.uk
W: www.jewersdoors.co.uk

Jim Hailstone Ltd
Broadfield, Church Lane, Coldwaltham, W Sussex RH20 1LW
T: 07860 478197
F: 01798 872892
E: jimhailstone@bluebottle.com
W: www.icrg.co.uk

JMJ Laboratories
See Synergy Health Plc

JMP Consultants Ltd
8th Floor, 3 Harbour Exchange Sq, London E14 9GE
T: 020 7536 8040
F: 020 7005 0462
E: docklands@jmp.co.uk
W: www.jmp.co.uk

Jobson James - Specialist Rail Supply Chain Insurance
30 St Pauls Square, Birmingham B3 1QZ
T: 0121 452 8450
F: 0121 452 8451
E: rail@jobson-james.co.uk
W: www.jobson-james.co.uk

John Fishwick & Sons
Golden Hill Lane, Leyland, Lancs PR25 3LE
T: 01772 421207
F: 01772 622407
E: enquiries@fishwicks.co.uk
W: www.fishwicks.co.uk

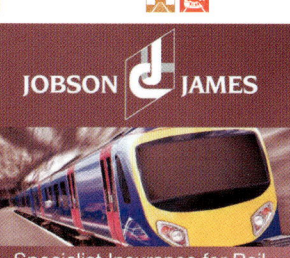

One of a few change management organisations with real hands on delivery experience in the rail industry. Driving change. Making it happen.
A: Bunch Meadows, Woodway, Princess Risborough, Buckinghamshire, HP27 0NW
T: 07919 386100
F: 0870 4602044
E: info@jba.uk.net
W: www.jba.uk.net
J BOYLE associates
J Boyle Associates ltd Management Consultants

John Headon Ltd
8 Green St East, Darwen, Lancs BB3 3HY
T: 01254 705001
E: john@johnheadonltd.co.uk
W: www.johnheadonltd.co.uk

John Prodger Recruitment
The Courtyard, Alban Park, Hatfield Rd, St Albans, Herts AL4 0LA
T: 01727 841101
F: 01727 838272
E: jobs@jprecruit.com
W: www.jprecruit.com

Johnson Rail
Orchard Ind Est, Toddington, Glos GL54 5EB
T: 01242 621362
F: 01242 621554
E: stephen.phillips@johnson-security.co.uk

Joint Line Railtours
15 The Greenway, Ickenham, Uxbridge, Middx UB10 8LS
M: 07905 023322
E: contact@jointlinerailtours.co.uk
W: www.jointlinerailtours.co.uk

Jonathan Lee Recruitment
3 Sylvan Court, Southfield Business Park, Basildon, Essex SS15 6TU
T: 01268 455520
F: 01268 455521
E: southfields@jonlee.co.uk
W: www.jonlee.co.uk

Jones Garrard Move Ltd
7 Beaker Close, Smeeton Westerby, Leics LE8 0RT
T: 07802 380 252
E: michael-rodber@jonesgarrardmove.com
W: www.jonesgarrardmove.com

JOBSON JAMES

Specialist Insurance for Rail Industry Supply Chain Companies
• Infrastructure • Contractors
• Maintenance • Rolling stock
• Manufacturers • Consultants
Jobson James Insurance Brokers Ltd
30 St Pauls Square Birmingham B3 1QZ
Tel. 0121 452 8450
E. rail@jobson-james.co.uk
www.jobson-james.co.uk

Jotun Paints (Europe) Ltd
Stather Rd, Flixborough, Scunthorpe, N. Lincs DN15 8RR
T: 01724 400000
F: 01724 400100
E: decpaints@jotun.co.uk
W: www.jotun.com/eu.com

Journeycall Ltd
Laurencekirk Business Park, Laurencekirk AB30 1AJ
T: 01561 376070
F: 01561 377983
M: 07545 696236
E: enquiries@journeycall.com
W: www.journeycall.com

JourneyPlan
12 Abbey Park Place, Dunfermline, Scotland KY12 7PD
T: 01383 731048
F: 01383 731788
W: www.journeyplan.co.uk

JPM Parry & Associates Ltd
Overend Rd, Cradley Heath, West Midlands B64 7DD
T: 01384 569171
F: 01384 637753
E: info@parryassociates.com
W: www.parryassociates.com/transport

JSD Research & Development Ltd
Old Carriage Works, Holgate Park Drive, York YO24 4EH
T: 01904 623500
E: info@jsdrail.com
W: www.jsdrail.com

Judge 3d
34 New St, St Neots, Cambs PE19 1AJ
T: 01480 211080
F: 05601 152019
E: admin@judge3dltd.com
W: www.judge3dltd.com

Kaba Door Systems Ltd
Door Automation, Halesfield 4, Telford, Shropshire TF7 4AP
T: 0870 000 5252
F: 0870 000 5253
E: info@kaba.co.uk
W: www.kabadoorsystems.co.uk

Karcher Vehicle Wash
Karcher UK Ltd, Karcher House, Beaumont Rd, Banbury OX16 1TB
T: 01295 752172
F: 01295 752040
W: www.karchervehiclewash.co.uk

Kavia Moulded Products Ltd
Rochdale Rd, Walsden, Todmorden, West Yorks OL14 6UD
T: 01706 816696
F: 01706 813822
E: enquiries@kavia.info
W: www.kavia.info

Kaymac Marine & Civil Engineering Ltd
Osprey Business Park, Byng St, Landore, Swansea SA1 2NR
T: 01792 301818
F: 01792 645698
E: claire.williamson@kaymacltd.co.uk
W: www.kaymacmarine.co.uk

Kelly Rail
Kelly House, Headstone Rd, Harrow, Middx HA1 1PD
T: 020 8884 6605
F: 020 8424 0509
E: info@kelly.co.uk
W: www.kelly.co.uk

Keltbray
St Andrews House, Portsmouth Rd, Esher, Surrey KT10 9TA
T: 020 7643 1000
F: 020 7643 1001
E: enquiries@keltbray.com
W: www.keltbray.com

Keltbray Aspire
Unit 4a/5b, Crewe Hall Enterprise Park, Weston Lane, Crewe CW1 6UA
T: 01270 254176
F: 01270 253267
E: keltbrayaspire@keltbray.com
W: www.keltbray.com

Kelvatek Ltd
Bermuda Innovation Centre, Bermuda Park, Nuneaton CV10 7SD
T: 02476 320100
F: 02476 641172
E: mail@kelman.co.uk
W: www.kelman.co.uk

Kendall Poole Consulting
Pinewood Business Park – TS2, Coleshill Rd, Marston Green, Solihull B37 7HG
T: 0121 779 0934
E: scm@kendallpoole.com
W: www.kendallpoole.com

Kennedy Solutions
1 Bromley Lane, Chislehurst, Kent BR7 6LH
T: 020 8468 1016
F: 01689 855261
E: martin@kennedy-solutions.com
W: www.kennedy-solutions.com

Kent Modular Electronics Ltd (KME)
621 Maidstone Rd, Rochester, Kent ME1 3QJ
T: 01634 835407
F: 01634 830619
E: sales@kme.co.uk
W: www.kme.co.uk

Kent PHK Ltd
Hermitage Way, Mansfield, Notts NG18 5ES
T: 01623 421202
F: 01623 421302
E: enquiries@kentphk.co.uk

Kent Stainless (Wexford) Ltd
Ardcavan, Wexford, Ireland
T: 0800 376 8377
F: 00353 53914 1802
E: info@kentstainless.com
W: www.kentstainless.com

Keolis (UK) Ltd
City Executive Centre, 344-354 Gray's Inn Rd, London WC1X 8BP
T: 020 7092 8240
E: communication@keolis.com
W: www.keolis.com

KeTech Ltd
Glaisdale Drive East, Bilborough, Nottingham NG8 4GU
T: 0115 900 5600
F: 0115 900 5601
E: info@ketech.com
W: www.ketech.com

Keyline Builders Merchants
National Rail Office, Unit 1, Electra Business Park, 160 Bidder St, London E16 4ES
T: 020 7473 5288
F: 020 7473 5171
E: rail@keyline.co.uk
W: www.keyline.co.uk

Kiel Seating UK Ltd
Regents Pavilion, 4 Summerhouse Road, Moulton Park, Northampton NN3 6BJ
T: 01604 641148
F: 01604 641149
E: p.scott@kiel-seating.co.uk
W: www.kiel-sitze.de

Kier Rail
Tempsford Hall, Sandy, Beds SG19 2BD
T: 01767 640111
F: 01767 641710
E: info@kier.co.uk
W: www.kier.co.uk

KILBORN CONSULTING
Kilborn Consulting Limited provides railway signalling and telecommunications consultancy services covering design, feasibility studies, auditing, maintenance strategy, site surveys, condition assessments and competency assessments.
Kilborn Consulting Limited
Kilborn House, 1 St Johns Street
Wellingborough, Northants NN8 4LG
T: 01933 279909
F: 01933 276629
E: pmcsharry@kilborn.co.uk
www.kilborn.co.uk

Kilborn Consulting Ltd
Kilborn House, 1 St Johns St, Wellingborough, Northants NN8 4LG
T: 01933 279909
F: 01933 276629
E: pmcsharry@kilborn.co.uk
W: www.kilborn.co.uk

Kilfrost Ltd
4th Floor, Time Central, 32 Gallowgate, Newcastle upon Tyne NE1 4SN
T: 01434 323182
F: 0191 230 0426
E: alex.stephens@kilfrost.com
W: www.kilfrost.com

Kilnbridge Construction Services Ltd
Mc Dermott House, Cody Rd. Business Park, South Crescent, London E16 4TL
T: 020 7511 1888
F: 020 7511 1114
E: sales@kilnbridge.com
W: www.kilnbridge.com

Kimberley-Clark Professional
1 Tower View, Kings Hill, West Malling, Kent ME19 4HA
T: 01732 594000
F: 01732 594060
E: marta.longhurst@kcc.com
W: www.kcprofessional.com/uk

King Rail
King Trailers Ltd, Riverside, Market Harborough, Leics LE16 7PX
T: 01858 467361
F: 01858 467161
E: info@kingtrailers.co.uk
W: www.kingtrailers.co.uk

Kingfisher Railtours
Felmersham, Mills Rd, Osmington Mills, Weymouth, Dorset DT3 6HE
T: 0845 053 3462
E: roger@kingfisher-prods.demon.co.uk
W: www.railwayvideo.com

Kingston Engineering Co (Hull) Ltd
Pennington St, Hull HU8 7LD
T: 01438 325676
F: 01438 216438
E: sales@kingston-engineering.co.uk
W: www.kingston-engineering.co.uk

KJ Hall Chartered Land & Engineering Surveyors
30 Church Rd, Highbridge, Somerset TA9 3RN
T: 01278 794600
F: 01278 785562
E: admin@kjhsurvey.co.uk
W: www.kjhsurvey.co.uk

Klaxon Signals Ltd
Wrigley St, Oldham OL4 1HW
T: 0161 287 5555
F: 0161 287 5511
E: sales@klaxonsignals.com
W: www.klaxonsignals.com

Klueber Lubrication GB Ltd
Hough Mills, Bradford Rd, Northowram, Halifax HX3 7BN
T: 01422 205115
F: 01422 207365
E: sales@uk.klueber.com
W: www.klueber.com

KM&T Ltd
The Techno Centre, Coventry University Technology Park, Puma Way, Coventry CV1 2TT
T: 02476 236275
E: info@kmandt.com
W: www.kmandt.com

KMC International
7 Old Park Lane, London W1K 1QR
T: 020 7317 4600
F: 020 7317 4620
W: www.kmcinternational.com

KME
See Kent Modular

Knights Rail Services Ltd (KRS)
The Bakery, 23 Church St, Coggeshall, Essex C06 1TX
T: 01376 561194
F: 01376 563992
E: bruce@knightsrail.fsnet.co.uk
W: www.rail-services.net

KNORR-BREMSE
Knorr-Bremse Rail Systems (UK) Limited operate their OE, and railservices and maintenance business divisions, serving the UK and Ireland, from their new, purpose built and equipped facility located at:
Westinghouse Way, Hampton Park East, Melksham, Wiltshire, SN12 6TL.
Tel: 01225 898700
Fax: 01225 898705
Enquiries via e-mail to: ian.palmer@knorr-bremse.com
www.knorr-bremse.co.uk
railservices

Knorr Bremse Rail Systems (UK) Ltd
Westinghouse Way, Hampton Park East, Melksham, Wilts SN12 6TL
T: 01225 898700
F: 01225 898705
E: ian.palmer@knorr-bremse.com
W: www.knorr-bremse.co.uk

Kone UK
Global House, Station Place, Chertsey, Surrey KT16 9HW
T: 0870 770 1122
F: 0870 770 1144
E: sales.marketinguk@kone.com
W: www.kone.com

Korec Group
34-44, Mersey View, Brighton le Sands, Liverpool L22 6QB
T: 0845 603 1214
F: 0151 931 5559
E: info@korecgroup.com
W: www.korecgroup.com

Kroy (Europe) Ltd
Unit 2, 14 Commercial Rd, Reading, Berks RG2 0QJ
T: 0118 986 5200
F: 0118 986 5205
E: sales@kroyeurope.com
W: www.kroyeurope.com

KV Mobile Systems Division
See Parker - KV

Kwik Step Ltd
Unit 5, Albion Dockside, Hanover Place, Bristol BS1 6UT
T: 0117 929 1400
F: 0117 929 1404
E: info@kwik-step.com
W: www.kwik-step.com

L.E.K Consulting
40 Grosvenor Place, London SW1X 7JL
T: 020 7389 7200
F: 020 7389 7440
E: surfacetransport@lek.com
W: www.lek.com

Laboursite Group Ltd (Rail)
See Wyse Rail

Lafarge Aggregates (UK) Ltd
Granite House, PO Box 7388, Watermead Business Park, Syston, Leicester LE7 1WA
T: 0870 336 8250
F: 0870 336 8602
W: www.lafarge.co.uk

Laing O'Rourke Infrastructure
Bridge Place, Anchor Blvd., Admirals Park, Crossways, Dartford, Kent DA2 6SN
T: 01322 296200
F: 01322 296262
E: info@laingorourke.com
W: www.laingorourke.com

Laing Rail
Western House, 14 Rickfords Hill, Aylesbury, Bucks HP20 2RX
T: 01296 332108
F: 01296 332126
W: www.laingrail.co.uk

Lancsville Rail Engineers
The Corner House, Joiners Lane, Wetwang, Driffield YO25 9YN
T: 01377 236700
F: 01377 236701

Lanes Group Plc - Lanes For Drains
17 Parkside Lane, Parkside Ind. Est, Leeds LS11 5TD
T: 0800 526488
F: 0161 788 2206
E: sales@lanesfordrains.co.uk
W: www.lanesfordrains.co.uk

Lankelma Limited
Cold Harbour Barn, Cold Harbour Lane, Iden, East Sussex TN31 7UT
T: 01797 280050
F: 01797 280195
E: info@lankelma.co.uk
W: www.lankelma.com

Lantern Engineering Ltd
Hamilton Rd, Maltby, Rotherham S66 7NE
T: 01709 813636
F: 01709 817130
W: www.lantern.co.uk

Laser Rail
Fitology House, Smedley St. East, Matlock, Derbys DE4 3GH
T: 01629 760750
F: 01629 760751
E: info@laser-rail.co.uk
W: www.laser-rail.co.uk

Lattix Solutions
Unit 5, Clarendon Drive, The Parkway, Tipton, West Midlands DY4 0QA
T: 0121 506 4770
F: 0121 506 4771
E: i.thomas@signfix.co.uk
W: www.signfix.co.uk

Leda Recruitment
See Mcginley Support Services

Leewood Projects
38 Deacon Rd, Kingston upon Thames, Surrey KT2 6LU
T: 020 8541 0715
F: 020 8546 4260
E: david.cockle@leewoodprojects.co.uk
W: www.leewoodprojects.co.uk

Legioblock (A Jansen B.V.)
Kanaaldijk Zuid 24, 5691 NL SON
T: 0845 689 0036
F: 0845 689 0035
M: 07725 853677
E: sales@legioblock.com
W: www.legioblock.com

Legion
22-26 Albert Embankment, Vauxhall, London SE1 7TJ
T: 020 7793 0200
F: 020 7793 8948
E: info@legion.com
W: www.legion.com

Leica Geosystems Ltd
Davy Avenue, Knowlhill, Milton Keynes MK5 8LB
T: 01908 256500
F: 01908 256509
E: uk.sales@leica-geosystems.com
W: www.leica-geosystems.co.uk

Leigh Fisher
16 Connaught Place, London W2 2ES
T: 020 7087 8777
E: richard.middleton@leighfisher.com
W: www.leighfisher.com

Leighs Paints
Tower Works, Kestor St, Bolton, Lancs BL2 2AL
T: 01204 521771
F: 01204 382115
E: enquiries@leighspaints.com
W: www.leighspaints.com

Lemon Consulting
See AMCL

Lesmac (Fasteners) Ltd
73 Dykehead St, Queenslie Ind. Est, Queenslie, Glasgow KA7 4SN
T: 0141 774 0004
F: 0141 774 2229
E: sales@lesmac.co.uk
W: www.lesmac.co.uk

Lexicraft Ltd
Unit 32, Woodside Business Park, Birkenhead, Wirral CH41 1EL
T: 0151 647 9281
F: 0151 666 1079
E: jeff.davies@lexicraft.co.uk
W: www.lexicraft.co.uk

HITACHI Inspire the Next
181

Directory

Ley Hill Solutions
Beech House, 9 Cheyne Walk,
Chesham,
Bucks HP5 1AY
T: 01494 772327
F: 0870 169 5984
E: graham.hull@leyhill.com
W: www.leyhill.com

Leyland & Birmingham Rubber Ltd
Unit 1, Bentley Ave,
Middleton,
Manchester M24 2GP
T: 0161 655 0300
F: 0161 655 0301
E: lh@leylandandbirminghamrubber.com
W: www.leylandandbirminghamrubber.com

LH Group Services
Graycar Business Park,
Barton-under-Needwood,
Burton upon Trent DE13 8EN
T: 01283 722600
F: 01283 722622
E: lh@lh-group.co.uk
W: www.lh-group.co.uk

LH Safety Footwear
Greenbridge, Rawtenstall,
Rossendale,
Lancs BB4 7NX
T: 01706 235100
F: 01706 235150
E: enquiries@lhsafety.co.uk
W: www.lhsafety.co.uk

Liebherr- Great Britain Ltd
Normandy Lane,
Stratton Business Park,
Biggleswade,
Beds SG18 8QP
T: 01767 602100
F: 01767 602110
E: info.lgb@liebherr.com
W: www.liebherr.com

Liebherr Sunderland
Works Ltd Ayres Quay,
Deptford Terrace,
Sunderland SR4 6DD
T: 0191 515 4930
F: 0191 515 4936
E: alan.lepatourel@liebherr.com
W: www.liebherr.com

Light Rail Transit Association (LRTA)
138 Radnor Ave, Welling, Kent DA16 2BY
T: 01179 517785
E: office@lrta.org
W: www.lrta.org

Lindapter International
Lindsay House, Brackenbeck Rd,
Bradford BD7 2NF
T: 01274 521444
F: 01274 521130
E: enquiries@lindapter.com
W: www.lindapter.com

Link Associates International
Trent House, RTC Business Park, London Rd,
Derby DE24 8UP
T: 01332 222299
F: 01332 222298
E: info@linkassociates.com
W: www.linkassociates.com

Link-up
See Achilles

Lionverge Civils Ltd
Unit 5, Ransome Rd, Far Cotton,
Northampton NN4 8AA
T: 01604 677227
F: 01604 677218
E: enquiries@lionverge.co.uk
W: www.lionverge.co.uk

Lloyds Register Rail Ltd
Edward Lloyd House, 8 Pinnacle Way,
Pride Park, Derby DE24 8ZS
T: 01332 268700
F: 01332 268799
E: martin.hayhoe@lr.org
W: www.lr.org/transportation

Lloyds TSB General Leasing (No 8) Ltd
c/o Rail Capital, Lloyds TSB Corporate Markets,
33 Old Broad St, London EC2N 1HW
T: 020 7158 2702
E: tim.durham@lloydsbanking.com
W: www.lloydsbankcorporatemarkets.com/railfinance

Llumar Anti-Grafitti Coating
See CP Films

LML Products Ltd
13 Portemarsh Rd, Calne, Wilts SN11 9BN
T: 01249 814271
F: 01249 812182
E: sales@lmlproducts.co.uk
W: www.lmlproducts.co.uk

LNWR Co Ltd
PO Box 111, Crewe,
Cheshire CW1 2FB
T: 01270 251467
F: 01270 251468
E: m.knowles@lnwr.com
W: www.lnwr.com

Logic Engagements Ltd
45-47 High St, Cobham, Surrey KT11 3DP
T: 01932 869869
F: 01932 864455
E: info@logicrec.com
W: www.logicrec.com

LogiKal Ltd
Fleet House, 8-12 New Bridge St, Blackfriars,
London EC4V 6AL
T: 020 7936 4403
E: admin@logikal.co.uk
W: www.logikal.co.uk

London Midland
PO Box 4323, Birmingham B3 4JB
T: 0121 634 2040
F: 0121 654 1234
E: comments@londonmidland.com
W: www.londonmidland.com

London Overground Rail Operations Ltd (LOROL)
Customer Services Centre, Overground House,
125 Finchley Rd, London NW3 6HY
T: 0845 601 4867
E: overgroundinfo@tfl.gov.uk
W: www.lorol.co.uk

London Rail
See Transport for London

London Underground Customer Service Centre,
55 Broadway,
London SW1W 0BD
T: 0845 330 9880
W: www.tfl.gov.uk/tube

LINK
Building emergency management capabilities
Business Continuity | Crisis | Risk | Emergency Safety | Communications

www.linkassociates.com

Training
Competence
Simulation
Consultancy

Crisis simulation facilities in London, Derby or client locations

Tel: +44(0) 1332 22 22 99 or +44(0) 207 5780 100
Email: info@linkassociates.com

Lloyd's Register LIFE MATTERS
Edward Lloyd House,
8 Pinnacle Way,
Pride Park, Derby,
DE24 8ZS

martin.hayhoe@lr.org
T: 01332 268727

Rail expertise you can trust

Lloyd's Register provides expert advice and assurance services to improve the safety, performance and management of the world's rail systems. Areas of expertise include strategy, infrastructure, rolling-stock, signalling, telecommunications, operations and management systems.

www.lr.org/rail

Look CCTV
Unit 4, Wyrefields, Poulton le Fylde,
Lancs FY6 8JX
T: 01253 891222
F: 01253 891221
E: enquiries@lookcctv.com
W: www.lookcctv.com

Lordgate Engineering
London Rd, St Ives, Cambs PE27 5EZ
T: 01480 300111
F: 01480 494880
E: paulbright@lordgate.com
W: www.lordgate.com

Lorne Stewart Plc
Stewart House, Orford Park, Greenfold Way,
Leigh, Lancs WN7 3XJ
T: 01942 683333
M: 07919 001767
E: andy.vickers@lornestewart.co.uk
W: www.lornestewart.co.uk

LPA Group
Todor Works, Debden Way, Saffron Walden,
Essex CB11 4AN
T: 01799 512800
F: 01799 512828
E: enquiries@lpa-niphan.com
W: www.lpa-group.com

Lucchini UK Ltd
Wheel Forge Way, Ashburton Park,
Trafford Park, Manchester M17 1EH
T: 0161 886 0342
F: 0161 872 2895
E: salesuk@lucchinis.co.uk
W: www.lucchinirs.co.uk

Lundy Projects Ltd
195 Chestergate, Stockport,
Cheshire SK3 0BQ
T: 0161 476 2996
F: 0161 476 3760
E: mail@lundy-projects.co.uk
W: www.lundy-projects.co.uk

Luxury Train Club
Benwell House, Preston,
Chippenham SN15 4DX
T: 01249 890176
E: info@luxurytrainclub.com
W: www.luxurytrainclub.com

M Buttkereit Ltd
Unit 2, Britannia Rd, Sale, Cheshire M33 2AA
T: 0161 969 5418
F: 0161 969 5419
E: sales@buttkereit.co.uk
W: www.buttkereit.co.uk

M H Southern & Co Ltd
Church Bank Sawmills, Jarrow,
Tyne & Wear NE32 3EB
T: 0191 428 0146
E: timber@mhsouthern.co.uk
W: www.mhsouthern.co.uk

M&M Rail Services Ltd
First Floor, Unit 7, Portland House, 1-7
Portland Place, Doncaster DN1 3DF
T: 01302 349888
F: 01302 349899

Mac Roberts LLP
Capella, 60 York St, Glasgow G2 8JX
T: 0141 303 1100
F: 0141 332 8886
E: alison.mcintosh@macroberts.com
W: www.macroberts.com

Mace Group
153 Moorgate, London EC2M 6XB
T: 020 3522 3000
E: info@macegroup.com
W: www.macegroup.com

Macemain + Amstad Ltd
Boyle Rd, Willowbrook Ind. Est., Corby,
Northants NN17 5XU
T: 01536 401331
F: 01536 401298
E: sales@macemainamstad.com
W: www.macemainamstad.com

Mack Brooks Exhibitions Ltd
Romelands House,
Romelands Hill,
St Albans AL3 4ET
T: 01727 814400
F: 01727 814401
E: infrarail@mackbrooks.co.uk
W: www.mackbrooks.co.uk

MacRail
Unit One, Marston Court, Aisecom Way,
Weston Super Mare BS22 8NG
T: 01934 319810
F: 01934 424139
E: info@macrail.co.uk
W: www.macrail.co.uk

Maddox Consulting Ltd
44 Wardour St,
London W1D 6QZ
T: 020 7292 8970
F: 020 7287 2905
E: info@maddoxconsulting.com
W: www.maddoxconsulting.com

Mainframe Communications Ltd
Network House, Journeymans Way,
Temple Farm Ind Est, Southend on Sea,
Essex SS2 5TF
T: 01702 443800
F: 01702 443801
E: info@mainframecomms.com
W: www.mainframecomms.com

MACK BROOKS exhibitions

Organising exhibitions for the rail industry in the UK:
Railtex and **Infrarail**
www.railtex.co.uk
railtex@mackbrooks.co.uk
www.infrarail.com
infrarail@mackbrooks.co.uk

As well as in France, Italy, Russia and India

Mack Brooks Exhibitions Ltd,
Romeland House, Romeland Hill,
St Albans AL3 4ET

Tel: +44 (0) 1727 814400
Fax: +44 (0) 1727 814401

www.mackbrooks.co.uk

Mainline Resourcing Ltd
Suite 214, Business Design Centre,
52 Upper St, London N1 0QH
T: 0845 083 0245
F: 020 7288 6685
E: info@mainlineresourcing.com
W: www.mainlineresourcing.com

Malcolm Rail
Tillyfrails, Laurieston Rd, Grangemouth,
Falkirk FK3 8XT
T: 01324 483681
F: 01324 665902
E: holwellj@whm.co.uk
W: www.malcolmgroup.co.uk

Mammoet (UK) Ltd
The Grange Business Centre, Belasis Ave,
Billingham, Cleveland TS23 1LG
T: 0800 111 4449
E: saleseurope@mammoet.com
W: www.mammoet.com

MAN Diesel Ltd
1 Mirrlees Drive, Hazel Grove,
Stockport SK7 5BP
T: 0161 483 1000
F: 0161 487 1438
E: primeserv-uk@mandiesel.com
W: www.mandieselturbo.com

Mane Rail
UCB House, 3 St George St, Watford WD18 0UH
T: 01923 470720
E: rail@mane.co.uk
W: www.mane.co.uk

Mansell Recruitment Group
Mansell House, Priestley Way, Crawley,
West Sussex RH10 9RU
T: 01293 404050
F: 01293 404122
E: neil@mansell.co.uk
W: www.mansell.co.uk

Maple Resourcing
Regus House, 1 Liverpool St,
London EC2M 7QD
T: 020 7048 0775
F: 0845 052 9357
E: infrarail@mackbrooks.co.uk
W: www.mapleresourcing.com

Marcroft Engineering Services
Whieldon Rd,
Stoke-on-Trent ST4 4HP
T: 01782 844075
F: 01782 843578
W: www.marcroft.co.uk

Maritime and Rail
E-Business Centre,
Consett Business Park,
Villa Real,
Consett DH8 6BP
T: 01207 693616
F: 01207 693917
W: www.maritimeandrail.com

Marl International
Marl Business Park,
Ulverston,
Cumbria LA12 9BN
T: 01229 582430
F: 01229 585155
E: sales@marl.co.uk
W: www.marlrail.com

Marsh Bellofram Europe Ltd
9 Castle Park, Queens Drive,
Nottingham NG2 1AH
T: 0115 993 3300
F: 0115 993 3301
E: bellofram@aol.com
W: www.marshbellofram.eu

Martek Power Ltd
Glebe Farm Technical Campus Knapwell,
Cambridge CB23 4GG
T: 01954 267726
F: 01954 267626
E: sales@martekpower.co.uk
W: www.martekpower.co.uk

Martin Higginson Transport Research & Consultancy
5 The Avenue, Clifton,
York YO30 6AS
T: 01904 636704
M: 07980 874126
E: mhrc@waitrose.com
W: www.martinhigginson.co.uk

Martineau
See SGH Martineau LLP

Masabi
56 Ayres St,
London SE1 1EU
T: 020 7089 8860
E: mobileticketing@masabi.com
W: www.masabi.com

Matchtech Group
1450 Park Way, Solent Business Park,
Whiteley, Fareham, Hants PO15 7AF
T: 01489 898989
F: 01489 898290
W: www.matchtech.com

Matisa (UK) Ltd
PO Box 202,
Scunthorpe DN15 6XR
T: 01724 877000
F: 01724 877001
E: melissa.came@matisa.co.uk
W: www.matisa.ch

Max Integrated Systems Ltd
Strathclyde Business Centre, 120 Carstairs St,
Glasgow G40 4JD
T: 0141 551 0921
F: 0141 556 0335
E: infrarail@mackbrooks.co.uk
W: www.maxgroup.co.uk

Maxim Power Tools (Scotland) Ltd
40 Couper St, Glasgow G4 0DL
T: 0141 552 5591
F: 0141 552 5064
E: akilpatrick@maximpower.co.uk
W: www.maxim-power.com

Maxmax Ltd
Beech Grove, Wootton, Eccleshall, Staffs
ST21 6HU
T: 01785 859106
E: sales@maxmaxltd.com
W: www.maxmaxltd.com

May Gurney Ltd
Rail Services, 312 Tadcaster Rd,
York YO24 1GS
T: 01904 770150
E: marketing@maygurney.co.uk
W: www.maygurney.co.uk

Mc Culloch Rail
Craigiemains, Main St, Ballantrae KA26 0NB
T: 01465 831350
F: 01465 831350
E: enquiries@mccullochrail.com
W: www.mccullochrail.com

MC Electronics
61, Grimsdyke Rd, Hatch End,
Middx HA5 4PP
T: 020 8428 2027
F: 020 8428 2027
E: mcelectron@aol.com
W: www.mcelectronics.co.uk

Mc Lellan & Partners
Sheer House, West Byfleet, Surrey KT14 6NL
T: 01932 343271
F: 01932 348037
E: hq@mclellan.co.uk
W: www.mclellan.co.uk

Mc Nicholas Rail
1st Floor, Consort House, Waterdale,
Doncaster DN1 3HR
T: 01302 380551
F: 01302 380591
E: mark.bugg@mcnicholas.co.uk
W: www.mcnicholas.co.uk

McGee Group Ltd
340-342 Athlon Rd, Wembley, Middx HA0 1BX
T: 020 8998 1001
F: 020 8997 7689
E: mail@mcgee.co.uk
W: www.mcgee.co.uk

McGeoch LED Technology
Unit 5, Daltongate Business Centre,
Daltongate, Ulverston, Cumbria LA12 7AJ
T: 01229 580180
E: info@mcgeochled.com
W: www.mcgeochled.com

McGinley Support Services
Ground Floor, Edward Hyde Building,
38 Clarendon Rd, Watford, Herts WD17 1JW
T: 0845 543 5953
F: 0845 543 5956
E: info@mcginley.co.uk
W: www.mcginley.co.uk

McKenzie Martin Partnership Ltd
126 Above Bar, Southampton SO14 7DW
T: 02380 216940
E: info@mmpartnership.co.uk
W: www.mmpartnership.co.uk

MCL (Martin Childs Ltd)
Wimbledon Ave, Brandon, Suffolk IP27 0NZ
T: 01842 812882
F: 01842 812002
W: www.martinchilds.com

McML Systems UK Ltd
3rd Floor, 34 Clarendon Rd, Watford WD17 1JJ
T: 01923 630871
F: 01923 226122
W: www.mcmlsystems.com

McNealy Brown Limited - Steelwork
Prentis Quay, Mill Way, Sittingbourne,
Kent ME10 2QD
T: 01795 470592
F: 01795 471238
E: info@mcnealybrown.co.uk
W: www.mcnealybrown.co.uk

MCT Brattberg Ltd
Commerce St, Carrs Ind. Est, Haslingden,
Lancs BB4 5JT
T: 01706 244890
F: 01706 244891
E: info@mctbrattberg.co.uk
W: www.brattberg.co.uk

MDL Laser Measurement Systems
Acer House, Hackness Rd,
Northminster Business Park, York YO26 6QR
T: 01904 791139
F: 01904 791532
E: privers@mdl.co.uk
W: www.laserace.com

MDM Transportation
Walkmill Lane, Bridgetown, Cannock, Staffs

MDS Transmodal Ltd
5-6 Hunters Walk, Canal St, Chester CH1 4EB
T: 01244 348301
F: 01244 348471
W: www.mdst.co.uk

Mechan Ltd
Sir John Brown Building, Davy Industrial Park,
Prince of Wales Rd, Sheffield S9 4EX
T: 0114 257 0563
F: 0114 245 1124
E: info@mechan.co.uk
W: www.mechan.co.uk

Mechan Technology Ltd
See Zonegreen

MEDC Ltd
Colliery Rd, Pinxton, Nottingham NG16 6FF
T: 01773 864100
F: 01773 582800
W: www.medc.com

In association with ATKINS

Medicals Direct
Buckingham House East, The Broadway,
Stanmore HA7 4EB
T: 020 8416 1401
F: 0871 900 2861
E: sales@medicalsdirect.com
W: www.medicalsdirect.com

Medscreen
Harbour Quay, 100 Prestons Rd,
London E14 9PH
T: 020 7712 8000
F: 020 7712 8001
E: sales@medscreen.com
W: www.medscreen.com

Melford Electronics Ltd
Cressex Business Park, Blenheim Rd,
High Wycombe HP12 3RS
T: 01494 638069
F: 01494 463358
E: info@melford-elec.co.uk
W: www.melford-elec.co.uk

Mendip Rail Ltd
Merehead, East Cranmore, Shepton Mallet,
Somerset BA4 4RA
T: 01749 881202
F: 01749 880141
E: karen.taylor@mendip-rail.co.uk
W: www.fosteryeoman.co.uk

Mennekes Electric Ltd
Unit 4, Crayfields Ind. Park, Main Rd,
St Pauls Cray, Orpington, Kent BR5 3HP
T: 01689 833522
F: 01689 833378
E: sales@mennekes.co.uk
W: www.mennekes.co.uk

Merc Engineering UK Ltd
Lower Clough Mill, Pendle St, Barrowford,
Lancs BB9 8PH
T: 01282 694290
F: 01282 613390
E: sales@merceng.co.uk
W: www.merceng.co.uk

Mercia Charters
PO Box 1926, Coventry CV3 6ZL
T: 07535 759344
E: team@merciacharters.co.uk
W: www.merciacharters.com

Merseyrail
Rail House, Lord Nelson St,
Liverpool L1 1JF
T: 0151 702 2534
F: 0151 702 3074
E: comment@merseyrail.org
W: www.merseyrail.org

Met Systems Ltd
Wool House,
74 Back Church Lane,
London E1 1AB
T: 020 3246 1000
F: 020 7712 2146
E: info@metsystems.co.uk
W: www.metsystems.co.uk

Meteo Group UK Ltd
292 Vauxhall Bridge Rd,
London SW1V 1AE
T: 020 7963 7534
F: 020 7963 7599
E: jeremy.fidlin@meteogroup.com
W: www.meteogroup.com

Metham Aviation Design ltd (MADCCTV Ltd)
Unit 5, Station Approach,
Four Marks, Alton,
Hants GU34 5HN
T: 01420 565618
F: 01420 565628
E: stuart@madcctv.com
W: www.madcctv.com

Metrolink (Manchester)
Serco Metrolink,
Metrolink House, Queens Rd,
Manchester M8 0RY
T: 0161 205 8665
W: www.metrolink.co.uk

Metronet
See Transport for London

Mettex Electronic Co Ltd
Beaumont Close,
Banbury,
Oxon OX16 1TG
T: 01295 250826
F: 01295 268643
E: sales@mettex.co.uk
W: www.mettex.co.uk

MF Hydraulics
The Brookworks,
174 Bromyard Rd, St Johns,
Worcester WR2 5EE
T: 01905 748569
F: 01905 420700
E: les@mfhydraulics.co.uk
W: www.mfhydraulics.co.uk

MGB Electrical Ltd
See Ilecsys

MGB Signalling Ltd
Tamar Science Park, 9
Research Way, Derriford,
Plymouth PL6 8BT
T: 0845 070 2490
F: 0845 070 2495
E: enquiries@mgbl.co.uk
W: www.mgbl.co.uk

Micro-Epsilon UK Ltd
Dorset House, West Derby Rd,
Liverpool L6 4BR
T: 0151 260 9800
F: 0151 261 2480
E: info@micro-epsilon.co.uk
W: www.micro-epsilon.co.uk

Micro-Mesh Filtration
60 Basford Rd, Old Basford,
Nottingham NG6 0JL
T: 01159 786348
F: 01159 422688
E: enquiries@micro-mesh.co.uk
W: www.micro-mesh.co.uk

Micromotive (A1 Results Ltd)
38 Coney Green Business Centre,
Wingfield View, Clay Cross,
Derbys S45 9JW
T: 01246 252360
F: 01246 252361
E: a1micromotive@btopenworld.com
W: www.a1micromotive.co.uk

Middle Peak Railways Ltd
PO Box 71, High Peak,
Derbys. SK23 7WL
T: 0870 881 6743
F: 0870 991 7350
E: info@middlepeak.co.uk
W: www.middlepeak.co.uk

Midland Metro
Travel Midland Metro,
Metro Centre, Potters Lane,
Wednesbury,
West Midlands WS10 0AR
T: 0121 502 2006
F: 0121 566 6299
W: www.travelmetro.co.uk

Mike Worbey Survey Consultancy
37 Ramblers Way, Welwyn Garden City,
Herts AL7 2JU
T: 01707 333677
F: 01707 333677
E: survey@mw-sc.co.uk
W: www.mw-sc.co.uk

Millar Bryce Ltd
5 Logie Mill, Beaverbank Office Park,
Logie Green Rd, Edinburgh EH7 4HH
T: 0131 556 1313
F: 0131 557 5960
E: marketing@millar-bryce.com
W: www.millar-bryce.com

Millcroft Services Plc
Salutation House, 1 Salutation Rd, Greenwich,
London SE10 0AT
T: 020 8305 1988
F: 020 8305 1986
E: sales@millcroft.co.uk
W: www.millcroft.co.uk

Mirror Technology Ltd
Redwood House, Orchard Ind Est, Toddington,
Glos GL54 5EB
T: 01242 621534
F: 01242 621529
E: malcolm@mirrortechnology.co.uk
W: www.mirrortechnology.co.uk

Mita (UK) Ltd
Manor Ind. Est., Bagillt,
Flint CH6 5UY
T: 01352 792300
F: 01352 792314
E: sales@mita.co.uk
W: www.mita.co.uk

MLM Rail Consulting Engineers Ltd
North Lodge, 25 London Rd,
Ipswich, Suffolk IP1 2HF
T: 01473 231100
F: 01473 231515
E: lee.bowker@mlm.uk.com
W: www.mlm.uk.com

Mono Design
4 St Andrews House, Vernon Gate,
Derby DE1 1UJ
T: 01332 361616
E: lynne@monodesign.co.uk
W: www.monodesign.co.uk

Moonbuggy Ltd
Solway Ind. Est, Maryport,
Cumbria CA15 8NF
T: 01900 815831
F: 01900 815553
E: r.smith@moonbuggy.com
W: www.moonbuggy.com

Moore Concrete Products Ltd
Caherty House, 41 Woodside Rd, Ballymena,
Co Antrim NI BT42 4QH
T: 028 2565 2566
F: 028 2565 8480
E: info@moore-concrete.com
W: www.moore-concrete.com

Morgan AM&T
Upper Fforest Way, Swansea Enterprise Park,
Swansea SA6 8PP
T: 01792 763052
F: 01792 763167
E: meclsales@morganplc.com
W: www.morganamt.com

Morgan Hunt
5th Floor, 16 Old Bailey, London EC4M 7EG
T: 020 7419 8968
F: 020 7419 8999
E: rail@morganhunt.com
W: www.morganhunt.com

Morgan Marine Ltd
Llandybie, Ammanford,
Carms SA18 3GY
T: 01269 850437
F: 01269 850656
E: sales@morgan-marine.com
W: www.morgan-marine.com

Morgan Sindall (infrastructure) Plc
Unit 9, Home Farm Ind. Est, Hundson Rd,
Stanstead Abbotts, Ware, Herts SG12 8LA
T: 01920 871047
F: 01920 871828
E: enquiries@morgansindall.com
W: www.morgansindall.com

Morris Material Handling
PO Box 7, North Rd, Loughborough,
Leics LE11 1RL
T: 01509 643200
F: 01509 610666
E: info@morriscranes.com
W: www.morriscranes.co.uk

Mors Smitt
Vrieslantlaan 6, 3526 AA Utrecht, Netherlands
T: 0031 30 288 1311
F: 0031 30 289 8816
E: sales@nieaf-smitt.nl
W: www.morssmitt.com

Mors Smitt UK Ltd
Doulton Rd, Cradley Heath,
West Midlands B64 5QB
T: 01384 567755
F: 01384 567710
E: sales@morssmitt.co.uk
W: www.morssmitt.com

Morson International
Stableford Hall,
Monton, Eccles,
Manchester M30 8AP
T: 0161 707 1516
F: 0161 788 8372
E: rail@morson.com
W: www.morson.com

Morson Projects Ltd
Adamson House,
Centenary Way, Salford,
Manchester M50 1RD
T: 0161 707 1516
F: 0161 786 2360
E: andy.hassall@morson-projects.com
W: www.morsonprojects.com

Motorail Logistics
The Control Tower,
Long Marston Storage Site,
Long Marston, Stratford upon Avon,
Warks CV37 8QR
T: 01789 721995
F: 01789 721396
E: ruth.dunmore@motorail.com
W: www.motorail.com

Mott MacDonald Group
Mott Macdonald House,
8-10 Sydenham Rd,
Croydon CR0 2EE
T: 020 8774 2000
F: 020 8681 5706
E: railways@mottmac.com
W: www.mottmac.com

Mouchel
4 Matthew Parker Street,
London SW1H 9NP
T: 020 7227 6800
F: 020 7277 6801
E: consultingsales@mouchel.com
W: www.mouchel.com

Moveright International Ltd
Dunton Park,
Dunton Lane, Wishaw,
Sutton Coldfield B76 9QA
T: 01675 475590
F: 01675 475591
E: andrew@moverightinternational.com
W: www.moverightinternational.com

Moxa Europe GmbH
Einsteinstrasse 7,
85716 Unterschleissheim,
Germany
T: 0049 8937003990
E: silke.boysen-korya@moxa.com
W: www.moxa.com

MPEC Technology Ltd
Wyvern House, Railway Terrace,
Derby DE1 2RU
T: 01332 363979
F: 08701 363958
E: andrew.whawell@mpec.co.uk
W: www.mpec.co.uk

MPI Ltd
International House,
Tamworth Rd,
Hertford SG13 7DQ
T: 01992 501111
F: 01992 535570
E: stuartg@mpi.ltd.uk
W: www.mpi.ltd.uk

MRO Software Now part of IBM UK Ltd
PO Box 41, North Harbour,
Portsmouth, PO6 3AU
T: 0870 542 6426
E: maximo@uk.ibm.com
W: www.maximo.com

MTR Corporation
Finland House, 56 Haymarket,
London SW1Y 4RN
T: 020 7766 3500
F: 020 7839 6217
E: europe@mtr.com.hk
W: www.mtr.com.hk

MTR Training Ltd
See HSS Training

MTU UK Ltd
Unit 29, The Birches Ind. Est,
East Grinstead,
West Sussex RH19 1XZ
T: 01342 335450
F: 01342 335475
E: firstname.lastname@mtu-online.com
W: www.mtu-online.com

Multicell
Swannington Rd, Broughton Astley,
Leicester LE9 6TU
T: 01455 283443
F: 01455 284250
E: help@multicell.com
W: www.multicell.com

Murphy Surveys
Head Office UK,
9 Devonshire Square,
London EC2M 4YF
T: 020 3178 6644
F: 020 3178 6642
E: london@murphysurveys.co.uk
W: www.murphysurveys.co.uk

MVA Consultancy
Seventh Floor, 15 Old Bailey,
London EC4M 7EF
T: 020 7342 7315
E: info@mvaconsultancy.com
W: www.mvaconsultancy.com

MWH Treatment Ltd
Biwater Place, Gregge St, Heywood,
Lancs OL10 2DX
T: 01706 626258
F: 01706 626294
E: info@mwhglobal.com
W: www.mwhglobal.com

National Car Parks Ltd (NCP)
6th Floor, Centre Tower, Croydon CR0 1LP
T: 0845 050 7080
E: derek.hulyer@ncp.co.uk
W: www.ncp.co.uk

National Express East Anglia
See Greater Anglia

National Express Group Plc
75, Davies St, London W1K 5HT
T: 020 7529 2000
F: 020 7529 2100
E: info@natex.co.uk
W: www.nationalexpressgroup.com

National Rail Enquiries
T: 08457 484950
W: www.nationalrail.co.uk

National Railway Museum
Leeman Rd, York YO26 4XJ
T: 0844 815 3139
E: nrm@nrm.org.uk
W: www.nrm.org.uk

Nationwide Healthcare Connect
See Healthcare Connections

Nazeing Glass Works Ltd
Nazeing New Rd, Broxbourne, Herts EN10 6SU
T: 01992 464485
F: 01992 450966
E: sales@nazeing-glass.co.uk
W: www.nazeing-glass.com

NCH (UK) Ltd – Chemsearch
Landchard House, Victoria St,
West Bromwich B70 8ER
T: 0121 5247300
F: 0121 500 5386
E: sales@chemsearch.co.uk
W: www.chemsearch.co.uk

NDT Services Ltd
Unit 10a, Victory Park, Victory Rd,
Derby DE24 2FJ
T: 01332 275700
F: 01332 275729
E: sales@ndtservices.co.uk
W: www.ndtservices.co.uk

Neale Consulting Engineers Ltd
Highfield, Pilcott Hill, Dogmersfield, Fleet,
Hants RG27 8SX
T: 01252 629199
F: 01252 815625
E: ncel@tribology.co.uk
W: www.tribology.co.uk

Neary Rail
6 Coal Pit Lane, Atherton,
Manchester M46 0RY
T: 0845 217 7150
F: 0845 217 7160
E: alex.riley@neary.co.uk
W: www.neary.co.uk

NedRailways
See Abellio

Nedtrain BV
Kantorencentrum Katereine 9, Stationshal 17,
3511 ED Utrecht
T: 0031 30 300 4929
F: 0031 30 300 4647
W: www.nedtrain.nl

MECHAN
Strength Behind Technology

RAIL DEPOT AND WORKSHOP EQUIPMENT

Davy Industrial Park
Prince of Wales Road
Sheffield S9 4EX

info@mechan.co.uk
www.mechan.co.uk
+44 (0)114 257 0563

MADE IN SHEFFIELD

Mors Smitt serves the railway rolling stock & signalling markets with (signalling) relays, vital / safety critical relays, protection components, safety critical electronics, traction energy measuring, train control solutions and test equipment.

Mors Smitt UK Ltd. info@morssmitt.co.uk
www.morssmitt.com

Mors Smitt – A Wabtec Company

SERVING SAFETY

Morgan AM&T™
Innovating tomorrow's solutions today

Morgan AM&T
(Morganite Electrical Carbon ltd)
Upper Fforest Way, Swansea SA6 8PP
Tel: 01792 763052
Fax: 01792 763167
meclsales@morganplc.com
www.morganamt.com

Morgan AM&T is a leading global supplier of products and services to the railway industry, offering:
- Pantograph carbons
- Carbon brushes
- Brush holders and springs
- Insulators
- Coupler contacts

Morganite

National

Morgan Crucible – The Advanced Materials Group
Morgan AM&T is a business of The Morgan Crucible Company plc.

HITACHI – Inspire the Next

183

Directory

Nelson Stud Welding UK
47/49 Edison Rd, Rabans Lane Ind. Est, Aylesbury HP19 8TE
T: 01296 433500
F: 01296 487930
E: enquiries@nelson-europe.co.uk
W: www.nelson-europe.co.uk

Nelsons Solicitors
Stone House, Lodge Lane, Derby DE1 3WP
T: 01332 372372
E: enquiries@nelsonslaw.co.uk
W: www.nelsonslaw.co.uk

Nenta Traintours
Railtour House, 10 Buxton Rd, North Walsham, Norfolk NR28 0ED
T: 01692 406152
F: 01692 406152
E: ray.davies@nentatraintours.co.uk
W: www.nentatraintours.co.uk

NES Track
Station House, Stamford New Rd, Altrincham, Cheshire WA14 1EP
T: 0161 942 4016
F: 0161 942 7969
E: nestrack.manchester@nes.co.uk
W: www.nestrack.co.uk

Network Construction Services Ltd
Ercall House, Pearson Rd, Central Park, Telford, Shropshire TF2 9TX
T: 01952 210243
F: 01952 290168
E: sales@ncsjob.co.uk
W: www.ncsjob.co.uk

Network Rail Infrastructure Ltd
Kings Place, 90 York Way, London N1 9AG
T: 020 3356 9595
W: www.networkrail.co.uk

Neway Training Solutions Ltd
Kelvin House, RTC Business Park, London Rd, Derby DE24 8UP
T: 01332 360033
F: 01332 366367
E: enquiries@neway-training.com
W: www.neway-training.com

Newbury Data Recording Ltd
T: 0870 224 8110
F: 0870 224 8177
E: ndsales@newburydata.co.uk
W: www.newburydata.co.uk

Newey & Eyre
Eagle Court 2, Hatchford Brook, Hatchford, Sheldon, Birmingham B26 3RZ
T: 0121 366 1000
F: 0121 366 1029
E: marc.roberts@rexel.co.uk
W: www.neweysonline.co.uk

NewRail, The Centre for Railway Research
Stephenson Building, Newcastle University, Claremont Rd, Newcastle upon Tyne NE1 7RU
T: 0191 222 5821
F: 0191 222 5821
E: newrail@ncl.ac.uk
W: www.newrail.org

Nexans
Nexans House, Chesney Wold, Bleak Hall, Milton Keynes MK6 1LF
T: 01908 250840
F: 01908 250841
E: iandi.sales@nexans.com
W: www.nexans.com

Nextiraone (UK) Ltd
Aldershaw Hall, Claypit Lane, Wall, Lichfield WS14 0AQ
T: 01543 414751
F: 01543 250159
E: enquiries@nextiraone.co.uk
W: www.nextiraone.co.uk

Nexus (Tyne & Wear Metro)
Nexus House, 33 St James Blvd, Newcastle upon Tyne NE1 4AX
T: 0191 203 3333
F: 0191 203 3180
E: contactus@twmetro.co.uk
W: www.tyneandwearmetro.co.uk

Nexus Alpha Low Power Systems Ltd
7 Prescott Place, Clapham, London SW4 6BS
T: 020 7622 6816
F: 020 7622 6817
E: commercialdept@lps.nexusalpha.com
W: www.lps.nexusalpha.com

Nexus Training
105 Sheffield Rd, Godley, Hyde, Cheshire SK14 2PLT
T: 0161 339 2190
E: info@nexustraining.org.uk
W: www.nexustraining.org.uk

Nichols Group Ltd
53 Davies St, London W1K 5JH
T: 020 7292 7000
F: 020 7292 5200
E: operations@nichols.uk.com
W: www.nicholsgroup.co.uk

NORGREN
PNEUMATIC MOTION & FLUID CONTROL SOLUTIONS
YOU CAN SEE OUR THINKING
ENGINEERING ADVANTAGE
T: 01543 265000
E: advantage@norgren.com
W: www.norgren.com/uk/rail

Nigel Nixon Consulting
Suite 1, AD Business Centre, Hithercroft Rd, Wallingford, Oxon OX10 9EZ
T: 01491 824030
F: 01491 824078
E: nigel@nigelnixon.com
W: www.nigelnixon.com

Nightsearcher Ltd
Unit 4, Applied House, Fitzherbert Spur, Farlington, Portsmouth PO6 1TT
T: 023 9238 9774
F: 023 9238 9788
E: carrie.f@nightsearcher.co.uk
W: www.nightsearcher.co.uk

Nitech Ltd
4-6 Highfield Business Park, St Leonards on Sea TN38 9UB
T: 01424 852788
F: 01424 851008
E: sales@nitech.co.uk
W: www.nitech.co.uk

NMB Minebea UK Ltd
Doddington Rd, Lincoln LN6 3RA
T: 01522 500933
F: 01522 500975
W: www.nmb-minebea.co.uk

NNN Ltd (Northcroft Group Ltd)
One Horseguards Ave, London SW1A 2HU
T: 020 7839 7858
F: 020 7930 2594
E: surv@northcroft.co.uk
W: www.northcroft.com

No1 Scaffolding Service
Swinbourne Rd, Burnt Mills Ind.Est., Basildon, Essex SS13 1EF
T: 01268 724793
F: 01268 725606
E: enquiries@no1scaffolders.co.uk
W: www.no1scaffolders.co.uk

Nomad Rail
First Floor, Baltic Chambers, 3 Broad Chare, Newcastle NE1 3DQ
T: 020 7096 6966
F: 0191 221 1339
E: enquiries@nomadrail.com
W: www.nomadrail.com

Nomix Enviro Ltd - A division of Frontier Agriculture Ltd
The Grain Silos, Weyhill Rd, Andover, Hants SP10 3NT
T: 01264 388050
F: 01264 337642
E: nomixenviro@frontierag.co.uk
W: www.nomix.co.uk

Nord-Lock Ltd
Room 9, Main Building, Aspire Business Centre, Ordnance Rd, Tidworth, Wilts SP9 7QD
T: 01980 847129
F: 01980 847674
E: enquiries@nord-lock.co.uk
W: www.nord-lock.com

Norgren Ltd
PO Box 22, Eastern Ave, Lichfield, Staffs WS13 6SB
T: 01543 265000
F: 01543 265827
E: advantage@norgren.com
W: www.norgren.com/rail

Norman Butcher & Jones (NBJ)
52 Lime St, London EC3M 7AF
T: 020 7337 4060
F: 020 7337 4061
E: jberry@normanbutcherjonesltd.co.uk
W: www.normanbutcherjonesltd.co.uk

North East Railtours
T: 0191 252 3774
W: www.srps.org.uk

North Star Consultancy Ltd
78 York St, London W1H 1DP
T: 020 7692 0936
F: 020 7692 0937
E: enquiries@northstarconsultancy.com
W: www.northstarconsultancy.com

Northern Ireland Railways
See Translink

Northern Rail Ltd
Northern House, 9 Rougier St, York YO1 6HZ
T: 0870 000 5151
E: firstname.lastname@northernrail.org
W: www.northernrail.org

Northwood Railway Eng. Ltd
9 Scot Grove, Pinner, Middx HA5 4RT
T: 020 8428 9890
E: davidnbradley@btopenworld.com

Norton & Associates
32a, High St, Pinner, Middx HA5 5PW
T: 020 8869 9237
F: 07005 964635
E: mail@nortonweb.co.uk
W: www.nortonweb.co.uk

Norton Rose
Kempson House, Camomile St, London EC3A 7AN
T: 020 7283 6000
F: 020 7283 6500
W: www.nortonrose.com

Norwest Holst Construction
See Vinci

Nottingham Trams Ltd
NET Depot, Wilkinson St, Nottingham NG7 7NW
T: 0115 942 7777
E: info@thetram.net
W: www.thetram.net

Novacroft
Harvest Barn, Spring Hill, Harborough Rd, Pitsford, Northants NN6 9AA
T: 0845 330 0601
F: 0845 330 0745
E: projects@novacroft.com
W: www.novacroft.com

Novah Ltd
Unit 3, Portside Business Park, Portside North, Ellesmere Port, Cheshire CH65 2HQ
T: 0151 357 1799
F: 0151 356 2811
E: sales@novah.co.uk
W: www.novah.co.uk

Novus Rail Ltd
Solaris Centre, New South Prom, Blackpool FY4 1RW
T: 01253 478027
F: 01253 478037
E: mmcm@novusrail.com
W: www.novusrail.com

NTM Sales & Marketing Ltd
PO Box 2, Summerbridge, Harrogate HG3 4XN
T: 01423 781010
F: 01423 781279
E: info@xl-lubricants.com
W: www.xl-lubricants.com

Nu Star Material Handling
Unit C, Ednaston Business Centre, Ednaston, Derby DE6 3AE
T: 0870 443 5646
F: 0870 443 5647
E: matt@nu-starmhl.com
W: www.nu-starmhl.com

Nusteel Structures
Lympne, Hythe, Kent CT21 4LR
T: 01303 268112
F: 01303 266098
E: general@nusteelstructures.com
W: www.nusteelstructures.com

Nuttall Finchpalm
See Bam Nuttall

NVR Fleet UK
See Hitachi Capital Vehicle Hire

O'Neill Transport Consultancy
87, Neville Rd, Darlington, Co.Durham DL3 8NQ
T: 01325 482193
E: rita.oneill@talk21.com
W: www.icrg.co.uk

Oce UK Ltd
Oce House, Chatham Way, Brentwood, Essex CM14 4DZ
T: 0870 600 5544
F: 0870 600 1113
E: salesinformation@oce.com
W: www.oce.com

Odgers Ray & Berndtson
11 Hanover Square, London W1S 1JJ
T: 020 7529 1111
F: 020 7529 1000
E: info@rayberndtson.co.uk
W: www.odgers.com

Office of Rail Regulation (ORR)
One Kemble St, London WC2B 4AN
T: 020 7282 2000
F: 020 7282 2040
E: contact.cct@orr.gsi.gov.uk
W: www.rail-reg.gov.uk

Ogier Electronics Ltd
Unit 13, Sandridge Park, Porters Wood, St Albans, Herts AL3 6PH
T: 01727 845547
F: 01727 852186
E: jacqui.robbins@ogierelectronics.com
W: www.ogierelectronics.com

Oil Analysis Services Ltd
Unit 6/7, Blue Chalet Ind. Park, London Rd, West Kingsdown, Kent TN15 6BQ
T: 01474 854450
F: 01474 854408
E: ihbrown@oas-online.co.uk
W: www.oas-online.co.uk

Oleo International
Grovelands, Longford Rd, Exhall, Coventry CV7 9ND
T: 02476 645555
F: 02476 645900
E: roy.hunt@oleo.co.uk
W: www.oleo.co.uk

Omega Red Group Ltd
Dabell Ave, Blenheim Ind.Est., Bulwell, Nottingham NG6 8WA
T: 0115 877 6666
F: 0115 876 7766
E: enquiries@omegaredgroup.com
W: www.omegaredgroup.com

Omnicom Engineering Ltd
292 Tadcaster Rd, York YO24 1ET
T: 01904 778100
F: 01904 778200
E: sales@omnicomengineering.co.uk
W: www.omnicomengineering.co.uk

On Track Design Solutions Ltd
1st Floor Suite, 11 Pride Point Drive, Pride Park, Derby DE24 8BX
T: 01332 204450
F: 01332 204458
E: brianchadwick@ontrackdesign.co.uk
W: www.ontrackdesign.co.uk

On Track Flooring Ltd
Unit E18, Laws Lane, Stanton by Dale, Derbys DE7 4RT
T: 01159 321691
E: t.carter@ontrackflooring.co.uk

Onboard Retail Solutions
See Iridium Onboard

One-On Ltd
7 Home farm Courtyard, Meriden Rd, Berkswell, West Midlands CV7 7SH
T: 0845 505 1955
F: 0845 505 1977
E: info@one-on.co.uk
W: www.one-on.co.uk

Open Access Rail (The Train Chartering Company Ltd)
Benwell House, Preston, Wilts SN15 4DX
T: 01249 890176
E: info@openaccessrail.com
W: www.openaccessrail.com

Optilan Communication Systems
Sibree Rd, Stonebridge Ind. Est, Coventry CV3 4FD
T: 01926 864999
F: 01926 851818
E: sales@optilan.com
W: www.optilan.com

Optimized Systems & Solutions Ltd
SIN D-7, PO Box 31, Derby DE24 8BJ
T: 01332 771700
F: 01332 770921
W: www.o-sys.com

Optimum Consultancy Ltd
Spencer House, Mill Green Rd, Haywards Heath, West Sussex RH16 1XQ
T: 01444 443551
F: 01444 448071
E: enquiries@optimum.uk.com
W: www.optimum.uk.com

Oracle Recruitment
See Exell Group

Orchard Consulting
See Optimum

Ordnance Survey
Romsey Rd, Southampton SO16 4GU
T: 02380 305030
F: 02380 792615
E: customerservice@ordnancesurvey.co.uk
W: www.ordnancesurvey.co.uk

Orient Express
T: 020 7921 4028
F: 020 7805 5908
E: oesales.uk@orient-express.com
W: www.orient-express.com

Orion Electrotech
4 Danehill, Lower Earley, Reading RG6 4UT
T: 0118 923 9239
F: 0118 975 3332
W: www.orionelectrotech.com

Orion Rail Services Ltd
29-31 Lister Road, Hillington Park, Glasgow G52 4BH
T: 0141 892 6666
F: 0141 892 6662
E: sales@orioneng.com
W: www.orioneng.com

Osborne Rail
Fonteyn House, 47-49 London Rd, Reigate, Surrey RH2 2PY
T: 01737 378200
F: 01737 378295
E: paul.williams@osborne.co.uk
W: www.osborne.co.uk

Park Signalling Limited

PSL supplies novel and conventional signalling equipment and provides design, development, repair and consultancy services for UK signalling, including re-engineering and support for legacy systems.

Address: Houldsworth Mill Business Centre, Houldsworth Street, Reddish, Stockport SK5 6DA

Telephone: 0161 975 6161
Fax: 0161 975 6160

Email: info@park-signalling.co.uk
Website: www.park-signalling.co.uk

OSL
Unit 1.3, Alexander House, 19 Fleming Way, Swindon SN1 2NG
T: 01793 600793
F: 08701 236249
E: enquiries@osl-rail.co.uk
W: www.osl-rail.co.uk

OTN Systems
E: info@otnsystems.com
W: www.otnsystems.com

Owen Williams
See Amey

Oxford Hydrotechnics Ltd
Baynards Green, Bicester, Oxon OX27 7SR
T: 01869 346001
F: 01869 345455
E: info@h2ox.net
W: www.h2ox.net

P T Rail & Civils Ltd
57A Dock Rd, London E16 1AG
T: 020 7511 0811
F: 0560 345 8060
E: contact@ptrail.co.uk
W: www.ptrail.co.uk

Panasonic Electric Works UK Ltd
Sunrise Parkway, Linford Wood, Milton Keynes MK14 6LF
T: 01908 231555
F: 01908 231599
E: info-uk@eu.pewg.panasonic.com
W: www.panasonic-electricworks.co.uk

Pandrol UK Ltd
Gateford Rd, Worksop, Notts S81 7AX
T: 01909 476101
F: 01909 500004
E: info@pandrol.com
W: www.pandrol.com

Panolin
Ripon Way, Harrogate, N Yorks HG1 2AU
T: 01423 522911
F: 01423 530043
E: admin@cardev.com
W: www.cardev.com

Pantrak Transportation Ltd
G&S Building, 5, Sholto Cresc., Righead Ind Est, Bellshill, Lanarkshire ML4 3LX
T: 01698 840465
F: 01698 749672
E: gavinroser@pantrak.com
W: www.pantrak.com

Parallel Project Training
Davidson House, Forbury Sq, Reading RG1 3EU
T: 0845 519 2305
F: 0118 900 0501
W: www.parallelprojecttraining.com

Parallel Studios
22 Balmoral Ave, Bedford MK40 2PT
T: 07872 307692
F: 01234 217200
E: rick@parallelstudios.co.uk
W: www.parellelstudios.co.uk

Park Signalling Ltd
Houldsworth Mill Business Centre, Houldsworth St, Reddish, Stockport SK5 6DA
T: 0161 975 6161
F: 0161 975 6160
E: info@park-signalling.co.uk
W: www.park-signalling.co.uk

Parkeon Ltd
10 Willis Way, Fleets Ind Est, Poole, Dorset BH15 3SS
T: 01202 339494
F: 01202 667293
E: sales_uk@parkeon.com
W: www.parkeon.com

Parker Hannifin (UK) Ltd
Brunel Way, Thetford, Norfolk IP24 1HP
T: 01842 763299
F: 01842 756300
E: filtrationinfo@parker.com
W: www.parker.com

Parker KV Division
Presley Way, Crownhill, Milton Keynes MK8 0HB
T: 01908 561515
F: 01908 561227
E: saleskv@parker.com
W: www.parker.com

Parry People Movers Ltd
Overend Rd, Cradley Heath, West Midlands B64 7DD
T: 01384 569553
F: 01384 637753
E: info@parrypeoplemovers.com
W: www.parrypeoplemovers.com

Parsons Brinckerhoff
6 Devonshire Square, London EC2M 4YE
T: 020 7337 1700
F: 020 7337 1701
E: railandtransit@pbworld.com
W: www.pbworld.co.uk

Parsons Brinckerhoff Ltd
Westbrook Mills, Godalming, Surrey GU7 2AZ
T: 01483 528400
F: 01483 528989
E: morrisj@pbworld.com
W: www.pbworld.com/pbltd

Parsons Transport Group
Holborn Gate, High Holborn, London WC1V 7QT
T: 020 7203 8440
F: 020 7203 8441
E: enquiries.pgil@parsons.com
W: www.parsons.com

Partsmaster Ltd (NCH Europe)
Landchard House, Victoria St, West Bromwich B70 8ER
T: 0121 525 8939
F: 0121 524 7379
E: victoria.summerfield@nch.com
W: www.partsmaster.com

Passcomm Ltd
Unit 24, Tatton Court, Kingsland Garage, Warrington WA1 4RR
T: 01925 821333
F: 01925 821321
E: info@passcomm.co.uk
W: www.passcomm.co.uk

Passenger Focus
2nd Floor, One Drummond Gate, Pimlico, London SW1V 2QY
T: 0300 123 0860
F: 020 7630 7355
E: info@passengerfocus.org.uk
W: www.passengerfocus.org.uk

Passenger Transport Networks
49, Stonegate, York YO1 8AW
T: 01904 611187
E: ptn@btconnect.com
W: www.passengertransportnetworks.co.uk

Pathfinder Services (UK) Ltd
Pathfinder House, 2 Cross Farm Rd, Draycott, Somerset BS27 3SE
T: 0845 017 1247
F: 0117 981 1352
E: james@pathfinderservicesuk.com
W: www.pathfinderservicesuk.com

Pathfinder Systems UK PTY Ltd
Unit 6, Bighams Park Farm, Waterend, Hemel Hempstead HP1 3BN
T: 07711 189366
F: 020 7328 8818
E: cel@pathfindersystems.com.au
W: www.pathfindersystems.com.au

Pathfinder Tours
Stag House, Gydynap Lane, Inchbrook, Woodchester, Glos GL5 5EZ
T: 01453 835414/834477
F: 01453 834053
E: office@pathfindertours.co.uk
W: www.pathfindertours.co.uk

Paul Fabrications Ltd
Unit 10a, Sills Rd, Willow Farm Business Park, Castle Donington DE74 2US
T: 01332 818000
F: 01332 818089
E: sales@paulfabs.co.uk
W: www.paulfabs.co.uk

Paul John Plant
Telford Way, Stephenson Ind. Est, Coalville, Leics LE67 3HE
T: 01530 513400
F: 01530 513446
E: coalvilleplant@pauljohngroup.com
W: www.pauljohngroup.com

PB – Consult GmbH
Am Plaerrer 12, 90429 Nuremburg, Germany
T: 0049 911 32239 0
F: 0049 911 32239 10
E: info@pbconsult.de
W: www.pbconsult.eu

PB Design & Development
Unit 9/10, Hither Green Ind. Est., Clevedon, Bristol BS21 6ZT
T: 01275 874411
E: sales@pbdesign.co.uk
W: www.pbdesign.co.uk

HITACHI
Inspire the Next

In association with ATKINS

PBL Training
53 Guildford St, Bagshot, Surrey GU19 5NG
T: 01276 477499
F: 01276 562726
E: mike@pbl-training.co.uk
W: www.pbl-training.com

PD Devices Ltd
Old Station Yard, South Brent, Devon TQ10 9AL
T: 01364 649248
F: 01364 649250
E: enquiries@pddevices.co.uk
W: www.pddevices.co.uk

Peacock Salt Ltd
North Harbour, Ayr KA8 8AE
T: 01292 292000
F: 01292 292001
E: info@peacocksalt.co.uk
W: www.peacocksalt.co.uk

Peek Traffic Ltd
Hazlewood House, Limetree Way, Chineham Business Park, Basingstoke RG24 8WZ
T: 01256 891800
E: sales@peek.co.uk
W: www.peekglobal.com

Peeping Ltd
See Tracsis

Pegasus Transconsult Ltd
17 North Court, Hassocks, West Sussex BN6 8JS
T: 01273 845 583
E: sales@pegasustransconsult.com
W: www.pegasustransconsult.com

PEI Genesis UK Ltd
George Curl Way, Southampton SO18 2RZ
T: 02380 621260
F: 0844 871 6070
E: peiuk@peigenesis.com
W: www.peigenesis.com

Peli Products (UK) Ltd
Peli House, Peakdale Rd, Brookfield, Glossop, Derbys SK13 6LQ
T: 01457 869999
F: 01457 569966
E: sales@peliproducts.co.uk
W: www.peliproducts.co.uk

Pell Frischmann
5 Manchester Square, London W1A 1AU
T: 020 7486 3661
F: 020 7487 4153
E: plondon@pellfrischmann.com
W: www.pellfrischmann.com

Pelma Services and Autobuild Ltd
Chestnut Tree Cottage, One Pin Lane, Farnham Common, Bucks SL2 3QY
T: 01753 648484
M: 07778 651876
E: pelma@btconnect.com
W: www.autobuilduk.co.uk

Pennant Consulting Ltd
1 Sopwith Cres., Wickford Business Park, Wickford, Essex SS11 8YU
T: 01268 493495
E: enquiries@pennant-recruit.com
W: www.pennant-consult.com

Pennant Information Services Ltd
Parkway House, Palatine Rd, Northenden, Manchester M22 4DB
T: 0161 947 6940
F: 0161 947 6959
E: john.churchman@pennantplc.co.uk
W: www.pennantplc.co.uk

Pennant International Group Plc
Pennant Court, Staverton Technology Park, Cheltenham GL51 6TL
T: 01452 714914
F: 01452 714920
E: sales@pennantplc.co.uk
W: www.pennantplc.co.uk

People 1st
Second Floor, Armstrong House, 38 Market Square, Uxbridge UB8 1LH
T: 01895 817000
F: 01895 817035
E: info@people1st.co.uk
W: www.people1st.co.uk

Perco Engineering Services Ltd
The Old Nurseries, Nottingham Rd, Radcliffe on Trent, Nottingham NG12 2DU
T: 0115 933 5000
F: 0115 933 4692
E: nick.sheehan@perco.co.uk
W: www.perco.co.uk

Permali Gloucester Ltd
Permali Park, Bristol Rd, Gloucester GL1 5TT
T: 01452 528282
F: 01452 507409
E: fraser.rankin@permali.co.uk
W: www.permali.co.uk

Permanent Way Institution
4 Coombe Rd, Folkestone CT19 4EG
T: 01303 274534
M: 07768 105691
E: secretary@permanentwayinstitution.com
W: www.permanentwayinstitution.com

Permaquip Ltd
Brierley Industrial Park, Stanton Hill, Sutton-in-Ashfield NG17 3JZ
T: 01623 513349
F: 01623 517742
E: sales@permaquip.co.uk
W: www.permaquip.co.uk

Petards Joyce-Loebl Ltd
390, Princesway North, Team Valley Est., Gateshead, Tyne & Wear NE11 0TU
T: 0191 423 3608
F: 0191 423 3604
E: sales@petards.com
W: www.petards.com

Peter Brett Associates
Caversham Bridge House, Waterman Place, Reading RG1 8DN
T: 0118 950 0761
F: 0118 959 7498
E: reading@pba.co.uk
W: www.pba.co.uk

Peter Davidson Consultancy
Brownlow House, Ravens Lane, Berkhamsted, Herts HP4 2DX
T: 01442 891665
F: 01442 879776
E: mail@peter-davidson.com
W: www.peter-davidson.com

Peter Staveley Consulting
247 Davidson Rd, Croydon CR0 6DQ
T: 07973 168742
F: 0800 471 5332
E: peter@peterstaveley.co.uk
W: www.peterstaveley.co.uk

Pfisterer
Unit 9, Ellesmere Business Park, off Swingbridge Rd, Grantham, Lincs NG31 7XT
T: 01476 578657
F: 01476 568631
E: beverley.stokes@pfisterer.com
W: www.pfisterer.com

Pfleiderer
See Railone

PFS Ltd
Unit 1, Parker House Est., Manor Rd, West Thurrock, Essex RM20 4EH
T: 01708 252960
F: 01708 864140
E: trevor.mason@pfsfueltec.com
W: www.pfsfueltec.com

Phi Group Ltd
Harcourt House, Royal Crescent, Cheltenham, Glos GL50 3DA
T: 0870 333 4126
F: 0870 333 4127
E: marketing@phigroup.co.uk
W: www.phigroup.co.uk

Phoenix Contact Ltd
Halesfield 13, Telford, Shropshire TF7 4PG
T: 0845 881 2222
F: 0845 881 2211
E: info@phoenixcontact.co.uk
W: www.phoenixcontact.co.uk

Phoenix Systems UK Ltd
Unit 48, Standard Way, Fareham Ind. Est., Fareham, Hants PO16 8XY
T: 0845 658 6111
F: 0845 658 6222
E: sales@phoenixsystemsuk.com
W: www.phoenixsystemsuk.com

PHS Besafe incorporating Hiviz Laundries Ltd
Western Ind. Est., Caerphilly CF83 1XH
T: 02920 851000
F: 02920 863288
E: enquiries@phs.co.uk
W: www.phs.co.uk/hiviz

Pilkington Glass Ltd
Prescot Rd, St Helens, Merseyside WA10 3TT
T: 01744 28882
F: 01744 692660
W: www.pilkington.com

Pinsent Masons
City Point, One Ropemaker St, London EC2Y 9AH
T: 020 7418 7000
F: 020 7418 7050
E: tracy.williams@pinsentmasons.com
W: www.pinsentmasons.com

Pipeline Drillers Ltd
10 Kirkford, Stewarton, Kilmarnock KA3 5HZ
T: 01560 482021
F: 01560 484809
E: info@pipelinedrillers.co.uk

Pipex PX
Pipex House, 1 Belliver Way, Roborough, Plymouth, Devon PL6 7BP
T: 01752 581200
F: 01752 581209
E: sales@pipexpx.com
W: www.pipexpx.com

Pirtek (UK) Ltd
35 Acton Park Estate, The Vale, Acton, London W3 7QE
T: 020 8749 8444
F: 020 8749 8333
E: info@pirtek.co.uk
W: www.pirtekuk.com

Pitchmastic PmB Ltd
Panama House, 184 Attercliffe Rd, Sheffield S4 7WZ
T: 0114 270 0100
F: 0114 276 8782
E: info@pitchmasticpmb.co.uk
W: www.pitchmasticpmb.co.uk

Plan Me Project Management
PO Box 281, Malvern WR14 9EP
T: 07906 439055
F: 0800 471 5332
E: info@planme.com
W: www.planme.com

Planet Platforms
Brunel Close, Century Park, Wakefield 41 Ind. Est, Wakefield WF2 0XG
T: 0800 085 4161
F: 01924 267090
E: info@planetplatforms.co.uk
W: www.planetplatforms.co.uk

Plasser Machinery, Parts & Services Ltd
Manor Rd, West Ealing, London W13 0PP
T: 020 8998 4781
F: 020 8997 8206
E: info@plasser.co.uk
W: www.plasser.co.uk

Platipus Anchors Ltd
Unit Q, Philanthropic Rd, Kingsfield Business Centre, Redhill, Surrey RH1 4DP
T: 01737 762300
F: 01737 773395
E: info@platipus-anchors.com
W: www.platipus-anchors.com

Plowman Craven Ltd
141 Lower Luton Rd, Harpenden, Herts AL5 5EQ
T: 01582 765566
F: 01582 765370
E: post@plowmancraven.co.uk
W: www.plowmancraven.co.uk

PM Safety Consultants Ltd
Suite D, 3rd Floor, Saturn Facilities, 101 Lockhurst Lane, Coventry CV6 5SF
T: 02476 665770
F: 02476 582401
E: info@pmsafety.com
W: www.pmsafety.com

PMA UK Ltd (Thomas & Betts Ltd)
Unit 4, Imperial Court, Magellan Close, Walworth Ind. Est., Andover, Hants SP10 5NT
T: 01264 333527
F: 01264 333643
E: sales@pma-uk.com
W: www.pma-uk.com

PMProfessional Learning
See Aikona

Pod-Track Ltd
Unit 8 Fleetway Business Park, 14-16 Wadsworth Rd, Perivale, Middx UB6 7LD
T: 020 8998 0010
E: info@pod-track.com
W: www.pod-track.com

Polyamp AB
Box 229, Atvidaberg, 597 25 Sweden
T: 0046 120 85410
F: 0046 120 85405
E: info@polyamp.se
W: www.polyamp.com

Polydeck Ltd
Unit 14, Burnett Ind Est, Cox's Green, Wrington, Bristol BS40 5QS
T: 01934 863678
F: 01934 863683
E: sales@gripfast.co.uk
W: www.gripfast.co.uk

Polyflor Ltd
Transport Flooring Division, PO Box 3, Radcliffe New Rd, Whitefield, Manchester M45 7NR
T: 0161 767 1111
F: 0161 767 2515
E: transport@polyflor.com
W: www.polyflor.com

Polypipe
Charnwood Business Park, North Rd, Loughborough, Leics LE11 1LE
T: 01509 615100
F: 01509 610215
E: emma.thompson@polypipe.com
W: www.polypipe.com

Polysafe Level Crossings
King St. Ind. Est., Langtoft, Peterborough PE6 9NF
T: 01778 560555
F: 01778 560773
E: sales@polysafe.co.uk
W: www.polysafe.co.uk

Portaramp UK Ltd
Units 3&4, Dolphin Business Park, Thetford, Norfolk IP24 2RY
T: 01953 681799
F: 01953 688153
E: sales@portaramp.co.uk
W: www.portaramp.co.uk

Portec Rail Group
Stamford Street, Sheffield S9 2TL
T: 0114 256 2225
F: 0114 261 7826
E: uk.sales@portecrail.co.uk
W: www.portecrail.com

Porterbrook Leasing Company Ltd
Ivatt House, 7 The Point, Pinnacle Way, Pride Park, Derby DE24 8ZS
T: 01332 285050
F: 01332 285051
E: enquiries@porterbrook.co.uk
W: www.porterbrook.co.uk

Portwest Clothing Ltd
Commercial Rd, Goldthorpe Ind. Est., Goldthorpe, S.Yorks S63 9BL
T: 01709 894575
F: 01709 880830
E: info@portwest.com
W: www.portwest.com

Postfield Systems
53, Ullswater Cres., Coulsdon, Surrey CR5 2HR
T: 020 8655 6080
F: 020 8655 6082
E: sales@postfield.co.uk
W: www.postfield.co.uk

Potensis Ltd
7th Floor, Froomsgate House, Rupert St, Bristol BS1 2QJ
T: 0117 910 7999
F: 0117 927 2722
E: office@potensis.com
W: www.potensis.com

Potter Group Logistics Ltd
Melmerby Ind. Est, Green Lane, Melmerby, Ripon, North Yorks HG4 5HP
T: 01353 646703
E: sales@pottergroup.co.uk
W: www.pottergroup.co.uk

Power 4 from Fox & Cooper
See Stuart Group

Power Electronics (PE Systems Ltd)
Victoria St, Leigh, Lancs WN7 5SE
T: 01942 260330
F: 01942 261835
E: sales@pe-systems.co.uk
W: www.power-electronics.co.uk

Power Jacks Ltd
Balmacassie Commercial Park, Ellon, Aberdeenshire AB41 8BX
T: 01358 285100
F: 01358 724105
E: sales@powerjacks.com
W: www.powerjacks.com

Powerbox Group
4/5 Knights Court, Magellan Close, Walworth Ind. Est, Andover, Hants SP10 5NT
T: 01264 337800
E: warren.venn@powerboxgroup.co.uk
W: www.powerbox.info

Powernetics International Ltd
Jason Works, Clarence St, Loughborough, Leics LE11 1DX
T: 01509 214153
F: 01509 262460
E: sales@powernetics.co.uk
W: www.powernetics.co.uk

Powertron Convertors Ltd
See Martek Power

Praxis
See Altran Praxis

Prayborne Ltd
Unit 11 Dunlop Road, Hunt End Ind. Est, Redditch B97 5XP
T: 0870 242 0004
F: 01527 543 752
E: enquiries@prayborne.co.uk
W: www.prayborne.co.uk

PRB Consulting
167 London Rd, Hailsham, E.Sussex BN27 3AN
T: 0845 557 6814
W: www.prbconsulting.co.uk

PRC Rail Consulting
10 Park Lane, Sutton Bonington, Loughborough LE12 5NH
T: 01509 670679
F: 01509 670679
E: piers.connor@railway-technical.com
W: www.railway-technical.com

Preformed Markings Ltd
Unit 6, Oyster Park, 109 Chertsey Rd, Byfleet KT14 7AX
T: 01932 359270
F: 01932 340936
E: info@preformedmarkings.co.uk
W: www.preformedmarkings.co.uk

Premier Calibration Ltd
Unit 3K/L, Lake Enterprise Park, Sandall Stores Rd, Kirk Sandall, Doncaster DN3 1QR
T: 01302 888448
F: 01302 881197
E: enquiries.premcal@btconnect.com
W: www.premier-calibration.co.uk

Premier Pits
Town Drove, Quadring, Spalding, Lincs PE11 4PU
T: 01775 821222
F: 01775 820914
E: info@premierpits.com
W: www.premierpits.com

Premier Stampings
Station St, Cradley Heath, West Midlands B64 6AJ
T: 01384 353100
F: 01384 353101
E: ashleyh@premierstampings.co.uk
W: www.premierstampings.co.uk

Premier Train Catering
See Creative Rail Dining

PremTech Solutions Ltd
9 Saffron Meadow, Harrogate, North Yorks HG3 2NU
M: 07778 981641
E: david@premtech.net
W: www.premtech.net

Preston Trampower Ltd
48 Watling St Rd, Fulwood, Preston PR2 8BP
T: 01772 713900
F: 0151 521 5509
M: 07831 337356
E: lincoln.shields@trampower.co.uk
W: www.prestontrampower.co.uk

Price Tool Sales Ltd
See Birchwood Price Tools

PricewaterhouseCoopers LLP
1 Embankment Place, London WC2N 6NN
T: 020 7583 5000
F: 020 7822 4652
E: julian.smith@uk.pwc.com
W: www.pwcglobal.com

Primarius UK Ltd
12b, Earlstrees Rd, Earlstrees Ind Est, Corby, Northants NN17 4AZ
T: 01536 263691
E: sales@primariusuk.com
W: www.primariusuk.com

Priority Vehicle Hire Ltd
Unit 4, Quaking Farm Buildings, Bestmans Lane, Kempsey, Worcester
T: 01905 821843/07939 038875
F: 01227 770035

Progress Rail Services
See Caterpillar

Prolec Ltd
25 Benson Rd, Nuffield Ind. Est., Poole, Dorset BH17 0GB
T: 01202 681190
F: 01202 677909
E: info@prolec.co.uk
W: www.prolec.co.uk

Prostaff Rail Recruitment
172, Buckingham Ave, Slough, Bucks SL1 4RD
T: 01753 575888
W: www.prostaff.com

Protec Fire Detection Plc
Protec House, Churchill Way, Nelson, Lancs BB9 6RT
T: 01282 717171
F: 01282 717273
E: sales@protec.co.uk
W: www.protec.co.uk

Proteq
96, High St, Epworth, Doncaster DN9 1JJ
T: 01427 872572
E: info@proteq.co.uk
W: www.proteq.co.uk

PRV Engineering
Pegasus House, Polo Grounds, New Inn, Pontypool, Gwent NP4 0TW
T: 01495 769697
F: 01495 769776
E: enquiries@prv-engineering.co.uk
W: www.prv-engineering.co.uk

Prysm Rail
See Archer Signs

Prysmian Cables & Systems
Chickenhall Lane, Bishopstoke, Hants SO50 6YU
T: 023 8029 5029
F: 023 8060 8769
E: marketing.telecom@prysmian.com
W: www.prysmian.co.uk

Psion Teklogix
Unit Q, Bourne End Business Centre, Cores End Rd, Bourne End, Bucks SL8 5AS
T: 01628 648800
F: 01628 648810
W: www.psionteklogix.co.uk

PSV Glass
16 Hill Bottom Rd, Sands Ind Est, High Wycombe, Bucks HP12 4HJ
T: 01494 533131\0845 600 9801
F: 01494 462675
E: rail@psvglass.co.uk
W: www.psvglass.com

Ptarmigan Transport Solutions Ltd
See Trainpeople.co.uk

PTH Group Ltd
Banham Court, Hanbury Rd, Stoke Prior, Bromsgrove, Worcs B60 4JZ
T: 01527 577242
F: 01527 832618
E: admin@pthgroup.co.uk
W: www.pthgroup.co.uk

PTM Design Ltd
Unit B2, Sovereign Park Ind Est, Lathkill St, Market Harborough LE16 9EG
T: 01858 463777
F: 01858 463777
E: ptmdesign@aol.com

PTP Associates
The Lodge, 21 Harcourt Rd., Dorney Reach, Berks SL6 0DT
T: 01628 776059
E: ces@ptpassociates.co.uk
W: www.ptpassociates.co.uk

Pullman Group
Train Maintenance Depot, Leckwith Rd, Cardiff CF11 8HP
T: 02920 368866
F: 02920 368874
E: colin@pullmans.net
W: www.pullmans.net

Pulsarail
See Prayborne Ltd

Pyeroy Group
Kirkstone House, St Omers Rd, Western Riverside Route, Gateshead, Tyne & Wear NE11 9EZ
T: 0191 493 2600
F: 0191 493 2601
E: mail@pyeroy.co.uk
W: www.pyeroy.co.uk

Pym & Wildsmith (Metal Finishers) Ltd
Bramshall Ind. Est, Bramshall, Uttoxeter, Staffs ST14 8TD
T: 01889 565653
F: 01889 567064
E: enquiries@pymandwildsmith.co.uk
W: www.pymandwildsmith.co.uk

Q'Straint
Unit 72-76, John Wilson Business Park, Whitstable, Kent CT5 3QT
T: 01227 773035
F: 01227 770035
E: info@qstraint.co.uk
W: www.qstraint.com

QC Data Ltd
Park House, 14 Kirtley Drive, Castle Marina, Nottingham NG7 1LD
T: 0115 941 5806
F: 0115 947 2901
E: rjohnson@qcdata.com
W: www.qcdata.com

QHI Rail
1 Allied Business Centre, Coldharbour Lane, Harpenden, Herts AL5 4UT
T: 01582 461123
F: 01582 461117
E: info@qhigroup.com
W: www.qhirail.com

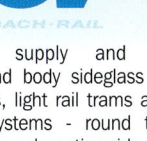

QinetiQ
Cody Technology Park, Building A7, Room 2008, Ively Road, Farnborough, Hants GU14 0LX
T: 01252 394786
F: 01252 397 298
E: jldavies1@qinetiq.com
W: www.qinetiq.com

QTS Plant
QTS Group, Rench Farm, Drumclog, Strathaven, S. Lanarks ML10 6QJ
T: 01357 440222
F: 01357 440364
E: enquiries@qtsgroup.com
W: www.qtsgroup.com

Qualter Hall & Co Ltd
PO Box 8, Johnson St, Barnsley S75 2BY
T: 01226 205761
F: 01226 286269
E: admin@qualterhall.co.uk
W: www.qualterhall.co.uk

Quasar Associates
8 Flitcroft St, London WC2H 8DJ
T: 020 7010 7700
F: 020 7010 7701
E: jonathan@quasarassociates.co.uk
W: www.quasarassociates.co.uk

Quattro Plant Ltd
Greenway Court, Canning Rd, Stratford, London E15 3ND
T: 020 8519 6165
F: 020 8503 0505
E: sales@quattroplant.co.uk
W: www.quattroplant.co.uk

Quest Diagnostics
Unit B1, Parkway West, Cranford Lane, Heston, Middx TW5 9QA
T: 020 8377 3378
F: 020 8377 3350
E: uksales@questdiagnostics.com
W: www.questdiagnostics.com

Quickbuild (UK) Ltd
Imperial House, 1 Factory Rd, Silvertown, London E16 2EL
T: 020 7473 2712
F: 020 7476 2713
E: davidbrowne@hiremasters.co.uk
W: www.hiremasters.co.uk/www.quickbuild.uk.com

Directory

Quickway Buildings
Hardys Yard, London Rd, Riverhead,
Sevenoaks, Kent TN13 2DN
T: 01304 612284
F: 01304 620012
E: sales@quickway-wingham.co.uk
W: www.quickway-wingham.co.uk

QW Rail Leasing
12 Plumtree Court, London EC4A 4HT

R&B Power Engineering Ltd
Switchgear House, The Courtyard, Green Lane,
Heywood, Lancs OL10 2EX
T: 01706 369933
F: 01706 364564
E: ian.penswick@rb-power.co.uk
W: www.rbswitch.org

R.S. Clare & Co Ltd
8-14, Stanhope St, Liverpool L8 5RQ
T: 0151 709 2902
F: 0151 709 0518
E: info@rsclare.co.uk
W: www.rsclare.com

Ra'alloy Ramps Ltd
Unit B8 Hortonwood 10, Telford,
Shropshire TF1 7ES
T: 01952 677877
F: 01952 677883
E: enquiries@raalloy.co.uk
W: www.raalloyramps.co.uk

Radio-Tech Ltd
U1/U2, The London Road Campus,
London Road, Harlow, Essex CM17 9NA
T: 01279 635 849
F: 01279 442 261
E: sales@radio-tech.co.uk
W: www.radio-tech.co.uk

Rail & Road Protec GmbH
Norderhofenden 12-13, Flensburg 24937,
Germany
T: 01628 635497
F: 004 61 500 33820
M: 07747 460509
E: balvinder.chana@r2protec.com
W: www.r2protec.com

Rail Accident Investigation Branch
Cullen House, Berkshire Copse Rd, Aldersot,
Hants GU11 2HH
T: 01932 440002
E: enquiries@raib.gov.uk
W: www.raib.gov.uk

Rail Alliance
The Control Tower, Long Marston Storage,
Campden Rd, Long Marston,
Stratford upon Avon,
Warks CV37 8QR
T: 01789 720626
E: info@railalliance.co.uk
W: www.railalliance.co.uk

Rail Door Solutions Ltd
Blackhill Drive, Wolverton Mill,
Milton Keynes MK12 5TS
T: 01908 224140
F: 01908 224149
E: sales@raildoorsolutions.co.uk
W: www.raildoorsolutions.co.uk

Rail Freight Group
7 Bury Place, London WC1 2LA
T: 020 3116 0007
F: 020 3116 0008
E: phillippa@rfg.org.uk
W: www.rfg.org.uk

Rail Gourmet Group
Mac Millan House,
Paddington Station,
London W2 1FT
T: 020 7313 0720
F: 020 7922 6596
E: jfleet@railgourmetuk.com
W: www.railgourmet.com

Rail Images & Rail Images Video
5 Sandhurst Crescent,
Leigh on Sea,
Essex SS9 4AL
T: 01702 525059
F: 01702 525059
E: info@railimages.co.uk
W: www.railimages.co.uk

Rail Industry Contractors Association Ltd (RICA)
Gin Gan House, Thropton, Morpeth,
Northumberland NE65 7LT
T: 01669 620569
E: enquiries@rica.com.uk
W: www.rica.com.uk

Rail Industry First Aid Association (RIFAA)
Room 103, Denison House South,
Hexthorpe Road,
Doncaster DN4 0BF
T: 01302 329 729
F: 01302 320 590
E: bookings@rifaa.com
W: www.rifaa.com

Rail Manche Finance EEIG
Times House, Bravingtons Walk,
Regent Quarter,
London N1 9AW
T: 020 7042 9961
F: 020 7833 3896
E: david.hiscock@rmf.co.uk
W: www.rmf.co.uk

Rail Measurement Ltd
The Mount, High St, Toft,
Cambridge CB23 2RL
T: 01223 264327
F: 01223 263273
E: enquiries@railmeasurement.com
W: www.railmeasurement.com

Rail Op UK Ltd
13 The Links Ind. Est, Raynham Rd,
Bishops Stortford, Herts CM23 5NZ
T: 0845 450 5332
E: info@railop.co.uk
W: www.railop.co.uk

Rail Operations Competence Solutions Ltd
40 Weston Lane, Shavington, Crewe,
Cheshire CW2 5AN
T: 07796 548651
E: info@rail-operations-competence-solutions.co.uk
W: www.rail-operations-competence-solutions.co.uk

Rail Operations Developments Ltd
Electra House, Electra Way,
Crewe Business Park,
Crewe CW1 6GL
T: 01270 588500
F: 01270 588500
E: enquiries@rodl.co.uk
W: www.railoperationsdevelopment.co.uk

Rail Order
Unit 3, Sherwood Networking Centre,
Sherwood Energy Village, Ollerton,
Notts NG22 9FD
T: 01623 862431
F: 01623 861881
E: sales@rail-order.co.uk
W: www.rail-order.co.uk

Rail Personnel Ltd
Level 26, Office Tower,
Convention Plaza, 1 Harbour Rd,
Wanchai, Hong Kong
T: 00 852 2753 5636
F: 00 852 2305 4512
E: info@railpersonnel.com
W: www.railpersonnel.com

Rail Photo Library
F: 0116 259 2068
E: studio@railphotolibrary.com

Rail Positive Relations
The Bothy,
18 Holloway Rd,
Duffield,
Derbys DE56 4FE
T: 020 7617 7018
M: 07973 950923
E: rupert@railpr.com
W: www.railpr.com

Rail Professional Development
Cranes House,
5 Paycocke Rd,
Basildon,
Essex SS14 3DP
T: 01268 822842
F: 01268 822841
E: info@rpd.co.uk
W: www.rpd.co.uk

Rail Research UK Association (RRUK-A)
Block 2,
Angel Square,
1 Torrens St,
London EC1V 1NY
T: 02380 598454
F: 02380 677519
E: secretariat@rruka.org.uk
W: www.rruka.org.uk

Rail Restorations North East Ltd
8A Hackworth Industrial Park,
Shildon DL4 1HF
T: 01388 777138
M: 07971 100092
E: enquiries@rail-restorations-north-east.co.uk
W: www.rail-restorations-north-east.co.uk

Rail Safety and Standards Board (RSSB)
Block 2, Angel Square,
1 Torrens St,
London EC1V 1NY
T: 020 3142 5300
F: 020 3142 5301
E: enquirydesk@rssb.co.uk
W: www.rssb.co.uk

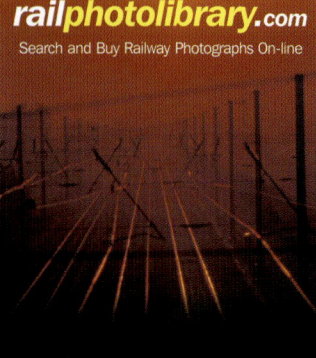

Rail Safety Solutions
Unit 27, Royal Scot Rd, Pride Park,
Derby DE24 8AJ
T: 01332 989593
F: 020 3142 5301
E: info@railsafetysolutions.com
W: www.railsafetysolutions.com

Rail Tech Group (Railway & Signalling Engineering) Ltd
91 Dales Rd, Ipswich IP1 4JR
T: 01473 242330
F: 01473 242379
E: reception@railtech.co.uk
W: www.railtech.co.uk

Rail Technology Ltd
Mill End Lane, Alrewas, Staffs DE13 7BY
T: 01283 790012
F: 01283 792371
M: 07715 374635
E: bg@track-man.co.uk
W: www.railtechnologyltd.com

Rail Training International Ltd
North Suite, Parsonage Offices, Church Lane,
Canterbury, Kent CT4 7AD
T: 01227 769096
F: 01227 479435
E: rtiuk@rti.co.uk
W: www.rti.co.uk

Rail Vision
2 Cygnus Court,
Beverley Rd,
Pegasus Business Park,
East Midlands Airport,
Castle Donnington,
Leics DE74 2UZ
T: 01509 672211
E: enquiries@rail-vision.com
W: www.rail-vision.com

Rail Waiting Structures
Dyffryn Business Park,
Llantwit Major Rd,
Llandow,
Vale of Glamorgan
T: 01446 795444
F: 01446 793344
E: lisa.brown@shelters.co.uk
W: www.shelters.co.uk

Rail-Ability Ltd
Tilcon Ave, Baswich,
Stafford ST18 0YJ
T: 01785 214747
F: 01785 214717
E: skelly@railability.co.uk
W: www.railability.co.uk

Rail-Blue Charters
32 Sydney Rd, Haywards Heath,
West Sussex RH16 1QA
T: 01444 450011
F: 01444 450011
E: ingrid.sluis@rail-bluecharters.co.uk
W: www.rail-bluecharters.co.uk

Railcare Ltd
Wolverton Works, Stratford Rd, Wolverton,
Milton Keynes MK12 5NT
T: 01908 574400
F: 01908 574414
E: info@railcare.co.uk
W: www.railcare.co.uk

Railcare Ltd
Springburn Depot, 79 Charles St,
Glasgow G21 2PS
T: 0141 548 8305
W: www.railcare.com

Raileasy
10 Station Parade, High St, Wanstead,
London E11 1QF
T: 0906 202 0002
E: admin@raileasy.co.uk
W: www.raileasy.co.uk

Railex Aluminium Ltd
12/26 Dry Drayton Ind. Est., Dry Drayton,
Cambridge CB3 8AT
T: 0845 612 9555
F: 01954 210352
E: tony@humanhi.com
W: www.railex.net

Railfuture
29 Granby Hill, Bristol BS8 4LT
M: 07759 557389
E: media@railfuture.org.uk
W: www.railfuture.org.uk

RailRoute Ltd
The Business and Innovation Centre,
Enterprise Park East, Sunderland SR5 2TA
T: 0191 516 6354
M: 0776 586 0998
E: michael.beaney@railroute.co.uk
W: www.railroute.co.uk

Railscape Ltd
15 Totman Cresc, Brook Rd Ind Est, Rayleigh,
Essex SS6 7UY
T: 01268 777795
F: 01268 777762
E: info@railscape.co.uk
W: www.railscape.co.uk

Railtex/Infrarail - Mack Brooks Exhibitions Ltd
Romelands House, Romelands Hill,
St Albans AL3 4ET
T: 01727 814400
F: 01727 814401
E: railtex@mackbrooks.co.uk
W: www.mackbrooks.co.uk

Railtourer Ltd
42 Kingston Rd, Willerby,
Hull HU10 6BH
T: 01482 659082
W: www.railtourer.co.uk

Railway Approvals Ltd
Derwent House,
rtc Business Park, London Rd,
Derby DE24 8UP
T: 01332 483800
F: 01332 483800
E: info@railwayapprovals.co.uk
W: www.railwayapprovals.co.uk

Railway Civil Engineers Association
One Great George St,
Westminster,
London SW1P 3AA
T: 020 7665 2233
F: 020 7799 1325
E: info@rcea.co.uk
W: www.rcea.co.uk

Railway Convalescent Home (RCH)
Bridge House, 2 Church St, Dawlish,
Devon EX7 9AU
T: 01626 863303
F: 01626 866676
E: sueg@rch.org.uk
W: www.rch.org.uk

Railway Drainage Ltd
The Steadings, Maisemore Court, Maisemore,
Glos GL2 8EY
T: 01452 422666
E: enquiries@rdlonline.co.uk
W: www.rdlonline.co.uk

Railway Engineering Associates Ltd
68 Boden St, Glasgow G40 3PX
T: 0141 554 3868
F: 0141 556 5091
E: postmaster@rea.uk.com
W: www.rea.uk.com

Railway Finance Ltd
Barrow Rd, Wincobank, Sheffield S9 1JZ
T: 01223 891300
F: 01223 891302
E: nick.preston@railwayfinance.co.uk
W: www.railwayfinance.co.uk

Railway Friendly Society
MacMillan House, Paddington Station,
London W2 1FT
T: 0800 032 4326
E: enquiries@railwayfs.co.uk
W: www.railwayfs.co.uk

Railway Industry Association
22 Headfort Place, London SW1X 7RY
T: 020 7201 0777
F: 020 7235 5777
E: ria@riagb.org.uk
W: www.riagb.org.uk

Railway Management Services
Kingfisher House, Suite 27,
21-23 Elmfield Rd, Bromley,
Kent BR1 1LT
T: 020 8315 6767
F: 020 8315 6766
E: peter.coysten@railwayms.com
W: www.railwayms.com

Railway Projects Ltd
Lisbon House, 5-7 St Marys Gate,
Derby DE1 3JA
T: 01332 349255
F: 01332 349261
E: enquiries@railwayprojects.co.uk
W: www.railwayprojects.co.uk

Railway Study Association (RSA)
37 Charlwood Rd, Burgess Hill,
West Sussex RH15 0RJ
T: 01444 246379
E: info@railwaystudyassociation.org
W: www.railwaystudyassociation.org

Railway Support Services
Montpellier House,
Montpellier Drive,
Cheltenham GL50 1TY
T: 0870 803 4651
F: 0870 803 4652
E: info@railwaysupportservices.co.uk
W: www.railwaysupportservices.co.uk

Railway Systems Engineering & Integration Group
Birmingham Centre for Railway Research and
Education College of Engineering Sciences,
University of Birmingham, Edgbaston,
Birmingham B15 2TT
T: 0121 414 4342
F: 0121 414 4291
E: j.grey@bham.ac.uk
W: www.eng.bham.ac.uk/civil/study/postgrad/railway.shtml

Railway Touring Company
14a Tuesday Market Place, Kings Lynn,
Norfolk PE30 1JN
T: 01553 661500
F: 01553 661800
E: enquiries@railwaytouring.co.uk
W: www.railwaytouring.co.uk

Railway Vehicle Engineering Ltd (RVEL)
RTC Business Park, London Rd,
Derby DE24 8UO
T: 01332 293035
F: 01332 331210
E: enquiries@rvel.co.uk
W: www.rvel.co.uk

Railweight
Foundry Lane, Smethwick,
Birmingham B66 2LP
T: 0121 568 1708
F: 0121 697 5655
E: sales@railweight.co.uk
W: www.averyweightronix.com/railweight

Railwork (UK) Ltd
1 Portway Close, Coventry CV4 9UY
T: 02476 695550
F: 02476 695040
E: info@railwork.co.uk
W: www.railwork.co.uk

Ramboll UK Ltd
Carlton House, Ringwood Rd, Woodlands,
Southampton SO40 7HT
T: 02380 817500
F: 02380 817600
E: tim.holmes@ramboll.co.uk
W: www.ramboll.co.uk

Rampart Carriage & Wagon Services Ltd
Brunel Gate, RTC Business Park, London Rd,
Derby DE24 8UP
T: 01332 263261
F: 01332 263181
E: admin@rampartderby.co.uk
W: www.rampartderby.co.uk

Ramtech Electronics Ltd
Abbeyfield House, Abbeyfield Rd, Nottingham
NG7 2SZ
T: 0115 988 7090
F: 0115 970 5415
E: matt.sadler@ramtech.co.uk
W: www.ramtech.co.uk

Ransome Engineering Services Ltd
Clopton Commercial Park, Clopton,
Woodbridge, Suffolk IP13 6QT
T: 01473 737731
F: 01473 737398
E: info@ransomeengineering.co.uk
W: www.ransomeengineering.co.uk

Ranstad CPE
Forum 4, Parkway, Solent Business Park,
Whiteley, Fareham PO15 7AD
T: 01489 560000
F: 01489 560001
E: info@ranstadcpe.com
W: www.ranstadcpe.com

Raspberry Software Ltd
9 Deben Mill Business Centre,
Old Maltings Approach,
Melton, Woodbridge,
Suffolk IP12 1BL
T: 01394 387386
F: 01394 387386
E: info@raspberrysoftware.com
W: www.raspberrysoftware.com

Ratdiff Palfinger
Bessemer Rd, Welwyn Garden City,
Herts AL7 1ET
T: 01707 325571
F: 01707 327752
E: info@ratcliffpalfinger.co.uk
W: www.ratcliffpalfinger.co.uk

Rayleigh Instruments
Raytel House, Brook Rd, Rayleigh,
Essex SS6 7XH
T: 01268 749300
F: 01268 749309
E: sales@rayleigh.co.uk
W: www.rayleigh.co.uk

RE: Systems
Systems House, Deepdale Business Park,
Bakewell, Derbys DE45 1FZ
T: 01629 815902
F: 01629 813349
E: steve.england@re-systems.co.uk
W: www.re-systems.co.uk

Reg Harman Consultancy Services Ltd
2 Valley Close,
Hertford SG13 8BD
T: 01992 415248
E: reg.harman@ntlworld.com

Rehau Ltd
Units 5J&K, Langley Business Centre,
Station Rd, Langley,
Slough SL3 8DS
T: 01753 588500
F: 01753 588501
E: jason.chapman@rehau.com
W: www.rehau.co.uk

RVEL
RAILWAY-VEHICLE-ENGINEERING-LIMITED
Specialist rolling stock engineering - design, build, heavy overhaul and maintenance capabilities. Design, fitment and modification of ETCS, ERTMS & TPWS systems on passenger and freight vehicles. RVAR compliance work.
Railway Vehicle Engineering Ltd
RTC Business Park, London Road
Derby DE24 8UP
Phone: 01332 293035
Fax: 01332 331210
Email: enquiries@rvel.co.uk
www.rvel.co.uk

REACT by Autoclenz
Stanhope Rd, Swadlincote, Derbys DE11 9BE
T: 08707 510422
F: 08707 510417
E: react@autoclenz.co.uk
W: www.react-decon.co.uk

React Engineering Ltd
Fleswick Court, Westlakes Science & Tech. Park,
Moor Row, Whitehaven, Cumbria CA24 3HZ
T: 01946 590511
F: 01946 591044
E: mail@react-engineering.co.uk
W: www.react-engineering.co.uk

Readypower
Readypower House, Molly Millars Bridge,
Wokingham, Berks RG41 2WY
T: 01189 774901
F: 01189 774902
E: info@readypower.co.uk
W: www.readypower.co.uk

Real Time Consultants Plc
118-120, Warwick St, Royal Leamington Spa,
Warks CV32 4QY
T: 01926 313133
F: 01926 422165
E: contract@rtc.co.uk
W: www.rtc.co.uk

Record Electrical Associates Ltd
Unit C1, Longford Trading Est., Thomas St.,
Stretford, Manchester M32 0JT
T: 0161 864 3583
F: 0161 864 3603
E: alanj@reauk.com
W: www.record-electrical.co.uk

Recruitrail (Recruit Engineers)
Bank Chambers, 36 Mount Pleasant Rd,
Tunbridge Wells, Kent TN1 1RA
T: 01909 540825
F: 0870 443 0453
W: www.recruitrail.com

Redex Rail Services Ltd
Unit 7, Abbey Way, North Anston Trading Est,
Sheffield S25 4JL
T: 01909 552070
F: 01909 569893
W: www.redexrail.co.uk

Redman Fisher Engineering Ltd
Birmingham New Rd, Tipton,
West Midlands DY4 9AQ
T: 01902 880880
F: 01902 880446
E: sales@redmanfisher.co.uk
W: www.redmanfisher.co.uk

Reid Lifting Ltd
Unit 1, Severnlink,
Newhouse Farm Ind. Est,
Chepstow,
Monmouthshire NP16 6UN
T: 01291 620796
F: 01291 626490
E: enquiries@reidlifting.com
W: www.reidlifting.com

Relec Electronics Ltd
Animal House, Justin Bus. Park,
Sandford Lane, Wareham, Dorset BH20 4DY
T: 01929 555700
F: 01929 555701
E: sales@relec.co.uk
W: www.relec.co.uk

Renaissance Trains Ltd
4 Spinneyfield, Ellington, Cambs PE28 0AT
T: 07977 917148
E: peter.wilkinson@renaissancetrains.com
W: www.renaissancetrains.com

Renown Training
Brookside House, Brookside Business Park,
Cold Meece, Staffs ST15 0RZ
T: 01785 764476
F: 01785 760896
E: enquiries@renownrailway.co.uk
W: www.renownrailway.co.uk

Replin Fabrics
March St Mills, Peebles EH45 8ER
T: 01721 724311
F: 01721 721893
E: enquiries@replin-fabrics.co.uk
W: www.replin-fabrics.co.uk

Resourcing Solutions
Vector House, 5 Ruscombe Park, Ruscombe,
Berks RG10 9JW
T: 0118 932 0100
F: 0118 932 1818
E: info@resourcing-solutions.com
W: www.resourcing-solutions.com

Retro Railtours Ltd
2 Brookfield Grove, Ashton-under-Lyne,
Lancashire OL6 6TL
T: 0870 312 1066
E: info@retrorailtours.co.uk
W: www.retrorailtours.co.uk

Revitaglaze
Unit 9, Park Industrial Estate, Frogmore, St
Albans Herts AL2 2DR
T: 0843 289 3901
F: 01372 200881
E: marketing@revitaglaze.com
W: www.revitaglaze.com

Rexquote Ltd
Broadgauge Business Park,
Bishops Lydeard, Taunton, Somerset TA4 3RU
T: 01823 433398
F: 01823 433378
E: sales@rexquote.co.uk
W: www.rexquote.co.uk

RGB Integrated Services Ltd
Unit 3007, Access House, Nestle Ave, Hayes,
Middlesex UB3 4UZ
T: 020 8573 9882
F: 020 8711 3916
E: info@rgb-services.com
W: www.rgb-services.com

RGS Rail
6 Clarendon St, Nottingham NG1 5HQ
T: 0115 959 9687
M: 07973 676323
E: enquiries@rgsexecutive.co.uk
W: www.rgsexecutive.co.uk

RIB Software (UK) Ltd
12 Floor, The Broadgate Tower,
20 Primrose St, London EC2A 2EW
T: 020 7596 2747
F: 020 7596 2701
W: www.rib-software.co.uk

Ricardo Plc
Midlands Technical Centre, Southam Rd,
Radford Semele, Leamington Spa,
Warks CV31 1FQ
T: 01926 477171
F: 01926 319352
E: jim.buchanan@ricardo.com
W: www.ricardo.com

Riello UPS Ltd
Unit 68, Clywedog Rd North,
Wrexham Ind.Est., Wrexham LL13 9XN
T: 01978 729297
F: 01978 729290
E: marketing@riello-ups.co.uk
W: www.riello-ups.co.uk

Riley & Son (E) Ltd
Baron St, Bury, Lancs BL9 0TY
T: 0161 764 2892
F: 0161 763 5191
E: ian.riley@btconnect.com

Ring Automotive
Gelderd Rd, Leeds LS12 6NA
T: 0113 213 2000
F: 0113 231 0266
E: autosales@ringautomotive.co.uk
W: www.ringautomotive.co.uk

RIQC Ltd
2 St Georges House, Vernon Gate,
Derby DE1 1UQ
T: 01332 221421
F: 01332 221401
E: enquiries@riqc.co.uk
W: www.riqc.co.uk

RISC Ltd – Railway & Industrial Safety Consultants Ltd
Harlyn House, 3 Doveridge Rd, Stapenhill,
Burton Upon Trent DE15 9GB
T: 0844 840 9420
F: 0871 247 2961
M: 07941 212568
E: enquiries@railwaysafety.co.uk
W: www.railwaysafety.co.uk

REVITAGLAZE
Revitaglaze is the supplier of choice for delivering glass restoration solutions to the Railway Industry, to include; anti-graffiti glass polishing and window filming initiatives.
A: Unit 9, Park Industrial Estate, Frogmore, St. Albans, Herts AL2 2DR
T: +44 (0) 843 289 3901
F: +44 (0) 1372 200 881
E: marketing@revitaglaze.com
www.revitaglaze.com

Risk Solutions
Dallam Court, Dallam Lane, Warrington
WA2 7LT
T: 01925 413984
E: enquiries@risksol.co.uk
W: www.risksol.co.uk

Ritelite Systems Ltd
Meadow Park, Bourne Rd, Essendine,
Stamford, Lincs PE9 4LT
T: 01780 765600
F: 01780 765700
E: sales@ritelite.co.uk
W: www.ritelite.co.uk

Rittal Ltd
Braithwell Way, Hellaby Ind Est, Hellaby,
Rotherham S66 8QY
T: 01709 704000
F: 01709 701217
E: information@rittal.co.uk
W: www.rittal.co.uk

Rittal is the world's largest manufacturer of enclosures and associated products for both indoor and outdoor applications with an extensive stock holding in the UK.
RITTAL
A: Rittal Ltd, Braithwell Way
Hellaby Industrial Estate
Hellaby, Rotherham
South Yorkshire S66 8QY
P: +44 (0)1709 704000
F: +44 (0)1709 701217
E: information@rittal.co.uk
W: www.rittal.co.uk

Riviera Trains
116, Ladbroke Grove,
London W10 5NE
T: 020 7727 4036
F: 020 7727 2083
E: enquiries@riviera-trains.co.uk
W: www.riviera-trains.co.uk

RJ Power Ltd
Unit 1,
Gaugemaster Ind. Est,
Gaugemaster Way,
Ford,
West Sussex BN18 0RX
T: 01903 868535
F: 01903 885932
E: info@rjpower.biz
W: www.rjpower.biz

RMT
National Union of Rail,
Maritime & Transport Workers,
Unity House,
39 Chalton St,
London NW1 1JD
T: 020 7387 4771
F: 020 7387 4123
E: info@rmt.org.uk
W: www.rmt.org.uk

Robel Bahnbaumaschmen GmbH
Industriestrasse 31, D 83395, Freilassing,
Germany
T: 0049 8654 6090
F: 0049 8654 609100
E: info@robel.info
W: www.robel.info

Robert West Consulting
West House, 46 High St, Orpington,
Kent BR6 0JQ
T: 01689 820216
F: 01689 831582
E: orpington@robertwest.co.uk
W: www.robertwest.co.uk

Rock Mechanics Technology Ltd
Bretby Business Park, Ashby Rd,
Stanhope Bretby, Burton on Trent DE15 0QP
T: 01283 522201
F: 01283 522279
E: rmt@rmtltd.com
W: www.rmtltd.com

ROCOL Acme Panels
Rocol House,
Wakefield Rd,
Swillington,
Leeds LS26 8BS
T: 0113 232 2800
F: 0113 232 2850
E: customer-service.safety@rocol.com
W: www.rocol.com

ROCOL Site Safety Systems
ROCOL Site Safety Systems
T: 0113 232 2800
F: 0113 232 2850
E: enquiries@rocol.com
W: www.rocol.com

Roechling Engineering Plastics (UK) Ltd
Waterwells Business Park,
Waterwells Drive, Quedgeley,
Glos GL2 2AA
T: 01452 727905
F: 01452 728056
E: david.ward@roechling-plastics.co.uk
W: www.roechling-plastics.co.uk

Roevin Engineering
4th Floor, Clydesdale Bank House,
33 Lower Regent St,
Piccadilly, London WC1Y 4NB
T: 0845 643 0486
F: 0870 759 8443
E: rail@roevin.co.uk
W: www.roevin.co.uk

Rollalong Ltd
Woolsbridge Ind. Park,
Three Legged Cross,
Wimborne, Dorset BH21 6SF
T: 01202 824541
F: 01202 826525
E: enquiries@rollalong.co.uk
W: www.rollalong.co.uk

Rolling Stock Services

Romac Technical Services Ltd
Clements House, Mount Ave,
Mount Farm, Bletchley,
Milton Keynes MK1 1LS
T: 01908 375845
F: 01908 270524
E: tom.appleton@romac.co.uk
W: www.romac.co.uk

Romag
Leadgate Ind. Est., Leadgate, Consett,
Co Durham DH8 7RS
T: 01207 500000
F: 01207 591979
W: www.romag.co.uk

Romic House
A1/M1 Business Centre, Kettering, Northants
NN16 8TD
T: 01536 414244
F: 01536 414245
E: sales@romic.co.uk
W: www.romic.co.uk

Ronfell Ltd
Challenge House, Pagefield industrial Est.,
Miry Lane, Wigan WN6 7LA
T: 01942 492200
F: 01942 492233
E: sales@ronfell.com
W: www.ronfell.com

Rose Hill P&OD Ltd
1a Queen St, Rushden, Northants NN10 0AA
T: 07771 612321
F: 01933 663846
E: info@rose-hill.co.uk
W: www.rose-hill.co.uk

Rosehill Polymers Ltd
Rosehill Mills, Beech Rd, Sowerby Bridge,
West Yorks HX6 2JT
T: 01422 839243
F: 01422 316952
E: stuart.wilson@rosehillpolymers.com
W: www.rosehillpolymers.com

Rosenqvist Rail AB
Box 334, 82427 Hudiksvall, Sweden
T: 0046 650 16505
F: 0046 650 16501
E: info@rosenqvist-group.se
W: www.rosenqvistrail.se

Rotabroach Ltd
Imperial Works, Sheffield Rd, Tinsley,
Sheffield S9 2YL
T: 0114 221 2510
F: 0114 221 2563
E: sales@rotabroach.co.uk
W: www.rotabroach.co.uk

Roughton Group
A2, Omega Park, Electron Way,
Chandlers Ford, Hants SO53 4SE
T: 023 8027 8600
F: 023 8027 8601
E: hq@roughton.com
W: www.roughton.com

Rowe Hankins Ltd
Power House, Parker St, Bury BL9 0RJ
T: 0161 765 3000
F: 0161 705 2900
E: sales@rowehankins.com
W: www.rowehankins.com

Roxtec Ltd
Unit C1, Waterfold Business Park,
Bury, Lancs BL9 7BQ
T: 0161 761 5280
F: 0161 763 6065
E: russell.holmes@uk.roxtec.com
W: www.roxtec.com

Royal British Legion Industries (RBLI)
Royal British Legion Village,
Hall Rd, Aylesford,
Kent ME20 7NL
T: 01622 795900
F: 01622 795978
E: sales.office@rbli.co.uk
W: www.rbli.co.uk/manufacturing/services/19/

Royal Haskoning Ltd
Rightwell House, Bretton,
Peterborough PE3 8DW
T: 01733 334455
F: 01733 262243
E: info@peterborough.royalhaskoning.com
W: www.royalhaskoning.com

RPS Planning and Development
RPS Planning and Development
T: 01636 605700
F: 01636 610696
E: alan.skipper@rpsgroup.com
W: www.rpsgroup.com

RS Components Ltd
Birchington Rd, Corby, Northants NN17 9RS
T: 0845 602 5226
W: www.rswww.com/purchasing

RSK STATS Health & Safety Ltd
Spring Lodge, 172 Chester Rd, Helsby,
Cheshire WA6 0AR
T: 01928 726006
F: 01928 725633
E: communications@rsk.com
W: www.rsk.com

RSK STATS Ltd
18 Frogmore Rd, Hemel Hempstead,
Herts HP3 9RT
T: 01442 437500
F: 01442 437550
E: info@stats.co.uk
W: www.stats.co.uk

RTI UK
35 Old Queen St,
London SW1H 9JD
T: 020 7340 0900
F: 020 7233 3411
E: rtiuk@rti.co.uk
W: www.rti.co.uk

RTS Solutions
Atlantic House, Imperial Way,
Reading RG2 0TD
T: 0118 903 6045
F: 0118 903 6100
E: stuart@rts-solutions.net
W: www.rts-solutions.net

Rugged Com Inc. (UK)
InfoLab21, Knowledge Business Centre,
Lancaster University, Lancaster LA1 4WA
T: 01524 510434
F: 01524 510433
E: ianpoulett@ruggedcom.com
W: www.ruggedcom.com

Rullion Engineering Personnel
2nd Floor, Unit 5, Bath Court, Islington Row,
Edgbaston, Birmingham B15 1NE
T: 0121 622 7720
F: 0121 622 7721
E: james.millward@rullion.co.uk
W: www.rullion.co.uk/rep

RVEL
See Railway Vehicle Engineering Ltd

RWD Technologies UK Ltd
Furzeground Way,
First Floor, Stockley Park,
Uxbridge UB11 1AJ
T: 020 8569 2787
F: 020 8756 3625
W: www.rwd.com

Rydon Signs
Unit 3, Peek House, Pinhoe Trading Est, Exeter,
Devon EX4 8JN
T: 01392 466653
F: 01392 466671
E: sales@rydonsigns.com
W: www.rydonsigns.com

S M Consult Ltd
3 High St, Stanford in the Vale,
Faringdon, Oxon SN7 8LH
T: 01367 710152
F: 01367 710152
W: www.smconsult.co.uk

S.E.T. Ltd
Atlas Works, Litchurch Lane,
Derby DE24 8AQ
T: 01332 346035
F: 01332 346494
E: sales@set.gb.com
W: www.set.gb.com

SA Viewcom (now Axion Technologies)
Lokesvej 7-9, 3400 Hilleroed,
Denmark
T: 0045 721 93500
F: 0045 721 93501
E: info@axiontech.dk
W: www.axiontech.dk

Sabre Rail Services Ltd
Grindon Way, Heighington Lane Business
Park, Newton Aycliffe,
Co Durham DL5 6SH
T: 01325 300505
F: 01325 300485
E: sales@sabre-rail.co.uk
W: www.sabre-rail.co.uk

Safe Aid supplies
Unit 16, Arnside Rd, Waterlooville,
Hants PO7 7UP
T: 02392 254442
F: 02392 257444
E: sales@safeaidsupplies.com
W: www.safeaidsupplies.com

Safeglass (Europe) Ltd
Nasmyth Building, Nasmyth Ave,
East Kilbride G75 0QR
T: 01355 272828
F: 01355 272788
E: sales@safeglass.co.uk
W: www.safeglass.co.uk

Safeguard Pest Control Ltd
6 Churchill Bus. Park, The Flyers Way,
Westerham, Kent TN16 1BT
T: 0800 195 7766
F: 01959 565888
E: info@safeguardpestcontrol.co.uk
W: www.safeguardpestcontrol.co.uk

Safeline Training Ltd
69-71, Haltwhistle Rd,
South Woodham Ferrers, Essex CM3 5ZA
T: 01245 425617
F: 01245 426042
E: info@safelinetraining.co.uk
W: www.safelinetraining.co.uk

Safestyle Security Services
Exe. Suite 1, Cardiff International Arena,
Mary Ann St, Cardiff CF10 2FQ
T: 02920 221711
F: 02920 234592
E: office@safestylesecurity.co.uk
W: www.safestylesecurity.co.uk

Safetech Environmental Care
4 Upton St, Hull HU8 7DA
T: 01482 224165
F: 01482 214522
E: info@safetechenv.com
W: www.safetechenv.com

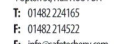

Safetell Ltd
Unit 46, Fawkes Ave, Dartford Trade Park,
Dartford DA1 1JQ
T: 01322 223233
F: 01322 277751
E: sales@safetell.co.uk
W: www.safetell.co.uk

Safetrack Baavhammar AB
1 Moleberga, S-245 93 Staffanstorp, Sweden
T: 0046 4044 5300
F: 0046 4044 5553
E: sales@safetrack.se
W: www.safetrack.se

Safetykleen UK Ltd
Profile West, 950 Great West Rd, Brentford,
Middx TW8 9ES
T: 01909 519300
E: skuk@sk-europe.com
W: www.safetykleen.co.uk

SAFT Ltd
1st Floor, Unit 5, Astra Centre, Edinburgh Way,
Harlow CM20 2BN
T: 01279 772550
F: 01279 420909
E: sarah.carter@saftbatteries.com
W: www.saftbatteries.com

SAFT Power Systems Ltd
See AEG

Saint Gobain Abrasives Ltd
Doxey Rd, Stafford ST16 1EA
T: 01785 279550
F: 01785 213487
E: sonia.uppal@saint-gobain.com
W: www.saint-gobain.com

Saltburn Railtours
16 Bristol Ave, Saltburn TS12 1BW
T: 01287 626572
E: r.dallara@btinternet.com
W: www.saltburnrailtours.co.uk

Samsung Electronics Hainan Fibreoptics
c/o Go Tel Communications Ltd, 4 Hicks Close,
Wroughton, Swindon SN4 9AY
T: 01793 813600
F: 01793 529380
E: robindash@gtcom.co.uk
W: www.samsungfiberoptics.com

HITACHI
Inspire the Next

Directory

Santon Switchgear Ltd
Unit 9, Waterside Court, Newport NP20 5NT
T: 01633 854111
F: 01633 854999
E: sales@santonswitchgear.com
W: www.santonswitchgear.com

Sartoria Corporatewear
Gosforth Rd, Derby DE24 8HU
T: 01332 342616
F: 01332 226940
W: www.sartorialtd.co.uk

Savigny Oddie Ltd
Wallows Ind. Est, Wallows Rd, Brierley Hill,
West Midlands DY5 1QA
T: 01384 481598
F: 01384 482383
E: keith@oddiefasteners.com
W: www.savigny-oddie.co.uk

SB Rail (Swietelsky Babcock)
Kintail House, 3 Lister Way, Hamilton
International Park, Blantyre G72 0FT
T: 01698 203005
F: 01698 203006
E: shona.jamieson@babcock.co.uk
W: www.babcock.co.uk/rail

SBC Rail Ltd
Littlewell Lane, Stanton by Dale, Ilkeston,
Derbys DE7 4QW
T: 0115 944 1448
F: 0115 944 1466
E: sbc@stanton-bonna.co.uk
W: www.stanton-bonna.co.uk

Schaeffler (UK) Ltd
Forge Lane, Minworth, Sutton Coldfield,
West Midlands B76 1AP
T: 0121 351 3833
F: 0121 351 7686
E: info.uk@schaeffler.com
W: www.schaeffler.co.uk

Schaltbau Machine Electrics
335/336, Springvale Industrial Estate,
Woodside Way, Cwmbran NP44 5BR
T: 01633 877555
F: 01633 873366
E: sales@schaltbau-me.com
W: www.schaltbau-me.com

Scheidt & Bachmann (UK) Ltd
7 Silverglade Business Park, Leatherhead Rd,
Chessington, Surrey KT9 2QL
T: 01372 230400
F: 01372 722053
E: info@scheidt-bachmann.de
W: www.scheidt-bachmann.de

schenck process

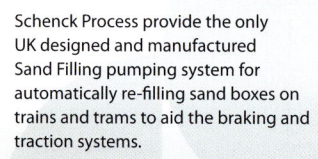

Schenck Process provide the only
UK designed and manufactured
Sand Filling pumping system for
automatically re-filling sand boxes on
trains and trams to aid the braking and
traction systems.

A: Carolina Court, Lakeside,
Doncaster, DN4 5RA
T: 01302 321 313
F: 01302 554 400
E: enquiries@schenckprocess.co.uk

www.schenckprocess.co.uk

Schenck Process UK
Carolina Court,
Lakeside,
Doncaster DN4 5RA
T: 01302 321313
F: 01302 554400
E: enquiries@schenckprocess.co.uk
W: www.schenckprocess.co.uk

Schneider Electric Ltd
Stafford Park 5, Telford,
Shropshire TF3 3BL
T: 01952 209226
F: 01952 292238
W: www.schneider-electric.co.uk

Schofield Lothian Ltd
Temple Chambers, 3-7 Temple Ave,
London EC4Y 0DT
T: 020 7842 0920
F: 020 7842 0921
E: enquiries@schofieldlothian.com
W: www.schofieldlothian.com

Schroff UK Ltd
Maylands Ave,
Hemel Hempstead,
Herts HP2 7DE
T: 01442 240471
F: 01442 213508
E: schroff.uk@pentair.com
W: www.schroff.co.uk

Schweerbau GmbH & Co KG
UK Branch Office,
20 Beattyville Gardens,
Ilford IG6 1JN
T: 07725 888933
F: 020 7681 3971
E: verheijen@schweerbau.de
W: www.schweerbau.de

Schweizer Electronic AG
Industriestrasse 3, CH-6260 Reiden,
Switzerland
T: 0041 6274 90707
F: 0041 6274 90700
E: info@schweizer-electronic.ch
W: www.schweizer-electronic.ch

Schwihag AG
Lebernstrasse 3, PO Box 152,
CH-8274 Tagerwilen,
Switzerland
T: 0041 71 666 8800
F: 0041 71 666 8801
E: info@schwihag.com
W: www.schwihag.com

Scientifics
ESG House, Bretby Business Park, Ashby Rd,
Burton upon Trent DE15 0YZ
T: 0845 603 2112
F: 01283 554401
E: sales@esg.co.uk
W: www.esg.co.uk

Scisys
Methuen Park, Chippenham,
Wilts SN14 0GB
T: 01249 466466
F: 01249 466666
E: marketing@scisys.co.uk
W: www.scisys.co.uk

Scotrail
See First Scotrail

Scott Bader
Wollaston,
Wellingborough,
Northants NN29 7RL
T: 01933 663100
E: composites@scottbader.com
W: www.scottbader.com

Scott Brownrigg – Design Research Unit
77 Endell St,
London WC2H 9DZ
T: 020 7240 7766
F: 020 7240 2454
E: enquiries@scottbrownrigg.com
W: www.scottbrownrigg.com

Scott White & Hookings
Fountain House, 26 St Johns St,
Bedford MK42 0AQ
T: 01234 213111
F: 01234 213333
E: bed@swh.co.uk
W: www.swh.co.uk

Scott Wilson Railways
See URS

Scotweld Employment Services
see sw global resourcing

Screwfast Foundations Ltd
7-14 Smallford Works, Smallford Way,
St. Albans, Herts AL4 0SA
T: 01727 821282
F: 01727 828098
E: info@screwfast.com
W: www.screwfast.com

SCT Europe Ltd
See Wabtec

SEA (Group) Ltd
SEA House, PO Box 800, Bristol BS16 1SU
T: 01373 852000
F: 01373 831133
E: info@sea.co.uk
W: www.sea.co.uk

Seaton Rail Ltd
Bridlington Business Centre, Enterprise Way,
Bridlington YO16 4SF
T: 01262 608313
F: 01262 604493
E: info@seaton-rail.com
W: www.seaton-rail.com

Secheron SA
Rue de pre-Bouvier 25, Zimeysa 1217 Meyrin,
Geneva, Switzerland
T: 0041 22 739 4111
F: 0041 22 739 4811
E: info@secheron.com
W: www.secheron.com

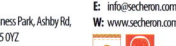

Sefac UK Ltd
Unit C211, Barton Rd, Water Eaton,
Bletchley MK2 3HU
T: 01908 821274
F: 01908 821275
E: info@sefac-lift.co.uk
W: www.sefac-lift.co.uk

Select Cables Ltd
Painter Close, Anchorage Park, Portsmouth
T: 02392 652552
F: 02392 655277
E: sales@selectcables.com
W: www.selectcables.com

Selectequip Ltd
Unit 7, Britannia Way,
Britannia Enterprise Park, Lichfield,
Staffs WS14 9UY
T: 01543 416641
F: 01543 416083
E: sales@selectequip.co.uk
W: www.selectequip.co.uk

Selex Elsag
Liverpool Innovation Park, Baird House,
Edge Lane, Fairfield, Liverpool L7 9NU
T: 0151 282 5304
F: 0151 282 5252
E: dave.byron@selexelsag.com
W: www.selexelsag.com

Selex Systems Integration
2 Falcon Way, Shire Park, Welwyn Garden City,
Herts AL7 1TW
T: 01707 391999
F: 01707 393909
E: info@selex-si-uk.com
W: www.selex-si-uk.com

Selux Lighting
10 Spartan Close, Leamington Spa,
Warks CV34 6RS
T: 01926 833455
F: 01926 339844
E: enquire@selux.co.uk
W: www.selux.com

Semikron Ltd
John Tate Rd, Foxholes Business Park,
Hertford SG13 7NW
T: 01992 584677
F: 01992 503847
E: sales.skuk@semikron.com
W: www.semikron.com

Semmco Ltd
9 Kestrel Way, Goldsworth Park Trading Est,
Woking, Surrey GU21 3BA
T: 01483 757200
F: 01483 740795
E: sales@semmco.com
W: www.semmco.com

Semperit Industrial Products
25 Cottesbrooke Park, Heartlands, Daventry,
Northants NN11 8YL
T: 01327 313144
F: 01327 313149
E: ian.rowlinson@semperit.co.uk
W: www.semperit.at

Sentripod Company Ltd
Honeystone, 13 The Hamlet,
Chippenham,
Wilts SN15 1BY
T: 01249 462039
F: 01249 462039
E: info@sentripod.com
W: www.sentripod.com

Serco Abellio (Abellio Site)
1 Ely Place, 2nd Floor, London EC1N 6RY
T: 020 7430 8270
E: anton.valk@abellio.com
W: www.sercorailways.com

Serco Integrated Transport
Serco House, 16 Bartley Wood Bus. Park,
Bartley Way, Hook,
Hants RG27 9XB
T: 01256 745900
F: 01256 744111
E: generalenquiries@serco.com
W: www.serco.com/markets/transport

Serco NedRailways
See Serco Abellio

Serco Rail Operations
Derwent House, RTC Business Park,
London Rd, Derby DE24 8UP
T: 01332 263340
F: 01332 262444
E: generalenquiries@serco.com
W: www.serco.com/sit/

Serco Technical & Assurance Services
Derwent House, RTC Business Park,
Derby DE24 8UP
T: 01332 262975
F: 01332 262405
E: john.benyon@serco.com
W: www.serco.com/assurance

Sersa (UK) Ltd
Sersa House, Auster Rd, Clifton Moor,
York YO30 4XA
T: 01904 479968
F: 01904 479970
E: sersa.uk@sersa-group.com
W: www.sersa-group.com

Severn Valley Railway
The Railway Station, Bewdley,
Worcs DY12 1BG
T: 01299 403816
F: 01299 400839
E: mktg@svr.co.uk
W: www.svr.co.uk

Severn-Lamb UK Ltd
Tything Rd, Alcester B49 6ET
T: 01789 400140
E: sales@severn-lamb.com
W: www.severn-lamb.com

SGA (Stuart Gray Associates)
88 Spring Hill, Arley,
Warks CV7 8FE
T: 01676 541402
E: info@stuartgrayassociates.com
W: www.stuartgrayassociates.com

SGH Martineau LLP
No.1 Colmore, Birmingham B4 6AA
T: 0800 763 1000
F: 0800 763 1001
W: www.sghmartineau.com

SGS Correl Rail Ltd
Gee House, Holborn Hill, Birmingham B7 5PA
T: 0121 326 3672
F: 0121 328 5343
E: gary.winstanley@sgs.com
W: www.sgs.com

SGS Engineering (UK) Ltd
Cranmer Rd, West Meadows Ind. Est,
Derby DE21 6JL
T: 01332 298126/01332 366552
F: 01332 366232
E: sales@sgs-engineering.com
W: www.sgs-engineering.com

SGS UK Ltd
Inward Way, Rossmore Business Park,
Ellesmere Port CH65 3EN
T: 0151 350 6666
F: 0151 350 6600
W: www.sgs.com

Shay Murtagh Precast Ltd
Rahamey, Mullingar, Co Westmeath,
Republic of Ireland
T: 0844 202 0263
E: sales@shaymurtagh.co.uk
W: www.shaymurtagh.co.uk

Sheerspeed Shelters Ltd
Unit 3, Diamond House, Reme Drive,
Heath Park, Honiton, Devon EX14 1SE
T: 01404 46006
F: 01404 45520
E: sales@sheerspeed.com
W: www.sheerspeed.com

Shere Ltd
See ATOS Origin

Sheridan Maine
Regus House, George Curl Way,
Southampton SO18 2RZ
T: 0871 218 0573
F: 0871 218 0173
E: southampton@sheridanmaine.com
W: www.sheridanmaine.com

Shield Batteries
277 Stansted Rd, Bishops Stortford,
Herts CM23 2BT
T: 01279 652067
F: 01279 758041
M: 07900 403716
E: paul.bowles@shieldbatteries.co.uk
W: www.shieldbatteries.co.uk

Shorterm Rail
The Barn, Philpotts Close, Yiewsley,
Middx UB7 7RY
T: 01895 427900
E: info@shortermgroup.com
W: www.shorterm.com

Shotcrete Services Ltd
Old Station Yard, Hawkhurst Rd, Cranbrook,
Kent TN17 2SR
T: 01580 714747
E: stuart.manning@shotcrete.co.uk
W: www.shotcrete.co.uk

SICK (UK) Ltd
39 Hedley Rd, St Albans AL1 5DN
T: 01727 831121
E: info@sick.co.uk
W: www.sick.co.uk

Siegrist-Orel Ltd
Pysons Rd Ind. Est., Broadstairs,
Kent CT10 2LQ
T: 01843 865241
F: 01843 867180
E: info@siegrist-orel.co.uk
W: www.siegrist-orel.co.uk

Siemens Rail Systems provides expertise and technology in the full range of rail vehicles – from heavy rail to metros to trams and light-rail vehicles. In the UK, Siemens Rail Systems employs around 650 people and maintains over 350 Siemens passenger trains.

Siemens Rail Systems, 2 Queen Anne's Gate Buildings, Dartmouth Street, London SW1H 9BP

Telephone: 020 7227 0722
Fax: 020 7227 4435

info.railsystems.gb@siemens.com
www.siemens.co.uk/rail

SIEMENS

Siemens Mobility
2 Queen Annes Gate Buildings,
Dartmouth Street,
London SW1H 9BP
T: 020 7227 0722
F: 020 7227 4435
E: info.railsystems.gb@siemens.com
W: www.siemens.com/mobility

Sig Cyclone
Unit 16,
Gerald House,
Sherwood Network Centre,
Sherwood Energy Village,
Newton Hill,
Ollerton,
Notts NG22 9FD
E: liane.launders@sigcyclone.com
W: www.sig-ukgroup.com

SigAssure UK Ltd
Gerald House (Office 25), Innovation House,
Retford Enterprise Centre, Randall Way,
Retford DN22 7GR
T: 020 7628 2020
F: 020 7628 2070
E: info@sig-ukgroup.com
W: www.sig-ukgroup.com

■ Consultant Project Engineering
■ Consultant Project Management
■ Fabrication and Engineering Services
■ Bespoke Fabrications and Prototypes
■ Signalling Design, Installation & Testing
■ Signalling Product Innovation

Gerald House (office 25), Innovation House, Retford Enterprise Centre, Randall Way, Retford DN22 7GR
T: +44 (0) 1777 712624
E: info@sigassure-uk.com
W: www.sig-ukgroup.com

sigMTIFS
modular technology interface system

Sigma Coachair Group UK Ltd
Unit 1, Queens Drive, Newhall, Swadlincote,
Derbys DE11 0EG
T: 01283 559140
F: 01283 225253
E: hsingh@sigmacoachair.com
W: www.sigmacoachair.com

Signal House Ltd
Cherrycourt Way, Stanbridge Rd,
Leighton Buzzard, Beds LU7 8UH
T: 01525 377477
F: 01525 850999
E: sales@signalhouse.co.uk
W: www.signalhousegroup.co.uk

Signalling Solutions Ltd
Bridge Foot House, Watling St, Radlett,
Herts WD7 7HT
T: 01923 635000
E: info@signallingsolutions.com
W: www.signallingsolutions.com

Signature Aromas Ltd
Signature House,
65-67 Gospel End St, Sedgley,
West Midlands DY3 3LR
T: 01902 678822
F: 01902 672888
E: enquiries@signaturearomas.co.uk
W: www.signaturearomas.co.uk

Signet Solutions
Kelvin House,
RTC Business Park,
London Rd, Derby DE24 8UP
T: 01332 343585
F: 01332 367132
E: enquiries@signet-solutions.com
W: www.signet-solutions.com

Sill Lighting UK
3 Thame Park Bus. Centre,
Wenman Rd, Thame,
Oxon OX9 3XA
T: 01844 260006
E: sales@sill-uk.com
W: www.sill-uk.com

Silver Atena
Cedar House, Riverside Business Park,
Swindon Rd, Malmesbury,
Wilts SN16 9RS
T: 01666 580000
F: 01666 580001
E: info@silver-atena.com
W: www.silver-atena.com

Silver Software
See Silver Atena

Silver Track Training
Fleet House, Pye Close,
Haydock,
St Helens WA11 9JT
T: 01942 728196
E: angela@silvertracktraining.co.uk
W: www.silvertracktraining.co.uk

Simmons & Simmons
City Point,
One Ropemaker St,
London EC2Y 9SS
T: 020 7628 2020
F: 020 7628 2070
E: juliet.reingold@simmons-simmons.com
W: www.simmons-simmons.com

Simona UK
Telford Drive, Brookmead Ind. Park,
Stafford ST16 3ST
T: 01785 222444
F: 01785 222080
E: mail@simona-uk.com
W: www.simona.de

SIMS
Fourth Floor, Roman Wall House,
1-2 Crutched Friars, London EC3N 2HT
T: 020 7481 9798
F: 020 7481 9657
E: inbox@sims-uk.com
W: www.simsrail.co.uk

Simulation Systems Ltd
Unit 12, Market Ind. Est, Yatton,
Bristol BS49 4RF
T: 01934 838803
F: 01934 876202
W: www.simulation-systems.co.uk

Sinclair Knight Merz
Victoria House, Southampton Row,
London WC1B 4EA
T: 020 7759 2600
F: 020 7759 2601
E: enquiries@globalskm.com
W: www.skmconsulting.com

Site Vision Surveys
19 Warwick St, Rugby,
Warks CV21 3DH
T: 01788 575036
F: 01788 576208
W: www.svsltd.net

Skanska UK
Maple Cross House, Denham Way, Maple
Cross, Rickmansworth, Herts WD3 9SW
T: 01923 423100
F: 01923 423111
E: www.cementation foundations.skanska.com

SKF UK Ltd
Railway Sales Unit, Sundon Park Rd,
Luton LU3 3BL
T: 01582 496490
F: 01582 496327
E: stewart.mclellan@skf.com
W: www.skf.com

SKM Colin Buchanan
The Metro Building, 33 Trafford Rd,
Salford Quays, Manchester M5 3NN
T: 0161 873 8500
F: 0161 873 8501
E: enquiries@globalskm.com
W: www.skmcolinbuchanan.com

Skymasts Antennas
Unit 4, Clayfield Close, Moulton Park Ind. Est,
Northampton NN3 6QF
T: 01604 494132
F: 01604 494133
E: info@skymasts.com
W: www.skymasts.com

Slender Winter Partnership
The Old School, London Rd, Westerham,
Kent TN11 1DN
T: 01959 564777
F: 01959 562802
E: swp@swpltd.co.uk
W: www.swpltd.co.uk

---

signalling solutions

excellence in train control

Signalling Solutions offers turnkey solutions to the rail industry's train control and resignalling markets from conceptual design to full project delivery.

a Balfour Beatty and Alstom company.

Signalling Solutions Limited
Bridgefoot House, Watling Street,
Radlett, Herts WD7 7HT

Tel: 01923 635000
Email: info@signallingsolutions.com

www.signallingsolutions.com

SMC Light & Power
Belchmire Lane, Spalding, Lincs PE11 4HG
T: 01775 840020
F: 01775 843063
E: info@smclightandpower.com
W: www.smclightandpower.com

SMC Pneumatics Ltd
Vincent Ave, Crownhill,
Milton Keynes MK8 0AN
T: 0845 121 5122
F: 01908 555064
E: sales@smcpneumatics.co.uk
W: www.smcpneumatics.co.uk

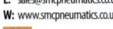

SMI Conferences
SMI Group Ltd, Unit 122,
Great Guildford Business Square,
30 Great Guildford St,
London SE1 0HS
T: 020 7827 6000
F: 020 7827 6001
E: info@smi-online.com
W: www.smi-online.co.uk

Smith Bros & Webb Ltd
Britannia House, Arden Forest Ind.Est, Alcester, Warks B49 6EX
T: 01789 400096
F: 01789 400231
E: sales@sbw-wash.com
W: www.sbw-wash.com

SML Resourcing
Unit 3.07, New Loom House,
101 Back Church Lane, London E1 1LU
T: 020 7423 4390
F: 020 7702 1097
E: jobs@sml-resourcing.com
W: www.sml-resourcing.com

SMP Electronics
Unit 6, Border Farm, Station Rd, Chobham, Surrey GU24 8AS
T: 01276 855166
F: 01276 855115
E: sales@smpelectronics.com
W: www.smpelectronics.com

Snap-On Rail Solutions
Distribution Centre, Telford Way, Kettering, Northants NN16 8SN
T: 01536 413904
F: 01536 413874
E: rail@snapon.com
W: www.snapon.com/industrialuk

Society of Operations Engineers (SOE)
22 Greencoat Place, London SW1P 1PR
T: 020 7630 1111
F: 020 7630 6677
E: soe@soe.org.uk
W: www.soe.org.uk

Socomec UPS (UK)
Units 7-9A, Lakeside Business Park, Broadway Lane, South Cerney, Cirencester, Glos GL7 5XL
T: 01285 863300
F: 01285 862304
E: rail.ups.uk@socomec.com
W: www.socomec.co.uk/ups

Softech Global Ltd
Softech House, London Rd, Albourne, West Sussex BN6 9BN
T: 01273 833844
F: 01273 833044
E: rail@softechglobal.com
W: www.softechglobal.com

SOLID Applications Ltd
Old Market Place, Market St,
Oldbury B69 4DH
T: 0121 544 1400
E: anton.plackowski@saplm.co.uk
W: www.saplm.co.uk/rail

Solo Fabrications
Landor St, Saltley, Birmingham B8 1AE
T: 0121 327 3378
F: 0121 327 3757
W: www.solofabs.com

Solution Rail
22 Somers Way, Bushey, Herts WD23 4HR
T: 07717 712272
F: 0871 989 5700
E: enquiries@solutionrail.co.uk
W: www.solutionrail.co.uk

Somers Totalkare
15 Forge Trading Est., Mucklow Hill, Halesowen B62 8TR
T: 0121 585 2700
F: 0121 501 1458
E: sales@somerstotalkare.co.uk
W: www.somerstotalkare.co.uk

Sonic Rail Service Ltd (SRS)
Unit 15, Springfield Ind. Est, Springfield Rd, Burnham-on-Crouch, Essex CM0 8UA
T: 01621 784688
F: 01621 786594
E: stewart.robinson@sonicrail.co.uk
W: www.sonicrail.co.uk

Sonic Windows Ltd
Unit 14/15, Beeching Park Ind.Est., Wainwright Rd, Bexhill on Sea, E Sussex TN39 3UR
T: 01424 223864
F: 01424 215859
E: enquiries@sonicwindows.co.uk
W: www.sonicwindows.co.uk

Sortimo International Ltd
Old Sarum Park, Salisbury, Wilts SP4 6EB
T: 01722 411585
F: 01722 320831
E: vanrack1@sortimo.co.uk
W: www.sortimo.co.uk

Sotera Risk Solutions Ltd
22 Glanville Rd, Bromley BR2 9LW
T: 07946 638 424
F: 01737 551203
E: chris.chapman@sotera.co.uk
W: www.sotera.co.uk

South West Trains
Stagecoach Group, 10 Dunkeld Rd, Perth PH1 5TW
T: 01738 442111
F: 01738 643648
E: mail@stagecoachgroup.com
W: www.stagecoachgroup.com

South Yorkshire Passenger Transport Executive
11 Broad St West, Sheffield S1 2BQ
T: 0114 276 7575
F: 0114 275 9908
E: comments@sypte.co.uk
W: www.sypte.co.uk

Southco Manufacturing Ltd
Touch Point, Wainwright Rd, Warndon, Worcs WR4 9FA
T: 01905 346722
F: 01905 346723
E: info@southco.com
W: www.southco.com

Southeastern
Friars Bridge Court, 41-45 Blackfriars Rd, London SE1 8PG
T: 020 7620 5000
W: www.southeasternrailway.co.uk

Southern Electric Contracting
55 Vastern Rd, Reading RG1 8BU
T: 0118 958 0100
F: 0118 953 4755
E: marketing@sec.eu.com
W: www.sec.eu.com

Southern/Gatwick Express
Go-Ahead House, 26-28 Addiscombe Rd, Croydon CR9 5GA
T: 020 8929 8600
F: 020 8929 8687
E: communications@southernrailway.com
W: www.southernrailway.com / www.gatwickexpress.com

Sovereign Planned Services On Line Ltd
Unit 3d, Forge Way, Brown Lees Ind Est, Biddulph, Stoke on Trent ST8 7DN
T: 01782 510600
F: 01782 510700
E: sales@sovonline.co.uk
W: www.sovonline.co.uk

Spartan Safety Ltd
Unit 3, Waltham Park Way, Walthamstow, London E17 5DU
T: 020 8527 5888
F: 020 8527 5999
E: ryan@spartansafety.co.uk
W: www.spartansafety.co.uk

Specialist Engineering Services Ltd (SES)
SES House, Harworth Park, Doncaster DN11 8DB
T: 01302 756800
E: info@ses-holdings.com
W: www.ses-holdings.com

Specialist Plant Associates
Airfield Rd, Hinwick, Wellingborough, Northants NN29 7JG
T: 01234 781882
F: 01234 781992
E: info@specialistplant.co.uk
W: www.specialistplant.co.uk

Spectro
Palace Gate, Odiham RG29 1NP
T: 01256 704000
F: 01256 704006
E: enquiries@spectro-oil.com
W: www.spectro-oil.com

Spectrum Technologies
Western Avenue, Bridgend, Mid Glamorgan CF31 3RT
T: 01656 655437
F: 01656 655920
E: ehardy@spectrumtech.com
W: www.spectrumtech.com

Speedy Hire Plc
Chase House, 16 The Parks, Newton le Willows, Merseyside WA12 0JQ
T: 01942 720000
F: 01942 720077
E: admin@speedyhire.co.uk
W: www.speedyhire.co.uk

Spence Ltd
Parcel Deck, Bamby St, Euston Station, London NW1 2RS
T: 020 7387 1268
F: 020 7380 1255
E: info@spenceltd.co.uk
W: www.spenceltd.co.uk

Speno International SA
26 Parc Chateau-Banquet POB 16, 1211 Geneva 21, Switzerland
T: 0041 22906 4600
F: 0041 22906 4601
E: info@speno.ch
W: www.speno.ch

Sperry Rail International Ltd
Trent House, RTC Business Park, London Rd, Derby DE24 8UP
T: 01332 262565
F: 01332 262541
W: www.sperryrail.com

Spescom Software Ltd
Woolbrook House, Crabtree Office Village, Eversley Way, Thorpe, Surrey TW20 8RY
T: 0870 890 8000
F: 0870 890 9000
W: www.spescomsoftware.com

Spitfire Tours
PO Box 824, Taunton TA1 9ET
T: 0870 879 3675
E: info@spitfirerailtours.co.uk
W: www.spitfirerailtours.co.uk

Spring Personnel
1 Canal Arm, Festival Park, Stoke on Trent ST1 5UR
T: 01782 221500
F: 01782 221600
E: personnel@spring.com
W: www.spring.com

SPX Rail Systems
Unit 7, Thames Gateway Park, Choats Rd, Dagenham, Essex RM9 6RH
T: 020 8526 7100
F: 020 8526 7151
E: brian.cannon@spx.com
W: www.spx.com

SRPS Railtours
3 South Cathkin Farm Cottages, Glasgow G73 5RG
T: 01698 263814/457777
E: railtours@srps.org.uk
W: www.srps.org.uk

SRS Rail Systems Ltd
3, Riverside Way, Gateway Business Park, Bolsover, Chesterfield S44 6GA
T: 01246 241312
F: 01246 825076
E: info@srsrailuk.co.uk
W: www.srsrailuk.com

SSDM
Freemantle Rd, Lowestoft, Suffolk NR33 0EA
T: 0845 052 5241
F: 01502 501234
E: talk2us@ssdm.co.uk
W: www.ssdm.co.uk

SSE Contracting
55 Vastern Rd, Reading, Berks RG1 8BU
T: 0118 958 0100
F: 0118 953 4996
E: enquiries@ssecontracting.com
W: www.ssecontracting.com

SSP
169, Euston Rd, London NW1 2AE
T: 020 7543 3300
F: 020 7543 3389
W: www.foodtravelexpert.com

St Pancras International Station Chaplaincy
Network Rail Station Reception, St Pancras Station, Euston Rd, London N1C 4QP
T: 020 7843 7518
F: 020 7843 7715
M: 07896 934881
E: jonathan.barker@networkrail.co.uk
W: www.stpancras.com

Stadler Pankow GmbH
Lessingstrasse 102, D-13158 Berlin, Germany
T: 0049 309191 1616
F: 0049 309191 2150
E: stadler.pankow@stadlerrail.de
W: www.stadlerrail.com

Stagecoach Group
10 Dunkeld Rd, Perth PH1 5TW
T: 01738 442111
F: 01738 643648
E: info@stagecoachgroup.com
W: www.stagecoachgroup.com

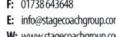

Stagecoach Supertram
Nunnery Depot, Woodbourn Rd, Sheffield S9 3LS
T: 0114 275 9888
F: 0114 279 8120
E: enquiries@supertram.com
W: www.supertram.com

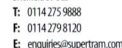

Stahlwille Tools Ltd
Unit 2D, Albany Park Ind. Est, Frimley Rd, Camberley, Surrey GU16 7PD
T: 01276 24080
F: 01276 24696
E: scottsheldon@stahlwille.co.uk
W: www.stahlwille.co.uk

Stanley Tools
Sheffield Business Park, Sheffield City Airport, Europa Link, Sheffield S3 9PD
T: 0114 244 8883
F: 0114 273 9038

Stannah Lifts
Anton Mill, Andover, Hants SP10 2NX
T: 01264 339090
E: liftsales@stannah.co.uk
W: www.stannahlifts.co.uk

Stansted Express
Enterprise House, Stansted Airport, Essex CM20 1QW
E: eleni.jordan@nationalexpress.com
W: www.stanstedexpress.com

Stanton Bonna Concrete Ltd
Littlewell Lane, Stanton by Dale, Ilkeston, Derbys DE7 4QW
T: 0115 944 1448
F: 0115 944 1466
E: sbc@stanton-bonna.co.uk
W: www.stanton-bonna.co.uk

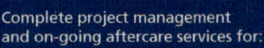

Star Fasteners (UK) Ltd
Unit 3, Gallows Ind. Est, Furnace Rd, Ilkeston, Derbys DE7 5EP
T: 0115 932 4939
F: 0115 944 1278
E: sales@starfasteners.co.uk
W: www.starfasteners.co.uk

Statesman Rail Ltd
PO Box 83, St Erth, Hayle, Cornwall TR27 9AD
T: 0845 310 2458
F: 0115 944 1278
W: www.statesmanrail.com

STATS
See RSK Stats

Stauff Ltd
500 Carlisle St East, Sheffield S4 8BS
T: 01142 518518
F: 01141 518519
E: sales@stauff.co.uk
W: www.stauff.co.uk

Staytite Ltd
Staytite House, Coronation Rd, Cressex Bus.Park, High Wycombe, Bucks HP12 3RP
T: 01494 462322
F: 01494 464747
E: fasteners@staytite.com
W: www.staytite.com

Steam Dreams
PO Box 169, Albury, Guildford, Surrey GU5 9YS
T: 01483 209888
F: 01483 209889
E: info@steamdreams.co.uk
W: www.steamdreams.com

Steelteam Construction (UK) Ltd
46 Goods Station Rd, Tunbridge Wells, Kent TN1 2DD
T: 01892 533677
F: 01892 511535
E: sales@steelteamconstruction.co.uk
W: www.steelteamconstruction.co.uk

Steelway Rail
Queensgate Works, Bilston Rd, Wolverhampton, West Midlands WV2 2NJ
T: 01902 451733
F: 01902 452256
E: sales@steelway.co.uk
W: www.steelway.co.uk

Steer Davies Gleave
28-32 Upper Ground, London SE1 9PD
T: 020 7910 5000
F: 020 7910 5001
E: sdginfo@sdgworld.net
W: www.steerdaviesgleave.com

Stego UK Ltd
Unit 12, First Quarter Bus. Park, Blenheim Rd, Epsom, Surrey KT19 9QN
T: 01372 747250
F: 01372 729854
E: info@stego.co.uk
W: www.stego.co.uk

Stent
Pavilion C2, Ashwood Park, Ashwood Way, Basingstoke, Hants RG23 8BG
T: 01256 366000
F: 01256 366001
E: neil.beresford@stent.co.uk
W: www.stent.co.uk

Stephenson Harwood LLP
1 Finsbury Circus, London EC2M 7SH
T: 020 7329 4422
F: 020 7003 8521
E: graeme.mdellan@shlegal.com
W: www.shlegal.com

Stewart Signs Rail
Trafalgar Close, Chandlers Ford Ind. Est, Eastleigh, Hants SO53 4BW
T: 023 8025 4781
F: 023 8025 5620
E: sales@stewartsigns.com
W: www.stewartsigns.com

Stirling Maynard
Construction Consultants, Stirling House, Rightwell, Bretton, Peterborough PE3 8DJ
T: 01733 262319
F: 01733 331527
E: enquiries@stirlingmaynard.com
W: www.stirlingmaynard.com

Stobart Rail
Solway Business Centre, Carlisle, Cumbria CA6 4BY
T: 01228 882300
F: 01228 882301
E: grant.mcnab@stobartrail.com
W: www.stobartrail.co.uk

Stock Redler Ltd
Redler House, Dudbridge, Stroud, Glos GL5 3EY
T: 01453 819461
F: 0049 6151 321043
E: cillsley@schenckprocess.com
W: www.schenckprocess.com

Stocksigns Ltd
43 Ormside Way, Holmethorpe Ind Est, Redhill, Surrey RH1 2LG
T: 01737 764764
F: 01737 763763
E: jgodden@stocksigns.co.uk
W: www.stocksigns.co.uk

Stockton Engineering Management Ltd
1 Warwick Row, London SW1E 5ER
T: 020 7808 7808
F: 020 7117 5253
E: info@stocktonlondon.com
W: www.stocktonlondon.com

Stored Energy Technology
See S.E.T.

Story Rail
Burgh Rd Ind Est, Carlisle CA2 7NA
T: 01228 640880
F: 01228 640881
E: info@storygroup.co.uk
W: www.storygroup.co.uk

STRAIL (UK) Ltd
Room 3, First Floor, 3 Tannery House, Tannery Lane, Send, Woking, Surrey GU23 7EF
T: 01483 222090
F: 01483 222095
E: richard@srsrailuk.co.uk
W: www.strail.com

Strainstall UK Ltd
9-10, Mariners Way, Cowes, IOW PO31 8PD
T: 01983 203600
F: 01983 201335
E: enquiries@strainstall.com
W: www.strainstall.co.uk

Strataform
See Technocover

Strategic Team Group Ltd
Head Office, Strategic Business Centre, Blue Ridge Park, Thunderhead Ridge, Glasshoughton, Castleford, West Yorks WF10 4UA
T: 01977 555550
E: contact@strategicteamgroup.com
W: www.strategicteamgroup.com

Strathclyde Partnership for Transport
Consort House, 12 West George St, Glasgow G2 1HN
T: 0141 332 6811
E: enquiry@spt.co.uk
W: www.spt.co.uk

Street Crane Co. Ltd
Chapel-en-le-Frith, High Peak, Derbys SK23 0PH
T: 01298 812456
E: sales@streetcrane.co.uk
W: www.streetcrane.co.uk

STS Signals
See Mors Smitt

Stuart Group
Lancaster Approach, North Killingholme, Immingham, NE Lincs DN40 3TZ
T: 0870 4141 400
F: 0870 4141 440
E: enquiries@stuartgroup.info
W: www.stuartgroup.info

Stuart Maher Ltd (SML)
Unit 3.07, New Loom House, 101 Back Church Lane, London SE1 1LU
T: 020 7423 4390
F: 07092 810 920
E: nick.stuart@stuart-maher.co.uk
W: www.stuart-maher.co.uk

Sulzer Dowding & Mills
Camp Hill, Bordesley, Birmingham B12 0JJ
T: 0121 766 6333
F: 0121 766 7247
E: engineering.birmingham@sulzer.com
W: www.sulzer.com

Superform Aluminium
Cosgrove Close, Worcester WR3 8UA
T: 01905 874300
F: 01905 874301
E: sales@superform-aluminium.com
W: www.superforming.com

Superjet London
Unit 5, Kennet Rd, Dartford, Kent DA1 4QN
T: 01322 554595
F: 01322 557773
E: chris@superjet.co.uk
W: www.jetchem.com

Supersine Duramark
see ssdm

Survey Inspection Systems Ltd (SIS)
Green Lane Ind. Est, Enterprise House, Meadowfield Ave, Spennymoor, Co Durham DL16 6JF
T: 01388 810308
F: 01388 819260
E: sales@survey-inspection.com
W: www.survey-inspection.com

Survey Systems Ltd
Willow Bank House, Old Road, Handforth, Wilmslow SK9 3AZ
T: 01625 533444
F: 01625 526815
E: enquiries@survsys.co.uk
W: www.survsys.co.uk/rail

SW Global Resourcing
270 Peters Hill Rd, Glasgow G21 4AY
T: 0141 557 6133
F: 0141 557 6143
E: admin@sw-gr.com
W: www.scotweld.com

Sweetnam & Bradley Ltd
Industrial Est, Gloucester Rd, Malmesbury, Wilts SN16 0DY
T: 01666 823491
F: 01666 826010
E: sales@sweetnam-bradley.com
W: www.sweetnam-bradley.com

Swietelsky Babcock
See SB Rail

Swietelsky International UK & Ireland
7 Clairmont Gardens, Glasgow G3 7LW
T: 0141 353 1915
W: www.swietelsky.com

Sydac Ltd
Derwent Business Centre, Clarke St, Derby DE1 2BU
T: 01332 299600
F: 01332 299624
E: paul.williamson@sydac.co.uk
W: www.sydac.co.uk

Synectic Systems Group Ltd
32 Alexandra Way, Tewkesbury, Glos GL20 8NB
T: 01684 295807
F: 01684 850011
E: sales@synx.com
W: www.synecticsystems.com

Synergy Health Plc
Gavenny Court, Brecon Rd, Abergavenny, Monmouthshire NP7 7RX
T: 01873 856688
F: 01873 585982
E: enquiries@synergyhealthplc.com
W: www.synergyhealthplc.com

Syntax Recruitment
1 College Place, Derby DE1 3DY
T: 01332 287720
F: 01332 296128
E: carl.veseles@syntaxnet.com
W: www.syntaxnet.com

Systecon (UK) Ltd
PO Box 4612, Weymouth, Dorset DT4 9YY
T: 0871 641 2202
F: 01305 768480
E: phil.sturgess@systecon.co.uk
W: www.systecon.co.uk

Directory

System Store Solutions Ltd
Ham Lane, Lenham, Maidstone,
Kent ME17 2LH
T: 01622 859522
F: 01622 858746
E: sales@systemstoresolutions.com
W: www.system-store.com

SYSTRA UK Branch
SYSTRA - World Leading Rail and Urban Transport Engineers
Contact us:
4th Floor
Dukes Court
Duke Street, Woking, Surrey
GU21 5BH
T: +44 (0)1483 742941
E: jonions@systra.com
www.systra.co.uk

Systra UK
Fourth Floor,
Dukes Court, Duke St,
Woking, Surrey GU21 5BH
T: 01483 742941
F: 01483 723899
E: jonions@systra.com
W: www.systra

T & R Williamson Ltd
36 Stonebridgegate,
Ripon, N Yorks HG4 1TP
T: 01765 607711
F: 01765 607908
E: info@trwilliamson.com
W: www.trwilliamson.co.uk

T J Thomson & Sons Ltd
Millfield Works,
Grangefield Rd,
Stockton on Tees TS18 4AE
T: 01642 672551
F: 01642 672556
E: postbox@tjthomson.co.uk
W: www.tjthomson.co.uk

TAC Europe
Matrix House,
Basing View,
Basingstoke,
Hants
T: 08700 600822
F: 01256 356371
E: enquiries@taceurope.com
W: www.taceurope.com

Talascend Ltd
First Floor,
Broadway Chambers,
Hammersmith Broadway,
London W6 7PW
T: 020 8600 1600
F: 020 8741 2001
E: info@talascend.com
W: www.talascend.com

Tanfield Engineering Systems
Tanfield Lea Ind. Est. North, Stanley,
Co Durham DH9 9NX
T: 01207 521111
F: 01207 523318
E: enquiries@tanfieldgroup.co.uk
W: www.tanfieldgroup.co.uk

Tangram Management Services Ltd
173 Yardley Fields Rd, Yardley,
Birmingham B33 8RP
T: 0121 783 9480
F: 07527 811700
E: mail@tangram-ms.co.uk
W: www.tangram-ms.co.uk

Tarmac Precast Concrete
Tallington, Stamford, Lincs PE9 4RL
T: 01778 381000
E: enquiries@tarmac.co.uk
W: www.tarmac.co.uk/precast

Tasty Plant Sales
Chipstead Farm, Amersham Rd,
Chalfont St Giles, Bucks HP8 4RT
T: 0845 677 4444
E: info@tastyplant.com
W: www.tastyplant.com

Tata Steel Projects
Meridian House, The Crescent,
York YO24 1AW
T: 01904 454600
F: 01904 454601
E: tatasteelprojects@tatasteel.com
W: www.tatasteeleurope.com

Tata Steel Rail
Rail Service Centre, PO Box 1, Brigg Rd,
Scunthorpe DN16 1BP
T: 01724 403398
E: rail@tatasteel.com
W: www.tatasteeleurope.com

Tate Rail Ltd
Station House, Station Hill, Cookham,
Berks SL6 9BP
T: 0844 381 9956
F: 0844 381 9957
E: info@taterail.com
W: www.taterail.com

Taylor Precision Plastics / Commercial Vehicle Rollers Ltd
Mile Oak Ind. Est,
Maesbury Rd, Oswestry,
Shropshire SY10 8GA
T: 01691 679516
F: 01691 670538
E: sales@cvrollers.co.uk
W: www.cvrollers.co.uk

Taylor Woodrow
See VINCI

Taziker Industrial Ltd t/a TI Protective Coatings
Unit 6, Lodge Bank,
Crown Lane, Horwich,
Bolton BL6 5HY
T: 01204 468080
F: 01204 695188
E: sales@ti-uk.com
W: www.ti-uk.com

TBM Consulting Group
Unit 8, H20 Business Complex,
Sherwood Business Park, Annesley,
Nottingham NG15 0HT
T: 01623 758298
F: 01623 755941
E: nfletcher@tbmcg.com
W: www.tbmcg.com

TDK-Lambda UK
Kingsley Ave, Ilfracombe, Devon EX34 8ES
T: 01271 856600
F: 01271 856741
E: powersolutions@emea.tdk-lambda.com
W: www.emea.tdk-lambda.com

TEAL Consulting Ltd
Deangate, Tuesley Lane, Godalming,
Surrey GU7 1SG
T: 01483 420550
F: 01483 420550
E: info@tealconsulting.co.uk
W: www.tealconsulting.co.uk

Team Surveys Ltd
Team House, St Austell Bay Business Park,
Par Moor Rd, St Austell PL25 3RF
T: 01726 816069
F: 01726 814611
E: email@teamsurveys.com
W: www.teamsurveys.com

Tecalemit Garage Equipment Co Ltd
Eagle Rd, Langage Business Park,
Plymouth PL7 5JY
T: 01752 219111
F: 01752 219128
E: sales@tecalemit.co.uk
W: www.tecalemit.co.uk

Tecforce
Litchurch Lane, Derby DE24 8AA
T: 01332 268000
F: 01332 268030
E: sales@tecforce.co.uk
W: www.tecforce.co.uk

Technical Cranes Ltd
Holmes Lock Works, Steel St, Holmes,
Rotherham S61 1DP
T: 01709 561861
F: 01709 556516
E: info@technicalcranes.co.uk
W: www.technicalcranes.co.uk

Technical Resin Bonders
See TRB Lightweight Structures Ltd

Technocover
See Technorail

Technology Project Services Ltd
1 Warwick Row,
London SW1E 5LR
T: 020 7963 1234
F: 020 7963 1299
E: mail@tps.co.uk
W: www.tps.co.uk

Technology Resourcing Ltd
The Technology Centre,
Surrey Research Park,
Guildford GU2 7YG
T: 01483 302211
F: 01483 301222
E: railways@tech-res.co.uk
W: www.railwayengineeringjobs.co.uk

TechnoRail (Technocover)
Henfaes Lane, Welshpool,
Powys SY21 7BE
T: 01938 555511
F: 01938 555527
E: admin@technocover.co.uk
W: www.technocover.co.uk

Tecnopali UK ltd
Unit 3, Headway Rd, Wobaston Rd,
Wolverhampton WV10 6PZ
T: 01902 788588
F: 01902 788589
E: sales@tecnopali.co.uk
W: www.tecnopali.co.uk

TEK Personnel Consultants Ltd
Norwich Union House, Irongate,
Derby DE1 3GA
T: 01332 360055
F: 01332 363345
E: derby@tekpersonnel.co.uk
W: www.tekpersonnel.co.uk

Telent – Rail
Point 3, Haywood Rd,
Warwick CV34 5AH
T: 01926 693569
F: 01926 693023
E: services@telent.com
W: www.telent.com

Telerail Ltd
9a New St, Carnforth, Lancs LA5 9BX
T: 01524 735774
F: 01524 736386
E: steve@telerail.co.uk
W: www.telerail.co.uk

Temple Group Ltd
Tempus Wharf, 33A Bermondsey Wall West,
London SE16 4TQ
T: 020 7394 3700
F: 020 7394 7871
E: enquiries@templegroup.co.uk
W: www.templegroup.co.uk

Ten 47 Ltd
Unit 2B, Frances Ind. Park, W
emyss Rd, Dysart,
Kirkcaldy KY1 2XZ
T: 01592 655725
F: 01592 651079
E: admin@ten47.com
W: www.ten47.com

Tenmat Ltd (Railko)
Ashburton Road West, Trafford Park,
Manchester M70 1RU
T: 0161 872 2181
F: 0161 872 7596
E: info@tenmat.com
W: www.tenmst.com

Tensar International
Cunningham Court, Shadsworth Business
Park, Shadsworth, Blackburn BB1 2QX
T: 01254 262431
F: 01254 266868
E: info@tensar-international.com
W: www.tensar.co.uk

Tension Control Bolts
Whitchurch Business Park,
Shakespeare Way, Whitchurch,
Shropshire SY13 1LJ
T: 01948 667700
F: 01948 667744
E: info@tcbolts.co.uk
W: www.tcbolts.co.uk

Terram Ltd
Mamhilad Park Estate, Pontypool,
Gwent NP4 0YR
T: 01495 757722
F: 01495 762383
E: info@terram.co.uk
W: www.terram.com

Terrawise Construction Ltd
104 The Court Yard, Radway Green Business
Centre, Radway Green, Crewe CW2 5PR
T: 01270 879011
F: 01270 875079
E: info@terrawise.co.uk
W: www.terrawise.co.uk

Testo Ltd
Newman Lane, Alton, Hants GU34 2QJ
T: 01420 544433
W: www.testo.co.uk

Tevo Ltd
Unit 14-16, Woobum Green Ind Est,
Thomas Rd, Woobum Green,
Bucks HP10 0PE
T: 01628 528034
E: sales@tevo.eu.com
W: www.tevo.eu.com

Tew Engineering Ltd
Crocus St, Nottingham NG2 3DR
T: 0115 935 4354
F: 0115 935 4355
E: sales@tew.co.uk
W: www.tew.co.uk

Thales
Ground Floor, Unit 4b,
Kenavon Drive, Forbury Park,
Reading RG1 3DH
T: 0118 908 6000
F: 0118 908 7732
E: uk.enquiries@thalesgroup.com
W: www.thalesgroup.com

The Bradley Group
Russell St, Heywood, Lancs OL10 1NU
T: 01706 360353
F: 01706 366154
E: pce@johnbradleygroup.com
W: www.johnbradleygroup.com

The Chartered Institute of Logistics and Transport (UK) (CILT)
Logistics and Transport Centre,
Earlstrees Court,
Earlstrees Rd,
Corby NN17 4AX
T: 01536 740100
F: 01536 740101
E: enquiry@ciltuk.org.uk
W: www.ciltuk.org.uk

The Deritend Group Ltd
Cyprus St, Off Upper Villiers St,
Wolverhampton WV2 4PA
T: 01902 392315
F: 01902 390186
E: sales@deritend.co.uk
W: www.deritend.co.uk

The Direct Group
Unit 1, Churnet Court,
Churnetside Business Park,
Harrison Way, Cheddleton,
Staffs ST13 7EF
T: 01538 360555
F: 01538 369100
E: dpl@direct-group.com
W: www.direct-group.com/direct link north

The Fenning Lovatt Partnership Ltd
69-71 Newington Causeway,
London SE1 6BD
T: 020 7378 4812
F: 020 7407 4612
E: mail@fenninglovatt.com
W: www.fenninglovatt.com

The Fire Service College
Moreton-in-Marsh,
Glos GL56 0RH
T: 01608 812130
F: 01608 651790
E: dluff@firservicecollege.ac.uk
W: www.fireservicecollege.ac.uk

The Haste Partnership
10 The Croft, Sheriff Hutton,
York YO60 6SQ
T: 01347 878034
E: richardhaste@aol.com
W: www.icrg.co.uk

The Highgate Partnership
Joel House, 19 Garrick St,
London WC2E 9AX
T: 020 7010 7750
F: 020 7010 7751
E: lucy@highgatepartners.com
W: www.highgatepartners.com

The Input Group
101 Ashbourne Road,
Derby DE22 3FW
T: 01332 348830
F: 01332 296342
E: info@inputgroup.co.uk
W: www.inputgroup.co.uk

The Mobile Catering Group
The Monkey House,
Kersoe, Pershore,
Worcs WR10 3JD
T: 01386 710123
F: 01386 710123
M: 07850 915959
E: fred@cateringcontracts.com
W: www.careingcontracts.com

The Nationwide Accreditation Bureau Ltd
The Olympic Office Centre, 8 Fulton Rd,
Wembley HA9 0NU
T: 08458 902902
F: 08458 903903
E: enquiries@thenab.co.uk
W: www.thenab.co.uk

The QSS Group Ltd
2 St Georges House, Vernon Gate,
Derby DE1 1UQ
T: 01332 221400
F: 01332 221401
E: enquiries@theqssgroup.co.uk
W: www.theqssgroup.co.uk

The Railway Consultancy Ltd
1st Floor, South Tower, Crystal Palace Station,
London SE19 2AZ
T: 020 8676 0395
F: 020 8778 7439
M: 07802 623548
E: info@railwayconsultancy.com
W: www.railwayconsultancy.com

The Railway Engineering Company Ltd
Manvers House, Kingston Rd,
Bradford-on-Avon, Wilts BA15 1AB
T: 01225 860140
F: 01225 867698
E: info@theraileng.com
W: www.theraileng.com

The Railway Mission
PO Box 495, Bedford MK41 9WQ
T: 01234 214790
F: 01124 214790
E: dick.crane@railwaychaplain.net
W: www.railwaymission.org

The Severn Partnership Ltd
The Maltings, 59 Lythwood Rd, Bayston Hill,
Shrewsbury SY3 0NA
T: 01743 874135
F: 01743 874716
E: mark.combes@severn-partnership.co.uk
W: www.severnpartnership.co.uk

The TAS Partnership Ltd.
Guildhall House, 59-61, Guildhall St,
Preston PR1 3NU
T: 01772 204998
E: info@taspartnership.co.uk
W: www.tas.uk.net

The Train Chartering Company Ltd
Benwell House, Preston, Wilts SN15 4DX
T: 01249 890176
E: info@trainchartering.com
W: www.trainchartering.com

The Trainline
Trainline Holdings Ltd, 498 Gorgie Rd,
Edinburgh EH11 3AF
T: 08704 111111
W: www.thetrainline.com

The Universal Improvement Company
17 Knowl Ave, Belper, Derbys DE56 2TL
T: 01773 826659
F: 01773 826659
E: info@theuic.com
W: www.theuic.com

The Welding Institute
See Institute of Rail Welding

Thermal Economics Ltd
Thermal House,
8 Cardiff Rd, Luton,
Beds LU1 1PP
T: 01582 450814
F: 01582 429305
E: info@thermal-economics.co.uk
W: www.thermal-economics.co.uk

Thermit Welding (GB) Ltd
87 Ferry Lane, Rainham,
Essex RM13 9YH
T: 01708 522626
F: 01708 553806
E: rsj@thermitwelding.com
W: www.thermitwelding.com

Thomas & Betts Ltd
See PMA

Thomson Rail Equipment Ltd
Valley Rd, Cinderford,
Glos GL14 2NZ
T: 01594 826611
F: 01594 825560
E: sales@thomsonrail.com
W: www.thomsonrail.com

Thurlow Countryside Management Ltd
2 Charterhouse Trading Est,
Sturmer Rd, Haverhill,
Suffolk CB9 7UU
T: 01440 760170
F: 01440 760171
E: info@t-c-m.co.uk
W: www.t-c-m.co.uk

Thurrock Engineering Supplies Ltd
Unit 1, Tes House,
Motherwell Way,
West Thurrock,
Essex RM20 3XD
T: 01708 861178
F: 01708 861158
E: info@thurrockengineering.com
W: www.thurrockengineering.co.uk

Thursfield Smith Consultancy
25 Grange Rd,
Shrewsbury SY3 9DG
T: 01743 246407
E: david@thursfieldsmith.co.uk
W: www.thursfieldsmith.co.uk

Thyssenkrupp GFT Gleistechnik GmbH
Altendorfstrasse 120, 45143 Essen,
Germany
T: 0049 201 188 3710
F: 0049 201 188 3714
E: gleistechnik@thyssenkrupp.com
W: www.tkgftgleistechnik.de

TI Protective Coatings
See Taziker Industrial Ltd

TICS Ltd
Oxford House, Sixth Avenue,
Robin Hood Airport,
Doncaster DN9 3GG
T: 01302 623074
F: 01302 623075
E: andrewmackenzie@tics-ltd.co.uk
W: www.tics-ltd.co.uk

Your route to passenger transport's vital statistics - now online

Our new TAS Business Monitor on-line subscription service gives you instant access to essential data about the financial and market performance of our ground public transport operations - constantly updated. Give us a click!

TAS Business Monitor — Monitoring the UK Public Transport Industry

head for
www.tas.uk.net
and follow the links

Ross Holme, West End,
Long Preston, Skipton,
BD23 4QL.
Tel: 01729 840756
info@TASpublications.co.uk

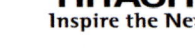

tie Ltd (Transport Initiatives Edinburgh)
Citypoint, 65 Haymarket Terrace, Edinburgh EH12 5HD
T: 0131 622 8300
F: 0131 622 8301
E: comms@tie.ltd.uk
W: www.tie.ltd.uk

Tiflex Ltd
Tiflex House, Liskeard, Cornwall PL14 4NB
T: 01579 320808
F: 01579 320802
E: sales@tiflex.co.uk
W: www.tiflex.co.uk

Time 24 Ltd
19 Victoria Gardens, Burgess Hill, West Sussex RH15 9NB
T: 01444 257655
F: 01444 259000
E: sales@time24.co.uk
W: www.time24.co.uk

Timeplan Ltd
12 The Pines, Broad St, Guildford, Surrey GU3 3BH
T: 01483 462340
F: 01483 462349
E: dave@timeplansolutions.com
W: www.timeplansolutions.com

TMD Friction UK Ltd
PO Box 18 Hunsworth Lane, Cleckheaton, West Yorks BD19 3UJ
T: 01274 854000
F: 01274 854001
E: info@tmdfriction.com
W: www.tmdfriction.com

TMP Worldwide
Chancery House, Chancery Lane, London WC2A 1QS
T: 020 7406 5075
W: www.tmpw.co.uk

Tony Gee and Partners LLP
Hardy House, 140 High St, Esher, Surrey KT10 9QJ
T: 01372 461600
F: 01372 461601
E: enquiries@tonygee.com
W: www.tonygee.com

TopDeck Parking
Springvale Business & Industrial Park, Bilston, Wolverhampton WV14 0QL
T: 01902 499400
F: 01902 494080
E: info@topdeckparking.co.uk
W: www.topdeckparking.co.uk

Topdrill
1 Seagrave Court, Walton Park, Milton Keynes MK7 7HA
T: 01908 666606
E: info@topdrill.co.uk
W: www.topdrill.co.uk

Toray Textiles Europe Ltd
Crown Farm Way, Forest Town, Mansfield, Notts NG19 0FT
T: 01623 415050
F: 01623 415070
E: sales@ttel.co.uk
W: www.ttel.co.uk

Torrent Trackside Ltd
Network House, Europa Way, Britannia Enterprise Park, Lichfield, Staffs WS14 9TZ
T: 01543 421900
F: 01543 421931
E: richard.donald@torrent.co.uk
W: www.torrent.co.uk

Total Access Training
Unit 5, Raleigh Hall Ind. Est, Eccleshall, Staffs ST21 6JL
T: 01785 850333
E: sales@totalaccess.co.uk
W: www.totalaccess.co.uk

Total Rail Solutions
Unit 1, Hazeley Enterprise Park, Twyford, Winchester SO21 1QA
T: 01962 711642
F: 01962 717330
E: info@totalrailsolutions.co.uk
W: www.totalrailsolutions.org

Total UK Ltd
Pottery Lane, Ferrybridge, West Yorks WF11 8JY
T: 01977 636100
E: tom.hyde@total.co.uk
W: www.lubricants.total.com

Totectors (UK) Ltd
9 Pondwood Close, Moulton Park Ind. Estate, Northampton NN3 6RT
T: 0870 600 5055
F: 0870 600 5056
E: sales@totectors.net
W: www.totectors.net

Touchstone Renard Ltd
123 Pall Mall, London SW1Y 5EA
T: 020 7101 0788
M: 07768 366744
E: paustin@touchstonerenard.com
W: www.touchstonerenard.com

Tower Surveys Ltd
Vivian House, Vivian Lane, Nottingham NG5 1AF
T: 0115 960 1212
F: 0115 962 1200
E: beverley.chiang@opusjoynespike.co.uk
W: www.towersurveys.co.uk

TPA Portable Roadways Ltd
Dukeries Mill, Claylands Ave, Worksop, Notts S81 7DJ
T: 0870 240 2381
F: 0870 240 2382
E: enquiries@tpa-ltd.co.uk
W: www.tpa-ltd.co.uk

TPK Consulting Ltd (RPS Group)
Centurion Court, 85, Milton Park, Abingdon, Oxon OX14 4RY
T: 01235 438151
F: 01235 438188
E: rpsab@rpsgroup.com
W: www.rpsplc.co.uk

TQ Catalis
Garden Court, Lockington Hall, Main St, Lockington, Derby DE74 2SJ
T: 0845 880 8108
E: hotline@catalis.co.uk
W: www.catalis.com

TRAC Engineering Ltd
Dovecote Rd, Eurocentral, North Lanarkshire ML1 4GP
T: 01698 831111
F: 01698 832222
E: engineering@trac.com
W: www.tracengineering.com

Track Maintenance Equipment Ltd
Witham Wood, Marley Lane, Haslemere, Surrey GU27 3PZ
T: 01428 651114
F: 01428 644727
E: info@tmeltd.co.uk
W: www.tmeltd.co.uk

Track Safe Telecom (TST)
See Centregreat

Tracklink UK Ltd
Unit 5, Miltons Yard, Petworth Rd, Witley, Surrey GU8 5LH
T: 01428 685124
F: 01428 687788
W: www.tklink.co.uk

Tracksure Ltd
8 Woburn St, Ampthill, Beds MK45 2HP
T: 01525 840557
F: 01525 403918
E: sales@tracksure.co.uk
W: www.tracksure.co.uk

Trackwork Ltd
PO Box 139, Kirk Sandall Lane, Kirk Sandall Ind. Est., Doncaster DN3 1WX
T: 01302 888666
F: 01302 888777
E: sales@trackwork.co.uk
W: www.trackwork.co.uk

Tracsis Plc
Unit 6, The Point, Pinnacle Way, Pride Park, Derby DE24 8ZS
T: 01332 226860
E: info@tracsis.com
W: www.tracsis.com

Tractel UK Ltd
Old Lane, Halfway, Sheffield S20 3GA
T: 0114 248 2266
F: 0114 247 3350
E: tracteluk.info@tractel.com
W: www.tractel.com

TracTruc Bi-modal
See TruckTrain

Traffic Management Services Ltd
PO Box 10, Retford, Notts DN22 7EE
T: 01777 705053
F: 01777 709878
E: info@traffic.org.uk
W: www.traffic.org.uk

Train FX Ltd
15 Melbourne Business Court, Millennium Way, Pride Park, Derby DE24 8HZ
T: 01332 366175
F: 01332 298761
E: enquiries@trainfx.com
W: www.trainfx.com

Train'd Up
Elmbank Mill, Menstrie Business Centre, Menstrie, Clackmannanshire FK11 7BU
T: 0845 602 9665
F: 0870 850 3397
E: enquiries@traindup.org
W: www.traindup.org

Trainpeople.co.uk Ltd
Arran House, Arran Rd, Perth PH1 3DZ
T: 01738 446110
F: 01738 622055
E: info@trainpeople.co.uk
W: www.trainpeople.co.uk

Trakside Systems Ltd
See High Voltage Maintenance Services Ltd

TRAM Power Ltd
99 Stanley Rd, Bootle, Merseyside L20 7DA
T: 0151 547 1425
F: 0151 521 5509
M: 07976 949618
E: lewis.lesley@trampower.co.uk
W: www.trampower.co.uk

Tramlink (Croydon)
See Transport for London

Tranect Ltd
Unit 4, Carraway Rd, Gilmoss Ind. Est, Liverpool L11 0EE
T: 0151 548 7040
F: 0151 546 6066
E: sales@tranect.co.uk
W: www.tranect.co.uk

Trans Pennine Express (TPE)
See First Trans Pennine

Transaction Systems Ltd
See Transys

Transdev Plc
401 King St, London W6 9NJ
T: 020 8600 5650
F: 020 8600 5651
E: information@transdevplc.co.uk
W: www.transdevplc.co.uk

Transec UK Ltd (Bowden Bros Ltd)
Brickworks House, Spook Hill, North Holmwood, Dorking, Surrey RH5 4HR
T: 01306 743355
F: 01306 876768
E: ian.bowden@bowden-bros.com
W: www.bowden-bros.com

Translec Ltd
Saddleworth Business Centre, Huddersfield Rd, Delph, Oldham OL3 5DF
T: 01457 878888
F: 01457 878887
E: mail@translec.co.uk
W: www.translec.co.uk

Translink NI Railways
Central Station, East Bridge St, Belfast BT1 3PB
T: 02890 666630
F: 02890 899452
E: feedback@translink.co.uk
W: www.translink.co.uk

Transmitton
See Siemens

Transport & Travel Research Ltd (TTR)
Minster House, Minster Pool Walk, Lichfield, Staffs
T: 01543 416416
F: 01543 416681
E: enquiries@ttr-ltd.com
W: www.ttr-ltd.com

Transport 2000
See Campaign for Better Transport

Transport Benevolent Fund
22 Lovat Lane, London EC3R 8EB
T: 0300 333 2000 (ETD 00 38571)
F: 0870 831 2882
E: help@tbf.org.uk
W: www.tbf.org.uk

TBF is a registered charity (No 1058032 in England & Wales, SC040013 in Scotland) which helps almost 40,000 members throughout the public transport industry.

22 Lovat Lane, LONDON, EC3R 8EB

T: 0300 333 2000
Railway internal 00 38571
F: 0870 831 2882
E: help@tbf.org.uk

www.tbf.org.uk

tbf Transport Benevolent Fund

Transport for London
55 Broadway, London SW1H 0BD
T: 020 7222 5600
E: enquire@tfl.gov.uk
W: www.tfl.gov.uk/rail

Transport iNet
SEIC, Holywell Business Park, Loughborough University LE11 3TU
T: 01509 635270
F: 01509 635231
E: a.m.wilkinson@lboro.ac.uk
W: www.eminnovation.org.uk/transport

Transport Interchange Consultants Ltd
1 Lochaline St, London W6 9ST
T: 020 8563 0555
F: 020 8563 0555
E: mw@ticonsultants.co.uk
W: www.ticonsultants.co.uk

Transport Scotland
Buchanan House, 58 Port Dundas Rd, Glasgow G4 0HF
T: 0141 272 7100
E: info@transportscotland.gsi.gov.uk
W: www.transportscotland.gov.uk

Transportation Planning International
International Design Hub, Colmore Plaza, 20 Colmore Circus, Birmingham B4 6AT
T: 0121 2125102
E: info@tpi-world.com
W: www.tpi-world.com

Transsol Ltd
32 Buxton Rd West, Disley, Cheshire SK12 2LY
T: 07775 893620
F: 0870 052 5838
E: enquiries@transsol.net
W: www.transsol.net

Transys Projects Ltd
See Vossloh Kiepe

Travel Info. Systems
Suite 1, Grand Union House, 20 Kentish Town Rd, London NW1 9NX
T: 020 7428 1288
F: 020 7267 2745
E: enquiries@travelinfosystems.com
W: www.travelinfosystems.com

Traxsydes Training
Room 11, E.L.O.C, 80-86 St Mary Rd, Walthamstow, London E17 9RE
T: 020 8223 1257
F: 020 8223 1258
E: bookings@traxsydes.co.uk
W: www.traxsydes.co.uk

TRB Lightweight Structures Ltd
12 Clifton Rd, Huntingdon, Cambs PE29 7EN
T: 01480 447400
F: 01480 414992
E: sales@trbls.com
W: www.trbls.com

TRE Ltd
See The Railway Engineering Company

Treadmaster Flooring
See Tiflex

Trelleborg Industrial AVS
1 Hoods Close, Leicester LE4 2BN
T: 0116 267 0300
F: 0116 267 0310
E: rail@trelleborg.com
W: www.trelleborg.com/industrialavs

Tremco Illbruck Limited
Coupland Rd, Hindley Green, Wigan WN2 4HT
T: 01942 251400
F: 01942 251410
E: uk.info@tremco-illbruck.com
W: www.tremco-illbruck.com

Trent Instruments Ltd
Unit 39, Nottingham South and Wilford Ind. Est, Ruddington Lane, Nottingham NG11 7EP
T: 0115 969 6188
F: 0115 945 5696
E: phillip@trentinstruments.co.uk
W: www.trentinstruments.co.uk

Triforce Security Solutions Ltd
Westmead House, Westmead, Farnborough, Hants GU14 7LP
T: 01252 373496
E: enquiries@triforcesecurity.co.uk
W: www.triforcesecurity.co.uk

Trimble UK
Trimble House, Meridian Office Park, Osborn Way, Hook, Hants RG27 9HX
T: 01256 760150
F: 01256 760148
W: www.trimble.com

Tritech Rail/Tritech Rail Training
See AECOM

TRL
Crowthorne House, Nine Mile Ride, Wokingham, Berks RG40 3GA
T: 01344 773131
F: 01344 770356
E: rail@trl.co.uk
W: www.trl.co.uk

Trojan Services Ltd
PO Box 675, Chichester, West Sussex PO19 9LG
T: 0845 074 0407
F: 01243 783654
E: info@trojan-services.com
W: www.trojan-services.com

TRS Staffing Solutions
8th Floor, York House, Kingsway, London WC2B 6UJ
T: 020 7419 5800
F: 020 7419 5801
E: info-uk@trsstaffing.com
W: www.trsstaffing.com

Truck Train Developments Ltd (and TracTruc Bi-Modal)
4 Elfin Grove, Bognor Regis, W.Sussex PO21 2RX
T: 01243 869118
E: pmtrucktrain@tiscali.co.uk

Truflame Welding
Truflame House, 56 Newhall Rd, Sheffield S9 2QL
T: 0114 243 3020
F: 0114 243 5297
E: sales@truflame.co.uk
W: www.truflame.co.uk

TSL Turton Ltd
Burton Rd, Sheffield S3 8DA
T: 0114 270 1577
F: 0114 275 6947
E: sales@tslturton.com
W: www.tslturton.com

TSSA (Transport Salaried Staff's Association)
Walkden House, 10 Melton St, London NW1 2EJ
T: 020 7387 2101
F: 020 7383 0656
E: enquiries@tssa.org.uk
W: www.tssa.org.uk

TT Electronics plc
Clive House, 12-18 Queens Rd, Weybridge, Surrey KT13 9XB
T: 01932 825300
F: 01932 836450
E: info@ttelectronics.com
W: www.ttelectronics.com

TTCI UK
13 Fitzroy St, London, W1T 4BQ
T: 020 7755 4080
F: 020 7755 4203
E: michele_johnson@aar.com
W: www.ttci.aar.com

TTG Transportation Technology (Europe) Ltd
The iD Centre, Lathkill House, rtc Business Park, London Rd, Derby DE24 8UP
T: 01332 258867
F: 01332 258823
E: enquiries@ttgeurope.com
W: www.ttgtransportationtechnology.com

TTR
See Transport & Travel Research

Tubelines
15 Westferry Circus, Canary Wharf, London E14 4HD
T: 0845 660 5466
E: enquiries@tubelines.com
W: www.tubelines.com

Tuchschmid Constructa AG
Cedar House, Glade Rd, Marlow SL7 1DQ
T: 01234 822821
F: 01234 822821
M: 07940 581623
E: derekbliss@bishamconsulting.com
W: www.intermodallogistics.co.uk

Tufcoat
Fox House, 8-10 Whimple St, Plymouth PL1 2DH
T: 01752 227333
F: 0871 264 5801
E: info@tufcoat.co.uk
W: www.tufcoat.co.uk

Tufnol Composites Ltd
Wellhead Lane, Perry Barr, Birmingham B42 2TB
T: 0121 356 9351
F: 0121 331 4235
E: sales@tufnol.co.uk
W: www.tufnol.com

Turbex Ltd
Unit 1, Riverwey Ind. Park, Newman Lane, Alton, Hants GU34 2QL
T: 01420 544909
F: 01420 542264
E: sales@turbex.co.uk
W: www.turbex.co.uk

Turbo Power Systems Ltd
1 Queens Park, Queensway North, Team Valley Trading Est, Gateshead, Tyne & Wear NE11 0NX
T: 0191 482 9200
F: 0191 482 9201
E: sales@turbopowersystems.com
W: www.turbopowersystems.com

Turkington Precast
James Park, Mahon Rd, Portadown, Co. Armagh, N.Ireland BT62 3EH
T: 028 38 332807
F: 028 38 361770
E: gary@turkington-precast.com
W: www.turkington-precast.com

Turner & Townsend
Low Hall, Calverley Lane, Horsforth, Leeds LS18 4GH
T: 0113 258 4400
F: 0113 258 2911
E: lee@turntown.com
W: www.turnerandtownsend.com

Turner Diesel Ltd
Unit 1A, Dyce Ind. Park, Dyce, Aberdeen AB21 7EZ
T: 01224 214200
F: 01224 723927
E: diesel.sales@turner.co.uk
W: www.turner-diesel.co.uk

TUV Product Service Ltd
Octagon House, Concorde Way, Segensworth, North Fareham, Hants PO15 5RL
T: 01489 558100
F: 01489 558101
E: info@tuvps.co.uk
W: www.tuvps.co.uk

TUV-SUD Rail GmbH
Ridlerstrasse 65, D-80339, Munich, Germany
T: 0049 89519 03537
F: 0049 89519 02933
W: www.tuv-sued.com

TXM Projects Ltd
1 St Peters Court, Church Lane, Bickenhill B92 0DN
M: 07814 422589
E: simon.pitt@txmprojects.co.uk
W: www.txmprojects.co.uk

TXM Recruit Ltd
Blackhill Drive, Wolverton Mill, Milton Keynes, Bucks MK12 5TS
T: 0845 2263454
F: 0845 2262453
E: info@txmrecruit.co.uk

Tyne & Wear Metro
See Nexus

Tyrone Fabrication Ltd (TFL)
Goland Rd, Ballygawley, Co Tyrone BT70 2LA
T: 028 8556 7200
F: 028 8556 7089
E: sales@tfl.eu.com
W: www.tfl.eu.com

UK Accreditation Service (UKAS)
21-47 High St, Feltham, Middx TW13 4UN
T: 020 8917 8400
E: info@ukas.com
W: info@ukas.com

We lead the way in rail electrical infrastructure.

HV engineering – traction supplies – station services – platform lighting

a: 237 Southwark Bridge Road, London, SE1 6NP
t: 0207 015 1676
e: rail@ukpowernetworks.co.uk
w: www.ukpowernetworks.co.uk/rail

UK Power Networks Services

UK Power Networks Services
237 Southwark Bridge Rd, London SE1 6NP
T: 0207 397 7695
E: rail@ukpowernetworks.co.uk
W: www.ukpowernetworks.co.uk/rail

UK Railtours
01438 715050
T: 01438 715050
E: john@ukrailtours.com
W: www.ukrailtours.com

UK Trade & Investment - Investment Services
1 Victoria St, London SW1H 0ET
T: 0845 539 0419/020 7333 5442
E: enquiries@ukti-invest.com
W: www.ukti.gov.uk

UK Ultraspeed
Warksburn House, Wark, Hexham, Northumberland NE48 3LS
T: 020 7861 2497
F: 020 7861 2497
E: ncameron@bell-pottinger.co.uk
W: www.500kmh.com

UKRS Projects Ltd
See Bowen Projects Ltd

Ultra Electronics PMES Ltd
Towers Business Park, Wheelhouse Rd, Rugeley, Staffs WS15 1UZ
T: 01889 503300
F: 01889 572929
E: enquiries@ultra-pmes.com
W: www.ultra-pmes.com

Ultra Electronics-Electrics
Kingsditch Lane, Cheltenham, Glos GL51 9PG
T: 01242 221166
F: 01242 221167
E: info@ultra-electrics.com
W: www.ultra-electrics.com

Underground Pipeline Services Ltd
See Integrated Water Services Ltd

Unic Cranes Europe
See GGR Group Ltd

UNIFE
Avenue Louise 221, B-1050 Brussels, Belgium
T: 0032 2642 2328
F: 0032 2626 1261
E: judit.sandor@unife.org
W: www.unife.org

HITACHI
Inspire the Next

Unilokomotive Ltd
Dunmore Rd, Tuam, Co. Galway, Ireland
T: 00353 93 52150
F: 00353 93 52227
E: omcconn@unilok.ie
W: www.unilok.ie

Unipart Dorman
see dorman

Unipart Rail (infrastructure)
Gresty Rd, Crewe CW2 6EH
T: 01270 847600
F: 01270 847601
E: enquiries@unipartrail.com
W: www.unipartrail.com

Unipart Rail (infrastructure)
Leeman Rd, York YO26 4ZD
T: 01904 544020
F: 01904 544021
E: enquiries@unipartrail.com
W: www.unipartrail.com

Unipart Rail (T&RS) Ltd
Jupiter Building, First Point, Balby Carr Bank,
Doncaster DN4 5JQ
T: 01302 731400
F: 01302 731401
E: trsenquiries@unipartrail.com
W: www.unipartrail.com

UNIPART RAIL

Unipart Rail is the UK's largest partner in infrastructure and T&RS materials supply & management, and lean business solutions

Unipart Rail (T&RS):
Jupiter House, First Point
Balby Carr Bank, Doncaster
DN4 5JQ

T: +44 (0) 1302 731 400
F: +44 (0) 1302 731 401
trsenquiries@unipartrail.com

Unipart Rail (Infrastructure):
Gresty Road, Crewe,
Cheshire CW2 6EH

Tel: +44 (0) 1270 847 600
Fax: +44 (0) 1270 847 601

Unipart Rail (Infrastructure):
Leeman Road, York
Yorkshire YO26 4ZD

T: +44 (0) 1904 544 020
F: +44 (0) 1904 544 021

enquiries@unipartrail.com

www.unipartrail.com

UNIPART RAIL

Unite - The Union
General Secretary, 35 King St, Covent Garden,
London WC2E 8JG
T: 020 7420 8900
F: 020 7420 8998
W: www.unitetheunion.com

United Kingdom Society for Trenchless Technology
38 Holly Walk, Leamington Spa,
Warks CV32 4LY
T: 01926 330935
E: admin@ukstt.org.uk
W: www.ukstt.org.uk

Universal Heat Transfer Ltd
Well Spring Close, Carlyon Rd, Atherstone,
Warks CV9 1QZ
T: 01827 722171
F: 01827 722174
E: sales@uhtltd.com
W: www.universalheattransfer.co.uk

Universal Railway Equipment Ltd
Princess Royal Buildings, Whitecroft Rd,
Bream, Lydney,
Glos GL15 6LY
T: 01594 560555
E: unirail@btconnect.com
W: www.peeway.co.uk

Up & Cuming Consultancy Ltd (UCCL)
74 Chenies Mews, London WC1E 6HU
T: 020 7388 2232
F: 020 7388 3730
E: info@ucd.net
W: www.ucd.net

Urban Hygiene Ltd
Sky Business Park,
Robin Hood Airport,
Doncaster DN9 3GA
T: 01302 623193
E: enquiries@urbanhygiene.com
W: www.urbanhygiene.co.uk

Urbis Lighting Ltd
Telford Rd, Houndmills, Basingstoke,
Hants RG21 6YW
T: 01256 354446
F: 01256 841314
E: sales@urbislighting.com
W: www.urbislighting.com

Uretek UK Ltd
Unit 6, Peel Rd, Skelmersdale,
Lancs WN8 9PT
T: 01695 50525
F: 01695 555212
E: sales@uretek.co.uk
W: www.uretek.co.uk

URS
Scott House, Alencon Link, Basingstoke,
Hants RG21 7PP
T: 01256 310200
F: 01256 310201
E: rail.marketing@scottwilson.com
W: www.urscorp.eu

URS Corporation Ltd
6-8 Greencoat Place, London SW1P 1PL
T: 0115 907 7086
F: 0115 907 7001
E: railways@scottwilson.com
W: www.urscorp.eu

VAE UK Ltd
Sir Harry Lauder Rd, Portobello,
Edinburgh EH15 1DJ
T: 0131 550 2297
F: 0131 550 2660
E: jim.gemmell@vae.co.uk
W: www.voestalpine.com/vae

Vaisala Ltd
351, Bristol Rd, Birmingham B5 7SW
T: 0121 683 1200
F: 0121 683 1299
E: liz.green@vaisala.com
W: www.vaisala.com

Van der Vlist UK Ltd
Burma Drive, Kingston upon Hull HU9 5SD
T: 01482 210100
F: 01482 216222
E: info@vandervlist.co.uk
W: www.vandervlist.co.uk

Variable Message Signs Ltd (VMS)
Unit 1, Monkton Business Park North,
Mill Lane, Hebburn, Tyne & Wear NE31 2JZ
T: 0191 423 7070
F: 0191 423 7071
E: aisaacs@vmslimited.co.uk
W: www.vmslimited.co.uk

Vector Management Ltd
Strathclyde House, Green Man Lane,
London Heathrow Airport, Feltham,
Middx TW14 0NZ
T: 020 8844 0444
F: 020 8844 0666
E: ju-liang.trigg@vecman.com
W: www.vecman.com

Vectra Group Ltd
See Arcadis

Verint Systems
241 Brooklands Rd, Weybridge,
Surrey KT13 0RH
T: 01932 839500
F: 01932 839501
E: marketing.emea@verint.com
W: www.verint.com

Veritec Sonomatic Ltd
Ashton House, The Village,
Birchwood Bus.Park, Warrington WA3 6FZ
T: 01925 414000
F: 01925 655595
E: jl@vsonomatic.com
W: www.veritecltd.co.uk

Vertex Systems
See AMD

Veryards Opus
See Opus International

Vi Distribution
Unit 7, Springvale Business Centre,
Millbuck Way, Sandbach, CW11 3HY
T: 01270 750520
F: 01270 750521
E: sales@vidistribution.co.uk
W: www.vidistribution.co.uk

Video 125 Ltd
Glade House, High St, Sunninghill,
Berks SL5 9NP
T: 01344 299551
E: sales@video125.co.uk
W: www.video125.co.uk

VINCI Construction UK Ltd
Astral House, Imperial Way,
Watford WD24 4WW
T: 01923 233433
F: 01923 800085
E: civils@vinciconstruction.co.uk
W: www.vinciconstruction.co.uk

Vinci Park Services UK Ltd
Oak House, Reeds Cres, Watford,
Herts WD24 4QP
T: 01908 223500
F: 01923 231914
E: info@vincipark.co.uk
W: www.vincipark.co.uk

Vintage Trains Ltd
670 Warwick Rd, Tyseley,
Birmingham B11 2HL
T: 0121 708 4960
F: 0121 708 4963
E: vintagetrains@btconnect.com
W: www.vintagetrains.co.uk

Virgin Trains (West Coast)
North Wing Offices. Euston Station,
London NW1 2HS
T: 0845 000 8000
E: firstname.lastname@virgintrains.co.uk
W: www.virgin.com/trains

Visimetrics (UK) Ltd
Skye House, Skye Rd, Prestwick,
Scotland
T: 01292 673770
F: 01292 677990
E: info@visimetrics.com
W: www.visimetrics.com

Vision Infrastructure Services Ltd
Unit 7, Durham Lane, West Moor Park,
Doncaster DN1 3FE
T: 01302 831730
F: 01302 832671
E: ian@visioninfrastructureservices.com
W: www.visioninfrastructureservices.com

Vistorm Ltd
See HP Information Security

Visul Systems
Kingston House,3 Walton Rd, Pattinson North,
Washington,Tyne & Wear NE38 8QA
T: 0191 402 1960
F: 0191 402 1906
E: ross.carty@usluk.com
W: www.visulsystems.com

Vita Safety Ltd
1 Gillingham Rd, Eccles, Manchester M30 8NA
T: 0161 789 1400
F: 0161 280 2528
E: ian.hutchings@vitasafety.com
W: www.vitasafety.com

Vital Rail
The Mill, South Hall St, Ordsall Lane,
Manchester M5 4TP
T: 0161 836 7000
F: 0161 836 7001
E: info@vital-rail.com
W: www.vital-rail.com

Vitec Webber Lenihan
3 Cae Gwrydd, Greenmeadow
Springs Bus. Park, Cardiff CF15 7AB
T: 02920 620232
F: 02920 624837
E: mail@vitecwebberlenihan.com
W: www.vitecwebberlenihan.com

VMS
See Variable Message Systems

Voestalpine UK Ltd
Voestalpine House, Albion Place,
Hammersmith, London W6 0QT
T: 020 8600 5800
E: catherine.crisp@voestalpine.com
W: www.voestalpine.com

Voith Turbo GmbH & Co.KG
Alexanderstrasse 2,
89522 Heidenheim,
Germany
T: 0044 7321 37 4069
F: 0044 7321 37 7616
E: rail.uk@voith.com
W: www.voith.com

Voith Turbo Ltd
Unit 49, Metropolitan Park,
Bristol Rd, Greenford,
Middx UB6 8UP
T: 020 8436 1060
F: 020 8569 1726
E: roger.everest@voith.com
W: www.uk.voithturbo.com

Volker Fitzpatrick Ltd
Hertford Rd, Hoddesden, Herts EN11 9BX
T: 01992 305000
F: 01992 305001
E: volkerfitzpatrickrail@volkerfitzpatrick.co.uk
W: www.volkerfitzpatrick.co.uk

Volker Rail
Carolina Court, Lakeside,
Doncaster DN4 5RA
T: 01302 791100
F: 01302 791200
E: marketing@volkerrail.co.uk
W: www.volkerrail.co.uk

Volo TV & Media Ltd
Departure Side Offices, Platform 1,
Paddington Station, Pread St, London W2 1F
T: 020 7193 0997
F: 020 7402 2498
E: findoutmore@volo.tv
W: www.volo.tv

Vortok International
Innovation House, 3 Western Wood Way,
Langage Science Park, Plymouth PL7 5BG
T: 01752 349200
F: 01752 338855
E: gfermie@vortok.co.uk
W: www.vortok.co.uk

Vossloh AG
Vosslohstrasse 4, 58791 Werdohl, Germany
T: 0049 2392 520
F: 0049 2392 520
W: www.vossloh.com

Vossloh Fastening Systems GmbH
Am Schimmersfeld 7a, D-40880 Ratingen,
Germany
T: 0049 2102 49090
F: 0049 2102 49094
W: www.vossloh-fastening-systems.de

Vossloh Kiepe
2 Priestley Wharf,
Birmingham Science Park, Holt St,
Aston,Birmingham B7 4BN
T: 0121 359 7777
F: 0121 359 1811
E: enquiries@vkb.vossloh.com
W: www.vossloh-kiepe.co.uk

VTG Rail UK Ltd
Sir Stanley Clarke House, 7 Ridgeway,
Quinton Business Park, Birmingham B32 1AF
T: 0121 421 9180
F: 0121 421 9192
E: ian.shaw@vtg.com
W: www.vtg.com

VTS Track Technology Ltd
80a Scotter Rd, Scunthorpe,
North Lincs DN15 8EF
T: 01724 862131
F: 01724 295243
E: info@vtstt.com
W: www.vtstt.com

Vossloh Kiepe UK vossloh KIEPE

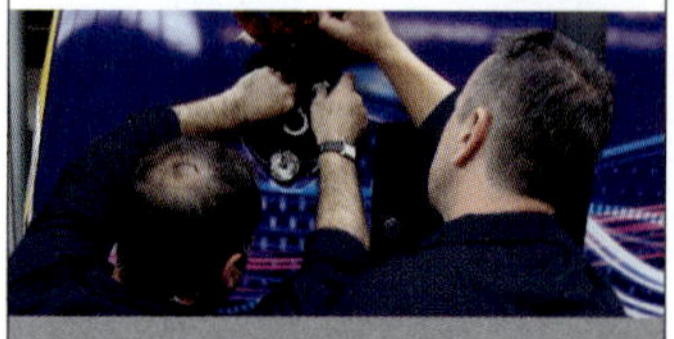

Assured rail vehicle solutions

Vossloh Kiepe UK Ltd
2 Priestley Wharf, Holt St,
Aston, Birmingham B7 4BN
T +44 (0)121 359 7777
E enquiries@vkb.vossloh.com
www.vossloh-kiepe.co.uk

Vulcascot Cable Protectors Ltd
Unit 12,
Norman-D-Gate, Bedford Rd,
Northampton NN1 5NT
T: 0800 035 2842
F: 01604 632344
E: sales@vulcascotcableprotectors.co.uk
W: www.vulcascotcableprotectors.com

W A Developments Ltd
see stobart rail

Wabtec Rail Ltd
PO Box 400, Doncaster Works,
Hexthorpe Rd,
Doncaster DN1 1SL
T: 01302 340700
F: 01302 790058
E: wabtecrail@wabtec.com
W: www.wabtecrail.co.uk

Wacker Neuson (GB) Ltd
Lea Rd, Waltham Cross,
Herts EN9 1AW
T: 01992 707228
F: 01992 707201
E: chris.pearce@eu.wackergroup.com
W: www.wackerneuson.com

VTS

Manufacturers of all types of Switch and Crossing systems and ancillary components for the **Heavy Rail**, **High Speed** and **Light Rail** markets.

VTS Track Technology Ltd
'The new name for Corus Cogifer'
80A Scotter Road,
Scunthorpe DN15 8EF
Tel: +44 0 1724 862131
Fax: +44 0 1724 295243
Web: vosslohtatasteel.com

VOITH

Voith Turbo Limited
17 Bristol Road, Unit 49
The Metropolitan Centre
UB6 8UP Greenford
Tel. +44 20 8436 1060
Fax +44 20 8569 1726
uk.voithturbo.com

Wabtec RAIL LIMITED

- Vehicles
- Wheelsets and Bogies
- Air Conditioning
- Door Systems
- Components

Now providing a wider than ever range of specialist skills, resources and technologies that are helping to make the country's railways better.

Wabtec Rail Ltd
PO Box 400, Doncaster DN1 1SL
T: 01302 340700
F: 01302 790058
E: wabtecrail@wabtec.com
W: www.wabtecrail.co.uk

Wagony Swidnica S.A.
UL. Strzelinska 35,
58-100 Swidnica,
Poland
T: 0048 74 856 2000
F: 0048 853 0323
E: secretariat@gbrx.com
W: www.gbrx.com

Washroom Joinery Ltd
The Loughton Seedbed Centre,
LangstonRd, Loughton,
Essex IG10 3TQ
T: 0700 492 7476
F: 08700 111860
E: info@washroomjoinery.co.uk
W: www.washroomjpinery.co.uk

Washtec UK Ltd
Unit 14A, Oak ind. Park, Great Dunmow,
Essex CM9 1XN
T: 01371 878800
F: 01371 878810
W: www.washtec-uk.com

Waterflow
12-16 David Rd, Poyle Trading Est,
Colnbrook SL3 0DG
T: 01753 810999
F: 01753 681442
E: sales@waterflow.co.uk
W: www.waterflow.co.uk

Waterman Transport & Development Ltd
Pickfords Wharf, Clink St,
London SE1 9DG
T: 020 7928 7888
F: 020 7902 0992
E: paul.worrall@watermangroup.com
W: www.waterman-group.co.uk

Waverley Rail Project
See Borders Railway

Wavesight Ltd
Talon House,
Presley Way, Crownhill,
Milton Keynes MK8 0ES
T: 01908 265223
F: 01908 265143
E: sales@wavesight.com
W: www.wavesight.com

Webasto AG
Kraillinger Strasse 5, 82131 Stockdorf,
Germany
T: 0049 89 857 948 444
F: 0049 89 899 217 433
E: tac3@webasto.com
W: www.rail.webasto.com

Webro Cable & Connectors Ltd
Vision House, Meadow Brooks Business Park,
Meadow Lane, Long Eaton, Notts NG10 2GD
T: 0115 972 4483
F: 0115 946 1230
E: info@webro.com
W: www.webro.com

WEC Group Ltd
Spring Vale House, Spring Vale Rd, Darwen,
Lancs BB3 2ES
T: 01254 773718
F: 01254 771109
E: stevecooke@wecl.co.uk
W: www.welding-eng.com

Weedfree
Holly Tree Farm,
Park Lane, Balne,
Goole DN14 0EP
T: 01405 860022
F: 01405 862283
E: sales@weedfree.net
W: www.weedfree.net

Weidmuller Ltd
Klippon House,
Centurion Court Office Park,
Meridian East,
Meridian Business Park,
Leicester LE19 1TP
T: 0116 282 3470
F: 0116 289 3582
E: marketing@weidmuller.co.uk
W: www.weidmuller.co.uk

Weightmans
High Holborn House,
52-54 High Holborn,
London WC1V 6RL
T: 020 7822 1900
F: 020 7822 1901
E: sarah.seddon@weightmans.com
W: www.weightmans.com

Weighwell Ltd
23 Orgreave Place,
Sheffield S13 9LU
T: 0114 269 9955
F: 0114 269 9256
E: rwood@weighwell.co.uk
W: www.weighwell.co.uk

Weld-A-Rail Ltd
Lockwood Close,
Top Valley,
Nottingham NG5 9JM
T: 0115 926 8797
F: 0115 926 4818
E: admin@weldarail.co.uk
W: www.weldarail.co.uk

Welfare Cabins UK (WCUK)
Martells Ind. Est,
Slough Lane, Ardleigh,
Colchester CO7 7RU
T: 01206 233270
E: sales@welfarecabinsuk.co.uk
W: www.welfarecabinsuk.co.uk

HITACHI
Inspire the Next

In association with ATKINS

West Coast Railway Co.
Jesson Way, Carnforth, Lancs LA5 9UR
T: 01524 732100
F: 01524 735518
E: info@wcrc.co.uk
W: www.wcrc.co.uk

West Midlands PTE
See Centro

West Yorkshire PTE (Metro)
Wellington House, 40-50 Wellington St, Leeds LS1 2DE
F: 0113 251 7272
W: www.wypte.gov.uk

Westcode Semiconductors
Langley Park Way, Langley Park, Chippenham, Wilts SN15 1GE
T: 01249 444524
F: 01249 659448
E: customer.services@westcode.com
W: www.westcode.com

Westermo Data Communications Ltd
Talisman Business Centre, Duncan Rd, Park Gate, Southampton SO31 7GA
T: 01489 580585
F: 01489 580586
E: sales@westermo.co.uk

Westinghouse Platform Screen Doors
Knorr-Bremse Rail Systems (UK) Ltd, Westinghouse Way, Hampton Park East, Melksham, Wilts SN12 6TL
T: 01225 898585
F: 01225 898710
E: mikael.baghammar@knorr-bremse.com
W: www.platformscreendoors.com

Westinghouse Rail Systems
See Invensys Rail

Westley Engineering Ltd
120 Pritchett St, Aston, Birmingham B6 4EH
T: 0121 333 1925
F: 0121 333 1926
E: g.dunne@westleyengineering.co.uk
W: www.westleyengineering.co.uk

Weston Williamson
43, Tannner St, London SE1 3PL
T: 020 7403 2665
F: 020 7403 2667
E: chris@westonwilliamson.com
W: www.westonwilliamson.com

Westquay Trading Co. Ltd
3F, Lyncastle Way, Appleton Thorn, Warrington, WA4 4ST
T: 01925 265333
F: 01925 211700
E: enquiries@westquaytrading.co.uk
W: www.westquaytrading.co.uk

Westshield Ltd
Waldron House, Drury Lane, Chadderton, Oldham OL9 8LU
T: 0161 682 6222
F: 0161 682 6333
E: mail@westshield.co.uk
W: www.westshield.co.uk

Wettons
Wetton House, 278-280 St James's Rd, London SE1 5JX
T: 020 7237 2007
F: 020 7252 3277
E: mark.hammerton@wettons.co.uk
W: www.wettons.co.uk

WH Davis Ltd
Langwith Rd, Langwith Junction, Mansfield, Notts NG20 9SA
T: 01623 741600
F: 01623 744474
W: www.whdavis.co.uk

Wheelsets UK
Unit 46, Denby Way, Hellaby Ind. Est, Rotherham S66 8NZ
T: 01302 322266
F: 01302 322299
E: martin@wheelsets.co.uk
W: www.wheelsets.co.uk

White & Case LLP
5 Old Broad St, London EC2N 1DW
T: 020 7532 2310
F: 020 7532 1001
E: twinsor@whitecase.com
W: www.whitecase.com

White Young Green
See Arney

Whiteley Electronics Ltd
See Gemma Lighting

Wicek Sosna Architects
Unit 15, 21 Plumbers Row, London E1 1EQ
T: 020 7655 4430
E: office@sosnaarchitects.co.uk
W: www.sosnaarchitects.co.uk

Wilcomatic Ltd
Unit 5, Commerce Park, 19 Commerce Way, Croydon CR0 4YL
T: 020 8649 5760
F: 020 8686 9571
E: sales@wilcomatic.co.uk
W: www.wilcomatic.co.uk

Wilkinson Star Ltd
Shield Drive, Wardsley Ind Est, Manchester M28 2WD
T: 0161 793 8127
F: 0161 727 8538
E: steve.ross@wilkinsonstar.com
W: www.wilkinsonstar.com

WillB Brand Consultants
Studio 17, Royal Victoria Patriotic Building, Trinity Rd, London SW18 3SX
T: 020 7112 8911
M: 07815 056026
E: will@willbaxter.com
W: www.willbaxter.com

William Bain Fencing Ltd
Lochrin Works, 7 Limekilns Rd, Blairlinn Ind. Est, Cumbernauld G67 2RN
T: 01236 457333
F: 01236 451166
E: sales@lochrin-bain.co.uk
W: www.lochrin-bain.co.uk

William Cook Rail
Cross Green, Leeds LS9 0SG
T: 0113 249 6363
F: 0113 249 1376
E: castproducts@william-cook.co.uk
W: www.william-cook.co.uk

Williamette Valley Company – WVCO Railroad Division
1075 Arrowsmith St, Eugene, OR 97402 USA
T: 001 541 484 9621
F: 001 541 284 2096
E: sales@wvlco.com
W: www.wvlco.com

Willie Baker Leadership & Development Ltd
Aggborough Farm, College Rd, Kidderminster, Worcs DY10 1LJ
T: 07789 943043
E: willie@williebaker.co.uk
W: www.williebaker.co.uk

Winckworth Sherwood
Minerva House, 5 Montague Close, London SE1 9BB
T: 020 7593 5000
F: 0207 593 5099
E: info@wslaw.co.uk
W: www.wslaw.co.uk

Wind River UK Ltd
Oakwood House, Grove Business Park, White Waltham, Maidenhead, Berks SL6 3HY
T: 01793 831831
F: 01793 831808
E: sue.woolley@windriver.com
W: www.windriver.com

Windhoff Bahn und Anlagentechnik GmbH
Hovestrasse 10, D-48431 Rheine, Germany
T: 0049 5971 580
F: 0049 5971 58209
E: aw@windhoff.de
W: www.windhoff.de

Winn & Coales (Denso) Ltd
Denso House, Chapel Rd, London SE27 0TR
T: 020 8670 7511
F: 020 8761 2456
E: mail@denso.net
W: www.denso.net

Winstanley & Co Ltd
Racecourse Rd, Pershore, Worcs WR10 2DF
T: 01386 552278
F: 01386 556531
E: info@winstanleyco.com
W: www.winstanleyco.com

Winsted Ltd
Units 7/8, Lovett Rd, Hampton Lovett Ind Est, Droitwich, Worcs WR9 0QG
T: 01905 770276
F: 01905 779791
E: info@winsted.co.uk
W: www.winsted.co.uk

Wintersgill
110 Bolsover St, London W1W 5NU
T: 020 7580 4499
F: 020 7436 8191
E: info@wintersgill.net
W: www.wintersgill.net

WM Plant Hire Ltd
Manor Farm Lane, Bridgnorth, Shropshire WV16 5HG
T: 01452 722200
F: 01452 769666
E: info@wmplanthire.com
W: www.wmplanthire.com

Woking Homes
Oriental Rd, Woking, Surrey GU22 7BE
T: 01483 763558
F: 01483 721048
E: www.uknursinghomes.org/wokinghomes

Wood & Douglas Ltd
Lattice House, Baughurst, Tadley, Hants RG26 5LP
T: 0118 981 1444
F: 0118 981 1567
E: sales@woodanddouglas.co.uk
W: www.woodanddouglas.co.uk

Wood & Wood Signs
Heron Rd, Sowton Estate, Exeter EX2 7LX
T: 01392 444501
F: 01392 252358
E: info@wwsigns.co.uk
W: www.wwsigns.co.uk

Woodstone Ltd
68 Houghton Rd, St Ives, Huntingdon PE27 6RL
T: 01480 469402
F: 01480 380280
E: mail@gripdeck.com
W: www.gripdeck.com

Woodward Diesel Systems
Lancaster Centre, Meteor Business Park, Cheltenham Rd East, Gloucester GL2 9QL
T: 01452 859940
F: 01452 855758
W: www.woodward.com/gloucester

Works infrastructure Ltd
Mallard House, 75 The Mount, York YO24 1AX
T: 01904 672233
F: 01904 672244
E: enquiries@worksinfrastructure.co.uk
W: www.worksinfrastructure.co.uk

Workthing
Beaumont House, Kensington Village, Avonmore Rd, London W14 8TS
T: 0870 898 0022
F: 0870 898 0033
E: info@workthing.com
W: www.workthing.com

Wor-Rail
Guild House, Sandy Lane, Wildmoor, Bromsgrove, Worcs B61 0QU
T: 0121 460 1113
F: 0121 460 1116
E: sales@wor-rail.co.uk
W: www.wor-rail.co.uk

Wrekin Circuits Ltd
29/30 Hortonwood 33, Telford, Shropshire TF1 7EX
T: 01952 670011
F: 01952 606565
E: sales@wrekin-circuits.co.uk
W: www.wrekin-circuits.co.uk

WSP UK
Mountbatten House, Basing View, Basingstoke, Hants RG21 4HJ
T: 01256 318802
F: 01256 318700
E: nicky.bushnell@wspgroup.com
W: www.wspgroup.com

WTB Geotechnics
Earl Russell Way, Lawrence Hill, Bristol BS5 0WT
T: 0845 600 5505
F: 0845 609 2525
E: geotechnics@wtbgroup.com
W: www.geotechnics-uk.com

WVCO Railroad Division
1075 Arrowsmith St, PO Box 2280, Eugene, OR 97402, USA
T: 001 541 484 9621
F: 001 541 284 2096
E: sales@wvcorailroad.com
W: www.wvcorailroad.com

WWP Consultants
5-15 Cromer St, London WC1H 8LS
T: 020 7833 5767
F: 020 7833 5766
E: admin@wwp-london.com
W: www.wwp-london.com

Wynnwith Rail
Wynnwith House, Church St, Woking, Surrey GU21 6DJ
T: 01483 748206
E: rail@wynnwith.com
W: www.wynnwith.com

Wyse Rail Ltd
Cressex Business Park, Lancaster Rd, Bucks HP12 3QP
T: 0870 145 0552
F: 01494 560929
E: wyserail@wysegroup.com
W: www.wysegroup.com

WyvernRail Plc
Wirksworth Station, Station Rd, Wirksworth, Derbys DE4 4FB
T: 01629 821828
E: wirksworth_station@wyvernrail.co.uk
W: www.mytesttrack.com

XiTRACK Ltd
See Dow Hyperlast

XI Lubricants Ltd
See Ntm Sales & Marketing Ltd

Yardene Engineering 2000 Ltd
Daux Rd, Billingshurst, West Sussex RH14 9SJ
T: 01403 783558
F: 01403 783104
E: sales@yardene.co.uk
W: www.yardene.co.uk

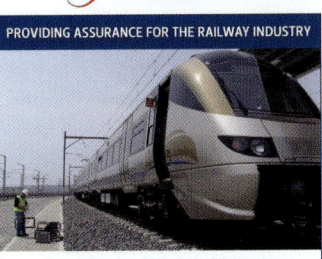

ZF Services UK
Abbeyfeld Rd, Lenton, Nottingham NG7 2SX
T: 0844 257 0555
F: 0115 986 9261
E: customerservices.zfgb@zf.com
W: www.zf.com/uk

Zigma Ground Solutions
Unit 11, M11 Business Link, Parsonage Lane, Stansted, Essex CM24 8TY
T: 0845 643 734
M: 07514 025121
E: amandacc@zigmagroundsolutions.com
W: www.zigmagroundsolutions.com

Zircon Software Ltd
Avon Court, Castle St, Trowbridge, Wilts BA14 8AS
T: 01225 764444
F: 01225 753087
E: info@zirconsoftware.co.uk
W: www.zirconsoftware.co.uk

Yellow Rail Ltd
The iD Centre, Lathkill House, rtc Business Park, London Rd, Derby DE24 8UP
T: 01332 258865
F: 01332 258823
E: enquiries@yellowrail.org.uk
W: www.yellowrail.org.uk

YJL Infrastructure Ltd
39 Cornhill, London EC3V 3ND
T: 020 7522 3220
F: 020 7522 3261
E: mccabep@yjli.co.uk
W: www.yjli.co.uk

York EMC Services Ltd
Market Square, University of York, Heslington, York YO10 5DD
T: 01904 324440
F: 01904 324434
E: enquiry@yorkemc.co.uk
W: www.yorkemc.co.uk

Yorkshire Rail Academy
National Railway Museum, Leeman Rd, York YO26 4XJ
T: 01904 770780
E: reception@yra.ac.uk
W: www.yorkcollege.ac.uk

Z+F UK Ltd
Unit 9, Derwent House, Clarence Ave, Trafford Park, Manchester M17 1Q
T: 0161 869 0450
F: 0161 869 0451
E: info@zf-uk.com
W: www.zf-uk.com

Zarges (UK) Ltd
Holdom Ave, Saxon Park Ind. Est, Bletchley, Milton Keynes MK1 1QU
T: 01908 641118
F: 01908 648176
E: sales@zargesuk.co.uk
W: www.zargesuk.co.uk

Zetica
Units 15/16, Hanborough Business Park, Long Hanborough, Oxon OX29 8LH
T: 01993 886682
F: 01993 886683
E: rail@zetica.com
W: www.zeticarail.com

Zollner UK Ltd
Clayton Business Ctr, Midland Rd, Leeds LS10 2RJ
T: 0113 270 3008
F: 0113 277 1007
E: frank.peters@zollner-uk.co.uk
W: www.zollner-uk.co.uk

Zonegreen
Sir John Brown Building, Davy Ind. Park, Prince of Wales Rd, Sheffield S9 4EX
T: 0114 230 0822
F: 0871 872 0349
E: info@zonegreen.co.uk
W: www.zonegreen.co.uk

ZTR Control Systems
8050 Country Rd, 101 East, Shakopee, Minneapolis, Minnesota 55379, USA
T: 001 952 233 4340
F: 001 952 233 4375
E: railinfo@ztr.com
W: www.ztr.com

Zuken
1500 Aztec West, Almondsbury, Bristol BS32 4RF
T: 01454 207800
F: 01454 207801
E: dionne.hayman@zuken.com
W: www.zuken.com

Zwicky Track Tools
See Arbil

ADDENDUM

Centinal Group
11 Brunel Close, 174 Bromyard Rd, St Johns, Worcester WR2 5EE
T: 01905 748569
F: 01905 420700
E: les@mfhydraulics.co.uk
W: www.mfhydraulics.co.uk

Central Engineering & Hydraulic Services Ltd
The Brookworks, 174 Brnley Road, St Johns, Worcester WR2 5EE
T: 01905 748569
F: 01905 420700
E: chris@cehsltd.co.uk
W: www.cehsltd.co.uk

ZF Services UK Ltd
The ZF Services UK Ltd team can provide maintenance solutions on Rail Final Drives of all makes. We work with you to provide the best preventative maintenance schedule to meet your needs.

ZF Services UK Ltd
Abbeyfield Road, Lenton,
Nottingham, NG7 2SX
Tel: 0844 257 0333
mark.doughty@zf.com
www.zf.com/uk

Advertisers Index

Photo Paul Bigland

Company	Page				
Aecom	170	Hima Sella	179	Rail Manche Finance	32,186
Alcatel	171	Hitachi	19,179	Rail Photolibrary	186
Angel Trains	37,171	Initial facilities	180	Rail Positive Relations	186
ACORP	32,172	Interfleet	127	Rail Research UK	153
Atkins	127, 149, 171	Invensys	141,180	Railway Industry Association (RIA)	186
Best Impressions	153	IRO	32,180	Revitaglaze	187
Bombardier	21,173	ISS	180	Rittal	187
CAF	55,173	ITIC	180	RVEL	187
Costain	128	J. Boyle Associates	181	Schenk Process	188
DCA	175	Jobson James	181	Siemens	23,188
Delta Rail	2,175	Kilborn	181	Shilling Media	193
Diamond Point International	175	Knorr Bremse	43,181	Sig Assure	188
Dilax	175	Leigh Fisher	182	Signalling Solutions	188
Direct Link North	175	Lexicraft	182	SSDM	189
Dorman	175	Link Associates	182	Stewart Signs	189
ERA	176	Lloyds Register	182	Systra	190
ESG	149	Lucchini	53	TAS	190
Eldapoint	176	Mack Brooks	8,182	Transport Benevolent Fund	191, Bookmark
Faiveley	57,177	MC Electronics	32	UK Power Networks	191
Finning	177, 195	Mechan	53, 183	Unipart Rail	192
Fourth Friday Club	178	Morgan AM&T	183	Voith Turbo	17,192
Hafren	178	Mors Smitt	183	Vossloh	67, 192
Halcrow	179	Moveright	57	VTS Track Technology	192
Harrington Generators	143	Norgren	184	Wabtec	192,196
Harry Needle Railroad Company	102	Park Signalling	184	Will B Brand Consultants	193
Hellerman Tyton	179	PSV Glass	185	Yellow Rail	193
		Rail Personnel	186	York EMC	193

194

HITACHI Inspire the Next